# SHAKESPEARE

# SHAKESPEARE

## THE INVENTION OF THE HUMAN

## HAROLD BLOOM

RIVERHEAD BOOKS

A MEMBER OF PENGUIN PUTNAM INC.

NEW YORK · 1998

Riverhead Books

a member of

Penguin Putnam Inc.

375 Hudson Street

New York, NY 10014

Library of Congress Cataloging-in-Publication Data

Bloom, Harold.

Shakespeare : the invention of the human / Harold Bloom.

p.   cm.

ISBN 1-57322-120-1 (acid-free paper)

1. Shakespeare, William, 1564–1616—Characters. 2. Shakespeare,

William, 1564–1616—Knowledge—Psychology. 3. Characters and

characteristics in literature. 4. Drama—Psychological aspects.

5. Personality in literature. 6. Humanism in literature.

I. Title.

PR2989.B58   1998                98-21325 CIP

822.3'3—dc21

Printed in the United States of America

10

This book is printed on acid-free paper. ∞

*Book design by Chris Welch*

That for which we find words is something already dead in our hearts. There is always a kind of contempt in the act of speaking.

Nietzsche, *The Twilight of the Idols*

Our wills and fates do so contrary run
That our devices still are overthrown,
Our thoughts are ours, their ends none of our own.

The Player King in *Hamlet*

# CONTENTS

# ACKNOWLEDGMENTS

Since there cannot be a definitive Shakespeare, I have employed a variety of texts, sometimes silently repunctuating for myself. In general, I recommend the Arden Shakespeare, but frequently I have followed the Riverside or other editions. I have avoided the New Oxford Shakespeare, which perversely seeks, more often than not, to print the worst possible text, poetically speaking.

Some of the material in this book was delivered, in much earlier drafts, as the Mary Flexner lectures at Bryn Mawr College, in October 1990, and as the Tanner Lectures at Princeton University, in November 1995.

John Hollander read and improved my manuscript, as did my devoted editor, Celina Spiegel. I have considerable debts also to my literary agents, Glen Hartley and Lynn Chu; to my copy editor, Toni Rachiele; and to my research assistants: Mirjana Kalezic, Jennifer Lewin, Ginger Gaines, Eric Boles, Elizabeth Small, and Octavio DiLeo. As always, I am grateful to the libraries and librarians of Yale University.

*H.B.*

*Timothy Dwight College*
*Yale University*
*April 1998*

# CHRONOLOGY

Arranging Shakespeare's plays in the order of their composition remains a disputable enterprise. This chronology, necessarily tentative, partly follows what is generally taken to be scholarly authority. Where I am skeptical of authority, I have provided brief annotations to account for my surmises.

Shakespeare was christened on April 26, 1564, at Stratford-on-Avon, and died there on April 23, 1616. We do not know when he first joined the London theatrical world, but I suspect it was as early as 1587. Probably in 1610, Shakespeare returned to live in Stratford, until his death. After 1613, when he composed *The Two Noble Kinsmen* (with John Fletcher), Shakespeare evidently gave up his career as dramatist.

My largest departure from most traditional Shakespeare scholarship is that I follow Peter Alexander's *Introduction to Shakespeare* (1964) in assigning the early *Hamlet* (written anytime from 1589 to 1593) to Shakespeare himself, and not to Thomas Kyd. I also dissent from the recent admission of *Edward III* (1592–95) into the Shakespeare canon, as I find nothing in the play representative of the dramatist who had written *Richard III.*

| | |
|---|---|
| *Henry VI, Part One* | 1589–90 |
| *Henry VI, Part Two* | 1590–91 |
| *Henry VI, Part Three* | 1590–91 |
| *Richard III* | 1592–93 |
| *The Two Gentlemen of Verona* | 1592–93 |

Most scholars date this 1594, but it is much less advanced than *The Comedy of Errors*, and seems to me Shakespeare's first extant comedy.

*Hamlet* (first version)    1589–93

This was added to the repertory of what became the Lord Chamberlain's Men when Shakespeare joined them in 1594. At the same time, *Titus Andronicus* and *The Taming of the Shrew* began to be performed by them. They never acted anything by Kyd.

*Venus and Adonis*        1592–93

*The Comedy of Errors*    1593

*Sonnets*                 1593–1609

The earliest of the Sonnets may have been composed in 1589, which would mean that they cover twenty years of Shakespeare's life, ending a year before his semi-retirement to Stratford.

*The Rape of Lucrece*     1593–94

*Titus Andronicus*        1593–94

*The Taming of the Shrew*  1593–94

*Love's Labour's Lost*    1594–95

It is so great a leap from Shakespeare's earlier comedies to the great feast of language that is *Love's Labour's Lost* that I doubt this early a date, unless the 1597 revision for a court performance was rather more than what generally we mean by a "revision." There is no printed version before 1598.

*King John*    1594–96

Another great puzzle in dating; much of the verse is so archaic that it suggests the Shakespeare of 1589 or so. And yet Faulconbridge the Bastard is Shakespeare's first character who speaks with a voice entirely his own.

*Richard II*                   1595

*Romeo and Juliet*             1595–96

*A Midsummer Night's Dream*    1595–96

*The Merchant of Venice*       1596–97

*Henry IV, Part One*           1596–97

*The Merry Wives of Windsor*   1597

*Henry IV, Part Two*           1598

*Much Ado About Nothing*       1598–99

*Henry V*                      1599

| | |
|---|---|
| *Julius Caesar* | 1599 |
| *As You Like It* | 1599 |
| *Hamlet* | 1600–1601 |
| *The Phoenix and the Turtle* | 1601 |
| *Twelfth Night* | 1601–2 |
| *Troilus and Cressida* | 1601–2 |
| *All's Well That Ends Well* | 1602–3 |
| *Measure for Measure* | 1604 |
| *Othello* | 1604 |
| *King Lear* | 1605 |
| *Macbeth* | 1606 |
| *Antony and Cleopatra* | 1606 |
| *Coriolanus* | 1607–8 |
| *Timon of Athens* | 1607–8 |
| *Pericles* | 1607–8 |
| *Cymbeline* | 1609–10 |
| *The Winter's Tale* | 1610–11 |
| *The Tempest* | 1611 |
| *A Funeral Elegy* | 1612 |
| *Henry VIII* | 1612–13 |
| *The Two Noble Kinsmen* | 1613 |

# TO THE READER

Literary character before Shakespeare is relatively unchanging; women and men are represented as aging and dying, but not as changing because their relationship to themselves, rather than to the gods or God, has changed. In Shakespeare, characters develop rather than unfold, and they develop because they reconceive themselves. Sometimes this comes about because they *overhear* themselves talking, whether to themselves or to others. Self-overhearing is their royal road to individuation, and no other writer, before or since Shakespeare, has accomplished so well the virtual miracle of creating utterly different yet self-consistent voices for his more than one hundred major characters and many hundreds of highly distinctive minor personages.

The more one reads and ponders the plays of Shakespeare, the more one realizes that the accurate stance toward them is one of awe. How he was possible, I cannot know, and after two decades of teaching little else, I find the enigma insoluble. This book, though it hopes to be useful to others, is a personal statement, the expression of a long (though hardly unique) passion, and the culmination of a life's work in reading, writing about, and teaching what I stubbornly still call imaginative literature. Bardolatry, the worship of Shakespeare, ought to be even more a secular religion than it already is. The plays remain the outward limit of human achievement: aesthetically, cognitively, in certain ways morally, even spiritually. They abide beyond the end of the mind's reach; we cannot catch up to them. Shakespeare will go on explaining us, in part because he invented us, which is the central argument of this book. I have repeated that argument throughout, because it will seem strange to many.

I offer a fairly comprehensive interpretation of all Shakespeare's plays, addressed to common readers and theatergoers. Though there are living Shakespearean critics I admire (and draw on here, by name), I am disheartened by much that now passes as readings of Shakespeare, whether academic or journalistic. Essentially, I seek to extend a tradition of interpretation that includes Samuel Johnson, William Hazlitt, A. C. Bradley, and Harold Goddard, a tradition that is now mostly out of fashion. Shakespeare's characters are roles for actors, and also they are considerably more than that: their influence upon life has been very nearly as enormous as their effect upon post-Shakespearean literature. No world author rivals Shakespeare in the apparent creation of personality, and I employ "apparent" here with some reluctance. To catalogue Shakespeare's largest gifts is almost an absurdity: where begin, where end? He wrote the best poetry and the best prose in English, or perhaps in any Western language. That is inseparable from his cognitive strength; he thought more comprehensively and originally than any other writer. It is startling that a third achievement should overgo these, yet I join Johnsonian tradition in arguing, nearly four centuries after Shakespeare, that he went beyond all precedents (even Chaucer) and invented the human as we continue to know it. A more conservative way of stating this would seem to me a weak misreading of Shakespeare: it might contend that Shakespeare's originality was in the *representation* of cognition, personality, character. But there is an overflowing element in the plays, an excess beyond representation, that is closer to the metaphor we call "creation." The dominant Shakespearean characters—Falstaff, Hamlet, Rosalind, Iago, Lear, Macbeth, Cleopatra among them—are extraordinary instances not only of how meaning gets started, rather than repeated, but also of how new modes of consciousness come into being.

We can be reluctant to recognize how much of our culture *was* literary, particularly now that so many of the institutional purveyors of literature happily have joined in proclaiming its death. A substantial number of

Americans who believe they worship God actually worship three major literary characters: the Yahweh of the J Writer (earliest author of Genesis, Exodus, Numbers), the Jesus of the Gospel of Mark, and Allah of the Koran. I do not suggest that we substitute the worship of Hamlet, but Hamlet is the only secular rival to his greatest precursors in personality. Like them, he seems not to be just a literary or dramatic character. His total effect upon the world's culture is incalculable. After Jesus, Hamlet is the most cited figure in Western consciousness; no one prays to him, but no one evades him for long either. (He cannot be reduced to a role for an actor; one would have to begin by speaking of "roles for actors" anyway, since there are more Hamlets than actors to play them.) Overfamiliar yet always unknown, the enigma of Hamlet is emblematic of the greater enigma of Shakespeare himself: a vision that is everything and nothing, a person who was (according to Borges) everyone and no one, an art so infinite that it *contains* us, and will go on enclosing those likely to come after us.

With most of the plays, I have attempted to be as straightforward as the oddities of my own consciousness allowed, within the limits of strongly favoring character over action, and of emphasizing what I call "foregrounding" in preference to the backgrounding of historicists old and new. The concluding section, "Foregrounding," is meant to be read in connection with any of the plays whatsoever, and could be printed at any point in this book. I cannot assert that I am straightforward upon the two parts of *Henry IV*, where I have centered obsessively upon Falstaff, the mortal god of my imaginings. In writing about *Hamlet*, I have experimented by employing a circling procedure, testing the mysteries of the play and its protagonist by returning always to my hypothesis (following the late Peter Alexander) that the young Shakespeare himself, and not Thomas Kyd, wrote the earlier version of *Hamlet* that existed more than a decade before the *Hamlet* we know. With *King Lear*, I have traced the fortunes of the four most disturbing figures—the Fool, Edmund, Edgar, and Lear himself—in order to track the tragedy of this most tragic of all tragedies.

Hamlet, Freud's mentor, goes about inducing all he encounters to reveal themselves, while the prince (like Freud) evades his biographers. What Hamlet exerts upon his fellow characters is an epitome of the effect of

Shakespeare's plays upon their critics. I have struggled, to the limit of my abilities, to talk about Shakespeare and not about myself, but I am certain that the plays have flooded my consciousness, and that the plays read me better than I read them. I once wrote that Falstaff would not accept being bored by us, if he was to deign to represent us. That applies also to Falstaff's peers, whether benign like Rosalind and Edgar, frighteningly malign like Iago and Edmund, or transcending us utterly, like Hamlet, Macbeth, and Cleopatra. We are lived by drives we cannot command, and we are read by works we cannot resist. We need to exert ourselves and read Shakespeare as strenuously as we can, while knowing that his plays will read us more energetically still. They read us definitively.

# SHAKESPEARE

# SHAKESPEARE'S UNIVERSALISM

The answer to the question "Why Shakespeare?" must be "Who else is there?"

Romantic criticism, from Hazlitt through Pater and A. C. Bradley on to Harold Goddard, taught that what matters most in Shakespeare is shared by him more with Chaucer and with Dostoevsky than with his contemporaries Marlowe and Ben Jonson. Inner selves do not exactly abound in the works of the creators of Tamburlaine and of Sir Epicure Mammon. Providing contexts that Shakespeare shared with George Chapman or Thomas Middleton will never tell you why Shakespeare, rather than Chapman or Middleton, changed us. Of all critics, Dr. Johnson best conveys the singularity of Shakespeare. Dr. Johnson first saw and said where Shakespeare's eminence was located: in a diversity of persons. No one, before or since Shakespeare, made so many separate selves.

Thomas Carlyle, dyspeptic Victorian prophet, must now be the least favored of all Shakespeare critics who once were respected. And yet the most useful single sentence about Shakespeare is his: "If called to define Shakespeare's faculty, I should say superiority of Intellect, and think I had included all under that." Carlyle was merely accurate; there are great poets who are not thinkers, like Tennyson and Walt Whitman, and great poets of shocking conceptual originality, like Blake and Emily Dickinson. But no Western writer, or any Eastern author I am able to read, is equal to Shakespeare as an intellect, and among writers I would include the principal philosophers, the religious sages, and the psychologists from Montaigne through Nietzsche to Freud.

This judgment, whether Carlyle's or mine, scarcely seems Bardolatry to me; perhaps it only repeats T. S. Eliot's observation that all we can hope for is to be wrong about Shakespeare in a new way. I propose only that we cease to be wrong about him by stopping trying to be right. I have read and taught Shakespeare almost daily for these past twelve years, and am certain that I see him only darkly. His intellect is superior to mine: why should I not learn to interpret him by gauging that superiority, which after all is the only answer to "Why Shakespeare?" Our supposed advances in cultural anthropology or in other modes of "Theory" are not advances upon *him*.

In learning, intellect, and personality, Samuel Johnson still seems to me first among all Western literary critics. His writings on Shakespeare necessarily have a unique value: the foremost of interpreters commenting upon the largest of all authors cannot fail to be of permanent use and interest. For Johnson, the essence of poetry was *invention*, and only Homer could be Shakespeare's rival in originality. Invention, in Johnson's sense as in ours, is a process of finding, or of finding out. We owe Shakespeare everything, Johnson says, and means that Shakespeare has taught us to understand human nature. Johnson does not go so far as to say that Shakespeare invented us, but he does intimate the true tenor of Shakespearean mimesis: "Imitations produce pain or pleasure, not because they are mistaken for realities, but because they bring realities to mind." An experiential critic above all, Johnson knew that realities change, indeed *are* change. What Shakespeare invents are ways of representing human changes, alterations not only caused by flaws and by decay but effected by the will as well, and by the will's temporal vulnerabilities. One way of defining Johnson's vitality as a critic is to note the consistent power of his inferences: he is always sufficiently *inside* Shakespeare's plays to judge them as he judges human life, without ever forgetting that Shakespeare's function is to bring life to mind, to make us aware of what we could not find without Shakespeare. Johnson knows that Shakespeare is not life, that Falstaff and Hamlet are larger than life, but Johnson knows also that Falstaff and

Hamlet have altered life. Shakespeare, according to Johnson, justly imitates *essential* human nature, which is a universal and not a social phenomenon. A. D. Nuttall, in his admirably Johnsonian *A New Mimesis* (1983), suggested that Shakespeare, like Chaucer, "implicitly contested the transcendentalist conception of reality." Johnson, firmly Christian, would not allow himself to say that, but he clearly understood it, and his uneasiness underlies his shock at the murder of Cordelia at the end of *King Lear.*

Only the Bible has a circumference that is everywhere, like Shakespeare's, and most people who read the Bible regard it as divinely inspired, if not indeed supernaturally composed. The Bible's center is God, or perhaps the vision or idea of God, whose location necessarily is unfixed. Shakespeare's works have been termed the secular Scripture, or more simply the fixed center of the Western canon. What the Bible and Shakespeare have in common actually is rather less than most people suppose, and I myself suspect that the common element is only a certain universalism, global and multicultural. Universalism is now not much in fashion, except in religious institutions and those they strongly influence. Yet I hardly see how one can begin to consider Shakespeare without finding some way to account for his pervasive presence in the most unlikely contexts: here, there, and everywhere at once. He is a system of northern lights, an aurora borealis visible where most of us will never go. Libraries and playhouses (and cinemas) cannot contain him; he has become a spirit or "spell of light," almost too vast to apprehend. High Romantic Bardolatry, now so much disdained in our self-defiled academies, is merely the most normative of the faiths that worship him.

I am not concerned, in this book, with how this happened, but with why it continues. If any author has become a mortal god, it must be Shakespeare. Who can dispute his good eminence, to which merit alone raised him? Poets and scholars revere Dante; James Joyce and T. S. Eliot would have liked to prefer him to Shakespeare, yet could not. Common readers, and thankfully we still possess them, rarely can read Dante; yet they can read and attend Shakespeare. His few peers—Homer, the Yahwist, Dante, Chaucer, Cervantes, Tolstoy, perhaps Dickens—remind us that the representation of human character and personality remains always the supreme literary value, whether in drama, lyric, or narrative. I am naïve enough to read incessantly because I cannot, on my own, get to know enough people profoundly enough. Shakespeare's own playgoers preferred Falstaff and Hamlet to all his other characters, and so do we, because Fat Jack and the Prince of Denmark manifest the most comprehensive consciousnesses in all of literature, larger than those of the biblical J Writer's Yahweh, of the Gospel of Mark's Jesus, of Dante the Pilgrim and Chaucer the Pilgrim, of Don Quixote and Esther Summerson, of Proust's narrator and Leopold Bloom. Perhaps indeed it is Falstaff and Hamlet, rather than Shakespeare, who are mortal gods, or perhaps the greatest of wits and the greatest of intellects between them divinized their creator.

What do Falstaff and Hamlet most closely share? If the question can be answered, we might get inside the man Shakespeare, whose personal mystery, for us, is that he seems not at all mysterious to us. Setting mere morality aside, Falstaff and Hamlet palpably are superior to everyone else whom they, and we, encounter in their plays. This superiority is cognitive, linguistic, and imaginative, but most vitally it is a matter of personality. Falstaff and Hamlet are the greatest of charismatics: they embody the Blessing, in its prime Yahwistic sense of "more life into a time without boundaries" (to appropriate from myself). Heroic vitalists are not larger than life; they are life's largeness. Shakespeare, who seems never to have made heroic or vitalistic gestures in his daily life, produced Falstaff and Hamlet as art's tribute to nature. More even than all the other Shakespearean prodigies—Rosalind, Shylock, Iago, Lear, Macbeth, Cleopatra—Falstaff and Hamlet are the invention of the human, the inauguration of personality as we have come to recognize it.

The idea of Western character, of the self as a moral agent, has many sources: Homer and Plato, Aristotle and Sophocles, the Bible and St. Augustine, Dante and Kant, and all you might care to add. Personality, in our sense, is a Shakespearean invention, and is not only Shakespeare's greatest originality but also the authentic cause of his perpetual pervasiveness. Insofar as we ourselves value, and deplore, our own personalities, we are the heirs of Falstaff and of Hamlet, and of all the other persons who throng Shakespeare's theater of what might be called the colors of the spirit.

How skeptical Shakespeare himself may have been of the value of personality, we cannot know. For Hamlet, the self is an abyss, the chaos of virtual nothingness. For Falstaff, the self is everything. Perhaps Hamlet, in Act V, transcends his own nihilism; we cannot be certain, in that ambiguous slaughter that reduces the court at Elsinore to the fop Osric, a few extras, and the inside outsider, Horatio. Is Hamlet self-divested of all his ironies at the end? Why does he give his dying vote to the bully boy Fortinbras, who wastes soldiers' lives in a battle for a barren bit of ground scarcely wide enough to bury their corpses? Falstaff, rejected and destroyed, remains an image of exuberance. His sublime personality, a vast value for us, has not saved him from the hell of betrayed and misplaced affection, and yet our final vision of him, related by Mistress Quickly in *Henry V*, remains a supreme value, evoking the Twenty-third Psalm and a child at play with flowers. It seems odd to observe that Shakespeare gives his two greatest personalities the oxymoron we call "a good death," but how else could we phrase it?

Are there *personalities* (in our sense) in the plays of any of Shakespeare's rivals? Marlowe deliberately kept to cartoons, even in Barabas, wickedest of Jews, and Ben Jonson as deliberately confined himself to ideograms, even in Volpone, whose final punishment so saddens us. I have a great taste for John Webster, but his heroines and villains alike vanish when juxtaposed to those of Shakespeare. Scholars attempt to impress upon us the dramatic virtues of George Chapman and of Thomas Middleton, but no one suggests that either of them could endow a role with human inwardness. It provokes considerable resistance from scholars when I say that Shakespeare invented us, but it would be a statement of a different order if anyone were to assert that our personalities would be different if Jonson and Marlowe had never written. Shakespeare's wonderful joke was to have his Ancient Pistol, Falstaff's follower in *Henry IV, Part Two*, identify himself with Marlowe's Tamburlaine; much slyer was Shakespeare's ironic yet frightening portrait of Marlowe as Edmund, the brilliantly seductive villain of *King Lear*. Malvolio in *Twelfth Night* is both a parodistic portrait of Ben Jonson and a personality so humanly persuasive as to remind the playgoer, unforgettably, that Jonson has no fully human beings in his own plays.

Shakespeare, not only witty in himself but the cause of wit in other men, absorbed his rivals in order to hint that their own extraordinary personalities far surpassed *their* creations, but not what Shakespeare could make of them. And yet Edmund's nihilistic intellect, like Iago's, is dwarfed by Hamlet's, and Malvolio's uneasily comic splendor is a teardrop alongside the cosmological ocean of Falstaff's laughter. We perhaps are too attentive to Shakespeare's theatrical metaphors, to his overt self-awareness as an actor-playwright. His models must have come more frequently from other spheres than his own, yet he may not have been "imitating life" but creating it, in most of his finest work.

What made his art of characterization possible? How can you create beings who are "free artists of themselves," as Hegel called Shakespeare's personages? Since Shakespeare, the best answer might be: "By an imitation of Shakespeare." It cannot be said that Shakespeare imitated Chaucer and the Bible in the sense that he imitated Marlowe and Ovid. He took hints from Chaucer, and they were more important than his Marlovian and Ovidian origins, at least once he had reached the creation of Falstaff. There are traces aplenty of fresh human personalities in Shakespeare before Falstaff: Faulconbridge the Bastard in *King John*, Mercutio in *Romeo and Juliet*, Bottom in *A Midsummer's Night's Dream*. And there is Shylock, at once a fabulous monster, the Jew incarnate, and also a troubling human uneasily joined with the monster in an uncanny blend. But there is a difference in kind between even these and Hamlet, and only a difference in degree between Falstaff and Hamlet. Inwardness becomes the heart of light and of darkness in ways more radical than literature previously could sustain.

Shakespeare's uncanny power in the rendering of personality is perhaps beyond explanation. Why do his personages seem so *real* to us, and how could he contrive that illusion so persuasively? Historical (and historicized) considerations have not aided us much in the answering of such questions. Ideals, both societal and individual, were perhaps more prevalent in Shakespeare's world than they appear to be in ours. Leeds Barroll notes that Renaissance ideals, whether Christian or philosophical or occult, tended to emphasize our need to join something personal that yet was larger than ourselves, God or a spirit. A certain strain or anxiety ensued, and Shakespeare became the greatest master at exploiting the void between persons and the personal ideal. Did his invention of what we recognize as "personality" result from that exploitation? Certainly we hear Shakespeare's influence upon his disciple John Webster, when Webster's Flamineo, dying at the close of *The White Devil*, cries out:

> While we look up to heaven we confound
> Knowledge with knowledge.

In Webster, even at his best, we can hear the Shakespearean paradoxes ably repeated, but the speakers have no individuality. Who can tell us the personality differences, in *The White Devil*, between Flamineo and Lodovico? Looking up to heaven and confounding knowledge with knowledge do not save Flamineo and Lodovico from being names upon a page. Hamlet, perpetually arguing with himself, does not seem to owe his overwhelming reality to a confounding of personal and ideal knowledge. Rather, Shakespeare gives us a Hamlet who is an agent, rather than an effect, of clashing realizations. We are convinced of Hamlet's superior reality because Shakespeare has made Hamlet free by making him know the truth, truth too intolerable for us to endure. A Shakespearean audience is like the gods in Homer: we look on and listen, and are not tempted to intervene. But we also are unlike the audience constituted by Homer's gods; being mortal, we too confound knowledge with knowledge. We cannot extract, from Shakespeare's era or from our own, social information that will explain his ability to create "forms more real than living men," as Shelley phrased it. Shakespeare's rival playwrights were subject to the same disjunctions between ideas of love, order, and the Eternal as he was, but they gave us eloquent caricatures, at best, rather than men and women.

We cannot know, by reading Shakespeare and seeing him played, whether he had any extrapoetic beliefs or disbeliefs. G. K. Chesterton, a wonderful literary critic, insisted that Shakespeare was a Catholic dramatist, and that Hamlet was more orthodox than skeptical. Both assertions seem to me quite unlikely, yet I do not know, and Chesterton did not know either. Christopher Marlowe had his ambiguities and Ben Jonson his ambivalences, but sometimes we can hazard surmises as to their personal stances. By reading Shakespeare, I can gather that he did not like lawyers, preferred drinking to eating, and evidently lusted after both genders. But I certainly do not have a clue as to whether he favored Protestantism or Catholicism or neither, and I do not know whether he believed or disbelieved in God or in resurrection. His politics, like his religion, evades me, but I think he was too wary to have any. He sensibly was afraid of mobs and of uprisings, yet he was afraid of authority also. He aspired after gentility, rued having been an actor, and might seem to have valued *The Rape of Lucrece* over *King Lear*, a judgment in which he remains outrageously unique (except, perhaps, for Tolstoy).

Chesterton and Anthony Burgess both stressed Shakespeare's vitality; I would go a touch farther and call Shakespeare a vitalist, like his own Falstaff. Vitalism, which William Hazlitt called "gusto," may be the ultimate clue to Shakespeare's preternatural ability to endow his personages with personalities and with utterly individuated styles of speaking. I scarcely can believe that Shakespeare preferred Prince Hal to Falstaff, as most scholars opine. Hal is a Machiavel; Falstaff, like Ben Jonson himself (and like Shakespeare?), is rammed with life. So, of course, are the great Shakespearean murderous villains: Aaron the Moor, Richard III, Iago, Edmund, Macbeth. So indeed are the comic villains: Shylock, Malvolio, and Caliban. Exuberance, well-nigh apocalyptic in its fervor, is as marked in Shakespeare as it is in Rabelais, Blake, and Joyce. The man Shakespeare, affable and shrewd, was no more Falstaff than he was Hamlet, and yet something in his readers and playgoers perpetually associates the dramatist with both figures. Only Cleopatra and the strongest of the villains—Iago, Edmund, Macbeth—hold on in our memories with the staying force of Falstaff's insouciance and Hamlet's intellectual intensity.

In reading Shakespeare's plays, and to a certain extent in attending their performances, the merely sensible procedure is to immerse yourself in the text and its speakers, and allow your understanding to move outward from what you read, hear, and see to whatever contexts suggest themselves as relevant. That was the procedure from the times of Dr. Johnson and David Garrick, of William Hazlitt and Edmund Kean, through the eras of A. C. Bradley and Henry Irving, of G. Wilson Knight and John Gielgud. Alas, sensible, even "natural" as this way was, it is now out of fashion, and has been replaced by arbitrary and ideologically imposed contextualization, the staple of our bad time. In "French Shakespeare" (as I shall go on calling it), the procedure is to begin with a political stance all your own, far out and away from Shakespeare's plays, and then to locate some marginal bit of English Renaissance social history that seems to sustain your stance. Social fragment in hand, you move in from outside upon the poor play, and find some connection, however established, between your supposed social fact and Shakespeare's words. It would cheer me to be persuaded that I am parodying the operations of the professors and directors of what I call "Resentment"—those critics who value theory over the literature itself—but I have given a plain account of the going thing, whether in the classroom or on the stage.

Substituting the name of "Shakespeare" for that of "Jesus," I am moved to cite William Blake:

I am sure this Shakespeare will not do
Either for Englishman or Jew.

What is inadequate about "French Shakespeare" is hardly that it is not "English Shakespeare," let alone Jewish, Christian, or Islamic Shakespeare: most simply, it is just not Shakespeare, who does not fit very easily into Foucault's "archives" and whose energies were not primarily "social." You can bring absolutely anything to Shakespeare and the plays will light it up, far more than what you bring will illuminate the plays. Though professional resenters insist that the aesthetic stance is itself an ideology, I scarcely agree, and I bring nothing but the aesthetic (in Walter Pater's and Oscar Wilde's language) to Shakespeare in this book. Or rather, he brings it to me, since Shakespeare educated Pater, Wilde, and the rest of us in the aesthetic, which, as Pater observed, is an affair of perceptions and sensations. Shakespeare teaches us how and what to perceive, and he also instructs us how and what to sense and then to experience as sensation. Seeking as he did to enlarge us, not as citizens or as Christians but as consciousnesses, Shakespeare outdid all his preceptors as an entertainer. Our resenters, who can be described (without malice) as gender-and-power freaks, are not much moved by the plays as entertainment.

Though G. K. Chesterton liked to think that Shakespeare was a Catholic, at least in spirit, Chesterton was too good a critic to locate Shakespeare's universalism in Christianity. We might learn from that not to shape Shakespeare by our own cultural politics. Comparing Shakespeare with Dante, Chesterton emphasized Dante's spaciousness in dealing with Christian love and Christian liberty, whereas Shakespeare "was a pagan; in so far that he is at his greatest in describing great spirits in chains." Those "chains" manifestly are not political. They return us to universalism, to Hamlet above all, greatest of all spirits, thinking his way to the truth, of which he perishes. The ultimate use of Shakespeare is to let him teach you to think too well, to whatever truth you can sustain without perishing.

2

It is not an illusion that readers (and playgoers) find more vitality both in Shakespeare's words and in the characters who speak them than in any other author, perhaps in all other authors put together. Early modern English was shaped by Shakespeare: the *Oxford English Dictionary* is made in his image. Later modern human beings are still being shaped by Shakespeare, not as Englishmen, or as American women, but in modes increasingly postnational and postgender. He has become the first universal author, replacing the Bible in the secularized consciousness. Attempts to historicize his ascendancy continue to founder upon the uniqueness of his eminence, for the cultural factors critics find relevant to Shakespeare are precisely as relevant to Thomas Dekker and to George Chapman. Newfangled expositions of Shakespeare do not persuade us, because their implicit program involves diminishing the difference between Shakespeare and the likes of Chapman.

What does not work, pragmatically, is any critical or theatrical fashion that attempts to assimilate Shakespeare to contexts, whether historical or here-and-now. Demystification is a weak technique to exercise upon the one writer who truly seems to have become himself only by representing other selves. I paraphrase Hazlitt upon Shakespeare; as the subtitle of this book indicates, I happily follow in Hazlitt's wake, seeking the Shakespearean difference, that which overcomes all demarcations between cultures, or within cultures. What allowed Shakespeare to be the supreme *magister ludi?* Nietzsche, like Montaigne a psychologist almost of Shakespeare's power, taught that pain is the authentic origin of human memory. Since Shakespeare is the most memorable of writers, there may be a valid sense in which the pain Shakespeare affords us is as significant as the pleasure. One need not be Dr. Johnson to dread reading, or attending a performance of, *King Lear,* particularly Act V, where Cordelia is murdered, and where Lear dies, holding her corpse in his arms. I myself dread *Othello* even more; its painfulness exceeds all measure, provided that we (and the play's director) grant to Othello his massive dignity and value that alone make his degradation so terrible.

I cannot solve the puzzle of the representation of Shylock or even of Prince Hal/King Henry V. Primal ambivalence, popularized by Sigmund Freud, remains central to Shakespeare, and to a scandalous extent was Shakespeare's own invention. Memorable pain, or memory engendered through pain, ensues from an ambivalence both cognitive and affective, an ambivalence that we associate most readily with Hamlet but that is prepared by Shylock. Perhaps Shylock began as a farcical villain—I once believed this, but now I rather doubt it. The play is Portia's, and not Shylock's, but Shylock is the first of Shakespeare's internalized hero-villains, as contrasted with such externalized forerunners as Aaron the Moor and Richard III. I take it that Prince Hal/Henry V is the next abyss of inwardness after Shylock, and so another hero-villain, a pious and patriotic Machiavel, but the piety and the kingly quality are modifiers, while the hypocrisy is the substantive. Even so, the tenacious and justice-seeking Shylock essentially is a would-be slaughterer, and Shakespeare painfully persuades us that Portia, another delightful hypocrite, prevents an atrocity through her shrewdness. One would hope that *The Merchant of Venice* is painful even for Gentiles, though the hope may be illusory.

What is not illusory is the frightening power of Shylock's will, his demand to have his bond. One surely can speak of the frightening power of Hal/Henry V's will, his demand to have his throne, and France, and absolute sway over everyone, including their hearts and minds. Hamlet's greatness, his transcending of the hero-villain's role, has much to do with his rejection of the will, including the will to avenge, a project he evades by negation, in him a revisionary mode that reduces every context to theater. Shakespeare's theatrical genius is less Iago than Hamlet. Iago is nothing if not critical, but he is, at most, a great criminal-aesthete, and his insight fails him utterly in regard to Emilia, his own wife. Hamlet is much the freer artist, whose insight cannot fail, and who converts his mousetrap into Theater of the World. Where Shylock is an obsessive, and Hal/Henry V an ingrate who fails to see Falstaff's uniqueness, and even Iago never quite gets beyond a sense of the injured self (his own passed-over military virtue), Hamlet consciously takes on the burden of the theater's mystery as augmented by Shakespeare's strength. Hamlet, too, ceases to represent himself and becomes something other than a single self—a something that is a universal figure and not a picnic of selves. Shakespeare became unique by representing other humans; Hamlet is the difference that Shakespeare achieved. I am not suggesting that Hamlet's beautiful disinterestedness in Act V ever was or became one of Shakespeare's personal qualities, but rather that Hamlet's final stance personifies Shakespeare's Negative Capability, as John Keats termed it. At the end, Hamlet is no longer a real personage condemned to suffer inside a play, and the wrong play at that. The personage and the play dissolve into each other, until we have only the cognitive music of "let be" and "Let it be."

3

It is difficult to describe Shakespeare's modes of representation without resorting to oxymorons, since most of these modes are founded upon seeming contradictions. A "naturalistic unreality" suggests itself, to meet Wittgenstein's annoyed comment that life is *not* like Shakespeare. Owen Barfield replied to Wittgenstein in advance (1928):

... there is a very real sense, humiliating as it may seem, in which what we generally venture to call *our* feelings are really Shakespeare's "meaning."

Life itself has become a naturalistic unreality, partly, because of Shakespeare's prevalence. To have invented our feelings is to have gone beyond psychologizing us: Shakespeare made us theatrical, even if we never attend a performance or read a play. After Hamlet literally has stopped the play—to joke about the War of the Theaters, to command the Player King to enact the absurd scene in which Aeneas recounts Priam's slaughter, to admonish the players to a little discipline—we more than ever regard Hamlet as *one of us,* somehow dropped into a role in a play, and the wrong play at that. The prince alone is real; the others, and all the action, constitute theater.

Can we conceive of ourselves without Shakespeare? By "ourselves" I do not mean only actors, directors, teachers, critics, but also you and everyone you know. Our education, in the English-speaking world, but in many other nations as well, has been Shakespearean. Even now, when our education has faltered, and Shakespeare is battered and truncated by our fashionable ideologues, the ideologues themselves are caricatures of Shakespearean energies. Their supposed "politics" reflect the passions of *his* characters, and insofar as they themselves possess any social energies, their secret sense of the societal is oddly Shakespearean. I myself would prefer them to be Machiavels and resenters on the Marlovian model of Barabas, Jew of Malta, but alas, their actual ideological paradigms are Iago and Edmund.

Do Shakespeare's modes of representation *in themselves* betray any ideological turn, whether Christian, skeptical, hermetic, or whatever? The question, difficult to frame, remains urgent in its implications: Is Shakespeare, in his plays, ultimately a celebrant of life, beyond tragedy, or is he pragmatically nihilistic? Since I myself am a heretical transcendentalist, gnostic in orientation, I would be happiest with a Shakespeare who seemed to hold on to at least a secular transcendence, a vision of the sublime. That seems not altogether true; the authentic Shakespearean litany chants variations upon the word "nothing," and the uncanniness of nihilism haunts almost every play, even the great, relatively unmixed comedies. As a play-wright, Shakespeare seems too wise to believe *anything*, and while he seems to know not less than everything, he is careful to keep that knowing several steps short of transcendence. Since his eloquence is comprehensive, and his dramatic concern almost unfaltering, one cannot assign precedence even to the plays' apparent nihilism, and to their clear sense of nature's indifference, alike, to human codes and to human suffering. Still, the nihilism has a peculiar reverberation. We remember Leontes in *The Winter's Tale* hardly at all for his closing repentance—"Both your pardons, / That e'er I put between your holy looks / My ill suspicion"—but for his great paean of "nothings":

> Is this nothing?
> Why then the world and all that's in't, is nothing,
> The covering sky is nothing, Bohemia nothing,
> My wife is nothing, nor nothing have these nothings,
> If this be nothing.

His nihilizing madness matters to us, and his restored sanity does not, since true poetry indeed is of the Devil's party, in William Blake's dialectical sense of the Devil. Nahum Tate's sanitized *King Lear*, with its happy ending of Cordelia married to Edgar, and Lear benignly beaming upon his daughter and his godson, cheered up Dr. Johnson but deprives us of the *kenoma*, the sensible emptiness or waste land in which the actual play by William Shakespeare concludes.

4

Few among us are qualified to testify as to whether God is dead, or alive, or wandering somewhere in exile (the possibility I tend to favor). Some authors indeed are dead, but not William Shakespeare. As for dramatic characters, I never know how to take the assurances (and remonstrances) I receive from Shakespeare's current critics, who tell me that Falstaff,

Hamlet, Rosalind, Cleopatra, and Iago are roles for actors and actresses but not "real people." Impressed as I (sometimes) am by these admonitions, I struggle always with the palpable evidence that my chastisers not only are rather less interesting than Falstaff and Cleopatra, but also are less persuasively alive than Shakespearean figures, who are (to steal from Ben Jonson) "rammed with life." When I was a child, and saw Ralph Richardson play Falstaff, I was so profoundly affected that I could never see Richardson again, on stage or on screen, without identifying him with Falstaff, despite this actor's extraordinary and varied genius. The reality of Falstaff has never left me, and a half century later was the starting point for this book. If a poor player struts and frets his hour upon the stage, and then is heard no more, we can say that a great player reverberates for a lifetime, most particularly if he acts not only a strong role, but a character deeper than life, a wit unmatched by anyone merely real whom we will ever know.

We ought to get these matters the right way round; *we* are not here to make moral judgments concerning Falstaff. Shakespeare perpsectivizes his dramas so that, measure for measure, we are judged even as we attempt to judge. If your Falstaff is a roistering coward, a wastrel confidence man, an uncourted jester to Prince Hal, well, then, we know something of you, but we know no more about Falstaff. If your Cleopatra is an aging whore, and her Antony a would-be Alexander in his dotage, then we know a touch more about you and rather less about them than we should. Hamlet's players hold the mirror up to nature, but Shakespeare's is a mirror within a mirror, and both are mirrors with many voices. Falstaff, Hamlet, Cleopatra, and the rest are not images of voice (as lyric poets can be), and they do not speak either for Shakespeare or for nature. An art virtually unlimited, Shakespearean representation offers us neither nature nor a second nature, neither cosmos nor heterocosm. "The art itself is nature" (*The Winter's Tale*) is a wonderfully ambiguous declaration. If I am right in finding true Shakespearean character first in Faulconbridge the Bastard in *King John* and last in *The Tempest*, that still sets aside superb plays with a very different sort of characterization, ranging from the perplexed triad of *Troilus and Cressida*, *All's Well That Ends Well*, and *Measure for Measure* on to the hieratic figures of *The Two Noble Kinsmen*. That is to say, Shakespearean characterization is finally so varied that we cannot call any one mode of it "true."

5

Pragmatically there is little difference between speaking of "Hamlet as a character" and "Hamlet as a role for an actor." Yet, mostly because of the peculiarities of modern criticism, the time has come around when it seems salutory to speak again of "literary and dramatic character" in order better to comprehend Shakespeare's men and women. Very little is gained by reminding us that Hamlet is made up of and by words, that he is "just" a grouping of marks upon a page. "Character" means both a letter of the alphabet, and also ethos, a person's habitual way of life. Literary and dramatic character is an imitation of human character, or so we once thought, on the premise that words were as much like people as they were like things. Words of course refer to other words, but their impact upon us emanates, as Martin Price says, from the empiric realm where we live, and where we attribute values and meanings, to our ideas of persons. Such attributions are a kind of fact, and so are our impressions that some literary and dramatic characters reinforce our ideas of persons and some do not.

There are two contradictory ways to account for Shakespeare's eminence. If, for you, literature is primarily language, then the primacy of Shakespeare is only a cultural phenomenon, produced by sociopolitical urgencies. In this view, Shakespeare did not write Shakespeare—his plays were written by the social, political, and economic energies of his age. But so was everything else, then and now, because certain more or less recent Parisian speculators have convinced many (if not most) academic critics that there are no authors anyway.

The other way of exploring Shakespeare's continued supremacy is rather more empirical: he has been universally judged to be a more adequate representer of the universe of fact than anyone else, before him or since. This judgment has been dominant since at least the mid–eighteenth century; it has been staled by repetition, yet it remains merely true, banal as resentful theorists find it to be. We keep returning to Shakespeare because we need him; no one else gives us so much of the world most of us take to be fact. But in the book that follows, I will not just begin with the assumption that Shakespeare palpably was much the best writer we ever will know. Shakespeare's originality in the representation of character will be demonstrated throughout, as will the extent to which we all of us were, to a shocking degree, pragmatically reinvented by Shakespeare. Our ideas as to what makes the self authentically human owe more to Shakespeare than ought to be possible, but then he has become a Scripture, not to be read as many of us read the Bible or the Koran or Joseph Smith's Doctrines and Covenants, but also not to be read as we read Cervantes or Dickens or Walt Whitman. *The Complete Works of William Shakespeare* could as soon be called *The Book of Reality*, fantastic as so much of Shakespeare deliberately intends to be. I have written elsewhere that Shakespeare is not only in himself the Western canon; he has become the universal canon, perhaps the only one that can survive the current debasement of our teaching institutions, here and abroad. Every other great writer may fall away, to be replaced by the anti-elitist swamp of Cultural Studies. Shakespeare will abide, even if he were to be expelled by the academics, in itself most unlikely. He extensively informs the language we speak, his principal characters have become our mythology, and he, rather than his involuntary follower Freud, is our psychologist. His persuasiveness has its unfortuante aspects; *The Merchant of Venice* may have been more of an incitement to anti-Semitism than *The Protocols of the Learned Elders of Zion*, though less than the Gospel of John. We pay a price for what we gain from Shakespeare.

# PART I

# THE EARLY COMEDIES

1

# THE COMEDY OF ERRORS

The shortest and most unified of all Shakespeare's plays, *The Comedy of Errors*, is regarded by many scholars as his very first, which I tend to doubt. It shows such skill, indeed mastery—in action, incipient character, and stagecraft—that it far outshines the three *Henry VI* plays and the rather lame comedy *The Two Gentlemen of Verona*. It is true that in comedy Shakespeare was free to be himself from the start, whereas the shadow of Marlowe darkens the early histories (*Richard III* included) and *Titus Andronicus*. Yet, even granted Shakespeare's comic genius, *The Comedy of Errors* does not read or play like apprentice work. It is a remarkably sophisticated elaboration of (and improvement upon) Plautus, the Roman comic dramatist whom most of our playgoers know through the musical adaptation *A Funny Thing Happened on the Way to the Forum*. Shakespeare himself was adapted splendidly by Rodgers and Hart, whose *The Boys from Syracuse* took *The Comedy of Errors* as their source, much as Cole Porter later was to utilize *The Taming of the Shrew* for his *Kiss Me Kate*.

In *The Comedy of Errors*, Shakespeare compounds Plautus's *The Two Menaechmuses* with hints from the same dramatist's *Amphitryon*, and gives us the wonderful absurdity of two sets of identical twins. We are in Greece, at Ephesus (where we will be again at the other end of Shakespeare's career, in *Pericles*), and we never go elsewhere, in this play so carefully confined in space and time (a single day). Antipholus of Syracuse arrives in Ephesus with his bondsman, Dromio. His twin brother, Antipholus of

Ephesus, also has a bondsman named Dromio, identical twin to the first.
The merchant of Syracuse and his servant have arrived in Ephesus not on
a commercial mission but on a familial quest to find their missing brothers. This quest is also the purpose of the merchant Egeon of Syracuse, father of the two Antipholuses, who enters Ephesus only to be immediately
arrested in the name of its Duke, who sentences the hapless Egeon to be
beheaded at sundown. Syracuse and Ephesus are fierce enemies. That gives
*The Comedy of Errors* a rather plangent opening, not at all Plautine:

> *Egeon.* Proceed, Solinus, to procure my fall,
>     And by the doom of death end woes and all.

Duke Solinus regretfully but firmly assures Egeon that indeed it will be
off with his head, unless a ransom of a hundred marks can be paid. In response to the Duke's questioning, Egeon tells us the fantastic, really outrageous yarn of a shipwreck some twenty-three years before, which
divided his family in half, separating husband and one of each set of twins
from the wife and the other infants. For the past five years, Egeon says, he
has searched for the missing trio, and his anguish at not finding them informs his wretched readiness to be executed:

> Yet this is my comfort; when your words are done,
> My woes end likewise with the evening sun.

These scarcely are the accents of comedy, let alone of the knockabout
farce soon to engulf us. But Shakespeare, who was to become the subtlest
of all dramatists, already is very ambiguous in *The Comedy of Errors*. The
twin Antipholuses are dead ringers but inwardly are very different. The
Syracusan Antipholus has a quasi-metaphysical temperament:

> He that commends me to mine own content
> Commends me to the thing I cannot get.
> I to the world am like a drop of water
> That in the ocean seeks another drop,

Who, falling there to find his fellow forth,
(Unseen, inquisitive) confounds himself.
So I, to find a mother and a brother,
In quest of them, unhappy, lose myself.

[I.ii.33–40]

These often-quoted lines belie our usual first impressions of *The Comedy of Errors* as a purely rambunctious farce, just as the laments of Egeon clearly transcend the expected situations of farce.

The Ephesian Antipholus is not a very interesting fellow, compared with his Syracusan twin, upon whom Shakespeare chooses to concentrate. Partly, the Antipholus of Syracuse benefits in our regard from what bewilders him: the strangeness of Ephesus. Since St. Paul's Epistle to the Ephesians makes reference to their "curious arts," a Bible-aware audience would expect the town (though clearly Shakespeare's London) to seem a place of sorcery, a kind of fairyland where anything may happen, particularly to visitors. Antipholus of Syracuse, already lost to himself before entering Ephesus, very nearly loses his sense of self-identity as the play proceeds.

Perhaps all farce is implicitly metaphysical; Shakespeare departs from Plautus in making the uneasiness overt. *The Comedy of Errors* moves toward madcap violence, in which, however, no one except the charlatan exorcist, Dr. Pinch, gets hurt. It is a play in which no one, even the audience, can be permitted to get matters right until the very end, when the two sets of twins stand side by side. Shakespeare gives the audience no hint that the Ephesian Abbess (presumably a priestess of Diana) is the lost mother of the Antipholuses until she chooses to declare herself. We can wonder, if we want to, why she has been in Ephesus for twenty-three years without declaring herself to her son who dwells there, but that would be as irrelevant as wondering how and why the two sets of twins happen to be dressed identically on the day that the boys from Syracuse arrive. Such peculiarities are the given of *The Comedy of Errors*, where the demarcations between the improbable and the impossible become very ghostly.

Exuberant fun as it is and must be, this fierce little play is also one of the starting points for Shakespeare's reinvention of the human. A role in a farce hardly seems an arena for inwardness, but genre never confined Shakespeare, even at his origins, and Antipholus of Syracuse is a sketch for the abysses of self that are to come. Even when he contemplates sightseeing, the visiting twin remarks: "I will go lose myself, / And wander up and down to view the city." You do not lose yourself to find yourself in *The Comedy of Errors*, which is hardly a Christian parable. At the play's close, the two Dromios are delighted with each other, but the mutual response of the two Antipholuses is left enigmatic, as we will see. Nothing could be more unlike the response of the Ephesian burgher, so indignant that his assured self-identity should ever be doubted, than the Syracusan quester's appeal to Luciana, sister-in-law to his brother:

> Sweet mistress, what your name is else I know not,
> Nor by what wonder you do hit of mine;
> Less in your knowledge and your grace you show not
> Than our earth's wonder, more than earth divine.
> Teach me, dear creature, how to think and speak;
> Lay open to my earthy gross conceit,
> Smother'd in errors, feeble, shallow, weak,
> The folded meaning of your words' deceit.
> Against my soul's pure truth why labour you
> To make it wander in an unknown field?
> Are you a god? would you create me new?
> Transform me then, and to your power I'll yield.
> But if that I am I, then well I know
> Your weeping sister is no wife of mine,
> Nor to her bed no homage do I owe;
> Far more, far more to you do I decline;
> O, train me not, sweet mermaid, with thy note,
> To drown me in thy sister's flood of tears;
> Sing, siren, for thyself, and I will dote;
> Spread o'er the silver waves thy golden hairs,
> And as a bed I'll take thee, and there lie,

And in that glorious supposition think
He gains by death that hath such means to die;
Let Love, being light, be drowned if she sink.

[III.ii.29–52]

The poignance of this inheres partly in its desperation; Antipholus of Syracuse falls in love to refind himself, presaging the erotic pattern that will be amiably satirized in *Love's Labour's Lost.* There the wit Berowne audaciously secularizes the Christian paradox that Shakespeare evades in *The Comedy of Errors:*

Let us once lose our oaths to find ourselves,
Or else we lose ourselves to keep our oaths.
It is religion to be thus forsworn;
For charity itself fulfils the law;
And who can sever love from charity?

[IV.iii.358–62]

That is not precisely what St. Paul meant by "he that loveth another hath fulfilled the law," but *Love's Labour's Lost* is of course no more Pauline than is *The Comedy of Errors.* Antipholus of Syracuse loves Luciana not to fulfill the law, even of his own lost being, but to achieve transformation, to be created new. Shakespeare does not let us linger in this plangency, but moves us to hilarity in a dialogue between the Syracusan Antipholus and Dromio, concerning the kitchen wench, Nell, who has confused the visiting Dromio with her husband, Dromio of Ephesus. Nell is a wench of an admirable girth, provoking marvelous geographical surmises:

*Syr. Ant.* Then she bears some breadth?
*Syr. Dro.* No longer from head to foot than from hip to hip; she is
    spherical, like a globe; I could find out countries in her.
*Syr. Ant.* In what part of her body stands Ireland?
*Syr. Dro.* Marry, sir, in her buttocks; I found it out by the bogs.
*Syr. Ant.* Where Scotland?

*Syr. Dro.* I found it by the barrenness, hard in the palm of the hand.

*Syr. Ant.* Where France?

*Syr. Dro.* In her forehead, armed and reverted, making war against her heir.

*Syr. Ant.* Where England?

*Syr. Dro.* I looked for the chalky cliffs, but I could find no whiteness in them. But I guess it stood in her chin, by the salt rheum that ran between France and it.

*Syr. Ant.* Where Spain?

*Syr. Dro.* Faith, I saw it not; but I felt it hot in her breath.

*Syr. Ant.* Where America, the Indies?

*Syr. Dro.* Oh, sir, upon her nose, all o'er-embellished with rubies, carbuncles, sapphires, declining their rich aspect to the hot breath of Spain, who sent whole armadoes of carracks to be ballast at her nose.

*Syr. Ant.* Where stood Belgia, the Netherlands?

*Syr. Dro.* Oh, sir, I did not look so low.

[III.ii.110–38]

This splendid tour de force is the epitome of *The Comedy of Errors*, whose laughter is always benign. The recognition scene, Shakespeare's first in what would become an extraordinary procession, prompts the astonished Duke of Ephesus to the play's deepest reflection:

One of these men is *genius* to the other;
And so of these, which is the natural man,
And which the spirit? Who deciphers them?

[V.i.332–34]

Though Antipholus of Syracuse cannot be called his brother's daemon or attendant spirit, one possible answer to the Duke's questions might be that the discerning playgoer would locate the spirit in the outlander, and the natural man in the Ephesian merchant. Shakespeare, who will perfect the art of ellipsis, begins here by giving the two Antipholuses no affective reactions whatsoever to their reunion. The Syracusan Antipholus commands his Dromio: "Embrace thy brother there; rejoice with him," but then exits with his own brother, sans embraces or joy. Doubtless, Antipholus of Syracuse is considerably more interested in pursuing Luciana, just as Antipholus of Ephesus wishes to get back to his wife, house, and commodities. Still, the coldness or dispassionateness of the Antipholuses is striking in contrast to the charming reunion of the Dromios, with which Shakespeare sweetly ends his comedy:

> *Syr. Dro.* There is a fat friend at your master's house,
>     That kitchen'd me for you to-day at dinner;
>     She now shall be my sister, not my wife.
> *Eph. Dro.* Methinks you are my glass, and not my brother:
>     I see by you I am a sweet-fac'd youth.
>     Will you walk in to see their gossiping?
> *Syr. Dro.* Not I, sir; you are my elder.
> *Eph. Dro.* That's a question, how shall we try it?
> *Syr. Dro.* We'll draw cuts for the senior; till then, lead thou first.
> *Eph. Dro.* Nay then, thus:
>     We came into the world like brother and brother,
>     And now let's go hand in hand, not one before another.
>                         *Exeunt.*
>
>                                         [V.i.414–26]

These two long-suffering clowns have had to sustain numerous blows from the Antipholuses throughout the play, and the audience is heartened to see them go out in such high good humor. When the Ephesian Dromio remarks: "I see by you I am a sweet-faced youth," we see it too, and the concluding couplet exudes a mutual affection clearly absent in the two Antipholuses. It would be absurd to burden *The Comedy of Errors* with sociopolitical or other current ideological concerns, and yet it remains touching that Shakespeare, from the start, prefers his clowns to his merchants.

## 2

# THE TAMING OF THE SHREW

The *Taming of the Shrew* begins with the very odd two scenes of the Induction, in which a noble practical joker gulls the drunken tinker, Christopher Sly, into the delusion that he is a great lord about to see a performance of Kate and Petruchio's drama. That makes their comedy, the rest of *The Taming of the Shrew*, a play-within-a-play, which does not seem at all appropriate to its representational effect upon an audience. Though skillfully written, the Induction would serve half a dozen other comedies by Shakespeare as well or as badly as it coheres with the *Shrew*. Critical ingenuity has proposed several schemes creating analogies between Christopher Sly and Petruchio, but I am one of the unpersuaded. And yet Shakespeare had some dramatic purpose in his Induction, even if we have not yet surmised it. Sly is not brought back at the conclusion of Shakespeare's *Shrew*, perhaps because his disenchantment necessarily would be cruel, and would disturb the mutual triumph of Kate and Petruchio, who rather clearly are going to be the happiest married couple in Shakespeare (short of the Macbeths, who end separately but each badly). Two points can be accepted as generally cogent about the Induction: it somewhat distances us from the performance of the *Shrew*, and it also hints that social dislocation is a form of madness. Sly, aspiring above his social station, becomes as insane as Malvolio in *Twelfth Night*.

Since Kate and Petruchio are social equals, their own dislocation may be their shared, quite violent forms of expression, which Petruchio "cures" in Kate at the high cost of augmenting his own boisterousness to an extreme where it hardly can be distinguished from a paranoid mania. Who cures, and who is cured, remains a disturbing matter in this marriage, which doubtless will maintain itself against a cowed world by a common front of formidable pugnacity (much more cunning in Kate than in her roaring boy of a husband). We all know one or two marriages like theirs; we can admire what works, and we resolve also to keep away from a couple so closed in upon itself, so little concerned with others or with otherness.

It may be that Shakespeare, endlessly subtle, hints at an analogy between Christopher Sly and the happily married couple, each in a dream of its own from which we will not see Sly wake, and which Kate and Petruchio need never abandon. Their final shared reality is a kind of conspiracy against the rest of us: Petruchio gets to swagger, and Kate will rule him and the household, perpetually acting her role as the reformed shrew. Several feminist critics have asserted that Kate marries Petruchio against her will, which is simply untrue. Though you have to read carefully to see it, Petruchio is accurate when he insists that Kate fell in love with him at first sight. How could she not? Badgered into violence and vehemence by her dreadful father Baptista, who vastly prefers the authentic shrew, his insipid younger daughter Bianca, the high-spirited Kate desperately needs rescue. The swaggering Petruchio provokes a double reaction in her: outwardly furious, inwardly smitten. The perpetual popularity of the *Shrew* does not derive from male sadism in the audience but from the sexual excitation of women and men alike.

The *Shrew* is as much a romantic comedy as it is a farce. The mutual roughness of Kate and Petruchio makes a primal appeal, and yet the humor of their relationship is highly sophisticated. The amiable ruffian Petruchio is actually an ideal—that is to say an overdetermined—choice for Kate in her quest to free herself from a household situation far more maddening than Petruchio's antic zaniness. Roaring on the outside, Petruchio is something else within, as Kate gets to see, understand, and control, with his final approval. Their rhetorical war begins as mutual sexual provocation, which Petruchio replaces, after marriage, with his hyperbolical game of childish tantrums. It is surely worth remarking that Kate, whatever her initial sufferings as to food, costume, and so on, has only one true moment of agony, when Petruchio's deliberately tardy arrival for the wedding makes her fear she has been jilted:

> *Bap.* Signor Lucentio, this is the 'pointed day
> That Katharine and Petruchio should be married,
> And yet we hear not of our son-in-law.
> What will be said? What mockery will it be
> To want the bridegroom when the priest attends
> To speak the ceremonial rites of marriage!
> What says Lucentio to this shame of ours?
> *Kath.* No shame but mine. I must forsooth be forc'd
> To give my hand, oppos'd against my heart,
> Unto a mad-brain rudesby, full of spleen,
> Who woo'd in haste and means to wed at leisure.
> I told you, I, he was a frantic fool,
> Hiding his bitter jests in blunt behaviour.
> And to be noted for a merry man
> He'll woo a thousand, 'point the day of marriage,
> Make feast, invite friends, and proclaim the banns,
> Yet never means to wed where he hath woo'd.
> Now must the world point at poor Katharine,
> And say 'Lo, there is mad Petruchio's wife,
> If it would please him come and marry her.'
> *Tra.* Patience, good Katharine, and Baptista too.
> Upon my life, Petruchio means but well,
> Whatever fortune stays him from his word.
> Though he be blunt, I know him passing wise;
> Though he be merry, yet withal he's honest.
> *Kath.* Would Katharine had never seen him though.
> *Exit weeping [followed by Bianca and attendants].*
>
> [III.ii.1–26]

No one enjoys being jilted, but this is not the anxiety of an unwilling bride. Kate, authentically in love, nevertheless is unnerved by the madcap

Petruchio, lest he turn out to be an obsessive practical joker, betrothed to half of Italy. When, after the ceremony, Petruchio refuses to allow his bride to attend her own wedding feast, he crushes what she calls her "spirit to resist" with a possessive diatribe firmly founded upon the doubtless highly patriarchal Tenth Commandment:

> They shall go forward, Kate, at thy command.
> Obey the bride, you that attend on her.
> Go to the feast, revel and domineer,
> Carouse full measure to her maidenhead,
> Be mad and merry, or go hang yourselves.
> But for my bonny Kate, she must with me.
> Nay, look not big, nor stamp, nor stare, nor fret;
> I will be master of what is mine own.
> She is my goods, my chattels, she is my house,
> My household stuff, my field, my barn,
> My horse, my ox, my ass, my any thing,
> And here she stands. Touch her whoever dare!
> I'll bring mine action on the proudest he
> That stops my way in Padua. Grumio,
> Draw forth thy weapon, we are beset with thieves,
> Rescue thy mistress if thou be a man.
> Fear not, sweet wench, they shall not touch thee, Kate.
> I'll buckler thee against a million.
> > *Exeunt PETRUCHIO, KATHARINA [and GRUMIO].*
> > > [III.ii.220–37]

This histrionic departure, with Petruchio and Grumio brandishing drawn swords, is a symbolic carrying-off, and begins Petruchio's almost phantasmagoric "cure" of poor Kate, which will continue until at last she discovers how to tame the swaggerer:

> *Pet.* Come on, a God's name, once more toward our father's.
> > Good Lord, how bright and goodly shines the moon!
> *Kath.* The moon? the sun! It is not moonlight now.

*Pet.* I say it is the moon that shines so bright.

*Kath.* I know it is the sun that shines so bright.

*Pet.* Now by my mother's son, and that's myself,

    It shall be moon, or star, or what I list,

    Or e'er I journey to your father's house.—

    [*To Servants.*] Go on, and fetch our horses back again.—

    Evermore cross'd and cross'd; nothing but cross'd.

*Hor.* Say as he says, or we shall never go.

*Kath.* Forward, I pray, since we have come so far,

    And be it moon, or sun, or what you please.

    And if you please to call it a rush-candle,

    Henceforth I vow it shall be so for me.

*Pet.* I say it is the moon.

*Kath.* I know it is the moon.

*Pet.* Nay, then you lie. It is the blessed sun.

*Kath.* Then, God be blest, it is the blessed sun.

    But sun it is not, when you say it is not,

    And the moon changes even as your mind.

    What you will have it nam'd, even that it is,

    And so it shall be so for Katharine.

                                [IV.v. 1–22]

From this moment on, Kate firmly rules while endlessly protesting her obedience to the delighted Petruchio, a marvelous Shakespearean reversal of Petruchio's earlier strategy of proclaiming Kate's mildness even as she raged on. There is no more charming a scene of married love in all Shakespeare than this little vignette on a street in Padua:

*Kath.* Husband, let's follow, to see the end of this ado.

*Pet.* First kiss me, Kate, and we will.

*Kath.* What, in the midst of the street?

*Pet.* What, art thou ashamed of me?

*Kath.* No, sir, God forbid; but ashamed to kiss.

*Pet.* Why, then, let's home again. Come, sirrah, let's away.

*Kath.* Nay, I will give thee a kiss. Now pray thee, love, stay.

*Pet.* Is not this well? Come, my sweet Kate.

Better once than never, for never too late.

Exeunt.

[V.i.130–38]

One would have to be tone deaf (or ideologically crazed) not to hear in this a subtly exquisite music of marriage at its happiest. I myself always begin teaching the *Shrew* with this passage, because it is a powerful antidote to all received nonsense, old and new, concerning this play. (One recent edition of the play offers extracts from English Renaissance manuals on wife beating, from which one is edified to learn that, on the whole, such exercise was not recommended. Since Kate does hit Petruchio, and he does not retaliate—though he warns her not to repeat this exuberance—it is unclear to me why wife beating is invoked at all.) Even subtler is Kate's long and famous speech, her advice to women concerning their behavior toward their husbands, just before the play concludes. Again, one would have to be very literal-minded indeed not to hear the delicious irony that is Kate's undersong, centered on the great line "I am asham'd that women are so simple." It requires a very good actress to deliver this set piece properly, and a better director than we tend to have now, if the actress is to be given her full chance, for she is advising women how to rule absolutely, while feigning obedience:

Fie, fie! Unknit that threatening unkind brow,
And dart not scornful glances from those eyes,
To wound thy lord, thy king, thy governor.
It blots thy beauty as frosts do bite the meads,
Confounds thy fame as whirlwinds shake fair buds,
And in no sense is meet or amiable.
A woman mov'd is like a fountain troubled,
Muddy, ill-seeming, thick, bereft of beauty,
And while it is so, none so dry or thirsty
Will deign to sip or touch one drop of it.

Thy husband is thy lord, thy life, thy keeper,
Thy head, thy sovereign; one that cares for thee,
And for thy maintenance; commits his body
To painful labour both by sea and land,
To watch the night in storms, the day in cold,
Whilst thou liest warm at home, secure and safe;
And craves no other tribute at thy hands
But love, fair looks, and true obedience;
Too little payment for so great a debt.
Such duty as the subject owes the prince
Even such a woman oweth to her husband.
And when she is froward, peevish, sullen, sour,
And not obedient to his honest will,
What is she but a foul contending rebel,
And graceless traitor to her loving lord?
I am asham'd that women are so simple
To offer war where they should kneel for peace,
Or seek for rule, supremacy, and sway,
When they are bound to serve, love, and obey.
Why are our bodies soft, and weak, and smooth,
Unapt to toil and trouble in the world,
But that our soft conditions and our hearts
Should well agree with our external parts?
Come, come, you froward and unable worms,
My mind hath been as big as one of yours,
My heart as great, my reason haply more,
To bandy word for word and frown for frown.
But now I see our lances are but straws,
Our strength as weak, our weakness past compare,
That seeming to be most which we indeed least are.
Then vail your stomachs, for it is no boot,
And place your hands below your husband's foot.
In token of which duty, if he please,
My hand is ready, may it do him ease.

[V.ii.137–80]

I have quoted this complete precisely because its redundancy and hyperbolical submissiveness are critical to its nature as a secret language or code now fully shared by Kate and Petruchio. "True obedience" here is considerably less sincere than it purports to be, or even if sexual politics are to be invoked, it is as immemorial as the Garden of Eden. "Strength" and "weakness" interchange their meanings, as Kate teaches not ostensible subservience but the art of her own will, a will considerably more refined than it was at the play's start. The speech's meaning explodes into Petruchio's delighted (and overdetermined) response:

Why, there's a wench! Come on, and kiss me, Kate.

If you want to hear this line as the culmination of a "problem play," then perhaps you yourself are the problem. Kate does not need to be schooled in "consciousness raising." Shakespeare, who clearly preferred his women characters to his men (always excepting Falstaff and Hamlet), enlarges the human, from the start, by subtly suggesting that women have the truer sense of reality.

# THE TWO GENTLEMEN
# OF VERONA

Though I have kept to the common ordering of the play, the weakest of all Shakespeare's comedies, *The Two Gentlemen of Verona*, also may be the earliest, if only because it is so much less impressive, in every register, than are *The Comedy of Errors* and *The Taming of the Shrew*. Never popular, whether in Shakespeare's time or our own, the *Two Gentlemen* might merit dismissal were it not partly rescued by the clown Launce, who leaps into life, and Launce's dog, Crab, who has more personality than anyone else in the play except Launce himself. Scholars esteem the *Two Gentlemen* as a presage of many better Shakespearean comedies, including the superb *Twelfth Night*, but that does not help much with the common playgoer or reader.

Directors and actors would do well to stage the *Two Gentlemen* as travesty or parody, the targets being the two Veronese friends of the title. Proteus, the protean cad, is almost outrageous enough to be interesting, but Valentine, aptly called a "lubber" (lout) by Launce, becomes worth consideration only when we take his perverseness seriously, since it appears to go considerably beyond a mere repressed bisexuality. The peculiar relationship between Valentine and Proteus *is* the play; one ought never to underestimate Shakespeare, and I uneasily sense that we have yet to understand *The Two Gentlemen of Verona*, a very experimental comedy. Exploring its equivocal aspects still will not raise the play to any eminence among Shakespearean comedies; only *The Merry Wives of Windsor* ranks lower, in my judgment, since it is a throwaway, with an impostor pretending to be Sir John Falstaff. Falstaff without titanic wit and metamorphic intelligence is not Falstaff, as Shakespeare himself best knew, and the *Merry Wives* is a scabrous exercise in sadomasochism, immensely popular forever on precisely that basis.

The plot of the *Two Gentlemen* is not even an absurdity. Proteus, more or less in love with the charming Julia (who more than reciprocates), departs unwillingly for the Emperor's court, there to join his best friend Valentine in learning the way of the world. Valentine, fiercely in love with Silvia (who secretly reciprocates), has a servant, Speed, a routine clown, whose friend is Proteus's man, Launce. To hear Launce go on about his dog is to apprehend the start of greatness in Shakespeare:

When a man's servant shall play the cur with him, look you, it goes hard: one that I brought up of a puppy; one that I saved from drowning, when three or four of his blind brothers and sisters went to it. I have taught him, even as one would say precisely 'thus I would teach a dog.' I was sent to deliver him as a present to Mistress Silvia from my master; and I came no sooner into the dining-chamber, but he steps me to her trencher, and steals her capon's leg. O, 'tis a foul thing when a cur cannot keep himself in all companies: I would have (as one should say) one that takes upon him to be a dog indeed, to be, as it were, a dog at all things. If I had not had more wit than he, to take a fault upon me that he did, I think verily he had been hanged for't; sure as I live he had suffered for't. You shall judge: he thrusts me himself into the company of three or four gentleman-like dogs, under the Duke's table; he had not been there (bless the mark) a pissing while, but all the chamber smelt him. 'Out with the dog', says one; 'What cur is that?' says another; 'Whip him out', says the third; 'Hang him up', says the Duke. I, having been acquainted with the smell before, knew it was Crab; and goes me to the fellow that whips the dogs: 'Friend,' quoth I, 'you mean to whip the dog?' 'Ay, marry, do I,' quoth he. 'You do him the more wrong,' quoth I; ''twas I did the thing you wot of.' He makes me no more ado, but whips me out of the chamber. How many masters would do this for his servant? Nay, I'll be sworn I have sat in the stocks, for puddings he hath stolen, otherwise he had been executed; I have stood on the pillory for geese he hath killed, otherwise he had suffered for't. Thou think'st not of this now. Nay, I remember the trick you served me, when I took my leave of Madam Silvia: did not I bid thee still mark me, and do as I do? When didst thou see me heave up my leg, and make water against a gentlewoman's farthingale? Didst thou ever see me do such a trick?

[IV.iv. 1–39]

Launce is so hearteningly a person (or rather person-with-dog) that I sometimes wonder why he is wasted upon *The Two Gentlemen of Verona*, which is not at all good enough for him. What remains of the plot is that Proteus, having fallen in love with Silvia's picture, slanders Valentine until the lout is sent into exile, where he is elected chief of an outlaw band. Julia, in what seems the first of Shakespeare's many such disguises, dresses as a boy to go in search of Proteus, and has the pleasure of hearing him proclaim his passion to Silvia, while he swears that his own love is deceased. Silvia, who has the good taste to scorn the cad, goes through the forest in quest of Valentine, accompanied by the brave Sir Eglamour, who in true Monty Python style runs for it when the outlaws capture the lady he supposedly defends. This farrago attains apotheosis when Proteus and the disguised Julia rescue Silvia, and Proteus immediately attempts to rape her, only to be frustrated by Valentine's entrance. What ensues between the two gentlemen is so manifestly peculiar that Shakespeare cannot have expected any audience to accept this, even as farce:

> *Val.* Thou common friend, that's without faith or love,
> For such is a friend now. Treacherous man,
> Thou hast beguil'd my hopes; nought but mine eye
> Could have persuaded me: now I dare not say
> I have one friend alive; thou wouldst disprove me.
> Who should be trusted now, when one's right hand

Is perjured to the bosom? Proteus,
I am sorry I must never trust thee more,
But count the world a stranger for thy sake.
The private wound is deepest: O time most accurst,
'Mongst all foes that a friend should be the worst!
*Pro.* My shame and guilt confounds me.
Forgive me, Valentine: if hearty sorrow
Be a sufficient ransom for offence,
I tender 't here; I do as truly suffer,
As e'er I did commit.
*Val.* Then I am paid;
And once again I do receive thee honest.
Who by repentance is not satisfied,
Is nor of heaven, nor earth; for these are pleas'd:
By penitence th' Eternal's wrath's appeased.
And that my love may appear plain and free,
All that was mine in Silvia I give thee.
*Jul.* O me unhappy!

                    *[She swoons.]*

                                    [V.iv.62–84]

Julia's reaction at least affords her some instant relief, while poor Silvia never utters another word in the play after she cries out 'O heaven!' when the lustful Proteus seizes her to commence his intended rape. What is the actress playing Silvia supposed to do with herself during the final hundred lines of *The Two Gentlemen of Verona*? She ought to whack Valentine with the nearest loose chunk of wood, but that would not knock any sense into the lummox, or into anyone else in this madness:

*Jul.* It is the lesser blot modesty finds,
Women to change their shapes, than men their minds.
*Pro.* Than men their minds? 'Tis true: O heaven, were man
But constant, he were perfect. That one error
Fills him with faults; makes him run through all th' sins;

Inconstancy falls off, ere it begins.
What is in Silvia's face but I may spy
More fresh in Julia's, with a constant eye?
*Val.* Come, come; a hand from either;
Let me be blest to make this happy close:
'Twere pity two such friends should be long foes.
*Pro.* Bear witness, heaven, I have my wish for ever.
*Jul.* And I mine.

[V.iv.107–19]

At least the nearly ravished Silvia is allowed to maintain her ambiguous silence; it is difficult to know whether Proteus or Valentine is the stupider here. In context, there is nothing in Shakespeare more unacceptable than the reformed Proteus's pragmatism: "What is in Silvia's face but I may spy / More fresh in Julia's, with a constant eye?" That means: any one woman will do as well as another. All men, Shakespeare hints, are invited to substitute any two women's names for Silvia and Julia.

Even the most solemn of Shakespearean scholars are aware that everything is amiss in the *Two Gentlemen*, but Shakespeare evidently could not have cared less. The cad and the booby, sent off to the Emperor's court by their severe fathers, somehow end up in Milan, or are they still in Verona? Clearly, it does not matter, nor do they matter, nor their unfortunate young women. Launce and his dog Crab matter; for the rest, I have to conclude that Shakespeare cheerfully and knowingly travesties love and friendship alike, thus clearing the ground for the greatness of his high romantic comedies, from *Love's Labour's Lost* through *Twelfth Night*.

PART II

THE FIRST HISTORIES

# HENRY VI

The chronology of Shakespeare's plays is only roughly a determined matter. In following Peter Alexander's suggestion that Shakespeare himself wrote the original version of *Hamlet*, presumably in 1588–89, I have extended Alexander by surmising that this earliest *Hamlet* could have been one of Shakespeare's first plays, and more a revenge history than a revenge tragedy. Something of the likely inadequacy of that inaugural *Hamlet* can be deduced from a consideration of what we now call (following the First Folio) *The First Part of King Henry the Sixth*. Written in 1589–90 (and then evidently revised in 1594–95), Shakespeare's play is bad enough that perhaps we should not lament the loss of the first *Hamlet*, which I suspect would have been at least as crude. Attempts by critics to ascribe much of *Henry VI, Part One*, to Robert Greene or George Peele, very minor dramatists, do not persuade me, though I would be pleased to believe that other botchers had been at work in addition to the very young Shakespeare. What I hear, though, is Marlowe's mode and rhetoric appropriated with great zest and courage but with little independence, as though the novice dramatist were wholly intoxicated by the *Tamburlaine* plays and *The Jew of Malta*. The laments for Henry V, whose funeral begins the play, sound rather like dirges for Tamburlaine the Great:

> *Bed.* Hung be the heavens with black, yield day to night!
> Comets, importing change of times and states,

Brandish your crystal tresses in the sky,
And with them scourge the bad revolting stars,
That have consented unto Henry's death!—
Henry the Fifth, too famous to live long!
England ne'er lost a king of so much worth.
*Glou.* England ne'er had a king until his time.
Virtue he had, deserving to command:
His brandish'd sword did blind men with his beams:
His arms spread wider than a dragon's wings:
His sparkling eyes, replete with wrathful fire,
More dazzled and drove back his enemies
Than mid-day sun fierce bent against their faces.
What should I say? His deeds exceed all speech:
He ne'er lift up his hand but conquered.
*Exe.* We mourn in black: why mourn we not in blood?
Henry is dead and never shall revive.
Upon a wooden coffin we attend;
And death's dishonourable victory
We with our stately presence glorify,
Like captives bound to a triumphant car.
What! shall we curse the planets of mishap
That plotted thus our glory's overthrow?

[I.i.1–24]

Change the names of the monarchs, substitute Scythia for England, and you would have passable Marlowe. Robert Greene was incapable of that good a Marlovian imitation, and George Peele shied away from too overt a tracking of Marlowe. The young Shakespeare, both here and in the first *Hamlet*, began with historical cartoons declaiming heroic bombast. There are some touches of lyricism and even of an intellectual music transcending Marlowe's, but these I assume came out of the 1594–95 revision, by which time Shakespeare had emerged into his own feast of language in *Love's Labour's Lost*. One rather doubts that Shakespeare's coarse travesty of Joan of Arc could chant like this in 1589–90:

Assign'd am I to be the English scourge,
This night the siege assuredly I'll raise:
Expect Saint Martin's summer, halcyon's days,
Since I have entered into these wars.
Glory is like a circle in the water,
Which never ceaseth to enlarge itself
Till by broad spreading it disperse to nought.
With Henry's death the English circle ends;
Dispersed are the glories it included.
Now am I like that proud insulting ship
Which Caesar and his fortune bare at once.

[I.ii.129–39]

Shakespeare's Joan is notoriously a Falstaffian wench rather than a
breath of Indian summer. Bawdy and unpleasant in certain scenes, courageous and direct in others, this version of Joan of Arc defeats criticism.
Shakespeare does not render her consistent; perhaps that was beyond his
powers at that moment in his development. Still, it is dangerous to undervalue even the novice Shakespeare, and Joan, though rather confusing, is
quirkily memorable. Why should she not be both a diabolic whore and a
political-military leader of peasant genius? Strident and shrewish, she gets
results, and being burned for a witch by English brutes is not calculated to
bring out the best in anyone. As a roaring girl, she has her own rancid
charm, and is certainly preferable to Shakespeare's protagonist, the brave
and tiresome Talbot. Joan is a virago, a warrior far more cunning than the
bully boy Talbot, and properly played she still has great appeal. Who
would want her to be as pompously virtuous as the current Amazons who
gratify male sadomasochism on television? Shakespeare is not so much
ambivalent toward his Joan as exploitative of her: she wants to win, and
whether victory comes in bed or on the battlefield is secondary. Moral
judgments, always foreign to Shakespeare's dramatic vision, are exposed by
*Henry VI, Part One,* as mere national prejudices. The French regard Joan as
the second coming of the biblical prophetess-warrior Deborah, while the
English condemn her as a Circe. What matter, Shakespeare pragmatically

implies, since either guise is incredibly potent, eclipsing every male personage, Talbot included. I differ considerably here from Leslie Fiedler,
who wrote that "everything about Joan enrages Shakespeare." Even near his
start, Shakespeare manifests no hostility toward any of his characters: his
Joan is uneasily comic yet essentially funny, and sometimes she effectively
satirizes male military vainglory. Her irony can be crude, even cruel, and
yet dramatically it always works, and though she is terribly burned by the
furious English, it is her spirit and not brave Talbot's that triumphs. We
never can quite catch up with Shakespeare's ironies; his Joan is a smudgy
cartoon compared with the human magnificence of his Falstaff, and yet she
anticipates something of Falstaff's grand contempt for time and the state.

If you judge Shakespeare to have maligned Joan of Arc, consider how
inadequate *Henry VI, Part One,* would be without her. She goes out cursing
(not very eloquently), but it remains her play, not Talbot's. That courageous captain-general expires, with his gallant son's corpse in his arms, but
Shakespeare fails dismally in Talbot's last words:

> Come, come, and lay him in his father's arms:
> My spirit can no longer bear these harms.
> Soldiers, adieu! I have what I would have,
> Now my old arms are young John Talbot's grave.
>
> [IV.vii.29–32]

Presumably this was intended as heroic pathos; either Shakespeare himself was unmoved by Talbot, which was likely, or else the poet-playwright
did not yet know how to express so oxymoronic an affect. King Henry VI
becomes a figure of authentic pathos, not at all heroic, in Parts Two and
Three, but in Part One his true piety and childlike decency are only hinted
at, as he rarely appears on stage, and then only as a presage of future disasters. Part Two is redeemed only by its fourth act (from Scene ii on),
which vividly depicts Jack Cade's Rebellion. Popular uprisings horrified
Shakespeare and yet freed his imagination; the comedy of the Cade scenes
is worthy of Shakespeare, bordering as it does upon both nightmare and
realistic representation:

*Cade.* Be brave then; for your captain is brave, and vows reformation.
There shall be in England seven half-penny loaves sold for a
penny; the three-hoop'd pot shall have ten hoops; and I will
make it felony to drink small beer. All the realm shall be in common, and in Cheapside shall my palfry go to grass. And when I
am king, as king I will be,—

*All.* God save your Majesty!

*Cade.* I thank you, good people—there shall be no money; all shall
eat and drink on my score, and I will apparel them all in one liv-
ery, that they may agree like brothers, and worship me their lord.

*But.* The first thing we do, let's kill all the lawyers.

*Cade.* Nay, that I mean to do. Is not this a lamentable thing, that of
the skin of an innocent lamb should be made parchment? that
parchment, being scribbled o'er, should undo a man? Some say
the bee stings; but I say, 'tis the bee's wax, for I did but seal once
to a thing, and I was never mine own man since. How now!
Who's there?

    *Enter some, bringing forward the Clerk of Chatham.*

*Wea.* The clerk of Chatham: he can write and read, and cast accompt.

*Cade.* O monstrous!

*Wea.* We took him setting of boys' copies.

*Cade.* Here's a villain!

*Wea.* H'as a book in his pocket with red letters in't.

*Cade.* Nay, then, he is a conjuror.

                                      [IV.ii.61–87]

    The mob will hang Cinna the poet in *Julius Caesar* for his name and his
bad verses; here they hang lawyers and anyone who is literate. "Hang him
with his pen and ink-horn about his neck" is Cade's command, and the
poor clerk is led forth to execution. Cade's splendid motto is: "But then are
we in order when we are most out of order," a wonderful anticipation of
Bakunin's Anarchist slogan: "The passion for destruction is a creative passion." Shakespeare grants Cade a zenith in the rebel leader's tirade to Lord
Say, antecedent to beheading Say and affixing his head to a pole:

Thou hast most traitorously corrupted the youth of the realm in erecting a grammar-school; and whereas, before, our forefathers had no other books but the score and the tally, thou hast caus'd printing to be used; and contrary to the King, his crown, and dignity, thou hast built a paper-mill. It will be prov'd to thy face that thou hast men about thee that usually talk of a noun, and a verb, and such abominable words as no Christian ear can endure to hear. Thou hast appointed justices of peace, to call poor men before them about matters they were not able to answer. Moreover, thou hast put them in prison; and because they could not read, thou hast hang'd them; when, indeed, only for that cause they have been most worthy to live.

(IV.vii.30–44)

"Grammar-school" and "a noun, and a verb" yield to the grand fun of "benefit of clergy" by which those who could read Latin escaped hanging and mutilation, even when convicted, as Ben Jonson did. Shakespeare, whatever his revulsion, manifests sufficient dramatic sympathy for Cade that the rebel makes a more eloquent dying speech than Talbot's:

Wither, garden; and be henceforth a burying-place to all that do dwell in this house, because the unconquered soul of Cade is fled.
[IV.x.65–67]

Jack Cade is to Part Two what Joan of Arc was to Part One: all that is memorable. Poor King Henry VI and his adulterous termagant wife, Queen Margaret, matter only when she chides him, "What are you made of? You'll nor fight nor fly." The Yorkists, even the monstrous Richard III-to-be, hardly can be distinguished from the loyalists. This changes in Part Three, which lacks a Joan or a Cade yet still seems to me the best of the three plays (Dr. Johnson preferred the second). Richard makes the difference; everyone else blends into a harmony of Marlovian rant, even the lamenting King Henry, while the sinister hunchback revises Marlowe so as to achieve a more individual tone:

And I,—like one lost in a thorny wood,
That rents the thorns and is rent with the thorns,
Seeking a way, and straying from the way;
Not knowing how to find the open air,
But toiling desperately to find it out—
Torment myself to catch the English crown:
And from that torment I will free myself,
Or hew my way out with a bloody axe.
Why, I can smile, and murder whiles I smile,
And cry 'Content!' to that that grieves my heart,
And wet my cheeks with artificial tears,
And frame my face to all occasions.
I'll drown more sailors than the Mermaid shall;
I'll slay more gazers than the basilisk;
I'll play the orator as well as Nestor,
Deceive more slily than Ulysses could,
And, like a Sinon, take another Troy.
I can add colors to the chameleon,
Change shapes with Proteus for advantages,
And set the murderous Machiavel to school.
Can I do this, and cannot get a crown?
Tut! were it further off, I'll pluck it down.

[III.ii.174–95]

We still hear in this Marlowe's Barabas, Jew of Malta, who will not abandon the Machiavel of *Richard III*, but the hyperboles convey considerably more cognitive zest than Shakespeare imparts to Queen Margaret's diatribes. She is at the borders of madness; Richard is madly charming, so long as he remains on stage or page. The butchery of King Henry VI, in the Tower of London, is carried out by Richard with commendable gusto, after which he rewards us with a secular prophecy of his future:

I that have neither pity, love, nor fear.
Indeed, 'tis true that Henry told me of:

For I have often heard my mother say
I came into the world with my legs forward.
Had I not reason, think ye, to make haste
And seek their ruin that usurp'd our right?
The midwife wonder'd, and the women cried
'O Jesu bless us, he is born with teeth!'
And so I was, which plainly signified
That I should snarl and bite and play the dog.
Then, since the heavens have shap'd my body so,
Let hell make crook'd my mind to answer it.
I have no brother, I am like no brother;
And this word 'love' which greybeards call divine,
Be resident in men like one another,
And not in me: I am myself alone.
Clarence, beware; thou keep'st me from the light,
But I will sort a pitchy day for thee;
For I will buzz abroad such prophecies
That Edward shall be fearful of his life;
And then, to purge his fear, I'll be thy death.
King Henry and the Prince his son are gone;
Clarence, thy turn is next, and then the rest,
Counting myself but bad till I be best.
I'll throw thy body in another room,
And triumph, Henry, in thy day of doom.

[V.vi.68–93]

"I am myself alone" is the Crookbackian motto, and seems to me the prime aesthetic justification for the *Henry VI* plays. They do not live now except for the triad of Joan, Jack Cade, and Richard, all Shakespearean exercises in the representation of evil, and all vivid comedians. *Richard III*, whether in its strengths or its limitations, owes its energy and brilliance to the laboratory of the three parts of *Henry VI*. That is justification enough for Shakespeare's immersion in the Wars of the Roses.

# KING JOHN

*The Life and Death of King John* may have been written as early as 1590, or as late as 1595 or even 1596. Since evidence continues to accumulate that Shakespeare was as facile a self-revisionist as he was a playmaker (the Elizabethan term for it), I suspect that Shakespeare first composed *King John* in 1590 and severely reworked it in 1594–95, saving the play by vitalizing the portrayal of Faulconbridge the Bastard, natural son of King Richard Coeur-de-Lion. What we think of as "Shakespearean character" does not begin with a Marlovian cartoon like Richard III, but with Faulconbridge in *King John*, who speaks his own highly individual language, combines heroism with comic intensity, and possesses a psychic interior. Even Faulconbridge cannot altogether redeem *King John*, which is a very mixed play, with Shakespeare fighting Marlowe's influence and winning only when Faulconbridge speaks. Though the Bastard is only a vivid sketch compared with the Hamlet of 1601, he shares Falstaff's and Hamlet's quality of being too large for the play he inhabits. Readers are likely to feel that the natural son of Richard the Lion Heart deserves a better play than the one in which he finds himself, and a better king to serve than his wretched uncle, John. Being a hopeless Romantic (my critical enemies would say, a sentimentalist), I would also like Falstaff at the end of *Henry IV, Part Two*, to forget the ungrateful Prince Hal and go off cheerfully to the Forest of Arden in *As You Like It*. And Hamlet clearly deserves a better life and death than the Elsinore of Claudius affords him. The

Bastard's greatness is not of the order of Falstaff's or of Hamlet's, but it is authentic enough to dwarf everyone else in *King John*.

There is already a touch of Falstaffian wit and irreverence in Faulconbridge; he is the first character in Shakespeare who fully can charm and arouse us, particularly because no one before in a Shakespearean play is so persuasive a representation of a person. It is not too much to say that the Bastard in *King John* inaugurates Shakespeare's invention of the human, which is the subject of this book. What made Faulconbridge's startling reality (or, if you prefer, the illusion of such reality) possible? The other characters in *King John*, including John himself, still have upon them the stigmata of Marlowe's high, vaunting rhetoric. With Faulconbridge the Bastard, Shakespeare's own world begins, and that originality, difficult as it is now to isolate, has become our norm for representation of fictive personages.

It is appropriate that the Bastard is not a historical figure but was developed by Shakespeare from a mere hint in the chronicler Holinshed. A few of Shakespeare's contemporaries, including Ben Jonson (much the greatest among them), ascribed his mode of representation to nature as much as to art. They saw in Shakespeare something of what we still see in him, and by calling it "nature" they prophesied our deepest tribute to Shakespeare, since the common reader continues to regard Shakespeare's persons as being more natural than those of all other authors. Shakespeare's language never merely purports accurately to represent nature. Rather, it reinvents "nature," in ways that, as A. D. Nuttall splendidly remarks, allow us to see much in human character that doubtless was there already but which we never could have seen had we not read Shakespeare, and seen him well performed (increasingly an unlikely happening, since directors, alas, have taken their cues from fashionable critics).

Faulconbridge is Shakespeare's only amiable bastard, unlike the Don John of *Much Ado About Nothing*, Thersites in *Troilus and Cressida*, and the sublimely fearsome Edmund of *King Lear*. It is wonderfully appropriate that Shakespeare's first truly "natural" character should be a natural son of Richard the Lion Heart, who had become a hero of English folklore. Faulconbridge is himself lionhearted, and indeed avenges his father by slaying the Duke of Austria, who had turned loose a lion upon his captive, the Crusader English king. Critics agree that Faulconbridge's appeal to English audiences is that he is both royal by blood and yet only gentry by upbringing and on his mother's side, seduced as she was by King Richard I. The Bastard thus stands in *King John* for all the popular virtues: loyalty to the monarchy, courage, plainspokenness, honesty, and a refusal to be deceived, whether by foreign princes or domestic churchmen, or by the Pope and his minions. Though Shakespeare has the Bastard vow that he will worship Commodity, or Machiavellian self-interest, neither Faulconbridge nor the audience believes this exasperated declaration. The authentic self-revelation by the Bastard comes in Act I, Scene i, when he has changed his identity from Philip Faulconbridge, heir to his supposed father's modest lands, to Sir Richard Plantagenet, landless but the son of his actual father, the demigod Richard the Lion Heart:

> A foot of honour better than I was,
> But many a many foot of land the worse.
> Well, now can I make any Joan a lady.
> "Good den, Sir Richard!"—"God-a-mercy, fellow!"—
> And if his name be George, I'll call him Peter;
> For new-made honour doth forget men's names:
> 'Tis too respective and too sociable
> For your conversion. Now your traveller,
> He and his toothpick at my worship's mess,
> And when my knightly stomach is suffic'd,
> Why then I suck my teeth and catechize
> My picked man of countries: "My dear sir,"—
> Thus, leaning on mine elbow, I begin,
> "I shall beseech you,"—that is Question now;
> And then comes Answer like an Absey book:
> "O sir," says Answer, "at your best command;
> At your employment; at your service, sir:"
> "No, sir," says Question, "I, sweet sir, at yours:"
> And so, ere Answer knows what Question would,

Saving in dialogue of compliment,
And talking of the Alps and Apennines,
The Pyrenean and the river Po,
It draws toward supper in conclusion so.
But this is worshipful society,
And fits the mounting spirit like myself;
For he is but a bastard to the time
That doth not smack of observation;
And so am I, whether I smoke or no.
And not alone in habit and device,
Exterior form, outward accoutrement,
But from the inward motion to deliver
Sweet, sweet, sweet poison for the age's tooth:
Which, though I will not practise to deceive,
Yet, to avoid deceit, I mean to learn;
For it shall strew the footsteps of my rising.

[I.i.182–216]

I follow Harold Goddard in hearing Shakespeare's own enterprise as poet-playwright in the Bastard's motto:

But from the inward motion to deliver
Sweet, sweet, sweet poison for the age's tooth:
Which, though I will not practise to deceive,
Yet, to avoid deceit, I mean to learn;

"Poison" here is not flattery but truth, and both the Bastard and Shakespeare assert their refusal to be deceived. How much of English literature comes out of the Bastard's monologue! In it one can hear, prophetically, Swift, Sterne, Dickens, and Browning, and a long tradition that reverberates still in the century now ending. The social humor of the Bastard, original with Shakespeare (try to interpolate this soliloquy anywhere into Marlowe), can be said to have invented the English satirist abroad, or the man of withdrawn sensibility returned home to observe, without deception or illusion. No one in Shakespeare before Faulconbridge speaks with so inward a motion, or with so subtly barbed an inflection. What helps make this character so formidable is that, more than Talbot in *Henry VI*, he is Shakespeare's first great captain, a soldier who preludes Othello in the Moor's prelapsarian greatness. "Keep up your bright swords or the dew will rust them" is Othello's single line that stops a street battle. That voice of authority is presaged when the Bastard warns a noble who rashly draws his sword, "Your sword is bright, sir, put it up again."

I return to my earlier question, as to what made the breakthrough of Faulconbridge possible for Shakespeare. Ben Jonson, rival yet close friend to his fellow actor-playmaker, in his tributary poem for the First Folio, says that nature herself was proud of Shakespeare's designs, a reference not only to Shakespeare's natural endowment but also to the way in which he exemplified a great metaphor in *The Winter's Tale*: "The art itself is nature." The Bastard himself is nature, and consciously is supremely artful, indeed theatrical. When the city of Angiers will not admit the army of either the King of England or of France, Faulconbridge sums up the moment in a mode that Shakespeare will exploit with ever-greater cunning:

> By heaven, these scroyles of Angiers flout you, kings,
> And stand securely on their battlements,
> As in a theatre, whence they gape and point
> At your industrious scenes and acts of death.

> [II.i.373–76]

No one before Faulconbridge in Shakespeare is overtly theatrical in this new way, which adds to the self-referential gloating of Marlowe's Barabas (repeated by Aaron the Moor and Richard III) a doubling effect, confronting the action with the actors, simultaneously destroying and enhancing illusion. But Tamburlaine and Barabas are firmly in the game, while praising themselves for their perceptual victories; the Bastard is both in and out of the game, watching and wondering at it.

Shakespearean protagonists from Faulconbridge on (Richard II, Juliet, Mercutio, Bottom, Shylock, Portia) prepare the way for Falstaff by manifesting an intensity of being far in excess of their dramatic contexts. They all suggest unused potentialities that their plays do not require of them. The Bastard ought to be king, because nobody else in *King John* is at all kingly. Richard II ought to be a metaphysical poet; Mercutio's vitalism deserves to find some expression beyond bawdry; Bottom's wonderfully good-humored, almost preternatural patience might weave an even more bottomless dream; Shylock's desperate will to avenge insults could get beyond evil farce by forsaking literalism; Juliet and Portia warrant lovers more equal to them than Romeo and Bassanio. Instead of fitting the role to the play, the post-Marlovian Shakespeare creates personalities who never could be accommodated by their roles: excess marks them not as hyperboles or Marlovian overreachers, but as overflowing spirits, more meaningful than the sum of their actions. Falstaff is their first culmination, because his mastery of language is so absolute, yet from the Bastard on they all have an eloquence individual enough to intimate what will come: characters who are "free artists of themselves" (Hegel on Shakespeare's personages), and who can give the impression that they are at work attempting to make their own plays. When we confront Hamlet, Iago, Edmund, Lear, Edgar, Macbeth, and Cleopatra, we cannot ever be certain that they are not carrying free artistry of the self beyond the limits that Shakespeare only *seems* to set for them. Trespassers defiant of formal and societal overdeterminations, they give the sense that all plot is arbitrary, whereas personality, however daemonic, is transcendent, and is betrayed primarily by what's within. They have an interior to journey out from, even if they cannot always get back to their innermost recesses. And they never are reduced to their fates; they are more, much more, than what happens to them. There is a substance to them that prevails; the major Shakespearean protagonists have souls that cannot be extinguished.

2

The character of Shakespeare's King John has few critical defenders; the most formidable is E.A.J. Honigmann, who deprecates the Bastard Faulconbridge so as to enhance John's status as the play's protagonist.

Honigmann's John is a brilliant politician, who attempts to know every-one's price and to buy everyone off, but who also possesses "ungovernable passion as well as cunning dissimulation in his heart." One can agree with Honigmann's shrewd observation that these irreconcilable psychological elements, properly played, keep John a "puzzle and a surprise" for the audience.

Alas, John is mostly a dour puzzle and an unhappy surprise: he is half-way between the Marlovian cartoon of his ranting, dreadful mother, Queen Eleanor, and the Shakespearean inwardness of the flamboyant Bastard.

John's peculiar interest for Shakespeare's audience was the king's am-biguous allusiveness to Queen Elizabeth's political dilemmas. Arthur, John's nephew, was the legitimate heir to Richard the Lion Heart, just as Mary Queen of Scots could have been regarded as the rightful heir to King Henry VIII, after the brief reigns of Elizabeth's half brother Edward VI and half sister Mary. The parallels are certainly there between King John and Queen Elizabeth I: papal excommunication, a foreign armada sent against England, even the plots against the "usurping" monarchs by English nobles, whom the invading forces intend to eliminate when their purpose has been served.

To compare, however implicitly, the ill-fated John and Elizabeth was rather dangerous, and Shakespeare is too circumspect to overwork the parallels. The Spanish Armada was defeated, and then wrecked by storm in the Hebrides, in the summer of 1588; in 1595 rumors swept London that a new Spanish Armada was coming together at Lisbon. Whether *King John*, as a kind of "Armada play," is likelier to have been written in 1590 or 1595 therefore cannot be determined by outward events alone. I tend to agree with Peter Alexander and with Honigmann that Shakespeare's *King John* is the source, not the heir, of *The Troublesome Raigne of John King of England* (1591), an anonymous play even more Marlovian than Shakespeare's.

Though Shakespeare's *King John* was a popular success, its fortunes through the centuries have been very mixed. Honigmann conjectures that in its first performances, by the combined Lord Strange's men and the Lord Admiral's men, Edward Alleyn (Marlowe's Tamburlaine) played John, and Richard Burbage (later, Shakespeare's Hamlet) appeared as the Bastard

Faulconbridge. The best *King John* I have seen was in 1948 at Stratford, with Anthony Quayle as the Bastard and Robert Helpmann as John. Though the play (because of the Bastard) seems to me far superior to *Richard III* (1592–93), it is no surprise that it receives, these days, infinitely fewer performances than the endlessly popular *Richard III*. There is something curiously antithetical about *King John*, with much in it that is Marlovian rant, yet much more that is very subtle and memorable. I associate this mystery of the play with the greatest mystery in Shakespeare, which is the missing first *Hamlet*, where I have followed Peter Alexander's lead in believing that "lost" work to be Shakespeare's own, partly embedded in the texts of *Hamlet* that we now possess. The common mystery is the nature of Shakespeare's complex apprenticeship to Marlowe's example, the only influence relationship that ever troubled the greatest and ultimately the most original of all writers.

3

One of the apparent faults of *King John* is that it divides into two plays, Acts I–III and IV–V. John Blanpied, analyzing this, usefully calls the Bastard a satiric improviser in I–III, who thus humanizes the drama for us. But in the chaotic world of IV–V, John falls apart, in a kind of hysteria, and the Bastard seems lost and confused, though always still a fighter and fiercely loyal to John. Blanpied does not say so, but Shakespeare hints that the Bastard's attachment to John (who is his uncle) is essentially filial and repeats the pattern of John's relation to his dreadful mother Eleanor, whose death helps precipitate John's collapse. When the two roles are properly interpreted and acted, I do not think either the Bastard's role or John's diminishes in interest or strength in Acts IV–V, and so I think the play's two-part division, while strange, is not ultimately a flaw. Faulconbridge ceases to delight us as much in the play's second part, but his inwardness (as I will show) is only augmented as he darkens. He opens a new mode for Shakespeare, one that will achieve apotheosis in the greatness of Sir John Falstaff. In Act II, in front of besieged Angiers, reacting to the dubious bargain struck by John and the King of France, the Bastard delivers the greatest of his monologues, an enlivening discourse upon "commodity": worldly self-interest and political payoff:

Mad world! mad kings! mad composition!
John, to stop Arthur's title in the whole,
Hath willingly departed with a part:
And France, whose armour conscience buckled on,
Whom zeal and charity brought to the field
As God's own soldier, rounded in the ear
With that same purpose-changer, that sly divel,
That broker, that still breaks the pate of faith,
That daily break-vow, he that wins of all,
Of kings, of beggars, old men, young men, maids,
Who, having no external thing to lose
But the word "maid," cheats the poor maid of that,
That smooth-fac'd gentleman, tickling commodity,
Commodity, the bias of the world,
The world, who of itself is peised well,
Made to run even upon even ground,
Till this advantage, this vile drawing bias,
This sway of motion, this commodity,
Makes it take head from all indifferency,
From all direction, purpose, course, intent:
And this same bias, this commodity,
This bawd, this broker, this all-changing word,
Clapp'd on the outward eye of fickle France,
Hath drawn him from his own determin'd aid,
From a resolv'd and honourable war,
To a most base and vile-concluded peace.
And why rail I on this commodity?
But for because he hath not woo'd me yet:
Not that I have the power to clutch my hand,
When his fair angels would salute my palm;
But for my hand, as unattempted yet,

Like a poor beggar, raileth on the rich.
Well, whiles I am a beggar, I will rail
And say there is no sin but to be rich;
And being rich, my virtue then shall be
To say there is no vice but beggary.
Since kings break faith upon commodity,
Gain, be my lord, for I will worship thee!

[II.i.561–98]

He will, of course, not worship gain, and will continue "from the inward motion to deliver / Sweet, sweet, sweet poison for the age's tooth," yet the shadow of "commodity" henceforward begins to darken his exuberance. Sent off by John to rob the English monasteries, he chants:

Bell, book, and candle shall not drive me back
When gold and silver becks me to come on:

[III.ii.22–23]

That is not exactly Faulconbridge at his best, but who in *King John*, except poor Arthur, is truly worth the Bastard's concern? Harold Goddard wisely compares Faulconbridge on Commodity with Shakespeare himself on Time and Policy in two magnificent sonnets, 123 and 124. Sonnet 124 in particular seems to me almost a gloss upon the Bastard's authentic defiance of timeserving:

If my dear love were but the child of state,
It might for Fortune's bastard be unfather'd,
As subject to Time's love, or to Time's hate,
Weeds among weeds, or flowers with flowers gather'd.
No, it was builded far from accident;
It suffers not in smiling pomp, nor falls
Under the blow of thralled discontent,
Whereto th' inviting time our fashion calls;
It fears not policy, that heretic,

Which works on leases of short-numb'red hours,
But all alone stands hugely politic,
That it nor grows with heat, nor drowns with show'rs.
    To this I witness call the fools of Time,
    Which die for goodness, who have liv'd for crime.

Except for the Bastard and the innocent Arthur, everyone in *King John* is among "the fools of Time," where "fools" means "victims." Desperate as the mother-dominated John is, neither he nor either of the two insanely driven royal women—Eleanor and Constance—is the prime fool of Time in the play. That has to be the Papal Legate, Cardinal Pandolph, a precursor of the Ulysses of *Troilus and Cressida*, and even more of Iago. Shakespeare sees to it that Pandolph alienates his audience every time he speaks, but it is Pandolph, high priest of Commodity and of Policy, who alone triumphs in this play. It is not that the Bastard is defeated, but the death of the boy Arthur, and the endless, twisted weakness of John finally have their effect upon even this most exuberant of Shakespeare's earliest inventors of the human:

*Hubert.* Who art thou?
*Bastard.* Who thou wilt: and if thou please
    Thou mayst befriend me so much as to think
    I come one way of the Plantagenets.

[V.vi.9–11]

That wry assertion of self-identity is extraordinarily unrepresentative of Faulconbridge, whose sense of himself as Richard the Lion Heart's natural son is everywhere else so celebratory and vehement. But loving John as king-father carries a high cost: John is not a mother's boy in the heroic mode of Coriolanus. Rather, John is a treacherous coward, even if one grants Honigmann his high evaluation of John as a politician. Historians remember John now only for his enforced granting of the Magna Carta to his barons, a matter so uninteresting to Shakespeare that he omits it altogether. Essentially, Shakespeare's John pragmatically abdicates to the Bastard when, at the worst of times, he appoints his nephew all power to exercise against the French and the rebel English nobles: "Have thou the ordering of this present time." The finest tribute to the Bastard as a fighter is made in some desperation by Salisbury, one of the rebels:

> That misbegotten devil, Faulconbridge,
> In spite of spite, alone upholds the day.
>
> [V.iv.4–5]

Against all odds, almost single-handedly, the Bastard maintains the glory of his actual father, the Lion Heart. Shakespeare concludes the play with a patriotic clarion call by the Bastard that reverberates against the dying music of John, who speaks most memorably out of the bodily tortures of having been poisoned:

> Poison'd, ill fare; dead, forsook, cast off:
> And none of you will bid the winter come
> To thrust his icy fingers in my maw,
> Nor let my kingdom's rivers take their course
> Through my burn'd bosom, nor entreat the north
> To make his bleak winds kiss my parched lips
> And comfort me with cold. I do not ask you much,
> I beg cold comfort; and you are so strait,
> And so ingrateful, you deny me that.
>
> [V.vii.35–43]

It is the only time that John moves us, though even here Shakespeare distances us from this pathos, since we also could offer only cold comfort. The distance departs with the Bastard's battle cry, which concludes the play:

> O, let us pay the time but needful woe,
> Since it hath been beforehand with our griefs.
> This England never did, nor never shall,

Lie at the proud foot of a conqueror,
But when it first did help to wound itself.
Now these her princes are come home again
Come the three corners of the world in arms
And we shall shock them! Nought shall make us rue
If England to itself do rest but true!

[V.vii.110–18]

This speech seems to me poetically preferable to such effusions as John of Gaunt's "this sceptred isle" and Henry V's "we happy few." Perhaps I am swayed by liking the Bastard Faulconbridge considerably more than I do Gaunt or the betrayer of Falstaff, but the image of self-wounding is of a higher order than any in the other two speeches. Overtly, the Bastard refers to the rebels returning to royal authority, but the image clearly comprehends John's hysterical personality and dubious moral character, at least in Shakespeare's own judgment. The spirit of Christopher Marlowe still dominates *King John*, and only Faulconbridge evades Marlowe's preference for outwardness. John himself is in part a Marlovian cartoon, and unsatisfactory as such, unable "from the inward motion to deliver / Sweet, sweet, sweet poison for the age's tooth."

# 6

# RICHARD III

Still not emancipated from Marlowe's influence, Shakespeare never-theless achieved a permanent success in *Richard III*, an immense im-provement over the *Henry VI* ranting contests. This melodrama retains astonishing vitality, though it is far more uneven than its reputation sug-gests. Richard *is* his play; no other role matters much, as Ralph Richardson seemed to learn in Laurence Olivier's effective film of *Richard III*, where Richardson did what he could with Buckingham, not a rewarding part. Clarence has some limited interest, but this drama centers more fully upon its hero-villain than anything by Shakespeare composed up to 1591, un-less the first *Hamlet* indeed existed by then. Marlowe seems to be taking back his own from the *Henry VI* plays in his *Edward II*, and it is very diffi-cult to decide whether *Richard III* parodies Marlowe or *Edward II* counter-parodies Shakespeare's play.

We do not know, but it is a safe surmise that the two rival dramatists consciously exchanged influences and suggestions. Tradition has left us no anecdotes concerning any encounters between Marlowe and Shake-speare, but they must have met frequently, sharing the leadership of the London stage until Marlowe's murder by the government in early 1593. Marlowe personally may have frightened Shakespeare rather in the way that Richard III shocks audiences; Shakespeare was anything but personally violent, while Marlowe was a veteran street fighter, a counterintelligence agent, and generally bad news, in ways that can remind us of Villon and

Rimbaud, neither of them pillars of society. I tend to interpret Shakespeare's Richard III as another parody of Barabas, Jew of Malta, like Aaron the Moor, and so as another step toward the brilliant portrait of the then long-dead Marlowe as Edmund in *King Lear*. Marlowe personally may have been fiercely parodistic, if we can believe the testimony extracted from Thomas Kyd under government torture.

What is certain is that Richard III is a grand parodist—of Marlowe, of stage conventions, and of himself. That is the secret of his outrageous charm; his great power over the audience and the other figures in his drama is a compound of charm and terror, hardly to be distinguished in his sadomasochistic seduction of the Lady Anne, whose husband and father-in-law alike he has slaughtered. His sadistic pleasure in manipulating Anne (and others) is related to his extreme version of skeptical naturalism, in no way like Montaigne's but perhaps like Marlowe's own. Richard's skepticism excludes piety; his naturalism makes us all beasts. Far cruder than Iago and Edmund, Richard nevertheless is their forerunner, particularly in his self-conscious triumphalism.

Josephine Tey's deft mystery novel *The Daughter of Time* (1951) is a useful guide to one aspect of Shakespeare's achievement in *Richard III*, which is his permanent imposition of the official Tudor version of history upon our imaginations. In Tey's story a bedridden Scotland Yard inspector, aided by a young American researcher, clears Richard of his crimes, including the murder of the little princes in the Tower. Tey makes the case for Richard very strong indeed, and some modern historians confirm her judgment, but as Tey herself implicitly concedes, you cannot fight Shakespeare and win. Richard III for all time will be an entertaining villain, and Henry VII (Richmond in the play) will be an heroic liberator, though it is most likely that *he* ordered the murder of the little princes in the Tower. As a dramatic achievement (within its limits) *Richard III* is unaffected by any historical revisions, but they are worth mentioning because Shakespeare's extraordinary excess in representing Richard's villainy may conceal ironic doubts in the playwright himself. Shakespeare viewed history not from the political perspectives of Sir Thomas More or Hall or Holinshed, let alone from those of modern scholarly historicists, old and new, but pretty much from the stance of Sir John Falstaff. Think of Falstaff as the author of *Richard III*, and you cannot go too far wrong. "Give me life" and "there's honor for you" are Shakespeare's superbly sane attitudes as he cheerfully contemplates the royal and noble butchers who infest his stage histories. Falstaff, like Shakespeare, loves play and plays, and prudently avoids the nonsense of dynastic loyalties. We will never know how Shakespeare truly regarded the historical Richard III; the Tudor cartoon was wonderful *materia poetica* for playful purposes, and that was more than enough.

Richard's zest, his antic glee in his own diabolism, ought to be infectious, unlike Iago's superior gusto, which authentically awes and frightens us. The best stage Richard I've seen, Ian McKellen, was perhaps too powerful in the part, rendering the comic villain as though he had been transformed into a blend of Iago and Macbeth. But Shakespeare's Richard is still overtly Marlovian, a master of persuasive language rather than a profound psychologist or a criminal visionary. This Richard has no inwardness, and when Shakespeare attempts to imbue him with an anxious inner self, on the eve of his fatal battle, the result is poetic bathos and dramatic disaster. Starting up out of bad dreams, Richard suddenly does not seem to be Richard, and Shakespeare scarcely knows how to represent the change:

> Give me another horse! Bind up my wounds!
> Have mercy, Jesu!—Soft, I did but dream.
> O coward conscience, how dost thou afflict me!
> The lights burn blue; it is now dead midnight.
> Cold fearful drops stand on my trembling flesh.
> What do I fear? Myself? There's none else by;
> Richard loves Richard, that is, I am I.
> Is there a murderer here? No. Yes, I am!
> Then fly. What, from myself? Great reason why,
> Lest I revenge? What, myself upon myself?
> Alack, I love myself. Wherefore? For any good
> That I myself have done unto myself?
> O no, alas, I rather hate myself
> For hateful deeds committed by myself.

I am a villain—yet I lie, I am not!
Fool, of thyself speak well! Fool, do not flatter.
My conscience hath a thousand several tongues,
And every tongue brings in a several tale,
And every tale condemns me for a villain:
Perjury, perjury, in the highest degree;
Murder, stern murder, in the direst degree;
All several sins, all us'd in each degree,
Throng to the bar, crying all, 'Guilty, guilty!'
I shall despair. There is no creature loves me,
And if I die, no soul will pity me—
And wherefore should they, since that I myself
Find in myself no pity to myself?
Methought the souls of all that I had murder'd
Came to my tent, and every one did threat
Tomorrow's vengeance on the head of Richard.

[V.iii.178–207]

I cannot think of another passage, even in the tedious clamor of much of the *Henry VI* plays, in which Shakespeare is so inept. Soon enough, the playwright of *Richard III* would transcend Marlowe, but here the urge to modify from speaking cartoon to psychic inwardness finds no art to accommodate the passage. Even if one alters line 184 to "Richard loves Richard, that is, I am I," it would remain dreadful, and the half dozen lines following are even worse. The peculiar badness is difficult to describe, though the fallacy of imitative form is nowhere better illustrated. The disjunctions in Richard's self-consciousness are meant to be reflected by the abrupt rhetorical questions and exclamations of lines 183–89, but no actor can salvage Richard from sounding silly in this staccato outburst. We can see what Shakespeare is trying to accomplish when we study the speech, but we cannot do for the poet what he has not yet learned to do for himself. And yet Shakespeare requires no defense; only Chaucer, at least in English, had mastered a rhetoric of self-overhearing, and only in a few places, with the Pardoner and with the Wife of Bath. Soon enough, in the

Romantic triad of *Romeo and Juliet, Richard II*, and *A Midsummer Night's Dream*,
Shakespeare leaps to perfection in the representation of inwardness and its
permutations. Compare Richard III to Bottom, awakening from his bottomless dream, and the glory of the transition is made manifest.

Another blemish of *Richard III* is the ghastly Margaret, widow of
Henry VI, for whom Shakespeare never could compose a decent line.
Since *Richard III* is of exorbitant length, Shakespeare would have been
much better without the long-winded Margaret, who curses in triplicate
and beyond. But then *Richard III* is any actress's nightmare, for none of the
women's parts are playable, whether poor Anne's, once Richard has seduced her through terror, or those of Elizabeth, Edward IV's queen and
widow, or the Duchess of York, Richard's mother. Declamation is all Shakespeare allows them, almost as though Margaret's rantings have set a gender style. From Juliet on, Shakespeare was to surpass all precursors, from
the Bible to Chaucer, in the representation of women, but no one could
surmise that on the basis of *Richard III*. The male characters of the play, except for the malformed Richard, are not particularly individualized either,
the one exception being the Duke of Clarence, who is rendered vivid by
his account of an astonishing dream. We remember Clarence for his unfortunate fate, first stabbed and then finished off by being drowned in a
butt of Malmsey wine, but also for his great dream—Shakespeare's dream,
as I would prefer to call it, since it is the most powerful in all his work. Pent
up in the Tower, Clarence tells the dream to his Keeper:

> Methoughts that I had broken from the Tower,
> And was embark'd to cross to Burgundy;
> And in my company my brother Gloucester,
> Who from my cabin tempted me to walk
> Upon the hatches, hence we look'd toward England,
> And cited up a thousand heavy times,
> During the wars of York and Lancaster,
> That had befall'n us. As we pac'd along
> Upon the giddy footing of the hatches,
> Methought that Gloucester stumbled, and in falling,

Struck me (that thought to stay him) overboard,
Into the tumbling billows of the main.
O Lord! Methought what pain it was to drown:
What dreadful noise of waters in my ears;
What sights of ugly death within my eyes!
Methoughts I saw a thousand fearful wrecks;
Ten thousand men that fishes gnaw'd upon;
Wedges of gold, great anchors, heaps of pearl,
Inestimable stones, unvalu'd jewels,
All scatter'd in the bottom of the sea.
Some lay in dead men's skulls, and in the holes
Where eyes did once inhabit, there were crept—
As 'twere in scorn of eyes—reflecting gems,
That woo'd the slimy bottom of the deep,
And mock'd the dead bones that lay scatter'd by.
*Keep.* Had you such leisure in the time of death
    To gaze upon these secrets of the deep?
*Cla.* Methought I had; and often did I strive
    To yield the ghost, but still the envious flood
    Stopp'd in my soul, and would not let it forth
    To find the empty, vast, and wand'ring air,
    But smother'd it within my panting bulk,
    Which almost burst to belch it in the sea.
*Keep.* Awak'd you not in this sore agony?
*Cla.* No, no; my dream was lengthen'd after life.
    O, then began the tempest to my soul:
    I pass'd, methought, the melancholy flood,
    With that sour ferryman which poets write of,
    Unto the kingdom of perpetual night.
    The first that there did greet my stranger-soul
    Was my great father-in-law, renowned Warwick,
    Who spake aloud, 'What scourge for perjury
    Can this dark monarchy afford false Clarence?'
    And so he vanish'd. Then came wand'ring by

A shadow like an angel, with bright hair
Dabbled in blood; and he shriek'd out aloud,
'Clarence is come: false, fleeting, perjur'd Clarence,
That stabb'd me in the field of Tewkesbury!
Seize on him, Furies! Take him unto torment!'
With that, methoughts, a legion of foul fiends
Environ'd me, and howled in mine ears
Such hideous cries, that with the very noise
I trembling wak'd, and for a season after
Could not believe but that I was in hell,
Such terrible impression made my dream.

[I.iv.9–63]

I have quoted all of this because its completeness defies selection; nothing else in *Richard III* matches it in poetic quality. Clarence, an unstable turncoat in the *Henry VI* plays, prophetically dreams his own death. He cannot drown by water, despite his own desire, but will "burst to belch" in the hellish wine of a parodistic sacrament of communion. Richard of Gloucester, too deep for Clarence consciously to unravel, "stumbles," and in aiding the fiend, Clarence is pushed into the sea. The irrealistic gold wedges and precious stones are emblematic of Clarence, a Trimmer, or political turncoat, many times bought and sold, and also hint at an Hermetic "near-death experience," ironically parodied. When the Prince of Wales, whom Clarence helped slaughter, shrieks an invocation to avenging Furies, they respond with howls that wake Clarence up to confront his actual murderers, sent by Richard. In the world of *Richard III*, your dreams are overdetermined by the evil genius of the nightmare Crookback, diabolic archon of his own play.

Shakespeare's greatest originality in *Richard III*, which redeems an otherwise cumbersome and overwritten drama, is not so much Richard himself as it is the hero-villain's startlingly intimate relationship with the audience. We are on unnervingly confidential terms with him; Buckingham is our surrogate, and when Buckingham falls out into exile and execution, we shudder at Richard's potential order directed at any one of us: "So much for the audience! Off with its head!" We deserve our possible beheading, because we have been unable to resist Richard's outrageous charm, which has made Machiavels of us all. Tamburlaine the Great bellows mighty cascades of blank verse at us, but Barabas again is Richard's authentic forerunner. The gleeful Jew of Malta, who skips about with proud ferocity as if he had just invented gunpowder, insists upon telling us everything, but still would rather provoke than seduce us. Richard leaps far beyond Barabas, and makes us all into the Lady Anne, playing upon the profound sadomasochism that any audience creates merely by assembling. We are there to be entertained by the suffering of others. Richard co-opts us as fellow torturers, sharing guilty pleasures with the added frisson that we may join the victims, if the dominant hunchback detects any failure in our complicity. Marlowe was sadomasochistic, but rather unsubtly, as in the gruesome execution of Edward II, murdered by the insertion of a white-hot poker into his anus. Shakespeare, reasonably free of such cruel prurience, shocks more profoundly by rendering us incapable of resisting Richard's terrifying charms.

These blandishments do not ensue from rhetorical magnificence, cognitive power, or analytical insight: Richard III is far distant from the complex genius of Iago, or the cold brilliance of Edmund. Nor is our intimacy with Richard more than a foreboding of Hamlet's comprehensive ability to turn the entire audience into so many Horatios. Buckingham cannot be played as Horatio; the Duke is merely a superior Catesby, another useful cat's-paw for the king of the cats. What, then, is Richard's peculiar charm, that alone rescues Shakespeare's perpetually popular melodrama? Sadomasochistic sexuality is certainly a crucial component: to surmise Richard III's bedroom behavior with wretched Anne is to indulge one's unhealthiest fantasies. We are not told how she dies, only that "Anne my wife hath bid this world good night," doubtless delivered with a certain relish. But kinkiness alone cannot account for Richard's exuberant appeal: endless gusto appears to be his secret, energy that delights and terrifies. He is like a Panurge turned from mischief to malevolence, vitalism transmogrified into the death drive. All of us, his audience, require periodical rest and recharging; Richard incessantly surges on, from victim to victim, in quest of more power to hurt. His alliance of gusto and triumphalism allows Shakespeare a new kind of nasty comedy, as in Richard's rejoicing after the seduction of Anne:

> Was ever woman in this humour woo'd?
> Was ever woman in this humour won?
> I'll have her, but I will not keep her long.
> What, I that kill'd her husband and his father:
> To take her in her heart's extremest hate,
> With curses in her mouth, tears in her eyes,
> The bleeding witness of her hatred by,
> Having God, her conscience, and these bars against me—
> And I, no friends to back my suit at all;
> But the plain devil and dissembling looks—
> And yet to win her, all the world to nothing!
> Ha!
> Hath she forgot already that brave prince,
> Edward, her lord, whom I, some three months since,
> Stabb'd in my angry mood at Tewkesbury?
> A sweeter and a lovelier gentleman,
> Fram'd in the prodigality of Nature,
> Young, valiant, wise, and no doubt right royal,
> The spacious world cannot again afford.
> And will she yet debase her eyes on me,
> That cropp'd the golden prime of this sweet prince,
> And made her widow to a woeful bed?
> On me, whose all not equals Edward's moiety?
> On me, that halts and am misshapen thus?
> My dukedom to a beggarly denier,
> I do mistake my person all this while!
> Upon my life, she finds—although I cannot—
> Myself to be a marvellous proper man.
> I'll be at charges for a looking-glass,
> And entertain a score or two of tailors
> To study fashions to adorn my body:

Since I am crept in favour with myself,
I will maintain it with some little cost.
But first I'll turn yon fellow in his grave,
And then return, lamenting, to my love.
Shine out, fair sun, till I have bought a glass,
That I may see my shadow as I pass.

[I.ii.232–68]

This brilliantly recapitulates Richard's speech that opened the play, where "I . . . / Have no delight to pass away the time, / Unless to spy my shadow in the sun." But now Richard takes command of the sun, and genially invites us to share in his triumph over Anne's virtue, expressed as only another element in the world's hypocrisy: "And yet to win her, all the world to nothing!" That subsequent "Ha!" is intoxicating, a grand expletive for a great actor. Richard's gusto is more than theatrical; his triumphalism blends into theatricalism, and becomes Shakespeare's celebration of his medium, and so of his rapidly developing art. To invent Richard is to have created a great monster, but one that will be refined into Shakespeare's invention of the human, of which Iago, to everyone's delight and sorrow, will constitute so central a part.

# PART III

# THE APPRENTICE
# TRAGEDIES

# TITUS ANDRONICUS

Both performances of *Titus Andronicus* that I have attended—one in New York, one in London—had similar effects upon their audiences, who never quite knew when to be horrified and when to laugh, rather uneasily. The young Shakespeare, emerging from the composition of *Richard III*, perhaps rebelled against Marlowe's still overwhelming influence by attempting a parody of Marlowe, and a kind of shock therapy for himself and his public. Something about *Titus Andronicus* is archaic, in an unpleasant way. Everything and everyone on stage is very remote from us, the rigid Titus most of all, except for the engaging Aaron the Moor, who is an improvement upon Richard III in the impossible contest to surpass Barabas, Jew of Malta, who is the most highly self-aware and self-amused of villains.

The best study of Marlowe remains Harry Levin's *The Overreacher* (1952), which commences by reminding us that Marlowe was accused by many of his contemporaries as being, at once, an atheist, a Machiavellian, and an Epicurean. As Levin says, the atheism was pagan or natural (as opposed to revealed) religion, while the Machiavellianism is today considered mere political realism. I would add to Levin that the Epicureanism, in our Age of Freud, assimilates easily to our common metaphysical materialism. Marlowe invented everything crucial to Shakespeare's art, except for the representation of the human, which was beyond both Marlowe's concern and his genius. Tamburlaine and Barabas are superb cartoons that chant remarkable hyperboles. Marlowe's hyperboles achieved some distinction from one another, but there are, and can be, no distinct among his characters. I have an intense enthusiasm for Barabas, but what delights me is an outrageous attitude, not the barely sketched personality. Under Marlowe's sway, Shakespeare emerged very slowly into the authentic representation of personality. If, as Peter Alexander argued, and I have tried to develop, the original *Hamlet* was one of Shakespeare's first plays, its protagonist would have been only a voice. The servant Launce in *The Two Gentlemen of Verona* was Shakespeare's inaugural personality, but most scholars believe that came after *Titus Andronicus*.

The young Shakespeare delighted himself, and his contemporary audiences, by both mocking and exploiting Marlowe in *Titus Andronicus*. "If they want bombast and gore, then they shall have it!" seems the inner impulse that activates this bloodbath, the Shakespearean equivalent of what we now respond to in Stephen King and in much cinema. I would hesitate to assert that there is one good line in the play that is straight; everything zestful and memorable clearly is a send-up. That judgment would now be disputed by many scholars, whose responses to *Titus Andronicus* rather baffle me. Thus Frank Kermode rejects the suggestion that the play is burlesque, though he concedes that "farcical possibilities" are invoked. Jonathan Bate, whose edition of the text is the most elaborate and useful, attempts an aesthetic defense of the indefensible, one that might have startled Shakespeare himself. Though I am fascinated by *Titus Andronicus*, I do see it as exploitative parody, with the inner purpose of destroying the ghost of Christopher Marlowe. If you read the play as authentic tragedy, then you confirm Dr. Johnson's disapproval: "The barbarity of the spectacles, and the general massacre which are here exhibited, can scarcely be conceived tolerable to any audience." Seeing both Laurence Olivier and Brian Bedford struggle with the role of Titus, many years apart, did not give me the impression that it was playable, except as parody.

The Elizabethan audience was at least as bloodthisty as the groundlings who throng our cinemas and gawk at our television sets, so the play was wildly popular, and it did well for Shakespeare, a success he may have accepted with considerable inner irony. Anything goes in the current scholarly criticism of Shakespeare, where there are defenses of the political sagacity of *Titus Andronicus*, and even feminist assertions that the sufferings of the unfortunate Lavinia, Titus's raped and mutilated daughter, testify to patriarchal society's ultimate oppression of its females. Some seriously find prefigurations of *King Lear* and of *Coriolanus*, and even compare Tamora, wicked Queen of the Goths, to Lady Macbeth and to Cleopatra. As perhaps the last High Romantic Bardolator, I am rendered incredulous, and still wish that Shakespeare had not perpetrated this poetic atrocity, even as a catharsis. Except for the hilarious Aaron the Moor, *Titus Andronicus* is ghastly bad if you take it straight, but I will demonstrate that Shakespeare knew it was a howler, and expected the more discerning to wallow in it self-consciously. If sadomasochism is your preferred mode, then *Titus Andronicus* is your meat, and you can join Tamora in her cannibal feast with the same gusto that you experience in raping Lavinia, slicing out her tongue, and chopping off her hands. A larger matter, whatever one's tastes, is how Titus himself is to be understood. Are we at all meant to sympathize with his endless, play-long sufferings, compared with which Job's are only noisy self-indulgences?

Shakespeare took care to estrange Titus from us early and late; Brecht could have done no better, and his celebrated "alienation effect" is plagiarized from Shakespeare. The play barely gets started before Titus commands that Tamora's eldest son is to be sacrificed to the memory of Titus's dead sons, twenty-one out of twenty-five of them having died bravely in battle. The sacrifice consists of throwing the prince of the Goths upon a woodpile, and then hewing his limbs to help feed the fire. After "Alarbus' limbs are lopp'd / And entrails feed the sacrificing fire," little time intervenes before Titus cuts down his own son, for standing in his way in a dispute as to who is to marry Lavinia. Before three hundred lines of Act I, Scene i, have gone by, Titus thus has to be regarded as a bizarre monster, a parody of Marlowe's Tamburlaine. From then until nearly the play's conclusion, the crimes are committed *against* Titus, including the ordeal of Lavinia, the execution of two out of his three surviving sons, and his consenting to let Aaron chop off his hand in a supposed bargain to save his sons. Yet all his vociferous sufferings do not prepare us for his murder of his own martyred daughter in the final scene:

*Tit.* Die, die, Lavinia, and thy shame with thee;
    And with thy shame thy father's sorrow die!
        *[He kills her.*
*Sat.* What hast thou done, unnatural and unkind?
*Tit.* Kill'd her for whom my tears have made me blind.

                                [V.iii.46–49]

At the least, one feels that the tormented Lavinia should have had some choice in the matter! Shakespeare in any case has done all he could to develop our antipathy for Titus, who is nearly as much a monster as Tamora and Aaron. Tamora has no redeeming aspects, but Aaron does, since he is very funny, and even moves us by his love for the black baby he has begotten upon Tamora. An aesthetic defense of *Titus Andronicus* is possible only if you center it upon Aaron, its most Marlovian character, and if you regard the entire play as a bloody farce, in the mode of Marlowe's *The Jew of Malta*.

2

Scholars of Shakespeare and his contemporaries always have been fascinated by the Roman tragedies ascribed to Nero's tutor, Seneca, since those frigid declamations had an indubitable effect upon Elizabethan drama. Shakespeare's first *Hamlet* doubtless had its Senecan qualities, and *Titus Andronicus* certainly derives much of its badness from Seneca. How any Roman audience ever sustained Seneca's tragedies we cannot guess, since they did not receive public performances, as far as we know. Their prestige among the Elizabethans doubtless stemmed from their lack of competition: Athenian tragedy was not available, and its travesty in Seneca had to serve. The Senecan plays are not exactly well made, but their author's interests had little to do with dramatic form; heightened rhetoric was very nearly his sole purpose. Marlowe, and Shakespeare after him, had recourse to Seneca as a stimulus to vaunting language and neo-Stoic sentiments, but Marlowe easily bettered Seneca's instruction. Shakespeare had been unable to cast off Marlowe in *Richard III; Titus Andronicus*, as I read it, is a ritual of exorcism in which Shakespeare carries on an agon with Marlowe. The contest involves taking Marlovian language to so extreme a point that it parodies itself, thus achieving a limit, and so an end to the Senecan mode. Aaron the Moor, like Richard III a version of Marlowe's Barabas, is Shakespeare's principal weapon in this struggle, as can most readily be seen when we directly juxtapose speeches by Barabas and by Aaron.

*Barabas.* As for myself, I walk abroad a-nights,
And kill sick people groaning under walls.
Sometimes I go about and poison wells;
And now and then, to cherish Christian thieves,
I am content to lose some of my crowns,
That I may, walking in my gallery,
See 'em go pinion'd along by my door.
Being young, I studied physic, and began
To practice first upon the Italian;
There I enrich'd the priests with burials,
And always kept the sexton's arms in ure
With digging graves and ringing dead men's knells.
And, after that, was I an engineer,
And in the wars 'twixt France and Germany
Under the pretence of helping Charles the Fifth,
Slew friend and enemy with my stratagems:
Then after that was I a usurer,

*Aar.* Ay, that I had not done a thousand more.
Even now I curse the day, and yet, I think,
Few come within the compass of my curse,
Wherein I did not some notorious ill:
As kill a man or else devise his death;
Ravish a maid, or plot the way to do it;
Accuse some innocent, and forswear myself;
Set deadly enmity between two friends;
Make poor men's cattle break their necks;
Set fire on barns and haystacks in the night,
And bid the owners quench them with their tears.
Oft have I digg'd up dead men from their graves,
And set them upright at their dear friends' door,
Even when their sorrows almost was forgot,
And on their skins, as on the bark of trees,

And with extorting, cozening,
forfeiting,
And tricks belonging unto brokery,
I fill'd the gaols with bankrupts in
a year,
And with young orphans planted
hospitals;
And every moon made some or
other mad,
And now and then one hang
himself for grief,
Pinning upon his breast a long
great scroll
How I with interest tormented him.
But mark how I am blest for
plaguing them:
I have as much coin as will buy the
town.
But tell me now, how hast thou
spent thy time?

Have with my knife carved in
Roman letters,
"Let not your sorrow die, though I
am dead."
But I have done a thousand
dreadful things
As willingly as one would kill a fly,
And nothing grieves me heartily
indeed
But that I cannot do ten thousand
more.

[V.i.124–44]

Shakespeare wins (though the agon remains Marlowe's), because Marlowe's wonderful hanged man with the long great scroll pinned upon his
breast is outdone by the Moor's carving his greetings directly on the skins
of dead men, and setting them upright at the door of their dear friends.
Aaron combines with Tamburlaine's rant Barabas's talent for making the audience his accomplices. The result is a Marlovian monster more outrageous than anyone in Marlowe. Without Aaron, *Titus Andronicus* would be
unendurable; the first act seems to stretch forever, because he does not
speak in it, though he is on stage. In Act II, he suggests to Tamora's sons
that they settle their quarrel about Lavinia by gang-raping her. They
blithely accomplish this, first killing her husband, and then using the
corpse as the bed for violating her. Slicing off her hands and tongue, they
thus render it rather difficult for her to identify her tormentors, and Aaron

successfully shifts the blame for murdering her husband to two of Titus's
three surviving sons. Even summarizing this wedges us between shock and
defensive laughter, though not to the extent of the antithetical reaction
that we undergo when Titus urges his brother and Lavinia to help him
carry off stage the severed heads of two of his sons, and his own severed
hand:

> *Tit.*     Come, brother, take a head;
> And in this hand the other will I bear.
> And, Lavinia, thou shalt be employ'd
> Bear thou my hand, sweet wench, between thy teeth.
>
>            [III.i.279–82]

This beggars commentary, but I do urge all scholars who think *Titus An-*
*dronicus* a sincere and serious tragedy to read these lines out loud several
times in a row, with particular emphasis upon "Bear thou my hand, sweet
wench, between thy teeth." Shakespeare, after all, already had written *The*
*Comedy of Errors* and *The Taming of the Shrew,* and was about to compose *Love's*
*Labour's Lost;* his genius for comedy was highly evident, both to the public
and himself. To call *Titus Andronicus* a mere send-up of Marlowe and Kyd
hardly seems sufficient; it is a blowup, an explosion of rancid irony carried
well past the limits of parody. Nothing else by Shakespeare is so sublimely
lunatic; it prophesies not *King Lear* and *Coriolanus,* but Artaud.

 As it moves toward its absurd conclusion, it becomes more surrealistic,
even irrealistic. In Act III, Scene ii, Titus and his brother use their knives
to kill a fly; their dialogue concerning this occupies thirty lines of fantasy.
Baroque as it is, it is tame in contrast to Act IV, Scene i, where the muted
Lavinia employs her stumps to turn the leaves of a volume of Ovid's *Meta-*
*morphoses,* until she comes to the tale of Philomel, ravished by Tereus. Holding a staff in her mouth, and guiding it with her stumps, she inscribes in
the sands *stuprum* (Latin for "rape") and the names of the culprit sons of Tamora, Chiron and Demetrius. Titus responds by quoting from Seneca's
*Hippolytus,* the same play that furnished Demetrius with a tag preluding the
rape and mutilation of Lavinia.

Ovid and Seneca serve not so much as literary allusions as they do further distancing from mimetic realism for the preposterous sufferings of Titus and his family. It therefore seems appropriate that Titus stages an attack upon the imperial palace in which visionary arrows rain down, each marked as being directed to a particular god. Curious as this is, Shakespeare surpasses the irreality when Tamora, disguised as a personified Revenge, makes a social call upon Titus, accompanied by her sons Demetrius, in the guise of Murder, and Chiron, as Rape. Their ostensible purpose is to urge Titus to give a banquet for Tamora and her husband, the dubious emperor Saturninus, at which Titus's one surviving son, Lucius, will also be present. Summarizing all this is like telling the plot of a soap opera, but the action of *Titus Andronicus* essentially is a horror opera, Stephen King turned loose among the Romans and the Goths. Titus allows Tamora-Revenge to depart, doubtless to get properly attired for the banquet, but he detains Murder and Rape. Bound and gagged, they stand ready even as we enjoy the frisson of a grand stage direction: *Enter Titus Andronicus with a knife, and Lavinia with a basin.* Titus's speech, his first cheerful utterance in the entire play, does not disappoint us:

> *Tit.* Hark, wretches, how I mean to martyr you.
> This one hand yet is left to cut your throats,
> Whiles that Lavinia 'tween her stumps doth hold
> The basin that receives your guilty blood.
> You know your mother means to feast with me,
> And calls herself Revenge, and thinks me mad.
> Hark, villains, I will grind your bones to dust,
> And with your blood and it I'll make a paste,
> And of the paste a coffin I will rear,
> And make two pasties of your shameful heads,
> And bid that strumpet, your unhallowed dam,
> Like to the earth swallow her own increase.
> This is the feast that I have bid her to,
> And this the banket she shall surfeit on;
> For worse than Philomel you us'd my daughter,

And worse than Progne I will be reveng'd.
And now prepare your throats—Lavinia, come,
Receive the blood: and when that they are dead,
Let me go grind their bones to powder small,
And with this hateful liquor temper it,
And in that paste let their vile heads be bak'd.
Come, come, be everyone officious
To make this banket, which I wish may prove
More stern and bloody than the Centaurs' feast.
  [*He cuts their throats.*
So, now bring them in, for I'll play the cook,
And see them ready against their mother comes.
      [*Exeunt.*

[V.ii.180–205]

As Titus indicates, he has Ovidian precedent in the supper served by
Progne, Philomela's sister, to the rapist Tereus, who unknowingly devoured
his own child, and there may hover also Seneca's *Thyestes*, with its climax
in the sinister feast of Atreus. Shakespeare improves upon his sources,
what with a coffin-like piecrust, and the amiable vision of Demetrius's and
Chiron's heads reduced to tasty meat pies. We are ready for the banquet,
with Titus in a chef's hat setting the table. First dispatching poor Lavinia,
Titus then stabs the more deserving Tamora, but only after informing her
that she has devoured her sons. Doubtless a touch sated, Shakespeare does
not allow Titus a grand death scene. Saturninus kills Titus, and in turn is
slain by Lucius, last of twenty-five brothers and the new emperor of Rome.
Aaron the Moor, after bravely saving the life of his black baby by Tamora,
is buried breast-deep in the earth, so as to starve to death. Shakespeare,
who probably shares our desperate affection for Aaron, allows him the
dignity of unrepentant last words, in the mode of Marlowe's Barabas:

*Aar.* Ah, why should wrath be mute, and fury dumb?
    I am no baby, I, that with base prayers
    I should repent the evils I have done;

Ten thousand worse than ever yet I did
Would I perform, if I might have my will.
If one good deed in all my life I did,
I do repent it from my very soul.

[V.iii.184–90]

The English production of *Titus Andronicus* that I attended was Peter Brook's abstractly stylized presentation in 1955, which at least had the virtue of keeping the gore at a symbolic distance, though at the expense of Shakespeare's parodistic excess. I don't think I would see the play again unless Mel Brooks directed it, with his company of zanies, or perhaps it could yet be made into a musical. Though there is a nasty power evident throughout the text, I can concede no intrinsic value to *Titus Andronicus*. It matters only because Shakespeare, alas, undoubtedly wrote it, and by doing so largely purged Marlowe and Kyd from his imagination. A remnant of Marlowe lingered, just long enough to help spoil *King John*, as we have seen, but with *Love's Labour's Lost* in comedy, *Richard II* in history, and *Romeo and Juliet* in tragedy, Shakespeare stood at last quite clear of his brilliantly heartless precursor. *Titus Andronicus* performed an essential function for Shakespeare, but cannot do very much for the rest of us.

# ROMEO AND JULIET

Shakespeare's first authentic tragedy has sometimes been critically undervalued, perhaps because of its popularity. Though *Romeo and Juliet*
is a triumph of dramatic lyricism, its tragic ending usurps most other aspects of the play and abandons us to unhappy estimates of whether, and
to what degree, its young lovers are responsible for their own catastrophe.
Harold Goddard lamented that the Prologue's "A pair of star-cross'd lovers
take their life" had "surrendered this drama to the astrologers," though
more than the stars in their courses are to blame for the destruction of the
superb Juliet. Alas, half a century after Goddard, the tragedy more frequently is surrendered to commissars of gender and power, who can thrash
the patriarchy, including Shakespeare himself, for victimizing Juliet.

Thomas McAlindon in his refreshingly sane *Shakespeare's Tragic Cosmos*
(1991) traces the dynamics of conflict in the dramatist back to the rival
worldviews of Heraclitus and Empedocles, as refined and modified in
Chaucer's *The Knight's Tale*. For Heraclitus, all things flowed, as Empedocles
visualized a strife between Love and Death. Chaucer, as I have remarked,
rather than Ovid or Marlowe, was the ancestor of Shakespeare's greatest
originality, that invention of the human that is my prime concern in this
book. Chaucer's ironic yet amiable version of the religion of love, more
perhaps in his *Troilus and Criseyde* than in *The Knight's Tale*, is the essential context for *Romeo and Juliet*. Time's ironies govern love in Chaucer, as they will
in *Romeo and Juliet*. Chaucer's human nature is essentially Shakespeare's: the

deepest link between the two greatest English poets was temperamental rather than intellectual or sociopolitical. Love dies or else lovers die: those are the pragmatic possibilities for the two poets, each of them experientially wise beyond wisdom.

Shakespeare, somewhat unlike Chaucer, shied away from depicting the death of love rather than the death of lovers. Does anyone, except Hamlet, ever fall out of love in Shakespeare? Hamlet denies anyway that he ever loved Ophelia, and I believe him. By the time the play ends, he loves no one, whether it be the dead Ophelia or the dead father, the dead Gertrude or the dead Yorick, and one wonders if this frightening charismatic ever could have loved anyone. If there were an Act VI to Shakespeare's comedies, doubtless many of the concluding marriages would approximate the condition of Shakespeare's own union with Anne Hathaway. My observation, of course, is nonsensical if you would have it so, but most of the Shakespearean audience—then, now, and always—goes on believing that Shakespeare uniquely represented realities. Poor Falstaff never will stop loving Hal, and the admirably Christian Antonio always will pine for Bassanio. Whom Shakespeare himself loved we do not know, but the Sonnets seem more than a fiction and, at least in this aspect of life, Shakespeare evidently was not so cold as his Hamlet.

There are mature lovers in Shakespeare, most notably Antony and Cleopatra, who cheerfully sell each other out for reasons of state, yet return to each other in their suicides. Both Romeo and Antony kill themselves because they falsely think their beloveds are dead (Antony bungles the suicide, as he does everything else). The most passionate marriage in Shakespeare, the Macbeths', subtly appears to have its sexual difficulties, as I will show, and ends in madness and suicide for Queen Macbeth, prompting the most equivocal of elegiac reflections by her usurping husband. "Yet Edmund was belov'd," the icy villain of *King Lear* overhears himself saying, when the bodies of Goneril and Regan are brought in.

The varieties of passionate love between the sexes are endlessly Shakespeare's concern; sexual jealousy finds its most flamboyant artists in Othello and Leontes, but the virtual identity of the torments of love and jealousy is a Shakespearean invention, later to be refined by Hawthorne and Proust. Shakespeare, more than any other author, has instructed the West in the catastrophes of sexuality, and has invented the formula that the sexual becomes the erotic when crossed by the shadow of death. There had to be one high song of the erotic by Shakespeare, one lyrical and tragicomical paean celebrating an unmixed love and lamenting its inevitable destruction. *Romeo and Juliet* is unmatched, in Shakespeare and in the world's literature, as a vision of an uncompromising mutual love that perishes of its own idealism and intensity.

There are a few isolated instances of realistic distincts in Shakespeare's characters before *Romeo and Juliet*: Launce in *The Two Gentlemen of Verona*, the Bastard Faulconbridge in *King John*, Richard II, self-destructive king and superb metaphysical poet. The fourfold of Juliet, Mercutio, the Nurse, and Romeo outnumber and overgo these earlier breakthroughs in human invention. *Romeo and Juliet* matters, as a play, because of these four exuberantly realized characters.

It is easier to see the vividness of Mercutio and the Nurse than it is to absorb and sustain the erotic greatness of Juliet and the heroic effort of Romeo to approximate her sublime state of being in love. Shakespeare, with a prophetic insight, knows that he must lead his audience beyond Mercutio's obscene ironies if they are to be worthy of apprehending Juliet, for her sublimity *is* the play and guarantees the tragedy of this tragedy. Mercutio, the scene stealer of the play, had to be killed off if it was to remain Juliet's and Romeo's play; keep Mercutio in Acts IV and V, and the contention of love and death would have to cease. We overinvest in Mercutio because he insures us against our own erotic eagerness for doom; he is in the play to some considerable purpose. So, in an even darker way, is the Nurse, who helps guarantee the final disaster. The Nurse and Mercutio, both of them audience favorites, are nevertheless bad news, in different but complementary ways. Shakespeare, at this point in his career, may have underestimated his burgeoning powers, because Mercutio and the Nurse go on seducing audiences, readers, directors, and critics. Their verbal exuberances make them forerunners of Touchstone and Jacques, rancid ironists, but also of the dangerously eloquent manipulative villains Iago and Edmund.

2

Shakespeare's greatness began with *Love's Labour's Lost* (1594–95, revised 1597) and *Richard II* (1595), superb achievements respectively in comedy and in history. Yet *Romeo and Juliet* (1595–96) has rightly overshadowed both, though I cannot quite place it for eminence with *A Midsummer Night's Dream*, composed simultaneously with Shakespeare's first serious tragedy. The permanent popularity, now of mythic intensity, of *Romeo and Juliet* is more than justified, since the play is the largest and most persuasive celebration of romantic love in Western literature. When I think of the play, without rereading and teaching it, or attending yet one more inadequate performance, I first remember neither the tragic outcome nor the gloriously vivid Mercutio and the Nurse. My mind goes directly to the vital center, Act II, Scene ii, with its incandescent exchange between the lovers:

> *Rom.* Lady, by yonder blessed moon I vow,
>     That tips with silver all these fruit-tree tops—
> *Jul.* O swear not by the moon, th'inconstant moon,
>     That monthly changes in her circled orb,
>     Lest that thy love prove likewise variable.
> *Rom.* What shall I swear by?
> *Jul.* Do not swear at all,
>     Or if thou wilt, swear by thy gracious self,
>     Which is the god of my idolatry,
>     And I'll believe thee.
> *Rom.* If my heart's dear love—
> *Jul.* Well, do not swear. Although I joy in thee,
>     I have no joy of this contract tonight:
>     It is too rash, too unadvis'd, too sudden,
>     Too like the lightning, which doth cease to be
>     Ere one can say 'It lightens'. Sweet, good night.
>     This bud of love, by summer's ripening breath,
>     May prove a beauteous flower when next we meet.

Good night, good night. As sweet repose and rest
Come to thy heart as that within my breast.
*Rom.* O wilt thou leave me so unsatisfied?
*Jul.* What satisfaction canst thou have tonight?
*Rom.* Th'exchange of thy love's faithful vow for mine.
*Jul.* I gave thee mine before thou didst request it,
And yet I would it were to give again.
*Rom.* Wouldst thou withdraw it? For what purpose, love?
*Jul.* But to be frank and give it thee again;
And yet I wish but for the thing I have.
My bounty is as boundless as the sea,
My love as deep: The more I give to thee
The more I have, for both are infinite.

[II.ii.107–35]

The revelation of Juliet's nature here might be called an epiphany in the religion of love. Chaucer has nothing like this, nor does Dante, since his Beatrice's love for him transcends sexuality. Unprecedented in literature (though presumably not in life), Juliet precisely does not transcend the human heroine. Whether Shakespeare reinvents the representation of a very young woman (she is not yet fourteen) in love, or perhaps does even more than that, is difficult to decide. How do you distance Juliet? You only shame yourself by bringing irony to a contemplation of her consciousness. Hazlitt, spurred by a nostalgia for his own lost dreams of love, caught better than any other critic the exact temper of this scene:

He has founded the passion of the two lovers not in the pleasures they had experienced, but on all the pleasures they had *not* experienced.

It is the sense of an infinity yet to come that is evoked by Juliet, nor can we doubt that her bounty is "as boundless as the sea." When Rosalind in *As You Like It* repeats this simile, it is in a tonality that subtly isolates Juliet's difference:

*Ros.* O coz, coz, coz, my pretty little coz, that thou didst know how many fathoms deep I am in love! But it cannot be sounded. My affection hath an unknown bottom, like the Bay of Portugal.

*Celia.* Or rather bottomless, that as fast as you pour affection in, it runs out.

*Rosalind.* No. That same wicked bastard of Venus, that was begot of thought, conceived of spleen and born of madness, that blind rascally boy that abuses everyone's eyes because his own are out, let him be judge how deep I am in love.

[IV.i.195–205]

This is the sublimest of female wits, who one imagines would advise Romeo and Juliet to "die by attorney," and who knows that women, as well as men, "have died from time to time and worms have eaten them, but not for love." Romeo and Juliet, alas, are exceptions, and die for love rather than live for wit. Shakespeare allows nothing like Rosalind's supreme intelligence to intrude upon Juliet's authentic rapture. Mercutio, endlessly obscene, is not qualified to darken Juliet's intimations of ecstasy. The play has already made clear how brief this happiness must be. Against that context, against also all of his own ironic reservations, Shakespeare allows Juliet the most exalted declaration of romantic love in the language:

*Juliet.* But to be frank and give it thee again;
    And yet I wish but for the thing I have.
    My bounty is as boundless as the sea,
    My love as deep: The more I give to thee
    The more I have, for both are infinite.

[II.ii.131–35]

We have to measure the rest of this play against these five lines, miraculous in their legitimate pride and poignance. They defy Dr. Johnson's wry remark on Shakespeare's rhetorical extravagances throughout the play: "his pathetick strains are always polluted with some unexpected depravations." Molly Mahood, noting that there are at least a hundred and seventy-five puns and allied wordplays in *Romeo and Juliet*, finds them appropriate to a riddling drama where "Death has long been Romeo's rival and enjoys Juliet at the last," an appropriate finale for doom-eager lovers. Yet little in the drama suggests that Romeo and Juliet are in love with death, as well as with each other. Shakespeare stands back from assigning blame, whether to the feuding older generation, or to the lovers, or to fate, time, chance, and the cosmological contraries. Julia Kristeva, rather too courageously not standing back, rushes in to discover "a discreet version of the Japanese *Realm of the Senses*," a baroque sadomasochistic motion picture.

Clearly Shakespeare took some risks in letting us judge this tragedy for ourselves, but that refusal to usurp his audience's freedom allowed ultimately for the composition of the final high tragedies. I think that I speak for more than myself when I assert that the love shared by Romeo and Juliet is as healthy and normative a passion as Western literature affords us. It concludes in mutual suicide, but not because either of the lovers lusts for death, or mingles hatred with desire.

3

Mercutio is the most notorious scene stealer in all of Shakespeare, and there is a tradition (reported by Dryden) that Shakespeare declared he was obliged to kill off Mercutio, lest Mercutio kill Shakespeare and hence the play. Dr. Johnson rightly commended Mercutio for wit, gaiety, and courage; presumably the great critic chose to ignore that Mercutio also is obscene, heartless, and quarrelsome. Mercutio promises a grand comic role, and yet disturbs us also with his extraordinary rhapsody concerning Queen Mab, who at first seems to belong more to *A Midsummer Night's Dream* than to *Romeo and Juliet*:

> *Mer.* O then I see Queen Mab hath been with you.
> *Benvolio.* Queen Mab, what's she?
> *Mer.* She is the fairies' midwife, and she comes
>  In shape no bigger than an agate stone

On the forefinger of an alderman,
Drawn with a team of little atomi
Over men's noses as they lie asleep.
Her chariot is an empty hazelnut made by the joiner squirrel or
old grub,
Time out o' mind the fairies' coachmakers;
Her wagon-spokes made of long spinners' legs;
The cover of the wings of grasshoppers,
Her traces of the smallest spider web,
Her collars of the moonshine's watery beams,
Her whip of cricket's bone, the lash of film,
Her waggoner, a small grey-coated gnat,
Not half so big as a round little worm
Prick'd from the lazy finger of a maid;
And in this state she gallops night by night
Through lovers' brains, and then they dream of love;
O'er courtiers' knees, that dream on curtsies straight;
O'er lawyers' fingers who straight dream on fees;
O'er ladies' lips, who straight on kisses dream,
Which oft the angry Mab with blisters plagues
Because their breaths with sweetmeats tainted are.
Sometime she gallops o'er a courtier's nose,
And then dreams he of smelling out a suit;
And sometime comes she with a tithe-pig's tail,
Tickling a parson's nose as a lies asleep;
Then dreams he of another benefice,
Sometime she driveth o'er a soldier's neck
And then dreams he of cutting foreign throats,
Of breaches, ambuscados, Spanish blades,
Of healths five fathom deep; and then anon
Drums in his ear, at which he starts and wakes,
And being thus frighted swears a prayer or two
And sleeps again. This is that very Mab
That plaits the manes of horses in the night

And bakes the elf-locks in foul sluttish hairs,
Which, once untangled, much misfortune bodes.
This is the hag, when maids lie on their backs,
That presses them and learns them first to bear,
Making them women of good carriage.
This is she—

[I.iv.53–94]

Romeo interrupts, since clearly Mercutio never stops once started. This
mercurial vision of Queen Mab—where "Queen" probably means a whore,
and Mab refers to a Celtic fairy, who frequently manifests as a will-o'-the-
wisp—is anything but out of character. Mercutio's Mab is the midwife of
our erotic dreams, aiding us to give birth to our deep fantasies, and she appears to possess a childlike charm for much of the length of Mercutio's description. But since he is a major instance of what D. H. Lawrence was to
call "sex-in-the-head," Mercutio is setting us up for the revelation of Mab
as the nightmare, the incubus who impregnates maids. Romeo interrupts
to say: "Thou talkst of nothing," where "nothing" is another slang term for
the vagina. Mercutio's bawdy obsessiveness is splendidly employed by
Shakespeare as a reduction of Romeo and Juliet's honest exaltation of their
passion. Directly before their first rendezvous, we hear Mercutio at his
most obscenely exuberant pitch:

If love be blind, love cannot hit the mark.
Now will he sit under a medlar tree
And wish his mistress were that kind of fruit
As maids call medlars when they laugh alone.
O Romeo, that she were, O that she were
An open-arse, and thou a poperin pear!

[II.i.33–38]

Mercutio's reference is to Rosaline, Romeo's beloved before he falls, at
first glance, in love with Juliet, who instantly reciprocates. The medlar, rotten with ripeness, popularly was believed to have the likeness of the female

genitalia, and "to meddle" meant to perform sexual intercourse. Mercutio happily also cites a popular name for the medlar, the open-arse, as well as the poperin pear, at once pop-her-in her open arse, and the slang name for a French pear, the Poperingle (named for a town near Ypres). This is the antithetical prelude to a scene that famously concludes with Juliet's couplet:

Good night, good night. Parting is such sweet sorrow
That I shall say good night till it be morrow.

Mercutio at his best is a high-spiritual unbeliever in the religion of love, reductive as he may be:

*Ben.* Here comes Romeo, here comes Romeo!
*Mer.* Without his roe, like a dried herring. O flesh, flesh, how art thou
   fishified! Now is he for the numbers that Petrarch flowed in. Laura,
   to his lady, was a kitchen wench—marry, she had a better love to
   berhyme her—Dido a dowdy, Cleopatra a gypsy, Helen and Hero
   hildings and harlots, Thisbe a grey eye or so, [. . .]
                                                        [II.iv.37–44]

Obsessed as he may be, Mercutio has the style to take his death wound as gallantly as anyone in Shakespeare:

*Romeo.* Courage, man, the hurt cannot be much.
*Mer.* No, 'tis not so deep as a well, nor so wide as a church door, but
   'tis enough, 'twill serve. Ask for me tomorrow and you shall find
   me a grave man. I am peppered, I warrant for this world. A plague
   o' both your houses.
                                                        [III.i.96–101]

That indeed is what in his death Mercutio becomes, a plague upon both Romeo of the Montagues and Juliet of the Capulets, since hencefor-ward the tragedy speeds on to its final double catastrophe. Shakespeare is already Shakespeare in his subtle patterning, although rather overlyrical still in his style. The two fatal figures in the play are its two liveliest comics, Mercutio and the Nurse. Mercutio's aggressivity has prepared the destruction of love, though there is no negative impulse in Mercutio, who dies by the tragic irony that Romeo's intervention in the duel with Tybalt is prompted by love for Juliet, a relationship of which Mercutio is totally unaware. Mercutio is victimized by what is most central to the play, and yet he dies without knowing what *Romeo and Juliet* is all about: the tragedy of authentic romantic love. For Mercutio, that is nonsense: love is an open arse and a poperin pear. To die as love's martyr, as it were, when you do not believe in the religion of love, and do not even know what you are dying for, is a grotesque irony that foreshadows the dreadful ironies that will destroy Juliet and Romeo alike as the play concludes.

4

Juliet's Nurse, despite her popularity, is altogether a much darker figure. Like Mercutio, she is inwardly cold, even toward Juliet, whom she has raised. Her language captivates us, as does Mercutio's, but Shakespeare gives both of them hidden natures much at variance with their exuberant personalities. Mercutio's incessant bawdiness is the mask for what may be a repressed homoeroticism, and like his violence may indicate a flight from the acute sensibility at work in the Queen Mab speech until it too transmutes into obscenity. The Nurse is even more complex; her apparent vitalism and her propulsive flood of language beguile us in her first full speech:

Even or odd, of all days in the year,
Come Lammas Eve at night shall she be fourteen.
Susan and she—God rest all Christian souls!—
Were of an age. Well, Susan is with God;
She was too good for me. But as I said,
On Lammas Eve at night shall she be fourteen.
That shall she; marry, I remember it well.
'Tis since the earthquake now eleven years,

And she was wean'd—I never shall forget it—
Of all the days of the year upon that day.
For I had then laid wormwood to my dug,
Sitting in the sun under the dovehouse wall.
My lord and you were then at Mantua—
Nay I do bear a brain. But as I said,
When it did taste the wormwood on the nipple
Of my dug and felt it bitter, pretty fool,
To see it tetchy and fall out with the dug.
Shake! quoth the dovehouse! 'Twas no need, I trow,
To bid me trudge.
And since that time it is eleven years.
For then she could stand high-lone. Nay, by th'rood,
She could have run and waddled all about;
For even the day before she broke her brow,
And then my husband—God be with his soul,
A was a merry man—took up the child,
'Yea,' quoth he, 'dost thou fall upon thy face?
Thou wilt fall backward when thou hast more wit,
Wilt thou not, Jule?' And, by my holidame,
The pretty wretch left crying and said 'Ay'.
To see now how a jest shall come about.
I warrant, and I should live a thousand years
I never should forget it. 'Wilt thou not, Jule?' quoth he,
And, pretty fool, it stinted, and said 'Ay'.

[I.iii.16–48]

Her speech is shrewd and not so simple as first it sounds, and comes short of poignance, because already there is something antipathetic in the Nurse. Juliet, like her late twin sister, Susan, is too good for the Nurse, and there is an edge to the account of the weaning that is bothersome, since we do not hear the accents of love.

Shakespeare delays any more ultimate revelation of the Nurse's nature until the crucial scene where she fails Juliet. The exchanges here need to be quoted at length, because Juliet's shock is a new effect for Shakespeare. The Nurse is the person who has been closest to Juliet for all the fourteen years of her life, and suddenly Juliet realizes that what has seemed loyalty and care is something else.

*Jul.* O God, O Nurse, how shall this be prevented?
　　My husband is on earth, my faith in heaven.
　　How shall that faith return again to earth
　　Unless that husband send it me from heaven
　　By leaving earth? Comfort me, counsel me.
　　Alack, alack, that heaven should practise stratagems
　　Upon so soft a subject as myself.
　　What sayst thou? Hast thou not a word of joy?
　　Some comfort, Nurse.
*Nurse.* Faith, here it is:
　　Romeo is banish'd, and all the world to nothing
　　That he dares ne'er come back to challenge you,
　　Or if he do, it needs must be by stealth.
　　Then, since the case so stands as now it doth,
　　I think it best you married with the County.
　　O, he's a lovely gentleman.
　　Romeo's a dishclout to him. An eagle, madam,
　　Hath not so green, so quick, so fair an eye
　　As Paris hath. Beshrew my very heart,
　　I think you are happy in this second match,
　　For it excels your first; or if it did not,
　　Your first is dead, or 'twere as good he were
　　As living here and you no use of him.
*Jul.* Speakest thou from thy heart?
*Nurse.* And from my soul too, else beshrew them both.
*Jul.* Amen.
*Nurse.* What?
*Jul.* Well, thou hast comforted me marvellous much.
　　Go in, and tell my lady I am gone,

Having displeas'd my father, to Laurence' cell,

To make confession and to be absolv'd.

*Nurse.* Marry, I will; and this is wisely done.

*Jul.* Ancient damnation! O most wicked fiend,

Is it more sin to wish me thus forsworn,

Or to dispraise my lord with that same tongue

Which she hath praised him with above compare

So many thousand times? Go, counsellor.

Thou and my bosom henceforth shall be twain.

I'll to the friar, to know his remedy.

If all else fail, myself have power to die.

[III.v.204–42]

The more-than-poignant: "that heaven should practise stratagems / Upon so soft a subject as myself" is answered by the Nurse's astonishing "comfort": "it excels your first; or if it did not, / Your first is dead." The Nurse's argument is valid if convenience is everything; since Juliet is in love, we hear instead an overwhelming rejection of the Nurse, proceeding from the eloquent "amen" on to the dry: "Well, thou hast comforted me marvellous much." The Nurse indeed is "Ancient damnation! O most wicked fiend," and we will hardly hear from her again until Juliet "dies" her first death in this play. Like Mercutio, the Nurse moves us at last to distrust every apparent value in the tragedy except the lovers' commitment to each other.

5

Juliet, and not Romeo, or even Brutus in *Julius Caesar,* dies her second death as a prefiguration of Hamlet's charismatic splendor. Romeo, though he changes enormously under her influence, remains subject to anger and to despair, and is as responsible as Mercutio and Tybalt are for the catastrophe. Having slain Tybalt, Romeo cries out that he has become "Fortune's fool." We would wince if Juliet called herself "Fortune's fool," since she is as nearly flawless as her situation allows, and we recall instead her wry prayer: "Be fickle, Fortune." Perhaps any playgoer or any reader remembers best Romeo and Juliet's aubade after their single night of fulfillment:

> *Jul.* Wilt thou be gone? It is not yet near day.
> It was the nightingale and not the lark
> That pierc'd the fearful hollow of thine ear.
> Nightly she sings on yond pomegranate tree.
> Believe me, love, it was the nightingale.
>
> *Rom.* It was the lark, the herald of the morn,
> No nightingale. Look, love, what envious streaks
> Do lace the severing clouds in yonder east.
> Night's candles are burnt out, and jocund day
> Stands tiptoe on the misty mountain tops.
> I must be gone and live, or stay and die.
>
> *Jul.* Yond light is not daylight, I know it, I.
> It is some meteor that the sun exhales
> To be to thee this night a torchbearer
> And light thee on thy way to Mantua.
> Therefore stay yet: Thou need'st not to be gone.
>
> *Rom.* Let me be ta'en, let me be put to death.
> I am content, so thou wilt have it so.
> I'll say yon grey is not the morning's eye,
> 'Tis but the pale reflex of Cynthia's brow.
> Nor that is not the lark whose notes do beat
> The vaulty heaven so high above our heads.
> I have more care to stay than will to go.
> Come death, and welcome. Juliet wills it so.
> How is't, my soul? Let's talk. It is not day.
>
> *Jul.* It is, it is. Hie hence, begone, away.
> It is the lark that sings so out of tune,
> Straining harsh discords and unpleasing sharps.
> Some say the lark makes sweet division.
> This doth not so, for she divideth us.
> Some say the lark and loathed toad change eyes.

O, now I would they had chang'd voices too,
Since arm from arm that voice doth us affray,
Hunting thee hence with hunt's-up to the day.
O now be gone, more light and light it grows.
*Rom.* More light and light: more dark and dark our woes.

[III.v.1–36]

Exquisite in itself, this is also a subtle epitome of the tragedy of this tragedy, for the entire play could be regarded as a dawn song that, alas, is out of phase. A bemused audience, unless the director is shrewd, is likely to become skeptical that event after event arrives in the untimeliest way possible. Romeo and Juliet's aubade is so disturbing precisely because they are not courtly love sophisticates working through a stylized ritual. The courtly lover confronts the possibility of a real-enough death if he lingers too long, because his partner is an adulterous wife. But Juliet and Romeo know that death after dawn would be Romeo's punishment, not for adultery, but merely for marriage. The subtle outrageousness of Shakespeare's drama is that everything is against the lovers: their families and the state, the indifference of nature, the vagaries of time, and the regressive movement of the cosmological contraries of love and strife. Even had Romeo transcended his anger; even if Mercutio and the Nurse were not quarrelsome busybodies, the odds are too great against the triumph of love. That is the aubade's undersong, made explicit in Romeo's great outcry against the contraries: "More light and light: more dark and dark our woes."

What was Shakespeare trying to do for himself as a playwright by composing *Romeo and Juliet*? Tragedy did not come easily to Shakespeare, yet all this play's lyricism and comic genius cannot hold off the dawn that will become a destructive darkness. With just a few alterations, Shakespeare could have transformed *Romeo and Juliet* into a play as cheerful as *A Midsummer Night's Dream*. The young lovers, escaped to Mantua or Padua, would not have been victims of Verona, or of bad timing, or of cosmological contraries asserting their sway. Yet this travesty would have been intolerable for us, and for Shakespeare: a passion as absolute as Romeo's and Juliet's cannot consort with comedy. Mere sexuality will do for comedy, but the shadow of death makes eroticism the companion of tragedy. Shakespeare, in *Romeo and Juliet*, eschews Chaucerian irony, but he takes from *The Knight's Tale* Chaucer's intimation that we are always keeping appointments we haven't made. Here it is the sublime appointment kept by Paris and Romeo at Juliet's supposed tomb, which soon enough becomes both her authentic tomb and their own. What is left on stage at the close of this tragedy is an absurd pathos: the wretched Friar Laurence, who fearfully abandoned Juliet; a widowed Montague, who vows to have a statue of Juliet raised in pure gold; the Capulets vowing to end a feud already spent in five deaths—those of Mercutio, Tybalt, Paris, Romeo, and Juliet. The closing curtain of any proper production of the play should descend upon these final ironies, presented as ironies, and not as images of reconciliation. As is *Julius Caesar* after it, *Romeo and Juliet* is a training ground in which Shakespeare teaches himself remorselessness and prepares the way for his five great tragedies, starting with the *Hamlet* of 1600–1601.

# 9

# JULIUS CAESAR

L ike so many others in my American generation, I read *Julius Caesar* in grade school, when I was about twelve. It was the first play by Shakespeare that I read, and though soon after I encountered *Macbeth* on my own, and the rest of Shakespeare in the next year or two, a curious aura still lingers for me when I come back to *Julius Caesar*. It was a great favorite for school use in those days, because it is so well made, so apparently direct, and so relatively simple. The more often I reread and teach it, or attend a performance, the subtler and more ambiguous it seems, not in plot but in character.

Shakespeare's stance toward Brutus, Cassius, and Caesar himself is very difficult to interpret, but that is one of the strengths of this admirable play. I say "Caesar himself," and yet his is only a supporting role in what could have been entitled *The Tragedy of Marcus Brutus*. Because Caesar is so crucial a figure in history, Shakespeare is obliged to call the play after him, its highest-ranking personage. The two parts of *Henry IV* are Falstaff's plays, and Hal's, yet they are named for their reigning monarch, which was Shakespeare's general practice as a dramatist. Caesar actually appears only in three scenes, speaks fewer than 150 lines, and is murdered in Act III, Scene i, at the exact center of the play. Nevertheless, he pervades all of it, as Brutus testifies when he beholds the self-slain Cassius:

O Julius Caesar, thou art mighty yet!
Thy spirit walks abroad, and turns our swords
In our own proper entrails.

*Brutus*

[V.iii.94–96]

Hazlitt considered Julius Caesar "inferior in interest to *Coriolanus*," and many modern critics agree, but I am not one of them. *Coriolanus*, as Hazlitt first demonstrated, is a profound meditation upon politics and power, but its protagonist fascinates more for his predicament than for his limited consciousness. Brutus is Shakespeare's first intellectual, and the enigmas of his nature are multiform. Hazlitt pioneered in observing that Shakespeare's Julius Caesar does not answer "to the portrait given of him in his *Commentaries*," an observation that George Bernard Shaw repeated in a severer tone:

It is impossible for even the most judicially minded critic to look without a revulsion of indignant contempt at this travestying of a great man as a silly braggart, whilst the pitiful gang of mischief-makers who destroyed him are lauded as statesmen and patriots. There is not a single sentence uttered by Shakespeare's Julius Caesar that is, I will not say worthy of him, but even worthy of an average Tammany boss.

Shaw was preparing the way for his own *Caesar and Cleopatra* (1898), which has not survived a century, while *Julius Caesar* has better than survived four. Shakespeare's play has faults, but Shaw's has little else. Shakespeare's source, North's Plutarch, did not show a Caesar in decline; with sure insight, Shakespeare decided that his play required exactly a waning Caesar, a highly plausible mixture of grandeurs and weaknesses.

Though a persuasive representation, this Caesar is difficult to understand. Why is it so easy for the conspirators to murder him? His power pragmatically is all but absolute; where is his security apparatus? Where indeed are his guards? There may even be a suggestion that this Julius Caesar on some level courts martyrdom, as a way both to godhood and to the permanent establishment of the empire. Yet that is left ambiguous, as is the question of Caesar's decline. Shakespeare does not foreground his *Julius Caesar* by reference to Plutarch. He foregrounds it by the affection for their leader not just of Mark Antony and the Roman populace, but of Brutus himself, who has a filial love for Caesar, which is strongly returned. What Brutus communicates to us in one way, Antony does in another, and Cassius in a third, with negative power: Caesar's greatness is not in question, whatever his decline, and however one reacts to his royal ambitions.

Caesar is the grandest figure Shakespeare ever will represent, the person of most permanent historical importance (except perhaps for Octavius, both here and in *Antony and Cleopatra*). Octavius, though, is not yet Augustus Caesar, and Shakespeare evades conferring greatness upon him, in both plays, and indeed makes him rather unsympathetic, the type of the highly successful politician. Though sometimes silly, even fatuous, Shakespeare's Julius Caesar is an immensely sympathetic character, benign yet dangerous. He is, of course, self-centered, and always conscious of being Caesar, perhaps even sensing his deification in advance. And though he can be very blind, his estimate of Cassius shows him to be the best analyst of another human being in all of Shakespeare:

*Caes.* Antonius.

*Ant.* Caesar?

*Caes.* Let me have men about me that are fat,
Sleek-headed men, and such as sleep a-nights.
Yond Cassius has a lean and hungry look;
He thinks too much: such men are dangerous.

*Ant.* Fear him not, Caesar, he's not dangerous.
He is a noble Roman, and well given.

*Caes.* Would he were fatter! But I fear him not:
Yet if my name were liable to fear,
I do not know the man I should avoid
So soon as that spare Cassius. He reads much,
He is a great observer, and he looks
Quite through the deeds of men. He loves no plays,

As thou dost, Antony; he hears no music.
Seldom he smiles, and smiles in such a sort
As if he mock'd himself, and scorn'd his spirit
That could be mov'd to smile at any thing.
Such men as he be never at heart's ease
Whiles they behold a greater than themselves,
And therefore are they very dangerous.
I rather tell thee what is to be fear'd
Than what I fear; for always I am Caesar.
Come on my right hand, for this ear is deaf,
And tell me truly what thou think'st of him.

*Caesar*

*left ear deaf*

[I.ii.188–211]

Caesar is accurate, and Antony is not; Shakespeare scarcely could have found a better way to demonstrate the psychological acuity that made Caesar as great a politician as he was a soldier. Yet the same speech indicates one of several gathering infirmities, deafness, and the increasing tendency for Caesar to regard himself in the third person: "for always I am Caesar." Cassius, like many Roman Epicureans, is a Puritan, and embodies the spirit of resentment, unhappy as he is at contemplating a greatness beyond him. Brutus, a Stoic, has no envy of Caesar's splendor yet fears the potential of unlimited power, even if exercised by the responsible and rational Caesar. The soliloquy in which this fear is voiced is the best thing of its kind that Shakespeare yet had written, and is marvelously subtle, particularly where I italicize it:

*Bru.* It must be by his death: and for my part,
    I know no personal cause to spurn at him,
    But for the general. He would be crown'd:
    How that might change his nature, there's the question.
    It is the bright day that brings forth the adder,
    And that craves wary walking. Crown him?—that;—
    And then, I grant, we put a sting in him,
    That at his will he may do danger with.

*Brutus*

Th' abuse of greatness is when it disjoins

Remorse from power; and, to speak truth of Caesar,

*Brutus*

I have not known when his affections sway'd

More than his reason. But 'tis a common proof,

That lowliness is young ambition's ladder,

Whereto the climber-upward turns his face;

But when he once attains the upmost round,

He then unto the ladder turns his back,

Looks in the clouds, scorning the base degrees

By which he did ascend. So Caesar may;

Then lest he may, prevent. *And since the quarrel*

*Will bear no colour for the thing he is,*

*Fashion it thus:* that what he is, augmented,

Would run to these and these extremities;

And therefore think him as a serpent's egg,

Which, hatch'd, would, as his kind, grow mischievous,

And kill him in the shell.

[II.i.10–34]

It is one thing to speculate, "So Caesar may," and to follow with "Then lest he may, prevent." But it is peculiarly shocking that Brutus practices the overt self-deception of *"And since the quarrel / Will bear no colour for the thing he is, / Fashion it thus."* That is to acknowledge that there is no plausible complaint to make against Caesar: "Fashion it thus" means to make up your own anxious fiction, and then believe in its plausibility. Caesar, contrary to his entire career, will become an unreasonable and oppressive tyrant, only because Brutus wants to believe this.

Why should Brutus knowingly fashion such a fiction? The instigations of Cassius aside, Brutus appears to need the role of leading the conspiracy to slay Caesar. One could regard Freud's *Totem and Taboo* as a rewriting of *Julius Caesar*: the totem father must be murdered, and his corpse divided and devoured by the horde of his sons. Though Caesar's nephew, Octavius, is his adopted son and heir, there is a tradition that Brutus was Caesar's natural son, and many critics have noted the similarities that Shakespeare portrays between the two. I firmly reject Freud's identification of Hamlet with Oedipus; it is Brutus, and Macbeth after him, who manifest Oedipal ambivalences toward their fatherly rulers.

Brutus's patriotism is itself a kind of flaw, since he overidentifies himself with Rome, just as Caesar does. It is uncanny that Brutus, awaiting the night visit of Cassius and the other conspirators, suddenly becomes a prophecy of Macbeth, in a further soliloquy that seems to belong in the first act of *Macbeth*:

*Brutus*

> *Bru.* Between the acting of a dreadful thing
> And the first motion, all the interim is
> Like a phantasma, or a hideous dream:
> The genius and the mortal instruments
> Are then in council; and the state of man,
> Like to a little kingdom, suffers then
> The nature of an insurrection.
>
> [II.i.63–69]

For a few moments Brutus anticipates Macbeth's proleptic imagination, with "the state of man" echoed by Macbeth in Act I, Scene iii, line 140: "My thought, whose murther yet is but fantastical, / Shakes so my single state of man." Macbeth has nothing like Brutus's rational powers; Brutus has nothing like the Scottish regicide's range of fantasy, yet they almost fuse together here. The difference is that Brutus's "state of man" is more unaided and lonesome than Macbeth's. Macbeth is the agent of supernal forces that transcend Hecate and the witches. Brutus, the Stoic intellectual, is affected not by preternatural forces, but by his ambivalence which he has managed to evade. His love of Caesar has in it a negative element darker than Cassius's resentment of Caesar. Masking his own ambivalence toward Caesar, Brutus chooses to believe in a fiction, a rather unlikely one in which a crowned Caesar becomes only another Tarquin. But that fiction is not the quality of being that we hear in Caesar's final speech, when he refuses the conspirators' hypocritical pleas that an exile be allowed to return:

*Caesar*

Caes. I could be well mov'd, if I were as you;
If I could pray to move, prayers would move me;
But I am constant as the northern star,
Of whose true-fix'd and resting quality
There is no fellow in the firmament.
The skies are painted with unnumber'd sparks,
They are all fire, and every one doth shine;
But there's but one in all doth hold his place.
So in the world: 'tis furnish'd well with men,
And men are flesh and blood, and apprehensive;
Yet in the number I do know but one
That unassailable holds on his rank,
Unshak'd of motion; and that I am he,
Let me a little show it, even in this,
That I was constant Cimber should be banish'd,
And constant do remain to keep him so.

[III.i.58–73]

Some critics interpret this as absurd or arrogant, but it is true gold;
Caesar may idealize himself, and yet he is accurate. He is the northern star
of his world, and his rule partly depends upon his consistency. The essence
of this speech is its exaltation of a natural hierarchy that has become political. Caesar has no natural superior, and his intrinsic rank has extended
itself outward to dictatorship. The skeptic could remark that actually the
political here masks itself as the natural, but natural ease is Caesar's great
gift, so much envied by Cassius. Julius Caesar, and not Brutus or Cassius,
is the free artist of himself in this play, in living and dying. The audience's
underlying impression that Caesar is the playwright gives us the unsettling
notion of his death as a willing sacrifice to the imperial ideal. I call this unsettling because it diminishes Brutus, whose story then ceases to be a
tragedy. Sometimes I entertain the notion that Shakespeare himself—a
specialist in kings, older men, and ghosts—played Julius Caesar. Caesar
wants the crown, and (according to North's Plutarch) fresh conquests in
Parthia; Shakespeare is on the threshold of writing the high tragedies:
*Hamlet, Othello, King Lear, Macbeth, Antony and Cleopatra.* The cool disengage-

ment of the dramatist's stance in *Julius Caesar* allows for an inner gathering of the forces, just as perhaps Caesar gathered himself for conquest. Caesarism and tragedy, the first true works in that kind since ancient Athens, will triumph together. The play's authentic victims are Brutus and Cassius, not Caesar, just as its victors are not Mark Antony and Octavius, tuning up for their cosmological contest in *Antony and Cleopatra*. Caesar and Shakespeare are the winners; it is appropriate that this tragedy's most famous lines show Caesar at his finest:

> *Caes.* Cowards die many times before their deaths;
> The valiant never taste of death but once.
> Of all the wonders that I yet have heard,
> It seems to me most strange that men should fear,
> Seeing that death, a necessary end,
> Will come when it will come.
>
> [II.ii.32–37]

*Caesar*

That is not quite Hamlet's "the readiness is all," for Hamlet means something more active, the willingness of the spirit though the flesh be weak. Caesar, gambling on eternity, falls back upon a rhetoric unworthy of him, one that Hamlet would have satirized:

> *Caes.* The gods do this in shame of cowardice:
> Caesar should be a beast without a heart
> If he should stay at home to-day for fear.
> No, Caesar shall not. Danger knows full well
> That Caesar is more dangerous than he.
> We are two lions litter'd in one day,
> And I the elder and more terrible,
> And Caesar shall go forth.
>
> [II.ii.41–48]

*Caesar*

That bombast, mocked by Ben Jonson, nevertheless is there to considerable purpose, lest Caesar become so sympathetic that Brutus alienate us wholly. Shakespeare's Brutus is difficult to characterize. To call him a hero-villain clearly is wrong; there is nothing Marlovian about him. Yet he does seem archaic, as archaic as Julius Caesar, in contrast to Mark Antony and Octavius. A stoic tragic hero may be an impossibility. Titus Andronicus, *contra* many critics, was no such being, as we have seen. Brutus may attempt to assert reason against emotion, but pragmatically he stabs Caesar (by some traditions, in the privates), and then endures the mob's initial outcry: "Let him be Caesar," after it has heard his peculiar oration explaining his murder of Julius Caesar, dear friend if not hidden father, but less dear to him than Rome.

Brutus is such a puzzle that he is wonderfully interesting, to Shakespeare as to us. To call Brutus a sketch for Hamlet destroys poor Brutus: he hasn't a trace of wit, insouciance, or charisma, though everyone within the play clearly regards him as the Roman charismatic, after Caesar. Mark Antony has considerably more zest, and Cassius rather more intensity; who and what is Brutus? His own reply would be that Brutus is Rome, Rome Brutus, which tells us at once too much and much too little. Roman "honor" is incarnated in Brutus; is it not at least as massively present in Julius Caesar? Caesar is a politician; Brutus becomes the leader of a conspiracy, which is politics at an extremity. And yet Brutus has no capacity for change; his curious blindness dominates him until the end:

> —Countrymen,
> My heart doth joy that yet in all my life
> I found no man but he was true to me.
>
> [V.v.33–35]

These twenty monosyllabic words are very moving, yet they compel the audience to the question: Were you true to Julius Caesar? Evidently Brutus is more troubled than he admits; his dying words are

> —Caesar, now be still;
> I kill'd not thee with half so good a will.
>
> [V.v.50–51]

Cassius dies, hardly in the same spirit, but with a parallel declaration:

> —Caesar, thou art reveng'd,
> Even with the sword that kill'd thee.

*Cassius*

[V.iii.45–46]

The Ghost of Caesar identifies himself to Brutus, quite wonderfully, as "Thy evil spirit, Brutus," and indeed Caesar and Brutus share one spirit. Shakespeare perhaps did not consider the spirit of Caesarism evil, yet he left that quite ambiguous. "We all stand up against the spirit of Caesar," Brutus stirringly tells his subordinate conspirators in Act II, but do they? Can they? Shakespeare's politics, like his religion, forever will be unknown to us. I suspect that he had no politics, and no religion, only a vision of the human, or the more human. Shakespeare's Julius Caesar is at once human-all-too-human and, as he suspects, more than human, a mortal god. His genius—in history, Plutarch, and Shakespeare—was to merge Rome into himself. Brutus vainly attempts to merge himself into Rome, but he necessarily remains Brutus, since Caesar has usurped Rome forever. I think part of Shakespeare's irony, in the play, is to suggest that no Roman, in good faith, could stand up against the spirit of Caesar, even as no Englishman could stand up against the spirit of Elizabeth. Rome was overripe for Caesarism, as England and then Scotland were for Tudor-Stuart absolutism. Harold Goddard charmingly enlisted Falstaff, Rosalind, and Hamlet as Shakespeare's surrogates on Caesar; Falstaff refers to "the hook-nosed fellow of Rome," Rosalind speaks of the "thrasonical brag," the boastful "I came, I saw, I conquered"; and Hamlet in the graveyard composes an irreverent epitaph:

> Imperious Caesar, dead and turn'd to clay,
> Might stop a hole to keep the wind away.

If Shakespeare identified himself with any of his characters, it might have been with these three, but that takes us no closer to Caesar and to Brutus. Still, I do not trust the scholars on Shakespeare's politics, and no one emerges from *Julius Caesar* looking very admirable. Caesar is coming apart, Brutus is dangerously confused, and there is little to choose between Cassius on the one side and Mark Antony and Octavius on the other: scurvy politicians all. Supposedly Brutus and Cassius stand for the Roman republic, but their actual plans seem to culminate in the butchery of Caesar; their subsequent outcries of "Liberty, freedom, and enfranchisement!" are ludicrous. Brutus, the noblest Roman of them all, is notoriously inept in his funeral oration, particularly when he tells the mob: "As Caesar loved me, I weep for him," rather than "As I loved Caesar." Mark Antony's masterpiece of an oration may be the most famous sequence in Shakespeare, yet it is a half step on the road to Iago. I never quite get out of my ears Antony's finest rhetorical flourish:

*Antony*

O, what a fall was there, my countrymen!
Then I, and you, and all of us fell down.

[III.ii.192–93]

There is Caesar's greatest triumph: the promulgation of his myth by Antony's dangerous eloquence. In death, Caesar devours all of Rome.

By the play's end, Brutus, with ambivalent yet "noble" motives, has murdered Caesar. Antony, in vengeance and in quest for power, creates an Iago-like furor: "Mischief, thou art afoot, / Take what course thou wilt!" Shakespeare, always wary of a state power that had murdered Marlowe and tortured Kyd into another early grave, makes a fine joke of the raging mob's dragging off the wretched Cinna the poet for having the wrong name: "Tear him for his bad verses, tear him for his bad verses," even as Cinna the poet suffers the same fate of Marlowe and of Kyd. Shakespeare, whatever his nonpolitics, did not want to be torn for his good verses, or even for his great ones. *Julius Caesar* was, and is, a deliberately ambiguous play.

2

*The Tragedy of Julius Caesar* is a beautifully made play, and magnificent in its poetry, and yet it seems cold to many good critics. The greatest of all critics, Samuel Johnson, shrewdly remarked that Shakespeare subdued himself to his subject:

> Of this tragedy many particular passages deserve regard, and the contention and reconcilement of Brutus and Cassius is universally celebrated; but I have never been strongly agitated in perusing it, and think it somewhat cold and unaffecting, comparing with some other of Shakespeare's plays; his adherence to the real story, and to Roman manners, seems to have impeded the natural vigor of his genius.

Johnson was massively right; something inhibited Shakespeare, though I cannot believe that it was North's Plutarch or Roman stoicism. We must look elsewhere, perhaps to the tyrannicide debate, as Robert Miola has suggested. By the time Shakespeare was at work on the play, the popes had excommunicated Elizabeth, and Catholics had plotted to murder her. Shakespeare's Caesar is at most a benign tyrant, certainly in comparison with the terror afterward practiced as policy by Antony and Octavius. It may be that Shakespeare subtly marks the limits of judgment on tyranny: who is to decide which monarch is or is not a tyrant? The people are a mob, and both sides in the civil war after Caesar's death seem worse than Caesar, which does suggest a pragmatic support for Elizabeth. Yet I am uncertain that the tyrannicide controversy was a prime inhibitor for Shakespeare in this play, wary as he always was of alarming state power.

I suspect that there is a curious gap in *Julius Caesar*; we want and need to know more about the Caesar-Brutus relationship than Shakespeare seems willing to tell us. Caesar accepts death when Brutus, *his* Brutus, inflicts the final wound: "Then fall Caesar!" Plutarch repeats the gossip of Suetonius that Brutus was Caesar's natural son. Shakespeare surprisingly makes no use of this superb dramatic possibility, and surely we need to ask why not. So far is Shakespeare from invoking the father-son relationship (known to all in his audience who, like himself, had read North's Plutarch) that he refuses to allow Caesar and Brutus any significant contact until the murder scene. In their only meeting before that, we get the outrageously banal exchange of Caesar's asking the time, Brutus's saying that it is eight in the morning, and Caesar's thanking Brutus "for your pains and courtesy"! Their very next exchange is their last: Brutus kneels and kisses Caesar's hand ("not in flattery," he fatuously insists) as part of the fraudulent petition to bring Publius Cimber back from exile. Caesar is shocked enough to cry out, "What, Brutus?" and later to note that even Brutus cannot sway him: "Doth not Brutus bootless kneel?" The Caesar–Brutus relationship is thus for Shakespeare a nonstarter; the playwright evades it, as though it would needlessly complicate the tragedy of Caesar, and the tragedy of Brutus.

Unfortunately, this may have been a rare Shakespearean error, for the audience, if it reflects, will sense a missing foreground in the play, as I think Dr. Johnson did. Brutus, in his orchard soliloquy and elsewhere, betrays an ambivalence toward Caesar, which Shakespeare nowhere adumbrates. If the dramatist feared to add patricide to regicide, then he should have given some alternative account of the special relationship between Caesar and Brutus, but he gives absolutely none. Antony, in his funeral oration, says that Brutus was "Caesar's angel" (his darling, perhaps even his genius), and adds that the populace knows this, but gives no hint as to why Brutus was so well beloved by Caesar. Evidently the mob, like the audience, was supposed to know. It is as though Edmund in *King Lear* himself were to gouge out Gloucester's eyes.

Shakespeare perhaps frustrated himself even as he baffles us by this evasion, and I wonder if the absence of the Caesar–Brutus complication does not help account for the baffled quality of the play. As things stand, the mysterious special relationship between Caesar and Brutus makes it seem as though Brutus and not Octavius is the authentic heir to Caesar. Certainly Brutus has a very high self-regard, and a sense of destiny that transcends his own official descent from the Brutus who expelled the Tarquins. If he knows that truly he is not a Brutus but a Caesar, he would possess both a double pride and a double ambivalence. Though Brutus, after the murder, says that "ambition's debt" has been paid, he seems to be thinking of quite another debt. Shakespeare excludes none of this, and includes nothing of it. But the explanation of a father-son relationship would illuminate the ambiguities of Brutus as nothing else does. I turn again to the question: Why did Shakespeare choose not to write this relationship into his play?

At the least, such a relationship would have given Brutus too personal a motive for letting himself be seduced into Cassius's conspiracy, a motive perhaps endless to speculation. Patriotism is Brutus's dominant theme; his function is to save an older and nobler Rome from Caesarism. Shakespeare refuses to foreground why Brutus should be "Caesar's angel," even though, as I will later attempt to show, foregrounding is one of the great Shakespearean originalities, and is the most elliptical element in Shakespeare's art. By refusing to foreground or give any hint as to why Brutus should be "Caesar's angel," the dramatist allows at least an elite in the audience to assume that Brutus is Caesar's natural son. Since Cassius is Brutus's brother-in-law, he can be presumed to know this also, which gives a particular edge to his famous speech that is pivotal in winning over Brutus:

> *Cassius.* Why, man, he doth bestride the narrow world
> Like a Colossus, and we petty men
> Walk under his huge legs, and peep about
> To find ourselves dishonourable graves.
> Men at some time are masters of their fates:
> The fault, dear Brutus, is not in our stars,
> But in ourselves, that we are underlings.
> Brutus and Caesar: what should be in that "Caesar"?
> Why should that name be sounded more than yours?
> Write them together, yours is as fair a name;
> Sound them, it doth become the mouth as well;
> Weigh them, it is as heavy; conjure with 'em,
> "Brutus" will start a spirit as soon as "Caesar".
> Now in the names of all the gods at once,
> Upon what meat doth this our Caesar feed,
> That he is grown so great? Age, thou art sham'd!
> Rome, thou hast lost the breed of noble bloods!
> When went there by an age, since the great flood,
> But it was fam'd with more than with one man?

Cassius    When could they say, till now, that talk'd of Rome,
That her wide walks encompass'd but one man?
Now is it Rome indeed, and room enough,
When there is in it but one only man.
O, you and I have heard our fathers say,
There was a Brutus once that would have brook'd
Th' eternal devil to keep his state in Rome
As easily as a king.

[I.ii.133–59]

In a play weighted with magnificent ironies, the most ironical line may
be " 'Brutus' will start a spirit as soon as 'Caesar,' " since the Ghost of Caesar will identify himself as "Thy evil spirit, Brutus." And there would be a
shrewd irony, an audacious one, when Cassius speaks of "our fathers." Brutus is an unfinished character because Shakespeare exploits the ambiguity
of the Caesar–Brutus relationship without in any way citing what may be
its most crucial strand. *Julius Caesar* has an implicit interest as a study in
what shades upon patricide, but Shakespeare declines to dramatize this implicit burden in the consciousness of Brutus.

PART IV

# THE HIGH COMEDIES

# 10

## LOVE'S LABOUR'S LOST

There has almost always been agreement as to which plays are Shakespeare's greatest, and that general consent still prevails. Critics, audiences, and common readers all prefer *A Midsummer Night's Dream*, *As You Like It*, and *Twelfth Night* among the pure comedies, and *The Merchant of Venice* as well, despite the darker shadings conveyed by Shylock. The two parts of *Henry the Fourth* have something of the same eminence among the histories, while *Antony and Cleopatra* rightly vies with the four high tragedies: *Hamlet*, *Othello*, *King Lear*, *Macbeth*. Of the late romances, *The Winter's Tale* and *The Tempest* are universally preferred. Many critics, myself included, exalt *Measure for Measure* among the problem comedies.

But we all have particular favorites, in literature as in life, and I take more unmixed pleasure from *Love's Labour's Lost* than from any other Shakespearean play. I could not argue that as an aesthetic achievement, it stands with the fourteen dramas just mentioned, but I entertain the illusion that Shakespeare may have enjoyed a particular and unique zest in composing it. *Love's Labour's Lost* is a festival of language, an exuberant fireworks display in which Shakespeare seems to seek the limits of his verbal resources, and discovers that there are none. Even John Milton and James Joyce, the greatest masters of sound and sense in the English language after Shakespeare, are far outdone by the linguistic exuberance of *Love's Labour's Lost*. Alas, I have never seen a production of this extravagant comedy that could begin to perform to its vocal magnificence, but I always live in hope that some director of genius will yet deliver it to us.

*Love's Labour's Lost* is itself an opera, rather than a libretto that an opera could enhance, though Thomas Mann projects just such a fictive composition in his *Doctor Faustus* (1947). There Adrian Leverkühn, the daemonic German modernist composer, sets *Love's Labour's Lost* to be:

> as un-Wagnerian as possible, and most remote from nature-daemony and the theatrical quality of the myth: a revival of opéra bouffe in a spirit of the most artificial parody and mockery of the artificial: something highly playful and highly precious; its aim the ridicule of affected asceticism and that euphuism which was the social fruit of classical studies. He spoke with enthusiasm of the theme, which gave opportunity to set the lout and "natural" alongside the comic sublime and make both ridiculous in each other. Archaic heroics, rodomontade, bombastic etiquette tower out of forgotten epochs in the person of Don Armado, whom Adrian rightly pronounced a consummate figure of opera.

Mann captures much of the tone and mode of *Love's Labour's Lost,* even though he imports something of his own irony into Shakespeare's play. Joyous as Shakespeare's exuberance is in the language of *Love's Labour's Lost,* there are several different kinds of irony in the comedy, and none is quite Mannian. Berowne, Shakespeare's protagonist, is a highly conscious male narcissist who seeks his own reflection in the eyes of women and meets his catastrophe in the dark lady, Rosaline, "with two pitch-balls stuck in her face for eyes." The centuries have conjectured that Rosaline is linked to the Dark Lady of the Sonnets, a surmise supported by the lack of any justification in the play's text for Berowne's anxiety of betrayal in regard to Rosaline:

> *Ber.* O! and I forsooth in love!
> I, that have been love's whip;
> A very beadle to a humorous sigh;
> A critic, nay a night-watch constable,
> A domineering pedant o'er the boy,

Than whom no mortal so magnificent!

This wimpled, whining, purblind, wayward boy,

This signor junior, giant-dwarf, dan Cupid;

Regent of love rhymes, lord of folded arms,

The anointed sovereign of sighs and groans,

Liege of all loiterers and malcontents,

Dread prince of plackets, king of codpieces,

Sole imperator and great general

Of trotting paritors: O my little heart!

And I to be a corporal of his field,

And wear his colours like a tumbler's hoop!

What! I love! I sue! I seek a wife!

A woman that is like a German clock,

Still a-repairing, ever out of frame,

And never going aright, being a watch,

But being watch'd that it may still go right!

Nay to be perjur'd, which is worst of all;

And among three, to love the worst of all;

A whitely wanton with a velvet brow,

With two pitch-balls stuck in her face for eyes;

Ay and by heaven, one that will do the deed

Though Argus were her eunuch and her guard:

And I to sigh for her! to watch for her!

To pray for her! Go to; it is a plague

That Cupid will impose for my neglect

Of his almighty dreadful little might.

Well, I will love, write, sigh, pray, sue, and groan:

Some men must love my lady, and some Joan.

[III.i.170–202]

Cupid's revenge promises cuckoldry (as in the Sonnets), and the enigmatic, aggressive Rosaline seems a clue to the story of the Sonnets. What
is mysterious about *Love's Labour's Lost* is not its supposed hermetism but its
occult relationship between Berowne and Rosaline, who seem to have a

prehistory that Shakespeare evades foregrounding except for a few delicious hints such as this, when they first meet in the play:

> *Ber.* Did not I dance with you at Brabant once?
>
> *Ros.* Did not I dance with you in Brabant once?
>
> *Ber.* I know you did.
>
> *Ros.* How needless was it then to ask the question!
>
> *Ber.* You must not be so quick.
>
> *Ros.* 'Tis 'long of you that spur me with such questions.
>
> *Ber.* Your wit's too hot, it speeds too fast, 'twill tire.
>
> *Ros.* Not till it leave the rider in the mire.
>
> *Ber.* What time o' day?
>
> *Ros.* The hour that fools should ask.
>
> *Ber.* Now fair befall your mask!
>
> *Ros.* Fair fall the face it covers!
>
> *Ber.* And send you many lovers!
>
> *Ros.* Amen, so you be none.
>
> *Ber.* Nay, then will I be gone.
>
> [II.i.114–28]

The essence of Berowne is in that insouciant line, uttered upon meeting a French lady-in-waiting in Navarre: "Did not I dance with you in Brabant once?"

*Love's Labour's Lost* is a superb and exact title, but *Did Not I Dance with You in Brabant Once?* would have done almost as well, since it conveys the outrageously high sophistication of this comedy. The play's opening speech, addressed by the King of Navarre to his fellow "scholars"—Berowne, Longaville, Dumain—has all the stigmata of a comic Baroque:

> *King.* Let fame, that all hunt after in their lives,
>
>  Live register'd upon our brazen tombs,
>
>  And then grace us in the disgrace of death;
>
>  When, spite of cormorant devouring Time,
>
>  Th' endeavour of this present breath may buy

That honour which shall bate his scythe's keen edge,
And make us heirs of all eternity.
Therefore, brave conquerors—for so you are,
That war against your own affections
And the huge army of the world's desires—
Our late edict shall strongly stand in force:
Navarre shall be the wonder of the world;
Our court shall be a little academe,
Still and contemplative in living art.

[I.i.1–14]

The mock eloquence, with its grandiose vocabulary of death, time, war, and desire, does not altogether conceal the Shakespearean undersong that makes these first fourteen lines almost a blank verse sonnet, akin to several of the Sonnets. Though he is careful to distance us from Berowne and all the other fantastics of *Love's Labour's Lost*, Shakespeare seems unable or unwilling to distance himself from the enchantingly negative Rosaline. At an emblematical level, the play opposes Berowne's vision—half Promethean, half narcissistic—of women's eyes, to the unreflecting "pitch-balls" so fascinatingly stuck in Rosaline's face. Protesting Navarre's proscription against women during the three years' term of the little academy, Berowne gives us his initial apotheosis of the female eye:

*Ber.* Why! all delights are vain, but that most vain,
    Which with pain purchas'd doth inherit pain:
    As, painfully to pore upon a book
    To seek the light of truth; while truth the while
    Doth falsely blind the eyesight of his look:
    Light seeking light doth light of light beguile:
    So, ere you find where light in darkness lies,
    Your light grows dark by losing of your eyes.
    Study me how to please the eye indeed,
    By fixing it upon a fairer eye,
    Who dazzling so, that eye shall be his heed,

And give him light that it was blinded by.
Study is like the heaven's glorious sun,
That will not be deep-search'd with saucy looks;
Small have continual plodders ever won,
Save base authority from others' books.
These earthly godfathers of heaven's lights,
That give a name to every fixed star,
Have no more profit of their shining nights
Than those that walk and wot not what they are.
Too much to know is to know nought but fame;
And every godfather can give a name.

[I.i.72–93]

The essence of this is in the dazzling line 77:

Light seeking light doth light of light beguile:

Harry Levin unpacked this as: *"intellect,* seeking *wisdom,* cheats *eyesight* out of *daylight,"* a sound deciphering of Berowne's polemic against solitary study. Pursuing "a fairer eye," Berowne is ambushed by Rosaline, who warns the other ladies: "His eye begets occasion for his wit." Shrewdly exploiting the play's insight that men fall in love primarily through visual stimulation, while women fall in love more comprehensively and subtly, Shakespeare pursues the ill-fated quest of his four light-dazzled young men for their wary and elusive objects of desire. Boyet, counselor to the Princess of France, discerns that Navarre, on first sight, has fallen in love with her:

*Boyet.* Why, all his behaviors did make their retire
    To the court of his eye, peeping thorough desire:
    His heart, like an agate, with your print impress'd,
    Proud with his form, in his eye pride express'd:
    His tongue, all impatient to speak and not see,
    Did stumble with haste in his eyesight to be;

All senses to that sense did make their repair,
To feel only looking on fairest of fair:
Methought all his senses were lock'd in his eye,
As jewels in crystal for some prince to buy;
Who, tend'ring their own worth from where they were glass'd,
Did point you to buy them, along as you pass'd:
His face's own margent did quote such amazes,
That all eyes saw his eyes enchanted with gazes.
I'll give you Aquitaine, and all that is his,
An you give him for my sake but one loving kiss.

                                          [II.i.234–49]

"All senses to that sense did make their repair" is a pithy summary of the erotic despotism of the male eye. Berowne, in his misdirected sonnet to Rosaline, says that her eye "Jove's lightning bears," a rueful and masochistic recognition that the lovelorn wit adumbrates in a prose reverie:

*Ber.* The king he is hunting the deer; I am coursing myself: they have pitched a toil; I am toiling in a pitch,—pitch that defiles: defile! a foul word. Well, set thee down, sorrow! for so they say the fool said, and so say I, and I the fool: well proved, wit! By the Lord, this love is as mad as Ajax: it kills sheep, it kills me, I a sheep: well proved again o' my side! I will not love; if I do, hang me; i' faith, I will not. O! but her eye,—by this light, but for her eye, I would not love her; yes, for her two eyes. Well, I do nothing in the world but lie, and lie in my throat. By heaven, I do love, and it hath taught me to rhyme, and to be melancholy; and here is part of my rhyme, and here my melancholy. Well, she hath one o' my sonnets already: the clown bore it, the fool sent it, and the lady hath it: sweet clown, sweeter fool, sweetest lady! By the world, I would not care a pin if the other three were in. Here comes one with a paper: God give him grace to groan!

                                          [IV.iii.1–20]

The other three grace to groan lyrically, the King first in a sonnet on the Princess of France's eye beams, followed by Longaville in a sonnet celebrating the heavenly rhetoric of his love's eye, and Dumain in an ode a little lacking in the ocular obsession. With all four scholars of the Navarrese Academe revealed as traitors to their ascetic ideal, Berowne sums up their joint conversion to Eros in what most scholars have agreed is the central speech of the play:

> *Ber.* Learning is but an adjunct to ourself,
> And where we are our learning likewise is:
> Then when ourselves we see in ladies' eyes,
> Do we not likewise see our learning there?
> O! we have made a vow to study, lords,
> And in that vow we have forsworn our books:
> For when would you, my liege, or you, or you,
> In leaden contemplation have found out
> Such fiery numbers as the prompting eyes
> Of beauty's tutors have enrich'd you with?
> Other slow arts entirely keep the brain,
> And therefore, finding barren practisers,
> Scarce show a harvest of their heavy toil;
> But love, first learned in a lady's eyes,
> Lives not alone immured in the brain,
> But, with the motion of all elements,
> Courses as swift as thought in every power,
> And gives to every power a double power,
> Above their functions and their offices.
> It adds a precious seeing to the eye;
> A lover's eyes will gaze an eagle blind;
> A lover's ear will hear the lowest sound,
> When the suspicious head of theft is stopp'd:
> Love's feeling is more soft and sensible
> Than are the tender horns of cockled snails:
> Love's tongue proves dainty Bacchus gross in taste.
> For valour, is not Love a Hercules,

Still climbing trees in the Hesperides?
Subtle as Sphinx; as sweet and musical
As bright Apollo's lute, strung with his hair;
And when Love speaks, the voice of all the gods
Make heaven drowsy with the harmony.
Never durst poet touch a pen to write
Until his ink were temper'd with Love's sighs;
O! then his lines would ravish savage ears,
And plant in tyrants mild humility.
From women's eyes this doctrine I derive:
They sparkle still the right Promethean fire;
They are the books, the arts, the academes,
That show, contain, and nourish all the world;
Else none at all in aught proves excellent.
Then fools you were these women to forswear,
Or, keeping what is sworn, you will prove fools.
For wisdom's sake, a word that all men love,
Or for love's sake, a word that loves all men,
Or for men's sake, the authors of these women,
Or women's sake, by whom we men are men,
Let us once lose our oaths to find ourselves,
Or else we lose ourselves to keep our oaths.
It is religion to be thus forsworn;
For charity itself fulfils the law;
And who can sever love from charity?

[IV.iii.311–62]


This is Berowne's rhetorical triumph, and a wonderful parody of all male erotic triumphalism—then, now, and in time to be. It needs no feminist critique to uncover the outrageous narcissism that Berowne gorgeously celebrates:

Then when ourselves we see in ladies' eyes,
Do we not likewise see our learning there?

Their study is of themselves, and what they study to love is also themselves. Somehow Berowne has seen his own reflection, more truly than
ever before, in Rosaline's pitch-black eyes, and so has fallen more deeply
in love with himself. Freud's version of this Shakespearean wisdom was the
grim observation that object-libido began as ego-libido and always could
be converted back to ego-libido again. Berowne, as much in love with language as he is with himself, exalts the pragmatic augmentation of sensuous
power that accompanies the Herculean and Promethean fall into love. His
rhapsody is superbly free of any concern for Rosaline, ostensible object of
his passion: the "double power" that love confers comes with the theft of
"the right Promethean fire" from women's eyes, a theft that parodies Romans 13:8, "For he that loveth another hath fulfilled the law." Berowne's
spirited blasphemy ("It is religion to be thus forsworn; / For charity itself
fulfils the law; / And who can sever love from charity?"), which concludes
Act IV, ends the Navarrese Academy, and takes us to the play's comic crisis, where love's labor will be lost. But there is more to the play than the
campaign of Berowne and his fellows to win the ladies of France, and so I
double back to the fantastic comedians of Shakespeare's joyous invention:
Don Adriano de Armado and his witty page, Moth; Holofernes the pedant
and Sir Nathaniel the curate; Costard the Clown and Constable Dull.

2

*Love's Labour's Lost* shares with *A Midsummer Night's Dream* and *As You Like It* an
amiable mingling of social classes. Prince Hal, in the *Henry IV* plays, is all
too aware that he is on holiday with the people, while poor Malvolio in
*Twelfth Night* is ruined by erotic aspirations that transcend his social status.
But in what C. L. Barber called Shakespeare's "festive comedies," there is a
kind of pragmatic idealization of class relations. Barber attributed this to
"the sense Shakespeare creates of people living in a settled group, where
everyone is known and to be lived with around the clock of the year."
That conveys very aptly the serenity between classes in *Love's Labour's Lost,*
where the only strife is the contest between eloquent lust and wise disdain.
The madness of language, triumphant in the proto-Falstaffian wit of

Berowne, is equally prevalent in the exchanges between Armado and
Moth, Holofernes and Nathaniel, and Costard the Clown with everyone
he encounters. Little Moth, a child genius of rhetoric, is particularly effective in his witty outracings of the quixotic Armado, who dotes upon the
boy:

*Arm.* I will hereupon confess I am in love; and as it is base for a soldier
to love, so am I in love with a base wench. If drawing my sword
against the humour of affection would deliver me from the reprobate thought of it, I would take Desire prisoner, and ransom him
to any French courtier for a new-devised courtesy. I think scorn
to sigh: methinks I should outswear Cupid. Comfort me, boy.
What great men have been in love?

*Moth.* Hercules, master.

*Arm.* Most sweet Hercules! More authority, dear boy, name more;
and, sweet my child, let them be men of good repute and carriage.

*Moth.* Samson, master: he was a man of good carriage, great carriage,
for he carried the town-gates on his back like a porter; and he
was in love.

*Arm.* O well-knit Samson! strong-jointed Samson! I do excel thee in
my rapier as much as thou didst me in carrying gates. I am in love
too. Who was Samson's love, my dear Moth?

*Moth.* A woman, master.

*Arm.* Of what complexion?

*Moth.* Of all the four, or the three, or the two, or one of the four.

*Arm.* Tell me precisely of what complexion.

*Moth.* Of the sea-water green, sir.

*Arm.* Is that one of the four complexions?

*Moth.* As I have read, sir; and the best of them too.

*Arm.* Green indeed is the colour of lovers; but to have a love of that
colour, methinks, Samson had small reason for it. He surely affected her for her wit.

*Moth.* It was so, sir, for she had a green wit.

*Arm.* My love is most immaculate white and red.

*Moth.* Most maculate thoughts, master, are masked under such colours.

*Arm.* Define, define, well-educated infant.

*Moth.* My father's wit and my mother's tongue assist me!

*Arm.* Sweet invocation of a child; most pretty and pathetical!

[I.ii.54–92]

"Define, define, well-educated infant" must be the most charming educational plea in all of Shakespeare, with its wonderful mixture of affection and incomprehension. Moth's dry "Most maculate thoughts, master, are masked under such colours" conceals, partly through its alliteration, the page's demolition of Armado's erotic idealism. The flamboyant Armado (whose name jovially alludes to the defeated Spanish Armada) and the incisive Moth are a grand comic duo, and their bantering is a foreshadowing of Falstaff and Hal's exchanges. A very different order of comedy enters with the obsessed Holofernes (named for Gargantua's Latin tutor in Rabelais), who touches an apotheosis in boasting of his own rhetorical talents:

*Hol.* This is a gift that I have, simple, simple; a foolish extravagant
    spirit, full of forms, figures, shapes, objects, ideas, apprehensions,
    motions, revolutions: these are begot in the ventricle of memory,
    nourished in the womb of *pia mater,* and delivered upon the mel-
    lowing of occasion. But the gift is good in those in whom it is
    acute, and I am thankful for it.

[IV.ii.66–72]

The pia mater, the fine membrane that encloses the brain, is more a linguistic than an anatomical entity here. The descendants of Holofernes, endearingly absurd, were once to be found profusely on academic faculties, and I have a certain nostalgia for them, as they did no harm.

The high comedy of fantastical language mounts to a crescendo in Act V, Scene i, the funniest in the play, and clearly a favorite with James Joyce, who alludes to it, and in some sense is invented by Shakespeare in what I am calling the cognitive music that rises from the coming together of Armado, Moth, Holofernes, Sir Nathaniel, Dull, and Costard. The six zanies give us a *Finnegans Wake* in miniature, best summarized by little Moth: "They have been at a great feast of languages, and stolen the scraps," rephrased by Costard as "O, they have lived long on the alms-basket of words" (the reference being to the refuse of aristocratic and mercantile meals, placed in a tub for the poor). Here is Holofernes commenting upon Armado, a mad wordman castigating another, while himself vocalizing into a fine frenzy:

> *Hol.* He draweth out the thread of his verbosity finer than the staple of his argument. I abhor such fanatical phantasimes, such insociable and point-devise companions; such rackers of orthography, as to speak dout, fine, when he should say doubt; det, when he should pronounce debt,—d, e, b, t, not d, e, t; he clepeth a calf, cauf; half, hauf; neighbour *vocatur* nebour; neigh abbreviated ne. This is ab-hominable, which he would call abominable, it insinuateth me of insanie: *ne intellegis domine?* to make frantic, lunatic.
>
> [V.i.17–27]

Risking the wrath of his friend and rival Ben Jonson, Shakespeare de-lightfully indulges himself by emphasizing what Samuel Johnson called "the longest word known": *honorificabilitudinitatibus*, or "the state of being loaded with honors." Costard has the honor of using the word to scoff at Moth:

> *Cost.* I marvel thy master hath not eaten thee for a word; for thou art not so long by the head as *honorificabilitudinitatibus*: thou art easier swallowed than a flapdragon.
>
> [V.i.40–43]

The flapdragon, a raisin floating in a Christmas drink, is after all a prize, as is Moth.

All the zanies, gathered together, resolve to stage an antic pageant of the Nine Worthies in order to entertain the Princess and her ladies. The pageant, a memorable disaster, is central to the long (more than 900 lines) Scene ii that ends Act V and Shakespeare's play, a scene in which love's labor indeed is lost. Before examining the debacle of Berowne and his fellows, I want to stand back from Shakespeare's great feast of language, so as to achieve some perspective upon the personages of this comedy, and the comedy's place in Shakespeare's development.

3

C. L. Barber called *Love's Labour's Lost* "a strikingly fresh start, a more complete break with what [Shakespeare] had been doing earlier" than anything in his career except for the transition from the tragedies to the late romances. The discovery that his verbal resources were limitless freed Shakespeare for the lyrical crescendo of 1595–97 that includes *Richard II, Romeo and Juliet, A Midsummer Night's Dream,* and the astonishing Act V of *The Merchant of Venice.* I myself would interpret this movement to lyrical drama as part of Shakespeare's final emancipation from Marlowe, since it was followed by the great enabling act of creating Falstaff, the anti-Machiavel and so anti-Marlowe. There is a continuity between Faulconbridge the Bastard in *King John* (probably 1595), a first anti-Machiavel in Shakespeare, and Falstaff, and a deeper link between Berowne's wit and Falstaff's, though the connection is purely linguistic.

Whether Berowne has any interests that transcend his language is disputable, since his passion for Rosaline may be no more than a play upon words, despite his own later convictions. Though he is the most eminent wit of the four male would-be lovers, Berowne's passion is individualized only by its ruefulness, which is suitable, since his Rosaline is the thorniest of the four resistant noblewomen. Yet Berowne is also the theoretician of male narcissism in the play; he understands and indeed celebrates what his friends can only act out. Barber eloquently comments that all four manifest "the folly of acting love and talking love, without being in love," but I think that falls short of Berowne's hapless fall into love, probably the only form of love he ever can know: lust of the eye fused with self-delighting wit. Berowne's linguistic self-intoxication foreshadows Richard II's meta-physical brilliance as a lyric poet, fatally unsuitable for a reigning king, yet astonishing in its fireworks display of linguistic invention. Shakespeare's ironizing of Richard II is acutely palpable: this is a dangerous mode of wit, from which we are to be distanced. Berowne is very different; charming and resourceful, though in love with the wrong woman, does he perhaps represent some aspect of the elusive Shakespeare himself, prey of the Dark Lady of the Sonnets? Some commentators have thought so, but the clues are lacking in the profusion we would need to make the identification, however tentative. With Falstaff, Shakespeare's empathy is more persuasive, and Berowne is certainly one of the roles that seem retrospectively to prefigure Falstaff's.

Something is held back in Berowne's role; a reserve is intimated, but we cannot participate in it:

At Christmas I no more desire a rose
Than wish a snow in May's new-fangled shows;
But like of each thing that in season grows.

[I.i.105–7]

That is Berowne, and it is also the speaker of the Sonnets. Harold God-dard, always a refreshing personalizer of Shakespeare (so few attempt it!), gave to Berowne "precisely Shakespeare's capacity to taste without swal-lowing, to dally with the tempter until he is intimately acquainted with him, only in the end to resist the temptation." That is a lovely idealization both of Berowne and of the speaker of the Sonnets, each of whom swal-lowed and yielded to temptations. Still, more than any other critic of all Shakespeare since Johnson and Hazlitt, Goddard is always interesting, and more often than not is right. The comic genius of Falstaff seems as much Shakespeare's own as Hamlet's cognitive powers and Macbeth's pro-leptic imaginings are their author's endowments pushed to their limits. Berowne is a superb wit, and no comic genius: you cannot find anything in Berowne that is endless to meditation, as so much is in the sublimely dis-reputable Falstaff. Berowne does not get away from Shakespeare, as Falstaff perhaps does. We cannot imagine Berowne outside the world of *Love's Labour's Lost*. Unimaginative critics scoff at the notion, but Falstaff is larger than the *Henry IV* plays, superb as they are, even as Hamlet seems to need a sphere greater than Shakespeare provides him. Berowne falls in love with the wrong woman, and his Promethean dream of love, stealing fire from a woman, is a knowing projection of male narcissism, and yet there is something legitimately Promethean in his ecstatic celebration of a woman's eyes. His zest, like his wit, marks him as possessing Hazlittian gusto, little as Hazlitt cared for *Love's Labour's Lost*. Berowne has a resonance that somewhat exceeds the play's requirements, and is worthy of an heroic wit, who nevertheless is one of the fools of love. As a wit, Berowne stands back and looks at the play, almost from outside it, but as a lover he is a catastrophe, and Rosaline is his folly.

4

Act V, Scene ii, of *Love's Labour's Lost* is Shakespeare's earliest triumph at closure, the first of those elaborate set pieces that surprise us by their fine excess. In length, this single scene constitutes almost a third of the play's text, and it affords Shakespeare astonishing scope for his gifts, while as action little more comes about than the announcement of the king of France's death and the subsequent loss of their love's labor of wooing by Berowne, Navarre, and their friends. The sustained eloquence and verve of this final scene rivals all the Shakespearean brilliances yet to come, at the closes of *As You Like It, Measure for Measure,* and the late romances.

The construction of Act V, Scene ii, of *Love's Labour's Lost* is adroitly worked through. It starts with the four women coolly analyzing their would-be lovers' tactics, after which their elderly counselor, Boyet, advises them to prepare for a visitation by their admirers disguised as Muscovites. The Muscovite invasion is beaten off with defensive wit and evasion, and is followed by the Masque of the Nine Worthies, as performed by the commoners, an entertainment disrupted by the rudeness of the frustrated noblemen, who thus forget the courtesy they owe to their inferiors in rank and status. A fine theatrical coup then intervenes, as a messenger announces the death of the French king. The ceremonial farewell of the ladies to their defeated suitors meets with the expected male protests, which are answered by severe conditions of a year's service and penance for each courtier, after which presumably their entreaties may find some acceptance. Berowne's skepticism as to the realism of such expectations preludes a final entertainment, in which the owl of winter and the cuckoo of spring debate rival versions of the way things are. That gives us an elaborate fivefold sequence, more a pageant than it is the completion of a plot, and it raises the erotic war between men and women to new levels of sophistication and ruefulness. The play ceases to be Berowne's, and threatens ever more intensely his sense of identity, since he becomes another fool of love, Rosaline's victim.

No other comedy by Shakespeare ends with such erotic defeat, since we can doubt, with Berowne, whether these particular Jacks and Jills ever will come together. This realization gives the festive rituals of the final scene a hollow undersong, one that emerges with fierce resonance in the final contest between the cuckoo and the owl. We hear throughout a countercelebration, since more than male vanity is vanquished. In the war of wits, women's sophistication exposes and overcomes the universal inability of young men fully to differentiate the objects of their desire, a trait that marks the haplessness of their lust. Shakespeare's florabundance of language modulates to plain (but utterly witty) talk between the ladies as Act V, Scene ii, begins:

Prin. We are wise girls to mock our lovers so.
Ros. They are worse fools to purchase mocking so.
That same Berowne I'll torture ere I go.
O! that I knew he were but in by the week.
How I would make him fawn, and beg, and seek,
And wait the season, and observe the times,
And spend his prodigal wits in bootless rimes,
And shape his service wholly to my hests
And make him proud to make me proud that jests!

[V.ii.58–66]

If that is the Dark Lady of the Sonnets speaking, then Shakespeare suffered perhaps even more than he intimates. The relationship of Berowne and Rosaline has sadomasochistic overtones that make us doubt the woman ever would yield the greater pleasures of her ambivalence to the simpler ones of acceptance. Disguised, the women discover that they are interchangeable to the men; Berowne woos the Princess, and Navarre courts Rosaline, to the chorus of Boyet's monitory guide for all perplexed males:

> *Boyet.* The tongues of mocking wenches are as keen
>   As is the razor's edge invisible,
> Cutting a smaller hair than may be seen;
>   Above the sense of sense; so sensible
> Seemeth their conference; their conceits have wings
> Fleeter than arrows, bullets, wind, thought, swifter things.
>
> [V.ii.256–61]

Boyet is the play's prophet; himself past love, he sounds forth the theme of a female anti-wit itself so fiercely witty as to destroy any possibility of erotic fulfillment. There is wonderful humor and charm, but also an authentic pathos when Berowne surrenders in the war of wit, only to find that Rosaline takes no prisoners:

> *Ber.* Thus pour the stars down plagues for perjury.
>   Can any face of brass hold longer out?
>   Here stand I, lady; dart thy skill at me;
>   Bruise me with scorn, confound me with a flout;
>   Thrust thy sharp wit quite through my ignorance;
>   Cut me to pieces with thy keen conceit;
>   And I will wish thee never more to dance,
>   Nor never more in Russian habit wait.
>   O! never will I trust to speeches penn'd
>   Nor to the motion of a school-boy's tongue,
>   Nor never come in visor to my friend,

Nor woo in rhyme, like a blind harper's song,
Taffeta phrases, silken terms precise,
Three-pil'd hyperboles, spruce affection,
Figures pedantical; these summer flies
Have blown me full of maggot ostentation:
I do forswear them; and I here protest,
By this white glove (how white the hand, God knows),
Henceforth my wooing mind shall be express'd
In russet yeas and honest kersey noes.

[V.ii.394–413]

Trading "taffeta phrases" for "russet yeas and honest kersey noes" allies Berowne with homespun English cloth, an alliance that inspires Berowne to a semi-reformed declaration that is instantly squelched by the remorseless Rosaline:

*Ber.* And, to begin: Wench,—so God help me, law!—
My love to thee is sound, sans crack or flaw.
*Ros.* Sans "sans," I pray you.

[V.ii.414–16]

Still irrepressible, Berowne erupts into the dangerous wit of comparing his friends' passion for Rosaline's companions to the plague in Shakespeare's London. This metaphor or conceit is so extreme that one wonders if Shakespeare's bitterness toward his own Dark Lady is not again contaminating the exuberant Berowne:

*Ber*.  Soft! let us see:
Write "Lord have mercy on us" on those three;
They are infected, in their hearts it lies;
They have the plague, and caught it of your eyes:
These lords are visited; you are not free,
For the Lord's tokens on you do I see.

[V.ii.418–23]

The Princess and Rosaline deny these "tokens" or plague symptoms and proceed to demonstrate the Muscovites' inabilities to distinguish one beloved from another. Discomfited, Berowne and his fellows proceed to disgrace themselves by converting their frustration into a rather nasty scorn of the Masque of the Nine Worthies, as acted by "the pedant, the braggart, the hedge-priest, the fool, and the boy." But it is the lords who behave like petulant, scorned boys, ragging their social inferiors with viciously false wit. In response, the pedantic Holofernes reproves them with an authentic dignity: "This is not generous, not gentle, not humble." Poor Armado, even more savagely derided, charmingly defends the Trojan hero Hector, whom he impersonates:

> The sweet war-man is dead and rotten; sweet chucks, beat not the
> bones of the buried; when he breathed, he was a man.
>
> [V.ii.651–55]

Shakespeare enhances the amiable pathos of Armado when the eloquent Spaniard reveals his shirtless poverty, thus provoking Boyet to a peculiarly low nastiness. A marvelous theatrical coup intervenes with Marcade, a messenger from the court of France, announcing to the Princess the sudden death of the King, her father. Since Berowne and his friends, and Boyet, are about to forfeit all of our humorous sympathy, Shakespeare could not have delayed the coup longer without marring *Love's Labour's Lost.* Death is also in Navarre, as it is in Arcady, and the war of wit is over none too soon, with the defeat of the suitors threatening to turn into a witless rout. In a wonderful recovery, Shakespeare salvages the dignity of all on stage, though at the expense of what Berowne and his fellows persist in calling "love."

The Princess begins the final movement with a gracious apology that comes a little short of accounting for Rosaline's bitterness:

> *Prin.* Prepare, I say. I thank you, gracious lords,
>     For all your fair endeavours; and entreat,
>     Out of a new-sad soul, that you vouchsafe

In your rich wisdom to excuse or hide
The liberal opposition of our spirits,
If over-boldly we have borne ourselves
In the converse of breath; your gentleness
Was guilty of it. Farewell, worthy lord!
A heavy heart bears not a humble tongue.
Excuse me so, coming too short of thanks
For my great suit so easily obtain'd.

[V.ii.719–29]

To say that Berowne's "gentleness" provoked Rosaline's overboldness is diplomatic, and somewhat askew. But Berowne's own entreaty hardly shows him as accepting the Princess's chastisement:

  *Ber.* Honest plain words best pierce the ear of grief;
      And by these badges understand the king.
      For your fair sakes have we neglected time,
      Play'd foul play with our oaths. Your beauty, ladies,
      Hath much deform'd us, fashioning our humours
      Even to the opposed end of our intents;
      And what in us hath seem'd ridiculous,—
      As love is full of unbefitting strains;
      All wanton as a child, skipping and vain;
      Form'd by the eye, and therefore, like the eye,
      Full of straying shapes, of habits, and of forms,
      Varying in subjects, as the eye doth roll
      To every varied object in his glance:
      Which party-coated presence of loose love
      Put on by us, if, in your heavenly eyes,
      Have misbecom'd our oaths and gravities,
      Those heavenly eyes, that look into these faults,
      Suggested us to make. Therefore, ladies,
      Our love being yours, the error that love makes
      Is likewise yours: we to ourselves prove false,

By being once false for ever to be true
To those that make us both,—fair ladies, you:
And even that falsehood, in itself a sin,
Thus purifies itself and turns to grace.

[V.ii.743–66]

"Honest plain words" rapidly elaborate here into Berowne's baroque style, which is the man. Rather splendidly, he has learned nothing (or very little), as befits a hero of extravagant comedy. We are back in his exalted rhapsody on "the right Promethean fire," to be stolen by men from their own images reflected in women's eyes. The faith of Eros is carried over here into a parody of Christian grace in the final lines of his speech. But Berowne's hymn, though it may alarm the audience, is turned aside by the Princess, who deftly denies the analogue of devoutness:

*Prin.* We have receiv'd your letters full of love;
    Your favours, the ambassadors of love;
    And in our maiden council, rated them
    At courtship, pleasant jest, and courtesy,
    As bombast and as lining to the time.
    But more devout than this in our respects
    Have we not been; and therefore met your loves
    In their own fashion, like a merriment.

[V.ii.767–74]

There is a note of fine desperation in Navarre's response:

Now, at the latest minute of the hour,
Grant us your loves.

The reply of the Princess is one of those Shakespearean apothegms perpetually invaluable to women resisting any premature ensnarement:

    A time, methinks, too short
To make a world-without-end bargain in.

Of Shakespeare's own marriage, we have just enough information to infer that it may have been about as amiable as that of Socrates. As I have noted, in the cosmos of the plays, the happiest marriages doubtless are those of the Macbeths, before their crimes, and of Claudius and Gertrude, before Hamlet's interventions. As I read Shakespeare, before-and-after is a legitimate inference, a vital aspect of the supreme dramatist's art. The marital futures of Helena and Bertram in *All's Well That Ends Well,* and of the Duke and Isabella in *Measure for Measure,* give cause for grimaces, nor does one contemplate cheerfully years of Beatrice and Benedick battling it out, in what follows the end of *Much Ado About Nothing.* All Shakespearean marriages, comic and otherwise, are zany or grotesque, since essentially the women must marry down, particularly the peerless Rosalind in *As You Like It.* Shakespeare, and his public, can take a curious delight in *Love's Labour's Lost,* where no one gets married, and where we are more than free to doubt that a year's service or penance by the men (unlikely to be performed) will bring about any unions. The Princess sends Navarre off to a year in a hermitage, while Rosaline, with diabolic glee, assigns Berowne a year as comic comforter in a hospital: "To enforce the pained impotent to smile." We need not, however, contemplate married life between Berowne and Rosaline, as a final exchange between Navarre and Berowne makes clear:

> *Ber.* Our wooing doth not end like an old play;
>     Jack hath not Jill: these ladies' courtesy
>     Might well have made our sport a comedy.
> *King.* Come, sir, it wants a twelvemonth and a day,
>     And then 'twill end.
> *Ber.*                 That's too long for a play.
>
> [V.ii.864–69]

Berowne ruefully destroys two illusions: erotic and representational. The play indeed is over, except for the songs of the cuckoo and the owl. Standing on stage, but outside the artifice of the player, Berowne more than ever speaks for Shakespeare himself, who revised *Love's Labour's Lost* in 1597 after having achieved Falstaff, and so after fully achieving himself. There are two voices in Berowne, as I hear him, one pre-Falstaffian, and the other in Sir

John's spirit, destroying illusions. That is also, to my understanding, the spirit of the final twenty-eight Sonnets, starting with 127: "In the old age black was not counted fair," which returns us to Rosaline's mysterious rancor, and to Berowne's apparently unfounded fear that she will cuckold him. One of the charming oddities of *Love's Labour's Lost* is the mock dispute as to Rosaline's beauty in Act IV, Scene iii, lines 228–73, argued between Berowne and his friends, where Berowne is rather clearly the author of Sonnet 127, which he either echoes or prefigures. I tend to agree with Stephen Booth that we learn nothing more certain about Shakespeare from the Sonnets than we do from the plays. I do not *know* whether Shakespeare was heterosexual, homosexual, or bisexual (presumably the last), nor do I know the identity of the Dark Lady or of the Young Man (though she seems to me much more than a fiction, and most likely he is the Earl of Southampton). Yet I hear the reluctant passion of Berowne when I read Sonnet 127:

In the old age black was not counted fair,
Or if it were, it bore not beauty's name;
But now is black beauty's successive heir,
And beauty slandered with a bastard shame:
For since each hand hath put on nature's power,
Fairing the foul with art's false borrow'd face,
Sweet beauty hath no name, no holy bower,
But is profaned, if not lives in disgrace.
Therefore my mistress' eyes are raven black,
Her eyes so suited, and they mourners seem
At such who, not born fair, no beauty lack,
Sland'ring creation with a false esteem;
    Yet so they mourn, becoming of their woe,
    That every tongue says beauty should look so.

Berowne never touches the agonies of later Dark Sonnets, such as the "desire is death" of 147, but his equivocal variations upon Rosaline's black eyes are incessant throughout the play. Rosaline seems sometimes to be in the wrong play, since her stance toward Berowne is so severe and vindictive, unlike anything in the Princess's attitude toward Navarre, or of the other women toward their lovers. When Rosaline orders Berowne to hospital service, so as "to enforce the pained impotent to smile," the wit replies with what could be Shakespeare's own realization of the limits of comedy:

> To move wild laughter in the throat of death?
> It cannot be; it is impossible:
> Mirth cannot move a soul in agony.
>
> [V.ii.845–47]

Impressive as these lines are, they in no way move the implacable Rosaline, whose sole concern is "to choke a gibing spirit." As the play's audience, we have no desire to see Berowne's wit choked, and we therefore take some relief from his last words in *Love's Labour's Lost*: "That's too long for a play." It has been Berowne's play, but Shakespeare chooses to end with two contending songs, Spring against Winter, in which Berowne departs, and we are clearly in the world of Shakespeare's own country youth. The land of Navarre has vanished as we listen to the cuckoo and the owl sing, and hear about "Dick the shepherd" and "greasy Joan." Barber finely remarked that, in the absence of marriages, the songs provide "an expression of the going-on power of life"; I would add to that our satisfaction at being returned to the common life after our sojourn with the courtly wits of Navarre. And this is an appropriate point to say that Shakespeare, who wrote the best blank verse and prose in the language, is also the most eminent of its song writers:

> *Spring.* When daisies pied and violets blue
> And lady-smocks all silver-white
> And cuckoo-buds of yellow hue
> Do paint the meadows with delight.
> The cuckoo then, on every tree,
> Mocks married men; for thus sings he,
> Cuckoo;
> Cuckoo, cuckoo: O word of fear,
> Unpleasing to a married ear!

When shepherds pipe on oaten straws,
    And merry larks are ploughman's clocks,
When turtles tread, and rooks, and daws,
    And maidens bleach their summer smocks,
The cuckoo then, on every tree,
Mocks married men; for thus sings he,
        Cuckoo;
Cuckoo, cuckoo; O word of fear,
Unpleasing to a married ear!

*Winter.* When icicles hang by the wall,
    And Dick the shepherd blows his nail,
And Tom bears logs into the hall,
    And milk comes frozen home in pail,
When blood is nipp'd, and ways be foul,
Then nightly sings the staring owl,
        Tu-whit;
Tu-who, a merry note,
While greasy Joan doth keel the pot.

When all aloud the wind doth blow,
    And coughing drowns the parson's saw,
And birds sit brooding in the snow,
    And Marian's nose looks red and raw,
When roasted crabs hiss in the bowl,
Then nightly sings the staring owl,
        Tu-whit;
Tu-who, a merry note,
While greasy Joan doth keel the pot.

[V.ii.884–921]

Berowne's vivid but oddly misplaced fear of being cuckolded by his Dark Lady, as Shakespeare is in the Sonnets, finds superb transmutation in the song of the Spring. Married or unmarried, we are alarmed by the re-

turn of nature's force, and we are receptive to the song's mockery of the immemorial male anxiety of being cuckolded. Lovely as the first song is, the
Winter's lyric is grander, with its celebration of a communal life conducted
around a fire and a stirred pot. The owl's note is merry only because it is
heard from snugly within, by men and women held together by needs, by
realities, and by the shared values represented by the parson's saw, drowned
out by country coughs. Shakespeare's most elaborately artificial comedy,
his great feast of language, antithetically subsides in natural simplicities and
in country phrases.

# 11

# A MIDSUMMER NIGHT'S DREAM

In the midst of the winter of 1595–96, Shakespeare visualized an ideal summer, and he composed *A Midsummer Night's Dream*, probably on commission for a noble marriage, where first it was played. He had written *Richard II* and *Romeo and Juliet* during 1595; just ahead would come *The Merchant of Venice* and Falstaff's advent in *Henry IV, Part One*. Nothing by Shakespeare before *A Midsummer Night's Dream* is its equal, and in some respects nothing by him afterward surpasses it. It is his first undoubted masterwork, without flaw, and one of his dozen or so plays of overwhelming originality and power. Unfortunately, every production of it that I have been able to attend has been a brutal disaster, with the exception of Peter Hall's motion picture of 1968, happily available on videotape. Only *The Tempest* is as much distorted in recent stagings as *A Midsummer Night's Dream* has been and is likely to go on being. The worst I recall are Peter Brook's (1970) and Alvin Epstein's (a Yale hilarity of 1975), but I cannot be the only lover of the play who rejects the prevailing notion that sexual violence and bestiality are at the center of this humane and wise drama.

Sexual politics is too much in fashion for me just to shudder and pass by; *A Midsummer Night's Dream* will reassert itself, at a better time than this, but I have much to say on behalf of Bottom, Shakespeare's most engaging character before Falstaff. Bottom, as the play's text comically makes clear, has considerably less sexual interest in Titania than she does in him, or than many recent critics and directors have in her. Shakespeare, here and elsewhere, is bawdy but not prurient; Bottom is amiably innocent, and not very bawdy. Sex-and-violence exalters really should look elsewhere; *Titus Andronicus* would be a fine start. If Shakespeare had desired to write an orgiastic ritual, with Bottom as "this Bacchic ass of Saturnalia and carnival" (Jan Kott), we would have a different comedy. What we do have is a gentle, mild, good-natured Bottom, who is rather more inclined to the company of the elves—Peaseblossom, Cobweb, Moth, and Mustardseed— than to the madly infatuated Titania. In an age of critical and theatrical absurdity, I may yet live to be told that Bottom's interest in the little folk represents a potential for child abuse, which would be no sillier than the ongoing accounts of *A Midsummer Night's Dream*.

It is a curious link between *The Tempest*, *Love's Labour's Lost*, and *A Midsummer Night's Dream* that these are the three plays, out of thirty-nine, where Shakespeare does not follow a primary source. Even *The Merry Wives of Windsor*, which has no definite source, takes a clear starting point from Ovid. *The Tempest* is essentially plotless, and almost nothing happens in *Love's Labour's Lost*, but Shakespeare uniquely took pains to work out a fairly elaborate and outrageous plot for *A Midsummer Night's Dream*. Inventing plot was not a Shakespearean gift; it was the one dramatic talent that nature had denied him. I think he prided himself on creating and intertwining the four different worlds of character in the *Dream*. Theseus and Hippolyta belong to ancient myth and legend. The lovers—Hermia, Helena, Lysander, and Demetrius—are of no definite time or place, since all young people in love notoriously dwell in a common element. The fairies—Titania, Oberon, Puck, and Bottom's four chums—emerge from literary folklore and its magic. And finally, the "mechanicals" are English rustic artisans— the sublime Bottom, Peter Quince, Flute, Snout, Snug, and Starveling— and so come out of Shakespeare's own countryside, where he grew up.

This mélange is so diverse that a defense of it becomes the hidden reference in the wonderfully absurd exchanges between Theseus and Hippolyta concerning the music of the hounds in Act IV, Scene i, lines 103–27, which I will consider in some detail later. "So musical a discord, such sweet thunder" has been widely and correctly taken as this play's description of itself. Chesterton, who sometimes thought the *Dream* the greatest of all

Shakespeare's plays, found its "supreme literary merit" to be "a merit of design."

As an epithalamium, the *Dream* ends with three weddings, and the reconciliation of Oberon and Titania. But we might not know that all this was an extended and elaborate marriage song if the scholars did not tell us, and from the title on we do know that it is (at least in part) a dream. Whose dream? One answer is: Bottom's dream or his weaving, because he *is* the protagonist (and the greatest glory) of the play. Puck's epilogue, however, calls it the audience's dream, and we do not know precisely how to receive Puck's apologia. Bottom is universal enough (like Joyce's Poldy Bloom or Earwicker) to weave a common dream for all of us, except insofar as we are Pucks rather than Bottoms. How are we meant to understand the play's title? C. L. Barber pointed out Dr. Johnson's error in believing that "the rite of May" must take place on May Day, since the young went Maying when the impulse moved them. We are neither at May Day nor at Midsummer Eve, and so the title probably should be read as *any* night at all in midsummer. There is a casual, throwaway gesture in the title: this could be anyone's dream or any night in midsummer, when the world is largest.

Bottom is Shakespeare's Everyman, a true original, a clown rather than a fool or jester. He is a wise clown, though he smilingly denies his palpable wisdom, as if his innocent vanity did not extend to such pretension. One delights in Falstaff (unless one is an academic moralist), but one loves Bottom, though necessarily he is the lesser figure of the two. No one in Shakespeare, not even Hamlet or Rosalind, Iago or Edmund, is more intelligent than Falstaff. Bottom is as shrewd as he is kind, but he is not a wit, and Falstaff is Monarch of Wit. Every exigency finds Bottom round and ready: his response is always admirable. The Puck-induced metamorphosis is a mere externality: the inner Bottom is unfazed and immutable. Shakespeare foregrounds Bottom by showing us that he is the favorite of his fellow mechanicals: they acclaim him as "bully Bottom," and we learn to agree with them.

Like Dogberry after him, Bottom is an ancestor of Sheridan's Mrs. Malaprop, and uses certain words without knowing what they signify. Though he is thus sometimes inaccurate at the circumference, he is always sound at the core, which is what Bottom the Weaver's name means, the center of the skein upon which the weaver's wool is wound. There are folkloric magical associations attendant upon weaving, and Puck's choice of Bottom for enchantment is therefore not as arbitrary as first it seems. Whether or not Bottom (very briefly) becomes the carnal lover of the Fairy Queen Shakespeare leaves ambiguous or elliptical, probably because it is unimportant compared with Bottom's uniqueness in the *Dream*: he alone sees and converses with the fairy folk. The childlike fourfold of Peaseblossom, Moth, Cobweb, and Mustardseed are as charmed by Bottom as he is by them. They recognize themselves in the amiable weaver, and he beholds much that is already his own in them. "On the loftiest of the world's thrones we still are sitting on our own Bottom," Montaigne taught Shakespeare and the rest of us in his greatest essay, "Of Experience." Bottom the natural man is also the transcendental Bottom, who is just as happily at home with Cobweb and Peaseblossom as he is with Snug and Peter Quince. For him there is no musical discord or confusion in the overlapping realms of the *Dream*. It is absurd to condescend to Bottom: he is at once a sublime clown and a great visionary.

2

There is no darkness in Bottom, even when he is caught up in an enchanted condition. Puck, his antithesis, is an ambivalent figure, a mischief maker at best, and something weirder also, though the play (and Oberon) confine him to harmlessness, and indeed bring benignity out of his antics. Puck's alternate name in both the play and in popular lore is Robin Goodfellow, more a prankster than a wicked sprite, though to call him "Goodfellow" suggests a need to placate him. The word *puck* or *pook* originally meant a demon out for mischief or a wicked man, and Robin Goodfellow was once a popular name for the Devil. Yet throughout the *Dream* he plays Ariel to Oberon's Prospero, and so is under firmly benign control. At the end of the play, Bottom is restored to his external guise, the lovers pair off sensibly, and Oberon and Titania resume their union. "But we are spirits of another sort," Oberon remarks, and even Puck is therefore benevolent in the *Dream*.

The Puck–Bottom contrast helps define the world of the *Dream*. Bottom, the best sort of natural man, is subject to the pranks of Puck, helpless to avoid them, and unable to escape their influence without Oberon's order of release: though the *Dream* is a romantic comedy, and not an allegory, part of its power is to suggest that Bottom and Puck are invariable components of the human. One of the etymological meanings of "bottom" is the ground or the earth, and perhaps people can be divided into the earthy and the puckish, and are so divided within themselves. And yet Bottom is human, and Puck is not; since he has no human feelings, Puck has no precise human meaning.

Bottom is an early Shakespearean instance of how meaning gets started, rather than merely repeated: as in the greater Falstaff, Shakespearean meaning comes from excess, overflow, florabundance. Bottom's consciousness, unlike Falstaff's and Hamlet's, is not infinite; we learn its circumferences, and some of them are silly. But Bottom is heroically sound in the goodness of his heart, his bravery, his ability to remain himself in any circumstance, his refusal to panic or even be startled. Like Launce and the Bastard Faulconbridge, Bottom is a triumphant early instance of Shakespeare's invention of the human. All of them are on the road to Falstaff, who will surpass them even in their exuberance of being, and vastly is beyond them as a source for meaning. Falstaff, the ultimate anarchist, is as dangerous as he is fascinating, both life-enhancing and potentially destructive. Bottom is a superb comic, and a very good man, as benign as any in Shakespeare.

3

Doubtless Shakespeare remembered that in Edmund Spenser's *The Faerie Queene* Oberon was the benevolent father of Gloriana, who in the allegory of Spenser's great epic represented Queen Elizabeth herself. Scholars believe it likely that Elizabeth was present at the initial performance of the *Dream*, where necessarily she would have been the Guest of Honor at the wedding. *A Midsummer Night's Dream*, like *Love's Labour's Lost*, *The Tempest*, and *Henry VIII*, abounds in pageantry. This aspect of the *Dream* is wonderfully analyzed in C. L. Barber's *Shakespeare's Festive Comedy*, and has little to do with my prime emphasis on the Shakespearean invention of character and personality. As an aristocratic entertainment, the *Dream* bestows relatively little of its energies upon making Theseus and Hippolyta, Oberon and Titania, and the four young lovers lost in the woods into idiosyncratic and distinct personages. Bottom and the uncanny Puck are protagonists, and are portrayed in detail. Everyone else—even the other colorful Mechanicals—are subdued to the emblematic quality that pageantry tends to require. Still, Shakespeare seems to have looked beyond the play's initial occasion to its other function as a work for the public stage, and there are small, sometimes very subtle touches of characterization that transcend the function of an aristocratic epithalamium. Hermia has considerably more personality than Helena, while Lysander and Demetrius are interchangeable, a Shakespearean irony that suggests the arbitrariness of young love, from the perspective of everyone except the lover. But then all love is ironical in the *Dream*: Hippolyta, though apparently resigned, is a captive bride, a partly tamed Amazon, while Oberon and Titania are so accustomed to mutual sexual betrayal that their actual rift has nothing to do with passion but concerns the protocol of just who has charge of a changeling human child, a little boy currently under Titania's care. Though the greatness of the *Dream* begins and ends in Bottom, who makes his first appearance in the play's second scene, and in Puck, who begins Act II, we are not transported by the sublime language unique to this drama until Oberon and Titania first confront each other:

> *Obe.* Ill met by moonlight, proud Titania.
> *Tita.* What, jealous Oberon? Fairies, skip hence; I have forsworn his
> bed and company.
> *Obe.* Tarry, rash wanton; am not I thy lord?
> *Tita.* Then I must be thy lady; but I know
> When thou hast stol'n away from fairy land,
> And in the shape of Corin, sat all day
> Playing on pipes of corn, and versing love
> To amorous Phillida. Why art thou here,

Come from the farthest step of India,
But that, forsooth, the bouncing Amazon,
Your buskin'd mistress and your warrior love,
To Theseus must be wedded, and you come
To give their bed joy and prosperity?
*Obe.* How canst thou thus, for shame, Titania,
Glance at my credit with Hippolyta,
Knowing I know thy love to Theseus?
Didst not thou lead him through the glimmering night
From Perigouna, whom he ravished;
And make him with fair Aegles break his faith,
With Ariadne and Antiopa?

[II.i.60–80]

In Plutarch's *Life of Theseus,* read by Shakespeare in Sir Thomas North's version, Theseus is credited with many "ravishments," cheerfully itemized here by Oberon, who assigns Titania the role of bawd, guiding the Athenian hero to his conquests, herself doubtless included. Though Titania will retort that "These are the forgeries of jealousy," they are just as persuasive as her visions of Oberon "versing love / To amorous Phillida," and enjoying "the bouncing Amazon," Hippolyta. The Theseus of the *Dream* appears to have retired from his womanizings into rational respectability, with its attendant moral obtuseness. Hippolyta, though championed as a victim by feminist critics, shows little aversion to being wooed by the sword and seems content to dwindle into Athenian domesticity after her exploits with Oberon, though she retains a vision all her own, as will be seen. What Titania magnificently goes on to tell us is that discord between herself and Oberon is a disaster for both the natural and the human realm:

*Tita.* These are the forgeries of jealousy:
And never, since the middle summer's spring,
Met we on hill, in dale, forest or mead,
By paved fountain, or by rushy brook,

Or in the beached margent of the sea,
To dance our ringlets to the whistling wind,
But with thy brawls thou hast disturb'd our sport.
Therefore the winds, piping to us in vain,
As in revenge have suck'd up from the sea
Contagious fogs; which, falling in the land,
Hath every pelting river made so proud
That they have overborne their continents.
The ox hath therefore stretch'd his yoke in vain,
The ploughman lost his sweat, and the green corn
Hath rotted ere his youth attain'd a beard;
The fold stands empty in the drowned field,
And crows are fatted with the murrion flock;
The nine-men's-morris is fill'd up with mud,
And the quaint mazes in the wanton green
For lack of tread are undistinguishable.
The human mortals want their winter cheer:
No night is now with hymn or carol blest.
Therefore the moon, the governess of floods,
Pale in her anger, washes all the air,
That rheumatic diseases do abound.
And thorough this distemperature we see
The seasons alter: hoary-headed frosts
Fall in the fresh lap of the crimson rose;
And on old Hiems' thin and icy crown,
An odorous chaplet of sweet summer buds
Is, as in mockery, set; the spring, the summer,
The childing autumn, angry winter, change
Their wonted liveries; and the mazed world,
By their increase, now knows not which is which.
And this same progeny of evils comes
From our debate, from our dissension;
We are their parents and original.

[II.i.81–117]

No previous poetry by Shakespeare achieved this extraordinary quality; he finds here one of his many authentic voices, the paean of natural
lament. Power in the *Dream* is magical rather than political; Theseus is ignorant when he assigns power to the paternal, or to masculine sexuality.
Our contemporary heirs of the materialist metaphysics of Iago, Thersites,
and Edmund see Oberon as only another assertion of masculine authority,
but they need to ponder Titania's lamentation. Oberon is superior in trickery, since he controls Puck, and he will win Titania back to what he considers his kind of amity. But is that a reassertion of male dominance, or
of something much subtler? The issue between the fairy queen and king
is a custody dispute: "I do but beg a little changeling boy / To be my
henchman"—that is, Oberon's page of honor in his court. Rather than the
unbounded prurience that many critics insist upon, I see nothing but an innocent assertion of sovereignty in Oberon's whim, or in Titania's poignant
and beautiful refusal to yield up the child:

> Set your heart at rest:
> The fairy land buys not the child of me.
> His mother was a votress of my order;
> And in the spiced Indian air, by night,
> Full often hath she gossip'd by my side;
> And sat with me on Neptune's yellow sands,
> Marking th'embarked traders on the flood:
> When we have laugh'd to see the sails conceive
> And grow big-bellied with the wanton wind;
> Which she, with pretty and with swimming gait
> Following (her womb then rich with my young squire),
> Would imitate, and sail upon the land
> To fetch me trifles, and return again
> As from a voyage rich with merchandise.
> But she, being mortal, of that boy did die;
> And for her sake do I rear up her boy;
> And for her sake I will not part with him.

[II.i.121–37]

Ruth Nevo accurately observes that Titania has so assimilated her votaries to herself that the changeling child has become her own, in a relationship that firmly excludes Oberon. To make the boy his henchman would be an assertion of adoption, like Prospero's initial stance toward Caliban, and Oberon will utilize Puck to achieve this object. But why should Oberon, who is not jealous of Theseus, and is willing to be cuckolded by Titania's enchantment, feel so fiercely in regard to the changeling's custody? Shakespeare will not tell us, and so we must interpret this ellipsis for ourselves.

One clear implication is that Oberon and Titania have no male child of their own; Oberon being immortal need not worry about an heir, but evidently he has paternal aspirations that his henchman Puck cannot satisfy. It may also be relevant that the changeling boy's father was an Indian king, and that tradition traces Oberon's royal lineage to an Indian emperor. What matters most appears to be Titania's refusal to allow Oberon any share in her adoption of the child. Perhaps David Wiles is correct in arguing that Oberon desires to parallel the pattern of Elizabethan aristocratic marriages, where the procreation of a male heir was the highest object, though Elizabeth herself as Virgin Queen undoes the tradition, and Elizabeth is the ultimate patroness of the *Dream*.

I think the quarrel between Titania and Oberon is subtler, and turns on the question of the links between mortals and immortals in the play. Theseus's and Hippolyta's amours with the fairies are safely in the past, and Oberon and Titania, however estranged from each other, have arrived in the wood near Athens to bless the wedding of their former lovers. Bottom, one of the least likely of mortals, will sojourn briefly among the fairies, but his metamorphosis, when it comes, is merely outward. The Indian child is a true changeling; he will live out his life among the immortals. That is anything but irrelevant to Oberon: he and his subjects have their mysteries, jealously guarded from mortals. To exclude Oberon from the child's company is therefore not just a challenge to male authority; it is a wrong done to Oberon, and one that he must reverse and subsume in the name of the legitimacy in leadership that he shares with Titania. As Oberon says, it is an "injury."

To torment Titania away from her resolution, Oberon invokes what becomes the most beautiful of Shakespeare's visions in the play:

*Obe.*                    Thou rememb'rest
     Since once I sat upon a promontory,
     And heard a mermaid on a dolphin's back
     Uttering such dulcet and harmonious breath
     That the rude sea grew civil at her song
     And certain stars shot madly from their spheres
     To hear the sea maid's music?
*Puck.*                              I remember.
*Obe.* That very time I saw (but thou couldst not),
     Flying between the cold moon and the earth,
     Cupid all arm'd: a certain aim he took
     At a fair vestal, throned by the west,
     And loos'd his love-shaft smartly from his bow
     As it should pierce a hundred thousand hearts.
     But I might see young Cupid's fiery shaft
     Quench'd in the chaste beams of the watery moon;
     And the imperial votress passed on,
     In maiden meditation, fancy-free.
     Yet mark'd I where the bolt of Cupid fell:
     It fell upon a little western flower,
     Before milk-white, now purple with love's wound:
     And maidens call it 'love-in-idleness'.
     Fetch me that flower; the herb I show'd thee once.
     The juice of it, on sleeping eyelids laid,
     Will make or man or woman madly dote
     Upon the next live creature that it sees.
     Fetch me this herb, and be thou here again
     Ere the leviathan can swim a league.
*Puck.* I'll put a girdle round about the earth
     In forty minutes.
*Obe.*                  Having once this juice.

I'll watch Titania when she is asleep,
And drop the liquor of it in her eyes:
The next thing then she waking looks upon
(Be it on lion, bear, or wolf, or bull,
On meddling monkey, or on busy ape)
She shall pursue it with the soul of love.
And ere I take this charm from off her sight
(As I can take it with another herb)
I'll make her render up her page to me.

[II.i.148–85]

The flower love-in-idleness is the pansy; the "fair vestal, throned by the west" is Queen Elizabeth I, and one function of this fairy vision is to constitute Shakespeare's largest and most direct tribute to his monarch during her lifetime. She passes on, and remains fancy-free; the arrow of Cupid, unable to wound the Virgin Queen, instead converts the pansy into a universal love charm. It is as though Elizabeth's choice of chastity opens up a cosmos of erotic possibilities for others, but at the high cost of accident and arbitrariness replacing her reasoned choice. Love at first sight, exalted in *Romeo and Juliet*, is pictured here as calamity. The ironic possibilities of the love elixir are first intimated when, in one of the play's most exquisite passages, Oberon plots the ensnarement of Titania:

I know a bank where the wild thyme blows,
Where oxlips and the nodding violet grows,
Quite over-canopied with luscious woodbine,
With sweet musk-roses, and with eglantine.
There sleeps Titania sometime of the night,
Lull'd in these flowers with dances and delight;
And there the snake throws her enamell'd skin,
Weed wide enough to wrap a fairy in;
And with the juice of this I'll streak her eyes,
And make her full of hateful fantasies.

[II.i.249–58]

The contrast between those first six lines and the four that come after grants us an aesthetic *frisson*; the transition is from Keats and Tennyson to Browning and the early T. S. Eliot, as Oberon modulates from sensuous naturalism to grotesque gusto. Shakespeare thus prepares the way for the play's great turning point in Act III, Scene i, where Puck transforms Bottom, and Titania wakens with the great outcry, "What angel wakes me from my flowery bed?" The angel is the imperturbable Bottom, who is sublimely undismayed that his amiable countenance has metamorphosed into an ass head.

This wonderfully comic scene deserves pondering: Who among us could sustain so weird a calamity with so equable a spirit? One feels that Bottom could have undergone the fate of Kafka's Gregor Samsa with only moderate chagrin. He enters almost on cue, chanting, "If I were fair, Thisbe, I were only thine," scattering his fellows. Presumably discouraged at his inability to frighten Bottom, the frustrated Puck chases after the Mechanicals, taking on many fearsome guises. Our bully Bottom responds to Peter Quince's "Bless thee, Bottom, bless thee! Thou art translated," by cheerfully singing a ditty hinting at cuckoldry, thus preparing us for a comic dialogue that even Shakespeare was never to surpass:

> *Tita.* I pray thee, gentle mortal, sing again:
> Mine ear is much enamour'd of thy note;
> So is mine eye enthralled to thy shape;
> And thy fair virtue's force perforce doth move me
> On the first view to say, to swear, I love thee.
>
> *Bot.* Methinks, mistress, you should have little reason for that. And yet, to say the truth, reason and love keep little company together nowadays. The more the pity that some honest neighbours will not make them friends. Nay, I can gleek upon occasion.
>
> *Tita.* Thou art as wise as thou art beautiful.
>
> *Bot.* Not so neither; but if I had wit enough to get out of this wood, I have enough to serve my own turn.
>
> *Tita.* Out of this wood do not desire to go:
> Thou shalt remain here, whether thou wilt or no.

[III.i.132–46]

Even C. L. Barber somewhat underestimates Bottom, when he says that Titania and Bottom are "fancy against fact," since "enchantment against Truth" is more accurate. Bottom is unfailingly courteous, courageous, kind, and sweet-tempered, and he humors the beautiful queen whom he clearly knows to be quite mad. The ironies here are fully in Bottom's control, and are kept gentle by his tact. Nothing else in the *Dream* is as pithy an account of its erotic confusions: "reason and love keep little company together nowadays." Bottom too can "gleek" (jest) upon occasion, which is the only other possibility, should poor Titania prove to be sane. Neither wise nor beautiful, Bottom sensibly wishes to get out of the wood, but he does not seem particularly alarmed when Titania tells him he is a prisoner. Her proud assertion of rank and self is hilarious in its absurd confidence that she can purge Bottom's "mortal grossness" and transform him into another "airy spirit," as though he could be another changeling like the Indian boy:

> *Tita.* I am a spirit of no common rate;
> The summer still doth tend upon my state;
> And I do love thee: therefore go with me.
> I'll give thee fairies to attend on thee;
> And they shall fetch thee jewels from the deep,
> And sing, while thou on pressed flowers dost sleep:
> And I will purge thy mortal grossness so,
> That thou shalt like an airy spirit go.
> Peaseblossom! Cobweb! Moth! And Mustardseed!
>
> [III.i.147–55]

Bottom, amiable enough to the infatuated Titania, is truly charmed by the four elves, and they by Bottom, who would be one of them even without benefit of Puckish translation:

> *Peas.* Ready.
> *Cob.*　　　And I.
> *Moth.*　　　　　And I.
> *Mus.*　　　　　　　And I.
> *All.*　　　　　　　　　Where shall we go?

*Tita.* Be kind and courteous to this gentleman;
  Hop in his walks, and gambol in his eyes;
  Feed him with apricocks and dewberries,
  With purple grapes, green figs, and mulberries;
  The honey-bags steal from the humble-bees,
  And for night-tapers crop their waxen thighs,
  And light them at the fiery glow-worms' eyes,
  To have my love to bed, and to arise;
  And pluck the wings from painted butterflies
  To fan the moonbeams from his sleeping eyes.
  Nod to him, elves, and do him courtesies.

*Peas.* Hail, mortal!

*Cob.* Hail!

*Moth.* Hail!

*Mus.* Hail!

*Bot.* I cry your worships mercy, heartily. I beseech your worship's name?

*Cob.* Cobweb.

*Bot.* I shall desire you of more acquaintance, good Master Cobweb: if I cut my finger, I shall make bold with you. Your name, honest gentleman?

*Peas.* Peaseblossom.

*Bot.* I pray you, commend me to Mistress Squash, your mother, and to Master Peascod, your father. Good Master Peaseblossom, I shall desire you of more acquaintance too. Your name, I beseech you sir?

*Mus.* Mustardseed.

*Bot.* Good Master Mustardseed, I know your patience well. That same cowardly giant-like ox-beef hath devoured many a gentleman of your house: I promise you, your kindred hath made my eyes water ere now. I desire you of more acquaintance, good Master Mustardseed.

[III.i.156–89]

Though Titania will follow this colloquy of innocents by ordering the elves to lead Bottom to her bower, it remains ambiguous exactly what transpires there amidst the nodding violet, luscious woodbine, and sweet musk roses. If you are not Jan Kott or Peter Brook, does it matter? Does one remember the play for "orgiastic bestiality" or for Peaseblossom, Cobweb, Moth, and Mustardseed? Undoubtedly played by children then, as they are now, these elves are adept at stealing from honeybees and butterflies, a precarious art emblematic of the entire *Dream*. Bottom's grave courtesy to them and their cheerful attentiveness to him help establish an affinity that suggests what is profoundly childlike (not childish, not bestial) about Bottom. The problem with reacting to resenters is that I sometimes hear the voice of my late mentor, Frederick A. Pottle, of Yale, admonishing me: "Mr. Bloom, stop beating dead woodchucks!" I will do so, and am content to cite Empson on Kott:

> I take my stand beside the other old buffers here. Kott is ridiculously indifferent to the Letter of the play and labors to befoul its spirit.

Fairies in general (Puck in particular) are likely to miss one target and hit another. Instructed by Oberon to divert Demetrius's passion from Hermia to Helena, Puck errs and transforms Lysander into Helena's pursuer. When Puck gets it right at second try, the foursome become more absurd than ever, with Helena, believing herself mocked, fleeing both suitors, while Hermia languishes in a state of amazement. Act III concludes with all four exhausted lovers being put to sleep by Puck, who carefully rearranges Lysander's affections to their original object, Hermia, while keeping Demetrius enthralled by Helena. This raises the happy irony that the play will never resolve: Does it make any difference at all who marries whom? Shakespeare's pragmatic answer is: Not much, whether in this comedy or another, since all marriages seem in Shakespeare to be headed for unhappiness. Shakespeare seems always to hold what I call the "black box" theory of object choice. The airliner goes down, and we seek out the black box to learn the cause of the catastrophe, but our black boxes are unfindable, and our marital disasters are as arbitrary as our successes. Perhaps this should be called "Puck's Law": who can say whether Demetrius-Helena or Lysander-Hermia will prove the better match? Act III of the *Dream* brushes aside any such question, ending as it does with Puck singing:

Jack shall have Jill,
Nought shall go ill.

[III.ii.461–62]

4

Everyone should collect favorite acts in Shakespeare; one of mine would
be Act IV of the *Dream*, where wonder crowds wonder and eloquence overflows, as Shakespeare manifests his creative exuberance without pause.
The orgiastic reading is prophetically dismissed by the first scene, where
Titania sits the amiable Bottom down upon a flowery bed, caresses his
cheeks, sticks musk roses in his head, and kisses his ears. This scarcely
arouses Bottom to lust:

*Bot.* Where's Peaseblossom?

*Peas.* Ready.

*Bot.* Scratch my head, Peaseblossom. Where's Mounsieur Cobweb?

*Cob.* Ready.

*Bot.* Mounsieur Cobweb, good mounsieur, get you your weapons in
your hand, and kill me a red-hipped humble-bee on the top of a
thistle; and good mounsieur, bring me the honey-bag. Do not fret
yourself too much in the action, mounsieur; and good mounsieur,
have a care the honey-bag break not; I would be loath to have you
overflowen with a honey-bag, signior. Where's Mounsieur Mustardseed?

*Mus.* Ready.

*Bot.* Give me your neaf, Mounsieur Mustardseed. Pray you, leave your
courtesy, good mounsieur.

*Mus.* What's your will?

*Bot.* Nothing, good mounsieur, but to help Cavalery Cobweb to scratch.
I must to the barber's, mounsieur, for methinks I am marvellous
hairy about the face; and I am such a tender ass, if my hair do but
tickle me, I must scratch.

*Tita.* What, wilt thou hear some music, my sweet love?

*Bot.* I have a reasonable good ear in music. Let's have the tongs and
   the bones.
*Tita.* Or say, sweet love, what thou desir'st to eat?
*Bot.* Truly, a peck of provender; I could munch your good dry oats.
   Methinks I have a great desire to a bottle of hay: good hay, sweet
   hay, hath no fellow.

                                                    [IV.i.5–33]

What hath Puck wrought: for Titania, a considerable indignity, no
doubt, but for Bottom a friendship with four elves. Since Bottom is getting
drowsy, we can understand his mixing up Cobweb with Peaseblossom,
but he is otherwise much himself, even if his eating habits perforce are altered. He falls asleep, entwined with the rapt Titania, in a charmingly innocent embrace. Oberon informs us that, since she has surrendered the
changeling boy to him, all is forgiven so that Puck can cure her enchantment, and in passing, Bottom's, though the weaver resolutely goes on sleeping. Shakespeare's touch here is astonishingly light; metamorphoses are
represented by the dance of reconciliation that restores the marriage of
Oberon and Titania:

       Come my queen, take hands with me,
   And rock the ground whereon these sleepers be.

                                                    [IV.i.84–85]

The four lovers and Bottom stay fast asleep even as Theseus, Hippolyta, and their train make a boisterous entry with a dialogue that is
Shakespeare's bravura defense of his art of fusion in this play:

*The.* Go one of you, find out the forester;
       For now our observation is perform'd,
       And since we have the vaward of the day,
       My love shall hear the music of my hounds.
       Uncouple in the western valley; let them go;
       Dispatch I say, and find the forester. [*Exit an Attendant.*]

We will, fair queen, up to the mountain's top,
And mark the musical confusion
Of hounds and echo in conjunction.
*Hip.* I was with Hercules and Cadmus once,
When in a wood of Crete they bay'd the bear
With hounds of Sparta; never did I hear
Such gallant chiding; for, besides the groves,
The skies, the fountains, every region near
Seem'd all one mutual cry; I never heard
So musical a discord, such sweet thunder.
*The.* My hounds are bred out of the Spartan kind,
So flew'd, so sanded; and their heads are hung
With ears that sweep away the morning dew;
Crook-knee'd and dewlapp'd like Thessalian bulls;
Slow in pursuit, but match'd in mouth like bells,
Each under each: a cry more tuneable
Was never holla'd to, nor cheer'd with horn,
In Crete, in Sparta, nor in Thessaly.
Judge when you hear. But soft, what nymphs are these?

[IV.i.102–26]

The musical discord holds together four different modes of representation: Theseus and Hippolyta, from classical legend; the four young lovers, from every place and every time; Bottom and his fellow English rustics; the fairies, who in themselves are madly eclectic. Titania is Ovid's alternate name for Diana, while Oberon comes out of Celtic romance, and Puck or Robin Goodfellow is English folklore. In their delightfully insane dialogue, Theseus and Hippolyta join in celebrating the wonderful nonsense of the Spartan hounds, bred only for their baying, so that they are "slow in pursuit." Shakespeare celebrates the "sweet thunder" of his comic extravagance, which like Theseus's hounds is in no particular hurry to get anywhere, and which still has superb surprises for us. I pass over the awakening of the four lovers (Demetrius now in love with Helena) to come at the finest speech Shakespeare had yet written, Bottom's sublime reverie upon waking up:

*Bot.* When my cue comes, call me and I will answer. My next is 'Most
fair Pyramus'. Heigh-ho! Peter Quince? Flute, the bellows-
mender? Snout, the tinker? Starveling? God's my life! Stolen
hence, and left me asleep! I have had a most rare vision. I have
had a dream, past the wit of man to say what dream it was. Man
is but an ass if he go about to expound this dream. Methought I
was—there is no man can tell what. Methought I was—and
methought I had—but man is but a patched fool if he will offer
to say what methought I had. The eye of man hath not heard, the
ear of man hath not seen, man's hand is not able to taste, his
tongue to conceive, nor his heart to report, what my dream was. I
will get Peter Quince to write a ballad of this dream: it shall be
called 'Bottom's Dream', because it hath no bottom; and I will
sing it in the latter end of a play, before the Duke. Peradventure,
to make it the more gracious, I shall sing it at her death.

[IV.i.199–217]

"The Spirite searcheth . . . the botome of Goddes secretes," is the
Geneva Bible's rendering of 1 Corinthians 2:9–10. Bottom's parody of
1 Corinthians 2:9 is audacious, and allows Shakespeare to anticipate
William Blake's Romantic vision, with its repudiation of the Pauline split
between flesh and spirit, though Bottom seems to have heard the text
preached to him in the Bishops' Bible version:

The eye hath not seene, and the eare hath not heard, neyther
have entered into the heart of man, the things which God hath
purposed . . .

For Bottom, "the eye . . . hath not heard, the ear . . . hath not seen, [the]
hand is not able to taste, his tongue to conceive, nor his heart to report"
the truths of his bottomless dream. Like William Blake after him, Bottom
suggests an apocalyptic, unfallen man, whose awakened senses fuse in a
synesthetic unity. It is difficult not to find in Bottom, in this his sublimest
moment, an ancestor not just of Blake's Albion but of Joyce's Earwicker, the
universal dreamer of *Finnegans Wake*. Bottom's greatness—Shakespeare upon

his heights—emerges most strongly in what could be called "Bottom's Vision," a mysterious triumph he is to enjoy before Theseus as audience, where the "play" cannot be the mere travesty, the play-within-the-play *Pyramus and Thisbe*:

> I will get Peter Quince to write a ballad of this dream: it shall be
> called 'Bottom's Dream', because it hath no bottom; and I will sing
> it in the latter end of a play, before the Duke. Peradventure, to make
> it the more gracious, I shall sing it at her death.

Whose death? Since we do not know the visionary drama playing out in Bottom's consciousness, we cannot answer the question, except to say that it is neither Titania nor Thisbe. When, in the next scene, sweet bully Bottom returns joyously to his friends, he will not speak in these tones. Shakespeare, though, has not forgotten this "more gracious" aspect of Bottom, and subtly opposes it to the famous speech of Theseus that opens Act V. Hippolyta muses on the strangeness of the story told by the four young lovers, and Theseus opposes his skepticism to her wonder.

> *The.* More strange than true. I never may believe
>  These antique fables, nor these fairy toys.
>  Lovers and madmen have such seething brains,
>  Such shaping fantasies, that apprehend
>  More than cool reason ever comprehends.
>  The lunatic, the lover, and the poet
>  Are of imagination all compact:
>  One sees more devils than vast hell can hold;
>  That is the madman: the lover, all as frantic,
>  Sees Helen's beauty in a brow of Egypt:
>  The poet's eye, in a fine frenzy rolling,
>  Doth glance from heaven to earth, from earth to heaven;
>  And as imagination bodies forth
>  The forms of things unknown, the poet's pen
>  Turns them to shapes, and gives to airy nothing

A local habitation and a name.
Such tricks hath strong imagination,
That if it would but apprehend some joy,
It comprehends some bringer of that joy:
Or, in the night, imagining some fear,
How easy is a bush suppos'd a bear!

[V.i.2–22]

Theseus himself could be called, not unkindly, "highly unimaginative," but there are two voices here, and one perhaps is Shakespeare's own, half-distancing itself from its own art, though declining also to yield completely to the patronizing Theseus. When Shakespeare writes these lines, the lover sees Helen's beauty in a gypsy girl's brow, and yet the prophetic consciousness somewhere in Shakespeare anticipates Antony seeing Helen's beauty in Cleopatra. "Imagination," to Shakespeare's contemporaries, was "fantasy," a powerful but suspect faculty of the mind. Sir Francis Bacon neatly stated this ambiguity:

Neither is the Imagination simply and only a messenger; but is invested with or at leastwise usurpeth no small authority in itself, besides the duty of the message.

"Usurpeth" is the key word there; the mind for Bacon is the legitimate authority, and imagination should be content to be the mind's messenger, and to assert no authority for itself. Theseus is more a Baconian than a Shakespearean, but Hippolyta breaks away from Theseus's dogmatism:

But all the story of the night told over,
And all their minds transfigur'd so together,
More witnesseth than fancy's images,
And grows to something of great constancy;
But howsoever, strange and admirable.

[V.i.23–27]

You could give Hippolyta's lines a rather minimal interpretation, stressing that she herself distrusts "fancy's images," but that seems to me a woeful reading. For Theseus, poetry is a furor, and the poet a trickster; Hippolyta opens to a greater resonance, to transfiguration that affects more than one mind at once. The lovers are her metaphor for the Shakespearean audience, and it is ourselves, therefore, who grow into "something of great constancy," and so are re-formed, strangely and admirably. Hippolyta's majestic gravity is an implicit rebuke to Theseus's scoffing at the poet's "fine frenzy." Critics rightly have expanded their apprehension of Shakespeare's "story of the night" beyond the *Dream*, marvelous as the play is. "No, I assure you; the wall is down that parted their fathers" is Bottom's final resonance in the play, and transcends Theseus's patronizing understanding. "The best in this kind are but shadows," Theseus says of all plays and playing—and while we might accept this from Macbeth, we cannot accept it from the dull Duke of Athens. Puck, in the Epilogue, only seems to agree with Theseus when he chants that "we shadows" are "but a dream," since the dream is this great play itself. The poet who dreamed Bottom was about to achieve a great dream of reality, Sir John Falstaff, who would have no interest in humoring Theseus.

# 12

# THE MERCHANT OF VENICE

One would have to be blind, deaf, and dumb not to recognize that Shakespeare's grand, equivocal comedy *The Merchant of Venice* is nevertheless a profoundly anti-Semitic work. Yet every time I have taught the play, many of my most sensitive and intelligent students become very unhappy when I begin with that observation. Nor do they accept my statements that Shylock is a comic villain and that Portia would cease to be sympathetic if Shylock were allowed to be a figure of overwhelming pathos. That Shakespeare himself was personally anti-Semitic we reasonably can doubt, but Shylock is one of those Shakespearean figures who seem to break clean away from their plays' confines. There is an extraordinary energy in Shylock's prose and poetry, a force both cognitive and passional, which palpably is in excess of the play's comic requirements. More even than Marlowe's Barabas, Jew of Malta, Shylock is a villain both farcical and scary, though time has worn away both qualities. Shakespeare's England did not exactly have a Jewish "problem" or "question" in our later modern terms; only about a hundred or two hundred Jews, presumably most of them converts to Christianity, lived in London. The Jews had been more or less expelled from England in 1290, three centuries before, and were not to be more or less readmitted until Cromwell made his revolution. The unfortunate Dr. Lopez, Queen Elizabeth's physician, was hanged, drawn, and quartered (possibly with Shakespeare among the mob looking on), having been more or less framed by the Earl of Essex and so perhaps falsely accused of a plot to poison the Queen. A Portuguese *converso*, whom Shakespeare may have known, poor Lopez lives on as a shadowy provocation to the highly successful revival of Marlowe's *The Jew of Malta* in 1593–94, and presumably to Shakespeare's eventual overcoming of Marlowe in *The Merchant of Venice*, perhaps in 1596–97.

Shakespeare's comedy is Portia's play, and not Shylock's, though some audiences now find it difficult to reach that conclusion. Antonio, the title's merchant, is the good Christian of the play, who manifests his piety by cursing and spitting at Shylock. For many among us now, that is at least an irony, but clearly it was no irony for Shakespeare's audiences. I have never seen *The Merchant of Venice* staged with Shylock as comic villain, but that is certainly how the play should be performed. Shylock would be very bad news indeed if he were not funny; since he doesn't provoke *us* to laughter, we play him for pathos, as he has been played since the early nineteenth century, except in Germany and Austria under the Nazis, and in Japan. I am afraid that we tend to make *The Merchant of Venice* incoherent by portraying Shylock as being largely sympathetic. Yet I myself am puzzled as to what it would cost (and not only ethically) to recover the play's coherence. Probably it would cost us Shakespeare's actual Shylock, who cannot have been quite what Shakespeare intended, if indeed we can recover such an intention. If I were a director, I would instruct my Shylock to act like a hallucinatory bogeyman, a walking nightmare flamboyant with a big false nose and a bright red wig, that is to say, to *look* like Marlowe's Barabas. We can imagine the surrealistic effect of such a figure when he begins to speak with the nervous intensity, the realistic energy of Shylock, who is so much of a personality as to at least rival his handful of lively precursors in Shakespeare: Faulconbridge the Bastard in *King John*, Mercutio and the Nurse in *Romeo and Juliet*, and Bottom the Weaver in *A Midsummer Night's Dream*. But these characters all fit their roles, even if we can conceive of them as personalities outside of their plays. Shylock simply does not fit his role; he is the wrong Jew in the right play.

I suggest that to understand the gap between the human that Shakespeare invents and the role that as playmaker he condemns Shylock to act, we regard the Jew of Venice as a reaction formation or ironic swerve away from Marlowe's Jew of Malta. All that Shylock and Barabas have in common is that both are supposed to be not Jews, but *the* Jew. Shakespeare's grim Puritan and Marlowe's ferocious Machiavel are so antithetical to each other that I have always wanted a mischievous director slyly to transfer crucial declarations between them. How disconcertingly splendid it would be to have Shylock suddenly burst out with Barabas's most outrageous parody of Jewish wickedness:

As for myself, I walk abroad a-nights,
And kill sick people groaning under walls;
Sometimes I go about and poison wells.

That is the superb cartoon that Shakespeare parodied again in Aaron the Moor of *Titus Andronicus*, and such savage zest cannot be repeated by Shylock, who is not a phantasmagoria, even when he behaves like one. The counterstroke would be to have Barabas cry out, "If you prick us, do we not bleed? If you tickle us, do we not laugh?" which may or may not be poignant when delivered by Shylock but certainly would destroy Barabas's antic irreality. Shakespeare, finished at last with Marlowe, contrasts against the cartoon Barabas Shylock's realistic mimesis, which is so overwhelming that it cannot be accommodated as a stage Jew. Yet Shakespeare wants it both ways, at once to push Marlowe aside, and also to so out-Marlowe Marlowe as to make our flesh creep. The stunning persuasiveness of Shylock's personality heightens our apprehension of watching a stage Jew slice off and weigh a pound of the good Antonio's flesh—"to bait fish withal." If the audience has a surrogate in this drama, it would appear to be Gratiano, whose anti-Semitic vulgarity reminds me of Julius Streicher, Hitler's favorite newspaper editor. The last two centuries of stage tradition have made Shylock a hero-villain, but the text cannot sustain such an interpretation. Since Shylock is a murderous villain, then Gratiano, though a touch crude, must be taken as a good fellow, cheerful and robust in his anti-Semitism, a kind of Pat Buchanan of Renaissance Venice.

Shakespearean skeptical irony, so pervasive elsewhere in *The Merchant of Venice*, perhaps goes into relative suspension whenever Shylock speaks.

Shylock's prose is Shakespeare's best before Falstaff's; Shylock's verse hews to the vernacular more than any in Shakespeare before Hamlet's. The bitter eloquence of Shylock so impresses us that it is always a surprise to be told how small a part of the play is spoken by him: only 360 lines and sentences. His utterances manifest a spirit so potent, malign, and negative as to be unforgettable. Yet it is spirit, albeit the spirit of resentment and revenge. I doubt that Shakespeare knew enough about the post-biblical history of the Jews to have meditated upon it, and therefore Shylock cannot be said to embody Jewish history, except for the unhappy truth that Shakespeare's power has converted much of later Jewish history into Shylock. It would have been better for the Jews, if not for most of *The Merchant of Venice*'s audiences, had Shylock been a character less conspicuously alive. What spurred Shakespeare to that liveliness, as I've already intimated, was the contest with Marlowe's Barabas. But what is it that provoked Shakespeare's inventiveness?

Perhaps it is the wicked small boy in me that so delights in Barabas; Marlowe certainly delighted in his Jew, who is as close to aspects of Marlowe's temperament as Shylock is distant from Shakespeare's, if Falstaff is as much the Shakespearean norm as I take him to be. Barabas, of course, is no more Jewish than the play's Christians are Christian or its Muslims Muslim. Shakespeare disturbs me because his influence has been so universal that Shylock seems Jewish to many audiences, though the figure they see has been converted into one of heroic pathos. When we think of the Jew in post-biblical literature, George Eliot's Daniel Deronda, Dickens's Fagin, and Joyce's half-Jewish Poldy, among others, come to mind only *after* we brood upon Shylock. No one, except the incessantly anti-Semitic T. S. Eliot, has tended to think of Barabas as a truly Jewish character. Barabas is a kind of wicked bottle imp or Jew-in-the-box; he is always jumping out at us, the audience. We can't help enjoying him, since his outrageousness is so cartoon-like. But I will return to Barabas later, in the context of Shakespeare's revision of Marlowe for his own rather different purposes.

We finally have a lucid and sound study of *The Merchant of Venice* in *Shakespeare and the Jews*, by James Shapiro (1996), whose "Conclusion" is worthy of much meditation:

I have tried to show that much of the play's vitality can be attributed to the ways in which it scrapes against a bedrock of beliefs about the racial, national, sexual, and religious difference of others. I can think of no other literary work that does so as unrelentingly and as honestly. To avert our gaze from what the play reveals about the relationship between cultural myths and peoples' identities will not make irrational and exclusionary attitudes disappear. Indeed, these darker impulses remain so elusive, so hard to identify in the normal course of things, that only in instances like productions of this play do we get to glimpse these cultural faultlines. This is why censoring the play is *always* more dangerous than staging it.

"Censoring," of course, is usually not the issue, except in Nazi Germany and in Israel, as Shapiro shows. What baffles us is how to stage a romantic comedy that rather blithely includes a forced Jewish conversion to Christianity, on penalty of death. When Shylock brokenly intones, "I am content," few of our audiences are going to be content, unless you can conjure up a cheerfully anti-Semitic audience somewhere. *King Lear* is a pagan play for a Christian audience, some scholars like to say. *The Merchant of Venice* is a Christian play for a Christian audience, according to Northrop Frye. I don't think that Shakespeare wrote Christian plays, or un-Christian ones either, and as I have written earlier, my sense of the endlessly perspectivizing Shakespeare would exclude the possibility that he was personally either anti-Semitic or philo-Semitic, which is also Shapiro's conclusion. It is difficult for me not to assent to Graham Bradshaw's fine contention that Shakespeare's "creative interiorization of Shylock" makes unlikely any views that see the Jewish merchant as being entirely a comic villain or only a figure of tragic pathos. What drives me back to a state of critical unhappiness is Shakespeare's disconcerting addition to the pound-of-flesh story: the forced conversion. It is Shakespeare's own invention, and I never find it dramatically persuasive that Shylock should consent to it. Portia may have broken Shylock, but she has not pulverized him, and it is no longer Shylock who stumbles off stage, soon to be a new Christian, or a false Christian, or whatever. Why did Shakespeare allow Antonio this final turn of the torturer's screw?

Had Shylock grown too large for the play, in Shakespeare's wary intuition, so that he needed to be removed, as Mercutio and Lear's Fool and Lady Macbeth are exiled? This seems dubious to me, if only because Shakespeare has waited too long in the play to exile Shylock. "He should have converted hereafter," we are likely to mutter, knowing that there would have been no such time. It is not like Shakespeare to blunder into a theatrical coup that makes even a comic villain behave with dramatic inconsistency. Malvolio, in a madman's cell, maintains his integrity, but Shylock, hemmed in by enemies, is not permitted to do so. Once I believed this to be a relatively rare Shakespearean error; now I suspect otherwise. Shakespeare needs the conversion, not so much to reduce Shylock as to take the audience off to Belmont without a Jewish shadow hovering in the ecstatic if gently ironic final act.

There is nothing lyrical about Shylock, and no place for him in Belmont. But what was Shakespeare to do with Shylock? Hanging, drawing, and quartering, or similar open-air entertainment, would be a poor prelude to Belmont. We cannot know precisely what Shakespeare the man thought of actual Jewish individual "conversions," but he was unlikely to be less skeptical of them than were almost all his contemporaries. It had been more than a century since the Spanish Expulsion of the Jews, a debacle partly caused by Christian awareness of massive Jewish recalcitrance and tendency to dissimulate when compelled to convert. Shapiro views Shylock's conversion as an answer to English Protestant anxieties, which contained the expectation of a mass conversion of the Jews, which would help confirm the Reformation's rightness. The relevance of such a Christian fantasy to *The Merchant of Venice* seems to me quite tenuous, since the Belmont joys of Act V are deliciously secular, nor is Shylock's forced conversion in any way a possible harbinger of a messianic age. We feel that Shakespeare intended an idiosyncratic end for Shylock, more as punishment than as redemption, and there may be the clue. Forced conversions on an individual basis were very rare phenomena, as Shapiro's researches confirm. Shakespeare, with Marlowe's Barabas in mind, does not give Shylock the option of declaring, "I will be no convertite," as Barabas does. His destroying Shylock's consistency as a character helps further to distinguish him from the unyielding Barabas, and helps also to augment the nihilistic element that is subtly present in the play. No one in *The Merchant of Venice* is what he or she seems to be—not Portia, Antonio, Bassanio, or Jessica—and can Shakespeare allow only Shylock to maintain a consistent stance? Who in this comedy can have his or her bond? A Sixth Act would dissolve Belmont into moonlight wiped away like mud. Shylock accepts conversion because the Venice of this play, like the Vienna of *Measure for Measure*, is too equivocal for any consistency to prevail. It is *The Merchant of Venice*'s finest irony that the alien Shylock is never more Venetian than when he sells himself out. What is his motive? Do we misread his "I am content" when we fail to hear a terrible irony in it? Has Shylock perhaps learned so much from Christian justice that he is prepared to move his struggle to a more inward mode of resistance?

We can only surmise, in this comedy set in a city of psychic dark corners. Despite the Belmont fifth act, *The Merchant of Venice* may be Shakespeare's first "dark comedy" or "problem play," forerunner of *All's Well That Ends Well, Troilus and Cressida*, and *Measure for Measure*, with their equivocal groupings of Helena, Bertram, and Parolles; Pandarus, Thersites, and Ulysses; Duke Vincentio, Isabella, and Lucio. Antonio, as so many critics observe, is Shylock's mirror image, bonded with him in mutual hatred, and no more cheerful than Shylock is. Portia, the play's center, is far more complex and shadowed than ever I have seen her played as being. Herself a sophisticated ironist, she settles happily for the glittering gold digger Bassanio, contemptuously sentences poor Morocco and Aragon to celibate existences, and is delighted with her Belmont and her Venice alike. More even than the vicious Gratiano, she incarnates the "anything goes" spirit of Venice, and her quality of mercy cheerfully tricks Shylock out of his life's savings in order to enrich her friends. Our directors go on instructing our actresses to play Portia as if she was Rosalind, which is a malfeasance. Bradshaw finds a touch of Henry James worldliness in Portia, but we would render her better by invoking Noël Coward or Cole Porter. I am not proposing that someone give us *The Merchant of Venice* as the first anti-Semitic musical comedy, but I do suggest that Portia, who knows better, consistently is delighted to fail all her own finely wrought self-awareness.

Her moral fiber is Jamesian, but her sense of the high life wryly allows her to settle for Bassanio and tricksterism. She is rather wonderful bad news, a slummer by joyous choice. Yes, she has the wit to flatten Shylock, Jew and alien, but her city, Venice, is completely on her side, and the obsessed Shylock is entirely on his own. He gets about what he deserves, except for that gratuitous forced conversion, which Portia happily endorses, but which is Antonio's idea, and not hers. She is at worst a happy hypocrite, far too intelligent not to see that she is not exactly dispensing Christian mercy, except by Venetian standards. Antonio is quite another matter; he is ironically the play's best Christian, a champion spitter-at and kicker-of Jews. If one is Jewish, one is hardly his intended audience, let alone his contemplated critic, even if one does not wish a pound of his Pauline heart or of his Venetian privates.

In this endlessly ironic play, the melancholy Antonio finishes with little except regained riches and his triumphant anti-Semitism to cheer him. Indeed, his sexual fate is precisely that of the Princes of Morocco and Aragon, perpetual celibacy, since Bassanio will be otherwise engaged in servicing Portia. Still, Antonio is at Belmont, surrounded by three pairs of lovers, while his enemy Shylock is in Venice, doubtless receiving instruction in Catholicism. Christian comedy triumphs, Jewish villainy is thwarted, and everything is for the best, if only Shylock's voice and presence would stop reverberating, which they never have and never will, four centuries after Shakespeare composed, and in the centuries to come. Had Hitler won the Second World War and gone on to add ten million more Jews to his achievement of six million Jewish corpses, then Shylock would have ceased to reverberate, but his unhappy persistence will extend as long as the history of the Jews, in which he has played an inglorious part, hardly one that Shakespeare ever could have contemplated. Early modern anti-Semitism was not pretty; the good Antonio and the loud Gratiano will stand as poor Shylock's godfathers at the baptismal font, though Gratiano would rather hang him, and Antonio is not at all likely to stop kicking and spitting, Venetian Christianity being what it was and is. Shakespeare, we can assume, was Shakespeare's most gifted critic, and he would have been aware that Shylock, comic or not, was a grander achievement than Antonio could be. Still, Antonio is a dark matter, and requires some contemplation if his adversary Shylock is to be properly perspectivized.

Antonio lives for Bassanio and indeed is willing to die for him, and mortgages his pound of flesh to Shylock solely so that Bassanio can deck his good looks out in order to wive it wealthily in Belmont. Bassanio is not a bad fellow, but no one would want to try the project of distinguishing between Bassanio and Lorenzo, two Venetian playboys in search of heiresses. It is true that all Shakespeare's heroines are condemned to marry down, but if you compare Portia's Bassanio to Rosalind's Orlando, obviously you will prefer the amiable young wrestler of *As You Like It* to the sincere fortune hunter of *The Merchant of Venice*. Notoriously, Portia's play, and Portia herself, and her friends, are all about money. Belmont is delightful, and obviously very expensive, and Portia, while wiser than Jessica, Nerissa, Gratiano, Lorenzo, and Bassanio, requires no loftier company than these well-dressed sophisticates. I never know what critics think they are talking about when they find transcendent virtues in Portia's Belmont. John Middleton Murry, admirable interpreter of Keats and of Blake, wrote a lesser study, *Shakespeare* (1936), in which he affirmed that *"The Merchant of Venice* is not a problem play; it is a fairy story." I murmur, when I read this, that I don't expect fairy stories to be anti-Semitic, though of course there are a few. More to the point is that Portia and her friends, in Act V, are not exactly partying in a pumpkin, or in a gingerbread house, but in a great hall, being serenaded by musicians, with a trumpet sounding at each fresh arrival. Once the pretty matter of the rings has been gotten through, thus reassuring Portia that she has priority over Antonio in Bassanio's affections, the only crucial question is whether to stay up partying until dawn or go to bed and get on with it. Everyone is a lot fresher than they were going to be four centuries later in *La Dolce Vita*, but basically they are the same set.

Antonio, though he is there in Belmont, will go to bed alone, presumably comforted by his altruism, his piety, and his triumph over Shylock. Bassanio, we have to assume, is bisexual, but Antonio clearly is not, and his homoeroticism is perhaps less relevant than his sadomasochism, the doom-eagerness that could allow him to make so mad a contract with Shylock.

If the comedy has a hero, to rival Portia as heroine, it has to be Antonio, and not the lightweight Bassanio, charming and harmless fellow. But I've never met anyone who much likes Antonio, quite aside from his compulsive tendency to kick and spit at passing Jews. We want for Shylock's antagonist a somewhat more engaging merchant of Venice, who has something other than his Christianity to recommend him. Leslie Fiedler once wrote that Antonio was a "projection of the author's private distress," which counts as interesting guesswork but no more. Various critics have found Antonio to be a gull, a Christ figure, a self-victimizer, and much else, and clearly he is rather an ambiguous character. But all that makes him vivid and memorable is the quality of the mutual hatred he shares with Shylock. As a hater, he is outclassed by Shylock, but then he achieves a certain stature by coming up with the idea of the forced conversion. That, and the notorious pound of flesh near his heart, are what matter about him, and one has to question whether Shakespeare, for whatever reason, failed to do enough with the interior Antonio.

However problematic, *The Merchant of Venice* essentially is a romantic comedy, and pathos is alien to it, as alien as Shylock the Jew. I myself find little pathos in Shylock, and am not moved by his "Hath not a Jew" litany, since what he is saying there is now of possible interest only to wavering skinheads and similar sociopaths. Perhaps it was a revelation for Shakespeare's audience, but it had better not be such for any audience now. Shylock matters where he is most formidable, as when he faces the Duke of Venice, and insists that he will have his bond. Let us dismiss the notion, Northrop Frye's weakest, that Shylock speaks for the Old Testament and Portia for the merciful New Covenant. Frye was a great critic but not when he mixed criticism with being a Low Church clergyman, just as T. S. Eliot's criticism did not benefit from his High Church proclivities. Deuteronomy forbids what Shylock seeks to do, and may God (and democracy) save me from Portia's mercy! Portia is dangerously theatrical, and not just when she is cross-dressing. She shares this trait with her lover, Bassanio, and with her rival, Antonio. Shylock oddly is not at all theatrical, dramatically superb as he is until his unlikely conversion. His menace and his now-lost comic force depend upon the contrast between his monomaniacal sincerity and the engaging frivolity of Portia's Venetian smart set. To reduce him to contemporary theatrical terms, Shylock would be an Arthur Miller protagonist displaced into a Cole Porter musical, Willy Loman wandering about in *Kiss Me Kate*.

Shakespeare specialized in such displaced spirits, and in this one regard Shylock has affinities with a strikingly varied company that includes Malvolio, Caliban, Lear's Fool, Barnardine, and even an aspect of Falstaff. Malvolio, in a play by Ben Jonson, almost would be Jonson, but in *Twelfth Night*, his displacement makes him the comic butt. I assume that Shylock began in *The Merchant of Venice* as a similar comic figure, in Shakespeare's design, but Shylock kindled Shakespeare's imagination and became enlarged beyond comedy, though into menace rather than pathos. The stimulus for Shylock's metamorphosis had to be Marlowe's Barabas, who had been haunting Shakespeare since his beginnings as a dramatist.

Shylock is an anti-Barabas, turned inward, as much a deep psyche as Barabas is a cartoon. Shakespeare's imitations of Barabas, Aaron the Moor and Richard III, do homage to Marlowe, but Shylock exposes Barabas as a mere caricature, however brilliant and ferocious. "I'll show you the Jew," Shakespeare says in reply to Marlowe, and so, alas, he has, to the everlasting harm of the actual Jewish people. This is hardly to say that Shylock is a valid representation of a Jew, let alone the Jew, but it does acknowledge the scandalous authority of Shakespeare in world culture, an authority that just this once is more of a sorrow than it is a benefit. *The Jew of Malta* is still a lively romp, much admired by T. S. Eliot, though I suspect for the wrong reasons, since Eliot doubtless treasured it as an anti-Semitic farce, which it is not. Its Christians and Muslims come off far worse than Barabas, since they would be just as wicked if they could but lack Barabas's genius for evil. Marlowe's Jew is simply Christopher Marlowe gone all out into lunatic zest and diabolic energy, overturning all values and sending up everything and everyone. A great holiday from reality, *The Jew of Malta* exalts active evil over passive good, and can be called the *Ubu Roi* of its time, the first Pataphysical drama. In his stage directions, Jarry remarked: "The action takes place nowhere—that is to say, in Poland," perhaps the first of modern Polish jokes. In the same spirit, Marlowe's action (such as it is) takes place in Malta—that is to say, nowhere. Marlowe had no literary or historical sources for *The Jew of Malta*, which could take place almost anywhere in the Mediterranean, in any one of several centuries, but only after Machiavel, who wonderfully steps forward in the play's prologue, to urge our acclaim of Barabas. Like his master, Machiavel, Marlowe's Jew is obsessed with "policy"—that is, with principles that undo Christ. The demoniac Barabas, madly exulting in his wickedness, has nothing in common with the bitter Shylock, whose revenge focuses so narrowly upon Antonio.

Shakespeare works assiduously to exclude any Marlovian element from Shylock, but that inevitably entails a journey to the Shylockian interior. Barabas is free of all inwardness; Shylock, in recoil, is so concentrated in his inward power that he reduces Portia and her friends, and even Antonio, to what can look like exercises in irony. The phenomenon of a "real" person entrapped in a play, surrounded by speaking shadows, is strongest in *Hamlet*, evidently by design. Yet the aesthetic experiment of the Pirandello-like mode, perfected in *Hamlet*, is first ventured in *The Merchant of Venice*, where the ontological weight of Shylock, from his first appearance through his last, places him as a representation of reality far distaining every other character in the play. Shylock, equivocal as he must be, is our best clue for tracing the process by which Shakespeare outdid Marlowe, and in doing so invented or reinvented the human.

Barabas is exuberant, but he is a monster, not a man. Shakespeare's obsessed Shylock is compulsive enough in his hatred of Antonio so that he would have performed monstrously, but for Portia; yet Shylock is no monster but an overwhelming persuasion of a possible human being. Shylock matters most not just in the historical world of anti-Semitism, but also in the inner world of Shakespeare's development, because no previous figure in the plays has anything like Shylock's strength, complexity, and vital potential. Shylock's pathos can be termed his *potentia*, his possible largeness on the scale of being. That so resourceful a spirit should have reduced itself to a lust for weighing out a pound of Antonio's flesh upon a literal scale is the most terrible of Shakespeare's ironies in this comedy of ironies.

There remains Shylock's largest puzzle, at least for me: Is he the first radical Shakespearean instance of Hobgoblin run off with the garland of

Apollo? Is Shylock of the literary race of Falstaff and of Dickens's Pickwick, the tribe in which Don Quixote, Sancho Panza, and Hamlet share with Falstaff the highest eminence? Can Shakespeare be said to have lost control of Shylock? Nothing after all sounds odder than to call Shylock a comic villain, like the zestful Barabas, even though *The Merchant of Venice*, however shaded, is still a comedy, and the Jewish moneylender is certainly its villain. In refusing to create another Aaron the Moor or Richard III, both imitations of Barabas, Shakespeare molded Shylock into someone rich and strange, in several senses. Barabas's principal affect is self-delight, a joy provoked by his own triumphant and antic villainy. Aaron and Richard Crookback also enjoy themselves to the highest degree, but Shylock takes little pleasure in himself or anything else, despite his pride in his self-identity. Critics frequently mark the sadness that is common to Antonio and to Shylock, an involuntary link between good haters of each other. Though the sadness be mutual, the causes are very different; Antonio, whatever his relations with Bassanio may have been, must lose him to Portia, while Shylock evidently has long mourned his wife Leah, mother of the insufferable Jessica, the Venetian Jewish princess who gets what she deserves in her playboy, Lorenzo. Shakespeare does not clarify Shylock's relationship to his thieving daughter, but he is certainly better off without her, and is accurate enough in grieving equally for his ducats and their appropriator.

We adore Barabas, Aaron, and even Richard III because their asides make us their accomplices. Shakespeare, to prevent this, never allows us to be alone with Shylock. Barabas dissembles, and consciously always gives a performance; Shylock is massively, frighteningly sincere and single-minded. He never acts a part: he *is* Shylock. Though this endows him with immense expressive force, it also makes him dreadfully vulnerable, and inevitably metamorphoses him into the play's scapegoat. He is capable of shattering irony, particularly in his speeches to the Duke, but the comedy's largest irony makes him its victim. Portia is the privileged ironist of *The Merchant of Venice*, but she becomes a brutal ironist at Shylock's expense, though not as brutal as the good Antonio, who offers Shylock a choice between a pauper's execution and a Christian's survival as a retired moneylender, since a converted Shylock by definition cannot engage in a purely Jewish business.

Shakespeare, rather more subtly than Marlowe, shows that though the Christians (except for Gratiano) are more refined than Shylock, they are hardly more merciful. Portia is a great charmer, but then Bassanio, Lorenzo, Nerissa, and Jessica are also charming, if rather emptier than Portia. Shylock is a candidate for the least charming character in all of Shakespeare, yet he fascinates us, and for reasons that transcend his transparent villainy. His language, an extraordinary instrument, had to impress Shakespeare as a dramatic breakthrough for the poet-playwright. We do not encounter Shylock until Act I, Scene iii, after we already know Antonio, Bassanio, and Portia, and we first hear Shylock speaking a virtuoso prose culminating in his refusal of Bassanio's civil invitation to dinner:

> Yes, to smell pork, to eat of the habitation which your prophet the
> Nazarite conjured the devil into: I will buy with you, sell with you,
> talk with you, walk with you, and so following: but I will not eat
> with you, drink with you, nor pray with you.
>
> [I.iii.29–33]

The reference to the Gospel of Mark, like the one to Luke when Shylock sees Antonio coming, provides the odd detail that Shakespeare's Jew has read the enemy Scripture. And indeed Shylock is a formidable polemicist against Christianity, particularly against what passes for Christian ethics in Venice. Less inflammatory than Marlowe's Jew, Shylock is at least as stubbornly loyal to his people as Barabas is, making his consent to the final, forced conversion almost absurdly inconsistent. His first speech in verse, a rare aside, invokes an archaic enmity, reaching back far beyond Antonio and Shylock:

> If I can catch him once upon the hip,
> I will feed fat the ancient grudge I bear him.
> He hates our sacred nation, and he rails
> (Even there where merchants most do congregate)

On me, my bargains, and my well-won thrift,
Which he calls interest: cursed be my tribe
If I forgive him!

[I.iii.41–47]

Shylock asserts his identity as *the* Jew, inheritor of the persecuted pride of fifteen centuries, in lines that burn with a terrifying spiritual rancor, and that are animated by what must be called a formidable spiritual intelligence. I greatly regret agreeing with the resentful legions of cultural materialists and cultural poeticians, all of whom have a particular grudge against the criticism of E.M.W. Tillyard, but no one ever has been more mistaken on Shylock than Tillyard, who allowed himself to speak of Shylock's "spiritual stupidity," and of Antonio's "disinterested kindness." That was in 1965, but it never seems too late in the day for English anti-Semitism to manifest itself. Disinterested kicking and spitting we can set aside; Shylock's spirit is diseased, distorted by hatred, however justified, but Shylock's intelligence, in any sphere, is unquestionable. He would not be so dreadfully dangerous as he is were he not a psychologist of some genius, a precursor of the great critic Iago, and of the superb nihilist Edmund in *King Lear*.

Shylock's companion in hatred is Antonio, whose anti-Semitism, though appropriate to the play's Venice, nevertheless is more viciously intense than anyone else's, even Gratiano's. Homosexual anti-Semitism is now too peculiar a malady for us to understand; from Proust onward the situations of Jews and homosexuals have tended to converge, symbolically and sometimes literally, as in Nazi Germany. Venice and Belmont alike float upon money, and Antonio's attempt to distinguish between his mercantilism and Shylock's usury persuades nobody. The merchant and the Jew perform a murderous dance of masochist and sadist, murderee and murderer, and the question of which is the merchant and which the Jew is resolved only by the unbelievable conversion. Antonio wins and has nothing except money; Shylock loses (and deserves to lose) and has nothing, not even an identity. We cannot interpret his "I am content" because we cannot get out of our ears his two greatest speeches, each directed against

Venice—the "gaping pig" rhapsody and the oration on Venetian slavery. Neither speech is necessary for comic completion, and neither is an exercise in pathos. Shakespeare drives his creation to its limit, as if to discover just what kind of character he has limned in Shylock, a night piece that was his best until he revised Hamlet from another wily trickster to a new kind of man.

The transformation of Shylock from a comic villain to a heroic villain (rather than a hero-villain, like Barabas) shows Shakespeare working without precedents, and for dramatic motives very difficult to surmise. Shylock always has been a great role: one thinks of Macklin, Kean, and Irving, though there does not appear to have been an overwhelming performance in our own time. I could never come to terms with Olivier's suave philo-Semitic Shylock, who seemed to emanate from Freud's Vienna and not at all from Shakespeare's Venice. The top hat and black tie had replaced the Jewish gaberdine, and the powerful speeches of menace were modulated into civilization and its discontents. Though the effect of this was quietly and persuasively irrealistic, the context for Shylock's passionate nihilism seemed withdrawn when the shocking lines came forth:

> You'll ask me why I rather choose to have
> A weight of carrion flesh than to receive
> Three thousand ducats: I'll not answer that!
> But say it is my humour, —is it answer'd?
> What if my house be troubled with a rat,
> And I be pleas'd to give ten thousand ducats
> To have it ban'd? what, are you answer'd yet?
> Some men there are love not a gaping pig!
> Some that are mad if they behold a cat!
> And others when the bagpipe sings i'th'nose,
> Cannot contain their urine—for affection
> [   ] of passion sways it to the mood
> Of what it likes or loathes,—now for your answer:
> As there is no firm reason to be rend'red
> Why he cannot abide a gaping pig,

Why he a harmless necessary cat,
Why he a woollen bagpipe, but of force
Must yield to such inevitable shame,
As to offend, himself being offended:
So can I give no reason, nor I will not,
More than a lodg'd hate, and a certain loathing
I bear Antonio, that I follow thus
A losing suit against him!—are you answered?

[IV.i.40–62]

The missing word is something like "master," and since Shylock's "affection" primarily means an innate antipathy, while his "passion" means any authentic feeling, he thus portrays himself, quite ironically, as being unable to govern his own will. But Shakespeare's irony goes against Shylock, since Shylock is playing the Christian's game, and cannot win at it: "A lodg'd hate, and a certain loathing" is an excellent definition of anti-Semitism, and Shylock, out of control, has become what he beheld in Antonio, a Jewish terrorist responding to incessant anti-Jewish provocations. But the images of Shylock's speech are more memorable than is his defense of his own vagaries. Antonio's anti-Shylockism and Shylock's anti-Antonioism are parallel instances to the madness of those who lose control when they encounter a gaping pig, become insane at seeing a harmless necessary cat, or involuntarily urinate when the bagpipe sings. What Shylock defiantly celebrates is compulsiveness for its own sake, or traumatic caprice. As a negative psychologist, Shakespeare's Jew prepares us for the abysses of the will in greater Shakespearean villains to come, but Shakespeare has divested Shylock of the grandeur of negative transcendence that will inform Iago, Edmund, and Macbeth. It is the "gaping pig" speech, more than the wounded cry "I will have my bond," that exposes Shylock's emptying-out of his self.

We know next to nothing about the dynamics of Shakespeare's personal relationships, if any, to the great roles he composed. The pattern of the Falstaff–Hal ambivalence seems not unlike the ambivalence sketched in the Sonnets, while the image of Shakespeare's son Hamnet Shakespeare may in some still unknown way contribute to the enigmas of Prince Hamlet. It is scarcely conceivable that Shylock was any kind of a personal burden to Shakespeare, who essentially belongs to his age, just this once, in regard to the Jews. Since he is not Marlowe, writing a bloody farce, Shakespeare is either vicious or ignorant (or both) when he has Shylock urge Tubal to meet him at the synagogue in order to work out the details for the judicial murder of Antonio. Still, both the viciousness and the ignorance were generic, which does not make them more forgivable. The plot required a Jew, Marlowe's Jew lingered on the stage, and Shakespeare needed to fight free of Marlowe. I surmise that Shakespeare's pride at having done just that increased his dramatic investment in Shylock, and helps account for the most astonishing speech in the play. When the Duke asks: "How shalt thou hope for mercy rend'ring none?" Shylock replies with preternatural power, invoking the ultimate foundation for the Venetian state economy, which is the ownership of slaves:

> What judgment shall I dread doing no wrong?
> You have among you many a purchas'd slave,
> Which (like your asses, and your dogs and mules)
> You use in abject and in slavish parts,
> Because you bought them—shall I say to you,
> Let them be free, marry them to your heirs?
> Why sweat they under burthens? let their beds
> Be made as soft as yours, and let their palates
> Be season'd with such viandes? you will answer
> "The slaves are ours,"—so do I answer you:
> The pound of flesh (which I demand of him)
> Is dearly bought, 'tis mine and I will have it:
> If you deny me, fie upon your law!
> There is no force in the decrees of Venice:
> I stand for judgment,—answer, shall I have it?
>
> [IV.i.89–103]

It is all too easy to get this speech wrong, as some recent Marxist critics have done. Shylock has no sympathy for the slaves, and he seems quite unaware of the irony his citation of the slaves evokes, since as a Jew he annually celebrates the Passover, with its opening reminder that his ancestors were slaves in Egypt until God liberated them. It is never wise to assume that Shakespeare did not know anything that was available in or near his world; his curiosity was unappeasable, his energy for information boundless. Shylock really does *mean* his ghastly parallel: one pound of Antonio's flesh is enslaved to him, and he will have his bond. What startles and delights us is Shylock's shrewd indictment of Christian hypocrisy, which he makes earlier in the play, but not with this shocking force. The Venetian slaves, like all slaves, are so many pounds of flesh; no more, no less. And in the context of Gingrich–Clinton America, the satire still works: our pious reformers of Welfare are determined to see that the descendants of our slaves do not lie down in beds as soft as theirs, and season their palates with such viands, let alone marry the heirs of the Contract with America. Yet Shylock does not care about his own fiercest point; he is, alas, not a prophet, just a would-be torturer and murderer. It is Shakespeare, exploiting the role of Shylock, who slyly provides the material for moral prophecy, which no one in this comedy is prepared or enabled to make.

Shylock, then, is a field of force larger than Shylock himself can encompass, and Shakespeare in *The Merchant of Venice*, as in the later *Measure for Measure*, severely qualifies his comedy by opening onto vistas that comedy rarely can accommodate. Unfortunately, Shakespeare's intimations do not alleviate the savagery of his portrait of the Jew, nor can we suppose they were meant to, for Shakespeare's own audience anyway. The Holocaust made and makes *The Merchant of Venice* unplayable, at least in what appear to be its own terms. With some relief, I turn to the question of what Shylock did for Shakespeare the poet-playwright. The surprising answer is that by completing his emancipation from Marlowe, Shylock made it possible to go on to *Henry IV, Part One*, with its two characters who surpass even Shylock in ambivalence: Prince Hal, and the height of Shakespeare's invention of the human, Sir John Falstaff.

Shakespeare's sense of ambivalence is not Freud's, though clearly Freud, himself so ambivalent about Shakespeare, founds his account of ambivalence upon materials initially supplied by Shakespeare. Primal ambivalence, whether in Shakespeare or in Freud, need not result from social overdeterminations. The antipathy between Antonio and Shylock transcends Jew baiting; Gratiano is an instance of that Christian sport, but Antonio cannot be let off so easily. His ambivalence, like Shylock's, is murderous, and unlike Shylock's, it is successful, for Antonio does end Shylock the Jew, and gives us Shylock the New Christian. Freudian ambivalence is simultaneous love and hatred directed toward the same person; Shakespearean ambivalence, subtler and more frightening, diverts self-hatred into hatred of the other, and associates the other with lost possibilities of the self. Hamlet, whatever his protestations, is truly not interested in revenge, since no one could be more aware that in revenge all persons blend into one another. To chop down Claudius is to become old Hamlet, the ghostly father and not the intellectual prince. It is horrible to say it, but the broken New Christian Shylock is preferable to a successful butcher of a Shylock, had Portia not thwarted him. What would be left for Shylock after hacking up Antonio? What is left for Antonio after crushing Shylock? In Shakespearean ambivalence, there can be no victories.

A. P. Rossiter, in his *Angel with Horns* (posthumously published in 1961), said that ambivalence was peculiarly the dialectic of Shakespeare's history plays, defining Shakespearean ambivalence as one mode of irony or another. Irony is indeed so pervasive in Shakespeare, in every genre, that no comprehensive account of it is possible. What in *The Merchant of Venice* is not ironical, including the Belmont celebration of Act V? The coexistence in Venice of Antonio and of Shylock is an unbearable irony, an ambivalence so acute that it must be ended, either by the barbarous mutilation of Antonio or the barbarous Christian revenge upon Shylock, who evidently is scarcely to be allowed time for instruction before he is baptized. Butchery or baptism is a nice dialectic: the merchant of Venice survives, but the Jew of Venice is immolated, since as a Christian he cannot continue to be a moneylender. Shakespeare's one law is change, and neither Shylock nor Antonio can change. Antonio darkens further and Shylock breaks, but then he is one man against a city.

I end by repeating that it would have been better for the last four centuries of the Jewish people had Shakespeare never written this play. So shadowed and equivocal is *The Merchant of Venice*, though, that I cannot be certain that there is any way to perform it now and recover Shakespeare's own art of representing Shylock. Shylock is going to go on making us uncomfortable, enlightened Jew and enlightened Christian, and so I close by wondering if Shylock did not cause Shakespeare more discomfort than we now apprehend. Malvolio is horribly treated, but that appears to be a theatrical in-joke directed against Ben Jonson. Parolles deserves exposure, but the humiliation displayed is withering. Lucio, whose caustic sanity gives us something against which to perspectivize the madnesses of *Measure for Measure,* is compelled by the dubious Duke to marry a whore, for having dared to tell the truth about the Duke of dark corners. Shylock surpasses all these in the outrage visited upon him, and Antonio's turn of the screw, calling for instant conversion, is Shakespeare's own invention, and no part of the pound-of-flesh tradition. Antonio's revenge is one thing, and Shakespeare's quite another. The playwright, capacious soul, would be aware that the gratuitous outrage of a forced conversion to Venetian Christianity surpasses all boundaries of decency. Shylock's revenge upon Shakespeare is that the Jew's dramatic consistency is destroyed when he accepts Christianity rather than death.

Shakespeare thus demeans Shylock, but who can believe Shylock's "I am content"? I remember once observing that Shylock's agreeing to become a Christian is more absurd than would be the conversion of Coriolanus to the popular party, or Cleopatra's consent to become a vestal virgin at Rome. We sooner can see Falstaff as a monk than Shylock as a Christian. Contemplate Shylock at Christian prayer, or confessing to a priest. It will not do; Shakespeare was up to mischief, but you have to be an anti-Semitic scholar, Old Historicist or New, to appreciate fully the ambition of such mischief.

13

# MUCH ADO ABOUT NOTHING

Though *Much Ado About Nothing* is not one of Shakespeare's comic masterworks, it continues to manifest extraordinary vitality in performance. I have not seen a Beatrice and Benedick who rival Peggy Ashcroft and John Gielgud, but that was almost half a century ago, and the play survives even the Kenneth Branagh film, in which Tuscan scenery was allowed to usurp our attention and distract us from hearing some of Shakespeare's best prose. Written just after the rejection of Falstaff in *Henry IV, Part Two,* and just before the rejecting Hal's equivocal triumph in *Henry V, Much Ado About Nothing* retains overtones of Falstaffian intelligence and wit, though no giant form takes the stage in his absence. Beatrice is not Rosalind, and Benedick is less than Beatrice. *Hamlet,* revised from Shakespeare's own *Hamlet* (if, as I have argued, Peter Alexander was right), carried on from Falstaff and Rosalind with a darker wit and with a ravening intelligence unequaled in literature. Beatrice and Benedick are slight in this sequence, but it is important to recognize that they dominate their play only because Shakespeare endows them with courtly versions of Falstaff's primal exuberance and cognitive power. Their mastery of prose owes something to the angrier duel of wit between Hal and Falstaff (angry only on Hal's part). Ambivalence, the peculiar mark of Hal's psyche, means something very different in the fencing relationship of Beatrice and Benedick. They have been more or less in love for some time, and Benedick had retreated:

*Bene.* O God, sir, here's a dish I love not! I cannot endure my Lady
   Tongue.

*Exit.*

*D. Pedro.* Come, lady, come; you have lost the heart of Signior Benedick.

*Beat.* Indeed, my lord, he lent it me awhile, and I gave him use for it, a
   double heart for his single one. Marry, once before he won it of me
   with false dice, therefore your grace may well say I have lost it.

[II.i.257–64]

The jilting they are referring to here ended nothing, as both are well
aware, since each is a great nihilist. *Much Ado About Nothing* is certainly the
most amiably nihilistic play ever written and is most appositely titled.
Nietzscheans long before Nietzsche, Beatrice and Benedick are also Con-
greveans before Congreve. With every exchange between the fencing
lovers, the abyss glitters, and their mutual wit does not so much defend
against other selves as it defends against meaninglessness. They make
much ado about nothing because they know that nothing will come of
nothing, and so they speak again. Beatrice will always win, or rather, win
what can be won, since she is much the wittier, formidable as Benedick can
be. Before we meet him, Beatrice already is triumphant:

I pray you, how many hath he killed and eaten in these wars? But how
many hath he killed? For indeed I promised to eat all of his killing.

[I.i.38–41]

"These wars" appear to be formalistic skirmishes, with the occasional
death of a common soldier, but almost never of a gentleman or a lord. Ostensibly, we are in Sicily, though everyone seems firmly English, the delightful Beatrice most of all. Her skirmishes of wit with Benedick are nearly
as formalized as the mimic wars fought by the men. The wit is real enough,
while love, in *Much Ado About Nothing,* is as superficial as war. Not even in
*Love's Labour's Lost* is the passion between women and men taken as lightly
as in this play, where even the underlying regard between Beatrice and
Benedick has its equivocal elements.

The noble young Claudio, Benedick's friend, casts a warm eye upon the beautiful young Hero, Beatrice's cousin, and declares, "That I love her, I feel." This feeling prompts the reasonable query as to whether she is her father's only heir. Reassured as to this crucial matter, Claudio applies to his commander, Don Pedro, the Prince of Arragon, who undertakes to woo the lady as Claudio's proxy. True love would thus be served, and there would be no play, but luckily there is Don John the Bastard, half brother to Don Pedro. "It must not be denied but I am a plain-dealing villain," Don John tells us, and he vows to disturb the match of Claudio and Hero. It is all as direct as that: we are to have a comedy without enigmas, except for gauging exactly what truly exists between Beatrice and Benedick. Shakespeare's art is exquisite in showing us what they themselves scarcely know: the wit in each desires the other, but neither trusts either the other or marriage. In addressing Hero, Beatrice anticipates Rosalind in her realism:

> The fault will be in the music, cousin, if you be not wooed in good time. If the Prince be too important, tell him there is measure in everything, and so dance out the answer. For hear me, Hero: wooing, wedding, and repenting is as a Scotch jig, a measure, and a cinque-pace: the first suit is hot and hasty, like a Scotch jig, and full as fantastical; the wedding, mannerly-modest as a measure, full of state and ancientry; and then comes repentance and, with his bad legs, falls into the cinque-pace faster and faster, till he sink into his grave.
>
> [II.i.63–73]

Rosalind's touch is lighter than that; Beatrice frequently is on the edge of bitterness. In the masked dance that is emblematic of the entire play, Don Pedro famously says to Hero, "speak low, if you speak love," where "love" means a masked dance. Dancing together, Beatrice wounds Benedick sufficiently so that the hurt lasts:

> But that my Lady Beatrice should know me, and not know me! The Prince's fool! Ha, it may be I go under that title because I am merry.

Yea, but so I am apt to do myself wrong. I am not so reputed: it is the base, though bitter, disposition of Beatrice that puts the world into her person, and so gives me out. Well, I'll be revenged as I may.

[II.i.189–95]

Putting the world into her person—making her own opinion into the general judgment—is Beatrice's largest flaw. "She speaks poniards, and every word stabs," Benedick cries out, and we begin to wonder at the perpetual aggressivity of her marvelous merriment. "You were born in a merry hour," Don Pedro compliments her, and she responds by enchanting the audience: "No, sure, my lord, my mother cried, but then there was a star danced, and under that was I born." Who could be a fit husband for a woman who "hath often dreamt of unhappiness and waked herself with laughing"?

Shakespeare's inventive exuberance in *Much Ado* is lavished upon Beatrice, who is a solitary eminence in the play. Benedick, the audience sympathetically feels, does his best to keep up, while Dogberry (alas) seems to me one of Shakespeare's few failures at comedy. The Dogberrian malapropisms constitute only one joke, which is repeated too often to be funny. I favor Beatrice enough that I want Benedick, Dogberry, and the play to be worthier of her. Don John's plot against Hero's happiness is a poor contrivance, reminding us that Shakespeare's interest in action frequently is merely tertiary to his powers of characterization and of language. What works to compensate for the relative weakness of the slandering of Hero is the gulling of Beatrice and Benedick by their friends, who help truth along by assuring both reluctant lovers of the other's infatuation. This engenders the splendor of Benedick's renunciation of his bachelorhood: "No, the world must be peopled."

2

Whatever the tediousness of the Hero subplot, it does allow Shakespeare one of his great comic scenes in the confrontation between the masterful Beatrice and the Benedick she is learning to control:

*Bene.* I do love nothing in the world so well as you—is not that
    strange?

*Beat.* As strange as the thing I know not. It were as possible for me to
    say I loved nothing so well as you, but believe me not; and yet I
    lie not; I confess nothing, nor I deny nothing. I am sorry for my
    cousin.

*Bene.* By my sword, Beatrice, thou lovest me.

*Beat.* Do not swear and eat it.

*Bene.* I will swear by it that you love me, and I will make him eat it
    that says I love not you.

*Beat.* Will you not eat your word?

*Bene.* With no sauce that can be devised to it. I protest I love thee.

*Beat.* Why then, God forgive me!

*Bene.* What offence, sweet Beatrice?

*Beat.* You have stayed me in a happy hour, I was about to protest I
    loved you.

*Bene.* And do it with all thy heart.

*Beat.* I love you with so much of my heart that none is left to protest.

*Bene.* Come, bid me do anything for thee.

*Beat.* Kill Claudio!

[IV.i.266–88]

Beatrice plays him with a skilled dramatist's art, until his vow to challenge Claudio becomes their pragmatic betrothal. The quality of Beatrice's
fury, intensely pure as is her wit, redeems the Hero ordeal simply because,
like Benedick, we are totally persuaded by Beatrice's will to power over her
play. Beatrice, to whom George Bernard Shaw owed too much for his
comfort, is not only the play's sole glory; she is as much its genius as Rosalind is the guiding spirit of *As You Like It*. *Much Ado About Nothing*, known
to many as *Beatrice and Benedick*, might as soon be called *As You Like Beatrice*
or *What Beatrice Wills*. The ambivalence in her will is the play's ultimate
strength, the fountain of its comic exuberance. The longer you ponder
Beatrice, the more enigmatic she becomes. Benedick has no such vital reserves: his defensive wit is wholly inspired by Beatrice. Without her, he
would blend back into Messina's festiveness, or go off to Aragon with Don

Pedro, in search of other battles. But even were there no intermediaries to insinuate the love of each to the other, Benedick at last would be Beatrice's, the best Messina could afford her. She takes her time to secure him, because her primary interest is herself; Benedick's self-love echoes hers, while Dogberry's self-intoxication parodies both the lovers.

The fascination of Beatrice is founded upon her extraordinary blend of merriment and bitterness, in contrast to the simpler Kate the Shrew. Beatrice has more affinity to the dark Rosaline of *Love's Labour's Lost*, though Rosaline's merriment is not very innocent. Shakespearean foregrounding rather subtly allows some clues for Beatrice's nature, and perhaps for her negative obsession with Benedick, who is at once the only threat to her freedom and the inevitable path out of her incessant toughness of spirit. Beatrice's most essential foreground is that she is an orphan; her uncle Leonato was her guardian, but clearly no foster father:

> *Leon.* Well then, go you into hell?
> *Beat.* No, but to the gate, and there will the Devil meet me like an old
>     cuckold with horns on his head, and say, 'Get you to heaven,
>     Beatrice, get you to heaven, here's no place for you maids.' So de-
>     liver I up my apes, and away to Saint Peter, for the heavens; he
>     shows me where the bachelors sit, and there live we as merry as
>     the day is long.
> *Ant.* [*To Hero*] Well, niece, I trust you will be ruled by your father.
> *Beat.* Yes, faith, it is my cousin's duty to make curtsy and say, 'Father,
>     as it please you': but yet for all that, cousin, let him be a hand-
>     some fellow, or else make another curtsy and say, 'Father, as it
>     please me'.
>
>                                                         [II.i.38–52]

Benedick's version of this paradise of bachelors (and maids) is less sublime:

> That a woman conceived me, I thank her: that she brought me up,
> I likewise give her most humble thanks: but that I will have a recheat
> winded in my forehead, or hang my bugle in an invisible baldrick,

all women shall pardon me. Because I will not do them the wrong
to mistrust any, I will do myself the right to trust none: and the fine
is, for the which I may go the finer, I will live a bachelor.

[I.i.221–28]

Whether or not Beatrice indeed is, as Benedick remarks, "possessed
with a fury," a permanent zeal for being on the attack, is not altogether
clear. The earlier jilting by Benedick, "a double heart for his single one,"
provides her starting point but does not explain her vitalizing firepower,
her continuous verve and drive, the "merriment" that at once dazzles and
wears out her world, though not her audience. We learn to listen to her
very carefully, as here when she responds to Claudio's having just called
Hero his betrothed "cousin" under the rights of alliance.

> *Beat.* Good Lord, for alliance! Thus goes everyone to the world but I,
>     and I am sunburnt. I may sit in a corner and cry 'Heigh-ho for a
>     husband!'
> *D. Pedro.* Lady Beatrice, I will get you one.
> *Beat.* I would rather have one of your father's getting. Hath your grace
>     ne'er a brother like you? Your father got excellent husbands, if a
>     maid could come by them.
> *D. Pedro.* Will you have me, lady?
> *Beat.* No, my lord, unless I might have another for working days: your
>     Grace is too costly to wear every day. But I beseech your Grace
>     pardon me, I was born to speak all mirth and no matter.

[II.i.299–311]

Going to the world is one of Beatrice's metaphors for marriage, while
"sunburnt" women attracted few suitors for marriage in Renaissance England. Don Pedro, a puzzling fellow, may mean his light proposal, and Beatrice's rejection carefully keeps to a line between compliment and the full
implications of "costly." Plainly, she perpetually intends to take Benedick,
and yet is sincerely reluctant to accept anyone, even the wittiest available
to her. Don Pedro's self-mockery seasons his self-love; her occasional ges-

tures at parodying herself are Beatrice's least persuasive moments. Her warranted regard for herself is partly why the audience delights in her; it echoes Falstaff's magnificent appreciation of his own comic intelligence. We are happy to see Sir John with Mistress Quickly and Doll Tearsheet; clearly there has not been and cannot be a Lady Falstaff! Only Chaucer's Wife of Bath might have been up to the task of being wife to Sir John, and there is some question as to which of the two would murder the other first, whether with language or with sexual exercise. We have to conclude that Beatrice and Benedick already have been lovers, and that her vitality, however expressed, has frightened him into flight. It is shrewd of Shakespeare to have Benedick react to his friends' gulling in prose—"Love? Why, it must be requited"—while Beatrice, at the same provocation, breaks into lyrical verse:

> What fire is in mine ears? Can this be true?
> Stand I condemn'd for pride and scorn so much?
>     Contempt, farewell, and maiden pride, adieu!
> No glory lives behind the back of such.
>     And, Benedick, love on, I will requite thee,
> Taming my wild heart to thy loving hand.
>     If thou dost love, my kindness shall incite thee
> To bind our loves up in a holy band;
>     For others say thou dost deserve, and I
>     Believe it better than reportingly.

Hero has told Ursula that Beatrice's spirits are as contemptuous (coy) as wild hawks ("haggards of the rock"). When Beatrice chants of "Taming my wild heart to thy loving hand," she does not imply that she will accept domestication. Her wildness is her freedom, and that sense of liberty, more even than her wit, captures her audience. The rather disappointing Branagh movie of *Much Ado About Nothing* was in part redeemed by Emma Thompson's Beatrice, with its nuances of a Brontë-like independence conveyed mostly through tone and facial expression. There is something in Beatrice's temperament that must always evade domestication. Her fury that she cannot be a man in order to avenge Claudio's slander upon Hero goes well beyond gender politics in authentic savagery:

> Is a not approved in the height a villain, that hath slandered, scorned, dishonoured my kinswoman? O that I were a man! What, bear her in hand until they come to take hands, and then with public accusation, uncovered slander, unmitigated rancour—O God that I were a man! I would eat his heart in the market-place.
>
> [IV.i.300–306]

### 3

How then does one answer the question: What is the definition of love in *Much Ado About Nothing?* The prime answer is there in the title: Love is much ado about nothing. What binds and will hold Beatrice and Benedick together is their mutual knowledge and acceptance of this benign nihilism. Doubtless the title has some reference also to the vexed transition of Hero and Claudio from noncourtship to a pragmatic marriage of mutual advantage. Tiresome and empty as Claudio is, he has a certain aplomb in his cheerful approach to his second betrothal to the supposedly dead Hero: "I'll hold my mind were she an Ethiope" and "Which is the lady I must seize upon?" This splendid unconcern is the prelude to the highest comedy in the play:

> *Bene.* Soft and fair, friar. Which is Beatrice?
> *Beat.* [*Unmasking.*] I answer to that name. What is your will?
> *Bene.* Do not you love me?
> *Beat.*                              Why, no, no more than reason.
> *Bene.* Why then, your uncle, and the Prince, and Claudio
>       Have been deceived—they swore you did.
> *Beat.* Do not you love me?
> *Bene.*                              Troth, no, no more than reason.
> *Beat.* Why then, my cousin, Margaret, and Ursula
>       Are much deceiv'd, for they did swear you did.
> *Bene.* They swore that you were almost sick for me.

*Beat.* They swore that you were well-nigh dead for me.
*Bene.* 'Tis no such matter. Then you do not love me?
*Beat.* No, truly, but in friendly recompense.

[V.iv.72–83]

This has gone beyond fencing into a wary exchange of tactics, brilliantly phrased, and climaxing in one of Shakespeare's finest comic epiphanies:

*Bene.* A miracle! Here's our own hands against our hearts. Come, I will have thee, but by this light I take thee for pity.
*Beat.* I would not deny you, but, by this good day I yield upon great persuasion, and partly to save your life, for I was told you were in a consumption.
*Bene.* Peace! I will stop your mouth.

[V.iv.91–97]

Protesting even while kissing, Beatrice will not speak again in *Much Ado About Nothing*. Shakespeare must have felt that, for now, she and the audience were at one. Benedick is allowed a spirited defense of his new status as "the married man," one that culminates in an obsessive Shakespearean mode of advice: get married and expect to be cuckolded:

*Bene.* First, of my word! Therefore play, music. Prince, thou art sad; get thee a wife! There is no staff more reverend than one tipped with horn.

Neither the prince's staff of authorization nor the staff of honored old age is more antique in vintage than the horned staff of the cuckold. Benedick jests in what is for us a light bad taste, but properly realistic for Shakespeare. Perhaps there is just a hint that like most Shakespeare marriages, the union of Beatrice and Benedick may not be a bower of bliss. In this comedy, more than ever, that does not matter. Two of the most intelligent and energetic of Shakespeare's nihilists, neither of them likely to be outraged or defeated, will take their chances together.

# 14

# AS YOU LIKE IT

The popularity of Rosalind is due to three main causes. First, she only speaks blank verse for a few minutes. Second, she only wears a skirt for a few minutes (and the dismal effect of the change at the end to the wedding dress ought to convert the stupidest champion of petticoats to rational dress). Third, she makes love to the man instead of waiting for the man to make love to her—a piece of natural history which has kept Shakespeare's heroines alive, whilst generations of properly governessed young ladies, taught to say "No" three times at least, have miserably perished.

That is George Bernard Shaw (hardly a Bardolator!) in 1896, when the reign of Rosalind was at one of its heights. When I saw Katharine Hepburn triumphing as Rosalind on Broadway in 1950, the role still maintained its long ascendancy, though now, nearly a half century later, Rosalind has been appropriated by our current specialists in gender politics, who sometimes even give us a lesbian Rosalind, more occupied with Celia (or with Phebe) than with poor Orlando. As the millennium goes by, and recedes into the past, we may return to the actual Shakespearean role, perhaps about the same time we wrest Caliban away from his "materialist" admirers and restore him to his bitter "family romance" (Freud's phrase) with the household of Prospero. Back in 1932, when Rosalind was all the rage, G. K. Chesterton, very much her admirer, nevertheless protested her popular reductions:

About three hundred years ago William Shakespeare, not knowing what to do with his characters, turned them out to play in the woods, let a girl masquerade as a boy and amused himself with speculating on the effect of feminine curiosity freed for an hour from feminine dignity. He did it very well, but he could do something else. And the popular romances of today cannot do anything else. Shakespeare took care to explain in the play itself that he did *not* think that life should be one prolonged picnic. Nor would he have thought that feminine life should be one prolonged piece of private theatricals. But Rosalind, who was then unconventional for an hour, is now the convention of an epoch. She was then on a holiday; she is now very hardworked indeed. She has to act in every play, novel or short story, and always in the same old pert pose. Perhaps she is even afraid to be herself: certainly Celia is now afraid to be herself.

Whether Shakespeare was as content as Chesterton would have him be to end the picnic in the forest of Arden (named, in part, for his mother, Mary Arden), I somewhat doubt. I think that Shakespeare must have been very fond of this play. We know that Shakespeare himself played the role of old Adam, Orlando's faithful retainer, an old Adam free of all sin and invested with original virtue. Of all Shakespeare's plays, the accurately titled *As You Like It* is as much set in an earthly realm of possible good as *King Lear* and *Macbeth* are set in earthly hells. And of all Shakespeare's comic heroines, Rosalind is the most gifted, as remarkable in her mode as Falstaff and Hamlet are in theirs. Shakespeare has been so subtle and so careful in writing Rosalind's role that we never quite awaken to her uniqueness among his (or all literature's) heroic wits. A normative consciousness, harmoniously balanced and beautifully sane, she is the indubitable ancestress of Elizabeth Bennet in *Pride and Prejudice*, though she has a social freedom beyond Jane Austen's careful limitations.

Daughter of Duke Senior, the rightful if usurped Duke, Rosalind is too far beyond Orlando (a poor gentleman) to accept him as husband, but the forest of Arden dissolves hierarchies, at least for a blessed time. The bad Duke, the younger brother of Duke Senior, absurdly yields up the usurped dukedom to the rightful Duke, Rosalind's father, while the wicked Oliver as surprisingly gives up their father's house to Orlando, his younger brother and Rosalind's lover. It is not possible to historicize so mixed a pattern, and social commentaries to *As You Like It* do not take us very far into this play's curious and charming ethos. We do not even know precisely where we are geographically in this comedy. Ostensibly, the usurped duchy is in France, and Arden is the Ardennes, but Robin Hood is invoked, and the forest seems very English. French and English names are haphazardly distributed among the characters, in a happy anarchy that works splendidly. Though critics can and do find many shadows in the forest of Arden, such discoveries obscure what matters most about this exquisite play. It is much Shakespeare's happiest: death has been in Arcadia, but not so that we can be oppressed by it, since nearly everything else is as we like it.

Shakespeare has some two dozen masterpieces among his thirty-nine plays, and no one would deny *As You Like It* eminence, though a few (wrongly) consider it the slightest of the masterpieces. If Rosalind cannot please us, then no one in Shakespeare or elsewhere in literature ever will. I love Falstaff and Hamlet and Cleopatra as dramatic and literary characters, but would not want suddenly to encounter them in actuality; yet falling in love with Rosalind always makes me wish that she existed in our subliterary realm. Edith Evans performed Rosalind before I was old enough to attend; according to one critic, she spoke to the audience as though everyone in it was Orlando, and so captured them all. A great role, like Rosalind's, is a kind of miracle: a universal perspective seems to open out upon us. Shakespeare makes even Falstaff and Hamlet victims, to some degree, of dramatic irony; we are afforded a few perspectives that are not available either to the greatest of comic protagonists or to the most troubling of tragic heroes. Rosalind is unique in Shakespeare, perhaps indeed in Western drama, because it is so difficult to achieve a perspective upon her that she herself does not anticipate and share. A stage play is virtually impossible without some degree of dramatic irony; that is the audience's privilege. We enjoy such an irony in regard to Touchstone, Jaques, and every other character in *As You Like It*, except for Rosalind. We forgive her for knowing what matters more than we do, because she has no will to power over us, except to exercise our most humane faculties in appreciating her performance.

2

I have remarked already that Shakespeare himself played the role of old Adam, the faithful servant who goes off with Orlando to the forest of Arden. The virtuous Adam is "not for the fashion of these times," as Orlando says, but represents rather "the constant service of the antique world." *As You Like It* is Shakespeare's sweetest-tempered play; there is *Twelfth Night,* but in that play everyone except the superb clown Feste is a zany. Orlando, a youthful Hercules, is certainly not Rosalind's human equal, but he is considerably saner than *Twelfth Night*'s loony Orsino, while Rosalind and Celia would be exemplary in any company, and in wisdom and wit are goddesses compared with those charming screwballs Viola and Olivia. I would grant to scholars that there are dark traces in the forest of Arden, for Shakespeare's overwhelming sense of reality does not allow him to depict an absolutely unmixed realm. Having made this point, I am delighted to observe that the forest of Arden is simply the best place to live, anywhere in Shakespeare. You cannot have an earthly paradise and still have a stage comedy that works, yet *As You Like It* comes closest. Old Adam (Shakespeare) is nearly eighty, and nothing is said of his (or any other) Eve. We are in a lapsed world, silver at best, but it has a woman beyond Eve, the sublime Rosalind. Eve, the mother of all living, is celebrated for her vitality and beauty, and not always for her intellect. The exuberant Rosalind is vital and beautiful, in spirit, in body, in mind. She has no equal, in or out of Arden, and deserves a better lover than the amiable Orlando, and better wits for her conversation than Touchstone and Jaques. Each time I read *As You Like It,* I indulge a favorite fantasy, that Shakespeare never had written *The Merry Wives of Windsor* (unworthy of Falstaff, who is represented there by an impostor), and did not kill Sir John off in *Henry V.* No, if Sir John was to be seen in love, then he, and not Touchstone, should have fled to the forest of Arden with Rosalind and Celia, there to exchange Mrs. Quickly and Doll Tearsheet for Audrey and Phebe. What prose Shakespeare might have written for Falstaff and Rosalind in their contests of wit, or for Sir John to flatten Jaques! There is a critical point to my fantasy, since Touchstone and Jaques combined do not make me miss Falstaff less.

Shakespeare sensibly would have rejected my suggestion: Falstaff, greatest of scene stealers, would have gotten in the way of our seeing Rosalind all round, as it were, and might have impeded Rosalind in her own educational venture, the instruction of Orlando, neither as brilliant nor as dangerous a student as Prince Hal.

Shakespeare's invention of the human, already triumphant through his creation of Falstaff, acquired a new dimension with Rosalind, his second great personality to date, beyond Juliet, Portia, and Beatrice. Rosalind's role was the best preparation for the revised Hamlet of 1600–1601, where wit achieves an apotheosis and becomes a kind of negative transcendence. Personality in Shakespeare always returns me to the difficult enterprise of surmising Shakespeare's own personality. Like Shylock, Shakespeare was a moneylender, and evidently became known as being rather sharp in his business dealings. Except for that, we do not encounter much that seems to find fault with Shakespeare, setting aside the early venom of the distraught Greene, failed rival dramatist. There are deep shadows on the speaker of the Sonnets, and some speculate that these are related to the anguish of bearing a wounded name in the later "Elegy" for Will Peter, if indeed that *is* Shakespeare's poem. Honigmann sensibly advises us to live with two antithetical images of Shakespeare, one genial and open, the other darkened and reclusive, Falstaff and Hamlet fused in a single consciousness. What, besides intellect, do Falstaff and Hamlet share? Nietzsche said of Hamlet that he thought too well, and so died of the truth. Can one joke too well? Falstaff dies because the order of play abandons him with Hal's betrayal; that is a death not by wit, but by the loss of love, akin to the little deaths that Shakespeare (or his speaker) endures in the Sonnets. Genre is a fluid dissolve in Shakespeare, but Falstaff was allowed only the mock comedy of *The Merry Wives of Windsor*, not the authentic comedy of *As You Like It* and *Twelfth Night*.

Rosalind's high good fortune—which exalts her over Falstaff, Hamlet, and Cleopatra—is to stand at the center of a play in which no authentic harm can come to anyone. We are permitted to relax into our apprehension of Rosalind's genius. Shakespeare the man seems to have had a healthy fear of being hurt or abused: the speaker of the Sonnets never gives himself away as fully as Falstaff does to Hal, or Hamlet to his dead father's memory. Cleopatra, until Antony dies, protects herself from too much abandonment to her love, and even Rosalind is careful to pace her relationship to Orlando. Yet the glory of Rosalind, and of her play, is her confidence, and ours, that all things will go well.

3

Touchstone and Jaques, in their very different ways, do not go well with Rosalind, or with her ideal context in Arden. Touchstone's indeliberate travesties far exceed his intentional fooleries; he is the total antithesis of *Twelfth Night*'s Feste, Shakespeare's wisest (and most humanly amiable) clown. Jaques, a more complex botcher, has withdrawn from the passions of existence, but not in the name of any values that Rosalind (or we) can honor. Many critics rightly note that Rosalind and even her Orlando (to a lesser extent) have remarkably few illusions about the nature of the high Romantic passion that they share. They do not merely play at love, or at courtship, but they are careful to entertain play as a crucial element in keeping love realistic. Poise is Rosalind's particular endowment, and Orlando learns it from her. Of Rosalind's poise, it can be remarked that this quality emanates neither from manners nor from morals. Rather, such balance ensues from an intricate spiritual choreography, denied to Falstaff only by his passion for Hal, and abandoned by Hamlet because he internalizes the open wound that is Elsinore. Cleopatra is always too much the actress, attempting the role of herself, to rival Rosalind in grace and in the control of perspective. Is it an accident that Rosalind is the most admirable personage in all of Shakespeare? The very name seems to have had a particular magic for him, though he named his actual daughters Susanna and Judith. *Love's Labour's Lost*'s Berowne fails in his campaign to win the formidable Rosaline, and Romeo, before he meets Juliet, is also infatuated with a Rosaline. But Rosalind is very different from both Rosalines, who resist their admirers. No one knows the name of the Dark Lady of the Sonnets, but we can be reasonably certain it was not Rosaline or Rosalind.

First in poise of all Shakespearean characters, the admirable Rosalind is also his most triumphant, both in her own fate and in what she brings about for others. *Twelfth Night* is *As You Like It*'s only rival among Shakespeare's Romantic comedies, but it lacks Rosalind. The difference may be that *As You Like It* directly precedes the *Hamlet* of 1600–1601, while *Twelfth Night* follows directly after it, and Hamlet made another Rosalind unlikely for Shakespeare. Nietzsche thought Hamlet to be the authentic Dionysiac hero. Though Camille Paglia boldly speculates that Rosalind is a Dionysiac heroine, I am not altogether persuaded. Paglia strongly emphasizes Rosalind's mercurial temperament, a somewhat different endowment than the one Nietzsche associates with Dionysus. Though anything but an academic feminist, Paglia shares in our current concern with the supposed androgyny of Shakespeare's heroines who adopt male disguises: Julia, Portia, Rosalind, Viola, Imogen. I cannot assert that I completely apprehend Shakespeare's vision of human sexuality, yet I distrust both G. Wilson Knight's and Paglia's notions as to a bisexual ideal in Shakespeare, though these critics are superb readers. Rosalind in any case hardly seems such a figure, since her sexual desires entirely center upon Orlando, a Herculean wrestler and by no means a diffident young man. Universally attractive, to women as to men (in or out of the audience), she is shrewdly absolute in her choice of Orlando, and she undertakes his amatory education in the role of a preceptor who is determined that he shall graduate. It is extraordinary that a dramatic character could be at once so interesting and so normative as Rosalind is: free of malice; turning her aggressivity neither against herself nor against others; free of all resentments, while manifesting a vital curiosity and an exuberant desire.

Orlando is a dreadfully bad poet:

Therefore Heaven Nature charg'd
   That one body should be fill'd
With all graces wide-enlarg'd.
   Nature presently distill'd
Helen's cheek, but not her heart,
   Cleopatra's majesty,
Atalanta's better part,

Sad Lucretia's modesty.
Thus Rosalind of many parts
   By heavenly synod was devis'd,
Of many faces, eyes, and hearts,
   To have the touches dearest priz'd.

                                        [III.ii.138–49]

And yet Rosalind is as integrated a personality as Shakespeare created: she is not a picnic of selves, as Hamlet sometimes becomes. Her changes unfold persuasively and only deepen the selfsame continuity of her nature. One of the most hideous of our current critical fashions, both academic and journalistic, calls itself sexual politics, and the sexual politicians all urge us to believe that Shakespeare abandons Rosalind to "patriarchal male bonds." It is not clear to me how Shakespeare could have avoided this supposed desertion of his heroine. Are Rosalind and Celia to marry each other? They don't want to; Rosalind rushes to Orlando, and Celia (with startling speed) leaps toward the reformed Oliver. Was Shakespeare to kill off the superb Duke Senior, Rosalind's affectionate father? Or was Rosalind to reject Orlando for Phebe? Let it suffice to affirm that no one else in the plays, not even Falstaff or Hamlet, represents Shakespeare's own stance toward human nature so fully as Rosalind does. If we can point to his unshadowed ideal, then it must be to Rosalind. His ironies, which are Rosalind's, are subtler and more capacious than ours, and more humane also.

4

Most commercial stagings of *As You Like It* vulgarize the play, as though directors fear that audiences cannot be trusted to absorb the agon between the wholesome wit of Rosalind and the rancidity of Touchstone, the bitterness of Jaques. I fear that this is not exactly the cultural moment for Shakespeare's Rosalind, yet I expect that moment to come again, and yet again, when our various feminisms have become even maturer and yet more successful. Rosalind, least ideological of all dramatic characters, surpasses every other woman in literature in what we could call "intelligibility." You never get far by terming her a "pastoral heroine" or a "Romantic comedian": her mind is too large, her spirit too free, to so confine her. She is as immensely superior to everyone else in her play as are Falstaff and Hamlet in theirs. The best starting point truly to apprehend her is a single grand sentence she speaks, when Orlando protests that he will die if she does not have him. I have heard this great line thrown away too often, when actresses suffered bad direction, but clearly delivered it is unforgettable: "Men have died from time to time, and worms have eaten them, but not for love." For wit and wisdom, that can compete with Falstaff at his greatest, after the Lord Chief Justice has chided him for speaking of his own "youth": "My lord, I was born about three of the clock in the afternoon, with a white head and something of a round belly." That affirmation of agelessness is a personal triumph; Rosalind's triumph is impersonal and overwhelming, and remains the best medicine for all lovesick males. "Men *have* died from time to time, and worms *have* eaten them": death is authentic and material, *"but not for love."* Falstaff takes the Lord Chief Justice's complaint, and explodes it with Falstaffian fantasia; Rosalind, an equal master of timing, deflates subtly and definitively the male refusal to grow up.

Chesterton said that "Rosalind did not go into the wood to look for her freedom; she went into the wood to look for her father." Though I worship Chesterton, that would have surprised Shakespeare; an undisguised Rosalind is not even in her father's presence until she reassumes female garments for her wedding. The search for the father has little importance in *As You Like It*, and Rosalind's freedom is central to her. Perhaps, as Marjorie Garber suggests, Rosalind goes into the forest in order to mature Orlando, to improve him both as person and as lover. Orlando actually is no more adolescent than most of Shakespeare's males: did Shakespeare or nature invent the emotional inferiority of men to women? Rosalind is too pragmatic to lament such inequality, and is content to educate Orlando. She shares with Falstaff the educator's role; Hamlet diagnoses everyone he encounters, and is too impatient to teach them. Rosalind and Falstaff both augment and enhance life, but Hamlet is the gateway through which supernal powers, many of them negative, enter as intimations of mortality. *As You Like It* is poised before the great tragedies; it is a vitalizing work, and Rosalind is a joyous representative of life's possible freedoms. The aesthetic representation of happiness demands a complex art; no drama of happiness ever has surpassed Rosalind's.

To be in love, and yet to see and feel the absurdity of it, one needs to go to school with Rosalind. She instructs us in the miracle of being a harmonious consciousness that is also able to accommodate the reality of another self. Shelley heroically thought that the secret of love was a complete going-out from our own nature into the nature of another; Rosalind sensibly regards that as madness. She is neither High Romantic nor a Platonist: love's illusions, for her, are quite distinct from the reality of maids knowing that "the sky changes when they are wives." One might venture that Rosalind as an analyst of "love" is akin to Falstaff as an analyst of "honor"—that is to say, of the whole baggage of state power, political intrigue, mock chivalry, and open warfare. The difference is that Rosalind herself is joyously in love and criticizes love from within its realm; Falstaff devastates the pretensions of power, but always from its periphery, and knowing throughout that he will lose Hal to the realities of power. Rosalind's wit is triumphant yet always measured to its object, while Falstaff's irreverent mockery is victorious but pragmatically unable to save him from rejection. Both are educational geniuses, and yet Rosalind is Jane Austen to Falstaff's Samuel Johnson; Rosalind is the apotheosis of persuasion, while Falstaff ultimately conveys the vanity of human wishes.

I have been urging us to see Rosalind in sequence, between Falstaff and Hamlet, just as witty and as wise but trapped neither in history with Falstaff nor in tragedy with Hamlet, and yet larger than her drama even as they cannot be confined to theirs. The invention of freedom must be measured against what encloses or threatens freedom: time and the state for Falstaff, the past and the enemy within for Hamlet. Rosalind's freedom may seem less consequential because *As You Like It* brushes aside time and the state, and Rosalind has no tragic sorrows, no Prince Hal, and no Gertrude or Ghost. Rosalind is her own context, unchallenged save for the melancholy Jaques and the rancid Touchstone.

5

Jaques, poseur as he is, gets some of the best speeches in Shakespeare, who must have had a certain fondness for this fake melancholic. Like Touchstone, Jaques is Shakespeare's own invention; neither of them figures in the play's source, Thomas Lodge's prose romance *Rosalynde* (1590). Whatever pleasure Shakespeare took in Jaques and in Touchstone, we are misled if we are persuaded by their negations (many scholars have been susceptible to Touchstone, in particular). Touchstone, authentically witty, is rancidly vicious, while Jaques is merely rancid (the Shakespearean pronunciation of his name plays upon a jakes, or privy). Both of them are in *As You Like It* to serve as touchstones for Rosalind's more congenial wit, and she triumphantly puts them in their places. Her amiable triumphalism prefigures Prospero's, as Marjorie Garber suggests, though Rosalind's mastery is a wholly natural magic, normative and humane, and shall we not call it Shakespeare's own? Jaques and Touchstone are different but related disasters that the speaker of the Sonnets avoids falling into, despite the provocations to despair amply provided by the fair young lord and the dark lady, the two loves of comfort and despair.

Reductionism, or the tendency to believe that only the worst truth about us is true, is a great irritation to Shakespeare, a grim joy to Jaques, and an obscene pleasure to Touchstone. Jaques is both a social satirist and a mocker of Arden; however, society is off stage, and we are in pastoral exile, so that the satirical stance of Ben Jonson is barely available to Jaques. That leaves only Arden, where Touchstone serves both as Jaques's rival and as his colleague, another malcontent. Touchstone, who is both funnier and cruder, sees country innocence as mere ignorance; Jaques is only a little kinder on this. The major target for both would-be satirists is erotic idealism, or romantic love. But their mutual critique is redundant; Rosalind is both an erotic realist and a superbly benign critic of romantic love, and she makes both malcontents seem inadequate to their chosen modes. She exposes Jaques's silliness and Touchstone's absurdity, and thus defends Arden and its affections from an unhealthy reductionism.

Yet Jaques has qualities that partly redeem his silliness, more for us than for Rosalind, since she does not need him. Shakespeare makes us need Jaques by assigning him two great speeches, the first celebrating his meeting with Touchstone:

A fool, a fool! I met a fool i' th' forest,
A motley fool: a miserable world!
As I do live by food, I met a fool,
Who laid him down and bask'd him in the sun,
And rail'd on Lady Fortune in good terms,
In good set terms, and yet a motley fool.
'Good morrow, fool', quoth I. 'No, sir', quoth he,
'Call me not fool, till heaven hath sent me fortune.'
And then he drew a dial from his poke,
And looking on it, with lack-lustre eye,
Says, very wisely, 'It is ten o'clock.
Thus we may see', quoth he, 'how the world wags:
'Tis but an hour ago since it was nine,
And after one hour more 'twill be eleven;
And so, from hour to hour, we ripe, and ripe,
And then from hour to hour, we rot, and rot,
And thereby hangs a tale.' When I did hear
The motley fool thus moral on the time,
My lungs began to crow like chanticleer,
That fools should be so deep-contemplative;
And I did laugh, sans intermission,
An hour by his dial. O noble fool!
A worthy fool! Motley's the only wear.

[II.vii.12–34]

Touchstone, a truant court jester or "motley fool," refuses the title of fool until fortune has favored him, and puns rather pungently on "hour" and "whore." Whatever tale hangs upon this rancid hint of venereal infection, we cannot be certain, but Touchstone's effect upon Jaques is both profound and enigmatic, since it releases Jaques from his obsessive melancholy, for an hour anyway, and revises his sense of his role as satirist:

> I must have liberty
> Withal, as large a charter as the wind,
> To blow on whom I please, for so fools have;
> And they that are most galled with my folly,
> They most must laugh. And why sir must they so?
> The why is plain as way to parish church.
> He that a fool doth very wisely hit
> Doth very foolishly, although he smart,
> Not to seem senseless of the bob. If not,
> The wiseman's folly is anatomiz'd
> Even by the squand'ring glances of the fool.
> Invest me in my motley. Give me leave
> To speak my mind, and I will through and through
> Cleanse the foul body of th'infected world,
> If they will patiently receive my medicine.
>
> [II.vii.47–61]

Shakespeare seems to glance slyly here at his friend Ben Jonson, and perhaps also conveys something of his own insight into the court fool's dramatic possibilities, an insight that will be developed in the Feste of *Twelfth Night* and the great nameless Fool of *King Lear.* Duke Senior is quick to retort that the Jonsonian Jaques himself has manifested the flaws he now would censure:

> Most mischievous foul sin, in chiding sin.
> For thou thyself hast been a libertine,
> As sensual as the brutish sting itself,
> And all th'embossèd sores and headed evils
> That thou with license of free foot hast caught
> Wouldst thou disgorge into the general world.
>
> [II.vii. 64–69]

Jaques defends himself with a Jonsonian apologia for the satirical play-wright, who attacks types and not individuals. This defense is the transi-tion to *As You Like It*'s most famous speech, where Jaques gives his own dramatic version of the Seven Ages of Man:

> All the world's a stage,
> And all the men and women merely players.
> They have their exits and their entrances,
> And one man in his time plays many parts,
> His acts being seven ages. At first, the infant,
> Mewling and puking in the nurse's arms.
> Then, the whining school-boy, with his satchel
> And shining morning face, creeping like snail
> Unwillingly to school. And then the lover,
> Sighing like furnace, with a woeful ballad
> Made to his mistress' eyebrow. Then a soldier,
> Full of strange oaths, and bearded like the pard,
> Jealous in honour, sudden, and quick in quarrel,
> Seeking the bubble reputation
> Even in the cannon's mouth. And then, the justice,
> In fair round belly with good capon lin'd,
> With eyes severe, and beard of formal cut,
> Full of wise saws, and modern instances,
> And so he plays his part. The sixth age shifts
> Into the lean and slipper'd pantaloon,
> With spectacles on nose, and pouch on side,
> His youthful hose well sav'd, a world too wide
> For his shrunk shank, and his big manly voice,
> Turning again toward childish treble, pipes
> And whistles in his sound. Last scene of all,
> That ends this strange eventful history,
> Is second childishness and mere oblivion,
> Sans teeth, sans eyes, sans taste, sans everything.

> [II.vii.139–66]

Powerful enough out of context, this speech has a very subtle reverberation within the play, since it enhances our sense of Jaques's reductionism. Jaques knows, as we do, that all infants do not incessantly bawl
and puke, and that all schoolboys do not whine. The lover and the soldier
are better served by Jaques's satirical eloquence, and we can imagine Falstaff laughing at those "seeking the bubble reputation / Even in the can-
non's mouth." Shakespeare, an inveterate litigator, invests considerable
gusto in the reference to the well-known practice of stuffing judges with
capons. Himself only in the middle of the journey, at thirty-five, Shakespeare (perhaps intuiting that two-thirds of his life was already over) en-
visions the silly old Pantalone of *commedia dell'arte* as a universal fate,
preluding the second childhood of all humans who survive long enough:
"sans teeth, sans eyes, sans taste, sans everything." That last line is Jaques's
triumph, it being a natural reductionism that even Sir John Falstaff could
not dispute, and yet Shakespeare does, by entering as old Adam (a part, as
I've noted, he himself performed). Orlando staggers onto the stage, carrying his benign old retainer, who has sacrificed everything for him, and
yet who is precisely not "sans everything." The rebuke to Jaques's reductionism scarcely could be more persuasive than Adam's quasi-paternal love
for and loyalty to Orlando.

Jaques's fine complexity abides in the charm and energy of his negations. When he should be rhetorically crushed by Rosalind's unanswerable
wit, he at first rebounds with a satiric gusto that wins our bemused affection:

> *Jaques.* I prithee, pretty youth, let me be better acquainted with
>      thee.
> *Ros.* They say you are a melancholy fellow.
> *Jaques.* I am so. I do love it better than laughing.
> *Ros.* Those that are in extremity of either are abominable fellows,
>      and betray themselves to every modern censure, worse than
>      drunkards.
> *Jaques.* Why, 'tis good to be sad and say nothing.
> *Ros.* Why then, 'tis good to be a post.

*Jaques.* I have neither the scholar's melancholy, which is emulation;
　　nor the musician's, which is fantastical; nor the courtier's, which is
　　proud; nor the soldier's, which is ambitious; nor the lawyer's,
　　which is politic; nor the lady's, which is nice; nor the lover's,
　　which is all these: but it is a melancholy of mine own, com-
　　pounded of many simples, extracted from many objects, and in-
　　deed the sundry contemplation of my travels, in which my often
　　rumination wraps me in a most humorous sadness.

　　　　　　　　　　　　　　　　　　　　　　　　[IV.i.1–19]

" 'Tis good to be a post" either goes right by Jaques, or else is evaded
by his insistence that his melancholy is original and individual. But his self-
affirmation is voided by Rosalind's next salvo:

*Ros.* A traveler! By my faith, you have great reason to be sad. I fear
　　you have sold your own lands to see other men's. Then to have
　　seen much and to have nothing is to have rich eyes and poor
　　hands.
*Jaques.* Yes, I have gained my experience.
*Ros.* And your experience makes you sad. I had rather have a fool to
　　make me merry than experience to make me sad—and to travel
　　for it too.

　　　　　　　　　　　　　　　　　　　　　　　　[IV.i.20–27]

The rather lame "Yes, I have gained my experience" is the mark of
Jaques's defeat, but Shakespeare grants his melancholic a dignified end.
With nearly everyone else in the play either getting married or returning
from pastoral exile, Jaques nevertheless departs with a flair: "So, to your
pleasures: / I am for other than dancing measures." He will go out with the
judgment that marriage is a "pastime," and we wonder again whether he
does not speak for a partial Shakespeare, perhaps for the man rather than
the poet-playwright. Jaques may be only what Orlando calls him, "either
a fool or a cipher," but his highly stylized linguistic gestures partly succeed
in saving him from himself.

6

Touchstone, despite so many of the critics, and the performance tradition, is truly rancid, in contrast to Jaques, and this more intense rancidity
works as a touchstone should, to prove the true gold of Rosalind's spirit.
Little as I love Touchstone, it is impossible to resist wholly a character who
can thus affirm his past (and future) career as courtier:

> I have trod a measure; I have flattered a lady; I have been politic
> with my friend, smooth with mine enemy; I have undone three
> tailors . . .
>
> [V.iv. 44–48]

Touchstone fascinates (and repels) because of his knowingness; he is
conscious of every duplicity, intended or not, his own or of others. He is
what Falstaff proudly (and accurately) insists the fat knight is not: a double man. Though Rosalind now provokes oceans of transvestite commentary, she floats over it quite untouched, precisely because she is not a
double woman. Endlessly volatile, she remains unitary, the perfect representation of what Yeats called Unity of Being. She may well be the least
nihilistic protagonist in all of Shakespeare, though Bottom the weaver is
her close rival, as are the great victims: Juliet, Ophelia, Desdemona,
Cordelia, and the near-victim yet troubled survivor Edgar. We cannot
imagine Rosalind (or Bottom!) in tragedy, because, as I have noted, she
seems not to be subject to dramatic irony, her mastery of perspective being
so absolute. Touchstone, an ironist even as Jaques is a satirist, is bested by
Rosalind, not only through her superiority in wit but also because she sees
so much more than he does. Jaques had quoted Touchstone, "a fool i' th'
forest," at his most characteristic: "From hour to hour, we ripe, and
ripe, / And then from hour to hour, we rot, and rot." After chanting a doggerel in response to Orlando's bad love verses, Touchstone addresses Rosalind:

*Touch.* This is the very false gallop of verses. Why do you infect your-
    self with them?

*Ros.* Peace, you dull fool! I found them on a tree.

*Touch.* Truly the tree yields bad fruit.

*Ros.* I'll graff it with you and then I shall graff it with a medlar. Then
    it will be the earliest fruit i' th' country; for you'll be rotten ere
    you be half ripe, and that's the right virtue of the medlar.

*Touch.* You have said; but whether wisely or no, let the forest judge.

                                         [III.ii.113–22]

The forest, as Touchstone knows, will judge as we judge: Rosalind has
impaled him. Rotten before he is half-ripe, Touchstone pursues his Audrey,
whose good-natured idiocy is sublimely conveyed by her: "I am not a slut,
though I thank the gods I am foul." Comparing himself to the exiled Ovid
among the Goths, Touchstone delivers Shakespeare's ultimate exorcism
of the spirit of Christopher Marlowe, who haunts a play wholly alien to his
savage genius:

*Touch.* When a man's verses cannot be understood, nor a man's good
    wit seconded with the forward child, understanding, it strikes a
    man more dead than a great reckoning in a little room. Truly, I
    would the gods had made thee poetical.

*Aud.* I do not know what 'poetical' is. Is it honest in deed and word? Is
    it a true thing?

*Touch.* No truly; for the truest poetry is the most feigning, and lovers
    are given to poetry; and what they swear in poetry may be said as
    lovers they do feign.

                                         [III.iii.9–18]

Many in the original audience must have appreciated Shakespeare's
audacity in alluding to Marlowe having been struck dead, supposedly on
account of "a great reckoning in a little room," the tavern in Deptford
where the poet-playwright was stabbed (in the eye) by one Ingram Frizer,
like Marlowe a member of Walsingham's royal Secret Service, the CIA of

Elizabethan England. The great reckoning ostensibly was a costly bill for liquor and food, in dispute between Marlowe, Frizer, and Walsingham's other thugs. Shakespeare hints strongly that it was a state-ordered execution, with maximum prejudice, and that the government's subsequent campaign against Marlowe's "atheism" had resulted in misunderstanding of the verses and "good wit" of the poet of *The Jew of Malta*, whose great line "infinite riches in a little room" is ironically echoed by Touchstone. Elsewhere in *As You Like It*, the "dead shepherd," Marlowe, is quoted with the famous tag from his lyric "The Passionate Shepherd to His Love": "Whoever loved that loved not at first sight." Touchstone, entrusted as Shakespeare's implicit defender of Marlowe, also states Shakespeare's own aesthetic credo: "for the truest poetry is the most feigning." Marlowe, true poet, feigned and was misread. Shakespeare, at last free of Marlowe's shadow, gives us *As You Like It* as the truest poetry, because it is the most inventive. Touchstone's final words in the play praise the "If" of poetical feigning. Asked by Jaques to name in order "the degrees of the lie" or contradiction that leads to the challenge to a duel, Touchstone achieves his most brilliant moment:

> O sir, we quarrel in print, by the book; as you have books for good manners. I will name you the degrees. The first, the Retort Courteous; the second, the Quip Modest; the third, the Reply Churlish; the fourth, the Reproof Valiant; the fifth, the Countercheck Quarrelsome; the sixth, the Lie with Circumstance; the seventh, the Lie Direct. All these you may avoid but the Lie Direct; and you may avoid that too, with an If. I knew when seven justices could not take up a quarrel, but when the parties were met themselves, one of them thought but of an If, as, 'If you said so, then I said so'. And they shook hands and swore brothers. Your If is the only peacemaker: much virtue in If.
>
> [V.iv.89–102]

"Much virtue in If" is a fine farewell for Touchstone, and teaches us to bear his nastiness to the shepherds, and his sordid exploitation of the too-willing Audrey. Jaques, in the presence of Rosalind, loses satiric dignity;

Touchstone, confronted by her, abandons the prestige of irony. The play belongs to Rosalind. To see the "how" and "why" of her greatness, the reason she must be the most remarkable and persuasive representation of a woman in all of Western literature, is also to apprehend how inadequate nearly every production of *As You Like It* has been to Rosalind.

7

*As You Like It* is a title addressed to Shakespeare's audience, yet the play also could be called *As Rosalind Likes It*, because she achieves all her purposes, which have little in common with the ambitions of the gender-and-power covens. Article after article deplores her "abandonment" of Celia for Orlando, or regrets the curbing of her "female vitality," or even insists that her appeal to males in the audience is "homoerotic" and not heterosexual. I have not yet seen an article chiding Rosalind for spurning the shepherdess Phebe, though I live in hope. Orlando, as all of us know, is not Rosalind's equal, but Shakespeare's heroines generally marry down, and Orlando is an amiable young Hercules, whom Rosalind is happy to educate, in her ostensible disguise as the forest-boy Ganymede. When Ganymede plays Rosalind in order to rehearse Orlando in life and love, are we to assume that her lover does not recognize her? Aside from straining credulity, it would be an aesthetic loss if Orlando were not fully aware of the charm of his situation. He is not brilliant, nor well educated, yet his natural wit is reasonably strong, and he is a livelier straight man for Rosalind than Horatio is for Hamlet:

> *Ros.* Come, woo me, woo me; for now I am in a holiday humour and like enough to consent. What would you say to me now, an I were your very very Rosalind?
>
> *Orl.* I would kiss before I spoke.
>
> *Ros.* Nay, you were better speak first, and when you were gravelled for lack of matter, you might take occasion to kiss. Very good orators when they are out, they will spit, and for lovers lacking— God warr'nt us!—matter, the cleanliest shift is to kiss.
>
> *Orl.* How if the kiss be denied?

*Ros.* Then she puts you to entreaty, and there begins new matter.

*Orl.* Who could be out, being before his beloved mistress?

*Ros.* Marry that should you, if I were your mistress, or I should think
my honesty ranker than my wit.

*Orl.* What, of my suit?

*Ros.* Not out of your apparel, and yet out of your suit. Am I not your
Rosalind?

*Orl.* I take some joy to say you are, because I would be talking of her.

*Ros.* Well, in her person, I say I will not have you.

*Orl.* Then in mine own person, I die.

*Ros.* No, faith, die by attorney. The poor world is almost six thousand years old, and in all this time there was not any man died in
his own person, videlicet, in a love-cause. Troilus had his brains
dashed out with a Grecian club, yet he did what he could to die
before, and he is one of the patterns of love. Leander, he would
have lived many a fair year though Hero had turned nun, if it
had not been for a hot mid summer night; for, good youth, he
went but forth to wash him in the Hellespont, and being taken
with the cramp, was drowned, and the foolish chroniclers of that
age found it was Hero of Sestos. But these are all lies: men have
died from time to time and worms have eaten them, but not for
love.

[IV.i. 65–103]

I have quoted the last sentence of this before, and wish I could find occasion to use it again, for it is Rosalind's best, and therefore very good indeed. The allusion to the Marlowe/Chapman *Hero and Leander* reinforces the
matrix of irony that celebrates Marlowe's influence as being absent from *As
You Like It*, where the courtship proceeds from splendor to splendor as Rosalind almost uniquely (even in Shakespeare) fuses authentic love with the
highest wit:

*Ros.* Now tell me how long you would have her, after you have possessed her?

*Orl.* For ever, and a day.

*Ros.* Say a day, without the ever. No, no, Orlando, men are April
when they woo, December when they wed. Maids are May when
they are maids, but the sky changes when they are wives. I will
be more jealous of thee than a Barbary cock-pigeon over his hen,
more clamorous than a parrot against rain, more new-fangled
than an ape, more giddy in my desires than a monkey. I will weep
for nothing, like Diana in the fountain, and I will do that when
you are disposed to be merry. I will laugh like a hyen, and that
when thou art inclined to sleep.

*Orl.* But will my Rosalind do so?

*Ros.* By my life, she will do as I do.

*Orl.* O but she is wise.

*Rosalind.* Or else she could not have the wit to do this. The wiser, the
waywarder. Make the doors upon a woman's wit, and it will out at
the casement; shut that, and 'twill out at the keyhole; stop that,
'twill fly with the smoke out at the chimney.

*Orl.* A man that had a wife with such a wit, he might say, 'Wit,
whither wilt?'

*Ros.* Nay, you might keep that check for it, till you met your wife's
wit going to your neighbour's bed.

*Orl.* And what wit could wit have to excuse that?

*Ros.* Marry to say she came to seek you there. You shall never take
her without her answer, unless you take her without her tongue.
O that woman that cannot make her fault her husband's occasion,
let her never nurse her child herself, for she will breed it like a
fool.

[IV.i.135–67]

She is marvelous here, but he (*pace* many critics) is no bumpkin: "But
will my Rosalind do so?" It is the wisest as well as the wittiest courtship in
Shakespeare, far eclipsing the mock carnage of Beatrice and Benedick.
Only Rosalind and Orlando could sustain their finest exchange, as their
play-of-two concludes:

*Ros.* Why then tomorrow I cannot serve your turn for Rosalind?
*Orl.* I can live no longer by thinking.

[V.ii.48–50]

Again despite the critics, Orlando's tone is light rather than desperate, but sexual urgency is well conveyed, and signals that he is ready to graduate from Rosalind's school. Are we? Rosalie Colie noted that "the love at the center of the play is not a particularly pastoral love," which helps save *As You Like It* from the death of the pastoral convention. William Empson, in his classic *Some Versions of Pastoral*, returns us to the First Folio text of Touchstone's ironic address to Audrey:

No trulie: for the truest poetrie is the most faining, and Lovers are given to Poetrie: and what they sweare in Poetrie, may be said as Lovers, they do feigne.

The pun on *faining* (desiring) and *feign* (simulate or pretend), highly appropriate for Touchstone and Audrey, would not work if we applied it to Rosalind and Orlando, since their desire and their playacting are one, even when Orlando cries out that he can live no longer by thinking. The subtlest moment in this masterpiece of all Shakespearean comedies comes in the Epilogue, where the boy actor playing Rosalind steps out before the curtain, still in costume, to give us her final triumph of affectionate wit, of faining and feigning in harmony:

It is not the fashion to see the lady the epilogue; but it is no more unhandsome than to see the lord the prologue. If it be true that good wine needs no bush, 'tis true that a good play needs no epilogue. Yet to good wine they do use good bushes; and good plays prove the better with the help of good epilogues. What a case am I in then, that am neither a good epilogue, nor cannot insinuate with you in the behalf of a good play? I am not furnished like a beggar, therefore to beg will not become me. My way is to conjure you, and I'll begin with the women. I charge you, O women, for the love you bear to men, to like as much of this play as please you. And I charge you, O men, for the love you bear to women—as I perceive by your simpering none of you hates them—that between you and the women the play may please. If I were a woman, I would kiss as many of you as had beards that pleased me, complexions that liked me, and breaths that I defied not. And I am sure, as many as have good beards, or good faces, or sweet breaths, will for my kind offer, when I make curtsy, bid me farewell.

In these curious days for literary criticism, this Epilogue stirs up the expected transports of transvestism and transgression, but such raptures have little to do with Shakespeare's Rosalind and her final words. I prefer Edward I. Berry, who is splendidly on target:

As the director and "busy actor" in her own "play," and the Epilogue in Shakespeare's, Rosalind becomes in a sense a figure for the playwright himself, a character whose consciousness extends in subtle ways beyond the boundaries of the drama.

Rosalind again makes a third with Falstaff and Hamlet, also figures for Shakespeare himself. "Play out the play!" Falstaff cries to Hal; "I have much to say in the behalf of that Falstaff." "Suit the action to the word, the word to the action," Hamlet admonishes the Player King. "I charge you, O men, for the love you bear to women," Rosalind adroitly pleads, "that between you and the women the play may please." The voice in all three, at just that moment, is as close as Shakespeare ever will come to letting us hear the voice of William Shakespeare himself.

# 15

# TWELFTH NIGHT

Despite my personal preference for *As You Like It*, which is founded upon my passion for Rosalind, I would have to admit that *Twelfth Night* is surely the greatest of all Shakespeare's pure comedies. No one in *Twelfth Night*, not even Viola, is so wholly admirable as Rosalind. *Twelfth Night or What You Will* probably was written in 1601–2, bridging the interval between the final *Hamlet* and *Troilus and Cressida*. There are elements of self-parody in *Twelfth Night*, not on the scale of *Cymbeline's* self-mockery, but holding a middle ground between Hamlet's ferocious ironies and the rancidity of *Troilus and Cressida*, most memorably expressed by Thersites.

Shakespeare, I suspect, himself acted the part of Antonio both in *The Merchant of Venice* and in *Twelfth Night*, where the homoerotic second Antonio travesties the first. But most of Shakespeare's earlier comedies are quarried in *Twelfth Night*, not because Shakespeare slackened at humorous invention, but because the zany spirit of "what you will" dominated him, if only as a defense against the bitterness of the three dark comedies just after: *Troilus and Cressida*, *All's Well That Ends Well*, and *Measure for Measure*. An abyss hovers just beyond *Twelfth Night*, and one cost of not leaping into it is that everyone, except the reluctant jester, Feste, is essentially mad without knowing it. When the wretched Malvolio is confined in the dark room for the insane, he ought to be joined there by Orsino, Olivia, Sir Toby Belch, Sir Andrew Aguecheek, Maria, Sebastian, Antonio, and even Viola, for the whole ninefold are at least borderline in their behavior. The largest fault of every staging of *Twelfth Night* I've attended is that the pace is not fast enough. It ought to be played at the frenetic tempo that befits this company of zanies and antics. I am a little sorry that Shakespeare used *Twelfth Night* as his primary title; *What You Will* is better, and among much else means something like "Have at You!"

Not that *Twelfth Night* is high farce. Like all the other strongest plays by Shakespeare, *Twelfth Night* is of no genre. It is not of *Hamlet's* cosmological scope, but in its own very startling way it is another "poem unlimited." One cannot get to the end of it, because even some of the most apparently incidental lines reverberate infinitely. Dr. Johnson, rather irritated with the play, complained that it rendered "no just picture of life," but by the grand Johnsonian test it certainly is "a just representation of general nature." I worship Johnson, particularly on Shakespeare, and suspect that his own perilous balance, the fear of madness, made him seek rational design where none exists:

> Viola seems to have formed a very deep design with very little premeditation: she is thrown by shipwreck on an unknown coast, hears that the prince is a bachelor, and resolves to supplant the lady whom he courts.

That is not at all like Viola, even though she evidently falls in love at first sight of the crazy Orsino. We wince at most Shakespearean matches, and this may be the silliest, altogether unworthy of the integral, good-natured, only somewhat wacky Viola. *Twelfth Night*, though, refuses to take itself seriously, and we would do it violence by such realistic expectations, except that Shakespeare's invention of the human surges with astonishing mimetic force in this play. Its most absurd characters, Orsino included, open inward, which is disconcerting in a farce, or a self-parody of previous farces. Malvolio obviously does not possess the infinitude of Falstaff or Hamlet, but he runs away from Shakespeare, and has a terrible poignance even though he is wickedly funny and is a sublime satire upon the moralizing Ben Jonson. Shakespeare is still closer to *Hamlet's* mode than to *Measure for Measure's*: subjectivity and individuality, his invented distincts, are the norm of *Twelfth Night*. I think the play is much Shakespeare's funniest, more so than *Henry IV, Part One*, where Falstaff, like Hamlet after him, is intelligent beyond intelligence, and so provokes thoughts that lie too deep for laughter. Only Feste in *Twelfth Night* has any mind, but everyone in the drama pulsates with vitality, most mindlessly Sir Toby Belch, the least truly Falstaffian of roisterers.

C. L. Barber classified *Twelfth Night* as another "festive comedy," but he accurately added so many qualifications as to place the festive motif in considerable doubt. A Feast of Fools touches its limits soon enough; *Twelfth Night* expands upon any rereading, or even in a less than brilliant performance. The play is decentered; there is almost no significant action, perhaps because nearly everyone behaves involuntarily. A much funnier Nietzsche might have conceived it, since forces somewhat beyond the characters seem to be living their lives for them.

The hidden heart of *Twelfth Night* lies in Shakespeare's seriocomic rivalry with Ben Jonson, whose comedy of humors is being satirized throughout. Ancient Greek medicine had posited four "humors": blood, choler, phlegm, and bile. In a person harmoniously balanced, none of these are evident, but the dominance of any indicated severe character disorders. By the time of Jonson and Shakespeare, pragmatically there was a simpler notion of just two humors, choler and blood. The choleric humor resulted in fury, while the sanguine temperament exercised itself in obsessive lust, frequently perverted. Popular psychology diffused this duality into easy explanations for every kind of flummery or affectation, Jonson's targets in his stage comedies.

In some ways, this debased theory of humors resembles our everyday vulgarizations of what Freud termed the unconscious. The choleric humor is roughly akin to Freud's Death Drive or Thanatos, while the sanguine humor is like the Freudian Eros.

Shakespeare generally mocks these mechanical operations of the spirit; his larger invention of the human scorns this reductiveness. He takes therefore the Feast of the Epiphany, the Twelfth Night after Christmas, as the occasion for an ambiguous comedy of revels that involves a practical joke upon the choleric Malvolio, a figure so Jonsonian as to suggest the choleric

Ben himself. The sanguine Will gives us *What You Will*, the spirit of Saturnalia that popular praxis had made out of the initially pious rejoicing of
Epiphany, the manifestation of the Christ child to the Magi. Cheerfully
secular, like almost all of Shakespeare, the play of "what you will" makes
no reference whatsoever to Twelfth Night. We are not at Christmas season in the very odd dukedom of Illyria, where the shipwrecked Viola pas-
sively and hilariously achieves perhaps not her happiness but certainly
ours. We open, though, not with the charming Viola but at the court of
Duke Orsino, where that sublimely outrageous lover of love, sanguine to
an insane degree, ravishes our ears with one of Shakespeare's most exquisite speeches:

> If music be the food of love, play on,
> Give me excess of it, that, surfeiting,
> The appetite may sicken, and so die.
> That strain again, it had a dying fall:
> O, it came o'er my ear like the sweet sound
> That breathes upon a bank of violets,
> Stealing and giving odour. Enough, no more;
> 'Tis not so sweet now as it was before.
> O spirit of love, how quick and fresh art thou,
> That notwithstanding thy capacity
> Receiveth as the sea, nought enters there,
> Of what validity and pitch soe'er,
> But falls into abatement and low price,
> Even in a minute! So full of shapes is fancy,
> That it alone is high fantastical.

> [I.i.1–15]

Shakespeare himself must have been pleased by Orsino's opening
metaphor, since Cleopatra, five years later, repeats it when she badly misses
Antony: "Give me some music; music, moody food / Of us that trade in
love." Orsino, far more in love with language, music, love, and himself than
he is with Olivia, or will be with Viola, tells himself (and us) that love is

too hungry ever to be satisfied by any person whatsoever. And yet the first eight lines of this rhapsody have more to do with music, and by extension, poetry, than with love. That "dying fall" is a cadence that echoes through-out subsequent English poetry, particularly in the Keats-Tennyson tradi-tion. Orsino, indeed "high fantastical" (very high), asks for excess of music, though not of love, but his metaphorical intensity implies that " 'Tis not so sweet now as it was before" pertains to sexual passion also. He will surpass even this self-revelation when speaking to Viola, in her disguise as his boyish go-between Cesario, appointed to carry his protestations of passion to Olivia. Supreme hyperbolist as he is, here Orsino touches the sublime of male fatuity:

> There is no woman's sides
> Can bide the beating of so strong a passion
> As love doth give my heart; no woman's heart
> So big, to hold so much: they lack retention.
> Alas, their love may be call'd appetite,
> No motion of the liver, but the palate,
> That suffers surfeit, cloyment, and revolt;
> But mine is all as hungry as the sea,
> And can digest as much. Make no compare
> Between that love a woman can bear me
> And that I owe Olivia.

[II.iv.94–104]

Out of context, this is even more magnificent than the opening chant, but as this merely is Orsino, it is wonderfully comic grandiloquence. Though he is minor compared with Viola, Olivia, Malvolio (how their names chime together), and the admirable Feste, Orsino's amiable erotic lunacy establishes the tone of *Twelfth Night*. Despite his amazing self-absorption, Orsino genuinely moves the audience, partly because his High Romanticism is so quixotic, but also because his sentimentalism is too uni-versal to be rejected:

O, fellow, come, the song we had last night.
Mark it, Cesario, it is old and plain;
The spinsters and the knitters in the sun,
And the free maids that weave their thread with bones
Do use to chant it: it is silly sooth,
And dallies with the innocence of love,
Like the old age.

[II.iv.42–48]

There is also Orsino's wonderful inconsistency, when he is moved to speak the truth:

For boy, however we do praise ourselves,
Our fancies are more giddy and unfirm,
More longing, wavering, sooner lost and worn
Than women's are.

[II.iv.32–35]

Poor Malvolio would be happier in some other play, while Viola, Olivia, and especially Feste would find appropriate contexts elsewhere in Shakespeare. Orsino is the genius of his place; he is the only character the exuberant madness of *Twelfth Night* accommodates.

2

The largest puzzle of the charming Viola is her extraordinary passivity, which doubtless helps explain her falling in love with Orsino. Anne Barton usefully comments that Viola's "boy's disguise operates not as a liberation but merely as a way of going underground in a difficult situation." There is an air of improvisation throughout *Twelfth Night*, and Viola's disguise is part of that atmosphere, though I rather doubt that even Shakespeare could have improvised this complex and beautiful play; his careful art works to give us the aesthetic effect of improvisation. Viola's personality is both receptive and defensive: she offers "the shield of a greeting"

(John Ashbery's phrase). Her diction has the widest range in the play, since she varies her language according to the vagaries of others' speech. Though she is as interesting in her subtle way as are the unfortunate Malvolio and the reluctant fool, Feste, Shakespeare seems to enjoy keeping her an enigma, with much held always in reserve. The "high fantastical" Orsino perhaps attracts her as an opposite; his hyperboles complement her reticences. If there is any true voice of feeling in this play, then it ought to be hers, yet we rarely hear that voice. When it does emerge, its pathos is overwhelming:

> Make me a willow cabin at your gate,
> And call upon my soul within the house;
> Write loyal cantons of contemned love,
> And sing them loud even in the dead of night;
> Halloo your name to the reverberate hills,
> And make the babbling gossip of the air
> Cry out 'Olivia!' O, You should not rest
> Between the elements of air and earth,
> But you should pity me.

[I.v.272–80]

The speech's effect is ironic, since it prompts Olivia's falling in love with the supposed Cesario. For Viola, this lament proceeds from a different irony: her absurd dilemma in urging Orsino's love upon Olivia, when her own desires are exactly contrary to such a match. What breaks through these ironies is the deepest, most plangent element in Viola, but also perhaps an intense suffering, ancient or recent, in Shakespeare himself. Call Viola a repressed vitalist, alive with Rosalind's intensity, but constrained from expressing her strength, perhaps because she mingles her identity with that of her twin brother, Sebastian. The "willow cabin" threnody beats with this innate strength, singing its rejected love songs "loud even in the dead of night." By this point in the play, we are accustomed to Viola's charm, but her personality, subdued on the surface, now intimates its resilience and its remarkable and persistent liveliness. "You might do much," Olivia responds to her chant, and speaks for the audience. In this cunning echo chamber of a play, Viola prophesies her imaginary sister in her own later dialogue with Orsino:

> *Viola.* My father had a daughter loved a man,
>     As it might be perhaps, were I a woman,
>     I should your lordship.
> *Duke.*                     And what's her history?
> *Viola.* A blank, my lord: she never told her love,
>     But let concealment like a worm i' the bud
>     Feed on her damask cheek: she pin'd in thought,
>     And with a green and yellow melancholy
>     She sat like Patience on a monument,
>     Smiling at grief. Was not this love indeed?
>
> [II.iv.108–16]

"Blank" is a Shakespearean metaphor that haunts poetry in English from Milton through Coleridge and Wordsworth on through Emily Dickinson to Wallace Stevens. Here it means primarily an unwritten page, a history never recorded; elsewhere in Shakespeare "blank" refers to the white mark at the center of a target. Since this pined-away sister is a surrogate invention of Viola's, there may be a hint also of an unhit target, an aim gone astray. The speech has in it the seeds of some of William Blake's most piercing lyrics, including "The Sick Rose" and "Never Seek to Tell Thy Love," dark visions of repression and its erotic consequences. Both elegiac utterances, made by Viola to Olivia and to Orsino, are powerfully apotropaic: they are meant to ward off a fate that she courts by her passivity, from which she seems not able to rally herself. That fate draws near in *Twelfth Night*'s oddest scene, totally inappropriate for comedy, when the frustrated Orsino vows to lead Viola-Cesario off stage to slaughter, with no resistance from the intended victim:

> *Duke.* Still so cruel?
> *Olivia.*         Still so constant, lord.

*Duke.* What, to perverseness? You uncivil lady,
    To whose ingrate and unauspicious altars
    My soul the faithfull'st off'rings hath breath'd out
    That e'er devotion tender'd—What shall I do?
*Olivia.* Even what it please my lord that shall become him.
*Duke.* Why should I not, had I the heart to do it,
    Like to th' Egyptian thief at point of death,
    Kill what I love?—a savage jealousy
    That sometime savours nobly. But hear me this:
    Since you to non-regardance cast my faith,
    And that I partly know the instrument
    That screws me from my true place in your favour,
    Live you the marble-breasted tyrant still.
    But this your minion, whom I know you love,
    And whom, by heaven, I swear I tender dearly,
    Him will I tear out of that cruel eye
    Where he sits crowned in his master's spite.
    Come, boy, with me; my thoughts are ripe in mischief:
    I'll sacrifice the lamb that I do love,
    To spite a raven's heart within a dove.
*Viola.* And I most jocund, apt, and willingly,
    To do you rest, a thousand deaths would die.

                   [V.i.109–31]

Orsino, not previously high in the audience's esteem, is a criminal madman if he means this, and Viola is a masochistic ninny if she is serious. Why
does Shakespeare push us to this perplexity? Would zaniness cross the
border into pathology if Sebastian did not suddenly appear and precipitate
the recognition scene? I do not find much useful commentary upon this
bad moment. Orsino's murderous rage is unsettling enough; Viola's swoon-
ing acceptance of a love death illuminates her entire role with unhappy
consequences. Wild with laughter, *Twelfth Night* is nevertheless almost always on the edge of violence. Illyria is not the healthiest of castaway
climes, located as it is in the Shakespearean cosmos between Hamlet's mi-
asmic Elsinore and the fierce wars and faithless loves of *Troilus and Cressida.*

3

Olivia, properly played, can dazzle us with her authority, and with her erotic arbitrariness, but no audience conceives for her the affection it accords to Viola, disconcerting as Viola turns out to be. The two heroines are oddly assorted, and Shakespeare must have delighted in the imaginative labor he gives us when we attempt to understand why Olivia falls in love with the supposed Cesario. There is little congruence between Viola's love for the egregious Orsino and Olivia's love for Orsino's witty but reserved go-between. Olivia's passion is more a farcical exposure of the arbitrariness of sexual identity than it is a revelation that mature female passion essentially is lesbian. I have been told of one production in which Sebastian pairs off with Orsino, while Olivia and Viola take each other. I do not want to see it, and Shakespeare did not write it. But here, as elsewhere, earlier and later, Shakespeare complexly qualifies our easier certainties as to sexual identity. In the dance of mating that concludes the play, Malvolio is not the only unfulfilled aspirant. Antonio does not speak again in the play after he cries out, "Which is Sebastian?" Like the Antonio of *The Merchant of Venice*, this second Antonio loves in vain.

Olivia, when we first encounter her, elaborately mourns a dead brother; doubtless this is authentic, but it serves also as a defense against Orsino's turbulence. Her mournfulness disappears when she meets Cesario and loves at first sight. Since Olivia is just as crazy as Orsino, perhaps any handsome young man without aggressive affect might have done as well as Cesario. Shakespeare's acute sense that all sexual love is arbitrary in its origins but overdetermined in its teleology is at the center of *Twelfth Night*. Freud thought that all object-choice (falling-in-love) was either narcissistic or a propping-against; Shakespeare's understanding is closer to a black-box theory, except that after erotic crashes, rather than airplane crashes, the box cannot be recovered. "Even so quickly may one catch the plague?" is Olivia's rhetorical question after Cesario's first exit, and she answers herself with: "Fate, show thy force; ourselves we do not owe," where "owe" means "control." Her second interview with the supposed Cesario gives us our largest sense of a nature that only heightens our interest and attraction as its self-indulgence touches sublimity. To possess Olivia's authority, and yet indulge in such a vulnerable self-surrender, is to excite the audience's sympathy, even its momentary love.

*Olivia.* Stay:

    I prithee tell me what thou think'st of me.
*Viola.* That you do think you are not what you are.
*Olivia.* If I think so, I think the same of you.
*Viola.* Then think you right; I am not what I am.
*Olivia.* I would you were as I would have you be.
*Viola.* Would it be better, madam, than I am?

    I wish it might, for now I am your fool.
*Olivia.* [*Aside*] O what a deal of scorn looks beautiful

    In the contempt and anger of his lip!

    A murd'rous guilt shows not itself more soon

    Than love that would seem hid. Love's night is noon.—

    Cesario, by the roses of the spring,

    By maidhood, honour, truth, and everything,

    I love thee so, that maugre all thy pride,

    Nor wit nor reason can my passion hide.

    Do not extort thy reasons from this clause,

    For that I woo, thou therefore hast no cause;

    But rather reason thus with reason fetter:

    Love sought is good, but given unsought better.
*Viola.* By innocence I swear, and by my youth,

    I have one heart, one bosom, and one truth,

    And that no woman has; nor never none

    Shall mistress be of it, save I alone.

    And so adieu, good madam; never more

    Will I my master's tears to you deplore.
*Olivia.* Yet come again: for thou perhaps mayst move

    That heart which now abhors, to like his love.

                                   [III.i.139–66]

It is a set piece that demands two great actresses skilled at romantic comedy, particularly in the exchange of the four monosyllabic lines (141–44), which admit of several meanings. The audience is likely to esteem both roles equally here: Viola's for its deftness in a deliciously absurd situation, Olivia's for its boldness. Shakespeare himself is highly outrageous, here as elsewhere in *Twelfth Night.* The proleptic self-parody is peculiarly jarring in Viola's "I am not what I am," to be appropriated from her by the least Viola-like of all characters, Iago. Both Viola and Iago travesty St. Paul's "By the grace of God, I am what I am." In Shakespeare's madly shrewd plot, Olivia is on the right course, since Viola's twin brother will yield to the countess with a readiness startling even in this play. The monosyllabic exchange turns upon issues of rank and of concealment. Viola reminds Olivia of her high status, and Olivia insinuates that Viola conceals her own noble birth. "I am not what I am" both concedes this and also alludes to Viola's sexual identity, which renders heavily ironic Olivia's "I would you were as I would have you be." That makes utterly ambiguous Viola's reply, an exasperation of spirit at the exhaustion of maintaining a drama-long lie. This superb dialogue is summed up by the climax of Olivia's aside: "Love's night is noon," which she intends to mean that love cannot be concealed, yet this line makes us wonder what, then, is "love's day"?

4

The revelers and practical jokers—Maria, Sir Toby Belch, Sir Andrew Aguecheek—are the least sympathetic players in *Twelfth Night,* since their gulling of Malvolio passes into the domain of sadism. Maria, the only mind among the three, is a high-spirited social climber, Olivia's woman-in-waiting. She is tough, a little shrill, fiercely resourceful, and immensely energetic. Sir Toby is Belch, just that; only an idiot (there have been many such) would compare this fifth-rate rascal to Shakespeare's great genius, Sir John Falstaff. The yet more dubious Sir Andrew is lifted bodily out of *The Merry Wives of Windsor,* where he is Slender. Both Belch and Aguecheek are caricatures, yet Maria, a natural comic, has a dangerous inwardness, and is the one truly malicious character in *Twelfth Night*. She coolly considers whether her stratagems will drive Malvolio mad and concludes: "The house will be the quieter."

Malvolio is, with Feste, Shakespeare's great creation in *Twelfth Night*; it has become Malvolio's play, rather like Shylock's gradual usurpation of *The Merchant of Venice*. Charles Lamb shrewdly considered Malvolio a tragi-comic figure, a Don Quixote of erotomania. That suggests a great truth about Malvolio; he suffers by being in the wrong play for him. In Ben Jonson's *Volpone* or *The Alchemist*, Malvolio would have been at home, except that he would have been another Jonsonian ideogram, caricature and not character. Shakespeare's Malvolio is more the victim of his own psychic propensities than he is Maria's gull. His dream of socio-erotic greatness— "To be Count Malvolio!"—is one of Shakespeare's supreme inventions, permanently disturbing as a study in self-deception, and in the spirit's sickness. As a satire upon Ben Jonson himself, Malvolio derives from the great comic playwright and satiric poet only a moral pugnacity. The depravity of the will in Malvolio is a flaw of the imagination, or what you will. Marxist criticism interprets Malvolio as a study in class ideology, but that reduces both the figure and the play. What matters most about Malvolio is not that he is Olivia's household steward but that he so dreams that he malforms his sense of reality, and so falls victim to Maria's shrewd insights into his nature.

The censorious Malvolio, or sham Puritan, is only a screen image that masks his desire to have greatness thrust upon him. Essentially, Malvolio is cursed by the dangerous prevalence of his imagination, and not by the rigid class structures of Shakespeare's world. He and Maria loathe each other, but actually would be a proper match of negative energies. Instead, Maria will achieve the brutally drunk Sir Toby, and Malvolio will find only alienation and bitterness. It is difficult to overestimate Malvolio's originality as a comic character; who else in Shakespeare, or elsewhere, resembles him? There are other grotesques in Shakespeare, but they do not begin as normative worthies and then undergo radical transformations.

Malvolio's downfall is prophesied when first we see him, in a grim exchange with his adversary, the wise fool Feste:

*Olivia.* What think you of this fool, Malvolio, doth he not mend?
*Mal.* Yes, and shall do, till the pangs of death shake him. Infirmity,
  that decays the wise, doth ever make the better fool.
*Clown.* God send you, sir, a speedy infirmity, for the better increasing
  your folly!

[I.v.71–77]

The infirmity is there already, as Maria surmises:

The devil a Puritan that he is, or anything constantly, but a time-
pleaser, an affectioned ass, that cons state without book, and utters
it by great swarths: the best persuaded of himself, so crammed (as
he thinks) with excellencies, that it is his grounds of faith that all
that look on him love him: and on that vice in him will my revenge
find notable cause to work.

[II.iii.146–53]

That accurate portrait of an affected time server is one of the most savage in Shakespeare. What happens to Malvolio is, however, so harshly
out of proportion to his merits, such as they are, that the ordeal of humiliation has to be regarded as one of the prime Shakespearean enigmas.
Even if a poet's war with Ben Jonson was the occasion for creating Malvolio, the social crucifixion of the virtuous steward passes the possible bounds
of playful literary rancor. Several other roles in *Twelfth Night* are technically
larger than Malvolio; he speaks only about a tenth of the play's lines. Like
Shylock, Malvolio captures his drama by his ferocious comic intensity,
and by the darkness of his fate. Yet Malvolio cannot be termed a comic villain, as Shakespeare evidently intended Shylock to be. *Twelfth Night* is not
primarily a satiric attack upon Jonson, and it seems clear that Malvolio,
again like Shylock, wonderfully got away from Shakespeare. The play
does not need Malvolio, but he has no choice: Shakespeare has inserted
him into a context where he must suffer.

Since Malvolio's very name indicates that he wishes no one well but
himself, our sympathy is bound to be limited, particularly because of the

high hilarity his discomfiture provokes in us. To see the self-destruction of a personage who cannot laugh, and who hates laughter in others, becomes an experience of joyous exuberance for an audience that is scarcely allowed time to reflect upon its own aroused sadism. Harry Levin, dissenting from Charles Lamb, thought it was weakness to feel sorry for Malvolio:

> As a sycophant, a social climber, and an officious snob, he well deserves to be put back in his place—or, as Jonson would have it, in his humor, for Malvolio seems to have a Jonsonian rather than a Shakespearean temperament.

That is unassailable, and yet there Malvolio is, in Shakespeare's superb comedy. Baiting Malvolio, Levin argued, was not sadistic but cathartic: it enacted again the ritual expulsion of a scapegoat. Well, yes and no: the comic spirit perhaps requires sacrifices, but need they be so prolonged?

Malvolio matters partly because he is so sublimely funny, in fearsome contrast to his total lack of what we, not being Jonsonians, call humor. But there is an excess in his role, which greatly challenges actors, who rarely can handle his enigmatic aspects, at their most complex after he reads Maria's forged note. Transported by the supposedly amorous hints of Olivia, he bursts into a rhapsody that is one of Shakespeare's finest outrages:

> Daylight and champaign discovers not more! This is open. I will be proud, I will read politic authors, I will baffle Sir Toby, I will wash off gross acquaintance, I will be point-device the very man. I do not now fool myself, to let imagination jade me; for every reason excites to this, that my lady loves me. She did commend my yellow stockings of late, she did praise my leg being cross-gartered, and in this she manifests herself to my love, and with a kind of injunction drives me to these habits of her liking. I thank my stars, I am happy. I will be strange, stout, in yellow stockings, and cross-gartered, even with the swiftness of putting on. Jove and my stars be praised!—Here is yet a postscript. [*Reads.*] *Thou canst not choose but know who I am. If thou entertain'st my love, let it appear in thy smiling, thy smiles become thee well. There-*

*fore in my presence still smile, dear my sweet, I prithee.* Jove, I thank thee, I will smile, I will do every thing that thou wilt have me.

[II.v.160–79]

Do we shudder a touch even as we laugh? The erotic imagination is our largest universal, and our most shameful, in that it must turn upon our overvaluation of the self as object. Shakespeare's uncanniest power is to press perpetually upon the nerve of the erotic universal. Can we hear this, or read this, without to some degree becoming Malvolio? Surely we are not as ridiculous, we should insist, but we are in danger of becoming so (or something worse) if we believe our own erotic fantasies, as Malvolio has been tricked into doing. His grand disaster comes in Act III, Scene iv, when he arrives in the presence of Olivia:

*Olivia.* How now, Malvolio!

*Mal.* Sweet lady, ho, ho!

*Olivia.* Smil'st thou? I sent for thee upon a sad occasion.

*Mal.* Sad, lady? I could be sad: this does make some obstruction in
    the blood, this cross-gartering; but what of that? If it please the
    eye of one, it is with me as the very true sonnet is: 'Please one,
    and please all'.

*Olivia.* Why, how dost thou, man? What is the matter with thee?

*Mal.* Not black in my mind, though yellow in my legs. It did come to
    his hands, and commands shall be executed. I think we do know
    the sweet Roman hand.

*Olivia.* Wilt thou go to bed, Malvolio?

*Mal.* To bed? Ay, sweetheart, and I'll come to thee.

*Olivia.* God comfort thee! Why dost thou smile so, and kiss thy hand
    so oft?

*Maria.* How do you, Malvolio?

*Mal.* At your request? Yes, nightingales answer daws!

*Maria.* Why appear you with this ridiculous boldness before my lady?

*Mal.* 'Be not afraid of greatness': 'twas well writ.

*Olivia.* What mean'st thou by that, Malvolio?

*Mal.* 'Some are born great'—

*Olivia.* Ha?

*Mal.* 'Some achieve greatness'—

*Olivia.* What say'st thou?

*Mal.* 'And some have greatness thrust upon them.'

*Olivia.* Heaven restore thee!

*Mal.* 'Remember who commended thy yellow stockings'—

*Olivia.* Thy yellow stockings?

*Mal.* 'And wished to see thee cross-gartered.'

*Olivia.* Cross-gartered?

*Mal.* 'Go to, thou art made, if thou desir'st to be so;'—

*Olivia.* Am I made?

*Mal.* 'If not, let me see thee a servant still.'

*Olivia.* Why, this is very midsummer madness.

[III.iv.16–55]

It is a duet for two great comedians, with Malvolio obsessed and Olivia incredulous. After Olivia departs, asking that Malvolio "be looked to," we hear in him the triumph of the depraved will:

Why, everything adheres together, that no dram of a scruple, no scruple of a scruple, no obstacle, no incredulous or unsafe circumstance—what can be said?—nothing that can be can come between me and the full prospect of my hopes. Well, Jove, not I, is the doer of this, and he is to be thanked.

[III.iv.78–84]

Shakespeare carefully keeps Malvolio a politic pagan here, as well as a dazed egomaniac, unable to distinguish "the full prospect of his hopes" from reality. Carried off by the plotters to be bound in a dark room, therapy for his madness, Malvolio is visited by Feste in the disguise of a Chaucerian curate, the good Sir Topas. The dialogue between the two constitutes an uncanny cognitive music:

*Mal.* [*Within*] Who calls there?

*Clown.* Sir Topas the curate, who comes to visit Malvolio the lunatic.

*Mal.* Sir Topas, Sir Topas, good Sir Topas, go to my lady.

*Clown.* Out, hyperbolical fiend! how vexest thou this man! talkest
thou nothing but of ladies?

*Sir Toby.* Well said, Master Parson.

*Mal.* Sir Topas, never was man thus wronged. Good Sir Topas, do not
think I am mad. They have laid me here in hideous darkness.

*Clown.* Fie, thou dishonest Satan! (I call thee by the most modest
terms, for I am one of those gentle ones that will use the devil
himself with courtesy.) Say'st thou that house is dark?

*Mal.* As hell, Sir Topas.

*Clown.* Why it hath bay-windows transparent as barricadoes, and the
clerestories toward the south-north are as lustrous as ebony: and
yet complainest thou of obstruction?

*Mal.* I am not mad, Sir Topas. I say to you, this house is dark.

*Clown.* Madman, thou errest. I say there is no darkness but ignorance,
in which thou art more puzzled than the Egyptians in their fog.

*Mal.* I say this house is as dark as ignorance, though ignorance were
as dark as hell; and I say there was never man thus abused. I am
no more mad than you are: make the trial of it in any constant
question.

*Clown.* What is the opinion of Pythagoras concerning wildfowl?

*Mal.* That the soul of our grandam might haply inhabit a bird.

*Clown.* What think'st thou of his opinion?

*Mal.* I think nobly of the soul, and no way approve his opinion.

*Clown.* Fare thee well: remain thou still in darkness. Thou shalt hold
th' opinion of Pythagoras ere I will allow of thy wits, and fear to
kill a woodcock, lest thou dispossess the soul of thy grandam.
Fare thee well.

*Mal.* Sir Topas, Sir Topas!

[IV.ii.21–62]

At once the funniest and the most unnerving passage in *Twelfth Night*,
this hardly shows us a defeated Malvolio. He retains dignity under great
duress and proudly states his stoic refusal to surrender the soul to
Pythagorean metempsychosis. Still, Feste bears off wit's honors, sagely

warning Malvolio against the ignorance of his Jonsonian moral pugnacity. There is a presage in this weird exchange of Lear's wild dialogues with the Fool and with Gloucester. Feste's wisdom, which Malvolio will not learn, is that identity is hopelessly unstable, as it is throughout *Twelfth Night*. Poor Malvolio, a great comic butt, has little of Jonson's wit but all of Ben's surliness and vulnerability to lampooning. That was Jonson not yet turned thirty, and the superb poet-playwright got beyond his own Malvolio phase. Shakespeare's Malvolio is perpetually trapped in the dark house of his obsessive self-regard and moral censoriousness, from which Shakespeare grants him no release. This is dreadfully unfair, but in the madness of *Twelfth Night*, does that matter? There can be no answer when Malvolio complains to Olivia that he has been "made the most notorious geck [butt] and gull / That e'er invention play'd on," and asks: "Tell me why?"

5

The genius of *Twelfth Night* is Feste, the most charming of all Shakespeare's fools, and the only sane character in a wild play. Olivia has inherited this court jester from her father, and we sense throughout that Feste, an accomplished professional, has grown weary of his role. He carries his exhaustion with verve and wit, and always with the air of knowing all there is to know, not in a superior way but with a sweet melancholy. His truancy is forgiven by Olivia, and in recompense he attempts to charm her out of her prolonged mourning for her brother. Feste is benign throughout the play, and does not participate in the gulling of Malvolio until he enters the dark house as Sir Topas. Even there, he is instrumental in bringing about the steward's release. A superb singer (his part was written for Robert Armin, who had an excellent voice), Feste keeps to a minor key: "Present mirth hath present laughter: / What's to come is still unsure." Though of Olivia's household, he is welcome at the music-loving Orsino's court, and gets Orsino right at one stroke:

Now the melancholy god protect thee, and the tailor make thy doublet of changeable taffeta, for thy mind is a very opal. I would have men of such constancy put to sea, that their business might be everything and their intent everywhere, for that's it that always makes a good voyage of nothing. Farewell.

[II.iv.73–78]

The fool's most revealing scene begins Act III, and is shared with the equally charming Viola, who gently provokes him to meditate upon his craft: "A sentence is but a chev'ril glove to a good wit—how quickly the wrong side may be turned outward!" That may be Shakespeare's playful admonition to himself, since the amiable Feste is one of his rare surrogates, and Feste is warning us to seek no moral coherence in *Twelfth Night*. Orsino, baffled by the sight of Viola and Sebastian together, utters a famous bewilderment:

One face, one voice, one habit, and two persons!
A natural perspective, that is, and is not!

[V.i.214–15]

In a useful gloss, Anne Barton calls this an optical illusion naturally produced, rather than presented by a disturbing perspective glass. The play's central toy is Feste's, when he sums up Malvolio's ordeal: "And thus the whirligig of time brings in his revenges." Dr. Johnson said of "a natural perspective" that nature so puts on "a show, where shadows seem realities; where that which 'is not' appears like that which 'is.'" That would seem contradictory in itself, unless time and nature merge into a Shakespearean identity, so that time's whirligig then would become the same toy as the distorting glass. Imagine a distorting mirror whirling in circles like a top, and you would have the compound toy that Shakespeare created in *Twelfth Night*. All of the play's characters, except the victimized Malvolio and Feste, are representations in that rotating glass.

At the play's end, Malvolio runs off stage shouting: "I'll be reveng'd on the whole pack of you!" Everyone else exits to get married, except for Feste, who remains alone to sing Shakespeare's most wistful song:

When that I was and a little tiny boy,
   With hey, ho, the wind and the rain,
A foolish thing was but a toy,
   For the rain it raineth every day.

But when I came to man's estate,
   With hey, ho, the wind and the rain,
'Gainst knaves and thieves men shut their gate,
   For the rain it raineth every day.

But when I came, alas, to wive,
   With hey, ho, the wind and the rain,
By swaggering could I never thrive,
   For the rain it raineth every day.

But when I came unto my beds,
   With hey, ho, the wind and the rain,
With toss-pots still 'had drunken heads,
   For the rain it raineth every day.

A great while ago the world begun,
   With hey, ho, the wind and the rain,
But that's all one, our play is done,
   And we'll strive to please you every day.

[V.i.389–408]

Whether or not Shakespeare was revising a folk song, this is clearly Feste's lyric farewell, and an epilogue to a wild performance, returning us to the wind and the rain of every day. We hear Feste's life story (and Shakespeare's?) told in erotic and household terms. "A foolish thing" probably is the male member, ironically still "but a toy" in the "man's estate" of knavery, marriage, ineffectual swaggering, drunken decline, and old age. "But that's all one" is Feste's beautiful sadness of acceptance, and the next afternoon's performance will go on.

# PART V

# THE MAJOR HISTORIES

# 16

# RICHARD II

This lyrical history makes a triad with *Romeo and Juliet*, a lyrical tragedy, and *A Midsummer Night's Dream*, the most lyrical of all comedies. Though the least popular of the three, *Richard II* is uneven but superb, and it is the best of all Shakespeare's histories, except for the Falstaffiad, the two parts of *Henry IV.* Scholars call the tetralogy of *Richard II*, the *Henry IV* plays, and *Henry V* the Henriad, but at the end of *Richard II* Prince Hal is merely lamented as a wastrel by his father, the usurper Bolingbroke, and in the two parts of *Henry IV* is secondary to the titanic Falstaff. Only *Henry V* is the Henriad, because there the living Falstaff is kept off stage, though the play's most poignant speech is Mistress Quickly's account of the great wit's death. *Richard II* also lacks Falstaff, robbing the drama of Shakespeare's greatest strength, comic invention of the human. Always experimenting, Shakespeare composed *Richard II* as an extended metaphysical lyric, which ought to be impossible for a history play, but for Shakespeare everything is possible.

*Richard II* is a bad king and an interesting metaphysical poet; his two roles are antithetical, so that his kingship diminishes even as his poetry improves. At the close, he is a dead king, first forced to abdicate and then murdered, but what stays in our ears is his metaphysical mock lyricism. A foolish and unfit king, victimized as much by his own psyche and its extraordinary language as he is by Bolingbroke, Richard wins not so much our sympathy as our reluctant aesthetic admiration for the dying fall of his cognitive music. He is totally incompetent as a politician, and totally a master of metaphor. If *Richard II* is inadequate as tragedy (Dr. Johnson's judgment), that is because it studies the decline and fall of a remarkable poet, who happens also to be an inadequate human being, and a hopeless king. It is better to think of *Richard II* as chronicle rather than tragedy, and of Richard himself neither as hero nor as villain but as victim, primarily of his own self-indulgence, yet also of the power of his imagination.

There is no prose whatsoever in *Richard II*, partly because there is no Falstaff to speak it. Though there are remarkable orations assigned to Gaunt and several others, Shakespeare centers almost entirely upon Richard. Bolingbroke, his usurper, is granted scarcely any inwardness, and marches inexorably through politics to power, without ever greatly arousing our interest. I return here to my very qualified endorsement of Graham Bradshaw's insistence that Shakespearean character depends upon internal connections and contrasts established within particular plays, the qualification being that Shakespearean representation, at its strongest, is able to break these connections and dim all contrasts. Richard is not that strong a representation, and therefore comes within what we might call Bradshaw's Law: Bolingbroke is the necessary contrast without whom Richard would not be Richard, lyrical self-destroyer.

Richard himself will make that point several times, by way of powerful metaphors. The transcendental horizon beyond which Bradshaw's Law will not altogether work does not exist in *Richard II*, which unlike *A Midsummer Night's Dream* and *Romeo and Juliet* contains no transcendent element akin to Bottom's dream or Juliet's bounty. Richard's imagination is trapped solipsistically in the prison of his petulant self, even when as an anointed king he invokes the sacredness of that anointing. Shakespeare, despite the argument of much scholarship, does not commit his art to any profound acknowledgment of kingship as a transcendence. The notion of the King's Two Bodies, one natural, the other virtually sacramental, is taken up by Richard more than once in the play, but Richard's testimony is at the least equivocal. Even the celebrations of kingship in *Henry V* and *Henry VIII* have their subtle ironies. One never can establish Shakespeare in a particular stance, whether political, religious, or philosophical. Something in the plays always prophesies Nietzsche's motive for metaphor: the desire to be different, the desire to be elsewhere.

An oddity of *Richard II*, for readers and playgoers now, is the extraordinary formalism of much of the play. Perhaps because its one action is deferred abdication, with the aftermath of the king's murder, *Richard II* is the most ceremonial of Shakespeare's plays before his coda in *Henry VIII* and *The Two Noble Kinsmen*. Sometimes the formalism works wonderfully, as in the actual abdication scene, but in other instances we are likely to be baffled. Here are Richard and his queen bidding a final farewell to each other:

*Queen.* And must we be divided? must we part?
*Rich.* Ay, hand from hand, my love, and heart from heart.
*Queen.* Banish us both, and send the king with me.
*North.* That were some love, but little policy.
*Queen.* Then whither he goes, thither let me go.
*Rich.* So two, together weeping, make one woe.
   Weep thou for me in France, I for thee here;
   Better far off than, near, be ne'er the near.
   Go count thy way with sighs; I mine with groans.
*Queen.* So longest way shall have the longest moans.
*Rich.* Twice for one step I'll groan, the way being short,
   And piece the way out with a heavy heart.
   Come, come, in wooing sorrow let's be brief,
   Since, wedding it, there is such length in grief:
   One kiss shall stop our mouths, and dumbly part;
   Thus give I mine, and thus take I thy heart.
*Queen.* Give me mine own again; 'twere no good part
   To take on me to keep and kill thy heart.
   So, now I have mine own again, be gone,
   That I may strive to kill it with a groan.
*Rich.* We make woe wanton with this fond delay.
   Once more, adieu; the rest let sorrow say.

                         [V.i.81–102]

That has a formal grace, and these ceremonial phrases can be read as a language of reserve and high dignity that the royal couple share. There is also a consistency of decorum that Shakespeare maintains throughout, and exploits by significant breakthroughs of tone whenever necessary, at times with ironical effect. In contrast to *Romeo and Juliet*, where the effect can be overwhelming, *Richard II* seeks to distance us from pathos as far as possible. We wonder at Richard, we admire his language, but we never suffer with him, even when he is deposed and subsequently murdered. Of all the histories, this is the most controlled and stylized. It is a radically experimental play, questing for the limits of a metaphysical lyricism, and brilliantly successful if we accept its rather stringent terms.

2

Walter Pater, amiably ignoring the Richard of Acts I and II, praised the royal masochist of Acts III to V as an "exquisite poet." One should never underestimate Pater's ironies; moralizings did not interest the great Aesthetic Critic, and he knew very well that Richard was a hollow man, yet he wished to judge a poet only as a poet. And as Pater said with a (for him) surprising gusto, "No! Shakespeare's kings are not, nor are meant to be, great men." Several astute critics have insisted that Richard II is not, nor is meant to be, a great or even a good poet. A. P. Rossiter thought Richard "surely a very bad poet," and Stephen Booth implied that Richard did not distinguish the manipulation of words from the manipulation of things. Ironies of syntax and of metaphor abound in *Richard II*, and Shakespeare seems intentionally to make us uneasy with not less than everything that is said by everyone in the play. In that respect at least, *Richard II* is an overture to *Hamlet*. Hamlet rarely means what he says or says what he means; as I have noted already, he anticipates Nietzsche's dictum that we find words only for what is already dead in our hearts, so there is always a kind of contempt in the act of speaking. When Richard, in Act V, begins to sound a little like a proleptic parody of Hamlet, we distrust the king as much as ever, and yet we also come to realize that he has been dazzling us since Act III, Scene ii, though with a purely verbal brilliance. So elaborate are Richard's conceits, from there to the end, that sometimes I wonder whether Shakespeare had read some of the earlier poems of Donne that were not published until *Songs and Sonnets* appeared in 1633, two years after Donne's death. This is, alas, most unlikely; *Richard II* was written in 1595, and while Shakespeare doubtless read some Donne, freely circulated in manuscript, it was likelier to have been the Ovidian Elegies than anything that eventually became the *Songs and Sonnets*. This hardly matters, since Shakespeare invents Metaphysical poetry in Richard's laments and soliloquies, and perhaps Donne attended a performance of *Richard II*, so that the influence (or parody) went in the other direction. Either way, the modes have much in common, though Donne is the real thing, and Richard is a troublesome and problematic rhapsode of royal martyrdom. His comparisons of himself to Jesus are unnerving—though technically not blasphemous, since Richard does not see himself as sharing in any aspect of Jesus except for being God's anointed.

Since we are not meant to like Richard, and no one could like the usurper Bolingbroke, Shakespeare has little trouble distancing us from the only actions of the play, abdication and murder. Whatever judgment an individual critic renders of Richard as poet, the last three acts of the play depend almost wholly upon the originality and vigor of Richard's language. Perhaps we could say that Richard has the language of a major poet but lacks range, since his only subject is his own sufferings, particularly the indignities he endures though he is the rightful king. His performance as king is early typified by his reaction, at the end of Act I, to the final illness of his uncle, John of Gaunt, the father of the just-exiled Bolingbroke, who will return from abroad to depose Richard. The historical John of Gaunt was just another robber baron more egregious than most, but Shakespeare, needing an oracle in this play, promotes John of Gaunt to be a patriotic prophet. Richard's callousness closes Act I:

Now put it, God, in the physician's mind
To help him to his grave immediately!
The lining of his coffers shall make coats
To deck our soldiers for these Irish wars.

Come, gentlemen, let's all go visit him,
Pray God we may make haste and come too late!

[I.iv.59–64]

This is a marvelous antithetical prologue to John of Gaunt's famous deathbed prophecy; its plain nastiness contrasts to Gaunt's unworldliness:

Methinks I am a prophet new inspir'd,
And thus expiring do foretell of him:
His rash fierce blaze of riot cannot last.
For violent fires soon burn out themselves;
Small showers last long, but sudden storms are short;
He tires betimes that spurs too fast betimes;
With eager feeding food doth choke the feeder;
Light vanity, insatiate cormorant,
Consuming means, soon preys upon itself.
This royal throne of kings, this scept'red isle,
This earth of majesty, this seat of Mars,
This other Eden, demi-paradise,
This fortress built by Nature for herself
Against infection and the hand of war,
This happy breed of men, this little world,
This precious stone set in the silver sea,
Which serves it in the office of a wall,
Or as a moat defensive to a house,
Against the envy of less happier lands;
This blessed plot, this earth, this realm, this England,
This nurse, this teeming womb of royal kings,
Fear'd by their breed, and famous by their birth,
Renowned for their deeds as far from home,
For Christian service and true chivalry,
As is the sepulchre in stubborn Jewry
Of the world's ransom, blessed Mary's son;
This land of such dear souls, this dear dear land,

Dear for her reputation through the world,
Is now leas'd out—I die pronouncing it—
Like to a tenement or pelting farm.
England, bound in with the triumphant sea,
Whose rocky shore beats back the envious siege
Of wat'ry Neptune, is now bound in with shame,
With inky blots and rotten parchment bonds;
That England, that was wont to conquer others,
Hath made a shameful conquest of itself.

[II.i.31–66]

This splendid patriotic rant, together with a similar declamation by John of Gaunt's grandson, Henry V, in his play, had their finest reverberations in the London of 1940–41, when England stood alone against Hitler. Both litanies can still be admired as eloquence, yet are troublesome when analyzed. Shakespeare makes us wonder that this other paradise should be the seat of Mars, not a deity we ordinarily associate with Eden. There is also the ironic prophecy—of royal crusades "for Christian service and true chivalry"—unintended by John of Gaunt, since his son Bolingbroke, confirmed as King Henry IV by his murder of Richard II, will vow at the play's close to expiate the murder by leading a Crusade:

I'll make a voyage to the Holy Land,
To wash this blood off from my guilty hand.

"Stubborn Jewry," already massacred by English kings both in York and in Jerusalem, had nothing to fear from Henry IV, whose Crusade reduced to his dying in the Jerusalem chamber of his palace. The Crusaders' zeal passed to Henry V, who took it out upon the French, not the Jews, as all in the audience knew. We like Gaunt less as a prophet than when he berates Richard quite directly for his commercial depredations: "Landlord of England art thou now, not king." Gaunt dead, Richard cheerfully confiscates "His plate, his goods, his money and his lands."

Vengeance arrives with Bolingbroke, who arrives in England with an armed force, to be welcomed by most of his fellow nobles. As Act II closes, we begin to understand the language of politics in this play. Bolingbroke and his supporters insist he has returned only for his inheritance, to become Duke of Lancaster as was his father, John of Gaunt. But everyone knows that the future Henry IV has come for the crown, and Shakespeare will explore this hypocrisy with marvelous skill until the moment of forced abdication. Thus, with Richard occupied with the Irish wars, Bolingbroke *in Richard's name* executes all of Richard's closest supporters that he can apprehend, and carefully sends messages of his affection to Richard's queen, which means that she is as good as imprisoned. Shakespeare has readied us for one of the play's great effects, the landing of Richard on the coast of Wales, returning from Ireland, perfectly ignorant that pragmatically he already has been deposed.

3

The self-destruction of Richard II, well advanced before his return, receives its seal in the speeches and gestures of his homecoming. His salute to the Welsh earth adjures it to rise against Bolingbroke, and his defense of his hyperbole is pathetic:

> Mock not my senseless conjuration, lords:
> This earth shall have a feeling, and these stones
> Prove armed soldiers ere her native king
> Shall falter under foul rebellion's arms.
>
> [III.ii.23–26]

The pathos increases when Richard compares himself to the rising sun, the most inappropriate image possible for a man upon whom the sun has gone down:

> So when this thief, this traitor, Bolingbroke,
> Who all this while hath revell'd in the night,
> Whilst we were wand'ring with the Antipodes,
> Shall see us rising in our throne the east,

His treasons will sit blushing in his face,
Not able to endure the sight of day,
But self-affrighted tremble at his sin.
Not all the water in the rough rude sea
Can wash the balm off from an anointed king;
The breath of worldly men cannot depose
The deputy elected by the Lord;
For every man that Bolingbroke hath press'd
To lift shrewd steel against our golden crown,
God for his Richard hath in heavenly pay
A glorious angel: then, if angels fight,
Weak men must fall, for heaven still guards the right.

[III.ii.47–62]

This vision of hosts of armed angels yields to Richard's anxious inquiry as to the whereabouts of his Welsh army, which has melted away the day before, on rumors that he was dead. When he realizes that all have abandoned him, he yields to a luxuriant despair so powerfully expressed as to transcend any previous eloquence in Shakespeare:

No matter where—of comfort no man speak.
Let's talk of graves, of worms, and epitaphs,
Make dust our paper, and with rainy eyes
Write sorrow on the bosom of the earth.
Let's choose executors and talk of wills.
And yet not so—for what can we bequeath
Save our deposed bodies to the ground?
Our lands, our lives, and all, are Bolingbroke's,
And nothing can we call our own but death;
And that small model of the barren earth
Which serves as paste and cover to our bones.
For God's sake let us sit upon the ground
And tell sad stories of the death of kings:
How some have been depos'd, some slain in war,
Some haunted by the ghosts they have deposed,

Some poisoned by their wives, some sleeping kill'd,
All murthered—for within the hollow crown
That rounds the mortal temples of a king
Keeps Death his court, and there the antic sits,
Scoffing his state and grinning at his pomp,
Allowing him a breath, a little scene,
To monarchize, be fear'd, and kill with looks;
Infusing him with self and vain conceit,
As if this flesh which walls about our life
Were brass impregnable; and, humour'd thus,
Comes at the last, and with a little pin
Bored thorough his castle wall, and farewell king!
Cover your heads, and mock not flesh and blood
With solemn reverence; throw away respect,
Tradition, form, and ceremonious duty;
For you have but mistook me all this while.
I live with bread like you, feel want,
Taste grief, need friends—subjected thus,
How can you say to me, I am a king?

[III.ii.144–77]

To see what this is not, think of Lear's "Take physic, pomp." In the great king's recognition of common mortality, there is an opening to all others, to poor naked wretches, wheresoever they are, who suffer the merciless storm with Lear. Richard opens only to Richard, and to other murdered kings before him. And yet he opens also to a greater poetry, with a vernacular intensity that astonishes:

For God's sake let us sit upon the ground
And tell sad stories of the death of kings.

Even better is that "and with a little pin," a touch of a new poetic greatness. The masochistic mode of this luxuriance is illuminated when Richard is told that the Duke of York, regent in the king's absence, also has gone over to Bolingbroke, so that Richard's party is reduced to a literal handful:

Beshrew thee, cousin, which didst lead me forth
Of that sweet way I was in to despair! [*To Aumerle.*]

[III.ii.204–5]

After this, Richard's despair leaps ahead of itself, perhaps inventing what has become another characteristic of the human, our tendency to speak as though matters could not be worse, and by overhearing such utterance, proceeding to make them worse. Richard becomes the antithesis of Edgar, the anti-Richard of *King Lear*, who moves us with his great speech that begins Act IV:

Yet better thus, and known to be contemn'd,
Than still contemn'd and flatter'd, to be worst.
The lowest and most dejected thing of Fortune,
Stands still in esperance, lives not in fear:
The lamentable change is from the best;
The worst returns to laughter. Welcome, then,
Thou unsubstantial air that I embrace:
The wretch that thou hast blown unto the worst
Owes nothing to thy blasts.

[*King Lear*, IV.i.1–9]

One wonders, here and in other places, if the contrasts between Richard II and King Lear are not deliberate. Richard is no more capable of "The worst returns to laughter" than he is of Lear's startled apprehensions of human otherness. Edgar transcends Richard even more sublimely when he beholds his blinded father: "The worst is not / So long as we can say 'This is the worst.' " But Richard never stops doing Bolingbroke's work for him, yielding up a kingdom while constructing metaphysical litanies:

What must the king do now? Must he submit?
The king shall do it. Must he be depos'd?
The king shall be contented. Must he lose
The name of king? a God's name, let it go.
I'll give my jewels for a set of beads;

My gorgeous palace for a hermitage;
My gay apparel for an almsman's gown;
My figur'd goblets for a dish of wood;
My sceptre for a palmer's walking staff;
My subjects for a pair of carved saints,
And my large kingdom for a little grave,
A little little grave, an obscure grave,
Or I'll be buried in the king's highway,
Some way of common trade, where subjects' feet
May hourly trample on their sovereign's head;
For on my heart they tread now whilst I live:
And buried once, why not upon my head?
Aumerle, thou weep'st (my tender-hearted cousin!),
We'll make foul weather with despised tears;
Our sighs and they shall lodge the summer corn,
And make a dearth in this revolting land.
Or shall we play the wantons with our woes,
And make some pretty match with shedding tears?
And thus to drop them still upon one place,
Till they have fretted us a pair of graves
Within the earth, and therein laid—there lies
Two kinsmen digg'd their graves with weeping eyes!
Would not this ill do well? Well, well, I see
I talk but idly, and you laugh at me.
Most mighty prince, my Lord Northumberland,
What says King Bolingbroke? Will his Majesty
Give Richard leave to live till Richard die?
You make a leg, and Bolingbroke says "ay".

[III.iii.143–75]

Once he starts, Richard cannot stop, as in "a little grave, / A little little grave, an obscure grave." This obsessive self-pity offends moralizing critics, but it thrilled the great Irish poet Yeats, who found in Richard an apocalyptic imagination. The brilliant fantasia that develops Richard's tears has in it a quality of visionary irony new in Shakespeare and anticipatory of Donne. The initial dialogue between the self-defeated King Richard and the victorious Bolingbroke carries this power of irony into a theatrical complexity again new to Shakespeare:

> *Bol.* Stand all apart,
> And show fair duty to his Majesty. [*He kneels down.*]
> My gracious lord.
> *Rich.* Fair cousin, you debase your princely knee
> To make the base earth proud with kissing it.
> Me rather had my heart might feel your love,
> Than my unpleased eye see your courtesy.
> Up, cousin, up; your heart is up, I know,
> Thus high at least, although your knee be low.
> *Bol.* My gracious lord, I come but for mine own.
> *Rich.* Your own is yours, and I am yours, and all.
> *Bol.* So far be mine, my most redoubted lord,
> As my true service shall deserve your love.
> *Rich.* Well you deserve. They well deserve to have
> That know the strong'st and surest way to get.
> Uncle, give me your hands; nay, dry your eyes—
> Tears show their love, but want their remedies.
> Cousin, I am too young to be your father,
> Though you are old enough to be my heir;
> What you will have, I'll give, and willing too,
> For do we must what force will have us do.
> Set on towards London, cousin, is it so?
> *Bol.* Yea, my good lord.
> *Rich.* Then I must not say no.
> > [*Flourish. Exeunt.*]
>
> > > [III.iii.187–209]

One might argue, "Well, but what else can Richard do?" To which the answer is "Anything at all, except to make Bolingbroke's job so much easier for him." Richard enjoys his ironies here, but they will be fatal for him, though aesthetically very satisfactory for Shakespeare and for us.

The exquisite garden interlude that follows (Act III, Scene iv) allows Richard's queen to speak of her husband's catastrophe as "A second fall of cursed man," but that is no more persuasive than Richard's attempts to align his ordeal with Christ's. What is troubling comes in the Bishop of Carlisle's courageous prophecy concerning Bolingbroke:

> My Lord of Herford here, whom you call king,
> Is a foul traitor to proud Herford's king,
> And if you crown him, let me prophesy—
> The blood of English shall manure the ground,
> And future ages groan for this foul act,
> Peace shall go sleep with Turks and infidels,
> And, in this seat of peace, tumultuous wars
> Shall kin with kin, and kind with kind, confound.
> Disorder, horror, fear, and mutiny,
> Shall here inhabit, and this land be call'd
> The field of Golgotha and dead men's skulls—
> O, if you raise this house against this house,
> It will be the woefullest division prove
> That ever fell upon this cursed earth.
> Prevent it, resist it, let it not be so,
> Lest child, child's children, cry against you woe.
>
> [IV.i.134–49]

The Bishop will suffer for this truthtelling, and yet Shakespeare is on no side or on all; Bolingbroke and his supporters are unholy thugs, and Richard, no Lear, was no inch a king. The Earl of Southampton helped arrange that Shakespeare's company give a performance of *Richard II* as prelude to the Essex Rebellion against Elizabeth in 1601, six years after the first performance of the play. Shakespeare cannot have been happy with this, but evidently he could not refuse, and he was fortunate that this elicited only Queen Elizabeth's ironic comment "I am Richard II, know ye not that?" Essex was no Bolingbroke, and Elizabeth not at all a Richard, and being dragged into potential danger was anything but Shakespeare's way, since he never forgot what the state had done to Marlowe and to Kyd.

Richard becomes more self-destructively eloquent with each scene. Summoned by Bolingbroke to surrender the Crown, Richard arrives, comparing himself to Christ yet once more, and converts the ceremony into a metaphysical dance of conceits and ironies:

> *Rich.* Give me the crown. Here, cousin, seize the crown.
>   Here, cousin,
>   On this side my hand, and on that side thine.
>   Now is this golden crown like a deep well
>   That owes two buckets, filling one another,
>   The emptier ever dancing in the air,
>   The other down, unseen, and full of water.
>   That bucket down and full of tears am I,
>   Drinking my griefs, whilst you mount up on high.
> *Bol.* I thought you had been willing to resign.
> *Rich.* My crown I am, but still my griefs are mine.
>   You may my glories and my state depose,
>   But not my griefs; still am I king of those.
> *Bol.* Part of your cares you give me with your crown.
> *Rich.* Your cares set up do not pluck my cares down.
>   My care is loss of care, by old care done;
>   Your care is gain of care, by new care won.
>   The cares I give, I have, though given away,
>   They 'tend the crown, yet still with me they stay.
> *Bol.* Are you contented to resign the crown?
> *Rich.* Ay, no; no, ay; for I must nothing be.
>
> [IV.i.181–201]

One could feel chagrin at Shakespeare's juxtaposition of a word man and a brutal politician if a critique of poetry were the issue, but of course it is not, and Richard's juggling with wordplays distracts him from any effective resistance. He cannot stop his own flood of eloquence, though he knows he must drown by it:

Therefore no "no", for I resign to thee.
Now, mark me how I will undo myself.
I give this heavy weight from off my head,
And this unwieldy sceptre from my hand,
The pride of kingly sway from out my heart;
With mine own tears I wash away my balm,
With mine own hands I give away my crown,
With mine own tongue deny my sacred state,
With mine own breath release all duteous oaths;
All pomp and majesty I do forswear;
My manors, rents, revenues, I forgo;
My acts, decrees, and statutes I deny.
God pardon all oaths that are broke to me,
God keep all vows unbroke are made to thee!
Make me, that nothing have, with nothing griev'd,
And thou with all pleas'd, that hast all achiev'd.
Long may'st thou live in Richard's seat to sit,
And soon lie Richard in an earthy pit.
God save King Henry, unking'd Richard says,
And send him many years of sunshine days!
What more remains?

                                          [IV.i.202–22]


An actor as well as a lyrical poet, Richard is more fit to join Shakespeare's company of players than he is to be martyred on behalf of an
anointing as king that he never could sustain by royal behavior. His high
theatricalism achieves an apotheosis when he utters his last command as
king, sending for a mirror so that he can behold whether he still is the selfsame being he was. Shakespeare both exploits this final caprice and criticizes it by flamboyantly exhibiting his own emancipation from Marlowe,
whose *Edward II* has hovered near throughout the play. What clearer signal of Shakespeare's achieved autonomy could he send to the audience
than this dazzling parody of one of Marlowe's most notorious purple passages, Faustus's acclamation of Helen of Troy: "Was this the face that

launched a thousand ships, / and burnt the topless towers of Ilium?" Shakespeare betters this by Richard's outrageous and desperate narcissism, as
the king's lost glory becomes his own Helen of Troy:

> *Rich.* Give me that glass, and therein will I read.
>      No deeper wrinkles yet? hath sorrow struck
>      So many blows upon this face of mine
>      And made no deeper wounds? O flatt'ring glass,
>      Like to my followers in prosperity,
>      Thou dost beguile me. Was this face the face
>      That every day under his household roof
>      Did keep ten thousand men? Was this the face
>      That like the sun did make beholders wink?
>      Is this the face which fac'd so many follies,
>      That was at last out-fac'd by Bolingbroke?
>      A brittle glory shineth in this face;
>      As brittle as the glory is the face,
>                    *[Dashes the glass against the ground.]*
>      For there it is, crack'd in an hundred shivers.
>      Mark, silent king, the moral of this sport—
>      How soon my sorrow hath destroy'd my face.
> *Bol.* The shadow of your sorrow hath destroy'd
>      The shadow of your face.
> *Rich.*                           Say that again.
>      The shadow of my sorrow? ha! let's see—
>      'Tis very true, my grief lies all within,
>      And these external manners of lament
>      Are merely shadows to the unseen grief
>      That swells with silence in the tortur'd soul.
>      There lies the substance. And I thank thee, king,
>      For thy great bounty, that not only giv'st
>      Me cause to wail, but teachest me the way
>      How to lament the cause.
>                                        [IV.i.276–302]

More than ever, the empty poetic-critical laurels go to Richard, and the
menacing political realism is entirely Bolingbroke's. But what a marvelous
poet-playwright/actor-critic is lost in Richard! The breaking of the glass,
the argument over "shadow" (at once sorrow and stage representation), and
the culmination of irony in thanking Bolingbroke for instruction—all these
constitute a theatrical breakthrough for Shakespeare. Richard is sent off to
Pomfret, to be murdered out of the way, and goes like the grand actor he
has become:

> *York.* As in a theatre the eyes of men,
>     After a well-grac'd actor leaves the stage,
>     Are idly bent on him that enters next,
>     Thinking his prattle to be tedious;
>     Even so, or with much more contempt, men's eyes
>     Did scowl on Richard. No man cried "God save him!"
>     No joyful tongue gave him his welcome home,
>     But dust was thrown upon his sacred head.
>
>                                         [V.ii.23–30]

What remains is the final scene, where Richard is murdered, but first he
speaks an extraordinary soliloquy, the height of Shakespeare's achievement in this difficult mode before Hamlet perfected it:

> *Rich.* I have been studying how I may compare
>     This prison where I live unto the world;
>     And, for because the world is populous
>     And here is not a creature but myself,
>     I cannot do it. Yet I'll hammer it out.
>     My brain I'll prove the female to my soul,
>     My soul the father, and these two beget
>     A generation of still-breeding thoughts,
>     And these same thoughts people this little world,
>     In humours like the people of this world;
>     For no thought is contented. The better sort,
>     As thoughts of things divine, are intermix'd

With scruples, and do set the word itself
Against the word,
As thus: "Come, little ones"; and then again,
"It is as hard to come as for a camel
To thread the postern of a small needle's eye".
Thoughts tending to ambition, they do plot
Unlikely wonders: how these vain weak nails
May tear a passage through the flinty ribs
Of this hard world, my ragged prison walls;
And for they cannot, die in their own pride.
Thoughts tending to content flatter themselves
That they are not the first of fortune's slaves,
Nor shall not be the last—like silly beggars
Who, sitting in the stocks, refuge their shame,
That many have and others must sit there;
And in this thought they find a kind of ease,
Bearing their own misfortunes on the back
Of such as have before indur'd the like.
Thus play I in one person many people,
And none contented. Sometimes am I king,
Then treasons make me wish myself a beggar,
And so I am. Then crushing penury
Persuades me I was better when a king;
Then am I king'd again, and by and by
Think that I am unking'd by Bolingbroke,
And straight am nothing. But whate'er I be,
Nor I, nor any man that but man is,
With nothing shall be pleas'd, til he be eas'd
With being nothing.
                    [*The music plays.*
                    Music do I hear?
Ha, ha! keep time—how sour sweet music is
When time is broke and no proportion kept!
So is it in the music of men's lives.
And here have I the daintiness of ear

To check time broke in a disordered string;
But for the concord of my state and time,
Had not an ear to hear my true time broke:
I wasted time, and now doth time waste me;
For now hath time made me his numb'ring clock;
My thoughts are minutes, and with sighs they jar
Their watches on unto mine eyes, the outward watch,
Whereto my finger, like a dial's point,
Is pointing still, in cleansing them from tears.
Now sir, the sound that tells what hour it is
Are clamorous groans which strike upon my heart,
Which is the bell—so sighs, and tears, and groans,
Show minutes, times, and hours. But my time
Runs posting on in Bolingbroke's proud joy,
While I stand fooling here, his Jack of the clock.
This music mads me. Let it sound no more;
For though it have holp mad men to their wits,
In me it seems it will make wise men mad.
Yet blessing on his heart that gives it me,
For 'tis a sign of love; and love to Richard
Is a strange brooch in this all-hating world.

[V.v.1–66]

Even here Shakespeare has us keep our distance from Richard, who is more interesting than before but still on the other side of poignance. No hidden greatness suddenly emerges from him; although he is an anointed king, as intellect and as spirit he counts for precious little—and yet he has just shaped his best poem. What Shakespeare is inventing here is another aspect of the human, possibly with Marlowe's personality rather than Marlowe's Edward II as the provocation. Overhearing his own reverie, Richard undergoes a change. He does not acquire any human dignity, but he does begin to incarnate what can be termed an aesthetic dignity. Richard is the first figure in Shakespeare who manifests this fissure between human and aesthetic stature, but greater personages will follow after, Iago, Edmund, Macbeth among them. They are free artists of themselves.

Richard cannot be that; he is bound within himself even as his body is imprisoned at Pomfret. Yet there is an aesthetic drive or impulse in Richard, which is new in Shakespeare: that is why Pater and Yeats were fascinated by Richard II. There are greater, freer artists of themselves in Shakespeare who preserve both human dignity and aesthetic dignity: Hamlet, Lear, Edgar, Prospero. Perhaps Shakespeare pondered great falls in his England—Essex and Raleigh among others—and perceived human and aesthetic dignity departing together. I do not believe that this fissure exists in literature earlier than Shakespeare.

Shakespeare did not invent the dignity of men and women: despite Renaissance enhancements, some of them Hermetic, that vision had developed across millennia. But aesthetic dignity, though not itself a Shakespearean phrase, is certainly a Shakespearean invention, as is the double nature of such dignity. It either coheres with human dignity, or survives isolated when the greater dignity is lost. That, I take it, is the importance of Richard's long prison soliloquy at the beginning of Act V. Something surprising to Shakespeare himself is coming to birth here, and it will change Shakespeare's art and the art and lives of many who will come after, who are in the wake of Richard II and of Hamlet.

Hamlet's intellect leaped to the realization that Denmark and the world were prisons for his spirit, but Richard hammers it out, since he is infinitely less swift in thought. His little world, his poor self, has no faith in salvation; his desperation can conceive of no escape, and so he recites the earliest Shakespearean litany of nihilism predating *Much Ado About Nothing* and prophesying Hamlet, Iago, and Leontes:

And straight am nothing. But whate'er I be,
Nor I, nor any man that but man is,
With nothing shall be pleas'd, till he be eas'd
With being nothing.

[V.v.38–41]

The equivocal easing by death is wonderfully startled by the music, which provokes Richard into a reverie on the metaphysics of time, his time:

I wasted time, and now doth time waste me.

[V.v.49]

The elaborate conceit of the deposed king turned into a timepiece is Richard's last and finest metaphysical image for himself, perhaps because it is much the most destructive, provoking him to the series of trapped rages that conclude his life. His grotesque denunciation of his horse, for consenting also to be usurped by Bolingbroke, is followed by his sudden rage against the jailer, and then by his death, with its rather lame concluding couplet:

Mount, mount, my soul! thy seat is up on high,
Whilst my gross flesh sinks downward, here to die.

[V.v.111–12]

Shakespeare ought to have done better than that for last words, but he probably intended a final regression to an earlier Richard. Though Richard dies with little dignity, his utterance is still preferable to Bolingbroke's absurd hypocrisy that closes the play:

Lords, I protest my soul is full of woe
That blood should sprinkle me to make me grow.
Come mourn with me for what I do lament,
And put on sullen black incontinent.
I'll make a voyage to the Holy Land,
To wash this blood off from my guilty hand.
March sadly after; grace my mournings here
In weeping after this untimely bier.

[V.vi.45–52]

Partly this is prelude to the two parts of *Henry IV*, where the usurper never enjoys an instant of peace, yet the dark taste it leaves badly requires a sweetening of wit. A year later more than that arrived, with the genius of Sir John Falstaff.

## 17

# HENRY IV

You cannot reduce Shakespeare to any single power, of all his myriad gifts, and assert that he matters most because of that one glory. Yet all his endowments issue from his extraordinary intelligence, which for comprehensiveness is unmatched, and not just among the greatest writers. The true Bardolatry stems from this recognition: Here at last we encounter an intelligence without limits. As we read Shakespeare, we are always engaged in catching up, and our joy is that the process is never-ending: he is still out ahead of us. I marvel at critics, of whatever persuasions, old and new, who substitute their *knowingness* (really their resentment) for Shakespeare's woe and wonder, which are among the prime manifestations of his cognitive power.

I have cited Hegel's fine observation that Shakespeare made his best characters "free artists of themselves." The freest of the free are Hamlet and Falstaff, because they are the most intelligent of Shakespeare's persons (or roles, if you prefer that word). Critics rarely condescend to Hamlet, though some, like Alistair Fowler, morally disapprove of him. With Falstaff, alas, it is different; many critics not only condemn him morally, they also lord it over him, as if Sir John knows less than they do. If one loves Falstaff (as I do, and as we all should, even as a role), they are likely to term one a "sentimentalist." I remember a graduate student in one of my Shakespeare seminars, a few years back, who informed me rather vehemently that Falstaff was not worthy of admiration, whereas the transformation of Prince

Hal into King Henry V was exemplary. Her point was that Hal represented rule and that Falstaff was a lord of misrule, and I could not persuade her that Falstaff transcended her categories, as he transcends virtually all our catalogings of human sin and error. That Shakespeare had an intensely personal relation to his Hamlet is clear enough, and he lavished all his powers upon the prince. Falstaff did not trouble Shakespeare for as many years as Hamlet did, and perhaps Falstaff did not at all perplex his creator. I would guess, though, that Falstaff surprised Shakespeare and ran away from the role originally intended for him, which may have been no larger than, say, Ancient Pistol's is in *Henry V*. The two parts of *Henry IV* do not belong to Hal, but to Falstaff, and even Hotspur, in the first part, is dimmed by Falstaff's splendor. I despair of ever again seeing a Falstaff to match Ralph Richardson's, half a century ago, because Richardson did not condescend to Falstaff or underestimate him. The Falstaff he played was neither coward nor jester, but infinite wit delighting in its own inventiveness, and transcending its own darkening pathos. Courage in Falstaff finds expression as a refusal to acknowledge rejection, even though Sir John is aware, as *Henry IV, Part One*, opens, that Hal's ambivalence has resolved itself into a murderous negativity. Hal's displaced paternal love is Falstaff's vulnerability, his one weakness, and the origin of his destruction. Time annihilates other Shakespearean protagonists, but not Falstaff, who dies for love. Critics have insisted that this love is grotesque, but they are grotesque. The greatest of all fictive wits dies the death of a rejected father-substitute, and also of a dishonored mentor.

Most of Shakespeare's mature plays implicitly demand that we provide them with a particular foreground, which we can arrive at by a kind of inference, as scholars from Maurice Morgann to A. D. Nuttall have indicated. The foreground of *Henry IV, Part One*, is only partly supplied by *Richard II*, the drama in which Bolingbroke usurps the crown and becomes King Henry IV. There, in Act V, Scene iii, the new King and Percy, soon to be known as Hotspur, have a prophetic conversation about Prince Hal:

> *Bol.* Can no man tell me of my unthrifty son?
> 'Tis full three months since I did see him last.
> If any plague hang over us, 'tis he.

I would to God, my lords, he might be found.
Inquire at London, 'mongst the taverns there,
For there, they say, he daily doth frequent
With unrestrained loose companions,
Even such, they say, as stand in narrow lanes
And beat our watch and rob our passengers,
Which he, young wanton, and effeminate boy,
Takes on the point of honor to support
So dissolute a crew.

*Percy.* My lord, some two days since I saw the prince,
And told him of those triumphs held at Oxford.

*Bol.* And what said the gallant?

*Percy.* His answer was, he would unto the stews.
And from the common'st creature pluck a glove,
And wear it as a favour; and with that
He would unhorse the lustiest challenger.

*Bol.* As dissolute as desperate! But yet
Through both I see some sparks of better hope,
Which elder years may happily bring forth.

[*Richard II*, V.iii.1–22]

The leader of this dissolute crew is Falstaff, whose pre-Shakespearean fortunes do not involve *him*—that is to say, the immortal Falstaff (as Bradley and Goddard rightly called him). Immortal Falstaff is Shakespeare's invention, the proverbial fat man who struggled triumphantly to get out of the thin Will Shakespeare. Many critics have pointed to the wordplay that is parallel: Fall/staff; Shake/spear. Others have found in the poet of the Sonnets a Falstaff figure suffering in relation to a Prince Hal–like noble youth. The personal link, though, seems to me strongest when one notes that Falstaff *is* Shakespeare's wit at its very limits, even as Hamlet *is* the farthest reach of Shakespeare's cognitive acuity. Whether we can surmise Shakespeare's human investment in Falstaff to the degree that we surmise it in Hamlet is a puzzle to me. A celebrated New Historicist critic of Shakespeare, responding to a talk I gave on value in the personalities of Hamlet and Falstaff, told the audience that my handling of those characters or roles was "a politics of identity." I don't know what politics have (or had) to do with this, but it is difficult not to speculate upon Shakespeare's identification both with his son Hamlet and with his other self, Falstaff. You don't write Hamlet and Falstaff into existence without something like Cervantes's own reactions to Don Quixote and Sancho Panza. Narrative fiction is not dramatic fiction, and so we cannot have Shakespeare's Cervantes-like expressions of pride and of mock dismay in what he had wrought. William Empson, first, and then C. L. Barber and Richard P. Wheeler, sought Shakespeare's oblique commentary on Falstaff in the Sonnets, with mixed but valuable enough results. I prefer to find Shakespeare's Falstaffian spirit in the plays, if I can, because the Sonnets, at their strongest, seem to me more equivocal than anything else by Shakespeare. Perhaps they can lead us into the plays, but Hamlet and Falstaff illuminate the Sonnets more often than the Sonnets give us new light upon those two giant forms.

In the chronicles of English history, a Sir John Falstolfe figures as a cowardly commander in the French wars, and as such enters *Henry VI, Part One* (Act I, Scene i, 130–40), where his flight leads to the brave Talbot's being wounded and captured. The character who became the Immortal Falstaff (no coward, as Morgann and Bradley insisted, against Prince Hal) was originally called Sir John Oldcastle. But in 1587 or so, the apprentice playwright Shakespeare may have helped botch *The Famous Victories of Henry IV,* a rousing, patriotic rant of a play, perhaps mostly written by the comic actor Dick Tarlton. In this drama, Prince Hal eventually reforms, and banishes his wicked companion, Sir John Oldcastle. But the historical Oldcastle died a Protestant martyr, and his descendants were not pleased to see him as a wicked glutton and walking vice. Shakespeare was compelled to change the name, and so came up with Falstaff instead. Shakespeare, a touch censured, allows Hal to call Falstaff "my old lad of the castle" but then adds to the Epilogue of *Henry IV, Part Two*, a blunt disclaimer: "for Oldcastle died a martyr, and this is not the man." How odd it would sound if Verdi's opera were called *Oldcastle!* Contingency governs the dramatist's choices, at many levels, and Oldcastle's annoyed progeny helped give us what now seems the one possible name for comic genius: Falstaff.

Sir John Oldcastle, in *The Famous Victories*, is only a minor roisterer. Shakespeare found Falstaff in Shakespeare, though the language and personalities of Berowne and of Faulconbridge the Bastard, of Mercutio and of Bottom, do not prepare us adequately for Falstaff, who speaks what is still the best and most vital prose in the English language. Sir John's mastery of language transcends even Hamlet's, since Falstaff has absolute faith both in language and in himself. Falstaff never loses faith either in himself or in language, and so seems to emanate from a more primordial Shakespeare than Hamlet does. Falstaff becomes Shakespeare's greatest and subtlest victory over Barabas and the other Marlovian overreachers, because the fat knight surpasses Marlowe's Machiavels as a rhetorician, yet never uses his magnificent language to persuade anyone of anything. Though Falstaff constantly has to defend himself against Hal's endless and well-nigh murderous aggressivity, even with Hal he seeks neither to persuade nor merely to defend. Wit is Falstaff's god, and since we must assume that God has a sense of humor, we can observe that Falstaff's vitalizing discourse, his beautiful laughing speech (as Yeats said of Blake), is truly Sir John's mode of devotion. Making others wittier is Falstaff's enterprise; not only witty in himself, he is the cause of Hal's wit as well. Sir John is a comic Socrates. What Shakespeare knew of Socrates, he would have learned from Montaigne, whose Plato and whose Socrates were skeptics. Falstaff is more than skeptical, but he is too much of a teacher (his true vocation, more than highwayman) to follow skepticism out to its nihilistic borders, as Hamlet does. Skeptical wit is not witty skepticism, and Sir John is not a master of negation, like Hamlet (or Iago). As the Socrates of Eastcheap, Falstaff need not concern himself with teaching virtue, because the struggle between the usurper Henry IV and the rebels has no possible relation to ethics or to morality. Falstaff jests of the rebels that "they offend only the virtuous," who clearly are not to be found in the England of Henry IV (or of Henry V).

What, then, are the teachings of the philosopher of Eastcheap? Eating, drinking, fornication, and the other obvious indulgences are not the heart of Falstaffianism, though they certainly take up much of the knight's time. This does not matter, because Falstaff, as Hal first tells us, has nothing to do with the time of the day. That which we are, that only can we teach; Falstaff, who is free, instructs us in freedom—not a freedom *in* society, but *from* society. The sage of Eastcheap inhabits Shakespearean histories but treats them like comedies. Scholars have named the tetralogy of *Richard II, Henry IV, Part One, Henry IV, Part Two,* and *Henry V* as the Henriad, but I regard the two middle plays as the Falstaffiad (to which I would not add *The Merry Wives of Windsor,* whose "Falstaff" is an operatic impostor). The Falstaffiad is tragicomedy; the Henriad is patriotic (with some shadings!) history. I wish that Shakespeare had not told us of the death of Falstaff in *Henry V* but instead had carried Sir John off to the forest of Arden, to exchange wit with Rosalind in *As You Like It.* Though he incarnates freedom, Falstaff's liberty is not absolute, like Rosalind's. As audience, we are given no perspective more privileged than Rosalind's own, whereas we can see Prince Hal's Machiavel-like qualities more clearly than Falstaff can bear to do, and we sense Falstaff's rejection, from Hal's opening speech on, in *Henry IV, Part One.* Edging the Falstaffiad's comic joy is its enclosure by the Henriad, and from one legitimate perspective, what is Hal except Falstaff's evil genius?

E. E. Stoll shrewdly compared Shakespeare's comic art of *isolation* in regard to Shylock and Falstaff. Shylock is never alone on stage; we are allowed only societal perspectives upon him. Falstaff, in the second part of his tragicomedy, is in Hal's company only twice, first to be seen by the prince in a tawdry scene of erotic pathos with Doll Tearsheet, and then to be brutally insulted and rejected by the newly crowned king. We would like Falstaff to enjoy absolute freedom, and something in Shakespeare would like that also, but Shakespearean mimesis is too artful for such a fantasy. Falstaff, as the comic Socrates, represents freedom only as an educational dialectic of conversion. If you come to Falstaff full of your own indignation and fury, whether directed at him or not, Falstaff will transform your dark affect into wit and laughter. If, like Hal, you come to Falstaff with ambivalence, now weighted to the negative side, Falstaff will evade you where he cannot convert you.

I don't believe that this makes Falstaff a pragmatist of economic exchange, as Lars Engle believes, when he says that Falstaff "is a figure not so much of freedom from value systems as of joyous participation in their in-evitably contingent and manipulable operation." You can exploit a value sys-tem, as Falstaff profits from the civil war, while seeing through and beyond it. The immortal Falstaff, never a hypocrite and rarely ambivalent, decidedly not a counterfeit like Hal, is essentially a satirist turned against all power, which means turned against all historicisms—explanations of history—rather than against history. A veteran warrior, now set against the chivalric code of honor, Falstaff knows that history is an ironic flux of reversals. Prince Hal refuses to learn this lesson from Falstaff, because as a mass of ambivalences toward everyone, including Falstaff, he cannot afford it.

Falstaff's energies are personal: his relative freedom is a dynamic one, which can be transferred to a pupil but at the cost of a dangerous distor-tion. Despite his current "materialist" critics, Falstaff declines to harvest his affections, but he certainly teaches Hal to harvest everyone: Hotspur, the King his father, and Falstaff himself. Hal is Falstaff's masterpiece: a student of genius who adopts his teacher's stance of freedom in order to exploit a universal ambivalence and turn it into a selective wit. Hal is totally am-bivalent toward everyone and everything—his wit is selective, while Fal-staff's is universal. Hotspur and King Henry IV are in Hal's way, but they do not menace him inwardly. Falstaff, once Hal is crowned, becomes a fig-ure to be dreaded, to be banished ten miles from the royal person. In the cruel speech of rejection, Henry V is at some trouble to ensure that Falstaff be given no opportunity for dialogue: "Reply not to me with a fool-born jest" (V. v.55). As "the tutor and the feeder of my riots" (V. v.62), poor Fal-staff is allowed no final evasions, and is essentially in receipt of a death sen-tence. Just as Shylock was ordered immediately to become a Christian, so Falstaff is enjoined to become "more wise and modest" (Prince John to the Lord Chief Justice), to undergo a severe diet, and presumably to get as close to God as Henry V now is. Squadrons of scholars, old-style and new, offer apologies for Henry V, while assuring us that Shakespeare realistically does not share our outrage: Order is in order, Henry V is an ideal monarch, the first authentic English king, the very model for Shakespeare's own po-litical ideal.

On the not unlikely grounds that Shakespeare himself was more

Falstaffian than Henrican, I join the now derided "humanist" critics—
including Dr. Johnson, Hazlitt, Swinburne, Bradley, and Goddard—in dismissing this idea of order as irrelevant nonsense. To reject Falstaff is to
reject Shakespeare. And to speak merely historically, the freedom Falstaff
represents is in the first case freedom from Christopher Marlowe, which
means that Falstaff is the signature of Shakespeare's originality, of his breakthrough into an art more nearly his own. Engle, speaking for most of his
historicizing contemporaries, tells us "that Shakespeare's work is subdued
to what it works in," but I wonder why the dyer's hand of tradition subdued
Shakespeare less than it did, say, Ben Jonson, let alone the several score
minor post-Marlovian dramatists. Falstaff, not a Marlovian, is quite
Chaucerian: he is the son of the vitalistic Wife of Bath. Marlowe, after an
initial inspiring effect, doubtless oppressed Shakespeare; Chaucer did not,
because Shakespeare's own genius for comedy came to him far more spon-
taneously than did an aptitude for tragedy.

2

Chronologically, *Henry IV, Part One*, comes directly after *The Merchant of
Venice*, yet the history and the comedy possess in common only a profound ambivalence, which may be Shakespeare's own, both toward himself and toward the young man and dark woman of the Sonnets. Hal's
ambivalence in regard to Falstaff, as every critic has seen, displaces the ambivalence provoked in him by his father, King Henry IV, from whom his
son already is in full flight at the close of *Richard II*. Shylock and Falstaff are
antithetical to each other: the Jew's bitter eloquence, life-denying and pu-
ritanical, is wholly other from the Falstaffian affirmation of a dynamic vitalism. And yet Shylock and Falstaff share an exuberance, negative in
Shylock, extravagantly positive in Falstaff. Both are anti-Marlovian emblems; their force is crucial to Shakespeare's invention of the human, of a
window onto reality.

Falstaff is anything but an elegiac figure; he would be fully present to
consciousness, if only we could summon up a consciousness in ourselves
to receive his. It is the comprehensiveness of Falstaff's consciousness that

puts him beyond us, not in Hamlet's way of transcendence but in Falstaff's way of immanence. Only a few characters in the world's literature can match the real presence of Falstaff, who in that regard is Hamlet's greatest rival in Shakespeare. Falstaff's presence is more than the presence of mind that Hazlitt praised in him. The illusion of being a real person—if you want to call it "illusion"—attends Falstaff as it does Hamlet. Yet somehow Shakespeare conveys to us that these two charismatics are *in* their plays, but not *of* them; Hamlet is a person, and Claudius and Ophelia are fictions—or Falstaff is a person, while Hal and Hotspur are fictions.

The Shakespearean charismatic has little in common with the sociological charismatic of Max Weber, but anticipates rather more Oscar Wilde's sense that comprehensiveness in consciousness is the sublime of value, when the representation of personality is at the center of one's concern. Shakespeare has other gorgeous triumphs—Rosalind, Iago, Cleopatra among them—but in circumference of consciousness, as I keep insisting, there are no rivals for Falstaff and Hamlet. The Edmund of *King Lear* perhaps is as intelligent as Falstaff and Hamlet, yet he is all but void of affect until he sustains his death wound, and so he must be judged as a negative charismatic in comparison with Sir John and the Prince of Denmark. Weber's sense of charisma, though derived from religion, has clear affinities with Carlyle's and Emerson's exaltation of heroic genius. Institution and routine, in Weber's vision, quickly absorb the effect of the charismatic individual on his followers. But Caesarism and Calvinism are not *aesthetic* movements; Falstaff and Hamlet scarcely can be routinized or institutionalized. Falstaff disdains any task or mission, and Hamlet cannot tolerate being the protagonist of a revenge tragedy. In both figures, charisma goes back beyond the model of Jesus to his ancestor King David, who uniquely held the blessing of Yahweh. Falstaff, though derided by virtuous scholars and rejected by the newly virtuous King Henry V, nevertheless retains the blessing, in its truest sense: more life.

Personality, even upon its deathbed, retains its unique value. I have known a number of intelligent philosophers and a vast multitude of poets, novelists, storytellers, playwrights. No one should expect them to talk as well as they write, yet even the best of them, on their best day, cannot equal those men made out of words, Falstaff and Hamlet. One wonders: Just how does the representation of cognition, in Shakespeare, differ from cognition itself? Pragmatically, can we tell the difference? One wonders again: Just how does the representation of charisma, in Shakespeare, differ from charisma itself? Charisma, by definition, is not a social energy; it originates outside society. Shakespeare's uniqueness, his greatest originality, can be described either as a charismatic cognition, which comes from an individual before it enters group thinking, or as a cognitive charisma, which cannot be routinized. The decisive theatrical experience of my life came half a century ago, in 1946, when I was sixteen, and watched Ralph Richardson play Falstaff. Even the bravura of Laurence Olivier, playing Hotspur in Part One, and Shallow in Part Two, could not divert me from the Richardsonian Falstaff. When he was off stage, then an absence in reality was felt by all the audience, and we waited, in helpless impatience, for Shakespeare to set Sir John before us again. W. H. Auden, commenting upon this phenomenon, rather oddly explained that Falstaff was "a comic symbol for the supernatural order of charity." Though I admire Auden's essays on Shakespeare, I am baffled by Auden's Christian Falstaff. The superb Sir John is neither Christ nor Satan, nor an imitation of either.

And yet a representation of secular immanence upon a stage, the most persuasive representation that we have, is going to tempt even the wisest critics into extravagant interpretations. I do not think that Shakespeare set out to show Falstaff as supremely immanent, or Hamlet as eminently transcendent. Ben Jonson composed ideograms and called them characters; at their best, as in Volpone and Sir Epicure Mammon, they are rammed with life, and yet they are not portrayals of persons. Though most current Shakespeare scholars in the Anglophonic academies refuse to confront Shakespeare's peopling of a world, that remains his appeal to almost all who attend performances of the plays, or who continue to read them. And while it is true that Shakespeare's persons are only images or complex metaphors, our pleasure in Shakespeare primarily comes from the persuasive illusion that these shadows are cast by entities as substantial as ourselves. Shakespeare's powers of persuading us of this magnificent illusion all stem from his astonishing ability to represent change, an ability un-

matched in the world's literature. Our own personalities may well reduce
to a flux of sensations, but that concourse of impressions requires presentation in detailed vividness if any one of us is to be distinguished from any
other. A Ben Jonson version of Falstaff would indeed be only a "trunk of humours," as Hal angrily terms Sir John when the prince acts the part of his
father in the skit of Act II, Scene iv, *Henry IV, Part One*. Not even Volpone,
greatest of Jonson's characters, undergoes significant change, but Falstaff,
like Hamlet, is always transforming himself, always thinking, speaking,
and overhearing himself in a quicksilver metamorphosis, always willing the
change and suffering the change that is Shakespeare's tribute to the reality of our lives.

Algernon Charles Swinburne, now mostly forgotten as both poet and
critic, yet frequently superb as both, adroitly compared Falstaff to his true
companions, the Sancho Panza of Cervantes and the Panurge of Rabelais.
He awarded the palm to Falstaff, not just for his massive intellect but for
his range of feeling and indeed even for his "possible moral elevation."
Swinburne meant a morality of the heart, and of the imagination, rather
than the social morality that is the permanent curse of Shakespearean
scholarship and criticism, afflicting historicists old and new, and Puritans
sacred and secular. Here Swinburne anticipated A. C. Bradley, who rightly
remarked that all adverse moral judgments upon Falstaff are antithetical to
the nature of Shakespearean comedy. One can add Chaucer's Wife of Bath
to form a foursome of great vitalists, all bearing the Blessing—which means
"more life"—and all impressing us as superb comedians. Shakespeare's
abandonment of judgment to his audience allows Falstaff to be even more
unsponsored and free than Sancho, Panurge, and the Wife. The will to live,
immense in all four, has a particular poignance in Sir John, a professional
soldier long since turned against the nonsense of military "glory" and
"honor." We have no reason to believe that Shakespeare set any supposed
societal good over an individual good, and considerable reason—based on
the plays and the Sonnets—to believe something close to the opposite.
After a lifetime surrounded by other professors, I question their experiential qualifications to apprehend, let alone judge, the Immortal Falstaff.
The late Anthony Burgess, who gave us a splendid, rather Joycean version

of Falstaff in his wastrel poet, Enderby, also gave us critical wisdom on Falstaff:

> The Falstaffian spirit is a great sustainer of civilization. It disappears when the state is too powerful and when people worry too much about their souls. . . . There is little of Falstaff's substance in the world now, and, as the power of the state expands, what is left will be liquidated.

The power of the state will be personified by King Henry V, whose attitude toward Falstaff differs scarcely a jot from that of academic puritans and professorial power freaks. Falstaff's irreverence is life-enhancing but state-destroying; it strains pragmatic sense to believe that Shakespeare shared the Henrican attitude toward Falstaff. To say that Shakespeare is also Hotspur, or Hal, or King Henry IV, is of little interest: he then also would be Romeo, Juliet, Mercutio, and the Nurse, and many hundreds of others. Falstaff, like and unlike Hamlet, has another kind of relation to his playwright. The instant popularity of Sir John with Shakespeare's audience prompted first *The Merry Wives of Windsor,* and next *Henry IV, Part Two.* Falstaff's death scene, brilliantly recounted by the Hostess in *Henry V,* testifies both to Shakespeare's inability to let the great wit's story go unfinished, and to the dramatist's shrewd awareness that the heroic posturings at Agincourt could not withstand a Falstaffian commentary, a counterchorus that would have sunk the play, however gloriously.

When Falstaff captured Queen Elizabeth and everyone else in Shakespeare's public, whatever had been the playwright's relation to his exorbitant comic character had to change. I hear a certain anxiety in *The Merry Wives of Windsor,* where Falstaff is travestied, and a struggle in *Henry IV, Part Two,* where Shakespeare seems, at moments, vexed as to whether to extend Falstaff's splendor or to darken it. Scholars can write what they will, but a diminished Falstaff is their creation, not Shakespeare's. Falstaff's festival of language cannot be reduced or melted down. Mind in the largest sense, more even than wit, is Falstaff's greatest power; who can settle which is the more intelligent consciousness, Hamlet's or Falstaff's? For all its comprehensiveness, Shakespearean drama is ultimately a theater of mind, and what matters most about Falstaff is his vitalization of the intellect, in direct contrast to Hamlet's conversion of the mind to the vision of annihilation.

I have suffered through recent performances of the *Henry IV* plays that debased Falstaff into a cowardly braggart, a sly instigator to vice, a fawner for the Prince's favor, a besotted old scoundrel, and much more of that sort of desecration of Shakespeare's actual text. The proper response is to give a brief cento of Sir John's own utterances:

O, thou hast damnable iteration, and art indeed able to corrupt a saint: thou hast done much harm upon me, Hal, God forgive thee for it: before I knew thee, Hal, I knew nothing, and now am I, if a man should speak truly, little better than one of the wicked.

But to say I know more harm in him than in myself were to say more than I know. That he is old, the more the pity, his white hairs do witness it, but that he is, saving your reverence, a whoremaster, that I utterly deny. If sack and sugar be a fault, God help the wicked! If to be old and merry be a sin, then many an old host that I know is damned: if to be fat be to be hated, then Pharaoh's lean kine are to be loved. No, my good lord; banish Peto, banish Bardolph, ban-ish Poins—but for sweet Jack Falstaff, kind Jack Falstaff, true Jack Falstaff, valiant Jack Falstaff, and therefore more valiant, being as he is old Jack Falstaff, banish not him thy Harry's company, banish not him thy Harry's company, banish plump Jack, and banish all the world.

Well, if Percy be alive, I'll pierce him. If he do come in my way, so: if he do not, if I come in his willingly, let him make a carbonado of me. I like not such grinning honour as Sir Walter hath. Give me life, which if I can save, so: if not, honour comes unlooked for, and there's an end.

Embowelled? If thou embowel me today, I'll give you leave to pow-der me and eat me too tomorrow. 'Sblood, 'twas time to counterfeit, or that hot termagant Scot had paid me, scot and lot too. Counterfeit? I lie, I am no counterfeit: to die is to be a counterfeit, for he is but the counterfeit of a man, who hath not the life of a man: but to counterfeit dying, when a man thereby liveth, is to be no counterfeit, but the true and perfect image of life indeed.

Call these four extracts Sir John Falstaff on popular piety, personal wickedness, military honor, and the blessing of life itself. I hear a great wit, but also an authentic sage, destroying illusions. I do not hear mere *knowingness*, which is the professional disease of resentful academic clerks, who see Falstaff, like themselves, as questing for room at the top. Sir John is anything but a lovable old darling; he personally is bad news, rather in the mode of certain great poets who were not exactly wholesome and productive citizens: Villon, Marlowe, Rimbaud among them. You wouldn't want to dine with any of them, or pick pockets with Villon, spy with Marlowe, work at gun running with Rimbaud, or go highway robbing with Falstaff. But like those reprobate poets, Sir John has genius, more of Shakespeare's own genius than any other character save Hamlet. As for exercising moral disapproval upon Falstaff—why, who is there in the Henriad whom we could prefer to Fat Jack? Henry IV, hypocrite and usurper, is not an option, nor is Hal/Henry V, hypocrite and brutal soldier, slaughterer of prisoners and of his old companion Bardolph. Are we to prefer Hotspur's "die all, die merrily" to Falstaff's "Give me life"? Is Falstaff morally inferior to the treacherous Prince John? There is, of course, the Lord Chief Justice, if you have a strong taste for law enforcement as such. Shakespeare, and his contemporary audience, got Falstaff right; it is much of the scholarly tradition that goes on getting Falstaff wrong. The Wife of Bath, Falstaff's literary mother, divides critics pretty much the way that Falstaff does. One wouldn't want to marry the Wife of Bath, or carouse with Falstaff, but if you crave vitalism and vitality, then you turn to the Wife of Bath, Panurge (in Rabelais), Sancho Panza (in Cervantes), but most of all to Sir John Falstaff, the true and perfect image of life itself.

Graham Bradshaw argues for a much more limited Falstaff, on the curious grounds that Falstaff speaks only in prose, like Thersites in *Troilus and Cressida*. But Shakespeare is not composing opera, and I do not think we as

yet know whether there were, for him, crucial intentions that accompany
a choice between prose or verse. Here is Bradshaw's contention:

> Like Iago, Falstaff prides himself on truth-telling but speaks a lan-
> guage in which it is only possible to tell some kinds of truth. His
> language speaks him, and its limited registers are placed within the
> incomparably large range of registers within the play as a whole (or
> two wholes: that issue need not distract us here). Our correspond-
> ing sense that various human potentialities and aspirations are en-
> tirely beyond Falstaff's range has important consequences. It should
> ensure that our delighted response to Falstaff's wonderful catechism
> on Honour commits us no further than Gloster's response to Edgar's
> 'Ripeness is all': 'And *that's* true *too*,' says Gloster.

The comparison to Iago is surprising in the astute Bradshaw, who is momentarily too invested in his prose/poetry hypothesis to remember that
Falstaff betrays and harms no one, and does not write with the lives of the
other characters, as Iago always does. The contrasts between the humane
wit of Fat Jack and the murderous ironies of Iago are almost too palpable
to be mentioned. But Bradshaw's true sin is elsewhere, in his quest to find
a middle path between Falstaffian celebrants and statist moralists. Who is
Bradshaw (or any other among us) to judge that "various human potentialities and aspirations are entirely beyond Falstaff's range," *because he speaks
prose,* and the best prose at that in any modern language? What are those
aspirations and potentialities?

They turn out to be what Hal/Henry V, King Henry IV, Prince John,
and Hotspur and company are all about: power, usurpation, rule, grand ex-
tortion, treachery, violence, hypocrisy, fake piety, the murder of prisoners
and of those who surrender under truce. For Bradshaw, all these come
under the category of Honor, to which Falstaff-Shakespeare responds: "I
like not such grinning honour as [the dead!] Sir Walter hath. Give me life,
which if I can save, so: if not, honour comes unlooked for, and there's an
end." Do we hear wider ranges of human aspirations and potentialities in
this, or in Hal's threat to Hotspur:

And all the budding honours on thy crest
I'll crop to make a garland for my head.

That is royal verse (and royal rant), but can anyone of sensibility prefer it to Falstaff's "Give me life"? Hal wins: He kills Hotspur, becomes Henry V, rejects Falstaff, conquers France, and dies young (in history, not on Shakespeare's stage), whereas Falstaff breaks, dies sadly (but to the astonishing music of Mistress Quickly's prose), resurrects perpetually in his own immortal prose, and haunts us ever since, as one of Shelley's "forms more real than living man." Shakespeare goes neither with the great wits nor with the big battalions, but we hardly can forget that he himself was the greatest of wits, a shrewd and peaceful scribbler, who perhaps sat quietly in the tavern and listened to Ben Jonson's truthful boasts that the author of *Volpone* had killed his man in single combat between, and in the sight of, two warring armies. Sir John, a battered old soldier, wanders about Shrewsbury battlefield with a bottle of sack in his holster, intending neither to kill nor to be killed, though he boldly takes his chances with his ragged recruits ("I have *led* my ragamuffins where they are peppered"). Shakespeare himself is neither an upholder of order nor a lord of disorder. I do not know why Shylock sometimes speaks verse and sometimes prose, but I don't *want* Sir John Falstaff to speak verse. The Falstaffian prose is suppler and ampler than Prince Hal's verse, and far more of the vast range of human potentiality is contained in it than in Hal's formulations.

3

Samuel Butler, Victorian novelist and independent thinker, observed in a notebook jotting that "the great characters live as truly as the memory of dead men. For the life after death, it is not necessary that a man or woman have lived." Falstaff—like Hamlet, Don Quixote, and Mr. Pickwick—is still alive because Shakespeare knew something like the Gnostic secret of resurrection, which is that Jesus first arose and *then* he died. Shakespeare shows Falstaff rising from the dead, and only later has Mrs. Quickly narrate the death of Sir John. The critic John Bayley wisely remarks that "character is what other people have, 'consciousness' is ourselves," but his

observation pertains more to life than to literature, since the miracle of
Hamlet and of Falstaff is that they manifest a consciousness that is and is
not "ourselves." The understanding of Falstaff must begin not necessarily
with affection for him, but with an acute apprehension of the nature and
extent of his consciousness. Immanent Falstaff and transcendent Hamlet
are the two largest representations of consciousness in Shakespeare, and indeed in all of literature. Consciousness must be consciousness of something; in Hamlet of all things in heaven or earth. Moralists and historicists
(two names for the same persons) see Falstaff's consciousness as being
rather more confined: food, drink, sex, power, money. We cannot know
whether Shakespeare was more Falstaff or Hamlet, though the formidable
E.A.J. Honigmann shakes me by arguing for Hamlet. Yet while dramatic
irony sometimes victimizes Hamlet, and we are allowed to see him as he
cannot see himself, Falstaff, like Rosalind, gazes in all directions, and beholds himself with a seriocomic self-acceptance that Hamlet is not allowed. Honigmann warns us that the Falstaff–Hal relationship does not
yield to psychological analysis. Not completely perhaps, but well enough.
Its paradigm for Shakespeare, by general consent, is his relationship to the
young nobleman of the Sonnets, whether Southampton or Pembroke. To
say that Shakespeare is Falstaff plainly is absurd; it was not a part he could
play, even on the stage. You can brood upon Shakespeare-as-Antonio in
The Merchant of Venice, should you want to; he probably acted the role, well
aware of all its implications. Yet both Falstaff's vivacity and his darkening
reaction to Hal's ambivalences have some connections to the Sonnets.
And it cannot be affirmed too often that Falstaff's most salient qualities are
his astonishing intellect and his exuberant vitality, the second probably not
so outward a personal endowment of the man William Shakespeare.

Shakespeare has Hal kill Hotspur at the close of Henry IV, Part One, but
Douglas fails to slay Falstaff. Consider how we would react if the "hot termagant Scot" indeed had carved up Sir John. We wince, and not just because we wish to preserve Part Two. The Epilogue to Part Two promises
that Falstaff will appear in what became Henry V, a pledge Shakespeare
thought better than to keep, though is there anything better in that play
than Mrs. Quickly's sketch of Falstaff's death scene? What would happen
to Sir John if he had appeared in Henry V? Would he be hanged, like poor

Bardolph, or beaten up like the wretched Pistol? Whatever the aesthetic virtues of *Henry V* may or may not be, it does not play itself out in the Theater of Mind, as do both parts of *Henry IV*. If you are greatly concerned with the history and theory of Renaissance kingship, then *Henry V* has a strong cognitive interest. But common readers and playgoers tend not to be spurred to deep thought by the Battle of Agincourt, its foregrounds and aftermath. King Henry V broods on the burdens of monarchy, and on the obligations of subjects, but most among us do not. Falstaff, to most scholars, is the emblem of self-indulgence, but to most playgoers and readers Sir John is the representative of imaginative freedom, of a liberty set against time, death, and the state, which is a condition that we crave for ourselves. Add a fourth freedom to timelessness, the blessing of more life, and the evasion of the state, and call it freedom from censoriousness, from the superego, from guilt. I hesitate to select any single power out of Shakespeare's infinite variety of powers as being foremost, but sometimes I would vote that eminence to confidence in his audience. You define who you are by your reaction to Falstaff, or to his younger sister, Cleopatra, even as Chaucer had you define yourself by your judgment of (or refusal to judge) the Wife of Bath. Those who do not care for Falstaff are in love with time, death, the state, and the censor. They have their reward. I prefer to love Falstaff, the image of freedom's wit, and the language of wit's freedom. There is a middle way, of being dispassionate about Falstaff, but it vanishes if you attend a good performance of the *Henry IV* plays. W. H. Auden caught this with great vividness:

> At a performance, my immediate reaction is to wonder what Falstaff is doing in this play at all. . . . As the play proceeds, our surprise is replaced by another kind of puzzle, for the better we come to know Falstaff, the clearer it becomes that the world of historical reality which a Chronicle Play claims to imitate is not a world which he can inhabit.

One can agree with this, and still dissent when Auden insists that the only world appropriate for Falstaff is Verdi's opera. Auden also, rather oddly, calls Falstaff a troll, in the Ibsenite sense of *Peer Gynt*, but that is an error. Trolls are daemonic, yet are more animal than human, and Falstaff dies a martyr to human love, to his unrequited affection for his displaced son, Prince Hal. Again, if you dislike Falstaff, you can dismiss this love as grotesque or as self-serving, but then you may as well dismiss the *Henry IV* plays. I hardly am determined to vindicate Falstaff, but to Shakespeare, clearly, the poet's own love for the young nobleman in the Sonnets was anything but grotesque or self-serving, and it does seem to be the paradigm for the Falstaff–Hal relationship. The personality of Shakespeare remains an enigma; some contemporaries thought him warm and open, though a touch ruthless in his financial dealings. Some, however, found him withdrawn, even a little cold. Perhaps he went from one kind of person to another, in his quarter century of a career. Shakespeare certainly never acted Falstaff upon a stage, any more than he acted Hamlet. Perhaps he played King Henry IV, or one of the older rebels. But his full exuberance of language, his festival self, is as present in Falstaff's prose as in Hamlet's verse. If you love language, then you love Falstaff, and Shakespeare palpably loved language. Falstaff's resourcefulness gathers together the florabundance of *Love's Labour's Lost* with the more aggressive verbal energies of Faulconbridge the Bastard and the negative exuberance of Shylock. After Falstaff's prose, Shakespeare was ready for Hamlet's prose, which rivals the Prince of Denmark's verse.

There are fewer than a double handful (at most) of Shakespearean characters who are truly endless to meditation: Falstaff, Rosalind, Hamlet, Iago, Lear, Edgar, Edmund, Macbeth, Cleopatra. A considerable portrait gallery of the others is not quite that profound and problematical: the Bastard Faulconbridge, Richard II, Juliet, Bottom, Portia, Shylock, Prince Hal/ Henry V, Brutus, Malvolio, Helena, Parolles, Isabella, Othello, Desdemona, Lear's Fool, Lady Macbeth, Antony, Coriolanus, Timon, Imogen, Leontes, Prospero, Caliban. These are two dozen great roles, but you cannot say of any of them what Milton's Satan says of himself, that "in every deep a lower deep opens." The great villains—Iago, Edmund, Macbeth— invent Western nihilism, and each is an abyss in himself. Lear and his godson Edgar are studies so profound in human torment and endurance that they carry biblical resonances in a pre-Christian, pagan play. But Falstaff, Rosalind, Hamlet, and Cleopatra are something apart in world literature: through them Shakespeare essentially invented human personality as we continue to know and value it. Falstaff has priority in this invention; not to appreciate his personal largeness, which surpasses even his sublime girth, would be to miss the greatest of Shakespearean originalities: the invention of the human.

How far back should we take our apprehension of Falstaff? Inference, as first practiced by Maurice Morgann in the eighteenth century, and refined by A. D. Nuttall in our era, is the mode offered us by Shakespeare himself. One of the neglected aspects of *Henry IV, Part Two*, is its subtle reach back to Falstaff's earlier years. It cannot be said that Shakespeare provides all the information we might hope for concerning the life and death of Sir John Falstaff, but we certainly are given more than enough to help us appreciate Falstaff's enormous personality. Shakespeare is no more a field anthropologist than his Prince Hal is: the Falstaffiad is intricately interwoven with the Henriad, each as the stuff of saga. What Shakespeare challenges us to imagine is left almost clueless by him: How did Hal and Falstaff enter upon their original friendship?

I am aware that partisans of supposed common sense will find my question mostly an irritant. But I am in no danger of believing that Sir John was a flesh-and-blood creature, merely as real as you and I. Falstaff would hardly matter if he did not greatly exceed all of us in vitality, exuberance, and wit. That is why Nuttall, mildly disputing Maurice Morgann, is so precise in his dissent:

> The objection to Morgann's speculations is not that Falstaff has no previous life but that Shakespeare does not give us enough clues to render Morgann's more detailed inferences probable.

The proper issue, then, is to judge just how many and how extensive the clues are, while accepting (as Nuttall wisely does), Morgann's notion of latent meaning, the Shakespearean play's undersong:

If the characters of Shakespeare are thus *whole*, and as it were original, whilst those of almost all other writers are mere imitation, it
may be fit to consider them rather as Historic than Dramatic beings;
and when occasion requires, to account for their conduct from the
*whole* of character, from general principles, from latent motives, and
from policies not avowed.

Morgann is calling for an *experiential* criticism of Shakespeare, which alas
is light-years away from nearly all current interpretation of Shakespeare.
Leo Salingar, who joins Nuttall as one of Morgann's few recent defenders,
nevertheless pursues Shakespeare's hints to discover a darker Falstaff than
Morgann, Hazlitt, and A. C. Bradley gave us. Though Salingar suggests
that critical agreement on Falstaff (and on Hal's rejection of him) is not
possible, I want to sketch as comprehensive a view of the Falstaff–Hal relationship as Shakespeare allows us to infer, from the origins of so unlikely
a friendship, on to the expulsion of Sir John from the righteously offended
royal presence. That returns me to my question: how might we give a
Shakespearean description of Prince Hal's initial choice of Falstaff as wayward mentor, as the alternative to Hal's mere repetition of his own usurping father?

When Hal's disaffection from Henry IV is first noted by Shakespeare,
in Act V, Scene iii, of *Richard II*, Falstaff is unmentioned. Presumably, he is
one of Hal's "unrestrained loose companions," highwaymen and tavern
denizens. Since King Richard II has not yet been murdered, Hal's flight
from his father can have reference only to evading the guilt of usurpation,
and not the still greater guilt of regicide. Still, what Hal flees from must be
his father's drive to power, an impulse the prince more than shares, so that
Hal represses his own ambitions—or is he merely postponing them, a
rather more conscious process? Shakespeare gives us more than enough evidence to suggest that part of Hal is a colder hypocrite than even his father Bolingbroke is and was. Yet another part of him is (or becomes)
Falstaffian, in the deepest sense of the Falstaffian: a genius for language and
its rhetorical control of others through psychological insight.

Falstaff is an outrageous version of Socrates, but then Socrates outraged his contemporaries to the point of provoking them to execute him. There is a link between Shakespeare's Falstaff and Montaigne's Socrates, a connection that may be a direct influence, since Shakespeare probably had access to John Florio's translation of Montaigne while it was still in manuscript. Scholars have recognized that Mistress Quickly's account of Falstaff's death, in *Henry V*, clearly alludes to Plato's story of the death of Socrates, in the *Phaedo*. Montaigne's Socrates resembles aspects of Falstaff in more than his death, and it may be that Prince Hal has a touch of Alcibiades in him, though hardly of Shakespeare's later Alcibiades as he appears in *Timon of Athens*. One can object that Falstaff teaches wit rather than wisdom, as Socrates did, but then Falstaff's wit is raffishly wise, and Socrates is so frequently witty.

Despite Hal's obsessive accusations of cowardice, I will vindicate Maurice Morgann's defense of Falstaff's courage, a pragmatic courage that scorns the pretenses of chivalric "honor," of the Hotspur variety. Falstaff's sensible courage resembles that of Socrates, who knew how to retreat intrepidly. Like Socrates, Falstaff will fight only so long as he sees reason, as Poins acknowledges to Hal.

The most authentic parallel between Falstaff and Montaigne's Socrates is in their shared contrast of outer deformity and inner genius. Socrates, Montaigne's hero throughout many of the *Essays*, is particularly lauded in the two final essays, "Of Physiognomy" and "Of Experience." We are reasonably certain that Shakespeare read "Of Physiognomy," because Hamlet almost certainly echoes it, while "Of Experience" is Montaigne's masterpiece and is profoundly Shakespearean in spirit. The ugliness of Socrates is the vessel that contains wisdom and knowledge, even as the grotesque Falstaff exceeds every Shakespearean character except Hamlet as an intellect.

Montaigne's Socrates is both skeptical and affirmative, questioning everything, while remaining positive in his values. Falstaff is both a superb ironist, like Hamlet, and a great vitalist, as that master of negations, Hamlet, might have been, except for the Ghost's intervention. In "Of Experience," Montaigne says he has a vocabulary, all his own, and so do Socrates and Falstaff, overwhelmingly. All three—Montaigne, Socrates, Falstaff—

are great educators, little as scholars credit Falstaff in this regard. What the three teach is the great lesson of experience, the perfection and virtual divinity of knowing how to enjoy our being rightfully.

One can surmise, then, that Hal first came to Falstaff as Alcibiades and so many other young men (Plato included) first came to Socrates: the disreputable sage was the authentic teacher of wisdom. But of Hal's earlier phase, or phases, in Falstaff's company, we know almost nothing. When we first see the two on stage together, Hal is on the attack, ambivalence toward Falstaff dominating every utterance he directs at him. Sir John parries nimbly, yet he must begin to recognize, as the audience does, that the prince's ambivalence has turned murderous. But such a turn argues implicitly for a prior relationship of great closeness and importance between the prince and the fat knight. Only Falstaff has maintained the positive affection of the earlier relationship, and yet why does Hal continue to seek Falstaff out? Evidently, the prince needs both to convict Falstaff of cowardice and to show himself that rhetorically he can not only hold his own against his teacher of wit but overgo Falstaff as well, bettering his instruction.

William Empson wrote brilliantly about a Falstaff not wholly different from the one I follow Morgann, Hazlitt, Bradley, and Goddard in reading. Empson's Falstaff is "a scandalous gentleman," descended among the lower orders:

> Falstaff is the first major joke by the English against their class system; he is a picture of how badly you can behave, and still get away with it, if you are a gentleman—a mere common rogue would not have been nearly so funny.

That seems to me a little reductive, yet behind it is Empson's sensible conviction that Falstaff's relation to Hal may well be influenced by Shakespeare's playing the role of Socrates to the Earl of Southampton's (or another nobleman's) Alcibiades, at least in the story intimated by the Sonnets. Shakespeare, we know, badly wished to restore his family's status as gentlemen, and was fiercely satirized by Ben Jonson for securing a coat of arms, with its motto, "Not without right," which became "Not without mustard" in Jonson's *Every Man Out of His Humor* (1599). But to center upon Falstaff as an exemplification of Shakespeare's class consciousness, while clearly not wrong, is ultimately inadequate. Empson's Falstaff is something of a patriotic Machiavel, and thus a fit teacher for the future Henry V. Going interestingly further, Empson sees Falstaff as a potential mob leader—charismatic, unscrupulous, and able to sway people lower in the social order than himself. Does that not wholly decenter the magnificent Falstaff?

Critics regularly have called Sir John one of the lords of language, which beggars him: he is the veritable monarch of language, unmatched whether elsewhere in Shakespeare or in all of Western literature. His superbly supple and copious prose is astonishingly attractive: Samuel Johnson and Oscar Wilde's Lady Bracknell (in *The Importance of Being Earnest*) alike are legatees of Falstaff's amazing resourcefulness of speech. What can a great teacher possess except high intellect and the language appropriate to it? Fluellen in *Henry V* happily compares his hero-king to Alexander the Great, pointing out that the former Prince Hal "turned away the fat knight with the great-belly doublet—he was full of jests, and gipes, and knaveries, and mocks" even as Alexander murdered his best friend, Cleitus. One feels that Fluellen did not get that right; Falstaff is no Cleitus, but as much Prince Hal's tutor as Aristotle was Alexander's. The implicit comparison to Aristotle is outrageous, yet it is Shakespeare's, not mine. What is the difference between Henry IV and Henry V? Falstaff, because the fat knight so "full of jests, and gipes, and knaveries, and mocks" taught the son how to transcend the usurping and joyless father without rejecting him. That is not exactly what Falstaff attempted to teach Hal, one can sensibly insist, but Hal (much as I dislike him) is almost as much a student of genius as Falstaff is a teacher of genius. Henry V is an authentic charismatic, who has learned the uses of charisma from his disreputable but endlessly gifted teacher. It is one of Shakespeare's harshest dramatic ironies that Falstaff prepares his own destruction not only by teaching too well but by loving much too well. Henry V is no man's teacher and loves no one; he is a great leader and exploiter of power, and destroying Falstaff causes him not an iota of regret.

The rejection of Falstaff possibly is a deep echo of Shakespeare's own sense of betrayal by the young nobleman of the Sonnets, except that Shakespeare manifests extraordinary ambivalence toward himself in the Sonnets, while Falstaff's almost innocent self-love is part of the secret of the fat knight's genius. Like his admirer Oscar Wilde, Sir John was always right, except in blinding himself to Hal's hypocrisy, just as the sublime Oscar was wrong only about Lord Alfred Douglas, poetaster and narcissist. Just before the battle of Shrewsbury, Falstaff, most probably the oldest and certainly the fattest soldier about to risk death, sensibly and rather movingly says, "I would 'twere bed-time, Hal, and all well." The prince grimly retorts, "Why, thou owest God a death," and exits, with the pun of "death" and "debt" (in Elizabethan pronunciation) still reverberating. I can still hear Ralph Richardson as Falstaff responding to the warlike Hal's nasty pun:

> 'Tis not due yet: I would be loath to pay him before his day—what need I be so forward with him that calls not on me? Well, 'tis no matter, honour pricks me on. Yea, but how if honour prick me off when I come on, how then? Can honour set to a leg? No. Or an arm? No. Or take away the grief of a wound? No. Honour hath no skill in surgery then? No. What is honour? A word. What is in that word honour? What is that honour? Air. A trim reckoning! Who hath it? He that died a-Wednesday. Doth he feel it? No. Doth he hear it? No. 'Tis insensible, then? Yea, to the dead. But will it not live with the living? No. Why? Detraction will not suffer it. Therefore I'll none of it. Honour is a mere scutcheon—and so ends my catechism.
>
> [V.i.127–41]

Can there be an audience that will not learn from this, in a society still given to military fantasies? Are there any societies not so given, past or present? Falstaff, like his reluctantly charmed admirer, Dr. Samuel Johnson, urges us to clear our minds of cant, and Falstaff is even freer of societal delusions than was the Grand Cham, Johnson. Shakespeare, we can surmise from his life as well as from his work, had a horror of violence, including the organized violence of warfare. *Henry V* hardly exalts battle; its ironies are subtle but palpable. "Honor" is the sphere of Hotspur, and of the Hal who slays Hotspur and thus usurps the throne of this "Air. A trim reckoning!" Going to the battle, Hotspur cries out, "Doomsday is near; die all, die merrily," while Falstaff, on the battlefield, says, "Give me life."

Shakespeare gave Sir John such abundant life that even Shakespeare had a very hard (and reluctant) time in ending Falstaff, who never owed Shakespeare a death. The debt (as Shakespeare knew) was to Falstaff, both for finally emancipating him from Marlowe, and for making him the most successful of Elizabethan dramatists, thus dwarfing Marlowe, Kyd, and all other rivals, Ben Jonson included. Ralph Richardson, exactly half a century ago, implicitly understood that Falstaff had absolute presence of mind, and could triumph over every challenger, until the terrible rejection by Hal. At sixty-seven, I again remember vividly my reactions as a boy of sixteen, educated by Richardson's Falstaff to a first understanding of Shakespeare. What Richardson played was the essence of playing, in every sense of playing, and his Falstaff (whether he knew it or not) was the Falstaff of A. C. Bradley, now absurdly deprecated but still the best English critic of Shakespeare since William Hazlitt:

> The bliss of freedom gained in humour is the essence of Falstaff. His humour is not directed only or chiefly against obvious absurdities; he is the enemy of everything that would interfere with his ease, and therefore of anything serious, and especially of everything respectable and moral. For these things impose limits and obligations, and make us the subjects of old father antic the law, and the categorical imperative, and our station and its duties, and conscience, and reputation, and other people's opinions, and all sorts of nuisances. I say he is therefore their enemy; but I do him wrong; to say that he is their enemy implies that he regards them as serious and recognises their power, when in truth he refuses to recognise them at all. They are to him absurd; and to reduce a thing ad absurdum is to reduce it to nothing and to walk about free and rejoicing. This

is what Falstaff does with all the would-be serious things of life, sometimes only by his words, sometimes by his actions too. He will make truth appear absurd by solemn statements, which he utters with perfect gravity and which he expects nobody to believe; and honour, by demonstrating that it cannot set a leg, and that neither the living nor the dead can possess it; and law, by evading all the attacks of its highest representative and almost forcing him to laugh at his own defeat; and patriotism, by filling his pockets with the bribes offered by competent soldiers who want to escape service, while he takes in their stead the halt and maimed and gaolbirds; and duty, by showing how he labours in his vocation— of thieving; and courage, alike by mocking at his own capture of Colevile and gravely claiming to have killed Hotspur; and war, by offering the Prince his bottle of sack when he is asked for a sword; and religion, by amusing himself with remorse at odd times when he has nothing else to do; and the fear of death, by maintaining perfectly untouched, in the face of imminent peril and even while he feels the fear of death, the very same power of dissolving it in persiflage that he shows when he sits at ease in his inn. These are the wonderful achievements which he performs, not with the sourness of a cynic, but with the gaiety of a boy. And therefore, we praise him, we laud him, for he offends none but the virtuous, and denies that life is real or life is earnest, and delivers us from the oppression of such nightmares, and lifts us into the atmosphere of perfect freedom.

I remember first reading this grand paragraph by Bradley a few months after seeing Richardson as Falstaff, and my shock of pleasure at recognizing how well the interpretations of this critic and this actor confirmed each other. Bradley's Falstaff is not sentimentalized; the critic knows full well that he would literally not be safe in Falstaff's company. But he knows also that Falstaff teaches us *not to moralize.* Hal's belated espousal of courage and honor is one kind of moralizing, and the Lord Chief Justice's is another; Falstaff wants childlike (not childish) play, which exists in another order than that of morality. As Bradley says, Falstaff simply refuses to recognize the social institutions of reality; he is neither immoral nor amoral but of another realm, the order of play. Hal entered that order as Falstaff's disciple, and sojourned there rather longer than he may have intended. Despite his presumably long-gathering ambivalence toward Falstaff, Hal struggles all through *Henry IV, Part One*, against the fascination exercised by the great wit. It seems just to observe that Falstaff charms the tough and resistant prince for many of the same reasons that Falstaff, properly played, dominates any audience.

4

Antithetical forces seem to drive Shakespeare's characterization of Falstaff in Part Two, if only to prepare us for Hal's climactic rejection. Still triumphant over the Lord Chief Justice and Prince John, the law and the state, Falstaff remains nimble at bidding the world of "honour" pass. Hal is the spokesperson for so-called honor's indictment of Falstaff, and he performs the rule with an exuberance learned from the teacher, though all the accusations fall flat. The sublime Falstaff simply is not a coward, a court jester or fool, a confidence man, a bawd, another politician, an opportunistic courtier, an alcoholic seducer of the young. Falstaff, as I remarked earlier, is the Elizabethan Socrates, and in the wit combat with Hal, the prince is a mere sophist, bound to lose. Falstaff, like Socrates, is wisdom, wit, self-knowledge, mastery of reality. Socrates too seemed disreputable to the powermongers of Athens, who finally condemned him to death. Hal, who plays with the possibility of hanging Falstaff, doubtless would have executed his mentor at Agincourt if the antics performed at Shrewsbury had been repeated there. Instead, Bardolph swings as the master's surrogate, and Sir John, heartbroken into acceptance of his old age, dies offstage to Mistress Quickly's loving, cockney elegy.

I wish that Shakespeare had put Socrates on stage in *Timon of Athens*, in company with Alcibiades, so as to give us an after-image of the Hal-Falstaff relationship. Perhaps Shakespeare felt that his Falstaff made Montaigne's Socrates redundant. Falstaff or Socrates? That may sound outrageous, since the two great challengers of moral values practiced very different styles: Socrates' dialectic, and Falstaff's perpetual reinvention of language. Socrates teases you into truth; Falstaff the parodist inundates you with wordplay. Those who detest Falstaff, in and out of his plays, insist that the fat knight drowns himself in his tidal wave of language. "The question is which is to be master?" Humpty Dumpty says to Alice, after that imitation Falstaff has boasted: "When I use a word it means just what I choose it to mean." Falstaff finishes at the head of Humpty Dumpty's class. Sir John is the master, as Hamlet and Rosalind are also masters. The witty knight is hardly the prisoner of his phonemes. Shakespeare gives Falstaff one of his own greatest gifts: the florabundant language of Shakespeare's own youth, not a style of old age.

For Hal, more than ironically, Falstaff is "the latter spring . . . all-hallown summer," ageless in his exuberance. Descending as a highwayman against travelers, Falstaff chants, "Ah, whoreson caterpillars, bacon-fed knaves, they hate us youth!" "What, ye knaves!" he adds, "young men must live." Outrageously parodistic, Falstaff mocks his own years, and persuasively continues a military career (when he has to) that he both scorns and indulges, primarily as *materia poetica* for further mockery, by others as by himself. "We must all to the wars," Hal tells his Eastcheap roisterers, and plans fresh exploits for Falstaff: "I'll procure this fat rogue a charge of foot, and I know his death will be a march of twelve score." Informed by the prince, Falstaff will not cease jesting: "Well God be thanked for these rebels, they offend none but the virtuous: I laud them, I praise them." "Rebellion lay in his way, and he found it" is the Falstaffian formula for civil war. Since Hal's kingdom (and his life) is at stake, the prince's growl of: "Peace, chewet, peace," is hardly excessive. Falstaff has outlived his function for a prince who means to conquer "honour," England, and France, in that order.

Yet Falstaff is the poem of Shakespeare's climate, not an idea of disorder but the essence of Shakespeare's dramatic art: the principle of play. If Falstaff's nature is subdued at all, it is to the element of play, without which he will die. This is the most intimate link between playwright and comedic genius: Falstaff's high theatricalism is prophetic of Hamlet, of Duke Vin-

centio in *Measure for Measure*, most darkly of Iago, most gloriously of
Cleopatra, Falstaff's truest child. Falstaff, always himself, surpasses the selfsame in the improvised but elaborate plays-within-the-play that present
shadows of the forthcoming confrontation between King Henry IV and
the prince. First, Falstaff portrays the king, while Hal plays himself. Parodying John Lyly's *Euphues*, of twenty years before, Falstaff leaves little of either father or son, while enjoying a vision of the greatness of Falstaff:

> *Fal.* Harry, I do not only marvel where thou spendest thy time, but also
> how thou art accompanied. For though the camomile, the more it
> is trodden on the faster it grows, yet youth, the more it is wasted
> the sooner it wears. That thou art my son I have partly thy mother's
> word, partly my own opinion, but chiefly a villainous trick of thine
> eye, and a foolish hanging of thy nether lip, that doth warrant me.
> If then thou be son to me, here lies the point—why, being son to
> me, art thou so pointed at? Shall the blessed sun of heaven prove a
> micher, and eat blackberries? A question not to be asked. Shall the
> son of England prove a thief, and take purses? A question to be
> asked. There is a thing, Harry, which thou hast often heard of, and
> it is known to many in our land by the name of pitch. This pitch (as
> ancient writers do report) doth defile, so doth the company thou
> keepest: for, Harry, now I do not speak to thee in drink, but in
> tears; not in pleasure, but in passion; not in words only, but in woes
> also. And yet there is a virtuous man whom I have often noted in
> thy company, but I know not his name.
> *Prince.* What manner of man, and it like your Majesty?
> *Fal.* A goodly portly man, i' faith, and a corpulent; of a cheerful look, a
> pleasing eye, and a most noble carriage; and, as I think, his age
> some fifty, or, by'r lady, inclining to threescore; and now I remem-
> ber me, his name is Falstaff. If that man should be lewdly given, he
> deceiveth me; for, Harry, I see virtue in his looks. If then the tree
> may be known by the fruit, as the fruit by the tree, then peremp-
> torily I speak it, there is virtue in that Falstaff; him keep with, the
> rest banish.
>
> [II.iv.393–425]

Falstaff, who has been absorbing much abuse from Hal, triumphantly betters the scoffing, though in a far finer tone than the prince's murderous aggressivity. Royal father and holidaying son are rendered charmingly foolish, while Falstaff's Falstaff is beheld in the light of Swinburne's "possible moral elevation." All this is play in its sweetest and purest sense, an exercise that heals and restores. Very different is Hal's thunderous version, after he commands that he is to play his own father, while Falstaff stands in for the prince:

*Prince.* Now, Harry, whence come you?

*Fal.* My noble lord, from Eastcheap.

*Prince.* The complaints I hear of thee are grievous.

*Fal.* 'Sblood, my lord, they are false: nay, I'll tickle ye for a young prince, i'faith.

*Prince.* Swearest thou, ungracious boy? Henceforth ne'er look on me. Thou art violently carried away from grace, there is a devil haunts thee in the likeness of an old fat man, a tun of man is thy companion. Why dost thou converse with that trunk of humours, that bolting-hutch of beastliness, that swoll'n parcel of dropsies, that huge bombard of sack, that stuffed cloak-bag of guts, that roasted Manningtree ox with the pudding in his belly, that reverend vice, that grey iniquity, that father ruffian, that vanity in years? Wherein is he good, but to taste sack and drink it? wherein neat and cleanly, but to carve a capon and eat it? wherein cunning, but in craft? wherein crafty, but in villainy? wherein villainous, but in all things? wherein worthy, but in nothing?

*Fal.* I would your Grace would take me with you: whom means your Grace?

*Prince.* That villainous abominable misleader of youth, Falstaff, that old white-bearded Satan.

*Fal.* My lord, the man I know.

*Prince.* I know thou dost.

*Fal.* But to say I know more harm in him than in myself were to say more than I know. That he is old, the more the pity, his white hairs do witness it, but that he is, saving your reverence, a whore-

master, that I utterly deny. If sack and sugar be a fault, God help
the wicked! If to be old and merry be a sin, then many an old
host that I know is damned: if to be fat be to be hated, then
Pharaoh's lean kine are to be loved. No, my good lord; banish
Peto, banish Bardolph, banish Poins—but for sweet Jack Falstaff,
kind Jack Falstaff, true Jack Falstaff, valiant Jack Falstaff, and
therefore more valiant, being as he is old Jack Falstaff, banish not
him thy Harry's company, banish plump Jack, and banish all the
world.

*Prince.* I do, I will.

[II.iv.434–75]

This is the glowing center of *Henry IV, Part One*, intense with Falstaff's
poignant wit and Hal's cold fury. Ambivalence explodes into positive hatred in Hal's final summation: "That villainous abominable misleader of
youth, Falstaff, that old white-bearded Satan." The Prince is not acting, and
speaks from his whole mind and heart. How are we to account for this un-
justified malevolence, this exorcism that transcends rejection? Whom do
we credit, Hal's "old white-bearded Satan" or "sweet Jack Falstaff, kind
Jack Falstaff, true Jack Falstaff, valiant Jack Falstaff, and therefore more
valiant, being as he is old Jack Falstaff"? Hal is so extreme that surely we
have no choice. Always Falstaff's student, he has one insult worthy of the
old professor: "that roasted Manningtree ox with the pudding in his belly,"
but that is hardly in a class with "if to be fat be to be hated, then Pharaoh's
lean kine are to be loved." No scholarly detractor of Falstaff, old- or new-
style, is so disgusted by Sir John as Hal reveals himself to be. I have mentioned Honigmann's assertion that Shakespeare does not allow us to
unravel the psychological perplexities of the Falstaff–Hal relationship, but
while a puzzling matter, it is not beyond all conjecture. Hal has fallen out
of love. Iris Murdoch remarks that this is one of the great human experiences, in which you see the world with newly awakened eyes. "But being
awak'd I do despise my dream," the newly crowned Henry V virtuously assures us. Alas, he has been awake as long as we have known him, since the
start of *Henry IV, Part One*, where he manifests three ambitions of equal
magnitude: wait for Henry IV to die (as quickly as possible), kill Hotspur

and appropriate his "honour," have Falstaff hanged. He very nearly does place Falstaff in the hangman's hands, but forbears, reasoning that it is more appropriate to kill the aged reprobate by a forced march, or even (honorably) in battle. Some residue of former affection for Falstaff could be argued, though I myself doubt it. Sir John has outlived his educational function, but he is annoyingly indestructible, as the marvelous Battle of Shrewsbury, so much livelier than the Falstaffless Agincourt, will demonstrate.

Shakespeare's charming disrespect for slaughter is frequently an undersong throughout the plays, but it is never quite as pungent as in Falstaff's audacious contempt at Shrewsbury:

> *Prince.* What, stands thou idle here? Lend me thy sword:
> Many a nobleman lies stark and stiff
> Under the hoofs of vaunting enemies,
> Whose deaths are yet unrevenged. I prithee lend me thy sword.
> *Fal.* O Hal, I prithee give me leave to breathe awhile—Turk Gregory
> never did such deeds in arms as I have done this day; I have paid
> Percy, I have made him sure.
> *Prince.* He is indeed, and living to kill thee:
> I prithee lend me thy sword.
> *Fal.* Nay, before God, Hal, if Percy be alive, thou gets not my sword,
> but take my pistol if thou wilt.
> *Prince.* Give it me: what, is it in the case?
> *Fal.* Ay, Hal, 'tis hot, 'tis hot; there's that will sack a city.
>> *The Prince draws it out, and finds it to be a bottle of sack.*
> *Prince.* What, is it a time to jest and dally now?
>> *He throws the bottle at him. Exit.*
> *Fal.* Well, if Percy be alive, I'll pierce him. If he do come in my way,
> so: if he do not, if I come in his willingly, let him make a car-
> bonado of me. I like not such grinning honour as Sir Walter hath.
> Give me life; which if I can save, so: honour comes unlooked for,
> and there's an end.
>> *[Exit.]*
>
> [V.iii.40–61]

In one sense, Falstaff here pays Hal back for many imputations of supposed cowardice, yet this is so fine a Falstaffian moment that it transcends their waning relationship. Having "led" his hundred and fifty men into their all-but-total destruction, the huge target Falstaff remains not only unscathed but replete with sublime mockery of the absurd slaughter. His grand contempt for Hotspurian "honour" allows him to take the risk of substituting a bottle of sack for the pistol his rank merits. After a half century, I retain the vivid image of Ralph Richardson gleefully and nimbly dodging the thrown bottle, with an expressive gesture indicating that indeed this was much the best time to jest and dally! Is there, in all Shakespeare, anything more useful than "I like not such grinning honour as Sir Walter hath. Give me life"? For Falstaff, Shrewsbury becomes an insane spectator sport, as when Sir John ironically cheers the prince on in the duel with Hotspur. Shakespeare's gusto is at its height when the ferocious Douglas charges on stage and forces Falstaff to fight. The wily Falstaff falls down as if dead, just as Hal gives Hotspur a death wound. Even as we wonder what the dying Hotspur "could prophesy" (the vanity of "honour"?), Shakespeare affords Hal his great moment when the prince believes that he beholds the corpse of Falstaff:

> What, old acquaintance, could not all this flesh
> Keep in a little life? Poor Jack, farewell!
> I could have better spared a better man:
> O, I should have a heavy miss of thee
> If I were much in love with vanity:
> Death hath not struck so fat a deer today,
> Though many dearer, in this bloody fray.
> Embowell'd will I see thee by and by,
> Till then in blood by noble Percy lie.
> *[Exit.]*
>
> [V.iv.101–9]

These intricate lines are not so much ambivalent as they are revelatory of Henry V, whose kingship is formed at Shrewsbury. "Poor Jack, farewell!"

is almost as much authentic grief as the warlike Harry can summon for the apostle of "vanity," who was so frivolous as to gambol about and jest upon a royal battleground. As an epitaph for Falstaff, this does not even achieve the dignity of being absurd, and is properly answered by the resurrection of "the true and perfect image of life," immortal spirit worth a thousand Hals. Here is the truest glory of Shakespeare's invention of the human:

> Embowelled? If thou embowel me today, I'll give you leave to powder me and eat me too tomorrow. 'Sblood, 'twas time to counterfeit, or that hot termagant Scot had paid me, scot and lot too. Counterfeit? I lie, I am no counterfeit: to die is to be a counterfeit, for he is but the counterfeit of a man, who hath not the life of a man: but to counterfeit dying, when a man thereby liveth, is to be no counterfeit, but the true and perfect image of life indeed. The better part of valor is discretion, in the which better part I have saved my life. 'Zounds, I am afraid of this gunpowder Percy, though he be dead; how if he should counterfeit too and rise? By my faith, I am afraid he would prove the better counterfeit; therefore I'll make him sure, yea, and I'll swear I killed him. Why may not he rise as well as I? Nothing confutes me but eyes, and nobody sees me: therefore, sirrah [*stabbing him*], with a new wound in your thigh, come you along with me.
>
> [V.iv.110–28]

To have seen Richardson bounding up was to have beheld the most joyous representation of secular resurrection ever staged: *Falstaff's Wake* would be an apt title for *Henry IV, Part One*. Maligned, threatened with hanging, hated (by the prince) where he had been loved, the great pariah rises in the flesh, having counterfeited death. As true and perfect image, he has seemed to the Christian critic Auden a type of Christ, but it is more than enough that he abides as Falstaff, mocker of hypocritical "honour," parodist of noble butchery, defier of time, law, order, and the state. He is still irrepressible, and is accurate, as Harold Goddard observed, in asserting that *he* killed the spirit of Hotspur: It is not the swordplay of Hal that upstages Hotspur; place Hotspur in any play not inhabited by Falstaff, and Hotspur would fascinate us, but he fades in the cognitive bonfire of Falstaff's exuberance and is exposed as only another counterfeit. Shakespearean secularists should manifest their Bardoaltry by celebrating the Resurrection of Sir John Falstaff. It should be made, unofficially but pervasively, an international holiday, a Carnival of wit, with multiple performances of *Henry IV, Part One.* Let it be a day for loathing political ambition, religious hypocrisy, and false friendship, and let it be marked by wearing bottles of sack in our holsters.

5

Falstaffians, derided by joyless scholars as "sentimentalists," actually are "pataphysicians," knowing that Falstaff's is the true science of imaginary solutions. Alfred Jarry, author of *Ubu Roi,* conceived of the Passion as an Uphill Bicycle Race. *Henry IV, Part Two,* is *The Passion of Sir John Falstaff,* who exuberantly surges on to his humiliation and destruction by the brutal hypocrite, the newly crowned Henry V. If you interpret the play otherwise, doubtless you will have your reward, since you stand with the Lord Chief Justice as he berates and admonishes Falstaff, who gives back much better than he receives, and yet at last will be conveyed to the Fleet, where the Chief Justice, hearing the case, is bound to have the last word. Shakespeare spares us the sadness of the hearing; perhaps we might venture that Shakespeare also spared himself, since nothing appropriate remains for Falstaff to experience, except for his beautiful death scene as reported by Mistress Quickly and his other survivors in *Henry V.*

Falstaff, still in his glory when first we see him in *Henry IV, Part Two,* memorably disputes his age with the Chief Justice:

> *Fal.* You that are old consider not the capacities of us that are young; you do measure the heat of our livers with the bitterness of your galls; and we that are in the vaward of our youth, I must confess, are wags too.

*Ch. Just.* Do you set down your name in the scroll of youth, that are
written down old with all the characters of age? Have you not a
moist eye, a dry hand, a yellow cheek, a white beard, a decreas-
ing leg, an increasing belly? Is not your voice broken, your wind
short, your chin double, your wit single, and every part about
you blasted with antiquity? And will you yet call yourself young?
Fie, fie, fie, Sir John!

*Fal.* My lord, I was born about three of the clock in the afternoon,
with a white head, and something a round belly. For my voice, I
have lost it with hallooing, and singing of anthems. To approve
my youth further, I will not: the truth is, I am only old in judgment and understanding; and he that will caper with me for a
thousand marks, let him lend me the money, and have at him!

[I.ii.172–93]

One can start with a good morning's moral disapproval of Falstaff (very
rueful if one is a fat man) and still contend that only a sensibility of stone
will not be charmed by "My lord, I was born about three of the clock in
the afternoon, with a white head, and something a round belly." Yet Shakespeare will show time darkening Falstaff, in the pathos of his aged lust for
Doll Tearsheet:

*Fal.* Thou dost give me flattering busses.
*Doll.* By my troth, I kiss thee with a most constant heart.
*Fal.* I am old, I am old.
*Doll.* I love thee better than I love e'er a scurvy young boy of them
all.
*Fal.* What stuff wilt have a kirtle of? I shall receive money a-
Thursday, shalt have a cap tomorrow. A merry song! Come, it
grows late, we'll to bed. Thou't forget me when I am gone.

[II.iv.266–74]

The play at perpetual youth yields to "I am old, I am old," in this giant
paradox of an exhausted vitalist, about to be dragged back to the civil

wars by a dozen sweating captains. Beneath Hal's savage banter and Falstaff's outrageous parries, there abides the prodigy of an ancient warrior still formidable enough to be of considerable if highly reluctant service. Coming upon the rebel Coleville, Falstaff observes his general praxis of playful pragmatism: "Do ye yield, sir, or shall I sweat for you?" Coleville surrenders, but it is clear that Falstaff would have sweated to defeat or kill Coleville had it been necessary. And yet Falstaff cheerfully mocks his own exploit of capturing Coleville: "But thou like a kind fellow gavest thyself away gratis, and I thank thee for thee." This is in the same spirit as Falstaff's insistence that he, not Hal, gave the death wound, not literally but in spirit. Hotspur, absurdly courageous and doom-eager, is one of Falstaff's antitheses; the other is John of Lancaster, Hal's warlike younger brother, who like Hal and the Chief Justice threatens Sir John with hanging. Lancaster, "sober-blooded boy," provokes Falstaff to his great rhapsody on the virtues of drinking sherry, but otherwise causes us to reflect that it was an ill hour when the sublime Sir John first became involved with the royal family. As the shadows of Hal's forthcoming rejection darken *Henry IV, Part Two*, Shakespeare distracts us (and himself) by the scenes shared by Falstaff with the two country justices, Shallow and Silence (Act III, Scene ii, and Act V, Scenes i and iii). Kenneth Tynan rightly remarked that "Shakespeare never surpassed these scenes in the vein of pure naturalism": the fatuousness of Shallow plays off deliciously against the Falstaffian wit, particularly when the appropriately named Shallow attempts to revive common memories dating back fifty-five years:

> *Shallow.* Ha, cousin Silence, that thou hadst seen that that this knight
>     and I have seen! Ha, Sir John, said I well?
> *Fal.* We have heard the chimes at midnight, Master Shallow.
>                                                  [III.ii.206–10]

Falstaff's dry response masks his resolution to return and fleece this country gull, which he will perform on the grand scale. Shallow is Hotspur turned inside out, as was beautifully demonstrated by Laurence Olivier, when he played Hotspur in the afternoon and Shallow in the evening, in the Old Vic productions of 1946. The eloquent swordsman mutated into the aged "forked radish," while Richardson maintained his exuberant wit in a long day's defiance of dying, only to suffer Hal's inevitable betrayal and pragmatic death sentence.

6

Sir John Falstaff is the greatest vitalist in Shakespeare, but while he is certainly not the most intense of Shakespeare's nihilists, his strain of nihilism is extraordinarily virulent. Indeed, Falstaff's nihilism seems to me his version of Christianity, and helps account for the darkest element in the grand wit, his realistic obsession with rejection, massively to be realized at the end of *Henry IV, Part Two*.

It is the image of rejection, rather than of damnation, that accounts for Falstaff's frequent allusions to the frightening parable of the purple-clad glutton, Dives, and poor Lazarus the beggar that Jesus tells in Luke 16:19–26:

> There was a certeine riche man, which was clothed in purple and fine linen, and fared wel and delicately everie day.
>
> Also there was a certeine begger named Lazarus, which was laied at his gate ful of sores,
>
> And desired to be refreshed with the crommes that fell from the riche mans table: yea, and the dogs came and licked his sores.
>
> And it was so that the begger dyed, and was caryed by the Angels into Abrahams bosome. The riche man also dyed and was buryed.
>
> And being in hel in torments, he lift vp his eyes, and sawe Abraham a farre of, & Lazarus in his bosome.
>
> Then he cryed, and sais, Father Abraham, gaue mercie on me, and send Lazarus that he may dippe y typ of his finger in water, and coole my tongue: for I am tormented in this flame.
>
> But Abraham said, Sonne, remember that thou in thy life time receiuedft thy pleasures, and likewise Lazarus paines: now therefore is he comforted, and thou art tormented.

Besides all this, betwene you and vs there is a great gulfe set, so that they which wolde go from hence to you, can not, nether can they come from thence to vs.

[Geneva Bible, Luke 16:19–26]

Three times Falstaff alludes to this fierce parable; I will suggest that there is a fourth, concealed allusion when Falstaff kneels and is rejected by King Henry V, in his new royal purple, and manifestly there is a fifth when the Hostess, describing Falstaff's death in the play he is not permitted to enter, *Henry V,* assures us that Falstaff is "in Arthur's bosom," with the British Arthur substituting for Father Abraham. To be sure, Henry V allows that Falstaff is to be fed crumbs from the royal table, but the initial feeding is held in prison, by order of the Lord Chief Justice. If we are to credit his Sonnets, Shakespeare knew what it was to be rejected, though I certainly do not wish to suggest an affinity between the creator of Falstaff and Falstaff himself. I wonder, though, at the affinities between Prince Hal and the Earl of Southampton, neither of them candidates for Abraham's bosom. What is Sir John's implicit interpretation of the parable of the rich man and the beggar?

Falstaff's first allusion to the parable is the richest and most outrageous, beginning as a meditation on Bardolph's fiery nose, which makes him "the Knight of the Burning Lamp." The hurt Bardolph complains, "Why, Sir John, my face does you no harm," to which Falstaff makes a massive reply:

No, I'll be sworn, I make as good use of it as many a man doth of a death's-head or a *memento mori*. I never see thy face but I think upon hell-fire, and Dives that lived in purple: for there he is in his robes, burning, burning. If thou wert any way given to virtue, I would swear by thy face; my oath should be "By this fire, that's God's angel!" But thou art altogether given over; and wert indeed, but for the light in thy face, the son of utter darkness. When thou ran'st up Gad's Hill in the night to catch my horse, if I did not think thou hadst been an *ignis fatuus*, or a ball of wildfire, there's no purchase in money. O, thou art a perpetual triumph, an everlasting bonfire-light! Thou hast saved me a thousand marks in links and torches, walking with thee in the night betwixt tavern and tavern: but the sack that thou hast drunk me would have bought me lights as good cheap at the dearest chandler's in Europe. I have maintained that salamander of yours with fire any time this two and thirty years, God reward me for it!

[III.iii.28–47]

"For there he is in his robes, burning, burning": of course we are to note that Falstaff himself is another glutton, but I do not believe we are to take seriously Falstaff's fear of hellfire, any more than we are to identify Bardolph with the Burning Bush. Sir John is at work subverting Scripture, even as he subverts everything else that would constrain him: time, the state, virtue, the chivalric concept of "honour," and all ideas of order whatsoever. The brilliant fantasia upon Bardolph's nose does not allow us much residual awe in relation to Jesus's rather uncharacteristic parable. What chance has the rhetorical threat of hellfire against the dazzling metamorphoses of Bardolph's nose, which goes from a *memento mori* to the Burning Bush to a will-o'-the-wisp to fireworks to a torchlight procession to a bonfire to a fiery salamander, seven amiable variants that far outshine the burning in Jesus's parable. Falstaff, the greatest of Shakespeare's prose poets, leaps from metaphor to metaphor so as to remind us implicitly that the parable's "burning, burning" is metaphor also, albeit a metaphor that Sir John cannot cease to empty out. He returns to it as he marches his wretched recruits on to the hellfire of the battle of Shrewsbury: "slaves as ragged as Lazarus in the painted cloth, where the glutton's dogs lick'd his sores."

Why does the allusion recur in this context? Hal, staring at Falstaff's troop, observes, "I did never see such pitiful rascals," prompting Falstaff's grand rejoinder: "Tut, tut, good enough to toss, food for powder, food for powder; they'll fill a pit as well as better; tush, man, mortal men, mortal men." Would it be more honorable if you tossed on a pike better-fed, better-clothed impressed men? How could one state it more tellingly: Falstaff's recruits have all the necessary qualities: food for powder, corpses to fill a pit, mortal men, who are there to be killed, only to be killed, like their betters, whose "grinning honour" Prince Hal will worship. Falstaff has drafted the poorest, like the beggar Lazarus, in contrast to the purple glutton he previously named as Dives, a name not to be found in the Geneva Bible or later in the King James. It is not likely that either Shakespeare or Falstaff had read Luke in the Vulgate, where the "certain rich man" is a *dives*, Late Latin for "rich man," but Dives by Shakespeare's day was already a name out of Chaucer and the common tongue. Sir John, after collecting the bribes of the affluent to release them from the service, has put together a fine crew of Lazaruses, who will be stabbed and blown up to serve the Henrys, father and son. Yet, true to his charismatic personality, Falstaff, marching with a bottle of sack in his pistol holster, observes, "I have led my ragamuffins where they are peppered; there's not three of my hundred and fifty alive, and they are for the town's end, to beg during life." All we can ask of Falstaff he has done; a mortal man, he *led* his Lazaruses to their peppering, taking his chances with them where the fire was hottest. Sir John's cognitive contempt for the entire enterprise is his true offense against time and the state; Prince Hal is never less hypocritical than when he bellows at Falstaff, "What, is it a time to jest and dally now?" while throwing at Sir John the bottle of sack the Prince has just drawn from the holster, in attempting to borrow a pistol.

Falstaff's last explicit allusion to Dives omits any mention of Lazarus, since it is turned against a tailor who has denied him credit: "Let him be damned like the glutton! Pray God his tongue be hotter!" Since Falstaff perpetually is in want of money, neither he nor we associate the fat knight with Dives. It is a fearful irony that Sir John must end like Lazarus, rejected by the newly crowned king in order to win admission to "Arthur's bosom," but clearly Shakespeare was not much in agreement with nearly all his modern critics, who mostly unite in defending the rejection of Falstaff, that spirit of misrule. They mistake this great representation of a personality not less than wholly, and I return again to Jesus's parable, for a final time. Falstaff's implicit interpretation of the text is nihilistic: one must either be damned with Dives, or else be saved with Lazarus, an antithesis that loses one either the world to come or this world. Emerson once said, "Other world? There is no other world; here or nowhere is the whole fact." Falstaff is more than pragmatic enough to agree with Emerson, and I find nothing in Shakespeare to indicate that he himself hoped to join Falstaff in Arthur's bosom, or Lazarus in Abraham's. Falstaff is the prose poet of "the whole fact," and I venture that for Sir John the "whole fact" is what we call "personality," as opposed to "character."

It is very difficult for me, even painful, to have done with Falstaff, for no other literary character—not even Don Quixote or Sancho Panza, not even Hamlet—seems to me so infinite in provoking thought and in arousing emotion. Falstaff is a miracle in the creation of personality, and his enigmas rival those of Hamlet. Each is first and foremost an absolutely individual *voice*; no other personages in Western literature rival them in mastery of language. Falstaff's prose and Hamlet's verse give us a cognitive music that overwhelms us even as it expands our minds to the ends of thought. They are beyond our last thought, and they have an immediacy that by the pragmatic test constitutes a real presence, one that all current theorists and ideologues insist literature cannot even intimate, let alone sustain. But Falstaff persists, after four centuries, and he will prevail centuries after our fashionable knowers and resenters have become alms for oblivion. Dr. Johnson, best and most moral of critics, loved Falstaff almost despite himself, partly because Sir John had cleared his mind of cant, but primarily because the fat knight's cheerfulness was contagious enough to banish, however momentarily, Johnson's vile melancholy. Schlegel, despite his high German seriousness, acutely noted Falstaff's freedom from malice; the critic should have gone further and emphasized that Sir John is also free of all censoriousness, free of what Freud came to call the *überich*, the superego. We all of us beat up upon ourselves; the sane and sacred Falstaff does not, and urges us to emulate him. Falstaff has nothing of Hamlet's savagery, or of Prince Hal's.

What Falstaff bears is the Blessing, in the original Yahwistic sense: more life. All the self-contradictions of his complex nature resolve themselves in his exuberance of being, his passion for being alive. Many of us become machines for fulfilling responsibilities; Falstaff is the largest and best reproach we can find. I am aware that I commit the Original Sin that all historicists—of all generations—decry, joined by all formalists as well: I exalt Falstaff above his plays, the two parts of *Henry IV* and Mistress Quickly's deathbed account in *Henry V.* This sin, like Bardolatry, to me seems salvation. No matter how often I reread Shakespeare, or teach him, or endure what currently passes for stagings, like everyone else I am left with memories, of language and of images, or of an image. I write these pages and Richardson's Falstaff rises before me, a vision of perfection in realizing a central Shakespearean role. But like Hamlet, Falstaff is more than a role. Hamlet and Falstaff have become our culture.

What can we do with dramatic and literary characters who are geniuses in their own right? We know in one sense far too little about Shakespeare himself, but in quite another sense we somehow apprehend that he invested himself very deeply in Hamlet and in Falstaff. They are—both of them—enigmatic and self-revelatory, and we never can mark precisely where what is hidden suddenly beacons to us. Hamlet, as I have remarked, sometimes seems a "real" person surrounded by actors; he has depths not suggested by anyone around him. Conversely, Falstaff can seem a great actor, a Ralph Richardson, surrounded by merely "real" people, since even Hotspur and Hal are trivialized when Falstaff stands on stage with them. They duel, and are a distraction, because we want to hear what Falstaff will say next. When Douglas dashes on and has at Falstaff, we wish the hot termagant Scot to get on with it and then leave us, so that we can enjoy the style of Falstaff's resurrection.

Shakespeare's largest tribute to Falstaff is that, belying his own promise to the audience, he dared not allow Sir John to appear on stage in *Henry V.* The playwright understood the magnitude of his creature. Scholars tend not to, which is why we have the nonsense of what they, and not Shakespeare, continue to call the Henriad. We do not need *Henry V,* and he does not need us. Falstaff needs an audience, and never fails to find it. We need Falstaff because we have so few images of authentic vitalism, and even fewer persuasive images of human freedom.

# 18

# THE MERRY WIVES OF WINDSOR

Though this competes, in my judgment, with *The Two Gentlemen of Verona* as Shakespeare's slightest comedy, nobody can wholly dislike what became the basis for Verdi's *Falstaff*. I begin, though, with the firm declaration that the hero-villain of *The Merry Wives of Windsor* is a nameless impostor masquerading as the great Sir John Falstaff. Rather than yield to such usurpation, I shall call him pseudo-Falstaff throughout this brief discussion.

The tradition is that Shakespeare wrote the *Merry Wives*, perhaps between the two parts of *Henry IV*, in response to Queen Elizabeth's request to show Sir John in love. Farce, natural to Shakespeare, dwindles into shallowness in *Merry Wives*, a tiresome exercise that I suspect the playwright revised from something older at hand, whether his own or another's. Russell Fraser shrewdly has puzzled out the autobiographical backgrounds of *Merry Wives*, in which Shakespeare may be paying back old slights and an injury or two. I would add that there is also a touch of satire at Ben Jonson's expense, though the target is more Jonson's art than Jonson himself. One of the uses of *Merry Wives* is to show us just how good Shakespeare's first farces, *The Comedy of Errors* and *The Taming of the Shrew*, really are, compared with the false energy unleashed in this humiliation of pseudo-Falstaff. There are hints throughout that Shakespeare is uncomfortable with what he is doing and wishes to get it over with as rapidly as possible.

This is about the best that the False Falstaff can manage:

O, she did so course o'er my exteriors with such a greedy intention that the appetite of her eye did seem to scorch me up like a burning-glass! Here's another letter to her; she bears the purse too: she is a region in Guiana, all gold and bounty. I will be cheaters to them both, and they shall be exchequers to me: they shall be my East and West Indies, and I will trade them both. Go bear this letter to Mistress Page; and thou this to Mistress Ford: we will thrive, lads, we will thrive.

[I.iii.61–70]

Is this the Immortal Falstaff? Or is this:

Go fetch me a quart of sack; put a toast in 't. [*Exit Bard.*] Have I lived to be carried in a basket, like a barrow of butcher's offal, and to be thrown in the Thames? Well, if I be served such another trick, I'll have my brains ta'en out and buttered, and give them to a dog for a New Year's gift. The rogues slighted me into the river with as little remorse as they would have drowned a blind bitch's puppies, fifteen i' th' litter; and you may know by my size that I have a kind of alacrity in sinking: if the bottom were as deep as hell, I should down. I had been drowned but that the shore was shelvy and shallow—a death that I abhor: for the water swells a man; and what a thing should I have been when I had been swelled! I should have been a mountain of mummy.

[III.v.3–17]

No longer either witty in himself or the cause of wit in other men, this Falstaff would make me lament a lost glory if I did not know him to be a rank impostor. His fascination, indeed, is that Shakespeare wastes nothing upon him. *The Merry Wives of Windsor* is Shakespeare's only play that he himself seems to hold in contempt, even as he indites it. Scorning the task, he tossed off a "Falstaff" fit only to be carried in a basket and thrown into the Thames. Such a diminishing is akin to reducing Cleopatra to a fishwife (in a recent British production brought to New York City) or giving us Juliet as a gang girl (on screen). You can cram any fat man into a bas-ket and get a laugh. He does not have to be Falstaff, nor need his creator be Shakespeare. By the time that Falstaff, disguised as a plump old woman, has absorbed a particularly nasty beating, one begins to conclude that Shakespeare loathes not only the occasion but himself for having yielded to it. The final indignity is a horned, chained pseudo-Falstaff, victim of sadomasochistic farce, and perhaps even of a quick burst of Shakespearean self-hatred. The wretched impostor, pinched and burned by mock fairies, is finally allowed a near-Falstaffian rejoinder to a Welsh parson:

> 'Seese' and 'putter'? Have I lived to stand at the taunt of one that
> makes fritters of English? This is enough to be the decay of lust and
> late-walking through the realm.
>
> [V.v.143–46]

That is only a tinge of the authentic Falstaff, but it is all we get. What we do receive is sadomasochistic carnival fit for Joyce's Nightown episode in *Ulysses* but unworthy of Joyce's superior wordplay (superior only to *The Merry Wives of Windsor*). Shakespeare's immortal Falstaff suffers the terrible final humiliation of public rejection but retains pathos, dignity, even a kind of nobility as he goes down, a Lazarus to Henry V's purple-clad Dives. All the False Falstaff retains is his tormented rump; I cannot better A. C. Bradley's indignation, in which I share:

> [Falstaff is] baffled, duped, treated like dirty linen, beaten, burnt,
> pricked, mocked, insulted, and, worst of all, repentant and didactic.
> It is horrible.

Commerce is commerce, but why did Shakespeare inflict this upon a character who represents his own wit at its most triumphant? I once saw a Yale production of this ritualistic farrago in what purported to be Shake-speare's pronunciation, and found a distinct gain in not always under-standing what was spoken. Some feminist critics suggest that Shakespeare, though only thirty-three, already dreaded the aging male's loss of sexual vitality, and punished the False Falstaff as a surrogate for himself. In their view, *The Merry Wives of Windsor* is a castration pageant, with the merry wives vastly enjoying their labors of emasculation. I eschew comment.

There remains the puzzle of why Shakespeare subjected the pseudo-Falstaff to so mindless a laceration, really a bear baiting, with "Sir John-in-love" as the bear. As a lifelong playwright, always quick to yield to subtle patrons, statist censors, and royal performances, Shakespeare in his deepest inwardness harbored anxieties and resentments that he rarely allowed expression. He knew that Walsingham's shadowy Secret Service had murdered Christopher Marlowe, and tortured Thomas Kyd into an early death. Hamlet dies upward, as it were, into a transcendence not available to Shakespeare, certainly not as a man, and the true Falstaff dies in bed, playing with flowers, smiling upon his fingertips, and evidently singing of a table prepared for him in the midst of his enemies. We do not know the mode or manner of Shakespeare's own death. Yet something in him, which he perhaps identified with the authentic Falstaff, rejected where he most loved, and solitary, like the poet of the Sonnets, may have feared further humiliations. I have to conclude that Shakespeare himself is warding off personal horror by scapegoating the false Falstaff in this weak play.

19

# HENRY V

This brilliant and subtle work will always be popular; I could say "for the wrong reasons," except that all reasons for Shakespeare's eternal popularity are correct, one way or another. And yet *Henry V* is clearly a lesser drama than the two parts of *Henry IV*. Falstaff is gone, and King Henry V, matured into the mastery of power, is less interesting than the ambivalent Prince Hal, whose potential was more varied. The great Irish poet W. B. Yeats made the classic comment on this aesthetic falling away in his *Ideas of Good and Evil*:

> [Henry V] has the gross vices, the coarse nerves, of one who is to rule among violent people, and he is so little "too friendly" to his friends that he bundles them out of door when their time is over. He is as remorseless and undistinguished as some natural force, and the finest thing in his play is the way his old companions fall out of it broken-hearted or on their way to the gallows.

I read the play that Yeats read, but much Shakespeare scholarship reads otherwise. *Henry V* is now most widely known because of the films quarried from it by Laurence Olivier and Kenneth Branagh. Both movies are lively, patriotic romps, replete with exuberant bombast, provided by Shakespeare himself, with what degree of irony we cannot quite tell but are free to surmise:

We few, we happy few, we band of brothers;
For he to-day that sheds his blood with me
Shall be my brother; be he ne'er so vile
This day shall gentle his condition:
And gentlemen in England, now a-bed,
Shall think themselves accurs'd they were not here,
And hold their manhoods cheap whiles any speaks
That fought with us upon Saint Crispin's day.

[IV.iii.60–67]

That is the King, just before the battle of Agincourt. He is very stirred;
so are we; but neither we nor he believes a word he says. The common
soldiers fighting with their monarch are not going to become gentlemen,
let alone nobles, and "the ending of the world" is a rather grand evocation
for an imperialist land grab that did not long survive Henry V's death, as
Shakespeare's audience knew too well. Hazlitt, with characteristic eloquence, joins Yeats as the true exegete of Henry V and his play:

He was a hero, that is, he was ready to sacrifice his own life for the
pleasure of destroying thousands of other lives. . . . How then do we
like him? We like him in the play. There he is a very amiable monster, a very splendid pageant. . . .

This cannot be bettered, but is that all Prince Hal matured into: an
amiable monster, a splendid pageant? Yes; for this, Falstaff was rejected,
Bardolph was hanged, and a great education in wit was partly thrown
away. Shakespeare's ironic insight remains highly relevant; power keeps
its habit through the ages. Our nation's Henry V (some might say) was
John Fitzgerald Kennedy, who gave us the Bay of Pigs and the enhance-
ment of our Vietnam adventure. Some scholars may moralize and historicize until they are purple with pride, but they will not persuade us that
Shakespeare (playwright *and* man) preferred his amiable monster to the
genius of Falstaff, and his splendid pageant to the varied and vital *Henry
IV* plays.

In *Henry V*, the two religious caterpillars, Canterbury and Ely, finance the French wars so as to save the Church's secular estates from royal confiscation; both praise Henry's piety, and he is careful to tell us how Christian a king he is. At Agincourt, he prays to God for victory, promising yet more contrite tears for his father's murder of Richard II, and he then proceeds to order the throats cut of all the French prisoners, a grace duly performed. Some recent attention has been devoted to this slaughter, but it will not alter Henry V's popularity with both scholars and moviegoers. Henry is brutally shrewd and shrewdly brutal, qualities necessary for his greatness as a king. The historical Henry V, dead at thirty-five, was an enormous success in power and war, and undoubtedly was the strongest English king before Henry VIII. Shakespeare has no single attitude toward Henry V, in the play, which allows you to achieve your own perspective upon the rejecter of Falstaff. My stance I derive from Yeats, whose views on Shakespeare and the state deliciously share little with old-style scholarly idealists and new-wave cultural materialists:

> Shakespeare cared little for the State, the source of all our judgments, apart from its shows and splendors, its turmoils and battles, its flamings-out of the uncivilized heart.

When Shakespeare thought of the state, he remembered first that it had murdered Christopher Marlowe, tortured and broken Thomas Kyd, and branded the unbreakable Ben Jonson. All that and more underlies the great lament in Sonnet 66:

> And right perfection wrongfully disgraced,
> And strength by limping sway disabled,
> And art made tongue-tied by authority.

The censor, external and internal, haunted Shakespeare, made cautious by Marlowe's terrible end. I agree, therefore, with Yeats's conclusion, which is that *Henry V*, for all its exuberance, is essentially ironic:

Shakespeare watched Henry V not indeed as he watched the greater souls in the visionary procession, but cheerfully, as one watches some handsome spirited horse, and he spoke his tale, as he spoke all tales, with tragic irony.

It is so much Henry V's play that the irony is not immediately evident: there is no substantial role for anyone except the warrior-king. Falstaff's death, narrated by Mistress Quickly, does not bring that great spirit upon stage, and ancient Pistol is only a shadow of his leader. Fluellen, the other comic turn, is a fine characterization but limited, except perhaps where Shakespeare slyly employs the Welsh captain to give us a properly ironic analogue for the rejection of Falstaff:

*Flu.* I think it is in Macedon where Alexander is porn. I tell you, captain, if you look in the maps of the 'orld, I warrant you sall find, in the comparisons between Macedon and Monmouth, that the situations, look you, is both alike. There is a river in Macedon, and there is also moreover a river at Monmouth: it is called Wye at Monmouth; but it is out of my prains what is the name of the other river; but 'tis all one, 'tis alike as my fingers is to my fingers, and there is salmons in both. If you mark Alexander's life well, Harry of Monmouth's life is come after it indifferent well; for there is figures in all things. Alexander, God knows, and you know, in his rages, and his furies, and his wraths, and his cholers, and his moods, and his displeasures, and his indignations, and also being a little intoxicates in his prains, did, in his ales and his angers, look you, kill his best friend, Cleitus.

*Gow.* Our King is not like him in that: he never killed any of his friends.

*Flu.* It is not well done, mark you now, to take the tales out of my mouth, ere it is made and finished. I speak but in the figures and comparisons of it: as Alexander killed his friend Cleitus, being in his ales and his cups, so also Harry Monmouth, being in his wits and his good judgments, turned away the fat knight with the great-

belly doublet: he was full of jests, and gipes, and knaveries, and
mocks; I have forgot his name.

*Gow.* Sir John Falstaff.

[IV.vii.23–53]

The drunken Alexander murdered his good friend Cleitus; Shakespeare
ironically reminds us that Hal, "being in his right wits and his good judgments," "killed" his best friend, the man "full of jests, and gipes, and knaveries, and mocks." One great conqueror or "pig" is much like another, as
Fluellen argues. *Henry V* certainly is not Falstaff's play; it belongs to "this star
of England," whose sword was made by Fortune. Yet its ironies are palpable and frequent, and transcend my own fierce Falstaffianism. Urging his
troops into the breach at Harfleur, King Henry had extolled their fathers
as "so many Alexanders." Distancing is not so much bewildering in *Henry V*
as it is suave and beguiling. Henry V is an admirable politician, a brave
basher of heads in battle, a peerless charismatic. With Shakespeare we are
delighted by him, and with Shakespeare we are rather chilled also, but
carefully so; we are not estranged from Falstaff's brilliant pupil. In some
ways, King Henry's hypocrisy is more acceptable than Prince Hal's, since
the warrior-king is in no way a clean and clever lad doing his best to get on.
Henry V has England and the English, captures France and its princess, if
not the French, and will die young like Alexander, another conqueror with
little left to conquer. Personal fidelities are shrugged off by so ideal a
monarch; Bardolph hangs, and perhaps Falstaff would too, had Shakespeare
risked that comic splendor on the French expedition. Something in us, attending or reading *Henry V,* is carefully rendered beyond care.

Henry is given to lamenting that as king he is not free, yet the former
Hal is himself a considerable ironist, and has learned one of Falstaff's most
useful lessons: Keep your freedom by seeing through every idea of order
and code of behavior, whether chivalrous or moral or religious. Shakespeare does not let us locate Hal/Henry V's true self; a king is necessarily
something of a counterfeit, and Henry is a great king. Hamlet, infinitely
complex, becomes a different role with each strong performer. Henry V is
veiled rather than complex, but the pragmatic consequence is that no actor

resembles another in the part. *Henry V or What You Will* might as well be the play's title. Shakespeare sees to it that even the most pungent ironies cannot resist the stance of the chorus, who adores "the warlike Harry," truly the model or "mirror of all Christian kings." Even if you wanted to hear duplicity in that, the chorus will charm you with: "A little touch of Harry in the night."

Shakespeare need not remind us that Falstaff, vastly intelligent and witty beyond all measure, was desperately in love with Hal. No one could fall in love with Henry V, but no one altogether could resist him either. If he is a monster, he is more than amiable. He is a great Shakespearean personality—hardly a Hamlet or a Falstaff, but more than a Hotspur. Henry V has the glamour of an Alexander who has staked everything upon one military enterprise, but this is an Alexander endowed with inwardness, keenly exploited for its pragmatic advantages. In Henry's vision, the growing inner self requires an expanding kingdom, and France is the designated realm for growth. Henry IV's guilt of usurpation and regicide is to be expiated by conquest, and the exploitation and rejection of Falstaff is to be enhanced by a new sense of the glory of Mars and kingship. The transcended fathers fade away in the dazzle of royal apotheosis. Ironies persist, but what are ironies in so flamboyant a pageant? More than Shakespeare's heart was with Falstaff; Falstaff is mind, while Henry is but policy. Yet policy makes for a superb pageant, and something in every one of us responds to the joyousness of *Henry V.* Militarism, brutality, pious hypocrisy all are outshone by England's charismatic hero-king. This is all to the good for the play, and Shakespeare sees to it that we will remember his play's limits.

PART VI

# THE "PROBLEM PLAYS"

# 20

# TROILUS AND CRESSIDA

Genre, frequently metamorphic in Shakespeare, is particularly uneasy in *Troilus and Cressida*, variously termed satire, comedy, history, tragedy, or what you will. The play is Shakespeare's most overtly bitter testament, nihilistic like the two comedies it directly preceded, *All's Well That Ends Well* and *Measure for Measure*. It is also the most difficult and elitist of all his works. Something of the aura of *Hamlet* lingers in *Troilus and Cressida*, which presumably was composed in 1601–2.

We have to assume that Shakespeare wrote it for performance at the Globe, where it seems, however, not to have played. Why? Only surmise is available, and the notion that Shakespeare and his company decided that they would have a failure with this drama seems unlikely, based both upon its intrinsic power and its stage history in the century now ending. Some scholars have argued that a private performance or two took place for the court or for an audience of lawyers, but Shakespeare's commercial sense renders such argument rather weak. It is possible to maintain that the play is Shakespeare's most sophisticated, and yet is it more intellectualized than *Love's Labour's Lost*, or *Hamlet* for that matter? Perhaps some high personage advised Shakespeare that *Troilus and Cressida* might seem too lively a satire upon the fallen Earl of Essex, who may be the model for the play's outrageous Achilles, or perhaps there are other political allusions that we no longer apprehend. Literary satire is more readily apparent; Shakespeare's language mocks the elaborate diction of George Chapman, who had compared Essex to Achilles, and more amiably teases the moral stance of Ben Jonson. But the mystery of why Shakespeare decided to give up on this marvelous work remains to be solved.

Homer's heroic men and suffering women, celebrated by Chapman in the commentary to his translation, are more savagely anatomized by Shakespeare than they are by Euripides, or by various satirists of our century. Thersites, identified in the Dramatis Personae as "a deformed and scurrilous Greek," pretty well speaks for the play, if not for Shakespeare:

Here is such patchery, such juggling, and such knavery! All the argument is a whore and a cuckold: a good quarrel to draw emulous factions, and bleed to death upon. Now the dry serpigo on the subject, and war and lechery confound all!

The Matter of Troy is reduced to "a whore and a cuckold," Helen and Menelaus, and to a company of rogues, fools, bawds, gulls, and politicians masquerading as sages—that is to say, to the public figures of Shakespeare's day, and of ours. Yet the play's bitterness surpasses the limits of satire, and leaves us with a more nihilistic impression than "heroic farce" or "travesty" would indicate. Some critics have traced the origins of *Troilus and Cressida* to the Poets' War fought between Ben Jonson on the one side and John Marston, Thomas Dekker, and perhaps Shakespeare on the other. Russell Fraser compares the "prologue armed" of *Troilus and Cressida* to the armed prologue—clearly resembling burly Ben himself (infamous for killing a fellow actor in a duel)—who begins Jonson's *Poetaster* (1601), an attack upon rival poet-playwrights. Shakespeare, mocking both Jonson and Chapman, may have commenced lightheartedly, intending an anti-*Poetaster*, stageworthy and brisk. But once started, this anti-tragedy, anti-comedy, anti-history ran away with its dramatist, and it is difficult to deny that a purely personal bitterness energizes the play. Perhaps we are back in the story of the Sonnets, as many have suggested, and Cressida is yet another version of the Dark Lady, like the mocking Rosaline in *Love's Labour's Lost*. War and lust, variations upon the one madness, alike are derided in the play, but the derision provoked by battle is wholehearted, and the rancor and anguish of the erotic life is represented with a far more equivocal response.

*Troilus and Cressida,* though a rigorously unified work for the stage, nevertheless is two plays. One is the tragicomedy of the death of Hector, murdered by the cowardly Achilles and his thugs. The other is the "betrayal" of Troilus by Cressida, who gives herself to Diomedes, when she is compelled to leave Troy and enter the camp of the Greeks. Shakespeare so estranges the audience from Hector and to some degree from Troilus that we are not much moved by the slaughter of Hector and only a little by the jealousy of Troilus. About the only true pathos the play could evoke would be if Shakespeare had altered either of the last appearances of Thersites and allowed him to be slain by Hector, or by Priam's bastard son, Margarelon. But quite wonderfully, Thersites survives both challenges:

*Hect.* What art thou, Greek? Art thou for Hector's match? Art thou of
    blood and honour?
*Thers.* No, no: I am a rascal, a scurvy railing knave: a very filthy rogue.
*Hect.* I do believe thee: live.

                                                [V.iv.26–30]

That is not really up to Thersites's standard, but this is:

*Marg.* Turn, slave, and fight.
*Thers.* What art thou?
*Marg.* A bastard son of Priam's.
*Thers.* I am a bastard, too; I love bastards. I am bastard begot, bastard
    instructed, bastard in mind, bastard in valour, in everything illegitimate. One bear will not bite another, and wherefore should
    one bastard? Take heed: the quarrel's most ominous to us—if the
    son of a whore fight for a whore, he tempts judgment. Farewell,
    bastard.
*Marg.* The devil take thee, coward.

                                                [V.vii.13–23]

I do not think that anyone could grow fond of Thersites, but we *need* him while we watch or read this play; he is its appropriate chorus. His slave status has not yet gained him support from our current Marxist and cultural materialist critics, but that may be because he is too foul-mouthed for professors, and besides his satire against lust is as politically incorrect as his animus against war is surpassingly correct. He belongs to the bottom layer of Shakespeare's cosmos, with companions in Parolles, Autolycus, Barnardine, and Pistol, among others. Presumably Thersites, like other slaves, has been dragged off to the Trojan War against his will, but his invective would be the same were he anywhere in the isles of Greece. His scabrous scoldings have a particular force at Troy, where, as he says, "All the argument is a whore and a cuckold."

It is important to recognize that Thersites, despite his scurrility, is pragmatically almost a normative moralist; his complaints against war and lechery depend upon our sense of some residual values in peace and in loyal love. To that degree, he is an authentic negative moralist, unlike Parolles in *All's Well That Ends Well*, or such varied figures as Lucio, Pompey, and Barnardine in *Measure for Measure*. Anne Barton argues strongly that Thersites sees his reductiveness—his negative view of everyone—as being endemic to the human condition, and not just as being appropriate for the thuggish Greek and Trojan heroes. Perhaps, but the dramatic effect seems otherwise; as both Shakespeare and Thersites portray them, the Homeric heroes are particularly egregious rascals. Barton usefully cites Euripides's *Orestes* as parallel to Shakespeare's play, but we have no evidence that Shakespeare knew the *Orestes*, in any form.

Euripides is also both less genial than Shakespeare and less savage; nearly everyone in *Troilus and Cressida* is at best a fool, so we should be surprised to be moved by the jealous sufferings of Troilus, and yet somehow we are. Shakespeare's largeness of temperament, his grand generosity of spirit, allows Troilus to become a figure of some limited pathos, and even a consciousness stunningly divided against itself.

And yet Shakespeare's art of characterization withdraws itself from *Troilus and Cressida*, even in the roles of Troilus, Cressida, Hector, and Ulysses. The interiorization of the self had given us Faulconbridge in *King John*; Richard II; Juliet, the Nurse, and Mercutio; Bottom; Portia, Shylock, and Antonio; Falstaff, Hal, and Hotspur; Brutus and Cassius; Rosalind; Hamlet; Malvolio and Feste. There are no such inwardnesses in the problematic comedies of *Troilus and Cressida*, *All's Well That Ends Well*, and *Measure for Measure*. The abyss of the deep self returns in Iago and Othello; Lear, the Fool, Edmund, and Edgar; and Macbeth. Before the forging of Iago, Shakespeare pauses in his journey to the interior, and the three "dark" comedies of 1601–4 give us neither accessible psychological depths nor Marlovian-Jonsonian caricatures and ideograms. Troilus and Thersites; Helena and Parolles; Isabella, Angelo, Duke Vincentio, and Barnardine—all of these abound in psychic complexities, but they keep themselves opaque from us, and Shakespeare will not tell us who and what they truly are.

Perhaps he himself, in that mood, did not care to know, or perhaps, for subtly dramatic purposes, he preferred that we should not know. One of the many consequences of this momentary turn away from the revelation of character is a certain lessening of character: we are invited, almost compelled, to care less for those figures than we care for Rosalind or for Feste. A more peculiar consequence is rhetorical: several speeches in each of these three "dark comedies" become much finer poetry when ripped from context. Ulysses on the idea of order at Troy, or on the transitoriness of reputation, gives one effect within the play and quite another outside it, rather like the difference between Duke Vincentio's "Be absolute for death" advice, when heard in or out of context. A scurvy politician, Ulysses seems eloquent beyond the play but only grandiose within its confines, while the Duke's sonorous vocables can persuade us in isolation but are exposed as inane and vacuous when they ring forth in the equivocal world of *Measure for Measure*.

Thersites, Parolles, and Barnardine are the grand exceptions: they so sublimely are at one with the contexts of their plays that they lose by citation. Coleridge, in expected distaste for Thersites, rather neatly dubbed him "the Caliban of demagogic life," and like Caliban, Thersites seems only half-human (whereas the uncanny Fool of *King Lear* seems scarcely human at all). What is least human about Thersites seems Shakespeare's ironic warning to us: the reductive tendency burns everything away, as it will, far more destructively, in the pyromaniac play-director, Iago. Graham Bradshaw calls Thersites "terminally reductive, sclerotically dogmatic."

"Dogmatic," from so evenhanded a critic, seems to me unfair: Thersites is an obsessed monomaniac, but he is also as outraged as he is outrageous. If you divide your time serving as Fool between Achilles and Ajax, between a vicious thug and a stupid one, you hardly can be reductive enough, particularly if your dramatic function is to be the chorus. Bradshaw also terms Thersites a nihilist, but the foul-mouthed Fool seems to me the only character in the play who truly has an outraged sense of intrinsic value. Nor is it fair to characterize poor Thersites as one of Alfred Adler's Inferiority Complexes (Bradshaw again). There is a weird self-reflective aspect to Thersites's highly conscious rankness, but it is difficult for us to receive, because of Thersites's otherness, his nonhuman aspect. If one can say to oneself, "How now, Thersites! What, lost in the labyrinth of thy fury?," then one is not quite lost. Thersites is by no means *pleased* to be the savage utterer of hateful truths, and I do not think Shakespeare wants us to take Thersites as other than a sufferer. If we can trust anyone in the play, then it must be Thersites, deranged as doubtless he is. But who else in the play is not both a self-deceiver and a deceiver of others? I have remarked upon the psychic opacities of *Troilus and Cressida*, and such blocked inwardness is most salient in Thersites.

As much as *Measure for Measure*, *Troilus and Cressida* is a play that defeats any wholly coherent interpretation, a defeat perhaps intended by Shakespeare himself, who more even than in *Hamlet* allowed himself to build his drama upon antithetical strains that could not accommodate each other. Since there is no Hamlet in these plays, no consciousness comprehensive enough to contain a wilderness of anomalies, we cannot altogether make sense either of Troilus or of Duke Vincentio in *Measure for Measure*. Troilus struggles with contraries that defy his intellect, but at least he somewhat engages our sympathies—unlike Vincentio, who is profoundly antipathetic in his moralizings. Troilus is fatuous, self-pitying, in love with love rather than with Cressida, and fiercely confused, but he remains rather more likable than Hector, his strenuously heroic brother, who alienates us by inconsistency, cupidity, and self-satisfaction. It isn't very useful to see Shakespeare's purposes as satiric, or even parodic in this play. He seems at moments to be mocking his rivals George Chapman and Ben Jonson, but he is not writing an anti-chivalric romance, as some critics have said. The matter of Troy does not matter to him, and while he quarries Chaucer, he deliberately distances himself from the amiable, even affectionate sophistication of Chaucer's great treatment of the same story.

There is a bitterness, somehow both personal and impersonal, in Shakespeare's version of this essentially medieval tale (of which Homer knew nothing). Thersites, Caliban of demagogic life, might have prompted Shakespeare himself to Prospero's gloomy final acceptance of Caliban: "this thing of darkness I / Acknowledge mine." Troilus is to love what Hector is to war, Ulysses to statecraft, Achilles to agonistic supremacy: they are all impostors, bad actors. For brainlessness, Agamemnon, Nestor, and Ajax are all nicely matched, while Cressida is as much the Trojan strumpet as Helen is the Spartan whore. That is all a little too strong for satire, even too extreme for parody. The tonalities of Shakespeare's *Troilus and Cressida* are not good-natured; no one smiles indulgently at the acts and torments, the posturings and speeches, of this rabblement. Pandarus, racked by venereal infection, is the counteremblem to Thersites: do we prefer the whinings of the bawd to the rantings of Thersites's invectorium?

2

The pleasures of *Troilus and Cressida*, though peculiar, are profuse: Shakespeare's exuberance of invention is manifest at every point. Troilus himself may well be the play's least interesting character. At the start, he is lovesick—that is to say, so consumed by his lust for Cressida that we cannot distinguish him from it. Coleridge, in his poorest comments upon Shakespeare, asked us to believe in Troilus's moral superiority to Cressida; Shakespeare shows such a judgment to be an absurdity. Cressida, in the vernacular, whether then or now, is for Troilus pragmatically what she is for Diomedes: a delicious dish. Anne Barton is finely precise upon this: "Cressida is regarded by her lover principally as matter for ingestion." Troilus, a vain and spoiled Trojan princeling, permits himself a certain idealizing as a lover, and Coleridge yields to it, even invoking the notion of "moral energy," whereas Coleridge allows himself to say that Cressida sinks into infamy.

Whatever the social distance between the lovers, Troilus nevertheless does not, for a moment, in this play, consider the possibility of a marriage to Cressida, or even of a permanent liaison. His jealousy—far more, of course, than that of Othello, or of Leontes in *The Winter's Tale*—prophesies the Proustian comedy of Swann's possessive desire for Odette and Marcel's for Albertine. Thersites and to some degree Ulysses see it as comic, but Troilus is hardly capable of saying, with Swann, "To think that I went through all this for a woman who did not suit me, who was not even my style!" Cressida suits Troilus very well, she is his style, and the style of Diomedes also, and of all those who will come after Diomedes. She is no better than Troilus, and why should she be? Shakespeare slyly revises Chaucer's Criseyde, in a manner splendidly noted by E. Talbot Donaldson in *The Swan at the Well* (1985), his study of Shakespeare's relation to his most authentic precursor. Chaucer's narrator in *Troilus and Criseyde* is madly in love with Criseyde, as Donaldson remarks, whereas Chaucer himself, though charmed with the lady, has a few amiable reservations. But then, his Criseyde is considerably more reluctant to take Troilus for a lover than Shakespeare's Cressida is.

Both heroines—Chaucer's and Shakespeare's—are socially isolated, with only Uncle Pandarus, eager pimp, as an adviser. Though Shakespeare's beauty is delightfully more forward, I agree with Donaldson that the two much maligned characters both enjoy the affectionate admiration of their poets—lustful admiration really, in Shakespeare's case. Yet Shakespeare necessarily is far more savage: if normative standards could apply to any-one in this play (and they can't), then Cressida is a whore, but who isn't, in *Troilus and Cressida*? Troilus, a callow self-deceiver, may not be a male whore like Achilles's beloved Patroclus, but he is military honor's whore, and masculine self-centeredness's whore, self-bought and self-sold. He wants one thing only from Cressida, and he wants it exclusively, and that essentially is his ideal of chivalric love. When he loses Cressida to circum-stances, he makes no effort to oppose those circumstances. He argues, and fights, to keep Helen for his brother Paris, but he clearly regards Cres-sida as being inferior to Helen, because possessing Helen brings more glory to Troy than holding on to Cressida can secure.

Shakespeare also emulates Chaucer in his characters' self-awareness of their role in literary history, but the dramatic effect, as contrasted with Chaucer's narrative cunning, is very curious, and makes us wonder just how Shakespeare apprehended his own play. Probably, we are still in the afterglow of *Hamlet*, with its audacious theatricality, particularly in the scene where Hamlet greets the players and suddenly thrusts us into the War of the Theaters. How ought a director to handle this?

*Troil.*                      O virtuous fight,
    When right with right wars who shall be most right!
    True swains in love shall, in the world to come,
    Approve their truth by Troilus; when their rhymes,
    Full of protest, of oath, and big compare,
    Wants similes, truth tir'd with iteration
    (As true as steel, as plantage to the moon,
    As sun to day, as turtle to her mate,
    As iron to adamant, as earth to th'centre)
    Yet, after all comparisons of truth,
    As truth's authentic author to be cited,
    'As true as Troilus' shall crown up the verse
    And sanctify the numbers.
*Cress.*                    Prophet may you be!
    If I be false, or swerve a hair from truth,
    When time is old and hath forgot itself,
    When water-drops have worn the stones of Troy,
    And blind oblivion swallow'd cities up,
    And mighty states characterless are grated
    To dusty nothing—yet let memory,
    From false to false, among false maids in love,
    Upbraid my falsehood. When they've said 'As false
    As air, as water, wind, or sandy earth,
    As fox to lamb, or wolf to heifer's calf,
    Pard to the hind, or stepdame to her son'—
    Yea, let them say, to stick the heart of falsehood,
    'As false as Cressid'.

*Pand.* Go to, a bargain made: seal it, seal it, I'll be the witness. Here I
hold your hand, here my cousin's. If ever you prove false one to
another, since I have taken such pains to bring you together, let
all pitiful goers-between be called to the world's end after my
name: call them all Pandars: let all constant men be Troiluses, all
false women Cressids, and all brokers-between Pandars. Say
'Amen'.

[III.ii.169–203]

"Amen" to pandars ever since, even if we do not find it worthwhile to
equate Troilus with constancy and Cressida with false women. Shakespeare
has stopped his play's action (such as it is) and raised our consciousness of
his (and our) debt to Chaucer. Not pathos but self-estrangement is conveyed by this tableau. Troilus, Cressida, and Pandarus see themselves as
players in a famous story, with much notoriety still to come. The effect is
neither comic nor satiric, and probably a director ought to advise the actors to play this scene quite straightforwardly, as if their characters were
unaware that they are affirming their own artificiality. Shakespeare has
prepared us for this dramatic freedom from self-consciousness earlier in the
scene, principally by creating an extraordinary gap between the remarkable
observations made both by Troilus and by Cressida and their palpable lack
of the cognitive and emotional powers, which make such eloquent insights possible. In context, we are astonished that these greedy lovers can
utter what is so powerful out of context:

*Troil.* This is the monstruosity in love, lady: that the will is infinite,
and the execution confined: that the desire is boundless, and the
act a slave to limit.
*Cress.* They say all lovers swear more performance than they are able,
and yet reserve an ability that they never perform: vowing more
than the perfection of ten, and discharging less than the tenth
part of one.

[III.ii.79–87]

Who, in or out of love, ever can forget "that the will is infinite, and the execution confined: that the desire is boundless, and the act a slave to limit"? I have a preternatural memory, for Shakespeare in particular, but rarely can identify Troilus as the speaker of this mordant observation. "Will" here also means "lust," and to the playwright had to be self-referential, as when he puns upon his name "Will" in the Sonnets. Troilus hardly seems to us an adequate metaphysician of love, or even of lust, but Shakespeare assigns him some extraordinary utterances. At their most intense, they transcend the play's sordid context in Act V, Scene ii, when Troilus and Ulysses spy upon the tryst between Cressida and Diomedes, while Thersites spies upon the spies. Shakespeare remains our greatest authority on the illness of falling in love, of being *in love* with someone, rather than simply loving another. Troilus, no authority but a sublimely sick case of still being in love with Cressida, appears a classical instance of the extreme defense against sexual jealousy, denial carried to its metaphysical limits: "Was Cressid here?" Ulysses coldly confirms that she was, provoking Troilus's most amazing outburst:

> *Troil.* This she?—No, this is Diomed's Cressida.
>     If beauty have a soul, this is not she;
>     If souls guide vows, if vows be sanctimonies,
>     If sanctimony be the gods' delight,
>     If there be rule in unity itself,
>     This is not she. O madness of discourse,
>     That cause sets up with and against itself!
>     Bifold authority! where reason can revolt
>     Without perdition, and loss assume all reason
>     Without revolt. This is, and is not, Cressid.
>     Within my soul there doth conduce a fight
>     Of this strange nature, that a thing inseparate
>     Divides more wider than the sky and earth;
>     And yet the spacious breadth of this division
>     Admits no orifex for a point as subtle
>     As Ariachne's broken woof to enter.

Instance, O instance! strong as heaven itself:
The bonds of heaven are slipp'd, dissolv'd and loos'd;
And with another knot, five-finger-tied,
The fractions of her faith, orts of her love,
The fragments, scraps, the bits, and greasy relics
Of her o'er-eaten faith are given to Diomed.

[V.ii.136–59]

From "Instance, O instance!" onward this is the rant of a "betrayed" lover, but until then it seems a crisis too severely metaphysical to be Troilus's. We are back at a central paradox of Shakespeare's "dark comedies" or "problem plays"; power of utterance transcends context. Thersites is the apt exegete for the context "Will a swagger himself out on's own eyes?" Troilus's negation of what is before him anticipates Hegelian negation, with its denial of the tyranny of fact. Troilus's dialectical Idealism is rather more drastic: "This is, and is not, Cressid." Psychological rather than philosophical, Troilus's double vision has less to do with debunking Petrarchan ecstasies of self-deception than with the common human blindness (or smugness) that enables sexual betrayal, as we oddly go on terming it. Shakespeare permits us a little sympathy for Troilus, but not much, particularly when the sanctimonious lover falls back into his customary mode of regarding Cressida as his private banquet:

The fractions of her faith, orts of her love,
The fragments, scraps, the bits, and greasy relics
Of her o'er-eaten faith are given to Diomed.

[V.ii.157–59]

The orts, or leftover meats, clearly designate the consubstantial Cressida as well as her pledge to Troilus; Troilus is about as chivalric as Cressida is constant. On our side of the play, we are abandoned to ambiguities: lust conquers all, and yet no specious standards are allowed to judge the energies of life. Shakespeare declines to be Chaucer, half in love with his

Cresyde, but (as always) Shakespeare also declines moralism. If Achilles the hero is just the cowardly leader of a gang of murdering thugs, if Ulysses is a speechmaking politician, if Hector cannot keep anything straight and dies for a gaudy suit of armor, if Troilus is no Romeo but only a witless version of Mercutio, then what should Cressida be except the Trojan strumpet? Except for Cassandra, who is insane, this is a play in which the women are whores, and the men are too. But with what exuberance they cavort! Shakespeare's generous rancidity here stems from a powerful insight that the mind itself is profoundly contaminated by lust, that what D. H. Lawrence condemned as "sex-in-the-head" is only another version of what William Blake satirized as "reasoning from the loins." The spirit at Troy, like the spirit everywhere and at every time, suffers the malaise that Hamlet anatomized. The motto of *Troilus and Cressida* might as well be the marvelous lines of Hamlet's Player King:

> For 'tis a question left us yet to prove,
> Whether love lead fortune or else fortune love.
>
> [*Hamlet*, III.ii.197–98]

Nothing is proved in *Hamlet*, or in *Troilus and Cressida*, in any sense of "proved." Hamlet, Nietzsche's precursor as a transvaluer of all value, still reigns at Troy, as he will do in all subsequent Shakespeare. In the movement from his first *Hamlet* (1588 or so) to *Hamlet* (1601), we see Shakespeare's Ghost change from one who is probably still part of a faith in resurrection to a Ghost intimating the illusory nature of resurrection. Himself bereft of both son and father, Shakespeare wrote a final *Hamlet* that seems to go beyond Christian belief into a purely secular transcendence. Nothing is got for nothing, and the nihilism of the Problem Comedies is part of the cost of this conversion. Yet it is a strangely joyous cost: What matters most about *Troilus and Cressida*, *All's Well That Ends Well*, and *Measure for Measure* is their negative exuberance, almost as though a fusion of Hamlet and Falstaff had written these plays.

3

If *Troilus and Cressida* has a villain, it cannot be the paltry Achilles. After Thersites, the genius of the play belongs to Ulysses, who says nothing that he believes, and believes nothing that he says. He is not Shakespeare's best portrait of a politician (various clerics dispute that eminence with various kings), but he might have dismayed any of several high personages at court, which again may account for Shakespeare's failure to stage the play at the Globe. Ulysses represents the state, its values and interests; he is the idea of order at Troy, the Contract with Greece, in the Gingrichian sense. His three great speeches, all undermined by their contexts, would qualify him to head our Republican Party, if not quite our Christian Coalition. Frankly a Machiavel, Ulysses nevertheless is more than a superb sophist. He possesses grand gusto; what other law-and-order demagogue has so persuasively defended the oppressiveness of hierarchy? We hear the eternal voice of the societal Right speak through him:

> Then everything includes itself in power,
> Power into will, will into appetite,
> And appetite, an universal wolf,
> So doubly seconded with will and power,
> Must make perforce an universal prey,
> And last eat up himself.
>
> [I.iii.119–24]

The language is very different from the scurvy rant of Thersites, but the pith is the same. Who is the true nihilist, Ulysses or Thersites? The authentic chill that emanates from Ulysses comes when he speaks as the Elizabethan spymaster, Walsingham or Cecil, whom Shakespeare must have suspected of terminating Christopher Marlowe with maximum prejudice, and of torturing Thomas Kyd. As we hear Ulysses, we can guess shrewdly why Shakespeare suppressed this brilliant play:

The providence that's in a watchful state

Knows almost every grain of Pluto's gold,

Finds bottom in th'uncomprehensive deep,

Keeps place with thought, and (almost like the gods)

Do thoughts unveil in their dumb cradles.

There is a mystery, with whom relation

Durst never meddle, in the soul of state,

Which hath an operation more divine

Than breath or pen can give expressure to.

All the commerce that you have had with Troy

As perfectly is ours as yours, my lord.

[III.iii.195–205]

This sublime passage is doubly blasphemous, set as it is both against the Intelligence Service and (by implication) against the divine mystery for which the state apparatus professes to work, Church and state being one, then and (increasingly) now. Perhaps Shakespeare wrote this dangerous speech only for his private pleasure, as a protest against the evil that had destroyed his playwright precursors. It may have been prompted by the frankly agonistic declaration Ulysses makes to Achilles just before this, perhaps the play's strongest poetry, when taken out of its context:

*Ulyss.* Time hath, my lord, a wallet at his back

Wherein he puts alms for oblivion,

A great-siz'd monster of ingratitudes.

Those scraps are good deeds past, which are devour'd

As fast as they are made, forgot as soon

As done. Perseverance, dear my lord,

Keeps honour bright: to have done is to hang

Quite out of fashion, like a rusty mail

In monumental mockery. Take the instant way;

For honour travels in a strait so narrow

Where one but goes abreast. Keep then the path;

For emulation hath a thousand sons

That one by one pursue; if you give way,
Or hedge aside from the direct forthright,
Like to an enter'd tide they all rush by
And leave you hindmost;
Or, like a gallant horse fall'n in first rank,
Lie there for pavement for the abject rear,
O'er-run and trampled on. Then what they do in present,
Though less than yours in past, must o'er-top yours;
For Time is like a fashionable host
That slightly shakes his parting guest by th'hand,
And with his arms out-stretch'd, as he would fly,
Grasps in the comer. Welcome ever smiles,
And farewell goes out sighing. O let not virtue seek
Remuneration for the thing it was;
For beauty, wit,
High birth, vigour of bone, desert in service,
Love, friendship, charity, are subjects all
To envious and calumniating Time.
One touch of nature makes the whole world kin—
That all with one consent praise new-born gauds,
Though they are made and moulded of things past,
And give to dust that is a little gilt
More laud than gilt o'er-dusted.
The present eye praises the present object.

[III.iii.145–80]

The epitome of this savage wisdom is the wonderfully sour "One touch of nature makes the whole world kin—," a reduction of all individuality and individual accomplishment that massively replies to the lament of Achilles: "What, are my deeds forgot?" It is ironic that Shakespeare has composed the definitive formulation of the sadness to which his own work has been least subject. In a sardonic play so overtly aware of Ben Jonson (he informs Ajax, even as he does Malvolio in *Twelfth Night*), perhaps the warning of Ulysses was another offhand smack at Jonson, whose desire for dramatic eminence was compounded by his resentment of Shakespeare's superiority. We only can surmise, as "gentle" Shakespeare slyly abstained from any overt ripostes to Jonson's acerbic allusions to Shakespeare's work. Time's envies and calumnies are universal, not merely Jonsonian, and clearly Shakespeare transcends the War of the Theaters when "love, friendship, charity" go down to oblivion, while "The present eye praises the present object."

There is a quality both exhilarating and disconcerting in this most powerful of Ulysses's utterances. To call oblivion, total forgetfulness, "a great-siz'd monster of ingratitudes" is to associate "those scraps [of] good deeds past, which are devour'd / As fast as they are made" with the ingestion of Cressida by her lovers, an association that underscores the generic imagery of the play, in which lechery and gluttony are fused. In a phantasmagoria of superb energy, Time's specious charity, "alms for oblivion," yields to time the fashionable host, who gives you a slight handshake as you go, and hugs your newcomer replacement. Everything in the play—the sexual delights of love, the rise and fall of reputations in battle, the persuasive orations of the "dog-fox" Ulysses—is summed up in the pungent formula "Welcome ever smiles, / And farewell goes out sighing." That embraces all action in the symbolic gesture of the panderer's craft, and proclaims the play's choices: Pandarus or Thersites. The audience cannot go mad with Cassandra, and has been alienated in turn from all the Greeks and all the Trojans. Thersites is a reductive truth teller, too horrible, too outcast for any audience's identification. As for Pandarus, Troilus rejects him, as though the poor bawd were responsible for Cressida's turn to Diomede, but by now Troilus himself is more than half-crazed and is wholly self-centered. No other play by Shakespeare closes with so explicit a rancidity, and indeed with a direct insult to the audience. But I wonder if even so sophisticated and intellectual an audience as the Inns of Court could have tolerated the outrageousness of the final identification that the syphilis-racked Pandarus proclaims to all of us:

> As many as be here of Pandar's hall,
> Your eyes, half out, weep out at Pandar's fall;
> Or if you cannot weep, yet give some groans,

Though not for me, yet for your aching bones.
Brethren and sisters of the hold-door trade,
Some two months hence my will shall here be made.
It should be now, but that my fear is this:
Some galled goose of Winchester would hiss.
Till then I'll sweat and seek about for eases,
And at that time bequeath you my diseases.

[V.x.48–57]

The "galled goose of Winchester," a syphilitic whore, is not a very appreciative audience for Pandarus, but then who would be? Perhaps Shakespeare had intended *Troilus and Cressida* for the Globe, or even for elsewhere, and perhaps also a version of the play had moved a highly placed person to warn the always circumspect Shakespeare that, for once, he had gone too far. All of Act V, increasingly violent and disaffected, might have been the playwright's reaction to his dilemma. We have (I repeat) no evidence whatsoever that Shakespeare's *Troilus and Cressida* ever was played anywhere before the twentieth century, though some scholars speculate that it failed at the Globe, which to me seems very unlikely. As a drama, it carries an odd aura of the forbidden, as though Shakespeare dares to trespass against the state, wholly contrary to his practice of a lifetime. I wonder whether Act V originally ended differently when Shakespeare still hoped to stage *Troilus and Cressida*? *Measure for Measure* goes further into societal alienation and nihilism, and yet seems to me the less personal work. Critics who have suggested that *Troilus and Cressida* shares the concerns and sufferings of the Sonnets seem to me correct. Magnificent in language, *Troilus and Cressida* nevertheless retreats from Shakespeare's greatest gift, his invention of the human. Something we cannot know drives him, in this play, against his own strength as a dramatist.

# 21

# ALL'S WELL THAT ENDS WELL

In proportion to its actual dramatic and literary merits, *All's Well That Ends Well* remains Shakespeare's most undervalued comedy, particularly when compared with such early works as *The Two Gentlemen of Verona* and *The Taming of the Shrew.* I have seen only one production of *All's Well That Ends Well,* and the play, alas, continues its long history of unpopularity, so I am unlikely to see many more. Fundamentally, we seem to misunderstand *All's Well That Ends Well,* from Samuel Johnson, master of all Shakespeare critics, down to the present. Like Dr. Johnson, we cannot abide Bertram, the caddish young nobleman whom the evidently admirable Helena loves. This is hardly the only unequal relationship in Shakespeare; generally his women choose inadequate men. But this does seem the most aggravating object choice in the plays. Bertram has no saving qualities; to call him a spoiled brat is not anachronistic. Dr. Johnson particularly resented the happy ending, with Bertram settling into supposed domestic bliss:

> I cannot reconcile my heart to Bertram; a man noble without generosity, and young without truth; who marries Helena as a coward, and leaves her as a profligate; when she is dead by his unkindness, sneaks home to a second marriage, is accused by a woman whom he has wronged, defends himself by falsehood, and is dismissed to happiness.

Shakespeare might have admired Johnson's bitter irony of "dismissed to happiness." *All's Well That Ends Well* is quite as rancid, in its courtly way, as *Troilus and Cressida* and *Measure for Measure;* even the play's title carries a sophisticated bitterness. Since Bertram is an empty-headed snob and nothing more, the drama's interest centers on Helena, and on Parolles, the fake soldier whose name aptly means "words," and who receives a demolition more in Ben Jonson's moral mode than in Shakespeare's. Many critics have disliked Parolles, but I cannot imagine why; he is a splendid scoundrel, perfectly transparent to anyone of good sense, which of course does not include Bertram. Parolles's and Helena's are the roles that matter most in this play. About all that a director can do with Bertram is to make him look like a juvenile Clark Gable, Trevor Nunn's solution in the production I recall seeing. Shakespeare's unpleasant young men are numerous; Bertram, as a vacuity, is authentically noxious.

Yeats, lamenting that his beloved Maud Gonne should have chosen to marry the gunman MacBride when she might have had Yeats, set down Shakespeare's own principle concerning all of his glorious women who select dreadful or empty men:

'Tis certain that fine women eat
A crazy salad with their meat
Whereby the horn of plenty is undone.

Since all of us know veritable instances of such Shakespearean mismatches, we should be delighted to turn to Shakespeare for insights into that "crazy salad." Portia happily settles for Bassanio, an amiable and perfectly useless fortune hunter, presumably because she thus implicitly gets back at her odd father, who imposed the casket ritual upon her, as she says:

O me the word "choose"! I may neither choose who I would, nor refuse who I dislike, so is the will of a living daughter curb'd by the will of a dead father.

[*The Merchant of Venice*, I.ii.22–25]

Julia, in *The Two Gentlemen of Verona*, is foolishly in love with Proteus, but a Protean lover comes in so many guises that a much wiser woman might make the same blunder. Hero, in *Much Ado About Nothing*, marries the feckless Claudio, but she is just too young to know that there is nothing to him. By *Twelfth Night*, Shakespeare has gone beautifully wild: the charming but zany Viola is delighted by the absurd Orsino, while Olivia snaps up Sebastian simply because he is Viola's twin; as another zany, he is pleased to be so devoured. Helena clearly is quite another matter, and her High Romantic passion for Bertram seems both an ironic culmination of Shakespeare's comic pairings and something well-nigh Keatsian:

> my imagination
> Carries no favour in't but Bertram's.
> I am undone; there is no living, none,
> If Bertram be away; 'twere all one
> That I should love a bright particular star
> And think to wed it, he is so above me.
> In his bright radiance and collateral light
> Must I be comforted, not in his sphere.
> Th' ambition in my love thus plagues itself:
> The hind that would be mated by the lion
> Must die for love. 'Twas pretty, though a plague,
> To see him every hour; to sit and draw
> His arched brows, his hawking eye, his curls,
> In our heart's table—heart too capable
> Of every line and trick of his sweet favour.
> But now he's gone, and my idolatrous fancy
> Must sanctify his relics.

> [I.i.80–96]

Keats's great, final sonnet, "Bright star, would I were steadfast as thou art!," echoes Helena's devotion to her "bright particular star," and the pathos of Keats's poem can be said to catch Shakespeare's irony. But Helena's ironies here are directed only against her own "idolatrous fancy," her Petrarchan worship of the young nobleman with whom she has been raised. By "imagination" and "fancy" here both she and Shakespeare mean a negative faculty, one that consciously self-deceives.

Shakespeare sees to it that we are moved (as Keats was) by Helena's capacity for love, while still apprehending that this splendid woman has eaten a crazy salad with her meat. Bertram is "above" her in social rank, and perhaps in good looks; otherwise she in fact is the "bright particular star" and Bertram is only a touch better than Parolles, since Bertram's only accomplishments are military, while Parolles is a mere braggart soldier, an impostor, a liar, a leech, considerably more interesting than the warring and whoring Bertram. The initial question of *All's Well That Ends Well* thus is: How can Helena be so massively wrong? You can salvage her bad judgment only by arguing that Bertram is immature, and will change, but Shakespeare indicates otherwise: this spoiled cad will grow up to be even more of a monster, despite his mother, his wife, and his king; almost, indeed, to spite them. The stubborn Helena triumphs, but only at her own expense, as the audience surely is compelled to conclude. With his uncanny mastery at representing women at least as persuasively as men, Shakespeare transforms the question into the much more interesting: Who is Helena?

We are told a great deal about Helena's late father, a distinguished physician and friend of the king's, but nowhere in the play do I recall any reference to Helena's actual mother. The Countess, Bertram's mother, has raised Helena as her foster child, and the love between the wretch's mother and Helena is the most admirable sentiment in the play. Shakespeare is very efficient at suppressing parents when they are, for his purposes, irrelevant. Of the mother of Goneril, Regan, and Cordelia we are told nothing, almost as though Lear's queen is as null as, say, Lady Macbeth's first husband or Iago's mother (even Iago presumably had one). I am not about to gratify formalists and materialists alike by speculating about Helena's childhood, let alone Iago's! But it is important to note Helena's love for the dowager Countess of Rossillion, protector of the orphaned Helena. Freud, Shakespearean in this also, divided object choices into two types, narcissistic and propped-against, and Helena's choice of Bertram participates strongly in both modes. Narcissistically Bertram, an earliest playfellow, is what Helena longed to be, the authentic child of her foster mother, while in the leaning-against mode, Bertram would have symbolized both lost fathers, his and hers. Helena's love therefore is overdetermined to a degree unusual even in Shakespeare, where the contingency of sexual passion is almost always established for us. It does not matter who Bertram inwardly is, or what he does: Helena is locked into loving him.

We therefore should begin apprehending *All's Well That Ends Well* by seeing that Helena's judgment is neither unsound nor sound; it is not a question of judgment at all. Helena, so long as she lives, will be in love with Bertram, because that is her selfsame identity, what she has been always. Shakespeare, who most certainly was unhappily married, shows us that marriage hardly is a matter of choice. I delight always in telling my students that the happiest marriage in all of Shakespeare is that of Macbeth and Lady Macbeth, who suit one another so admirably! Why do Othello and Desdemona marry, in a mismatch that gives Iago his terrible opportunity? We no more can answer that definitively than we can choose among Iago's many motives for his malignity. Something seems to be missing in both Othello's and Desdemona's accounts of their love, but that something is fundamental to the nature of marriage, the most peculiar of human institutions, both in and out of Shakespeare. Marriage, Shakespeare always implies, is where we are written, and not where we write.

2

It will not do to mention Parolles in relation to Falstaff, monarch of wit and freedom, though many critics fall into such error. The magnificent Falstaff is larger than the *Henry IV* plays and, as I intimate throughout this book, comes closer than any other character to representing Shakespeare's own vital center as a person. Not a cosmos like Falstaff, Parolles is the spiritual center of *All's Well That Ends Well*, the emblem of the rancidity that underlies its courtly surfaces. The play's bitterness is condensed into Parolles's vow to survive after his exposure and ruin:

*Par.* Yet am I thankful. If my heart were great
    'Twould burst at this. Captain I'll be no more,
    But I will eat and drink and sleep as soft
    As captain shall. Simply the thing I am
    Shall make me live. Who knows himself a braggart,
    Let him fear this; for it will come to pass
    That every braggart shall be found an ass.
    Rust, sword; cool, blushes; and Parolles live
    Safest in shame; being fool'd, by fool'ry thrive.
    There's place and means for every man alive.
    I'll after them.

                               [IV.iii.319–29]

We wince at, yet cannot quarrel with "Simply the thing I am / Shall make me live." "Who cannot be crush'd with a plot?" Parolles says a moment earlier, and that might make us flinch also. In context, "There's place and means for every man alive" has a particular aura to it, which can induce a shudder too. In his downfall, Parolles does not so much excite our sympathies as extend his range of possible identity with us. We may not be braggart soldiers, cowardly and wordy, but all of us share the terrible fear of disgrace and deprivation, of going down like Robert Frost's Abishag, or like Parolles. Frost's "Provide, Provide" is in the spirit of Parolles's "I'll after them."

Yet why are Parolles and Helena in the same play? Why, indeed, do they share it as opposites, if not quite mighty opposites? Their link is Bertram, who cannot be blamed upon Parolles, since Bertram hardly is improved after Parolles's exposure. Had Parolles not existed, Bertram would have fallen in with some other hanger-on, some other flattering rascal. The only authentic element in Bertram is his desire for military glory, since even his womanizing seems more an adjunct of his soldiering than a quest in itself. A few defenders of Bertram attempt to see him as the victim of his parasite Parolles, but that will not sustain scrutiny. Parolles is not in the play as Bertram's dark angel; rather he represents what Shakespeare always loathed, mindless fashion, time-serving mock gentility, false courage, the domain of the lie. What is singular and important about Parolles is his transparency; every person of good will in the play sees through Parolles at a glance. Bertram's blindness is the index of worthlessness, and is akin to Bertram's aversion from Helena, which must go a long way back into their shared childhood. We have—all of us—known a Parolles or two; what is astonishing again is Shakespeare's tolerance for the wordy rascal, whose abject but tough survivalism is acceptable to the playwright, and indeed is rendered instrumental in the undoing of Bertram and triumph of Helena. Parolles, and in a far more complex way Helena, are the keys to what is strongest and subtlest about *All's Well That Ends Well*, a dark vision of human nature that is also profoundly accepting of the darkness. It is as though Shakespeare, by an act of will, holds himself back from the nihilistic abysses of *Troilus and Cressida* and *Measure for Measure*, but only at the cost of assigning most value to an aged generation—the King, the Countess, the Lord Lafew, the clown Lavatch—and to Helena as a throwback to their principles. By going with the old order, Shakespeare gives us a possible wisdom, best expressed in the play by a prose observation of one of the French lords:

> The web of our life is of a mingled yarn, good and ill together; our virtues would be proud if our faults whipp'd them not, and our crimes would despair if they were not cherish'd by our virtues.
>
> [IV.iii.68–71]

Few sentences in the language are subtler or finally more disconcerting than this. There is no mingled yarn in the webs either of Bertram or of Parolles; the observation pertains to Helena, as our surrogate. Much admired by George Bernard Shaw as an aggressive, post-Ibsenite woman, Helena has little laughter in her, and so is not very Shavian. She is formidable indeed, well-nigh monomaniacal in her fixation upon the glittering emptiness of Bertram. Since her high-handedness in obtaining him is so outrageous, we can wonder why we are not moved to some sympathy for him, despite the usurpation of his choice by Helena's alliance with the King, who simply threatens the young man into an arranged marriage. Humanly, Bertram has been wronged to an extreme; he is the prize set by Helena as her fairy-tale reward for curing the King of France. This ought to be abominable, but since Bertram is abominable, we are not distressed. Shakespeare's art in handling Helena's outrageousness is extraordinary: she carries off her weird project with verve and *sprezzatura*:

> *Ber.* I cannot love her nor will strive to do't.
> *King.* Thou wrong'st thyself if thou should'st strive to choose.
> *Hel.* That you are well restor'd, my lord, I'm glad.
>     Let the rest go.
>
> [II.iii.145–48]

"Let the rest go" is wonderful, in its admixture of despair and cunning, since Helena knows, as does the King, that the royal honor and power alike are at stake. Provoked, authority speaks out in tones that prophesy the admonishing God of Milton's *Paradise Lost*:

> Obey our will which travails in thy good;
> Believe not thy disdain, but presently
> Do thine own fortunes that obedient right
> Which both thy duty owes and our power claims;
> Or I will throw thee from my care for ever
> Into the staggers and the careless lapse
> Of youth and ignorance; both my revenge and hate
> Loosing upon thee in the name of justice,
> Without all terms of pity.
>
> [II.iii.158–66]

Bertram's revenge, after he has capitulated, is properly childish: "I'll to the Tuscan wars and never bed her." The play's most poignant moment, at the close of Act II, juxtaposes Bertram's wounded petulance and Helena's dignified despair:

> *Hel.*          Sir, I can nothing say
>     But that I am your most obedient servant.

*Ber.* Come, come; no more of that.

*Hel.*                       And ever shall

    With true observance seek to eke out that

    Wherein toward me my homely stars have fail'd

    To equal my great fortune.

*Ber.*                   Let that go.

    My haste is very great. Farewell. Hie home.

*Hel.* Pray sir, your pardon.

*Ber.*                Well, what would you say?

*Hel.* I am not worthy of the wealth I owe,

    Nor dare I say 'tis mine—and yet it is;

    But, like a timorous thief, most fain would steal

    What law does vouch mine own.

*Ber.*                  What would you have?

*Hel.* Something, and scarce so much; nothing indeed.

    I would not tell you what I would, my lord.

    Faith, yes:

    Strangers and foes do sunder and not kiss.

*Ber.* I pray you, stay not, but in haste to horse.

*Hel.* I shall not break your bidding, good my lord.

                                  [II.v.71–88]

He is the wealth she owes (owns), sexually speaking, but his rejection of her renders her "a timorous thief," longing to steal what is only legally hers. The starts and stops of her voice here are immensely artful, and restore much of our fondness for her, if not for her judgment. His subsequent farewell letter to her completes both our contempt for him and our enforced complicity with her:

*When thou canst get the ring upon my finger, which never shall come off, and show me a child begotten of thy body that I am father to, then call me husband; but in such a "then" I write a "never."*

                                  [III.ii.56–59]

Pragmatically, this is Shakespeare's invitation to the bed trick, the sub-stitution of one woman for another in the dark, that helps bring about a rancid resolution, both here and in *Measure for Measure*. The sportive formula—in the dark they are all alike—is partly Shakespeare's satire upon the male propensity scarcely to distinguish one woman from another, but it also carries a burden of bitterness with it. When Isabella accepts the bed trick, with Mariana substituting for her, in *Measure for Measure*, at the insti-gation of "the Duke of dark corners," we are not startled at her moral complicity because, like nearly every other character in the play, she is at least half crazy. But we necessarily are bothered when Helena herself proposes the bed trick, where she is to be the sexual performer under an-other person's name. Our uneasiness ought to augment when we ponder Helena's language as she anticipates her impending union with the gulled Bertram:

> But, O strange men!
> That can such sweet use make of what they hate,
> When saucy trusting of the cozen'd thoughts
> Defiles the pitchy night; so lust doth play
> With what it loathes for that which is away.
> But more of this hereafter.
>
> [IV.v.21–26]

The superb rancidity of this resides in its pragmatism; does literature af-ford a cooler, more dispassionate female view of male lust? Helena's pun-gent phrase, "saucy trusting," will reverberate in *Measure for Measure* when the hypocrite Angelo equates murder with illicit procreation: "Their saucy sweetness that do coin heaven's image / In stamps that are forbid." "Saucy" in each case means both "insolent" and "lascivious," and the strength of He-lena's insight turns, in part, upon her mingled sense that male lust is at once pungent, undifferentiated, and misogynistic. Though Helena promises us "more of this hereafter," we will not (alas) listen to her again upon this mat-ter. As she tells us instead, the entire play must inform us, even as she cites its title:

> Yet, I pray you;
> But with the word: "the time will bring on summer"—
> When briars shall have leaves as well as thorns
> And be as sweet as sharp. We must away;
> Our wagon is prepar'd, and time revives us.
> All's well that ends well; still the fine's the crown.
> Whate'er the course, the end is the renown.
>
> [IV.iv.30–36]

This deliberate mishmash of proverbs is properly bittersweet, and is intended to justify Helena's audacity, itself a sauciness we need not underestimate. The bed trick is one thing, and fair game if you want to play it, but is it not a very different matter to pretend death, so as to grieve the foster mother Countess, the King, and LaFew? Helena's tactics here prelude those of the more-than-dubious Duke in *Measure for Measure*, when he cruelly deceives Isabella and everyone else as to Claudio's death. Not that Helena, like the Duke, is a sadist, but rather that she is relentless in her drive to make all's well for herself by ensnaring the inedible Bertram. This quest must strike the audience as singularly unwholesome, and Shakespeare gives every sign that he is well aware of our ambivalence, not toward Helena but toward her unrepentant mission.

The play protects Helena from our skepticism by presenting her monomania in heroic dimensions. Does anyone else in Shakespeare, woman or man, struggle so incessantly and at last so successfully to surmount every impediment to the fulfillment of an ambition? Only the hero-villains rival Helena—Richard III, Iago, Edmund, Macbeth—and they all at last are slain or undone. Helena triumphs, even if we are dismayed by her choice of reward. Yet what a complex struggle she has undergone; to recapitulate, it is to see that her agon to win Bertram is the total structure of the play, except for the saga of Parolles, whose defeat and subsequent will to survive constitute the parodic echo of Helena's victory and will to marry. Freud learned a scandalous proportion of his own supposed originalities from Shakespeare; one of them is the idea that fulfillment, if not happiness, depends upon the bringing to realization of our deepest ambitions when we were still children. Helena attains completion, and so presumably will be content. And yet Shakespeare deliberately makes us uneasy with the final exchange between wife and husband:

> *Hel.* O my good lord, when I was like this maid
>   I found you wondrous kind. There is your ring,
>   And, look you, here's your letter. This it says:
>   *When from my finger you can get this ring*
>   *And is by me with child, &c.* This is done;
>   Will you be mine now you are doubly won?
> *Ber.* If she, my liege, can make me know this clearly
>   I'll love her dearly, ever, ever dearly.
> *Hel.* If it appear not plain and prove untrue
>   Deadly divorce step between me and you!
>
> [V.iii.303–12]

These edgy couplets are among Shakespeare's most rancid, and provoke an alienating comic effect. Of all Helena's audacities, the most outrageous is "O my good lord, when I was like this maid / I found you wondrous kind," an innuendo so distasteful, in context, that something in our spirits abandons Helena. As for the insufferable Bertram, he goes out on the right note of ludicrous insincerity: "I'll love her dearly, ever, ever dearly," which is at least one "ever" too many. The King's final couplet, except for the Epilogue, expresses the saving reservations both of Shakespeare and the audience:

> All yet *seems* well, and *if* it end so meet,
> The bitter past, more welcome is the sweet.
>   [italics mine]
>
> [V.iii.327–28]

The Epilogue goes beyond this, by making *us* the actors, so that *our* applause becomes an ironic celebration of the play, the players, and the playwright's own ironic reservations. A curious dying fall accompanies Shakespeare's withdrawal from a resolution that remains purely Helena's:

*The king's a beggar, now the play is done;*
*All is well ended if this suit be won,*
*That you express content; which we will pay*
*With strife to please you, day exceeding day.*
*Ours be your patience then and yours our parts;*
*Your gentle hands lend us and take our hearts.*

[Epilogue 1–6]

The players become audience, and must take their contentment, if any, from us. Though the compositional sequence of the three problem comedies is disputed among scholars, *All's Well That Ends Well*, to me, is seen best as a crossing between *Troilus and Cressida* and *Measure for Measure*. It is not the equal of either nihilist masterwork, yet it carries us, via Helena and Parolles, from Ulysses and Thersites to Lucio and Barnardine, from the idea of order at Troy to the idea of order at Vienna. There is no idea of order in the France and Italy of *All's Well That Ends Well*. Either, like Helena, you break through every barrier and have your will, or like Parolles you are found out and have the will to survive despite it. Is this a difference that veritably makes a difference? Shakespeare, in this freest if also slightest of his trinity of problematic comedies, will not give us any unequivocal answer.

# 22

# MEASURE FOR MEASURE

Composed probably in the span from late spring through late summer 1604, the astonishing *Measure for Measure* can be regarded as Shakespeare's farewell to comedy, since one needs to term it something other than comedy. Traditionally called a "problem play," or "dark comedy," like its immediate predecessors, *Troilus and Cressida* and *All's Well That Ends Well*, *Measure for Measure* exceeds them in rancidity and seems to purge Shakespeare of whatever residual idealism Thersites and Parolles had not expunged in him. I have argued that Thersites is the center, as well as the chorus, of *Troilus and Cressida*, and that Parolles similarly centers *All's Well That Ends Well*. The parallel figure in *Measure for Measure* would be Lucio, except that he is too good-natured and scabrously sane to be the emblem of the corrupt cosmos of *Measure for Measure*. The emblematic role here belongs to the sublime Barnardine, perpetual drunkard and convicted murderer, who speaks only seven or eight sentences in a single scene, yet who can be called the particular comic genius of this authentically outrageous play. Zaniness, a proper term for the celebratory *Twelfth Night*, is inadequate when we try to characterize *Measure for Measure*, a play so savagely bitter as to be unmatched in that regard.

Everyone has (or I presume should have) particular favorites among Shakespeare's plays, however much they worship Falstaff, Hamlet, Lear, and Cleopatra. Mine are *Measure for Measure* and *Macbeth*: The high rancidity of the first and the ruthless economy of the second captivate me as no other works of literary art do. The Vienna of Lucio and Barnardine, and the hell of Macbeth, are unsurpassable visions of human disease, of sexual malaise in *Measure for Measure*, and of the imagination's horror of itself in *Macbeth*. Why *Measure for Measure*, though not neglected, is not truly popular has something to do with its equivocal tonalities: we never can be certain as to just how we ought to receive the play. Certainly the crazy last scene, when we come to it, abandons us to our astonishment. Isabella, the apocalyptically chaste heroine, does not speak once during the final 85 or so lines, which conclude with the Duke's startling proposal of marriage to her, a notion as insane as anything else in this unbelievable yet persuasive drama. Shakespeare, piling outrage upon outrage, leaves us morally breathless and imaginatively bewildered, rather as if he would end comedy itself, thrusting it beyond all possible limits, past farce, long past satire, almost past irony at its most savage. The comic vision, to which Shakespeare turned (for relief?) after triumphantly revising *Hamlet* in 1601, ends itself with this wild scherzo, after which tragedy comes back again in *Othello* and its successors. For me, at least, something of Iago's spirit hovers in *Measure for Measure*, suggesting that Shakespeare was already at work on *Othello*. Iago's impotent yet destructive sense of human sexuality is appropriate to the Vienna of *Measure for Measure*, city of Lucio, a fantastic; of Mistress Overdone, a bawd; of Pompey Bum, a bawd turned apprentice to Abhorson, an executioner; above all, of the convict Barnardine, who has the wisdom to stay perpetually drunk because to be sober in this mad play is to be madder than the maddest.

*Measure for Measure*, more specifically than any other work by Shakespeare, involves his audience in what I am compelled to call the dramatist's simultaneous invocation and evasion of Christian belief and Christian morals. The evasion decidedly is more to the point than the invocation, and I scarcely see how the play, in regard to its Christian allusiveness, can be regarded as other than blasphemous. Ultimately that includes the title, with its clear reference to the Sermon on the Mount: "With what measure ye mete, it shall be measured to you again," a reverberation of "Judge not, that ye be not judged." This has suggested an interpretation as crazy as the play but much less interesting: certain Christianizing scholars ask us to be-

lieve that *Measure for Measure* is an august allegory of the Divine Atonement, in which the dubious Duke is Christ, amiable Lucio is the Devil, and
the sublimely neurotic Isabella (who is unable to distinguish any fornication whatsoever from incest) is the human soul, destined to marry the
Duke, and thus become the Bride of Christ! Such Christian critics as Dr.
Johnson and Coleridge knew better, as did Hazlitt, himself no believer but
the son of a Dissenting minister. Sanity concerning *Measure for Measure* begins with Hazlitt's recognition that insofar as the play shows Shakespeare
as a moralist, he is "a moralist in the same sense in which nature is one." Nature, as a moralist (at least in this drama), seems to follow the Duke's dubious admonition to Angelo:

> nor nature never lends
> The smallest scruple of her excellence
> But, like a thrifty goddess, she determines
> Herself the glory of a creditor,
> Both thanks and use.
>
> [I.i.36–40]

Vincentio, Duke of Vienna, is taking a holiday from reality, and leaves
his city-state under the proxy rule of Angelo. "Mortality and mercy in Vienna" are deputized to Angelo, a whited sepulchre who proclaims virtue:
fornication and its begetting of illegitimate children are to be punished by
beheading. Mistress Overdone, the bawd, is called "Madame Mitigation"
by the witty Lucio, but the mitigation of desire is now a capital offense in
Vienna. Claudio is doomed to death, a consequence of "Groping for trouts,
in a peculiar river." Betrothed to Juliet but not yet married to her, Claudio
states the morality of nature:

> Our natures do pursue,
> Like rats that ravin down their proper bane,
> A thirsty evil, and when we drink we die.
>
> [I.ii.120–22]

A law, improbably placed upon Vienna's books by Shakespeare, promises death for unsanctioned lovemaking, and the peculiar Duke Vincentio pretends to leave town so that this mad statute can be enforced by his surrogate, Angelo, whose own sexual correctness could withstand no deep scrutiny. Shakespeare does not bother to provide the Duke with any motivations; Vincentio's antics, throughout the play, make him a kind of anarchistic precursor of Iago. There is no Othello for the Duke to bring down, but he seems to plot, quite impartially, against all his subjects, for ends in no way political or moral. Is he, as Anne Barton adroitly suggests, Shakespeare's own surrogate as a comic dramatist? If so, comedy goes beyond rancidity into Marxist mischief (Groucho's, not Karl's), and Shakespeare's purposes are only a touch clearer than the Duke's. This scherzo ends comedy for Shakespeare, though strange laughters erupt in the remaining range of his work.

Sexual desire, a disaster in *Troilus and Cressida*, becomes very unhappy comedy in *Measure for Measure*. A considerable despair richly informs the play, and it is not unreasonable to suppose that the despair was Shakespeare's, at least imaginatively. I myself, rereading the play, hear in it an experiential exhaustion, a sense that desire has failed, as in Ecclesiastes, where "all the daughters of music have been brought low." Whether Isabella, in her revulsion from a vision of universal incest, somehow speaks for the play, we cannot know, though this is the implicit conclusion of Marc Shell's *The End of Kinship* (1988), the best full-length study of *Measure for Measure*. Something is very wrong with Vincentio's Vienna, yet to suggest that "a withering of the incest taboo" (Shell) would be a remedy for any Vienna— Freud's included—is charmingly drastic. Still, Shakespeare is very drastic in this play, which almost rivals *Hamlet* as a "poem unlimited," breaking through traditional forms of representation.

We have seen Shakespeare, in *Troilus and Cressida*, refuse inwardness to his characters, thus going against the grain of his mature art as a dramatist. In *Measure for Measure*, everyone is an abyss of inwardness, but since Shakespeare takes care to keep each character quite opaque, we are frustrated at being denied an entry into anyone's consciousness. This has the singular effect of giving us a play without any minor characters: Barnardine's somehow is as large a role as the Duke's or Isabella's. Even Lucio, the "fantastic," who is saner than anyone else on stage (as Northrop Frye remarked), rails on with an intent we cannot grasp. I used to brighten my viewing of bad movies by fantasizing the effect of arbitrarily inserting Groucho Marx into the action. In the same spirit (though *Measure for Measure* is as great as it is, finally, opaque), I sometimes envision placing Sir John Falstaff in Vincentio's Vienna. The sage of Eastcheap, a fierce discursive intelligence as well as the monarch of wit, would destroy the entire cast by mockery, and yet might leave the stage sadly baffled by even *his* inability to reduce the Duke's project to some realistic, Epicurean sense. The Falstaffian scorn would be a proper reaction to the Duke's sanctimonious poem that sets up the bed trick by which Angelo will "perform an old contracting" to Mariana:

He who the sword of heaven will bear
Should be as holy as severe:
Pattern in himself to know,
Grace to stand, and virtue, go.

[III.ii.254–57]

Shakespeare cannot be serious, we rightly feel, and yet the Duke enforces the irony of the play's title. Coleridge, Shakespeare's fiercest Bardolator, said that only *Measure for Measure*, among all the plays, was painful for him. Walter Pater, in what remains, after more than a century, the best essay on the play, slyly contrasted it to *Hamlet*:

It deals, not like *Hamlet* with the problems which beset one of exceptional temperament, but with mere human nature. It brings before us a group of persons, attractive, full of desire, vessels of the genial, seed-bearing powers of nature, a gaudy existence flowering out over the old court and city of Vienna, a spectacle of the fulness and pride of life which to some may seem to touch the verge of wantonness. Behind this group of people, behind their various action, Shakespeare inspires in us the sense of a strong tyranny of nature and circumstance. Then what shall there be on this side of

it—on our side, the spectators' side, of this painted screen, with its
puppets who are really glad or sorry all the time? What philosophy
of life, what sort of equity?

"Mere human nature," "the genial, seed-bearing powers of nature," "the
verge of wantonness," "a strong tyranny of nature": Pater's subtle litany intimates just what being "full of desire" comes to in this play, to a force that
compels both public order and Christian morality to choices between nullity and hypocrisy. The "philosophy of life" on our "spectators' side" is the
Epicurean flux of sensations; the "sort of equity" is, as Marc Shell adumbrates, retaliation, the law of talion, or the giving back of like for like. Measure for measure is reduced to like for like, Claudio's head for Juliet's
maidenhead, Vincentio's bed trick for Angelo's attempt upon Isabella's impregnable chastity, Lucio's enforced marriage to the whore Kate Keepdown for Lucio's mockeries of the Duke-turned-false-friar. Perhaps
Shakespeare should have called the play *Like for Like*, but he chose not to
forgo his hidden blasphemy of the Sermon on the Mount, just sufficiently
veiled to escape his own regime's frightening version of the law of talion,
which had murdered Marlowe and broken Kyd, barbarities that we can assume still weighed upon Shakespeare, even as he lived through his too-
brief final days in Stratford.

The forerunners of nineteenth-century European nihilism, of Nietzsche's prophecies and Dostoevsky's obsessives, are Hamlet and Iago, Edmund and Macbeth. But *Measure for Measure* surpasses the four High
Tragedies as the masterpiece of nihilism. Thersites, in *Troilus and Cressida*, in
his scabrous invectives, still relies upon absent values, values that implicitly condemn the moral idiocy of everyone else in the play, but there are
no values available in Vincentio's Vienna, since every stated or implied vision of morality, civil or religious, is either hypocritical or irrelevant. So
thoroughgoing is Shakespeare's comic rebellion against authority that the
play's very audacity was its best shield against censorship or punishment.
Shell argues, with real brilliance, that the mad law against fornication is
Shakespeare's paradigm for *all* societal laws, his make-believe foundation
for civilization and its discontents. Though I find that extreme, Shell

catches, better than anyone else since Pater, the essential wildness of *Measure for Measure*. No other work by Shakespeare is so fundamentally alienated from the Western synthesis of Christian morality and Classical ethics, and yet the estrangement from nature itself seems even sharper to me. The spiritual despair of *King Lear* and of *Macbeth*, as I read them, removes them further from Christianity than we are in *Hamlet* and *Othello*, and further also from the naturalistic skepticism of Montaigne, which is firmly insulated from nihilism. *Measure for Measure*, the threshold to *Othello*, *King Lear*, and *Macbeth*, harbors a deeper distrust of nature, reason, society, and revelation than the ensuing tragedies manifest. In every deep of this comedy a lower deep opens, a way down and out that rules out return. That must be why (as we will see) the play's final scene is so little concerned with convincing either itself or us of the resolutions and reconciliations brought about by the equivocal Duke.

2

In terms of the plot, it can be said that poor Claudio causes all the trouble, by suggesting to Lucio that Isabella be recruited to move Angelo to mercy:

> Implore her, in my voice, that she make friends
> To the strict deputy: bid herself assay him.
> I have great hope in that. For in her youth
> There is a prone and speechless dialect
> Such as move men; beside, she hath prosperous art
> When she will play with reason and discourse,
> And well she can persuade.
>
> [I.ii.170–76]

Perhaps Claudio is not altogether conscious of what he implies, particularly since "prone" does not mean "lying down." But what does it mean? What are we to make of "assay"? "Move" and "play" are certainly ambiguous, and Claudio's diction prefigures the strong, sexual effect that Isabella

has upon men, virtually each time she speaks. Angelo's sadomasochistic desire for the novice nun is more palpable than the Duke's lust, but the difference between the two is in degree, not in kind. When we first encounter
Isabella, we hear her "wishing a more strict restraint / Upon the sister-
hood" she is soon to join. Something of her unconscious sexual power is
suggested by that desire for sterner discipline, presaging her rejection of
Angelo's offer to trade her brother's head for her maidenhead, measure for
measure:

> were I under the terms of death,
> Th'impression of keen whips I'd wear as rubies,
> And strip myself to death, as to a bed
> That longing have been sick for, ere I'd yield
> My body up to shame.

> [II.iv.100–104]

Had the Marquis de Sade been able to write so well, he might have
hoped to compete with that, but in fact he wrote abominably. Yet it is his
peculiar accent that Isabella anticipates, even as she further excites Angelo's
sadism (and ours, if we would admit it). It is one of Shakespeare's most effective outrages that Isabella is his most sexually provocative female character, far more seductive even than Cleopatra, the professional seductress.
Lucio, the flaneur or "fantastic," testifies to the perverse power of her innocence, which reminds the audience perpetually that a novice nun, in *their*
vocabulary, is a novice whore, and a nunnery a synonym for a leaping
house. Angelo and the Duke, in uncanny association, alike are moved to
sublime lust by Isabella's pleas, Angelo when she petitions him, and the
Duke when he watches, as false friar, the scene of high sexual hysteria in
which Isabella and Claudio clash as to the price of her virtue. It is difficult
to decide who is more antipathetic, Angelo or Duke Vincentio, but males
in the audience are likely to echo Angelo's "She speaks, and 'tis such
sense / That my sense breeds with it." Empson, reading "sense" as both rationality and sensuality, said that "the real irony . . . is that her coldness,
even her rationality, is what has excited him." Perhaps, but her holiness ex-

cites him more, and the pleasures of profanation are his deepest desire. What, to a repressed sadomasochist, could be more moving than Isabella's offer to bribe him:

> with true prayers
> That shall be up at heaven and enter there
> Ere sunrise: prayers from preserved souls,
> From fasting maids, whose minds are dedicate
> To nothing temporal.
>
> [II.ii.152–56]

To dedicate Isabella's body to the wholly temporal gratification of his lust is Angelo's inevitable response:

> Never could the strumpet
> With all her double vigour, art and nature,
> Once stir my temper: but this virtuous maid
> Subdues me quite.
>
> [II.ii.183–86]

One feels that Angelo's heaven would be a nunnery, where he might serve as visiting (and punishing) father-confessor, and that one hears the man for the first time when he plainly (and zestfully) cries out his ultimatum to the sensually maddening novice nun:

> I have begun,
> And now I give my sensual race the rein:
> Fit thy consent to my sharp appetite;
> Lay by all nicety and prolixious blushes
> That banish what they sue for. Redeem thy brother
> By yielding up thy body to my will;
> Or else he must not only die the death,
> But thy unkindness shall his death draw out

To ling'ring sufferance. Answer me tomorrow,
Or, by the affection that now guides me most,
I'll prove a tyrant to him. As for you,
Say what you can: my false o'erweighs your true.

[II.iv.58–69]

This splendid Return of the Repressed makes for wonderful melodrama, particularly when its theatrical context is comic, however rancidly so. Angelo is bad news, and Shakespeare happily sees to it that the news gets no better, right down to the end of the play. We need not doubt that, at least at this point, the infatuated Angelo would be willing to substitute torturing the brother for ravishing the sister. That, too, would be measure for measure, and outraged virtue (Angelo's) would be appeased! Again the Grand Marquis de Sade could match Shakespeare neither in psychic conception nor in eloquence of execution. Sade's fusion of political authority, spiritual dominance, and sexual torture is also anticipated by Angelo, whose name is no more ironic than his delegated office or his mission to stamp out fornication and bastardy.

Angelo alone might suffice as a peculiar admirer for the curious Isabella, but Shakespeare is determined to overgo himself, and so passes on to the disguised Duke, in the central scene of the play (Act III, Scene i), which is dominated by an uncanny eloquence that reverberates far more magnificently out of context than in it. We have encountered this oddity before in Ulysses's set pieces in *Troilus and Cressida*, but not on the scale of the Duke's response to Claudio's "I have hope to live, and am prepar'd to die." Here is the spiritual advice of the supposed Friar, a litany of sorrows that profoundly moved two very different sensibilities, those of Dr. Samuel Johnson and T. S. Eliot:

*Cla.* I have hope to live, and am prepar'd to die.
*Duke.* Be absolute for death: either death or life
    Shall thereby be the sweeter. Reason thus with life:
    If I do lose thee, I do lose a thing
    That none but fools would keep. A breath thou art,

Servile to all the skyey influences
That dost this habitation where thou keep'st
Hourly afflict. Merely, thou art Death's fool;
For him thou labour'st by thy flight to shun,
And yet run'st toward him still. Thou art not noble;
For all th'accommodations that thou bear'st
Are nurs'd by baseness. Thou'rt by no means valiant;
For thou dost fear the soft and tender fork
Of a poor worm. Thy best of rest is sleep;
And that thou oft provok'st, yet grossly fear'st
Thy death, which is no more. Thou art not thyself;
For thou exists on many a thousand grains
That issue out of dust. Happy thou art not;
For what thou hast not, still thou striv'st to get,
And what thou hast, forget'st. Thou art not certain;
For thy complexion shifts to strange effects
After the moon. If thou art rich, thou'rt poor;
For, like an ass whose back with ingots bows,
Thou bear'st thy heavy riches but a journey,
And Death unloads thee. Friend hast thou none;
For thine own bowels which do call thee sire,
The mere effusion of thy proper loins,
Do curse the gout, serpigo, and the rheum
For ending thee no sooner. Thou hast nor youth, nor age,
But as it were an after-dinner's sleep
Dreaming on both; for all thy blessed youth
Becomes as aged, and doth beg the alms
Of palsied eld: and when thou art old and rich,
Thou hast neither heat, affection, limb, nor beauty
To make thy riches pleasant. What's yet in this
That bears the name of life? Yet in this life
Lie hid moe thousand deaths; yet death we fear
That makes these odds all even.

[III.i.4–41]

Johnson and Eliot alike centered upon the most haunting cognitive music in this great (but in context greatly empty) speech:

> Thou hast nor youth, nor age,
> But as it were an after-dinner's sleep
> Dreaming on both.

Johnson commented:

This is exquisitely imagined. When we are young we busy ourselves in forming schemes for succeeding time, and miss the gratifications that are before us; when we are old we amuse the languor of age with the recollection of youthful pleasures or performances; so that our life, of which no part is filled with the business of the present time, resembles our dreams after dinner, when the events of the morning are mingled with the designs of the evening.

"Dinner" for Shakespeare and Johnson is our "lunch"; Johnson's sense of the unlived life was never stronger.

The Duke-Friar's speech is blasphemously anything but Christian comfort. It *sounds* impressive to the highest degree, and owes its general aura to Hamlet's soliloquies, but the emptiness at our core that harried Hamlet appears to be rather a good thing to the Duke-Friar. If he is serious, then he is half-crazed, which may very well be the case. Northrop Frye summed up this speech by saying that it advised Claudio to die as soon as possible, because if he lived he might catch several unpleasant diseases. Yet to dismiss the Duke's oration is hardly possible; it moves with a grandeur that enhances its nihilism, with a sonority that is eternal. The speech's stance is Epicurean, and suggests the polemic against the fear of death in Lucretius, with just a dash of Senecan Stoicism tossed in for flavoring. With music so pompously irrelevant, the Duke's eloquence nevertheless momentarily inspires Claudio to an appropriately answering double talk, which, like the Duke's speech, does not say what it means, nor mean what it says.

I humbly thank you.
To sue to live, I find I seek to die,
And seeking death, find life. Let it come on.

[III.i.41–43]

We can make immediate sense neither of the Duke nor of his ghostly
advice, because Shakespeare will not have it so. Vincentio indeed is what
Lucio calls him: "the duke of dark corners," addicted to disguises, sadistic
teasings, and designs hopelessly duplicitous. Since Lucio is the only rational and sympathetic character in this absurdist comedy (except for the superb Barnardine), it seems safe to assume that his constant verbal assaults
on the Duke speak for us, the audience, and for Shakespeare, if anyone except for Barnardine can represent the playwright's economy of affection
amidst such folly. Let us assume that Lucio gets everything right, as several critics have said before me, Marc Shell most fully. The Duke's lust for
Isabella then takes on its proper resonance; what in Angelo was a Return
of the Repressed becomes in Vincentio a desperate drive away from liber-
tinism, from the sexual malaise that he amply shares with his seething city
of bawds and whores. His flight from the city's stew of sexual corruption
is manifestly a flight from himself, and his cure, as he sees it, is the innocent temptress Isabella, whose passion for chastity is perhaps reversible, or
so he hopes. Shell rightly observes that Lucio portrays the Duke's own bad
intentions, and I think we can go further than that. No one else in Shakespeare is as weirdly motivated (or nonmotivated) as Vincentio, and many
if not most of his opacities vanish if Lucio is a truth teller and not a slan-
derer. Lucio will not let Vincentio alone: "Nay, friar, I am a kind of burr, I
shall stick." One fantastic sees himself in the other: a gallant of the light
finding a gallant of dark corners. Who knows better than Lucio the Vienna
of Mistress Overdone, Kate Keepdown, and Pompey Bum? Are we to believe Lucio, who tells the Friar, "Thou knowest not the Duke so well as I
do. He's a better woodman than thou tak'st him for," or do we believe Vincentio's overdefense:

O place and greatness! Millions of false eyes
Are stuck upon thee: volumes of report

Run with these false, and most contrarious guest
Upon thy doings: thousand escapes of wit
Make thee the father of their idle dream
And rack thee in their fancies.

[V.i.60–65]

It is the lament of all modern celebrities, political and theatrical, in the era of instant journalism. Lucio the flaneur is the journalist of Vincentio's Vienna, and his lies ring out some wounding truths. Who can believe the Duke's protestations to the authentic Friar Thomas: "Believe not that the dribbling dart of love / Can pierce a complete bosom," and "Even like an o'er-grown lion in a cave / That goes not out to prey." Vincentio is his own Vienna; he is the disease he purports to cure. I borrow this splendid formulation from Karl Kraus, who did not gratify Sigmund Freud by mordantly observing that psychoanalysis itself was the malady it attempted to alleviate. Shakespeare's Vienna is a pre-Freudian joke against Freud, a Shakespearean revenge for Freud's ardent support of the delightful argument that the low-born "man from Stratford" had stolen all his plays from the mighty Earl of Oxford. Vincentio is the type of all those Freudian heretics who rebelled against their patriarch, and seduced their female patients even as they proclaimed the scientific purity of the psychoanalytic transference. That would make Isabella the type of all those gifted and beautiful, disturbed and disturbing hysterical muses of psychoanalysis, the women of Vienna whom Freud and his disciples both exalted and exploited. Vincentio's handling of Isabella—between persuading her to assist in plotting the bed trick, and then deceiving her as to Claudio's execution—is very much a transference manipulation, a psychic conditioning intended to prepare her to fall in love with her ghostly father, the false Friar and wayward Duke.

That returns us to the "Be absolute for death" oration, an early phase of the Duke's campaign to seduce Isabella, by first working her brother into a terror that will provoke the saintly sister into an answering rapture of angry hysteria against her wretched sibling. Again we can see Vincentio as a prelude to Iago, though he lacks Iago's fierce clarity. The undersong of "Be absolute for death" is caught by Eliot when he uses "Thou hast nor

youth, nor age, / But as it were an after-dinner's sleep / Dreaming on both"
as the epigraph to his *Gerontion*, a hymn to the desiccation of death-in-life,
a rhapsody of negations. The Duke speaks for the Duke, for a savage reductionist who has emptied life of all value. Each of us is a servile breath,
a fool or victim, base, cowardly, sleepy, a concourse of atoms, caught between past and future in an illusory present, poor, moon-crazed, friendless,
and subject to a thousand little deaths. We are our anxieties; no more, no
less, and so we are well out of it all. That is Isabella's suitor, and it is small
wonder that we never know whether she will take the Duke or not, maddest of Vienna's mad as she is. But we know why he wants her; he is so vast
a sensible emptiness that her zealous chastity at least might spur him to
some zest of his own.

With us, Vincentio eavesdrops on the remarkable exchange between
brother and sister that is Shakespeare's most rancid salute to the joys of sib-
linghood. To Isabella's stern "Dar'st thou die?" Claudio renders a falsely
magnificent answer:

> If I must die,
> I will encounter darkness as a bride
> And hug it in mine arms.
>
> [III.i.82–84]

Were that said by Antony or Coriolanus, it would be something. In
context it receives its proper reply in Isabella's deathly tribute:

> There spake my brother: there my father's grave
> Did utter forth a voice. Yes, thou must die.
>
> [III.i.85–86]

Had Hamlet a sister, she might have spoken to him thus. Isabella is
nothing but the voice of the dead father, feeding upon life. And Claudio,
at his most eloquent, begs for his life, even at the expense of his sister's
virtue, in a speech that Milton remembered (perhaps involuntarily) when
he had the crafty Belial counsel passivity in *Paradise Lost*'s debate in Hell:

*Cla.* Ay, but to die, and go we know not where;
To lie in cold obstruction, and to rot;
This sensible warm motion to become
A kneaded clod; and the delighted spirit
To bathe in fiery floods, or to reside
In thrilling region of thick-ribbed ice;
To be imprison'd in the viewless winds
And blown with restless violence round about
The pendent world: or to be worse than worst
Of those that lawless and incertain thought
Imagine howling,—'tis too horrible.
The weariest and most loathed worldly life
That age, ache, penury and imprisonment
Can lay on nature, is a paradise
To what we fear of death.

[III.i.117–31]

This Lucretian ecstasy of dread goes past Isabella's sadism to reply primarily to the Duke's "Be absolute for death," as though Claudio has needed some time to absorb that admonition. Isabella, however, needs no time whatsoever to react with all her pent-up force:

*Isab.*                    O, you beast!
O faithless coward! O dishonest wretch!
Wilt thou be made a man out of my vice?
Is't not a kind of incest, to take life
From thine own sister's shame? What should I think?
Heaven shield my mother play'd my father fair:
For such a warped slip of wilderness
Ne'er issued from his blood. Take my defiance,
Die, perish! Might but my bending down
Reprieve thee from thy fate, it should proceed.
I'll pray a thousand prayers for thy death;
No word to save thee.

[III.i.135–46]

Setting aside Isabella's rather clear preference for her father over her mother, and firmly fending off her plain nastiness, this astonishing outburst could be judged the play's true center (as it is judged by Marc Shell). Yet this is not the hysteria it may seem: as I have stated earlier, for Isabella every act of coition is "a kind of incest," and her desire to become a bride of Christ is certainly authenticated. Does she speak for herself only, or is this also *Measure for Measure*'s true voice of cognition and of feeling? In Vincentio's Vienna, as in Freud's, reality comes down to sex and death, though Vincentio's city is even closer to the formula: sex equals incest equals death. That equation is the only idea of order in *Measure for Measure*, as it was also Hamlet's reductive idea of order until his sea change and emergence into disinterestedness in Act V. But in *Measure for Measure* we are given nothing like Hamlet's intellectual consciousness. Rather, we are halfway between Hamlet and Iago. Vincentio has neither Hamlet's transcendent mind nor Iago's diabolical will, yet he seethes with Hamlet's sexual malaise and with Iago's drive to manipulate others, to weave his own web. Hamlet composes *The Mousetrap*, Iago an Othello-trap, and Vincentio, a would-be comic dramatist, arranges marriages: Claudio and Juliet, Angelo and Mariana, Lucio and Kate Keepdown, Vincentio and Isabella. Shakespeare employs Vincentio as the ultimate parody of the comic play-botcher, bringing order to a Vienna that cannot endure order. Yet what is the Duke's Vienna except Shakespeare's London, or our New York City, or any other vital disorder of the human?

3

Barnardine is the genius of that disorder, and qualifies as the imaginative center (and greatest glory) of *Measure for Measure*. Claudio pleads in Act I that all he and Juliet lack is "outward order"; except for that, they truly are husband and wife. Angelo, grimly allowing the "fornicatress," Juliet, "needful, but not lavish means," adds, "There shall be order for't." The Duke also intricately plays upon "order," as he commands the beheading of Barnardine:

By the vow of mine order, I warrant you, if my instructions may be your guide: let this Barnardine be this morning executed, and his head borne to Angelo.

Sublimely, Barnardine refuses to cooperate: "I swear I will not die today for any man's persuasion." The idea of order in Vincentio's Vienna ultimately is an idea of death; Barnardine, refusing all order, declines to die, and Shakespeare seconds Barnardine, when he has the Duke finally pardon this confessed murderer. But who is Barnardine, and why is he in this most peculiar of Shakespearean dramas? He is introduced to us by way of an ironic allusion to Ecclesiastes: "The slepe of him that travaileth is swete, whether he eate little or much" (5:11, Geneva Bible). Claudio, presented by the Provost with his death warrant, answers the question "Where's Barnardine?":

> *Cla.* As fast lock'd up in sleep as guiltless labour
> When it lies starkly in the traveller's bones.
> He will not wake.
>
> [IV.ii.64–66]

The "traveller" is also the "travailer," the poor man or laborer, whose sleep is sweet. Barnardine is guilty, and drunk, but the "good" the Provost intends ("who can do good on him?") is just a beheading in the afternoon, the idea of order in Vienna. Of Barnardine we learn more just before we at last first hear and then see him:

> *Duke.* What is that Barnardine, who is to be executed in th'afternoon?
> *Prov.* A Bohemian born, but here nursed up and bred; one that is a
> prisoner nine years old.
> *Duke.* How came it that the absent Duke had not either delivered him
> to his liberty, or executed him? I have heard it was ever his manner to do so.
> *Prov.* His friends still wrought reprieves for him; and indeed, his fact
> till now in the government of Lord Angelo came not to an undoubtful proof.

*Duke.* It is now apparent?

*Prov.* Most manifest, and not denied by himself.

*Duke.* Hath he borne himself penitently in prison? How seems he to
be touched?

*Prov.* A man that apprehends death no more dreadfully but as a
drunken sleep; careless, reckless, and fearless of what's past,
present, or to come: insensible of mortality, and desperately
mortal.

*Duke.* He wants advice.

*Prov.* He will hear none. He hath evermore had the liberty of the
prison: give him leave to escape hence, he would not. Drunk
many times a day, if not many days entirely drunk. We have very
oft awaked him, as if to carry him to execution, and showed him
a seeming warrant for it; it hath not moved him at all.

[IV.ii.126–51]

The superb Barnardine will not play by the rules of Vincentio's Vienna,
and is equally unaffected both by its mortality and its mercy. For Barnardine, nine years have gone by in a drunken slumber, from which he wakes
only to refuse escape and execution alike. Perhaps nothing is more dreadfully funny in *Measure for Measure* than the Duke-Friar's perturbed "He wants
advice," meaning more ghostly comfort of the "Be absolute for death" variety. With marvelous dramatic cunning, Shakespeare prepares us for the
hilarity of Barnardine's one great scene, by letting Vincentio delude himself as to his power over Barnardine: "Call your executioner, and off with
Barnardine's head. I will give him a present shrift, and advise him for a better place." But we could as well be in *Alice in Wonderland* or *Through the Looking Glass* when we hear "off with Barnardine's head." Vincentio invariably
speaks nonsense, as the audience comes to understand. Part of Barnardine's function is to expose this nonsense; the convicted murderer's other
use is to represent, with memorable starkness, the unregenerate human
nature that is Vienna or the world, invulnerable to all the oppressions of
order. The authentic comedy in *Measure for Measure* touches its limit in
Barnardine's apotheosis, which requires to be quoted complete:

*Abhor.* Sirrah, bring Barnardine hither.

*Pom.* Master Barnardine! You must rise and be hanged, Master Barnardine.

*Abhor.* What hoa, Barnardine!

*Barnardine.* [*within.*] A pox o' your throats! Who makes that noise there? What are you?

*Pom.* Your friends, sir, the hangman. You must be so good, sir, to rise and be put to death.

*Barnardine.* [*within.*] Away, you rogue, away; I am sleepy.

*Abhor.* Tell him he must awake, and that quickly too.

*Pom.* Pray, Master Barnardine, awake till you are executed, and sleep afterwards.

*Abhor.* Go in to him and fetch him out.

*Pom.* He is coming, sir, he is coming. I hear his straw rustle.

*Enter BARNARDINE.*

*Abhor.* Is the axe upon the block, sirrah?

*Pom.* Very ready, sir.

*Barnardine.* How now, Abhorson? What's the news with you?

*Abhor.* Truly, sir, I would desire you to clap into your prayers; for look you, the warrant's come.

*Barnardine.* You rogue, I have been drinking all night; I am not fitted for't.

*Pom.* O, the better, sir; for he that drinks all night, and is hanged betimes in the morning, may sleep the sounder all the next day.

*Enter DUKE [disguised].*

*Abhor.* Look you, sir, here comes your ghostly father. Do we jest now, think you?

*Duke.* Sir, induced by my charity, and hearing how hastily you are to depart, I am come to advise you, comfort you, and pray with you.

*Barnardine.* Friar, not I. I have been drinking hard all night, and I will have more time to prepare me, or they shall beat out my brains with billets. I will not consent to die this day, that's certain.

*Duke.* O sir, you must; and therefore I beseech you
Look forward on the journey you shall go.

*Barnardine.* I swear I will not die today for any man's persuasion.

*Duke.* But hear you—

*Barnardine.* Not a word. If you have anything to say to me, come to
    my ward: for thence will not I today. *Exit.*

*Enter PROVOST.*

*Duke.* Unfit to live or die! O gravel heart.

*Prov.* After him, fellows, bring him to the block!

[IV.iii.21–64]

I have never seen this delicious and profound outrageousness properly
directed and acted. Now that legal executions multiply daily in the United
States, I would recommend Barnardine's example to our hosts of residents
of Death Row: they simply should refuse the obscene dignity of our decorous gassings, fatal injections, and electrocutions, hangings and firing
squads being (momentarily, doubtless) out of fashion. Let them not consent to die, for any man's persuasion, and so force us to beat out their
brains with blocks of wood, as Barnardine aptly suggests. *That* is the Shakespearean insight, conveyed here by a stubbornly ironic Barnardine, and by
the vastly perturbed gang of Abhorson, Pompey, the prison Provost, and
the egregious Duke, who totally forgets that he only acts the part of a Friar,
most of all when he yields to Barnardine's refusal to cooperate in a proper
execution:

*Duke.* A creature unprepar'd, unmeet for death;
    And to transport him in the mind he is
    Were damnable.

That bland idiocy, so expressive of Vincentio, is light-years away from
Pompey's exposure of our societal madness: "Pray, Master Barnardine,
awake till you are executed, and sleep afterwards." Barnardine never will be
fitted for his execution, and his eloquence illuminates everything that is
wonderfully wrong about the world of *Measure for Measure*: "I will not consent to die this day, that's certain." Only that is certain in this play, where
Vincentio makes no sense whether as Duke or as Friar, where Isabella's

passionate chastity is an irresistible goad to lust, and where the bed trick
is sanctified well beyond Helena's venture in *All's Well That Ends Well*. For
me, the best moment in the play is the interchange when the Duke says,
"But hear you—" and Barnardine responds: "Not a word." The moral comedy of this comedy is Shakespeare's riposte to anyone in the audience capable of being taken in by Vincentio. It is after we have absorbed
Barnardine's dissent that Shakespeare has the Duke-Friar descend to the
sadistic degradation of lying to Isabella that her brother has been executed. Angelo, of all men, gets it right when he says of Vincentio, "His actions show much like to madness."

*Measure for Measure* ends with the perfectly mad coda of the long, single
scene that constitutes Act V, in which the Duke pardons Angelo, Barnardine, and Claudio and turns into everyone's matchmaker, vindictively in
regard to Lucio. Nothing is more meaningful in this scene than the total
silence of Barnardine, when he is brought upon stage to be pardoned, and
of Isabella, once she has joined Mariana in pleading for Angelo's life. She
does not reply to the Duke's marriage proposal, which sets aside her obsessive drive to become a nun. But then her final lines, on behalf of Angelo,
are as peculiar as anything else in the play:

> For Angelo,
> His act did not o'ertake his bad intent,
> And must be buried but as an intent
> That perish'd by the way. Thoughts are no subjects;
> Intents, but merely thoughts.

[V.i.448–52]

Isabella, being crazed, must be serious; Shakespeare cannot be. A murderous intention is pragmatically dismissed, when indeed it was far more
than a thought: Angelo had ordered Claudio's beheading, and this *after*
Angelo's supposed deflowering of Isabella. What does not take place, Isabella says, and for whatever reason, is only a thought and not a subject—
that is, someone ruled by Vincentio. The imagery of burial and of perishing
on the way evidently pertains to *all* intents, all thoughts. Nothing is alive

in Isabella, and Shakespeare will not tell us why and how she has suffered such a vastation. Pragmatically mindless, she need not respond to the Duke's proposal, and her nullity means that presumably he will have his way with her. Contemplating the future marriages of Vincentio and Isabella, of Angelo and Mariana, is not a happy occupation. Even Lucio's enforced union with the punk Kate Keepdown is not likely to be less salubrious. I do not know any other eminent work of Western literature that is nearly as nihilistic as *Measure for Measure*, a comedy that destroys comedy. All that remains is the marvelous image of the dissolute murderer Barnardine, who gives us a minimal hope for the human as against the state, by being unwilling to die for any man's persuasion.

# PART VII

# THE GREAT TRAGEDIES

# 23

# HAMLET

The origins of Shakespeare's most famous play are as shrouded as *Hamlet's* textual condition is confused. There is an earlier *Hamlet* that Shakespeare's drama revises and overgoes, but we do not have this trial work, nor do we know who composed it. Most scholars believe that its author was Thomas Kyd, who wrote the archetypal revenge play *The Spanish Tragedy*. I think, though, that Peter Alexander was correct in his surmise that Shakespeare himself wrote the *Ur-Hamlet*, no later than 1589, when he was first starting as a dramatist. Though scholarly opinion is mostly against Alexander on this, such a speculation suggests that *Hamlet*, which in its final form gave its audience a new Shakespeare, may have been gestating in Shakespeare for more than a decade.

The play is huge: uncut, it is nearly four thousand lines, and is rarely acted in its (more or less) complete form. T. S. Eliot's once-fashionable judgment that *Hamlet* is "certainly an artistic failure" (what literary work then is an artistic success?) seems to have been prompted by the disproportion between the prince and the play. Hamlet appears too immense a consciousness for *Hamlet;* a revenge tragedy does not afford the scope for the leading Western representation of an intellectual. But *Hamlet* is scarcely the revenge tragedy that it only pretends to be. It is theater of the world, like *The Divine Comedy* or *Paradise Lost* or *Faust,* or *Ulysses,* or *In Search of Lost Time*. Shakespeare's previous tragedies only partly foreshadow it, and his later works, though they echo it, are very different from *Hamlet,* in spirit and in tonality. No other single character in the plays, not even Falstaff or Cleopatra, matches Hamlet's infinite reverberations.

The phenomenon of Hamlet, the prince without the play, is unsurpassed in the West's imaginative literature. Don Quixote and Sancho Panza, Falstaff, and perhaps Mr. Pickwick approximate Hamlet's career as literary inventions who have become independent myths. Approximation can extend here to a few figures of ancient literature: Helen of Troy, Odysseus (Ulysses), Achilles among them. Hamlet remains apart; something transcendent about him places him more aptly with the biblical King David, or with even more exalted scriptural figures. Charisma, an aura of the preternatural, attends Hamlet, both within and beyond Shakespeare's tragedy. Rare in secular literature, the charismatic is particularly (and strangely) very infrequent in Shakespeare. Henry V is apparently meant to have charisma, but he vulgarizes it, even as Shakespeare's Julius Caesar did before him. Lear largely has lost it before we first encounter him, and Antony rapidly becomes a case study in its evanescence. So histrionic and narcissistic is Cleopatra that we cannot quite be persuaded by her charismatic apotheosis as she dies, and Prospero is too compromised by his hermetic magic to achieve any unequivocal charisma. Hamlet, first and last, vies with King David and the Jesus of Mark as a charismatic-of-charismatics. One could add the Joseph of the Yahwist or J Writer, and who else? There is Tolstoy's Hadji Murad, the surrogate of his creator's dreaming old age, and outrageously there is Sir John Falstaff, who offends only the virtuous, but these virtuous scholars send out so perpetual a chorus of disapproval that they have made the great wit's charisma appear dimmer than actually it is.

Hamlet's eminence never has been disputed, which raises again the hard query "Did Shakespeare know how much he had lavished upon the prince?" Many scholars have held that Falstaff got away from Shakespeare, which seems clear enough even if we cannot know whether Shakespeare had anticipated Falstaff's wild, instant popularity. Henry IV, Part Two, is just as much Falstaff's play as Part One is, yet Shakespeare must have known that the Fat Jack of The Merry Wives of Windsor is a mere impostor, and not Falstaff the charismatic genius. Can we envision Hamlet, even a mock

Hamlet, in another Shakespearean play? Where could we locate him; what context could sustain him? The great villains—Iago, Edmund, Macbeth— would be destroyed by Hamlet's brilliant mockery. No one in the late tragedies and romances could stand on stage with Hamlet: they can sustain skepticism, but not an alliance of skepticism and the charismatic. Hamlet would always be in the wrong play, but then he already is. Elsinore's rancid court is too small a mousetrap to catch Hamlet, even though he voluntarily returns to it, to be killed and to kill.

Yet largeness alone is not the full problem; *King Lear* is Shakespeare's widest psychic cosmos, but it is deliberately archaic, while Hamlet's is the least archaic role in all of Shakespeare. It is not just that Hamlet comes after Machiavelli and Montaigne; rather, Hamlet comes after Shakespeare, and no one yet has managed to be post-Shakespearean. I hardly intend to imply that Hamlet *is* Shakespeare, or even Shakespeare's surrogate. More than a few critics have rightly seen the parallel between Falstaff's relation to Hal, and Shakespeare's to the noble youth (probably the Earl of Southampton) in the Sonnets. Moralists don't want to acknowledge that Falstaff, more than Prospero, catches something crucial in Shakespeare's spirit, but if I had to guess at Shakespeare's self-representation, I would find it in Falstaff. Hamlet, though, is Shakespeare's ideal son, as Hal is Falstaff's. My assertion here is not my own; it belongs to James Joyce, who first identified Hamlet the Dane with Shakespeare's only son, Hamnet, who died at the age of eleven in 1596, four to five years before the final version of *The Tragedy of Hamlet, Prince of Denmark,* in which Hamnet Shakespeare's father played the role of the Ghost of Hamlet's father.

When we attend a performance of *Hamlet,* or read the play for ourselves, it does not take us long to discover that the prince transcends his play. Transcendence is a difficult notion for most of us, particularly when it refers to a wholly secular context, such as a Shakespearean drama. Something in and about Hamlet strikes us as demanding (and providing) evidence from some sphere beyond the scope of our senses. Hamlet's desires, his ideals or aspirations, are almost absurdly out of joint with the rancid atmosphere of Elsinore. "Shuffle," to Hamlet, is a verb for thrusting off "this mortal coil," where "coil" means "noise" or "tumult." "Shuffling," for

Claudius, is a verb for mortal trickery; "with a little shuffling," he tells Laertes, you can switch blades and destroy Hamlet. "There is no shuffling" there, Claudius yearningly says of a heaven in which he neither believes nor disbelieves. Claudius, the shuffler, is hardly Hamlet's "mighty opposite," as Hamlet calls him; the wretched usurper is hopelessly outclassed by his nephew. If Shakespeare (as I am convinced) was revising his own *Ur-Hamlet* of a decade or so before, it may be that he left his earlier Claudius virtually intact, even as his Hamlet underwent a metamorphosis beyond recognition. There is in Claudius's villainy nothing of the genius of Iago, Edmund, and Macbeth.

Shakespeare's Devil, Iago, father of Milton's Satan, is the author of the tragic farce *The Jealousy of Othello, and His Murder of his Wife Desdemona*. This play, by no means identical with Shakespeare's *Othello*, is only partly embedded in Shakespeare's tragedy, because Iago doesn't finish it. Frustrated by Emilia's balking of his last act, he murders her, and then refuses all interpretation: "From this time forth I never will speak word." Hamlet, an even more metaphysical dramatist than Iago, writes his own Act V, and we never are quite certain whether Shakespeare or Hamlet composes more of Shakespeare's and Hamlet's play. Whoever Shakespeare's God may have been, Hamlet's appears to be a writer of farces, and not of a comedy in the Christian sense. God, in the Hebrew Bible, particularly in Job, composes best in rhetorical questions. Hamlet is much given to rhetorical questions, but unlike God's, Hamlet's do not always seek to answer themselves. The Hebrew God, at least in the Yahwist's text, is primarily an ironist. Hamlet, certainly an ironist, does not crave an ironical God, but Shakespeare allows him no other.

Harry Levin, brooding on this, aptly described *Hamlet* as a play obsessed with the word "question" (used seventeen times), and with the questioning of "the belief in ghosts and the code of revenge." I would want to get at this obsession with questioning a little differently. Shakespeare's principal departure from the Hamlet of legend and of history is to alter, quite subtly, the grounds of action for the prince. In the Danish chronicler Saxo Grammaticus and in the French tale by Belleforest, Prince Amleth from the start is in real danger from his murderous uncle, and cunningly feigns idiocy and madness in order to preserve his life. Perhaps in the *Ur-Hamlet* Shakespeare had followed this paradigm, but little remains of it in our *Hamlet*. Claudius is all too content to have his nephew as heir; rotten as the state of Denmark is, Claudius has everything that ever he wanted, Gertrude and the throne. Had Hamlet remained passive, after the Ghost's visitation, then Polonius, Ophelia, Laertes, Rosencrantz, Guildenstern, Claudius, Gertrude, and Hamlet himself would not have died violent deaths. Everything in the play depends upon Hamlet's response to the Ghost, a response that is as highly dialectical as everything else about Hamlet. The question of *Hamlet* always must be Hamlet himself, for Shakespeare created him to be as ambivalent and divided a consciousness as a coherent drama could sustain.

Shakespeare's first Hamlet must have been Marlovian, and would have been (as I've intimated already) an overreacher, a self-delighting counter-Machiavel, and a rhetorician whose metaphors persuaded others to action. The mature Hamlet is far more complex, outrageously so. With fascinated and (fascinating) cunning, Shakespeare did not follow his source by naming Hamlet's father Horwendil but gave father and son the same name, the name borne by Shakespeare's own (and only) son. Peter Alexander, with his customary shrewdness, notes in his *Hamlet, Father and Son* (1955) that the Ghost is a warrior fit for Icelandic saga, while the prince is a university intellectual, representative of a new age. Two Hamlets confront each other, with virtually nothing in common except their names. The Ghost expects Hamlet to be a version of himself, even as young Fortinbras is a reprint of old Fortinbras. Ironically, the two Hamlets meet as if the Edda were encountering Montaigne: the Archaic Age faces the High Renaissance, with consequences as odd as any we might expect.

The Ghost, as we come to see, is not Horwendil, but has more of the characteristics of the Amleth of Danish saga: tough, warlike, but as cunning in the attempted manipulation of his scholarly son as he was in fending off his enemies. Prince Hamlet, Renaissance wit and skeptic, reader of Montaigne and London playgoer, breaks both with the Belleforest Hamlet and the Hamlet of Shakespeare's original drama: Shakespeare, playing the Ghost's role in 1601, addresses what he might have hoped his own son

Hamnet, on the verge of manhood, to have been. The Ghost speaks of his uxorious passion for Gertrude, and we realize with a start that this refers back not to the father Horwendil but to Amleth, who in the old story is undone at last by his excessive love for his treacherous second wife. In so confounding the generations, Shakespeare gives us a hint of levels of complexity that may leave us only more baffled by the final *Hamlet*, but that also can guide us partway out of the labyrinth.

With more than Joycean wit, the Hamlet of 1588–89 becomes the father of the Hamlet of 1600–1601, and appears in the later play quite properly as the Ghost who demands an immediate revenge but receives instead the deferred blood atonement that consumes five acts and four thousand lines. As for the Ghost of 1588–89, let us call him Horwendil, and then observe that there is no room for him in 1600–1601. Horwendil the Ghost evidently was rather repetitious, and his cries of "Hamlet! Revenge!" evidently became a playgoer's joke. Hamlet the Ghost is no joke; he is Amleth the Danish Heracles, a spirit as wily as he is bloody-minded. It is Shakespeare's transcendent irony that this King Hamlet has fathered the most intelligent character in all of literature. It does not take supreme intellect and capacious consciousness to cut down Claudius, and Prince Hamlet is more aware than we are that he has been assigned a task wholly inappropriate for him. Had Hotspur or Douglas killed Henry IV, Hal would have been overqualified for the avenger's role, but he would have performed it at top speed. Henry V, compared with the Hamlet of 1601, is only a hypocrite and Machiavel—though a superb wit, thanks to the teaching of Sir John Falstaff. Hamlet, very much his own Falstaff, has not been grafted onto a revenge tragedy. Instead, rather like Falstaff only more so, Hamlet takes up all the mental space that any play can hope to occupy. The two-thirds of the lines that Hamlet does not speak are all in effect written about him, and might as well have been written by him. *"Hamlet without the Prince of Denmark"* has become a proverbial joke for emptiness or insignificance. Falstaff, as I observed earlier, was Shakespeare's first great experiment in the question as to how meaning gets started. Hamlet is the perfected experiment, the demonstration that meaning gets started not by repetition nor by fortunate accident nor error, but by a new transcendentalizing of the secular, an apotheosis that is also an annihilation of all the certainties of the cultural past.

About a dozen years later (from 1588–89 to 1600–1601), Shakespeare probably again acted the part of the Ghost in *Hamlet*. About all we know for sure of the first *Hamlet* is that it featured the Ghost of Hamlet's father. I suspect that Shakespeare cut the part severely in revision: on my guess, the Ghost was more important in the first play than the second because he got crowded out by the augmenting internalization of Hamlet. Not that it ever was the Ghost's play; Shakespeare was what we now call "a character actor," and perhaps was never wholehearted enough as a player to take on a protagonist's role. Why did he play the Ghost? Evidently, Shakespeare specialized in playing older men, including kings (though the only part we know for certain, besides the senior Hamlet's Ghost, is old Adam in *As You Like It*). Could there have been some personal investment in playing the Ghost? James Joyce's Stephen Dedalus thought so, in his brilliant fantasia on *Hamlet* in the Library scene of *Ulysses*, which Richard Ellmann insisted always remained Joyce's serious interpretation of the play. I think we need to start further back. How should we understand Shakespeare's naming of his own son after the Amleth of Belleforest, or rather of Hamlet the Green Man, as he had become in English folklore?

When Shakespeare was a boy, a young woman named Kate Hamlet or Hamnet drowned herself in the Avon River, near Stratford, supposedly because she was disappointed in love. What relation she might have to Ophelia is speculative, but any relation to Hamnet Shakespeare is only accidental; he hardly can have been named for her. Ostensibly, he was named for Shakespeare's friend, Hamnet or Hamlet Sadler, but any English Hamnet/Hamlet ultimately was named for the legendary Amleth, as the bookish young Shakespeare would have known. Amleth was proverbial for his trickery, for his famed idiocy, upon which his overwhelming triumph was based. Was the first *Hamlet* a tragedy at all? Did the prince die, or did that only come later, the price of his apotheosis as an intellectual consciousness? The Amleth of tradition, reported by Belleforest, marries the daughter of the king of Britain, and after that revenges his father upon his uncle.

He thus becomes a kind of British hero, and one can fantasize Shakespeare writing a first *Hamlet* with some connected hopes for his little son, then only three or four. When the mature *Hamlet* is written, Hamnet Shakespeare has been dead four years, and the ghost of the eleven-year-old certainly is not in the play. Joyce/Stephen, however, does not quite agree: for him Hamlet the Dane and Hamnet Shakespeare are twins, and the ghostly Shakespeare is therefore the father of his most notorious character.

Yet is the Ghost the author of the play? Shakespeare, with great care, even guile, gives us a father and a son totally unlike each other, in the elder Hamlet and the prince. Of King Hamlet we know that he was a formidable fighter and war leader, much in love (or lust) with his wife. Of the qualities that make the prince so remarkable, the warrior father seems to have possessed none whatsoever. How did Hamlet and Gertrude engender a son so intellectual that he cannot be contextualized, even by Shakespeare's play? Prince Hamlet actually has no more resemblance to his father than he has to his usurping uncle. Shakespeare gives Hamlet a pragmatic foster father in the king's jester, Yorick, because Hamlet is himself a nonstop joker, a step short of the most dangerous of jokers, Iago.

We do not know whether the mysterious movement from Act IV to Act V of *Hamlet* constituted Shakespeare's farewell to his own youth, but it certainly was a farewell to the Hamlet of his youth. The name Amleth derives from the Old Norse for an idiot, or for a tricky Fool who feigns idiocy. Nothing of Hamlet's "antic disposition" lingers after the graveyard scene, and even there the madness has evolved into an intense irony directed at the gross images of death. Why did Shakespeare compose the graveyard scene, since the evocation of Yorick scarcely advances the action of the play? The question has interest only if we apply it to a number of other scenes in this astonishing work, which at nearly four thousand lines is far too long for stage presentation. (One doubts that it was ever acted uncut in Shakespeare's London, though purported university performances at Oxford and at Cambridge may have been at full length.)

The possibility remains—though this is heresy to virtually all modern Shakespeareans—that just this once Shakespeare wrote partly out of a purely private compulsion, knowing he would have to slash his text with every staging. That may account for the difference between the Second

Quarto's 3,800 lines and First Folio's omission of 230 of those lines. That the First Folio contains an additional 80 lines not found in the Second Quarto may indicate that Shakespeare went on revising *Hamlet* after 1604–5, when the Second Quarto appeared. I take it that the Folio may have been Shakespeare's last acting version, though at 3,650 lines it would still have been remarkably long for the London stage. Our complete *Hamlet*, of 3,880 lines, has the virtue of reminding us that the play is not only "the Mona Lisa of literature" but also is Shakespeare's white elephant, and an anomaly in his canon.

I do suggest that Shakespeare *never* stopped rewriting it, from the early version, circa 1587–89, almost down to his retreat back to Stratford. Presumably the Second Quarto was printed directly from his manuscript, while the First Folio text was the final sense of the play that abode with his surviving fellow actors. Obsession certainly is suggested by this most personal and persistent of all Shakespeare's thirty-nine plays. Perhaps, master ironist as Kierkegaard called him, Shakespeare ironically enjoyed the peculiarity that only Kyd's *The Spanish Tragedy*, which some scholars believe to have influenced *Hamlet*, was as much a public success as *Hamlet* and the Falstaff plays. Except among scholars, *The Spanish Tragedy* is now dead; I have never seen a performance, rarely have heard of one, and doubt I could tolerate it, though I have gotten through stagings of *Titus Andronicus*. *Hamlet* has survived everything, even Peter Brook, and Falstaff's immortality transcends even Verdi's best opera. Can we surmise something of what Hamlet meant to Shakespeare?

2

It seems likely that no one ever will establish Shakespeare's religious sentiments, whether early in his life or late. Unlike his father, who died a Catholic, Shakespeare maintained his usual ambiguity in this dangerous area, and *Hamlet* is neither a Protestant nor a Catholic work. It seems to me indeed neither Christian nor non-Christian, since Hamlet's skepticism does not merely exceed its possible origin in Montaigne but passes into something very rich and strange in Act V, something for which we have no name. The audience wishes to dispute neither Fortinbras, who commands the soldier's music and the rites of war, nor Horatio, who invokes flights of angels. Whose soldier was Hamlet, and why are ministering angels not inappropriate? The play ends with a highly original, quite secular point-of-epiphany, as a transcendental splendor seems to break outward from the eminence up to which the soldiers carry Hamlet's body. In the background is Horatio's startling suicide attempt, forestalled by Hamlet only so that his follower can become his memorialist, healing the prince's wounded name. Yet not Horatio, but Fortinbras, is granted the last word, which is "shoot." The volley will be part of the rites of war, celebrating Hamlet presumably as another Fortinbras. It is difficult to believe that Shakespeare is not ending with an irony wholly appropriate to Hamlet, who was not only ironical in himself but also the cause of irony in other men. Neither Horatio nor Fortinbras is an ironist, and Shakespeare abandons us, with some regret on our part, when Hamlet is not there to speak a final commentary upon what seems ironic and yet perhaps transcends irony as we have known it.

I have been arguing that what critics like Empson and Graham Bradshaw regard as "grafting problems" will not illuminate *Hamlet*, because Shakespeare was not grafting onto a Kydian melodrama but was revising his own earlier play. From J. M. Robertson until now, there have been many speculations about the *Ur-Hamlet* (whoever wrote it), but not as many about the earlier Hamlet. Even if the original play was Shakespeare's creation, the prince in 1587 or 1588 could have been only a crude cartoon compared with the Hamlet of 1600–1601. Shakespeare's problem was less that of placing his Hamlet in an inadequate context than of showing a subtler Hamlet inside a grosser one. It seems sensible to suspect that Shakespeare's first Hamlet was much more like Belleforest's Amleth: a fortunate trickster out of archaic heroism, and reflecting not so much upon himself as upon the dangers he had to evade. The second or revisionary Hamlet is not a dweller in an inadequate vehicle, but he is at least two beings at once: a folkloric survivor and a contemporary of Montaigne's. This is all to the good: Hamlet's endless charm dissolves the distinction between Saxo Grammaticus and Montaigne's *Essays*. Whether this began as Shakespeare's private joke (or in-joke?) we cannot hope to tell, but it worked, and still does.

Hamlet, by 1601, cannot strike us as a likely avenger, because his intellectual freedom, his capaciousness of spirit, seems so at odds with his

Ghost-imposed mission. This may be the right point to wonder if the idea of Shakespeare's revising his own earlier Hamlet will not help clear up a permanent puzzle of the final play. As in Belleforest, the Hamlet of Shakespeare's first four acts is a young man of about twenty or less, a student at Wittenberg University, where he wishes to return, and where his friends evidently include the noble Horatio and the ill-fated Rosencrantz and Guildenstern. Laertes, of the same generation, presumably wishes to return to the University of Paris. But the Hamlet of Act V (after an interval of a few weeks, at most) is thirty years old (according to the gravedigger) and seems at least as old as the thirty-seven-year-old Shakespeare. Going back to his old play, the dramatist may have started with a Hamlet not yet come of age (like Belleforest's, and the Shakespearean *Ur-Hamlet's*), but the revisionary process may have yielded the mature Hamlet of Act V. Attached, to some degree, to the conception of Hamlet in his own earlier play, Shakespeare confidently let the contradiction stand. When he named his son Hamnet, Shakespeare himself was only twenty-one, and only twenty-five or so (at most) when he wrote his *Ur-Hamlet*. He wanted it both ways: to hold on to his youthful vision of Hamlet, and to show Hamlet as being beyond maturity at the close.

In *The Birth of Tragedy* (1873), Nietzsche memorably got Hamlet right, seeing him not as the man who thinks too much but rather as the man who thinks too well:

> For the rapture of the Dionysian state with its annihilation of the ordinary bounds and limits of existence contains, while it lasts, a *lethargic* element in which all personal experiences of the past become immersed. This chasm of oblivion separates the worlds of everyday reality and of Dionysian reality. But as soon as this everyday reality re-enters consciousness, it is experienced as such, with nausea: an ascetic, will-negating mood is the fruit of these states.
>
> In this sense the Dionysian man resembles Hamlet: both have once looked truly into the essence of things, they have *gained knowledge*, and nausea inhibits action; for their action could not change anything in the eternal nature of things; they feel it to be ridiculous or humiliating that they should be asked to set right a world that is

out of joint. Knowledge kills action; action requires the veils of illusion: that is the doctrine of Hamlet, not that cheap wisdom of Jack
the Dreamer who reflects too much and, as it were, from an excess
of possibilities does not get around to action. Not reflection, no—
true knowledge, an insight into the horrible truth, outweighs any
motive for action, both in Hamlet and in the Dionysian man.

How peculiar (though how illuminating) it might be if we tried Nietzsche's terms upon another apparent Dionysian man, the only Shakespearean rival to Hamlet in comprehensiveness of consciousness and
keenness of intellect: Sir John Falstaff. Clearly Falstaff *had* once looked
truly into the essence of things, long before we ever meet him. The veteran warrior saw through warfare and threw away its honor and glory as
pernicious illusions, and gave himself instead to the order of play. Unlike
Hamlet, Falstaff gained knowledge without paying in nausea, and knowledge in Falstaff does not inhibit action but thrusts action aside as an irrel-
evancy to the timeless world of play. Hotspur is accurate on this:

> where is his son,
> The nimble-footed madcap Prince of Wales,
> And his comrades, that daft the world aside
> And bid it pass?
>
> [*Henry IV, Part One*, IV.i.94–97]

As his own Falstaff, Hamlet rarely ceases to play, even though Hamlet
is so savage and Falstaff, for all his roistering, is so gentle. Marxist critics
confuse their materialism with Sir John's materiality, and so see the great
wit as an opportunist. Falstaff's investment, unlike Hamlet's, is in wit for its
own sake. Contrast the two at their greatest, Hamlet in the graveyard,
Falstaff in the tavern:

*Ham.* That skull had a tongue in it, and could sing once. How the
knave jowls it to th' ground, as if 'twere Cain's jawbone, that did
the first murder. This might be the pate of a politician which this
ass now o'er-offices, one that would circumvent God, might it not?

*Hor.* It might, my lord.

*Ham.* Or of a courtier, which could say, 'Good morrow, sweet lord.
How dost thou, sweet lord?' This might be my Lord Such-a-one,
that praised my Lord Such-a-one's horse when a [meant] to beg
it, might it not?

*Hor.* Ay, my lord.

*Ham.* Why, e'en so, and now my Lady Worm's, chopless, and knocked
about the [mazard] with a sexton's spade. Here's fine revolution
and we had the trick to see't. Did these bones cost no more the
breeding but to play at loggets with 'em? Mine ache to think on't.

[V.i.74–91]

*Fal.* O, thou hast damnable iteration, and art indeed able to corrupt a
saint: thou hast done much harm upon me, Hal, God forgive thee
for it: before I knew thee, Hal, I knew nothing, and now am I, if a
man should speak truly, little better than one of the wicked. I
must give over this life, and I will give it over: by the Lord, and I
do not I am a villain, I'll be damned for never a king's son in
Christendom.

[*Henry IV, Part One,* I.iii.88–95]

How can we set "before I knew thee, Hal, I knew nothing, and now am
I, if a man should speak truly, little better than one of the wicked" against
"Here's fine revolution and we had the trick to see't"? Surpassing wit against
surpassing wit, but how little these wits share! Falstaff's comic genius at
once turns the joke upon himself, yet also transcends that turning, by a
marvelous thrust at Puritan sanctimoniousness. Falstaff's sheer joy is coun-
tered by Hamlet's uncanny gallows humor, that thrusts at once against
mortality and against all our pretensions. In Falstaff's wit we hear the in-
junction "It must give pleasure," but in Hamlet's we hear "It must change,
and there is only one final form of change."

The *Ur-Hamlet* of Thomas Kyd, that authentic ghost of Shakespeare scholarship, never has been found because it never existed. Thomas Nashe, in
a blurb for his hapless friend Robert Greene, wrote an obscure passage that

has been weakly misread by most scholars, who fail to see that Nashe was attacking what he (and Greene) must have considered to be the School of Marlowe, comprising Marlowe, Shakespeare, and Kyd:

> I will turne backe to my first text of Studies of delight, and talke a little in friendship with a few of our triviall translators. It is a common practise now a dayes amongst a sort of shifting companions, that rune through every Art and thrive by none, to leave the trade of *Noverint*, whereto they were borne, and busie themselves with the indevours of Art, that could scarcely Latinize their neck verse if they should have neede; yet English *Seneca* read by Candle-light yeelds many good sentences, as *Blood is a begger*, and so forth; and if you intreate him faire in a frostie morning, he will affoord you whole Hamlets, I should say handfuls of Tragicall speeches. But O griefe! *Tempus edax rerum*, whats that will last alwayes? The Sea exhaled by droppes will in continuance bee drie, and *Seneca*, let blood line by line and page by page, at length must needes die to our Stage; which makes his famished followers to imitate the Kid in *Aesop*, who, enamoured with the Foxes newfangles, forsooke all hopes of life to leape into a new occupation; and these men, renouncing all possibilities of credite or estimation, to intermeddle with Italian Translations: Wherein how poorely they have plodded, (as those that are neither provenzall men, nor are able to distinguish of Articles) let all indifferent Gentlemen that have travelled in that tongue discerne by their two-pennie Pamphlets.

Here is Peter Alexander's wise comment upon this deliberate obscurity:

> From this hub-bub it is hard to extract any precise information; it seems clear however that among the productions of the unscholarly dramatists is a play *Hamlet*, which seems to Nashe to owe a great deal to Seneca in translation, and further, that one of these dramatists was Kyd, for Nashe drags in the name regardless of the fact that neither Aesop nor Spenser (to whose *Shepheard's Calendar*, the May

eclogue, he is referring) supplies an adequate parallel to the situation now being described. To conclude from this, as many do, that Kyd was the author of the early *Hamlet* is an assumption that the text does not justify and that later evidence makes questionable. Nashe is referring to 'a sort,' that is a group, of writers; that Kyd was one of them and a *Hamlet* one of their productions is as far as this deliberately teasing passage can by itself take us.

On the basis of this I want to propose a new shape to our vision of Shakespeare's career. Leeds Barroll, in his *Politics, Plague, and Shakespeare's Theater: The Stuart Years* (1991), usefully cautions us against dating Shakespeare's plays by supposed topical allusions, and suggests instead that the later Shakespeare composed only when theaters were available, and alternated, therefore, between lying fallow and then engaging in astonishing bursts of rapid writing, including the supreme feat of producing *King Lear, Macbeth,* and *Antony and Cleopatra* in just fourteen consecutive months.

Barroll also calls into question the scholarly myth of Shakespeare's "retirement" into Stratford subsequent to *The Tempest* in 1611, when the playwright was only forty-seven. Shakespeare lived another five years and, aided by John Fletcher, wrote three more plays by 1613 (*Henry VIII,* the apparently lost *Cardenio,* and *The Two Noble Kinsmen*). In his fiftieth year, Shakespeare evidently refused further labor for the theater, and doubtless we can regard him as retired during the last two and a half years of his life. What killed Shakespeare at fifty-two we don't know, though one contemporary source suggests that the immediate cause was a Stratford drinking binge with two old friends, Ben Jonson and Michael Drayton, which seems in character for the amiable Falstaffian Shakespeare. Tradition speaks also of a previous long illness, which may have been venereal, again likely enough. Perhaps augmenting disease weakened the professional will to compose. Whatever the reason for cessation, Barroll's point stands: *The Tempest* was not a valedictory work, and Shakespeare never wrote better than in his portions of *The Two Noble Kinsmen,* which only accidentally became a final work.

Somewhat in Barroll's spirit, I propose a similar (though more radical) revision in our sense of Shakespeare's beginnings as a playwright. The

*Ur-Hamlet* would seem to have been composed no later than early 1589, and perhaps in 1588. It preceded, then, all of apprentice Shakespeare, including the three parts of *Henry VI* (1589–91), *Richard III* (1592–93), and *Titus Andronicus* (1593–94). We simply do not know when Kyd wrote *The Spanish Tragedy*, but it may have been anytime from 1588 to 1592. I have never understood why and how Shakespeare scholars could consider that *The Spanish Tragedy* was a serious influence upon *Hamlet*. Popular as it was, *The Spanish Tragedy* is a dreadful play, hideously written and silly; common readers will determine this for themselves by starting to read it. They will not get much past the opening, and will find it hard to credit the notion that this impressed Shakespeare. The more rational supposition is that Shakespeare's first *Hamlet* influenced *The Spanish Tragedy*, and that any effect of Kyd's squalid melodrama on the mature *Hamlet* was merely Shakespeare's taking back of what initially had been his own.

Probably no one ever will be able to prove that Peter Alexander was right in his argument that Shakespeare wrote the *Ur-Hamlet*, but circumstantial evidence reinforces Alexander's surmise. When Shakespeare joined what became the Lord Chamberlain's men in 1594, the three plays newly added to the group's repertory were *The Taming of the Shrew*, *Titus Andronicus*, and *Hamlet*, and at no time did the company stage *The Spanish Tragedy*, or anything else by Kyd. We cannot know what, besides the Ghost, was part of the first *Hamlet*, but pre–*Titus Andronicus* Shakespeare is not exactly post-Falstaffian Shakespeare, and I doubt that we would be much intrigued by earliest *Hamlet*. Shakespeare must have been chagrined when he went back to what could have been his very first play; as I have noted, contemporary references indicate that the Ghost's outcry of "Hamlet! Revenge!" had become a matter for general derision. More interesting is the question as to just what had attracted Shakespeare to the Hamlet story.

Hamlet's first chronicler was Saxo Grammaticus, in his twelfth-century Latin *Danish History*, available in a Parisian edition from 1514 on. Shakespeare is not likely to have read Saxo, but he certainly began with the French storyteller Belleforest's *Histoire Tragiques*, the fifth volume of which (1570) contained Hamlet's saga, elaborated from Saxo's story. The heroic Horwendil, having slain the King of Norway in single combat, wins

Gerutha, the daughter of the King of Denmark, who bears him Amleth. Horwendil's jealous brother Fengon murders Horwendil and incestuously marries Gerutha. Amleth, to preserve his life, pretends to be mad, resists a woman sent to tempt him, stabs a friend of Fengon's hidden in Gerutha's bedchamber, berates his mother into repentance, and is sent off by Fengon to be executed in England. On the voyage, Amleth alters Fengon's letter and thus sends his two escorting retainers to their deaths. Returning home, Amleth kills Fengon with the usurper's own sword, and then is hailed as king by the Danish populace.

Belleforest's Amleth, except in this plot pattern, does not much resemble Shakespeare's Hamlet, and we can assume that Hamlet resembled the savage source less and less as Shakespeare revised. Whatever it was that first attracted Shakespeare to the figure of Amleth/Hamlet began early, because in 1585 the playwright named his infant son Hamnet, presumably with some reference to the Danish hero. Since I firmly believe Peter Alexander to be correct in assigning the *Ur-Hamlet* to Shakespeare, the question of what attracted Hamnet's father to the plot and character before the start of his writing career takes on considerable importance.

Belleforest's Amleth has a certain exemplary resourcefulness; he is hard to kill, persists in his project of revenge, and finally achieves the throne of Denmark. That toughness does not seem enough to name one's only son for, and one feels that we may be missing something.

Belleforest's Amleth, despite his handicaps, carries a primitive or Northern version of the blessing, the spirit of "more life," which pragmatically becomes his freedom. Shakespeare may have perceived in Amleth a Northern version of the biblical King David, a charismatic hero who must begin by enduring considerable travail on his way to the throne and the Blessing. Yet King Saul is no Fengon, and the biblical David is far closer to Shakespeare's Hamlet than he is to the legendary Amleth, whose wit and bravery are authentic but grotesque, with Eddic mythology hovering in the background. Shakespeare, always sensitive to suggestions of a lost social status, may have named his son Hamnet as a kind of talisman of family restoration, taking Amleth as a model of persistence in the quest for familial honor and of vindication of the relation between fathers and sons.

We surely can assume that Shakespeare's first Hamlet of 1588–89 was very close to Belleforest's Amleth, a Senecan or Roman avenger in a Northern context. Inwardness in Shakespeare's plays does not assume its characteristic strength before the comic triumph of Falstaff, though there are poignant traces of it in Bottom, and a grotesque, ambivalent version of it in Shylock. We need not suppose that Shakespeare's Ur-Hamlet was a transcendent intellectual. After Falstaff, Hal, and Brutus, Shakespeare chose to make a revisionary return to his own origins as a dramatist, perhaps in commemoration of his son Hamnet's death. There is a profoundly elegiac temper to the matured *Hamlet*, which may have received its final revisions after the death of Shakespeare's father, in September 1601. A mourning for Hamnet and for John Shakespeare may reverberate in Horatio's (and the audience's) mourning for Hamlet. The mystery of Hamlet, and of *Hamlet*, turns upon mourning as a mode of revisionism, and possibly upon revision itself as a kind of mourning for Shakespeare's own earlier self. At thirty-six, he may have realized that a spiritual culmination was upon him, and all his gifts seemed to fuse together, as he turned to a more considerable revisionary labor than he attempted before or after.

Marlowe had long since been exorcised; with the *Hamlet* of 1600–1601, Shakespeare becomes his own precursor, and revises not only the *Ur-Hamlet* but everything that came after it, through *Julius Caesar*. The inner drama of the drama *Hamlet* is revisionary: Shakespeare returns to what was beyond his initial powers, and grants himself a protagonist who, by Act V, has a relation to the Hamlet of Act I that is an exact parallel to the playwright's relation to the *Ur-Hamlet*. For Hamlet, revisioning the self replaces the project of revenge. The only valid revenge in this play is what Nietzsche, theorist of revision, called the will's revenge against time, and against time's "It was." "Thus I willed it," Shakespeare is able to imply, even as *Hamlet* becomes an implicit model for Nietzsche's *Towards a Genealogy of Morals*. Nietzsche's most Shakespearean realization is pure Hamlet: we can find words only for what already is dead in our hearts, so that necessarily there is a kind of contempt in every act of speaking. The rest is silence; speech is agitation, betrayal, restlessness, torment of self and of others. Shakespeare, with *Hamlet*, arrives at an impasse still operative in the high comedy of *Twelfth Night*, where Hamlet's inheritor is Feste.

There is no "real" Hamlet as there is no "real" Shakespeare: the character, like the writer, is a reflecting pool, a spacious mirror in which we needs must see ourselves. Permit this dramatist a concourse of contraries, and he will show us everybody and nobody, all at once. We have no choice but to permit Shakespeare, and his Hamlet, everything, because neither has a rival.

Anne Barton makes the point that *Hamlet* owes at least as much to Shakespeare's previous plays as it does to the *Ur-Hamlet*. Even if Peter Alexander was right (as I insist) and the *Ur-Hamlet* was one of those prior works, *Hamlet* and Hamlet are more indebted to the *Henry IV* plays and Falstaff than to an embryonic Hamlet. Inwardness as a mode of freedom is the mature Hamlet's finest endowment, despite his sufferings, and wit becomes another name for that inwardness and that freedom, first in Falstaff, and then in Hamlet. Even the earliest Shakespeare, in the *Henry VI* plays, shows the inward impulse, though he is too crude to accomplish it. Marlowe could not help Shakespeare to develop an art of inwardness (although Barabas is a wonderful monster, the only stage role I perpetually long to essay). Chaucer could and did: Chaucer's Pardoner is a human abyss, as inward as Iago, or as Edmund. The Wife of Bath provided a paradigm for Falstaff, and the Pardoner might have done as much for Iago. But there is no Chaucerian figure who could help in shaping Hamlet, not as we now see him, though the irony of the Hamlet of 1600–1601 has Chaucerian elements in it. These ironic components help inform the odd effect that Graham Bradshaw compares to Pirandello: Hamlet can seem an actual person who somehow has been caught inside a play, so that he has to perform even though he doesn't want to. Bradshaw, because he himself is caught in the bad tradition that Kyd wrote the *Ur-Hamlet*, relates this odd sensation to the Globe audience's reaction to watching Hamlet trapped in Kyd's old potboiler. The Pirandellian effect (not to mention the Beckettian, as in *Endgame*) is greatly enhanced if Shakespeare's new protagonist is trapped inside Shakespeare's earliest play, now blasted apart to admit the fiercest inwardness ever achieved in a literary work.

The idea of *play* is as central to Falstaff as the idea of *the play* is to Hamlet. These are not the same idea: Falstaff is infinitely more playful than Hamlet, and the prince is far more theatrical than the fat knight. The new Hamlet is self-consciously theatrical; the old one presumably was (as Bradshaw says) immersed in melodramatic theatricality. We can say that Hamlet the intellectual ironist is somehow conscious that he has to live down his crude earlier version. Indeed, we might say that there is a peculiar doubling: Hamlet contends not only with the Ghost but with the ghost of the first Ghost as well, and with the ghost of the first Hamlet. That out-Pirandellos Pirandello, and helps explain why Hamlet, who questions everything else, scarcely bothers to question revenge, even though pragmatically he has so little zest for it.

But that is typical of Hamlet's consciousness, for the prince has a mind so powerful that the most contrary attitudes, values, and judgments can coexist within it coherently, so coherently indeed that Hamlet nearly has become all things to all men, and to some women. Hamlet incarnates the value of personality, while turning aside from the value of love. If Hamlet is his own Falstaff (Harold Goddard's fine formulation), he is a Falstaff who doesn't need Hal, any more than he needs poor Ophelia, or even Horatio, except as a survivor who will tell the prince's story. The common element in Falstaff's ludic mastery and in Hamlet's dramaturgy is the employment of great wit as a counter-Machiavel, as a defense against a corrupted world.

We do not know how playful Shakespeare himself was, but we do know his plays, and so again we can find him more readily in some of Hamlet's observations than we can in Falstaff's. We cannot envision Falstaff giving instructions to the actors, or even watching a play, since reality *is* a play to Sir John. We delight in Falstaff's acting of King Henry IV and then of Hal, but we would gape at Falstaff acting Falstaff, since he is so at one with himself. One of our many perplexities with Hamlet is that we never can be sure when he is acting Hamlet, with or without an antic disposition. Mimesis, or the player's imitation of a person, is a concern for Hamlet, but could not be a problem for Falstaff. Hal, despite his brutality to Falstaff, which is inconceivable in Hamlet (contemplate Hamlet rejecting Horatio), shares in Hamlet's mimetic interests—he, too, calls for plays-within-the-play—though with a hypocrisy that Hamlet would have scorned. But had he become king, Hamlet would not have been a wittier Fortinbras, which is to say a Henry V. As his own Falstaff, Hamlet presumably would have entered the higher mode of play that is art. We return to the paradox that Hamlet could write *Hamlet*, while Falstaff would find redundant the composing of a Falstaffiad. Falstaff is wholly immanent, as overflowing with being as Iago and Edmund are deficient in it. As I have remarked, Falstaff is how meaning gets started. Hamlet, as negative as he is witty, blocks or baffles meaning, except in the beyond of transcendence.

Auden, a Christian wit who greatly preferred Falstaff to Hamlet, found in Falstaff "a comic symbol for the supernatural order of Charity," a discovery that makes me very uneasy, since Auden goes so far as to find Christlike implications in the world-rejected Falstaff. You can prefer Don Quixote to Hamlet, as Auden also does, if you wish to follow Kierkegaard's choice of the apostle over the genius. It does seem odd, though, that Auden tugs Falstaff away from genius to apostle, because there are no apostles in Shakespeare. Kierkegaard, as witty and as melancholy a Dane as Hamlet, is not a very Shakespearean character, because Kierkegaard indeed was an apostle. Auden, refreshingly, was not, and truly was Falstaffian enough in spirit to be forgiven his abduction of Sir John for the Christian order of Charity.

Are there any other figures in Shakespeare who are as autonomous as Falstaff and Hamlet? A panoply of the greatest certainly would include Bottom, Shylock, Rosalind, Iago, Lear, Macbeth, Cleopatra, and Prospero. Yet all of these, though they sustain meditation, depend more upon the world of their plays than do Falstaff and Hamlet. Falstaff surely got away from Shakespeare, but I would be inclined to judge that Shakespeare could not get away from Hamlet, who was built up from within, whereas Falstaff began as an external construction and then went inward, perhaps against Shakespeare's initial will. Hamlet, I surmise, is Shakespeare's will, long pondered and anything but the happy accident that became Falstaff. If anyone in Shakespeare takes up all the space, it is these two, but only Hamlet was destined for that role. Usurping the stage is the only role he has; unlike Falstaff, Hamlet is not a rebel against the idea of time and the idea of order. Falstaff is happy in his consciousness, of himself and of reality; Hamlet is unhappy in those same relations. Between them, they occupy the center of Shakespeare's invention of the human.

3

It is a peculiarity of Shakespearean triumphalism that the most original literary work in Western literature, perhaps in the world's literature, has now become so familiar that we seem to have read it before, even when we encounter it for the first time. Hamlet, as a character (or as a role, if you prefer), remains both as familiar, and as original, as is his play. Dr. Johnson, to whom *Hamlet* scarcely seemed problematical, praised the play for its "variety," which is equally true of its protagonist. Like the play, the prince stands apart from the rest of Shakespeare, partly because custom has not staled his infinite variety. He is a hero who pragmatically can be regarded as a villain: cold, murderous, solipsistic, nihilistic, manipulative. We can recognize Iago by those modifiers, but not Hamlet, since pragmatic tests do not accommodate him. Consciousness is his salient characteristic; he is the most aware and knowing figure ever conceived. We have the illusion that nothing is lost upon this fictive personage. Hamlet is a Henry James who is also a swordsman, a philosopher in line to become a king, a prophet of a sensibility still out ahead of us, in an era to come.

Though Shakespeare composed sixteen plays after *Hamlet*, putting the work just past the midpoint of his career, there is a clear sense in which this drama was at once his alpha and his omega. All of Shakespeare is in it: history, comedy, satire, tragedy, romance—one starts to sound like Polonius if one wants to categorize this "poem unlimited." Polonius only meant that such a poetic drama need not adhere to Ben Jonson's neoclassical sense of the unities of time and place, and *Hamlet* ironically destroys any coherent idea of time even more drastically than *Othello* will do. But "poem unlimited," as Shakespeare seems to have known, is the best phrase available for the genre of the completed *Hamlet*, which both is and is not the prince's tragedy. Goethe, whose *Faust* owed rather too much to *Hamlet*, is the best teacher as to what a "poem unlimited" might be. The daemonic apocalypse that is the Second Part of *Faust* is scandalously unlimited, and yet loses much of its aura when juxtaposed too directly with *Hamlet*. Shakespeare's "poem unlimited," I suggest, is as personal, capricious, arbitrary as the Second Part of *Faust*, and is weirdly more capacious even than Goethe's weird work. The "lost" *Ur-Hamlet* was doubtless as much Shakespeare's revenge tragedy as *Titus Andronicus* or *Julius Caesar* was (if one wants to regard that play as *The Revenge of Mark Antony*), but the triumphal *Hamlet* is cosmological drama of man's fate, and only masks its essential drive as revenge. We can forget Hamlet's "indecision" and his "duty" to kill the usurping king-uncle. Hamlet himself takes a while to forget all that, but by the start of Act V he no longer needs to remember: the Ghost is gone, the mental image of the father has no power, and we come to see that hesitation and consciousness are synonyms in this vast play. We might speak of the hesitations of consciousness itself, for Hamlet inaugurates the drama of heightened identity that even Pirandello and Beckett could only repeat, albeit in a more desperate tone, and that Brecht vainly sought to subvert. Brecht's Marxist impulse is now also only a repetition, as in Tony Kushner's *Angels in America*, which seeks to demonstrate that there are no single individuals as such, but achieves authentic pathos only when the hero-villain Roy Cohn takes the stage, as isolated as any tormented consciousness in Hamlet's tradition.

We hardly can think about ourselves as separate selves without thinking about Hamlet, whether or not we are aware that we are recalling him. His is not primarily a world of social alienation, or of the absence (or presence) of God. Rather, his world is the growing inner self, which he sometimes attempts to reject, but which nevertheless he celebrates almost continuously, though implicitly. His difference from his legatees, ourselves, is scarcely historical, because here too he is out ahead of us, always about to be. Tentativeness is the peculiar mark of his endlessly burgeoning consciousness; if he cannot know himself, wholly, that is because he is a breaking wave of sensibility, of thought and feeling pulsating onward. For Hamlet, as Oscar Wilde saw, the aesthetic is no mystification, but rather constitutes the only normative or moral element in consciousness. Wilde said that because of Hamlet, the world had grown sad. Self-consciousness, in Hamlet, augments melancholy at the expense of all other affects.

No one ever is going to call Hamlet "the joyous Dane," yet a consciousness so continuously alive at every point cannot be categorized simply as "melancholy." Even at its darkest, Hamlet's grief has something tentative in it. "Hesitant mourning" is almost an oxymoron; still, Hamlet's quintessence is never to be wholly committed to any stance or attitude, any mission, or indeed to anything at all. His language reveals this throughout; no other character in all of literature changes his verbal decorum so rapidly. He has no center: Othello has his "occupation" of honorable warfare, Lear has the majesty of being every inch a king, Macbeth a proleptic imagination that leaps ahead of his own ambition. Hamlet is too intelligent to be at one with any role, and intelligence in itself is decentered when allied with the prince's ultimate disinterestedness. Categorizing Hamlet is virtually impossible; Falstaff, who pragmatically is as intelligent, identifies himself with the freedom of wit, with play. One aspect of Hamlet is free, and entertains itself with bitter wit and bitterly intended play, but other aspects are bound, and we cannot find the balance.

If the play were Christian, or even un-Christian, then we could say that Hamlet bears the Blessing, as David and Joseph and the wily Jacob carry it away in the Bible. Hamlet, more than Falstaff or Cleopatra, is Shakespeare's great charismatic, but he bears the Blessing as though it were a curse. Claudius ruefully tells us that Hamlet is loved by the Danish populace, and most audiences have shared in that affection. The problem necessarily arises that the Blessing is "more life into a time without boundaries," and while Hamlet embodies such a heroic vitalism, he is also the representative of death, an undiscovered country bounded by time. Shakespeare created Hamlet as a dialectic of antithetical qualities, unresolvable even by the hero's death. It is not too much to say that Hamlet is Shakespeare's own creativity, the poet-playwright's art that itself is nature. Hamlet is also Shakespeare's death, his dead son and his dead father. That may sound fanciful, but temporally it is factual. If you represent both your author's living art and his prospect of annihilation, you are likely to play the most equivocal and multivalent of roles, a hero-villain's. Hamlet is a transcendental hero, as much a new kind of man as the Book of Samuel's King David was, and Hamlet is also a new kind of villain, direct precursor of Iago and Edmund, the villain-as-playwright, writing with the lives of others as much as with words. It might be better to call Hamlet a villain-hero, because his transcendence finally triumphs, even though pragmatically he is the agency of eight deaths, his own included. A stage left empty except for the colorless Horatio, the bully boy Fortinbras, and the fop Osric is the final consequence of the pragmatic Hamlet.

Shakespeare's shrewdness in composing Hamlet as a dance of contraries hardly can be overpraised, even if the result has been four centuries of misreadings, many of them highly creative in themselves. Red herrings abound in the inky seas of Hamlet interpretation: the man who thinks too much; who could not make up his mind; who was too good for his task, or his world. We have had High Romantic Hamlet and Low Modernist Hamlet, and now we have Hamlet-as-Foucault, or subversion-and-containment Hamlet, the culmination of the French Hamlet of Mallarmé, Laforgue, and T. S. Eliot. That travesty Hamlet was prevalent in my youth, in the critical Age of Eliot. Call him neo-Christian Hamlet, up on the battlements of Elsinore (or of Yale), confronting the Ghost as a nostalgic reminder of a lost spirituality. Manifestly, that is absurd, unless you take the Eliotic line that the Devil is preferable to a secular meaninglessness. Auden was wiser in seeing Hamlet (with some distaste) as the genius of secular transcendence, which is fairly close to Shakespeare's enigmatic intellectual, himself more subtly corrupt than the rotten court and state that dismay him. That doubleness of attitude, both secular and transcendent, is Shakespeare's own, throughout the Sonnets, and is strangely more personal in *Hamlet* than in the splendidly rancid triad of *Troilus and Cressida, All's Well That Ends Well,* and *Measure for Measure.* Falstaff may have been dearer to Shakespeare (as he should be to us), but Hamlet evidently was more a personal matter for his creator. We may surmise that Hamlet is Shakespeare's own consciousness (with some reservations) without fearing that we are those horrid entities, the High Romantic Bardolaters.

Hamlet will not do anything prematurely; something in him is determined not to be overdetermined. His freedom partly consists in not being too soon, not being early. In *that* sense, does he reflect Shakespeare's ironic regret at having composed the *Ur-Hamlet* too soon, almost indeed at his own origins as a poet-playwright? Whether or not we are to believe that Hamlet wrote the Player King's great speech (III.ii.186–215), does it perhaps have the same relation both to *The Murder of Gonzago* and to the *Ur-Hamlet?* Its negations undo everything. It might be a commentary, then, on Shakespeare's wry debacle in his premature *Hamlet*. To read (and attend) the mature *Hamlet* as a revisionary work is to take up something of the stance of Hamlet himself as self-revisionist. How charming the ironies of literary history might have seemed to Shakespeare! I suspect that Shakespeare's first *Hamlet* preceded and helped to spark Kyd's *The Spanish Tragedy*, so that Shakespeare was both the inventor and the great revisionist of revenge tragedy. It is another lovely irony that Ben Jonson, starting out as an actor, went on to play Hieronomo the avenger in *The Spanish Tragedy*, a drama for which he later composed revisions. Shakespeare played the Ghost of Hamlet's father at the Globe (and perhaps also the Player King). Did he grimace at having played the Ghost in the *Ur-Hamlet*, with his derision-provoking "Hamlet! Revenge!"?

Revisionism, in *Hamlet*, can be viewed very differently if Shakespeare is revising not that mythical play, Kyd's *Hamlet*, but Shakespeare's own earlier *Hamlet*. Self-revision is Hamlet's mode; was it imposed on him by Shakespeare's highly self-conscious confrontation with his own botched beginning as a tragic dramatist? Aside from the parody aspects of *Titus Andronicus*—its send-ups of Kyd and Marlowe—there is also a recoil in this charnel house of a play from any sympathetic identification with anyone on stage. The Brechtian "alienation effect" evidently was learned by that grand plagiarist from *Titus Andronicus*, whose protagonist estranges us from the start by his ghastly sacrifice of Tamora's son followed by his butchery of his own son. Any playgoer or reader is likely to prefer Aaron the Moor to Titus, since Aaron is savagely humorous, and Titus savagely dolorous.

I suspect that Shakespeare wrote in response not only to Marlowe and Kyd, but also to his own sympathy for his first Hamlet, a presumably wily avenger. Part of the definitive Hamlet's mystery is why the audience and readership, rather like the common people of Denmark in the play, should love him. Until Act V, Hamlet loves the dead father (or rather, his image) but does not persuade us that he loves (or ever loved) anyone else. The prince has no remorse for his manslaughter of Polonius, or for his vicious badgering of Ophelia into madness and suicide, or for his gratuitous dispatch of Rosencrantz and Guildenstern to their undeserved deaths. We do not believe Hamlet when he blusters to Laertes that he loved Ophelia, since the charismatic nature seems to exclude remorse, except for what has not yet been done. The skull of poor Yorick evokes not grief, but disgust, and the son's farewell to his dead mother is the heartless "Wretched Queen, adieu." There is the outsize tribute to the faithful and loving Horatio, but it is subverted when Hamlet angrily restrains his grieving follower from suicide, not out of affection but so as to assign him the task of telling the prince's story, lest Hamlet bear forever a wounded name. There is indeed a considerable "case against Hamlet," urged most recently by Alistair Fowler, but even if Hamlet is a hero-villain, he remains the Western hero of consciousness.

The internalization of the self is one of Shakespeare's greatest inventions, particularly because it came before anyone else was ready for it. There is a growing inner self in Protestantism, but nothing in Luther prepares us for Hamlet's mystery; his real interiority will abide: "But I have that within which passes show." Perhaps learning from his first *Hamlet*, Shakespeare never directly dramatizes Hamlet's quintessence. Instead, we are given the seven extraordinary soliloquies, which are anything but hackneyed; they are merely badly directed, badly played, badly read. The greatest, the "To be or not to be" monologue, so embarrassed director and actor in the most recent *Hamlet* I've attended, Ralph Fiennes's travesty, that Fiennes mumbled much of it offstage and came on only to mouth the rest of it as quickly as possible. Nevertheless, this soliloquy is the center of Hamlet, at once everything and nothing, a fullness and an emptiness playing off against each other. It is the foundation for nearly everything he will say in Act V, and can be called his death-speech-in-advance, the prolepsis of his transcendence.

It is very difficult to generalize about Hamlet, because every observation will have to admit its opposite. He is the paradigm of grief, yet he expresses mourning by an extraordinary verve, and his continuous wit gives the pragmatic effect of making him seem endlessly high-spirited, even as he mourns. Partly this is the result of a verbal energy that rivals Falstaff's.

Sometimes I amuse myself by surmising the effect, if Shakespeare had confronted Falstaff with Prince Hamlet rather than Prince Hal. But as I have cited earlier, Harold Goddard charmingly says Hamlet is his own Falstaff, and trying to imagine Falstaff as Horatio is dumbfounding. And yet Falstaff now seems to me Shakespeare's bridge from an *Ur*-Hamlet to Hamlet. It was because he had created Falstaff, from 1596 to 1598, that Shakespeare was able to revise the Hamlet (whether his own or another's) of circa 1588 into the Hamlet of 1600–1601. As Swinburne noted, Falstaff and Hamlet are the two most comprehensive consciousnesses in Shakespeare, or in anyone else. Each figure allies the utmost reach of consciousness with what W. B. Yeats praised in William Blake as "beautiful, laughing speech." The difference is that Falstaff frequently laughs with a whole heart, with faith both in language and in himself. Hamlet's laughter can unnerve us because it issues from a total lack of faith, both in language and in himself. W. H. Auden, who seems rather to have disliked Hamlet, made perhaps the best case against the prince of Denmark:

> Hamlet lacks faith in God and in himself. Consequently he must define his existence in terms of others, e.g., I am the man whose mother married his uncle who murdered his father. He would like to become what the Greek tragic hero is, a creature of situation. Hence his inability to act, for he can only "act," i.e., play at possibilities.

That is monstrously shrewd: Hamlet might like to be Oedipus or Orestes but (*contra* Freud) he is not at all similar to either. Yet I find it difficult to conceive Hamlet as "a creature of situation," because others scarcely matter to this hero of interiorization. That is why there is no central scene or passage in *Hamlet*. As the freest artist of himself in all of Shakespeare, Hamlet never knows what it might mean to be imprisoned by any contingency, even when imposed upon by the Ghost. Though he protests that he is not free, how can we believe that (or anything else) from a consciousness that seems to overhear itself, even when not bothering to speak? Since Hamlet baffles us by altering with nearly every phrase he utters, how can we reconcile his metamorphoses with his being "a creature of situation"? Auden subtly says that Hamlet would *like* to become such a creature, and so presumably does *not*, even though his desire reduces him to an actor or player. But is he so reduced? Richard Lanham concludes that Hamlet's self-consciousness cannot be distinguished from the prince's theatricality; like Auden's contention, this is difficult to refute, and very painful (for me anyway) to accept. Iago and Edmund (in *King Lear*) are great and murderous players; Hamlet is something else, though pragmatically he is quite murderous. A play in which the only survivors are Horatio, Fortinbras, and Osric is bloody enough for anyone, and cannot be particularly playful. The Hamlet of Act V has stopped playing; he has aged a decade in a brief return from the sea, and if his self-consciousness is still theatrical, it ensues in a different kind of theater, eerily transcendental and sublime, one in which the abyss between *playing* someone and *being* someone has been bridged.

That returns us to where the matured Hamlet always takes us, to the process of self-revision, to change by self-overhearing and then by the will to change. Shakespeare's term for our "self" is "selfsame," and *Hamlet*, whatever its first version was like, is very much the drama in which the tragic protagonist revises his sense of the selfsame. Not self-fashioning but self-revision; for Foucault the self is fashioned, but for Shakespeare it is given, subject to subsequent mutabilities. The great *topos*, or commonplace, in Shakespeare is change: his prime villains, from Richard III on to Iago, Edmund, and Macbeth, all suffer astonishing changes before their careers are ended. The *Ur-Hamlet* never will be found, because it is embedded in the palimpsest of the final *Hamlet*. Mockery, of others and of himself, is one of Hamlet's crucial modes, and he so mocks vengeance as to make it impossible for us to distinguish revenge tragedy from satire. Hamlet comes to understand that his grief and his comic genius are at odds, until both are subdued at sea. He is neither funny nor melancholy in Act V: the readiness or willingness is all. Shakespeare, disarming moral criticism, thus absolves Hamlet of the final slaughter. The deaths of Gertrude, Laertes, Claudius, and Hamlet himself are all caused by Claudius's "shuffling," unlike the deaths of Polonius, Ophelia, Rosencrantz, and Guildenstern. Those earlier deaths can be attributed to Hamlet's murderous theatricality, to his peculiar blend of the roles of comedian and avenger. But even Claudius is not slain as an act of vengeance—only as the final entropy of the plotted shuffling.

There is, then, no case to be made against Hamlet in his death scene, and this revisionary release is experienced by the audience as a transcendental music, with Horatio invoking angelic song and Fortinbras the rites of war. Is it wholly fanciful to suggest that Shakespeare, revising himself, also knows an order of release from his mourning for his own son Hamnet? The late Kenneth Burke taught me to ask, always, What is the writer trying to do for himself or herself by writing this work? Burke primarily meant for oneself as a person, not as a writer, but he genially tolerated my revision of his question. He taught me also to apply to *Hamlet* Nietzsche's powerful apothegm: "That which we can find words for is something already dead in our hearts; there is always a kind of contempt in the act of speaking." Nothing could be closer to Hamlet, and farther away from Falstaff. What Falstaff finds words for is still alive in his heart, and for him there is no contempt in the act of speaking. Falstaff possesses wit lest he perish of the truth; Hamlet's wit, thrown over by him in the transition to Act V, vanishes from the stage, and so Hamlet becomes the sublime personality whose fate must be to perish of the truth. Revising Hamlet, Shakespeare released himself from Hamlet, and was free to be Falstaff again.

There is something different about the finished *Hamlet* (to call it that), which sets it apart from Shakespeare's three dozen other plays. This sense of difference always may have been felt, but our record of it begins in 1770, with Henry MacKenzie's emphasis on Hamlet's "extreme sensibility of mind." For Mackenzie, Hamlet's was "the majesty of melancholy." Dr. Johnson seems to have been more moved by Ophelia than by Hamlet, and rather coldly remarked that the prince "is, through the whole play, rather an instrument than an agent." That is an observation not necessarily contrary to what the German and English Romantics made of Hamlet, but Johnson is light-years from Hamlet Romanticized. In our overenthusiastic embrace of the Romantic Hamlet, the hero of hesitation who dominates criticism from Goethe and Hazlitt through Emerson and Carlyle, and on to A. C. Bradley and Harold Goddard, we have been too ready to lose our apprehension of Hamlet's permanent strangeness, his continued uniqueness despite all his imitators. Whatever his precise relation to Shakespeare might have been, Hamlet is to other literary and dramatic characters what

Shakespeare is to other writers: a class of one, set apart by cognitive and aesthetic eminence. The prince and the poet-playwright are the geniuses of change; Hamlet, like Shakespeare, is an agent rather than an instrument of change. Here Dr. Johnson nodded.

In a lifetime of playgoing, one can encounter some samenesses among Lears, Othellos, and Macbeths. But every actor's Hamlet is almost absurdly different from all the others. The most memorable Hamlet that I have attended, John Gielgud's, caught the prince's charismatic nobility, but perhaps too much at the sacrifice of Hamlet's restless intellectuality. There will always be as many Hamlets as there are actors, directors, playgoers, readers, critics. Hazlitt uttered a more-than-Romantic truth in his: "It is we who are Hamlet." "We" certainly included Dostoevsky, Nietzsche, and Kierkegaard, and in a later time, Joyce and Beckett. Clearly, Hamlet has usurped the Western literary consciousness, at its most self-aware thresholds, gateways no longer crossable by us into transcendental beyonds. Yet most of us are not imaginative speculators and creators, even if we share in an essentially literary culture (now dying in our universities, and perhaps soon enough everywhere). What seems most universal about Hamlet is the quality and graciousness of his mourning. This initially centers upon the dead father and the fallen-away mother, but by Act V the center of grief is everywhere, and the circumference nowhere, or infinite.

Shakespeare of course had his own griefs, rather more in 1600–1601, when *Hamlet* was completed, than in 1587–89, when perhaps it was first tentatively composed. Still, if his major mourning was for the child Hamnet Shakespeare, it was transmuted beyond recognition in Hamlet's sorrows. Part of Hamlet's fascination is his *carelessness*; though an absolutely revisionary consciousness, he seems, throughout Act V, to be carried on a flood tide of disinterestedness or quietism, as though he is willing to accept every permutation in his own self but refuses to will the changes. Shakespeare, as a playwright, has his own kind of apparent carelessness, yet like Hamlet's this is more an open stance toward change than it is an artlessness. The parallel is there again between the universal-but-scattered Hamlet, and the dramatist fully achieving universality by returning to an earlier work, perhaps an earliest effort, that had defeated him. *Hamlet*, so far as I can tell, always had been Shakespeare's idea of a play, *his* play, and it seems no accident that the successful revision of *Hamlet* opened Shakespeare to the great tragedies that followed: *Othello, King Lear, Macbeth, Antony and Cleopatra, Coriolanus*. There is a savage triumphalism in Hamlet's nature, at least before Act V, and the prince's tragic apotheosis seems to have released a certain triumphalism in Shakespeare the poet-dramatist. Hamlet somehow has gotten it right in the high style of his death, and Shakespeare clearly at last has gotten *Hamlet* (and Hamlet) right, and has liberated himself into tragedy.

Shakespeare's only son and his father were both dead when the mature *Hamlet* was composed, but the play does not seem to me any more obsessed by mortality than is the rest of Shakespeare, before and after. Nor does Hamlet seem as preoccupied with death as many other Shakespearean protagonists; his are, as Horatio finally observes, "casual slaughters." If *Hamlet* differs from earlier Shakespeare (including a possible first *Hamlet*), the change inheres in change itself, because Hamlet incarnates change. The final form of change is death, which may be why we tend to think of *Hamlet* as having a highly individual relationship with death. We have to be bewildered by a dramatic character who changes every time he speaks and yet maintains a consistent enough identity so that he cannot be mistaken for anyone else in Shakespeare.

   Attempts to surmise the shape of the *Ur-Hamlet* almost always founder on the assumption that Kyd was the author, and so the play is seen as another *Spanish Tragedy*. Since the play was Shakespeare's, and his first, our best clues are in the earliest Shakespeare, excluding comedy: the tetralogy of the three parts of *Henry VI* and *Richard III*, and also *Titus Andronicus*, which may have been Shakespeare's parodistic rebellion against that fiercely Marlovian tetralogy. Only two characters are memorable in these five plays: Richard, and Aaron the Moor in *Titus*, and both are versions of Barabas the Machiavel, hero-villain of Marlowe's *Jew of Malta*. My guess is that the young Shakespeare, overwhelmed by the two parts of *Tamburlaine*, both on stage by late 1587, began his *Hamlet* in 1588 as an imitation of *Tamburlaine*, and then absorbed the grand shock of *The Jew of Malta* in 1589, and so went on to finish the *Ur-Hamlet* under the shadow of Barabas. Aaron the Moor (as I have shown) is manifestly a knowing travesty of Barabas, and though many scholars would disagree with me on this, all of *Titus Andronicus* seems an outrageous send-up of Marlowe. The hero Hamlet, even in 1600–1601, is very much a hero-villain, anticipating Iago, and in 1588–89 he is likely to have imitated the wiliness of Barabas, though in a legitimate quest for self-preservation and revenge.

4

Was Shakespeare's first *Hamlet* a tragedy? Did Hamlet survive triumphantly, as he does in the old stories, or did he die, as he did in 1601? We cannot know, but I suspect this first *Hamlet* could have been called *The Revenge of Hamlet*, rather than *The Tragical History of Hamlet, Prince of Denmark*. Except for Hamlet's end, there may have been little enough difference in the plots of the first and the final *Hamlet;* the great difference would have been in the character of Hamlet himself. In 1588–89, he could have been little more than a Marlovian cartoon, akin to Richard III and Aaron the Moor. In 1600–1601, Hamlet is the heir of Shakespearean inwardness, the culmination of the sequence that began with Faulconbridge the Bastard in *King John*, Richard II, Mercutio, Juliet, Bottom, Portia, and Shylock, and reached a first apotheosis with Falstaff. Henry V, Brutus, and Rosalind then prepared for the second apotheosis with Hamlet, which in turn made possible Feste, Malvolio, Iago, Lear, Edgar, Edmund, Macbeth, Cleopatra, Imogen, and Prospero. Our sense that Hamlet is far too large for his play may result from the enormous change in the protagonist, and the relatively smaller changes in the plot of the first four acts. Act V, though, probably has very little resemblance to what it was in 1589, which again may help explain why sometimes it seems a different play from the first four acts.

Harry Levin noted that "the line between the histories and the tragedies need not be quite so sharply drawn as it is by the classifications of the Folio." The definitive *Hamlet* is indisputably tragedy, by any definition; Hamlet's death has to be described as tragic. Since the Amleth of folklore and chronicle was a trickster, a Fool feigning idiocy in order first to survive, and then to win back his kingdom, it took a considerable twist to convert him into a tragic hero, and I doubt that Shakespeare, at no more than twenty-five, was capable of so decisive a swerve away from Marlowe. We might envision a revenge history, with strong comic overtones, in which a very young Hamlet outwits his enemies and at last burns down the court at Elsinore, thus ending happily, unlike the usurper Richard III and his fellow Machiavels, Barabas the Jew and Aaron the Moor. But like Richard III and Aaron, this first Hamlet would have owed as much to Barabas as to Tamburlaine. The debt to Barabas would be in a brazen self-delight, shared with the audience. To Tamburlaine, the debt would be a rhetoric, an aggressivity of high language, that itself was a mode of action, a "poetical persuasion" perfectly capable of converting or overcoming enemies.

Richard III and Aaron the Moor retain something of their sinister appeal for us, though they fall short of Barabas, in zest and sublime outrageousness. Perhaps the first Hamlet would have seemed rather problematical to us, since he must have been heroic (as in Belleforest) but with something of the northern uncanniness of the ferocious protagonists of Edda and saga. Tamburlaine's heaven-storming audacity and the cunning of Barabas could have blended quite effectively into that uncanniness. What probably was lacking was not less than nearly everything we associate with Hamlet: the central consciousness that has illuminated us these past four centuries. The final Hamlet is post-Falstaffian, and also comes after Rosalind and Brutus, all precursors of the prince's intellectual power. Hamlet the wily trickster may have had something Puckish about him; the Hamlet who battles supernal powers more than he does Claudius, and who knows that the corruption is within him as much as in the state of Denmark, has progressed well beyond wit and self-delight. Nothing *sounds* odder than the notion that *Hamlet*, in whatever form, began as Shakespeare's first play, because the enigmatic masterwork of 1601 seems more a finality than a revised point of origin.

Hamlet, as a character, bewilders us because he is so endlessly suggestive. Are there any limits to him? His *inwardness* is his most radical originality; the ever-growing inner self, the dream of an infinite consciousness, has never been more fully portrayed. Shakespeare's great figures, before his revised Hamlet, are comic creations, and I argue elsewhere in this book that Shylock and Henry V are among them. Hamlet is himself a great comedian, and there are elements of tragic farce in the tragedy *Hamlet*. Yet Hamlet, almost throughout the play, insists upon regarding himself as a failure, indeed as a failed tragic protagonist, which was how he may have begun, for Shakespeare. The all-but-universal illusion or fantasy that somehow Hamlet competes with Shakespeare in writing the play may well reflect Shakespeare's struggle with his recalcitrant protagonist.

What does it do to our vision of Shakespeare if we conceive of him as having begun his writing career with what he and the better sort considered as failed *Hamlet*, and then as having achieved aesthetic apotheosis with another *Hamlet*, a dozen or so years later? In one sense, very little, since we still would have a Shakespeare who had to develop, rather than just unfold. Yet it does make a difference if Shakespeare founded his mature *Hamlet* upon what he judged as an earlier defeat. There is, then, another ghost in the play, the wraith of the first Hamlet. We love too much the partial truth of a purely commercial Shakespeare, who took the cash and let renown go; like his good friend Ben Jonson, Shakespeare understood that the highest art was hard work, so he and Jonson had to challenge the ancients, while yet following in their tracks. Great comedy came fairly easily to Shakespeare, and Falstaff may have descended upon him like a revelation. But *Hamlet* and *King Lear* resulted from fierce revisionary processes, in which an earlier self died and a new self was born. Of that new being, we have the evidence only of Shakespeare's plays after *Hamlet*, a series of achievements from which unmixed comedy has been banished. If Hamlet dies as a sacrifice to transcendent powers, the powers were altogether Shakespeare's own, or rather became his, in exchange for Hamlet's tragic disinterestedness.

5

"Denmark's a prison" Hamlet says, yet no one else in all Shakespeare seems potentially so free as the crown prince of Denmark. I have remarked already that of all Shakespeare's "free artists of themselves" (Hegel), Hamlet is the freest. Shakespeare's play figuratively is at once bondage and liberation for its tragic protagonist, who sometimes feels he can do nothing at Elsinore, and also fears doing much too much, lest he become a Nero and make Gertrude into Agrippina, at once mother, lover, and victim. There is a bewildering range of freedoms available to Hamlet: he could marry Ophelia, ascend the throne after Claudius if waiting was bearable, cut Claudius down at almost any time, leave for Wittenberg without permission, organize a coup (being the favorite of the people), or even devote himself to botching plays for the theater. Like his father, he could center upon being a soldier, akin to the younger Fortinbras, or conversely he could turn his superb mind to more organized speculation, philosophical or hermetic, than has been his custom. Ophelia describes him, in her lament for his madness, as having been courtier, soldier, and scholar, the exemplar of form and fashion for all Denmark. If *The Tragedy of Hamlet, Prince of Denmark* is "poem unlimited," beyond genre and rules, then its protagonist is character unlimited, beyond even such precursors as the biblical David or the classical Brutus. But how much freedom can be afforded Hamlet by a tragic play? What project can be large enough for him? Ending Claudius does not require the capacity of a Hamlet, and revenge palpably is in any case insufficient motive for the central hero of Western consciousness. What was Shakespeare to do with a new kind of human being, one as authentically unsponsored as Hamlet is?

Nietzsche, in Hamlet's shadow, spoke of the will's revenge upon time, and upon time's: "It was." Such a revenge must revise the self, must grant it what Hart Crane called "an improved infancy." Hamlet's infancy, like everyone else's, could use considerable improvement. The prince evidently will go to his death having kissed Yorick the king's jester, his substitute father, rather more often than he is likely to have kissed Gertrude or Ophelia, let alone his awesome warrior-father. "Take him for all in all," Hamlet's judgment upon his father, implies some considerable reservations, though we do not doubt that Hamlet shall not look upon King Hamlet's like again. Whose son was Hamlet? How far back in time did Gertrude's "incest" and "adultery" begin? Since the play refuses to say (though in its earlier version it may have been less ambiguous), neither we nor Hamlet knows. Claudius has, in effect, adopted his nephew as his son, even as the Roman emperor Claudius adopted Nero when he married Nero's mother, Agrippina. Is Hamlet, on whatever level, fearful that to kill Claudius is to kill his natural father? That is part of Marc Shell's subtle argument in his *Children of the Earth* (1993): "What is really unique about Hamlet is not his unconscious wish to be patricidal and incestuous, but rather his conscious refusal to actually become patricidal and incestuous." Gertrude dies with Hamlet (and with Claudius and Laertes), but it is remarkable that Hamlet will not kill Claudius until he knows that he himself is dying, and that his mother is already dead.

A. D. Nuttall, amiably dismissing those who insist that Hamlet is not a person but a sequence of images, remarked that "a dramatist faced with an entire audience who austerely repressed all inferences and bayed for image-patterns might well despair." Going a touch beyond Nuttall, I would suggest that Shakespeare's art from the 1600–1601 *Hamlet* on to the end depended upon a more radical mode of inference than ever before employed, and not just by dramatists. Hamlet's freedom can be defined as *the freedom to infer*, and we learn this intellectual liberty by attending to Hamlet. Inference in Hamlet's praxis is a sublime mode of surmise, metaphoric because it leaps ahead with every change in circumstance, and inference becomes the audience's way to Hamlet's consciousness. We sound his circumstances, trust his drives more than he does, and we thus surmise his greatness, his difference from us both in degree and in kind. Hamlet is much more than Falstaff and Prince Hal fused into one; he adds to that fusion a kind of inferential negation that Iago and Edmund will turn into the way down and out, but that in Hamlet abandons the will, and so is free.

Hamlet now seems no more fictive than Montaigne; four centuries have established both as authentic personalities, rather in the same way that Falstaff appears to be as historical a reality as Rabelais. Western culture, if it is to survive its current self-hatred, must become only more Hamlet-like. We have no equally powerful and influential image of human cognition pushed to its limits; Plato's Socrates comes closest. Both think too well to survive. Socrates, at least in Montaigne, almost becomes a pragmatic alternative to Jesus. Hamlet's relation to Jesus is enigmatic;

Shakespeare, as always, evades both faith and doubt. Since the Jesus of the Gospel of Mark, like the Yahweh of the J Writer, is a literary character now worshiped as God (I speak only pragmatically), we have the riddle that Hamlet can be discussed in some of the ways we might employ to talk about Yahweh, or Socrates, or Jesus. University teachers of what once we called "literature" no longer regard dramatic and literary characters as "real"; this does not matter at all, since common readers and playgoers (and common believers) rightly continue to quest for personality. It is idle to warn them against the errors of identifying with Hamlet, or Jesus, or Yahweh. Shakespeare's most astonishing achievement, however unintended, is to have made available in Hamlet a universal instance of our will-to-identity. Hamlet, to some of us, offers the hope of a purely secular transcendence, but to others he intimates the spirit's survival in more traditional modes. Perhaps Hamlet has replaced Plato's and Montaigne's Socrates as the intellectual's Christ. Auden disagreed, and preferred Falstaff for that role, but I cannot see the defiant Sir John, in love with freedom, as atoning for anyone.

The largest enigma of Hamlet is the aura of transcendence he emanates, even at his most violent, capricious, and insane moments. Some critics have rebelled against Hamlet, insisting that he is, at best, a hero-villain, but they blow the sand against the wind, and the wind blows it back again. You cannot demystify Hamlet; the sinuous enchantment has gone on too long. He has the place among fictive characters that Shakespeare occupies among writers: the center of centers. No actor that I have seen—not even John Gielgud—has usurped the role to the exclusion of all others. Is this centrality only a back-formation of cultural history, or is it implicit in Shakespeare's text? Hamlet and Western self-consciousness have been the same for about the last two centuries of Romantic sensibility. There are many signs that global self-consciousness increasingly identifies with Hamlet, Asia and Africa included. The phenomenon may no longer be cultural, in the sense that rock music and blue jeans constitute international culture. Hamlet, the prince more than the play, has become myth, gossip matured into legend.

As with Falstaff, we can say more aptly what Hamlet is not than what he is. He ends a quietist rather than a man of active faith, but his passivity itself is a mask for something inexpressible, though it can be suggested. It is not his earlier nihilism, which foregrounds the play, and yet it is hardly a purposiveness, even in playing. The stage, at the close, is strewn with clues as well as corpses. Why does Hamlet care about his posthumous reputation? He is never more passionate than when he commands Horatio to go on living, not for pleasure and despite the pain of existence, only in order to ensure that his prince not bear a wounded name. Not until the end does the audience matter to Hamlet; he needs us to give honor and meaning to his death. His story must be told, and not just to Fortinbras, and it must be reported by Horatio, who alone knows it truly. Does Horatio then understand what we do not? Hamlet, as he dies, loves nobody— not father or mother, Ophelia or Yorick—but he knows that Horatio loves him. The story can only be told by someone who accepts Hamlet totally, beyond judgment. And despite the moral protests of some critics, Hamlet has had his way. It is we who are Horatio, and the world mostly has agreed to love Hamlet, despite his crimes and blunders, despite even his brutal, pragmatically murderous treatment of Ophelia. *We forgive Hamlet precisely as we forgive ourselves,* though we know we are not Hamlet, since our consciousness cannot extend as far as his does. Yet we worship (in a secular way) this all-but-infinite consciousness; what we have called Romanticism was engendered by Hamlet, though it required two centuries before the prince's self-consciousness became universally prevalent, and almost a third century before Nietzsche insisted that Hamlet possessed "true knowledge, an insight into the horrible truth," which is the abyss between mundane reality and the Dionysian rapture of an endlessly ongoing consciousness. Nietzsche was fundamentally right; Horatio is a stoic, Hamlet is not. The audience, like its surrogate, Horatio, is more or less Christian, and perhaps far more stoic than not. Hamlet, toward the close, employs some Christian vocabulary, but he swerves from Christian comfort into a Dionysian consciousness, and his New Testament citations become strong misreadings of both Protestant and Catholic understandings of the text. Had he but time, Hamlet says, he could tell us—what? Death intervenes, but we receive the clue in his next words: "Let it be."

"Let be" has become Hamlet's refrain, and has a quietistic force uncanny in its suggestiveness. He will not unpack his heart with words, since only his thoughts, not their ends, are his own. And yet there is something far from dead in his heart, something ready or willing, strong beyond the weakness of flesh. When Jesus spoke kindly to the sleep-prone Simon Peter, he did not say that the readiness was all, since Jesus's stance was for Yahweh alone, and only Yahweh was all. For Hamlet there is nothing but the readiness, which translates as a willingness to let everything be, not out of trust in Yahweh but through a confidence in a final consciousness. That consciousness sets aside both Jesus's Pharisaic trust in the resurrection of the body, and also the skeptical reality principle of annihilation. "Let be" is a setting aside, neither denial nor affirmation. What Hamlet could tell us is his achieved awareness of what he himself represents, a dramatist's apprehension of what it means to incarnate the tragedy one cannot compose.

6

Falstaff, in Shakespeare's lifetime, seems to have been more popular even than Hamlet; the centuries since have preferred the prince not only to the fat knight but to every other fictive being. Hamlet's universalism seems our largest clue to the enigma of his personality; the less he cares for anyone, including the audience, the more we care for him. It seems the world's oddest love affair; Jesus returns our love, and yet Hamlet cannot. His blocked affections, diagnosed by Dr. Freud as Oedipal, actually reflect a transcendental quietism for which, happily, we lack a label. Hamlet is *beyond* us, beyond everyone else in Shakespeare or in literature, unless indeed you agree with me in finding the Yahweh of the J Writer and the Jesus of the Gospel of Mark to be literary characters. When we reach Lear, we understand that Hamlet's beyondness has to do with the mystery of kingship, so dear to Shakespeare's patron, James I. But we have trouble seeing Hamlet as a potential king, and few playgoers and readers tend to agree with Fortinbras's judgment that the prince would have joined Hamlet Senior and Fortinbras as another great royal basher of heads. Clearly, Hamlet's sublimity is a question of personality; four centuries have so understood it. August Wilhelm von Schlegel accurately observed in 1809 that "Hamlet has no firm belief either in himself or in anything else"—including God and language, I would add. Of course there is Horatio, whom Hamlet notoriously overpraises, but Horatio seems to be there to represent the audience's love for Hamlet. Horatio is our bridge to the beyond, to that curious but unmistakable negative transcendence that concludes the tragedy.

Hamlet's linguistic skepticism coexists with a span and control of language greater even than Falstaff's, because its range is the widest we have ever encountered in a single work. It is always a shock to be reminded that Shakespeare used more than 21,000 separate words, while Racine used fewer than 2,000. Doubtless some German scholar has counted up just how many of the 21,000 words Hamlet had in his vocabulary, but we scarcely need to know the sum. The play is Shakespeare's longest because Hamlet speaks so much of it, and I frequently wish it even longer, so that Hamlet could have spoken on even more matters than he already covers. Falstaff, monarch of wit, nevertheless is something short of an authorial consciousness in his own right; Hamlet bursts through that barrier, and not just when he revises *The Murder of Gonzago* into *The Mousetrap*, but almost invariably as he comments upon all things between earth and heaven. G. Wilson Knight admirably characterized Hamlet as death's ambassador to us; no other literary character speaks with the authority of the undiscovered country, except for Mark's Jesus. Harry Levin pioneered in analyzing the *copiousness* of Hamlet's language, which utilizes the full and unique resources of English syntax and diction. Other critics have emphasized the mood shifts of Hamlet's linguistic decorum, with its startling leaps from high to low, its mutability of cognition and of affect. I myself always am struck by the varied and perpetual ways in which Hamlet keeps *overhearing himself speak*. This is not just a question of rhetoricity or word consciousness; it is the essence of Shakespeare's greatest originalities in the representation of character, of thinking, and of personality. Ethos, Logos, Pathos—the triple basis of rhetoric, psychology, and cosmology—all bewilder us in Hamlet, because he changes with every self-overhearing.

It is a valuable commonplace that *The Tragedy of Hamlet, Prince of Denmark* is an overwhelmingly theatrical play. Hamlet himself is even more self-consciously theatrical than Falstaff tends to be. Falstaff is more consistently attentive to his audience, both on stage and off, and yet Falstaff, though he vastly amuses himself, plays less *to* himself than Hamlet does. This difference may stem from Falstaff's greater playfulness; like Don Quixote and Sancho Panza, Falstaff is *homo ludens*, while anxiety dominates in Hamlet's realm. Yet the difference seems still greater; the counter-Machiavel Hamlet could almost be called an anti-Marlovian character, whereas Falstaff simply renders Marlowe's mode irrelevant. My favorite Marlovian hero-villain, Barabas, Jew of Malta, is a self-delighting fantastic, but being a cartoon, like nearly all Marlovian protagonists, he frequently speaks as though his words were wrapped up in a cartoonist's balloon floating above him. Hamlet is something radically new, even for and in Shakespeare: his theatricality is dangerously nihilistic because it is so paradoxically *natural* to him. More even than his parody Hamm in Beckett's *Endgame*, Hamlet is a walking mousetrap, embodying the anxious expectations that are incarnating the malaise of Elsinore. Iago may be nothing if not critical; Hamlet is criticism itself, the theatrical interpreter of his own story. With a cunning subtler than any other dramatist's, before or since, Shakespeare does not let us be certain as to just which lines Hamlet himself has inserted in order to revise *The Murder of Gonzago* into *The Mousetrap*. Hamlet speaks of writing some twelve or sixteen lines, but we come to suspect that there are rather more, and that they include the extraordinary speech in which the Player King tells us that ethos is not the daemon, that character is not fate but accident, and that eros is the purest accident. We know that Shakespeare acted the ghost of Hamlet's father; it would have been expedient if the same actor rendered the part of the Player King, another representation of the dead father. There would be a marvelous twist to Shakespeare himself intoning lines that his Hamlet can be expected to have written:

> Purpose is but the slave to memory,
> Of violent birth but poor validity,
> Which now, the fruit unripe, sticks on the tree,
> But fall unshaken when they mellow be.
> Most necessary 'tis that we forget

To pay ourselves what to ourselves is debt.
What to ourselves in passion we propose,
The passion ending, doth the purpose lose.
The violence of either grief or joy
Their own enactures with themselves destroy.
Where joy most revels, grief doth most lament;
Grief joys, joy grieves, on slender accident.
This world is not for aye, nor 'tis not strange
That even our loves should with our fortunes change,
For 'tis a question left us yet to prove,
Whether love lead fortune, or else fortune love.
The great man down, you mark his favorite flies;
The poor advanc'd makes friends of enemies;
And hitherto doth love on fortune tend:
For who not needs shall never lack a friend,
And who in want a hollow friend doth try
Directly seasons him his enemy.
But orderly to end where I begun,
Our wills and fates do so contrary run
That our devices still are overthrown:
Our thoughts are ours, their ends none of our own.

                                      [III.ii.183–209]

How any audience could take in these 26 closely packed lines of a psychologized metaphysic through the ear alone, I scarcely know. They are as dense and weighted as any passage in Shakespeare; the plot of *The Mousetrap* does not require them, and I assume that Hamlet composed them as his key signature, as what that other melancholy Dane, Kierkegaard, called "The Point of View of My Work as an Author." They center upon their final lines:

Our wills and fates do so contrary run
That our devices still are overthrown:
Our thoughts are ours, their ends none of our own.

Our "devices" are our intended purposes, products of our wills, but our fates are antithetical to our characters, and what we think to do has no relation to our thoughts' "ends," where "ends" means both conclusions and harvests. Desire and destiny are contraries, and all thought thus must undo itself. Hamlet's nihilism is indeed transcendent, surpassing what can exist in the personages of Dostoevsky, or in Nietzsche's forebodings that what we can find words for must be already dead in our hearts, and that only what cannot be said is worth the saying. Perhaps *that* is why Shakespeare bothered Wittgenstein so much. Rather oddly, Wittgenstein compared Shakespeare to dreams: all wrong, absurd, composite, things *aren't like that*, except by the law that belonged to Shakespeare alone, or to dreams alone. "He is *not* true to life," Wittgenstein insisted of Shakespeare, while evading the truth that Shakespeare had made us see and think what we could not have seen or thought without him. Hamlet emphatically is *not* true to life, but more than any other fictive being Hamlet makes us think what we could not think without him. Wittgenstein would have denied this, but that was his motive for so distrusting Shakespeare: Hamlet, more than any philosopher, actually makes us see the world in other ways, deeper ways, than we may want to see it. Wittgenstein wants to believe that Shakespeare, as a creator of language, made a heterocosm, a dream. But the truth is that Shakespeare's cosmos became Wittgenstein's and ours, and we cannot say of Hamlet's Elsinore or Falstaff's Eastcheap that things aren't like that. They *are* like that, but we need Hamlet or Falstaff to illuminate the "like that," to more than flesh out the similes. The question becomes rather: Is life true to Hamlet, or to Falstaff? At its worst, sometimes, and at its best, sometimes, life can or may be, so that the real question becomes, Is Wittgenstein true to Hamlet, or Bloom to Falstaff?

I grant that you don't need to be a formalist or a historicist to assert that being true to Hamlet or to Falstaff is a nonsensical quest. If you read or attend Shakespeare in order to improve your neighbor or your neighborhood, then doubtless I am being nonsensical, a kind of Don Quixote of literary criticism. The late Anthony Burgess, in his *Nothing Like the Sun*, a wonderful novel about Shakespeare, has the Bard make a fine, somewhat Nietzschean remark: "Tragedy is a goat and comedy a village Priapus and *dying* is the word that links both." Hamlet and Falstaff would have said it better, but the sexual play on *dying* is redemptive of the prose, and we are well reminded that Shakespeare writ no genre, and used poor Polonius to scorn those who did. Tragedy, Aldous Huxley once essayed, must omit the whole truth, yet Shakespeare comes close to refuting Huxley. John Webster wrote revenge tragedy; Shakespeare wrote *Hamlet*. There are no personalities in Webster, though nearly everyone manages to die with something like Shakespearean eloquence. Life must be true to Shakespeare if personality is to have value, is to *be* value. Value and pathos do not commune easily with each other, yet who but Shakespeare has reconciled them so incessantly? What, after all, is personality? A dictionary would say the quality that renders one a person, not a thing or an animal, or else an assemblage of characteristics that makes one somehow distinctive. That is not very helpful, particularly in regard to Hamlet or Falstaff, mere roles for actors, as formalists tell us, and perhaps players fall in love with roles, but do we, if we never mount a stage? What do we mean by "the personality of Jesus," whether we think of the Gospel of Mark or of the American Jesus? Or what might we mean by "the personality of God," whether we think of the Yahweh of the J Writer or of the American God, so notoriously fond of Republicans and of neo-conservatives? I submit that we know better what it is we mean when we speak of the personality of Hamlet as opposed to the personality of our best friend, or the personality of some favorite celebrity. Shakespeare persuades us that we know something in Hamlet that is the best and innermost part of him, something uncreated that goes back farther than our earliest memories of ourselves. There is a breath or spark to Hamlet that is his principle of individuation, a recognizable identity whose evidence is his singularity of language, and yet not so much language as diction, a cognitive choice between words, a choice whose drive always is toward freedom: from Elsinore, from the Ghost, from the world. Like Falstaff, Hamlet implicitly defines personality as a mode of freedom, more of a matrix of freedom than a product of freedom. Falstaff, though, as I intimated, is largely free of the censorious superego, while Hamlet in the first four acts suffers very terribly from it. In the beautiful metamorphosis of purgation that is Act V, Hamlet almost is freed from what is over or above the ego, though at the price of dying well before his death.

In *The Great Gatsby*, Fitzgerald's Conradian narrator, Nick Carraway, observes that personality is a series of successful gestures. Walter Pater would have liked that description, but its limits are severe. Perhaps Jay Gatsby exemplifies Carraway's definition, but who could venture that Hamlet's personality comprises a series of successful gestures? William Hazlitt, as I've said, cast his own vote for inwardness: "It is we who are Hamlet." Hamlet's stage, Hazlitt implied, is the theater of mind, and Hamlet's gestures therefore are of the inmost self, very nearly everyone's inmost self. It was in confronting this baffling representation, at once universal and solitary, that T. S. Eliot rendered his astonishing judgment that the play was an aesthetic failure. I assume that Eliot, with his own wounds, reacted to Hamlet's sickness of the spirit, certainly the most enigmatic malaise in all of Western literature. Hamlet's own poetic metaphysic, as we have seen, is that character and fate are antithetical, and yet, at the play's conclusion, we are likely to believe that the prince's character was his fate. Do we have a drama of the personality's freedom, or of the character's fate? The Player King says that all is accident; Hamlet in Act V hints that there are no accidents. Whom are we to believe? The Hamlet of Act V appears to have cured himself, and affirms that the readiness or willingness is all. I interpret that as meaning personality is all, once personality has purged itself into a second birth. And yet Hamlet has little desire to survive.

The canonical sublime depends upon a strangeness that assimilates us even as we largely fail to assimilate it. What is the stance toward life, the attitude, of the Hamlet who returns from the sea at the start of Act V? Hamlet himself veers dizzily between being everything and nothing, an alternation that haunts our lives as much as it does our literature. Like Shakespeare, Hamlet takes up no stance, which is why comparisons of either to Montaigne have been so misleading. We know what we mean when we speak of Montaigne's skepticism, but we tend to mean both too much and too little when our emphasis is on Hamlet's skepticism or Shakespeare's. There is no absolutely accurate term (or terms) for Hamlet's attitudes toward life and death in Act V. One can try them all out—stoicism, skepticism, quietism, nihilism—but they don't quite work. I tend to favor "disinterestedness," but then find I can define the word only with reference to Hamlet. Quietism, half a century after *Hamlet*, meant a certain Spanish mode of religious mysticism, but Hamlet is no mystic, no stoic, and hardly a Christian at all. He goes into the final slaughter scene in the spirit of a suicide, and prevents Horatio's suicide with a selfish awareness that Horatio's felicity is being postponed in order that the prince's own story can be told and retold. And yet he cares for his reputation as he dies; his "wounded name," if Horatio does not live to clear it, is his final anxiety. Since he has murdered Polonius, driven Ophelia to madness and to suicide, and quite gratuitously sent the wretched Rosencrantz and Guildenstern off to execution, his anxiety would seem justified, except that in fact he has no consciousness of culpability. His fear of a "wounded name" is one more enigma, and hardly refers to the deaths of Claudius and of Laertes, let alone of his mother, for whom his parting salute is the shockingly cold "Wretched Queen, adieu." His concern is properly theatrical; it is for us, the audience:

> You that look pale and tremble at this chance,
> That are but mutes or audience to this act . . .

That seems to me a playwright's concern, proper to the revisionist author of *The Mousetrap*. Joyce's Stephen, in the Library scene of *Ulysses*, scarcely distinguishes between Shakespeare and Hamlet, and as I have noted, Richard Ellmann assured us that Stephen's fantasia remained always Joyce's serious reading of the play. Hamlet himself seems quite free of the audience's shock that so vast a consciousness should expire in so tangled and absurd a mesh of poisoned sword and poisoned cup. It outrages our sensibility that the Western hero of intellectual consciousness dies in this grossly inadequate context, yet it does not outrage Hamlet, who has lived through much too much already. We mourn a great personality, perhaps the greatest; Hamlet has ceased to mourn in the interval between Acts IV and V. The profoundest mysteries of his personality are involved in the nature of his universal mourning, and in his self-cure. I will not bother with Oedipal tropes here, even to dismiss them, having devoted a chapter to just such a dismissal in a book on the Western canon, where I gave a Shakespearean reading of Freud. Hamlet's spiritual despair transcends a father's murder, a mother's hasty remarriage, and all the miasma of Elsinore's corruption, even as his apotheosis in Act V far transcends any passing of the Oedipus complex. The crucial question becomes, How ought we to characterize Hamlet's melancholia in the first four acts, and how do we explain his escape from it into a high place in Act V, a place at last entirely his own, and something like a radically new mode of secular transcendence?

Dr. Johnson thought that the particular excellence of *Hamlet* as a play was its "variety," which seems to me truer of the prince than of the drama. What most distinguishes Hamlet's personality is its metamorphic nature: his changes are constant, and continue even after the great sea change that precedes Act V. We have the perpetual puzzle that the most intensely theatrical personality in Shakespeare centers a play notorious for its anxious expectations, for its incessant delays that are more than parodies of an endlessly delayed revenge. Hamlet is a great player, like Falstaff and Cleopatra, but his director, the dramatist, seems to punish the protagonist for getting out of hand, for being Hobgoblin run off with the garland of Apollo, perhaps for having entertained even more doubts than his creator had. And if Hamlet is imaginatively sick, then so is everyone else in the play, with the possible exception of the audience's surrogate, Horatio. When we first encounter him, Hamlet is a university student who is not being permitted to return to his studies. He does not appear to be more than twenty years old, yet in Act V he is revealed to be at least thirty, after a passage of a few weeks at most. And yet none of this matters: he is always both the youngest and the oldest personality in the drama; in the deepest sense, he is older than Falstaff. Consciousness itself has aged him, the catastrophic consciousness of the spiritual disease of his world, which he has internalized, and which he does not wish to be called upon to remedy, if only because the true cause of his changeability is his drive toward freedom. Critics have agreed, for centuries now, that Hamlet's unique appeal is that no other protagonist of high tragedy still seems paradoxically so free. In Act V, he is barely still in the play; like Whitman's "real me" or "me myself" the final Hamlet is both in and out of the game while watching and wondering at it. But if his sea change has cured him of the Elsinore illness, what drives him back to the court and to the final catastrophe? We feel that if the Ghost were to attempt a third appearance in Act V, Hamlet would thrust it aside; his obsession with the dead father is definitely over, and while he still regards his maligned mother as a whore, he has worn out his interest there also. Purged, he allows himself to be set up for Claudius's refined, Italianate version of *The Mousetrap*, on the stated principle of "Let be." Perhaps the best comment is Wallace Stevens's variation: "Let be be finale of seem." And yet once more, we must return to the Elsinore illness, and to the medicine of the sea voyage.

Every student of the imagery of the play *Hamlet* has brooded on the imposthume, or abscess, which Robert Browning was to pun on brilliantly with his "the imposthume I prick to relieve thee of,—Vanity." Hamlet himself, precursor of so many Browning *personae*, may be punning on the abscess as imposture:

This is th'imposthume of much wealth and peace,
That inward breaks, and shows no cause without
Why the man dies.

Elsinore's disease is anywhere's, anytime's. Something is rotten in every state, and if your sensibility is like Hamlet's, then finally you will not tolerate it. Hamlet's tragedy is at last the tragedy of personality: The charismatic is compelled to a physician's authority despite himself; Claudius is merely an accident; Hamlet's only persuasive enemy is Hamlet himself. When Shakespeare broke away from Marlovian cartooning, and so became Shakespeare, he prepared the abyss of Hamlet for himself. Not less than everything in himself, Hamlet also knows himself to be nothing in himself. He can and does repair to that nothing at sea, and he returns disinterested, or nihilistic, or quietistic, whichever you may prefer. But he dies with great concern for his wounded name, as if reentering the maelstrom of Elsinore partly undoes his great change. But only in part: the transcendental music of cognition rises up again in a celebratory strain at the close of Hamlet's tragedy, achieving the secular triumph of "The rest is silence." What is not at rest, or what abides before the silence, is the idiosyncratic value of Hamlet's personality, for which another term is "the canonical sublime."

# 24

# OTHELLO

The character of Iago . . . belongs to a class of characters common to Shakspeare, and at the same time peculiar to him—namely, that of great intellectual activity, accompanied with a total want of moral principle, and therefore displaying itself at the constant expense of others, and seeking to confound the practical distinctions of right and wrong, by referring them to some overstrained standard of speculative refinement.—Some persons, more nice than wise, have thought the whole of the character of Iago unnatural. Shakspeare, who was quite as good a philosopher as he was a poet, thought otherwise. He knew that the love of power, which is another name for the love of mischief, was natural to man. He would know this as well or better than if it had been demonstrated to him by a logical diagram, merely from seeing children paddle in the dirt, or kill flies for sport. We might ask those who think the character of Iago not natural, why they go to see it performed, but from the interest it excites, the sharper edge which it sets on their curiosity and imagination? Why do we go to see tragedies in general? Why do we always read the accounts in the newspapers of dreadful fires and shocking murders, but for the same reason? Why do so many persons frequent executions and trials, or why do the lower classes almost universally take delight in barbarous sports and cruelty to animals, but because there is a natural tendency in the mind to strong excitement, a desire to have its faculties roused and stimulated to the utmost? Whenever this principle is not under the restraint of humanity, or the sense of moral obligation, there are no excesses to which it will not of itself give rise, without the assistance of any other motive, either of passion or self-interest. Iago is only an extreme instance of the kind; that is, of diseased intellectual activity, with an almost perfect indifference to moral good or evil, or rather with a preference of the latter, because it falls more in with his favourite propensity, gives greater zest to his thoughts, and scope to his actions.—Be it observed, too, (for the sake of those who are for squaring all human actions by the maxims of Rochefoucault), that he is quite or nearly as indifferent to his own fate as to that of others; that he runs all risks for a trifling and doubtful advantage; and is himself the dupe and victim of his ruling passion—an incorrigible love of mischief—an insatiable craving after action of the most difficult and dangerous kind. Our "Ancient" is a philosopher, who fancies that a lie that kills has more point in it than an alliteration or an antithesis; who thinks a fatal experiment on the peace of a family a better thing than watching the palpitations in the heart of a flea in an air-pump; who plots the ruin of his friends as an exercise for his understanding, and stabs men in the dark to prevent *ennui.*

—William Hazlitt

Since it is Othello's tragedy, even if it is Iago's play (not even Hamlet or Edmund seem to compose so much of their dramas), we need to restore some sense of Othello's initial dignity and glory. A bad modern tradition of criticism that goes from T. S. Eliot and F. R. Leavis through current New Historicism has divested the hero of his splendor, in effect doing Iago's work so that, in Othello's words, "Othello's occupation's gone." Since 1919 or so, generals have lost esteem among the elite, though not always among the groundlings. Shakespeare himself subjected chivalric valor to the superb comic critique of Falstaff, who did not leave intact very much of the nostalgia for military prowess. But Falstaff, although he still inhabited a corner of Hamlet's consciousness, is absent from *Othello.*

The clown scarcely comes on stage in *Othello*, though the Fool in *Lear*, the drunken porter at the gate in *Macbeth*, and the fig-and-asp seller in *Antony and Cleopatra* maintain the persistence of tragicomedy in Shakespeare after *Hamlet*. Only *Othello* and *Coriolanus* exclude all laughter, as if to protect two great captains from the Falstaffian perspective. When Othello, doubtless the fastest sword in his profession, wants to stop a street fight, he need only utter the one massive and menacingly monosyllabic line "Keep up your bright swords, for the dew will rust them."

To see Othello in his unfallen splendor, within the play, becomes a little difficult, because he so readily seems to become Iago's dupe. Shakespeare, as before in *Henry IV, Part One*, and directly after in *King Lear*, gives us the responsibility of foregrounding by inference. As the play opens, Iago assures his gull, Roderigo, that he hates Othello, and he states the only true motive for his hatred, which is what Milton's Satan calls "a Sense of Injured Merit." Satan (as Milton did not wish to know) is the legitimate son of Iago, begot by Shakespeare upon Milton's Muse. Iago, long Othello's "ancient" (his ensign, or flag officer, the third-in-command), has been passed over for promotion, and Cassio has become Othello's lieutenant. No reason is given for Othello's decision; his regard for "honest Iago," bluff veteran of Othello's "big wars," remains undiminished. Indeed, Iago's position as flag officer, vowed to die rather than let Othello's colors be captured in battle, testifies both to Othello's trust and to Iago's former devotion. Paradoxically, that quasi-religious worship of the war god Othello by his true believer Iago can be inferred as the cause of Iago's having been passed over. Iago, as Harold Goddard finely remarked, is always at war; he is a moral pyromaniac setting fire to all of reality. Othello, the skilled professional who maintains the purity of arms by sharply dividing the camp of war from that of peace, would have seen in his brave and zealous ancient someone who could not replace him were he to be killed or wounded. Iago cannot stop fighting, and so cannot be preferred to Cassio, who is relatively inexperienced (a kind of staff officer) but who is courteous and diplomatic and knows the limits of war.

Sound as Othello's military judgment clearly was, he did not know Iago, a very free artist of himself. The catastrophe that foregrounds Shakespeare's play is what I would want to call the Fall of Iago, which sets the paradigm for Satan's Fall in Milton. Milton's God, like Othello, pragmatically demotes his most ardent devotee, and the wounded Satan rebels. Unable to bring down the Supreme Being, Satan ruins Adam and Eve instead, but the subtler Iago can do far better, because his only God is Othello himself, whose fall becomes the appropriate revenge for Iago's evidently sickening loss of being at rejection, with consequences including what may be sexual impotence, and what certainly is a sense of nullity, of no longer being what one was. Iago is Shakespeare's largest study in ontotheological absence, a sense of the void that follows on from Hamlet's, and that directly precedes Edmund's more restricted but even more affectless excursion into the uncanniness of nihilism. Othello was everything to Iago, because war was everything; passed over, Iago is nothing, and in warring against Othello, his war is against ontology.

Tragic drama is not necessarily metaphysical, but Iago, who says he is nothing if not critical, also is nothing if not metaphysical. His grand boast "I am not what I am" deliberately repeals St. Paul's "By the grace of God I am what I am." With Iago, Shakespeare is enabled to return to the Machiavel, yet now not to another Aaron the Moor or Richard III, both versions of Barabas, Jew of Malta, but to a character light-years beyond Marlowe. The self-delight of Barabas, Aaron, and Richard III in their own villainy is childlike compared with Iago's augmenting pride in his achievement as psychologist, dramatist, and aesthete (the first modern one) as he contemplates the total ruin of the war god Othello, reduced to murderous incoherence. Iago's accomplishment in revenge tragedy far surpasses Hamlet's revision of *The Murder of Gonzago* into *The Mousetrap*. Contemplate Iago's achievement: his unaided genius has limned this night piece, and it was his best. He will die under torture, silently, but he will have left a mutilated reality as his monument.

Auden, in one of his most puzzling critical essays, found in Iago the apotheosis of the practical joker, which I find explicable only by realizing that Auden's Iago was Verdi's (that is, Boito's), just as Auden's Falstaff was operatic, rather than dramatic. One should not try to restrict Iago's genius; he is a great artist, and no joker. Milton's Satan is a failed theologian and a great poet, while Iago shines equally as nihilistic death-of-God theologue and as advanced dramatic poet. Shakespeare endowed only Hamlet, Falstaff, and Rosalind with more wit and intellect than he gave to Iago and Edmund, while in aesthetic sensibility, only Hamlet overgoes Iago. Grant Iago his Ahab-like obsession—Othello is the Moby-Dick who must be harpooned—and Iago's salient quality rather outrageously is his freedom. A great improviser, he works with gusto and mastery of timing, adjusting his plot to openings as they present themselves. If I were a director of *Othello*, I would instruct my Iago to manifest an ever-growing wonder and confidence in the diabolic art. Unlike Barabas and his progeny, Iago is an inventor, an experimenter always willing to try modes heretofore unknown. Auden, in a more inspired moment, saw Iago as a scientist rather than a practical joker. Satan, exploring the untracked Abyss in *Paradise Lost*, is truly in Iago's spirit. Who before Iago, in literature or in life, perfected the arts of disinformation, disorientation, and derangement? All these combine in Iago's grand program of uncreation, as Othello is returned to original chaos, to the Tohu and Bohu from which we came.

Even a brief glance at Shakespeare's source in Cinthio reveals the extent to which Iago is essentially Shakespeare's radical invention, rather than an adaptation of the wicked Ensign in the original story. Cinthio's Ensign falls passionately in love with Desdemona, but wins no favor with her, since she loves the Moor. The unnamed Ensign decides that his failure is due to Desdemona's love for an unnamed Captain (Shakespeare's Cassio), and so he determines to remove this supposed rival, by inducing jealousy in the Moor and then plotting with him to murder both Desdemona and the Captain. In Cinthio's version, the Ensign beats Desdemona to death, while the Moor watches approvingly. It is only afterward, when the Moor repents and desperately misses his wife, that he dismisses the Ensign, who thus is first moved to hatred against his general. Shakespeare transmuted the entire story by giving it, and Iago, a different starting point, the foreground in which Iago has been passed over for promotion. The ontological shock of that rejection is Shakespeare's original invention and is the trauma that truly creates Iago, no mere wicked Ensign but rather a genius of evil who has engendered himself from a great Fall.

Milton's Satan owes so much to Iago that we can be tempted to read the Christian Fall of Adam into Othello's catastrophe, and to find Lucifer's decline into Satan a clue to Iago's inception. But though Shakespeare's Moor has been baptized, *Othello* is no more a Christian drama than *Hamlet* was a doctrinal tragedy of guilt, sin, and pride. Iago playfully invokes a "Divinity of Hell," and yet he is no mere diabolist. He is War Everlasting (as Goddard sensed) and inspires in me the same uncanny awe and fright that Cormac McCarthy's Judge Holden arouses each time I reread *Blood Meridian, Or, The Evening Redness in the West* (1985). The Judge, though based on an historic filibuster who massacred and scalped Indians in the post–Civil War Southwest and in Mexico, is War Incarnate. A reading of his formidable pronunciamentos provides a theology-in-little of Iago's enterprise, and betrays perhaps a touch of Iago's influence upon *Blood Meridian*, an American descendant of the Shakespeare-intoxicated Melville and Faulkner. "War," says the Judge, "is the truest form of divination . . . War is god," because war is the supreme game of will against will. Iago is the genius of will reborn from war's slighting of the will. To have been passed over for Cassio is to have one's will reduced to nullity, and the self's sense of power violated. Victory for the will therefore demands a restoration of power, and power for Iago can only be war's power: to maim, to kill, to humiliate, to destroy the godlike in another, the war god who betrayed his worship and his trust. Cormac McCarthy's Judge Holden is Iago come again when he proclaims war as the game that defines us:

> Wolves cull themselves, man. What other creature could? And is the race of man not more predacious yet? The way of the world is to bloom and flower and die but in the affairs of men there is no waning and the moon of his expression signals the onset of night. His spirit is exhausted at the peak of its achievement. His meridian is at once his darkening and the evening of his day. He loves games? Let him play for stakes.

In Iago, what was the religion of war, when he worshiped Othello as its god, has now become the game of war, to be played everywhere except upon the battlefield. The death of belief becomes the birth of invention, and the passed-over officer becomes the poet of street brawls, stabbings in the dark, disinformation, and above all else, the uncreation of Othello, the sparagmos of the great captain-general so that he can be returned to the original abyss, the chaos that Iago equates with the Moor's African origins. That is not Othello's view of his heritage (or Shakespeare's), but Iago's interpretation wins, or almost wins, since I will argue that Othello's much-maligned suicide speech is something very close to a recovery of dignity and coherence, though not of lost greatness. Iago, forever beyond Othello's understanding, is not beyond ours, because we are more like Iago than we resemble Othello; Iago's views on war, on the will, and on the aesthetics of revenge inaugurate our own pragmatics of understanding the human.

We cannot arrive at a just estimate of Othello if we undervalue Iago, who would be formidable enough to undo most of us if he emerged out of his play into our lives. Othello is a great soul hopelessly outclassed in intellect and drive by Iago. Hamlet, as A. C. Bradley once observed, would have disposed of Iago very readily. In a speech or two, Hamlet would discern Iago for what he was, and then would drive Iago to suicide by lightning parody and mockery. Falstaff and Rosalind would do much the same, Falstaff boisterously and Rosalind gently. Only humor could defend against Iago, which is why Shakespeare excludes all comedy from Othello, except for Iago's saturnine hilarity. Even there, a difference emerges; Barabas and his Shakespearean imitators share their triumphalism with the audience, whereas Iago, at the top of his form, seems to be sending us postcards from the volcano, as remote from us as he is from all his victims. "You come next," something in him implies, and we wince before him. "With all his poetic gift, he has no poetic weakness," Swinburne said of Iago. The prophet of Resentment, Iago presages Smerdyakov, Svidrigailov, and Stavrogin in Dostoevsky, and all the ascetics of the spirit deplored by Nietzsche.

Yet he is so much more than that; among all literary villains, he is by merit raised to a bad eminence that seems unsurpassable. His only near-rival, Edmund, partly repents while dying, in a gesture more enigmatic than Iago's final election of silence. Great gifts of intellect and art alone could not bring Iago to his heroic villainy; he has a negative grace beyond cognition and perceptiveness. The public sphere gave Marlowe his Guise in *The Massacre at Paris*, but the Guise is a mere imp of evil when juxtaposed to Iago. The Devil himself—in Milton, Marlowe, Goethe, Dostoevsky, Melville, or any other writer—cannot compete with Iago, whose American descendants range from Hawthorne's Chillingworth and Melville's Claggart through Mark Twain's Mysterious Stranger on to Nathanael West's Shrike and Cormac McCarthy's Judge Holden. Modern literature has not surpassed Iago; he remains the perfect Devil of the West, superb as psychologist, playwright, dramatic critic, and negative theologian. Shaw, jealous of Shakespeare, argued that "the character defies all consistency," being at once "a coarse blackguard" and also refined and subtle. Few have agreed with Shaw, and those who question Iago's persuasiveness tend also to find Othello a flawed representation. A. C. Bradley, an admirable critic always, named Falstaff, Hamlet, Iago, and Cleopatra as Shakespeare's "most wonderful" characters. If I could add Rosalind and Macbeth to make a sixfold wonder, then I would agree with Bradley, for these are Shakespeare's grandest inventions, and all of them take human nature to some of its limits, without violating those limits. Falstaff's wit, Hamlet's ambivalent yet charismatic intensity, Cleopatra's mobility of spirit find their rivals in Macbeth's proleptic imagination, Rosalind's control of all perspectives, and Iago's genius for improvisation. Neither merely coarse nor merely subtle, Iago constantly re-creates his own personality and character: "I am not what I am." Those who question how a twenty-eight-year-old professional soldier could harbor so sublimely negative a genius might just as soon question how the thirty-nine-year-old professional actor, Shakespeare, could imagine so convincing a "demi-devil" (as Othello finally terms Iago). We think that Shakespeare abandoned acting just before he composed *Othello*; he seems to have played his final role in *All's Well That Ends Well*. Is there some link between giving up the player's part and the invention of Iago? Between *All's Well That Ends Well* and *Othello*, Shakespeare wrote *Measure for Measure*, a farewell to stage comedy. *Measure for Measure*'s enigmatic Duke Vincentio, as I have observed, seems to have some Iago-like qualities, and may also relate to Shakespeare's release from the burden of performance. Clearly a versatile and competent actor, but never a leading one, Shakespeare perhaps celebrates a new sense of the actor's energies in the improvisations of Vincentio and Iago.

Bradley, in exalting Falstaff, Hamlet, Iago, and Cleopatra, may have been responding to the highly conscious theatricalism that is fused into their roles. Witty in himself, Falstaff provokes wit in others through his performances. Hamlet, analytical tragedian, discourses with everyone he encounters, driving them to self-revelation. Cleopatra is always on stage—living, loving, and dying—and whether she ceases to perform, when alone with Antony, we will never know, because Shakespeare never shows them alone together, save once, and that is very brief. Perhaps Iago, before the Fall of his rejection by Othello, had not yet discovered his own dramatic genius; it seems the largest pragmatic consequence of his Fall, once his sense of nullity has passed through an initial trauma. When we first hear him, at the start of the play, he already indulges his actor's freedom:

> O, sir, content you!
> I follow him to serve my turn upon him.
> We cannot all be masters, nor all masters
> Cannot be truly followed. You shall mark
> Many a duteous and knee-crooking knave
> That, doting on his own obsequious bondage,
> Wears out his time much like his master's ass,
> For nought but provender, and, when he's old, cashiered.
> Whip me such honest knaves! Others there are
> Who, trimmed in forms and visages of duty,
> Keep yet their hearts attending on themselves
> And, throwing but shows of service on their lords,
> Do well thrive by them, and, when they have lined their coats,
> Do themselves homage: these fellows have some soul
> And such a one do I profess myself.
>
> [I.i.40–54]

Only the actor, Iago assures us, possesses "some soul"; the rest of us wear our hearts upon our sleeves. Yet this is only the start of a player's career; at this early point, Iago is merely out for mischief, rousing up Brabantio, Desdemona's father, and conjuring up street brawls. He knows that he is exploring a new vocation, but he has little sense as yet of his own genius. Shakespeare, while Iago gathers force, centers instead upon giving us a view of Othello's precarious greatness, and of Desdemona's surpassing human worth. Before turning to the Moor and his bride, I wish further to foreground Iago, who requires quite as much inferential labor as do Hamlet and Falstaff.

Richard III and Edmund have fathers; Shakespeare gives us no antecedents for Iago. We can surmise the ancient's previous relationship to his superb captain. What can we infer of his marriage to Emilia? There is Iago's curious mistake in his first mention of Cassio: "A fellow almost damned in a fair wife." This seems not to be Shakespeare's error but a token of Iago's obsessive concern with marriage as a damnation, since Bianca is plainly Cassio's whore and not his wife. Emilia, no better than she should be, will be the ironic instrument that undoes Iago's triumphalism, at the cost of her life. As to the relationship between this singular couple, Shakespeare allows us some pungent hints. Early in the play, Iago tells us what neither he nor we believe, not because of any shared regard for Emilia but because Othello is too grand for this:

> And it is thought abroad that 'twixt my sheets
> He's done my office. I know not if't be true,
> But I for mere suspicion in that kind
> Will do as if for surety.

> [I.iii.386–89]

Later, Iago parenthetically expresses the same "mere suspicion" of Cassio: "For I fear Cassio with my night-cap too." We can surmise that Iago, perhaps made impotent by his fury at being passed over for promotion, is ready to suspect Emilia with every male in the play, while not particularly caring one way or the other. Emilia, comforting Desdemona after Othello's initial rage of jealousy against his blameless wife, sums up her own marriage also:

'Tis not a year or two shows us a man.
They are all but stomachs, and we all but food:
They eat us hungerly, and when they are full
They belch us.

[III.iv.104–7]

That is the erotic vision of *Troilus and Cressida*, carried over into a greater realm, but not a less rancid one, because the world of *Othello* belongs to Iago. It is not persuasive to say that Othello is a normal man and Iago abnormal; Iago is the genius of his time and place, and is all will. His passion for destruction is the only creative passion in the play. Such a judgment is necessarily very somber, but then this is surely Shakespeare's most painful play. *King Lear* and *Macbeth* are even darker, but theirs is the darkness of the negative sublime. The only sublimity in *Othello* is Iago's. Shakespeare's conception of him was so definitive that the revisions made between the Quarto's text and the Folio's enlarge and sharpen our sense primarily of Emilia, and secondly of Othello and Desdemona, but hardly touch Iago. Shakespeare rightly felt no need to revise Iago, already the perfection of malign will and genius for hatred. There can be no question concerning Iago's primacy in the play: he speaks eight soliloquies, Othello only three.

Edmund outthinks and so outplots everyone else in *King Lear*, and yet is destroyed by the recalcitrant endurance of Edgar, who develops from credulous victim into inexorable revenger. Iago, even more totally the master of his play, is at last undone by Emilia, whom Shakespeare revised into a figure of intrepid outrage, willing to die for the sake of the murdered Desdemona's good name. Shakespeare had something of a tragic obsession with the idea of a good name living on after his protagonists' deaths. Hamlet, despite saying that no man can know anything of whatever he leaves behind him, nevertheless exhorts Horatio to survive so as to defend what might become of his prince's wounded name. We will hear Othello trying to recuperate some shred of reputation in his suicidal final speech, upon which critical agreement no longer seems at all possible. If the *Funeral Elegy* for Will Peter indeed was Shakespeare's (I think this probable), then the poet-dramatist in 1612, four years before his own death at fifty-two, was much preoccupied with his own evidently blemished name.

Emilia's heroic victory over Iago is one of Shakespeare's grandest ironies, and appropriately constitutes the play's most surprising dramatic moment:

*Emilia.* O God, O heavenly God!

*Iago.*                    Zounds, hold your peace!

*Emilia.* 'Twill out, 'twill out! I peace?

    No, I will speak as liberal as the north.

    Let heaven and men and devils, let them all,

    All, all cry shame against me, yet I'll speak.

*Iago.* Be wise, and get you home.

*Emilia.* I will not.

             *[IAGO tries to stab EMILIA.]*

*Gratiano.* Fie! Your sword upon a woman?

*Emilia.* O thou dull Moor, that handkerchief thou speak'st of

    I found by fortune and did give my husband,

    For often, with a solemn earnestness—

    More than indeed belonged to such a trifle—

    He begged of me to steal't.

*Iago.*                    Villainous whore!

*Emilia.* She give it to Cassio? No, alas, I found it

    And I did give't my husband.

*Iago.*                    Filth, thou liest!

*Emilia.* By heaven, I do not, I do not, gentlemen!

    O murderous coxcomb, what should such a fool

    Do with so good a wife?

        *[OTHELLO runs at IAGO. IAGO stabs his wife.]*

*Othello.*                 Are there no stones in heaven

    But what serves for the thunder? Precious villain!

*Gratiano.* The woman falls, sure he hath killed his wife.

*Emilia.* Ay, ay; O lay me by my mistress' side.

             *Exit IAGO.*

*Gratiano.* He's gone, but his wife's killed.

                      [V.ii.216–36]

We are surprised, but Iago is shocked; indeed it is his first reversal since being passed over for Cassio. That Emilia should lose her worldly wisdom, and become as free as the north wind, was the only eventuality that Iago could not foresee. And his failure to encompass his wife's best aspect—her love for and pride in Desdemona—is the one lapse for which he cannot forgive himself. That is the true undersong of the last lines he ever will allow himself to utter, and which are directed as much to us as to Othello or to Cassio:

> *Othello.* Will you, I pray, demand that demi-devil
>    Why he hath thus ensnared my soul and body?
> *Iago.* Demand me nothing. What you know, you know.
>    From this time forth I never will speak word.
>
> [V.ii.298–301]

What is it that we know, beyond what Othello and Cassio know? Shakespeare's superb dramatic irony transcends even that question into the subtler matter of allowing us to know something about Iago that the ancient, despite his genius, is incapable of knowing. Iago is outraged that he could not anticipate, by dramatic imagination, his wife's outrage that Desdemona should be not only murdered but perhaps permanently defamed. The aesthete's web has all of war's gamelike magic, but no place in it for Emilia's honest indignation. Where he ought to have been at his most discerning—within his marriage—Iago is blank and blind. The superb psychologist who unseamed Othello, and who deftly manipulated Desdemona, Cassio, Roderigo, and all others, angrily falls into the fate he arranged for his prime victim, the Moor, and becomes another wife murderer. He has, at last, set fire to himself.

2

Since the world is Iago's, I scarcely am done expounding him, and will examine him again in an overview of the play, but only after brooding upon the many enigmas of Othello. Where Shakespeare granted Hamlet, Lear, and Macbeth an almost continuous and preternatural eloquence, he chose instead to give Othello a curiously mixed power of expression, distinct yet divided, and deliberately flawed. Iago's theatricalism is superb, but Othello's is troublesome, brilliantly so. The Moor tells us that he has been a warrior since he was seven, presumably a hyperbole but indicative that he is all too aware his greatness has been hard won. His professional self-awareness is extraordinarily intense; partly this is inevitable, since he is technically a mercenary, a black soldier of fortune who honorably serves the Venetian state. And yet his acute sense of his reputation betrays what may well be an uneasiness, sometimes manifested in the baroque elaborations of his language, satirized by Iago as "a bombast circumstance, / Horribly stuffed with epithets of war."

A military commander who can compare the movement of his mind to the "icy current and compulsive course" of the Pontic (Black) Sea, Othello seems incapable of seeing himself except in grandiose terms. He presents himself as a living legend or walking myth, nobler than any antique Roman. The poet Anthony Hecht thinks that we are meant to recognize "a ludicrous and nervous vanity" in Othello, but Shakespeare's adroit perspectivism evades so single a recognition. Othello has a touch of Shakespeare's Julius Caesar in him; there is an ambiguity in both figures that makes it very difficult to trace the demarcations between their vainglory and their grandeur. If you believe in the war god Caesar (as Antony does) or in the war god Othello (as Iago once did), then you lack the leisure to contemplate the god's failings. But if you are Cassius, or the postlapsarian Iago, then you are at pains to behold the weaknesses that mask as divinity. Othello, like Caesar, is prone to refer to himself in the third person, a somewhat unnerving habit, whether in literature or in life. And yet, again like Julius Caesar, Othello believes his own myth, and to some extent we must also, because there is authentic nobility in the language of his soul. That there is opacity also, we cannot doubt; Othello's tragedy is precisely that Iago should know him better than the Moor knows himself.

Othello is a great commander, who knows war and the limits of war but who knows little else, and cannot know that he does not know. His sense of himself is very large, in that its scale is vast, but he sees himself from afar as it were; up close, he hardly confronts the void at his center. Iago's apprehension of that abyss is sometimes compared to Montaigne's; I sooner would compare it to Hamlet's, because like one element in the infinitely varied prince of Denmark, Iago is well beyond skepticism and has crossed into nihilism. Iago's most brilliant insight is that if *he* was reduced to nothingness by Cassio's preferment, then how much more vulnerable Othello must be, lacking Iago's intellect and game-playing will. Anyone can be pulverized, in Iago's view, and in this drama he is right. There is no one in the play with the irony and wit that alone could hold off Iago: Othello is consciously theatrical but quite humorless, and Desdemona is a miracle of sincerity. The terrible painfulness of *Othello* is that Shakespeare shrewdly omits any counterforce to Iago. In *King Lear,* Edmund also confronts no one with the intellect to withstand him, until he is annihilated by the exquisite irony of having created the nameless avenger who was once his gull, Edgar. First and last, Othello is powerless against Iago; that helplessness is the most harrowing element in the play, except perhaps for Desdemona's double powerlessness, in regard both to Iago and to her husband.

It is important to emphasize the greatness of Othello, despite all his inadequacies of language and of spirit. Shakespeare implicitly celebrates Othello as a giant of mere being, an ontological splendor, and so a natural man self-raised to an authentic if precarious eminence. Even if we doubt the possibility of the purity of arms, Othello plausibly represents that lost ideal. At every point, he is the antithesis of Iago's "I am not what I am," until he begins to come apart under Iago's influence. Manifestly, Desdemona has made a wrong choice in a husband, and yet that choice testifies to Othello's hard-won splendor. These days, when so many academic critics are converted to the recent French fashion of denying the self, some of them happily seize upon Othello as a fit instance. They undervalue how subtle Shakespeare's art can be; Othello indeed may seem to prompt James Calderwood's Lacanian observation:

> Instead of a self-core discoverable at the center of his being, Othello's "I am" seems a kind of internal repertory company, a "we are."

If Othello, at the play's start, or at its close, is only the sum of his self-descriptions, then indeed he could be judged a veritable picnic of souls. But his third-person relation to his own images of self testifies not to a "we are" but to a perpetual romanticism at seeing and describing himself. To some degree, he is a self-enchanter, as well as the enchanter of Desdemona. Othello desperately wants and needs to be the protagonist of a Shakespearean romance, but alas he is the hero-victim of this most painful Shakespearean domestic tragedy of blood. John Jones makes the fine observation that Lear in the Quarto version is a romance figure, but then is revised by Shakespeare into the tragic being of the Folio text. As Iago's destined gull, Othello presented Shakespeare with enormous problems in representation. How are we to believe in the essential heroism, largeness, and loving nature of so catastrophic a protagonist? Since Desdemona is the most admirable image of love in all Shakespeare, how are we to sympathize with her increasingly incoherent destroyer, who renders her the unluckiest of all wives? Romance, literary and human, depends on partial or imperfect knowledge. Perhaps Othello never gets beyond that, even in his final speech, but Shakespeare shrewdly frames the romance of Othello within the tragedy of *Othello*, and thus solves the problem of sympathetic representation.

*Othello* is not a "poem unlimited," beyond genre, like *Hamlet*, but the romance elements in its three principal figures do make it a very uncommon tragedy. Iago is a triumph because he is in exactly the right play for an ontotheological villain, while the charitable Desdemona is superbly suited to this drama also. Othello cannot quite fit, but then that is his sociopolitical dilemma, the heroic Moor commanding the armed forces of Venice, sophisticated in its decadence then as now. Shakespeare mingles commercial realism and visionary romance in his portrait of Othello, and the mix necessarily is unsteady, even for this greatest of all makers. Yet we do Othello wrong to offer him the show of violence, whether by unselfing him or by devaluing his goodness. Iago, nothing if not critical, has a keener sense of Othello than most of us now tend to achieve:

The Moor is of a free and open nature
That thinks men honest that but seem to be so.

There are not many in Shakespeare, or in life, that are "of a free and open nature": to suppose that we are to find Othello ludicrous or paltry is to mistake the play badly. He is admirable, a tower among men, but soon enough he becomes a broken tower. Shakespeare's own Hector, Ulysses, and Achilles, in his *Troilus and Cressida*, were all complex travesties of their Homeric originals (in George Chapman's version), but Othello is precisely Homeric, as close as Shakespeare desired to come to Chapman's heroes. Within his clear limitations, Othello indeed is "noble": his consciousness, prior to his fall, is firmly controlled, just, and massively dignified, and has its own kind of perfection. Reuben Brower admirably said of Othello that "his heroic simplicity was also heroic blindness. That too is part of the 'ideal' hero, part of Shakespeare's metaphor." The metaphor, no longer quite Homeric, had to extend to the professionalism of a great mercenary soldier and a heroic black in the service of a highly decadent white society. Othello's superb professionalism is at once his extraordinary strength and his tragic freedom to fall. The love between Desdemona and Othello is authentic, yet might have proved catastrophic even in the absence of the daemonic genius of Iago. Nothing in Othello is marriageable: his military career fulfills him completely. Desdemona, persuasively innocent in the highest of senses, falls in love with the pure warrior in Othello, and he falls in love with her love for him, her mirroring of his legendary career. Their romance is his own pre-existent romance; the marriage does not and cannot change him, though it changes his relationship to Venice, in the highly ironic sense of making him more than ever an outsider.

Othello's character has suffered the assaults of T. S. Eliot and F. R. Leavis and their various followers, but fashions in Shakespeare criticism always vanish, and the noble Moor has survived his denigrators. Yet Shakespeare has endowed Othello with the authentic mystery of being a radically flawed hero, an Adam too free to fall. In some respects, Othello is Shakespeare's most wounding representation of male vanity and fear of female sexuality, and so of the male equation that makes the fear of cuckoldry and the fear of mortality into a single dread. Leontes, in *The Winter's Tale*, is partly a study in repressed homosexuality, and thus his virulent jealousy is of another order than Othello's. We wince when Othello, in his closing apologia, speaks of himself as one not easily jealous, and we wonder at his blindness. Still we never doubt his valor, and this makes it even stranger that he at least matches Leontes in jealous madness. Shakespeare's greatest insight into male sexual jealousy is that it is a mask for the fear of being castrated by death. Men imagine that there never can be enough time and space for themselves, and they find in cuckoldry, real or imaginary, the image of their own vanishing, the realization that the world will go on without them.

Othello sees the world as a theater for his professional reputation; this most valiant of soldiers has no fear of literal death-in-battle, which only would enhance his glory. But to be cuckolded by his own wife, and with his subordinate Cassio as the other offender, would be a greater, metaphorical death-in-life, for his reputation would not survive it, particularly in his own view of his mythic renown. Shakespeare is sublimely daemonic, in a mode transcending even Iago's genius, in making Othello's vulnerability exactly consonant with the wound rendered to Iago's self-regard by being passed over for promotion. Iago says, "I am not what I am"; Othello's loss of ontological dignity would be even greater, had Desdemona "betrayed" him (I place the word between quotation marks, because the implicit metaphor involved is a triumph of male vanity). Othello all too self-consciously has risked his hard-won sense of his own being in marrying Desdemona, and he has an accurate foreboding of chaotic engulfment should that risk prove a disaster:

Excellent wretch! Perdition catch my soul
But I do love thee! and when I love thee not
Chaos is come again.

[III.iii.90–92]

An earlier intimation of Othello's uneasiness is one of the play's subtlest touches:

For know, Iago,
But that I love the gentle Desdemona
I would not my unhoused free condition
Put into circumscription and confine
For the sea's worth.

[I.ii.24–28]

Othello's psychological complexity has to be reconstructed by the audience from his ruins, as it were, because Shakespeare does not supply us with the full foreground. We are given the hint that but for Desdemona, he never would have married, and indeed he himself describes a courtship in which he was essentially passive:

> This to hear
> Would Desdemona seriously incline,
> But still the house affairs would draw her thence,
> Which ever as she could with haste dispatch
> She'd come again, and with a greedy ear
> Devour up my discourse; which I, observing,
> Took once a pliant hour and found good means
> To draw from her a prayer of earnest heart
> That I would all my pilgrimage dilate,
> Whereof by parcels she had something heard
> But not intentively. I did consent,
> And often did beguile her of her tears
> When I did speak of some distressful stroke
> That my youth suffered. My story being done
> She gave me for my pains a world of kisses.
> She swore in faith 'twas strange, 'twas passing strange,
> 'Twas pitiful, 'twas wondrous pitiful;
> She wished she had not heard it, yet she wished
> That heaven had made her such a man. She thanked me
> And bade me, if I had a friend that loved her,
> I should but teach him how to tell my story
> And that would woo her. Upon this hint I spake:
> She loved me for the dangers I had passed
> And I loved her that she did pity them.
>
> [I.iii.146–69]

That is rather more than a "hint," and nearly constitutes a boldly direct proposal, on Desdemona's part. With the Venetian competition evidently confined to the likes of Roderigo, Desdemona is willingly seduced by Othello's naïve but powerful romance of the self, provocative of that "world of kisses." The Moor is not only noble; his saga brings "a maiden never bold" (her father's testimony) "to fall in love with what she feared to look on." Desdemona, a High Romantic centuries ahead of her time, yields to the fascination of quest, if *yields* can be an accurate word for so active a surrender. No other match in Shakespeare is so fabulously unlikely, or so tragically inevitable. Even in a Venice and a Cyprus without Iago, how does so improbable a romance domesticate itself? The high point of passion between Othello and Desdemona is their reunion on Cyprus:

*Othello.* O my fair warrior!
*Desdemona.*                 My dear Othello.
*Othello.* It gives me wonder great as my content
    To see you here before me. O my soul's joy,
    If after every tempest come such calms
    May the winds blow till they have wakened death,
    And let the labouring bark climb hills of seas,
    Olympus-high, and duck again as low
    As hell's from heaven. If it were now to die
    'Twere now to be most happy, for I fear
    My soul hath her content so absolute
    That not another comfort like to this
    Succeeds in unknown fate.
*Desdemona.*              The heavens forbid
    But that our loves and comforts should increase
    Even as our days do grow.
*Othello.*                Amen to that, sweet powers!
    I cannot speak enough of this content,
    It stops me here, it is too much of joy.
    And this, and this the greatest discords be [*They kiss.*]
    That e'er our hearts shall make.
                                 [II.i.180–96]

From such an apotheosis one can only descend, even if the answering chorus were not Iago's aside that he will loosen the strings now so well tuned. Shakespeare (as I have ventured before, following my master, Dr. Johnson) came naturally to comedy and to romance, but violently and ambivalently to tragedy. *Othello* may have been as painful for Shakespeare as he made it for us. Placing the precarious nobility of Othello and the fragile romanticism of Desdemona upon one stage with the sadistic aestheticism of Iago (ancestor of all modern literary critics) was already an outrageous coup of self-wounding on the poet-dramatist's part. I am delighted to revive the now scoffed-at romantic speculation that Shakespeare carries a private affliction, an erotic vastation, into the high tragedies, *Othello* in particular. Shakespeare is, of course, not Lord Byron, scandalously parading before Europe the pageant of his bleeding heart, yet the incredible agony we rightly undergo as we observe Othello murdering Desdemona has a private as well as public intensity informing it. Desdemona's murder is the crossing point between the overflowing cosmos of Hamlet and the cosmological emptiness of Lear and of Macbeth.

### 3

The play *Hamlet* and the mind of Hamlet verge upon an identity, since everything that happens to the Prince of Denmark already seems to be the prince. We cannot quite say that the mind of Iago and the play *Othello* are one, since his victims have their own greatness. Yet, until Emilia confounds him, the drama's action is Iago's; only the tragedy of their tragedy belongs to Othello and Desdemona. In 1604, an anonymous storyteller reflected upon "Shakespeare's tragedies, where the Comedian rides, when the Tragedian stands on Tip-toe." This wonderful remark was made of Prince Hamlet, who "pleased all," but more subtly illuminates *Othello*, where Shakespeare-as-comedian rides Iago, even as the dramatist stands on tiptoe to extend the limits of his so painful art. We do not know who in Shakespeare's company played Iago against Burbage's Othello, but I wonder if it was not the great clown Robert Armin, who would have played the drunken porter at the gate in *Macbeth*, the Fool in *King Lear*, and the asp bearer in *Antony and Cleopatra*. The dramatic shock in Othello is that we delight in Iago's exuberant triumphalism, even as we dread his villainy's consequences. Marlowe's self-delighting Barabas, echoed by Aaron the Moor and Richard III, seems a cruder Machiavel when we compare him with the refined Iago, who confounds Barabas with aspects of Hamlet, in order to augment his own growing inwardness. With Hamlet, we confront the ever-growing inner self, but Iago has no inner self, only a fecund abyss, precisely like his descendant, Milton's Satan, who in every deep found a lower deep opening wide. Satan's discovery is agonized; Iago's is diabolically joyous. Shakespeare invents in Iago a sublimely sadistic comic poet, an archon of nihilism who delights in returning his war god to an uncreated night. Can you invent Iago without delighting in your invention, even as we delight in our ambivalent reception of Iago?

Iago is not larger than his play; he perfectly fits it, unlike Hamlet, who would be too large even for the most unlimited of plays. I have noted already that Shakespeare made significant revisions to what is spoken by Othello, Desdemona, and Emilia (even Roderigo) but not by Iago; it is as though Shakespeare knew he had gotten Iago right the first time round. No villain in all literature rivals Iago as a flawless conception, who requires no improvement. Swinburne was accurate: "the most perfect evildom, the most potent demi-devil," and "a reflection by hell-fire of the figure of Prometheus." A Satanic Prometheus may at first appear too High Romantic, yet the pyromaniac Iago encourages Roderigo to a

> dire yell
> As when by night and negligence the fire
> Is spied in populous cities.

[I.i.74–76]

According to the myth, Prometheus steals fire to free us; Iago steals us, as fresh fodder for the fire. He is an authentic Promethean, however negative, because who can deny that Iago's fire is poetic? The hero-villains of John Webster and Cyril Tourneur are mere names on the page when we contrast them with Iago; they lack Promethean fire. Who else in Shakespeare, except for Hamlet and Falstaff, is so creative as Iago? These three alone can read your soul, and read everyone they encounter. Perhaps Iago is the recompense that the Negative demanded to counterbalance Hamlet, Falstaff, and Rosalind. Great wit, like the highest irony, needs an inner check in order not to burn away everything else: Hamlet's disinterestedness, Falstaff's exuberance, Rosalind's graciousness. Iago is nothing at all, except critical; there can be no inner check when the self is an abyss. Iago has the single affect of sheer gusto, increasingly aroused as he discovers his genius for improvisation.

Since the plot of *Othello* essentially is Iago's plot, improvisation by Iago constitutes the tragedy's heart and center. Hazlitt's review of Edmund Kean's performance as Iago in 1814, from which I have drawn my epigraph for this chapter, remains the finest analysis of Iago's improvisatory genius, and is most superb when it observes that Iago "stabs men in the dark to prevent *ennui.*" That prophetic insight advances Iago to the Age of Baudelaire, Nietzsche, and Dostoevsky, an Age that in many respects remains our own. Iago is not a Jacobean Italian malcontent, another descendant of Marlowe's Machiavels. His greatness is that he is out ahead of us, though every newspaper and television newscast brings us accounts of his disciples working on every scale, from individual crimes of sadomasochism to international terrorism and massacre. Iago's followers are everywhere: I have watched, with great interest, many of my former students, undergraduate and graduate, pursue careers of Iagoism, both in and out of the academy. Shakespeare's great male intellectuals (as contrasted to Rosalind and Beatrice, among his women) are only four all together: Falstaff and Hamlet, Iago and Edmund. Of these, Hamlet and Iago are also aesthetes, critical consciousnesses of near-preternatural power. Only in Iago does the aesthete predominate, in close alliance with nihilism and sadism.

I place particular emphasis upon Iago's theatrical and poetic genius, as an appreciation of Iago that I trust will be aesthetic without also being sadomasochistic, since that danger always mingles with any audience's enjoyment of Iago's revelations to us. There is no major figure in Shakespeare with whom we are less likely to identify ourselves, and yet Iago is as beyond vice as he is beyond virtue, a fine recognition of Swinburne's. Robert B. Heilman, who perhaps undervalued Othello (the hero, not the play), made restitution by warning that there was no single way into Iago:

"As the spiritual have-not, Iago is universal, that is, many things at once, and of many times at once." Swinburne, perhaps tinged with his usual sadomasochism in his high regard for Iago, prophesied that Iago's stance in hell would be like that of Farinata, who stands upright in his tomb: "as if of Hell he had a great disdain." There is hardly a circle in Dante's *Inferno* that Iago could not inhabit, so vast is his potential for ill.

By interpreting Iago as a genius for improvising chaos in others, a gift born out of his own ontological devastation by Othello, I am in some danger of giving us Iago as a negative theologian, perhaps too close to the Miltonic Satan whom he influenced. As I have tried to emphasize throughout this book, Shakespeare does not write Christian or religious drama; he is not Calderón or (to invoke lesser poet-playwrights) Paul Claudel or T. S. Eliot. Nor is Shakespeare (or Iago) any kind of a heretic; I am baffled when critics argue as to whether Shakespeare was Protestant or Catholic, since the plays are neither. There are gnostic heretical elements in Iago, as there will be in Edmund and in Macbeth, but Shakespeare was not a gnostic, or a hermeticist, or a Neo-Platonic occultist. In his extraordinary way, he was the most curious and universal of gleaners, possibly even of esoteric spiritualities, yet here too he was primarily an inventor or discoverer. Othello is a Christian, by conversion; Iago's religion is war, war everywhere—in the streets, in the camp, in his own abyss. Total war is a religion, whose best literary theologian I have cited already, Judge Holden in Cormac McCarthy's frightening *Blood Meridian*. The Judge imitates Iago by expounding a theology of the will, whose ultimate expression is war, against everyone. Iago says that he has never found a man who knew how to love himself, which means that self-love is the exercise of the will in murdering others. That is Iago's self-education in the will, since he does not start out with the clear intention of murder. In the beginning was a sense of having been outraged by a loss of identity, accompanied by the inchoate desire to be revenged upon the god Iago had served.

Shakespeare's finest achievement in *Othello* is Iago's extraordinary mutations, prompted by his acute self-overhearing as he moves through his eight soliloquies, and their supporting asides. From tentative, experimental promptings on to excited discoveries, Iago's course develops into a tri-

umphal march, to be ended only by Emilia's heroic intervention. Much of
the theatrical greatness of *Othello* inheres in this triumphalism, in which we
unwillingly participate. Properly performed, *Othello* should be a momentary
trauma for its audience. *Lear* is equally catastrophic, where Edmund triumphs consistently until the duel with Edgar, but *Lear* is vast, intricate, and
varied, and not just in its double plot. In *Othello*, Iago is always at the center of the web, ceaselessly weaving his fiction, and snaring us with dark
magic. Only Prospero is comparable, a luminous magus who in part is
Shakespeare's answer to Iago.

You can judge Iago to be, in effect, a misreader of Montaigne, as opposed to Hamlet, who makes of Montaigne the mirror of nature. Kenneth
Gross shrewdly observes that "Iago is at best a nightmare image of so vig-
ilant and humanizing a pyrrhonism as Montaigne's." Pyrrhonism, or radical skepticism, is transmuted by Hamlet into disinterestedness; Iago turns
it into a war against existence, a drive that seeks to argue that there is no
reason why anything should be, at all. The exaltation of the will, in Iago,
emanates from an ontological lack so great that no human emotion possibly could fill it:

> Virtue? A fig! 'tis in ourselves that we are thus, or thus. Our bodies
> are gardens, to the which our wills are gardeners. So that if we will
> plant nettles or sow lettuce, set hyssop and weed up thyme, supply
> it with one gender of herbs or distract it with many, either to have
> it sterile with idleness or manured with industry—why, the power
> and corrigible authority of this lies in our wills. If the balance of our
> lives had not one scale of reason to poise another of sensuality, the
> blood and baseness of our natures would conduct us to most pre-
> posterous conclusions. But we have reason to cool our raging mo-
> tions, our carnal stings, our unbitted lusts; whereof I take this, that
> you call love, to be a sect or scion.
>
> [I.iii.320–33]

"Virtue" here means something like "manly strength," while by "reason" Iago intends only his own absence of significant emotion. This prose

utterance is the poetic center of *Othello*, presaging Iago's conversion of his leader to a reductive and diseased vision of sexuality. We cannot doubt that Othello loves Desdemona; Shakespeare also may suggest that Othello is amazingly reluctant to make love to his wife. As I read the play's text, the marriage is never consummated, despite Desdemona's eager desires. Iago derides Othello's "weak function"; that seems more a hint of Iago's impotence than of Othello's, and yet nothing that the Moorish captain-general says or does reflects an authentic lust for Desdemona. This certainly helps explain his murderous rage, once Iago has roused him to jealousy, and also makes that jealousy more plausible, since Othello literally does not know whether his wife is a virgin, and is afraid to find out, one way or the other. I join here the minority view of Graham Bradshaw, and of only a few others, but this play, of all Shakespeare's, seems to me the most weakly misread, possibly because its villain is the greatest master of misprision in Shakespeare, or in literature. Why did Othello marry anyway, if he does not sexually desire Desdemona? Iago cannot help us here, and Shakespeare allows us to puzzle the matter out for ourselves, without ever giving us sufficient information to settle the question. But Bradshaw is surely right to say that Othello finally testifies Desdemona died a virgin:

> Now: how dost thou look now? O ill-starred wench,
> Pale as thy smock. When we shall meet at compt
> This look of thine will hurl my soul from heaven
> And fiends will snatch at it. Cold, cold, my girl,
> Even like thy chastity.
>
> [V.ii.270–74]

Unless Othello is merely raving, we at least must believe he means what he says: she died not only faithful to him but "cold . . . Even like thy chastity." It is a little difficult to know just what Shakespeare intends Othello to mean, unless his victim had never become his wife, even for the single night when their sexual union was possible. When Othello vows not to "shed her blood," he means only that he will smother her to death, but the frightening irony is there as well: neither he nor Cassio nor anyone else has ever ended her virginity. Bradshaw finds in this a "ghastly tragicomic parody of an erotic death," and that is appropriate for Iago's theatrical achievement.

I want to shift the emphasis from Bradshaw's in order to question a matter upon which Iago had little influence: Why was Othello reluctant, from the start, to consummate the marriage? When, in Act I, Scene iii, the Duke of Venice accepts the love match of Othello and Desdemona, and then orders Othello to Cyprus, to lead its defense against an expected Turkish invasion, the Moor asks only that his wife be housed with comfort and dignity during his absence. It is the ardent Desdemona who requests that she accompany her husband:

> So that, dear lords, if I be left behind,
> A moth of peace, and he go to war,
> The rites for which I love him are bereft me,
> And I a heavy interim shall support
> By his dear absence. Let me go with him.
>
> [I.iii.256–60]

Presumably by "rites" Desdemona means consummation, rather than battle, and though Othello seconds her, he rather gratuitously insists that desire for her is not exactly hot in him:

> Let her have your voice.
> Vouch with me, heaven, I therefore beg it not
> To please the palate of my appetite,
> Nor to comply with heat, the young affects
> In me defunct, and proper satisfaction,
> But to be free and bounteous to her mind.
> And heaven defend your good souls that you think
> I will your serious and great business scant
> When she is with me. No, when light-winged toys
> Of feathered Cupid seel with wanton dullness
> My speculative and officed instrument,
> That my disports corrupt and taint my business,

Let housewives make a skillet of my helm
And all indign and base adversities
Make head against my estimation.

[I.iii.261–75]

These lines, hardly Othello at his most eloquent, exceed the measure that decorum requires, and do not favor Desdemona. He protests much too much, and hardly betters the case when he urges her off the stage with him:

Come, Desdemona, I have but an hour
Of love, of worldly matter and direction
To spend with thee. We must obey the time.

[I.iii.299–301]

If that "hour" is literal, then "love" will be lucky to get twenty minutes of this overbusy general's time. Even with the Turks impending, the state would surely have allowed its chief military officer an extra hour or two for initially embracing his wife. When he arrives on Cyprus, where Desdemona has preceded him, Othello tells us: "Our wars are done, the Turks are drowned." That would seem to provide ample time for the deferred matter of making love to his wife, particularly since public feasting is now decreed. Perhaps it is more proper to wait for evening, and so Othello bids Cassio command the watch, and duly says to Desdemona: "Come, my dear love, / The purchase made, the fruits are to ensue: / That profit's yet to come 'tween me and you," and exits with her. Iago works up a drunken riot, involving Cassio, Roderigo, and Montano, governor of Cyprus, in which Cassio wounds Montano. Othello, aroused by a tolling bell, enters with Desdemona following soon afterward. We are not told whether there has been time enough for their "rites," but Othello summons her back to bed, while also announcing that he himself will supervise the dressing of Montano's wounds. Which had priority, we do not precisely know, but evidently the general preferred his self-imposed obligation toward the governor to his marital obligation.

Iago's first insinuations of Desdemona's supposed relationship with Cassio would have no effect if Othello knew her to have been a virgin. It is because he does not know that Othello is so vulnerable. "Why did I marry!" he exclaims, and then points to his cuckold's horns when he tells Desdemona: "I have a pain upon my forehead, here," which his poor innocent of a wife attributes to his all-night care of the governor: "Why, that's with watching," and tries to bind it hard with the fatal handkerchief, pushed away by him, and so it falls in Emilia's way. By then, Othello is already Iago's, and is incapable of resolving his doubts through the only sensible course of finally bringing himself to bed Desdemona.

This is a bewildering labyrinth for the audience, and frequently is not overtly addressed by directors of *Othello*, who leave us doubtful of their interpretations, or perhaps they are not even aware of the difficulty that requires interpretation. Shakespeare was capable of carelessness, but not upon so crucial a point, for the entire tragedy turns upon it. Desdemona and Othello, alas, scarcely know each other, and sexually do not know each other at all. Shakespeare's audacious suggestion is that Othello was too frightened or diffident to seize upon the opportunity of the first night in Cyprus, but evaded and delayed the ordeal by devoting himself to the wounded Montano. The further suggestion is that Iago, understanding Othello, fomented the drunken altercation in order to distract his general from consummation, for otherwise Iago's manipulations would have been without consequence. That credits Iago with extraordinary insight into Othello, but no one should be surprised at such an evaluation. We can wonder why Shakespeare did not make all this clearer, except that we need to remember his contemporary audience was far superior to us in comprehending through the ear. They knew how to listen; most of us do not, in our overvisual culture. Shakespeare doubtless would not have agreed with Blake that what could be made explicit to the idiot was not worth his care, but he had learned from Chaucer, in particular, how to be appropriately sly.

Before turning at last to Iago's triumphalism, I feel obliged to answer my own question: Why did Othello marry when his love for Desdemona was only a secondary response to her primary passion for him? This prelude to tragedy seems plausibly compounded of her ignorance—she is still only a child, rather like Juliet—and his confusion. Othello tells us that he had been nine consecutive months in Venice, away from the battlefield and the camp, and thus he was not himself. Fully engaged in his occupation, he would have been immune to Desdemona's charmed condition and to her generous passion for his living legend. Their shared idealism is also their mutual illusion: the idealism is beautiful, but the illusion would have been dissolved even if Othello had not passed over Iago for promotion and so still had Iago's loving worship, rather than the ancient's vengeful hatred. The fallen Iago will teach Othello that the general's failure to know Desdemona, sexually and otherwise, was because Othello did not want to know. Bradshaw brilliantly observes that Iago's genius "is to persuade others that something they had not thought was something they had not *wanted* to think." Iago, having been thrown into a cosmological emptiness, discovers that what he had worshiped as Othello's warlike fullness of being was in part another emptiness, and Iago's triumph is to expand that part into very nearly the whole of Othello.

4

Iago's terrible greatness (what else can we term it?) is also Shakespeare's triumph over Christopher Marlowe, whose Barabas, Jew of Malta, had influenced the young Shakespeare so fiercely. We can observe that Iago transcends Barabas, just as Prospero is beyond Marlowe's Dr. Faustus. One trace of Barabas abides in Iago, though transmogrified by Shakespeare's more glorious villain: self-delight. Exuberance or gusto, the joy of being Sir John Falstaff, is parodied in Iago's negative celebrations, and yet to considerable purpose. Emptied out of significant being, Iago mounts out of his sense of injured merit in his new pride of attainments: dramatist, psychologist, aesthetic critic, diabolic analyst, countertherapist. His uncreation of his captain-general, the return of the magnificent Othello to an original chaos, remains the supreme negation in the history of Western literature, far surpassing the labors of his Dostoevskian disciples, Svidrigailov and Stavrogin, and of his American pupils, Claggart in Melville's *Billy Budd* and Shrike in Nathanael West's *Miss Lonelyhearts*. The only near-rivals to Iago are also his students, Milton's Satan and Cormac McCarthy's Judge in *Blood Meridian*. Compared with Iago, Satan is hampered by having to work on too cosmic a scale: all of nature goes down with Adam and Eve. McCarthy's Judge, the only character in modern fiction who genuinely frightens me, is too much bloodier than Iago to sustain the comparison. Iago stabs a man or two in the dark; the Judge scalps Indians and Mexicans by the hundreds. By working in so close to his prime victim, Iago becomes the Devil-as-matador, and his own best aficionado, since he is nothing if not critical. The only first-rate Iago I have ever seen was Bob Hoskins, who surmounted his director's flaws in Jonathan Miller's BBC television *Othello* of 1981, where Anthony Hopkins as the Moor sank without a trace by being faithful to Miller's Leavisite (or Eliotic) instructions. Hoskins, always best as a gangster, caught many of the accents of Iago's underworld pride in his own preternatural wiliness, and at moments showed what a negative beatification might be, in the pleasure of undoing one's superior at organized violence. Perhaps Hoskins's Iago was a shade more Marlovian than Shakespearean, almost as though Hoskins (or Miller) had *The Jew of Malta* partly in mind, whereas Iago is refined beyond that farcical an intensity.

Triumphalism is Iago's most chilling yet engaging mode; his great soliloquies and asides march to an intellectual music matched in Shakespeare only by aspects of Hamlet, and by a few rare moments when Edmund descends to self-celebration. Iago's inwardness, which sometimes echoes Hamlet's, enhances his repellent fascination for us: How can a sensible emptiness be so labyrinthine? To trace the phases of Iago's entrapment of Othello should answer that question, at least in part. But I pause here to deny that Iago represents something crucial in Othello, an assertion made by many interpreters, the most convincing of whom is Edward Snow. In a reading too reliant upon the Freudian psychic mythology, Snow finds in Iago the overt spirit that is buried in Othello: a universal male horror of female sexuality, and so a hatred of women.

The Age of Freud wanes, and joins itself now, in many, to the Age of Resentment. That all men fear and hate women and sexuality is neither Freudian nor true, though an aversion to otherness is frequent enough, in women as in men. Shakespeare's lovers, men and women alike, are very various; Othello unfortunately is not one of the sanest among them. Stephen

Greenblatt suggests that Othello's conversion to Christianity has augmented the Moor's tendency to sexual disgust, a plausible reading of the
play's foreground. Iago seems to see this, even as he intuits Othello's reluctance to consummate the marriage, but even that does not mean Iago
is an inward component of Othello's psyche, from the start. Nothing can
exceed Iago's power of contamination once he truly begins his campaign,
and so it is truer to say that Othello comes to represent Iago than to suggest we ought to see Iago as a component of Othello.

Shakespeare's art, as manifested in Iago's ruination of Othello, is in
some ways too subtle for criticism to paraphrase. Iago suggests Desdemona's infidelity by at first not suggesting it, hovering near and around it:

*Iago.*                    I do beseech you,
    Though I perchance am vicious in my guess—
    As I confess it is my nature's plague
    To spy into abuses, and of my jealousy
    Shape faults that are not—that your wisdom
    From one that so imperfectly conceits
    Would take no notice, nor build yourself a trouble
    Out of his scattering and unsure observance:
    It were not for your quiet nor your good
    Nor for my manhood, honesty and wisdom
    To let you know my thoughts.
*Othello.*                    Zounds! What dost thou mean?
*Iago.* Good name in man and woman, dear my lord,
    Is the immediate jewel of their souls:
    Who steals my purse steals trash—'tis something-nothing,
    'Twas mine, 'tis his, and has been slave to thousands—
    But he that filches from me my good name
    Robs me of that which not enriches him
    And makes me poor indeed.
*Othello.*          By heaven, I'll know thy thoughts!
*Iago.* You cannot, if my heart were in your hand,
    Nor shall not whilst 'tis in my custody.
*Othello.* Ha!

*Iago.*      O, beware, my lord, of jealousy!
    It is the green-eyed monster, which doth mock
    The meat it feeds on. That cuckold lives in bliss
    Who, certain of his fate, loves not his wronger,
    But O, what damned minutes tells he o'er
    Who dotes yet doubts, suspects yet strongly loves!
*Othello.* O misery!

                                          [III.iii.147–73]

This would be outrageous if its interplay between Iago and Othello were not so persuasive. Iago manipulates Othello by exploiting what the Moor shares with the jealous God of the Jews, Christians, and Muslims, a barely repressed vulnerability to betrayal. Yahweh and Othello alike are vulnerable because they have risked extending themselves, Yahweh to the Jews and Othello to Desdemona. Iago, whose motto is "I am not what I am," will triumph by tracking this negativity to Othello, until Othello quite forgets he is a man and becomes jealousy incarnate, a parody of the God of vengeance. We underestimate Iago when we consider him only as a dramatist of the self and a psychologist of genius; his greatest power is as a negative ontotheologian, a diabolical prophet who has a vocation for destruction. He is not the Christian devil or a parody thereof, but rather a free artist of himself, uniquely equipped, by experience and genius, to entrap spirits greater than his own in a bondage founded upon their inner flaws. In a play that held a genius opposed to his own—a Hamlet or a Falstaff—he would be only a frustrated malcontent. Given a world only of gulls and victims—Othello, Desdemona, Cassio, Roderigo, even Emilia until outrage turns her—Iago scarcely needs to exercise the full range of powers that he keeps discovering. A fire is always raging within him, and the hypocrisy that represses his satirical intensity in his dealings with others evidently costs him considerable suffering.

That must be why he experiences such relief, even ecstasy, in his extraordinary soliloquies and asides, where he applauds his own performance. Though he rhetorically invokes a "divinity of hell," neither he nor we have any reason to believe that any demon is listening to him. Though married, and an esteemed flag officer, with a reputation for "honesty," Iago is as solitary a figure as Edmund, or as Macbeth after Lady Macbeth goes mad. Pleasure, for Iago, is purely sadomasochistic; pleasure, for Othello, consists in the rightful consciousness of command. Othello loves Desdemona, yet primarily as a response to her love for his triumphal consciousness. Passed over, and so nullified, Iago determines to convert his own sadomasochism into a countertriumphalism, one that will commandeer his commander, and then transform the god of his earlier worship into a degradation of godhood. The chaos that Othello rightly feared if he ceased to love Desdemona has been Iago's natural element since Cassio's promotion. From that chaos, Iago rises as a new Demiurge, a master of uncreation.

In proposing an ontotheological Iago, I build upon A. C. Bradley's emphasis on the passed-over ancient's "resentment," and add to Bradley the idea that resentment can become the only mode of freedom for such great negations as Iago's Dostoevskian disciples, Svidrigailov and Stavrogin. They may seem insane compared with Iago, but they inherited his weird lucidity, and his economics of the will. René Girard, a theoretician of envy and scapegoating, feels compelled to take Iago at his word, and so sees Iago as being sexually jealous of Othello. This is to be yet again entrapped by Iago, and adds an unnecessary irony to Girard's reduction of all Shakespeare to "a theater of envy." Tolstoy, who fiercely resented Shakespeare, complained of Iago, "There are many motives, but they are all vague." To feel betrayed by a god, be he Mars or Yahweh, and to desire restitution for one's wounded self-regard, to me seems the most precise of any villain's motives: return the god to the abyss into which one has been thrown. Tolstoy's odd, rationalist Christianity could not reimagine Iago's negative Christianity.

Iago is one of Shakespeare's most dazzling performers, equal to Edmund and Macbeth and coming only a little short of Rosalind and Cleopatra, Hamlet and Falstaff, superb charismatics. Negative charisma is an odd endowment; Iago represents it uniquely in Shakespeare, and most literary incarnations of it since owe much to Iago. Edmund, in spite of his own nature, has the element of Don Juan in him, the detachment and freedom from hypocrisy that is fatal for those grand hypocrites, Goneril and Regan. Macbeth, whose prophetic imagination has a universal force, excites our sympathies, however bloody his actions. Iago's appeal to us is the power of the negative, which is all of him and only a part of Hamlet. We all have our gods, whom we worship, and by whom we cannot accept rejection. The Sonnets turn upon a painful rejection, of the poet by the young nobleman, a rejection that is more than erotic, and that seems to figure in Falstaff's public disgrace at Hal's coronation. Foregrounding *Othello* requires that we imagine Iago's humiliation at the election of Cassio, so that we hear the full reverberation of

> Though I do hate him as I do hell-pains,
> Yet for necessity of present life
> I must show out a flag and sign of love,
> Which is indeed but sign.
>
> [I.i.152–55]

The ensign, or ancient, who would have died faithfully to preserve Othello's colors on the battlefield, expresses his repudiation of his former religion, in lines absolutely central to the play. Love of the war god is now but a sign, even though revenge is as yet more an aspiration than a project. The god of war, grand as Othello may be, is a somewhat less formidable figure than the God of the Jews, Christians, and Muslims, but by a superb ontological instinct, Iago associates the jealousy of one god with that of the other:

> I will in Cassio's lodging lose this napkin
> And let him find it. Trifles light as air
> Are to the jealous confirmations strong
> As proofs of holy writ. This may do something.
> The Moor already changes with my poison:
> Dangerous conceits are in their natures poisons
> Which at the first are scarce found to distaste
> But with a little art upon the blood
> Burn like the mines of sulphur. I did say so.
> *Enter OTHELLO.*
>
> [III.iii.324–32]

The simile works equally well the other way round: proofs of Holy Writ are, to the jealous God, strong confirmations, but the airiest trifles can provoke the Yahweh who in Numbers leads the Israelites through the wilderness. Othello goes mad, and so does Yahweh in Numbers. Iago's marvelous pride in his "I did say so" leads on to a critical music new even to Shakespeare, one which will engender the aestheticism of John Keats and Walter Pater. The now obsessed Othello stumbles upon the stage, to be greeted by Iago's most gorgeous outburst of triumphalism:

> Look where he comes. Not poppy nor mandragora
> Nor all the drowsy syrups of the world
> Shall ever medicine thee to that sweet sleep
> Which thou owedst yesterday.
>
> [III.iii.333–36]

If this were only sadistic exultation, we would not receive so immortal a wound from it; masochistic nostalgia mingles with the satisfaction of uncreation, as Iago salutes both his own achievement and the consciousness that Othello never will enjoy again. Shakespeare's Iago-like subtle art is at its highest, as we come to understand that Othello *does not know* precisely because he has not known his wife. Whatever his earlier reluctance to consummate marriage may have been, he now realizes he is incapable of it, and so cannot attain to the truth about Desdemona and Cassio:

> I had been happy if the general camp,
> Pioneers and all, had tasted her sweet body,
> So I had nothing known. O now for ever
> Farewell the tranquil mind, farewell content!
> Farewell the plumed troops and the big wars
> That makes ambition virtue! O farewell,
> Farewell the neighing steed and the shrill trump,
> The spirit-stirring drum, th'ear-piercing fife,
> The royal banner, and all quality,
> Pride, pomp and circumstance of glorious war!

And, O you mortal engines whose rude throats
Th'immortal Jove's dread clamours counterfeit,
Farewell: Othello's occupation's gone.

[III.iii.348–60]

This Hemingwayesque farewell to the big wars has precisely Hemingway's blend of masculine posturing and barely concealed fear of impotence. There has been no time since the wedding, whether in Venice or on
Cyprus, for Desdemona and Cassio to have made love, but Cassio had
been the go-between between Othello and Desdemona in the play's foregrounding. Othello's farewell here essentially is to any possibility of consummation; the lost music of military glory has an undersong in which the
martial engines signify more than cannons alone. If Othello's occupation
is gone, then so is his manhood, and with it departs also the pride, pomp,
and circumstance that compelled Desdemona's passion for him, the "circumstance" being more than pageantry. Chaos comes again, even as Othello's ontological identity vanishes, in Iago's sweetest revenge, marked by the
villain's sublime rhetorical question: "Is't possible? my lord?" What follows
is the decisive moment of the play, in which Iago realizes, for the first time,
that Desdemona must be murdered by Othello:

Othello. Villain, be sure thou prove my love a whore,
   Be sure of it, give me the ocular proof,
   Or by the worth of man's eternal soul [catching hold of him]
   Thou hadst been better have been born a dog
   Than answer my waked wrath!
Iago.                              Is't come to this?
Othello. Make me to see't, or at the least so prove it
   That the probation bear no hinge nor loop
   To hang a doubt on, or woe upon thy life!
Iago. My noble lord—
Othello. If thou dost slander her and torture me
   Never pray more, abandon all remorse;
   On horror's head horrors accumulate,

Do deeds to make heaven weep, all earth amazed,
For nothing canst thou to damnation add
Greater than that!

[III.iii.362–76]

Iago's improvisations, until now, had as their purpose the destruction of Othello's identity, fit recompense for Iago's vastation. Suddenly, Iago confronts a grave threat that is also an opportunity: either he or Desdemona must die, with the consequences of her death to crown the undoing of Othello. How can Othello's desire for "the ocular proof" be satisfied?

*Iago.* And may—but how? how satisfied, my lord?
    Would you, the supervisor, grossly gape on?
    Behold her topped?
*Othello.*               Death and damnation! O!
*Iago.* It were a tedious difficulty, I think,
    To bring them to that prospect. Damn them then
    If ever mortal eyes do see them bolster
    More than their own. What then? how then?
    What shall I say? where's satisfaction?
    It is impossible you should see this
    Were they as prime as goats, as hot as monkeys,
    As salt as wolves in pride, as fools as gross
    As ignorance made drunk. But yet, I say,
    If imputation and strong circumstances
    Which lead directly to the door of truth
    Will give you satisfaction, you might have't.

[III.iii.397–411]

The only ocular proof possible is what Othello will not essay, as Iago well understands, since the Moor will not try his wife's virginity. Shakespeare shows us jealousy in men as centering upon both visual and temporal obsessions, because of the male fear that there will not be enough time and space for him. Iago plays powerfully upon Othello's now monumental aversion from the only door of truth that could give satisfaction, the entrance into Desdemona. Psychological mastery cannot surpass Iago's control of Othello, when the ensign chooses precisely this moment to introduce "a handkerchief, / I am sure it was your wife's, did I today / See Cassio wipe his beard with." Dramatic mastery cannot exceed Iago's exploitation of Othello's stage gesture of kneeling to swear revenge:

> *Othello.* Even so my bloody thoughts with violent pace
>     Shall ne'er look back, ne'er ebb to humble love
>     Till that a capable and wide revenge
>     Swallow them up. Now by yond marble heaven
>     In the due reverence of a sacred vow
>     I here engage my words.
> *Iago.*                     Do not rise yet. *Iago kneels.*
>     Witness, you ever-burning lights above,
>     You elements that clip us round about,
>     Witness that here Iago doth give up
>     The execution of his wit, hands, heart,
>     To wronged Othello's service. Let him command
>     And to obey shall be in me remorse
>     What bloody business ever.
> *Othello.*                   I greet thy love
>     Not with vain thanks but with acceptance bounteous,
>     And will upon the instant put thee to't.
>     Within these three days let me hear thee say
>     That Cassio's not alive.
> *Iago.*                   My friend is dead.
>     'Tis done—at your request. But let her live.
> *Othello.* Damn her, lewd minx: O damn her, damn her!
>     Come, go with me apart; I will withdraw
>     To furnish me with some swift means of death
>     For the fair devil. Now art thou my lieutenant.
> *Iago.* I am your own for ever.

[III.iii.460–82]

It is spectacular theater, with Iago as director: "Do not rise yet." And it is also a countertheology, transcending any Faustian bargain with the Devil, since the stars and the elements serve as witnesses to a murderous pact, which culminates in the reversal of the passing over of Iago in the play's foreground. "Now art thou my lieutenant" means something very different from what Othello can understand, while "I am your own for ever" seals Othello's starry and elemental fate. What remains is only the way down and out, for everyone involved.

5

Shakespeare creates a terrible pathos for us by not showing Desdemona in her full nature and splendor until we know that she is doomed. Dr. Johnson found the death of Cordelia intolerable; the death of Desdemona, in my experience as a reader and theatergoer, is even more unendurable. Shakespeare stages the scene as a sacrifice, as grimly countertheological as are Iago's passed-over nihilism and Othello's "godlike" jealousy. Though Desdemona in her anguish declares she is a Christian, she does not die a martyr to that faith but becomes only another victim of what could be called the religion of Moloch, since she is a sacrifice to the war god whom Iago once worshiped, the Othello he has reduced to incoherence. "Othello's occupation's gone"; the shattered relic of Othello murders in the name of that occupation, for he knows no other, and is the walking ghost of what he was.

Millicent Bell recently has argued that Othello's is an epistemological tragedy, but only Iago has intellect enough to sustain such a notion, and Iago is not much interested in how he knows what he thinks he knows. *Othello*, as much as *King Lear* and *Macbeth*, is a vision of radical evil; *Hamlet* is Shakespeare's tragedy of an intellectual. Though Shakespeare never would commit himself to specifically Christian terms, he approached a kind of gnostic or heretic tragedy in *Macbeth*, as I will attempt to show. Othello has no transcendental aspect, perhaps because the religion of war does not allow for any. Iago, who makes a new covenant with Othello when they kneel together, had lived and fought in what he took to be an old covenant with his general, until Cassio was preferred to him. A devout adherent to the fire of battle, his sense of merit injured by his god, has degraded that god into "an honourable murderer," Othello's oxymoronic, final vision of his role. Can such degradation allow the dignity required for a tragic protagonist?

A. C. Bradley rated *Othello* below *Hamlet*, *Lear*, and *Macbeth* primarily because it gives us no sense of universal powers impinging upon the limits of the human. I think those powers hover in *Othello*, but they manifest themselves only in the gap that divides the earlier, foregrounded relationship between Iago and Othello from the process of ruination that we observe between them. Iago is so formidable a figure because he has uncanny abilities, endowments only available to a true believer whose trust has transmuted into nihilism. Cain, rejected by Yahweh in favor of Abel, is as much the father of Iago as Iago is the precursor of Milton's Satan. Iago murders Roderigo and maims Cassio; it is as inconceivable to Iago as to us that Iago seeks to knife Othello. If you have been rejected by your god, then you attack him spiritually or metaphysically, not merely physically. Iago's greatest triumph is that the lapsed Othello sacrifices Desdemona in the name of the war god Othello, the solitary warrior with whom unwisely she has fallen in love. That may be why Desdemona offers no resistance, and makes so relatively unspirited a defense, first of her virtue and then of her life. Her victimization is all the more complete, and our own horror at it thereby is augmented.

Though criticism frequently has blinded itself to this, Shakespeare had no affection for war, or for violence organized or unorganized. His great killing machines come to sorrowful ends: Othello, Macbeth, Antony, Coriolanus. His favorite warrior is Sir John Falstaff, whose motto is: "Give me life!" Othello's motto could be "Give me honor," which sanctions slaughtering a wife he hasn't known, supposedly not "in hate, but all in honour." Dreadfully flawed, even vacuous at the center as Othello is, he still is meant to be the best instance available of a professional mercenary. What Iago once worshiped was real enough, but more vulnerable even than Iago suspected. Shakespeare subtly intimates that Othello's prior nobility and his later incoherent brutality are two faces of the war god, but it remains the same god. Othello's occupation's gone partly because he married at all. Pent-up resentment, and not repressed lust, animates Othello as he avenges his lost autonomy in the name of his honor. Iago's truest triumph comes when Othello loses his sense of war's limits, and joins Iago's incessant campaign against *being*. "I am not what I am," Iago's credo, becomes Othello's implicit cry. The rapidity and totality of Othello's descent seems at once the play's one weakness and its most persuasive strength, as persuasive as Iago.

Desdemona dies so piteously that Shakespeare risks alienating us forever from Othello:

> *Des.* O, banish me, my lord, but kill me not!
> *Oth.* Down, strumpet!
> *Des.* Kill me tomorrow, let me live tonight!
> *Oth.* Nay, if you strive—
> *Des.* But half an hour!
> *Oth.*                    Being done, there is no pause—
> *Des.* But while I say one prayer!
> *Oth.* It is too late.

[V.ii.77–82]

Rather operatically, Shakespeare gives Desdemona a dying breath that attempts to exonerate Othello, which would indeed strain credulity if she were not, as Alvin Kernan wonderfully put it, "Shakespeare's word for love." We are made to believe that this was at once the most natural of young women, and also so loyal to her murderer that her exemplary last words sound almost ironic, given Othello's degradation: "Commend me to my kind lord—O, farewell!" It seems too much more for us to bear that Othello should refuse her final act of love: "She's like a liar gone to burning hell: / 'Twas I that killed her." The influential modern assaults upon Othello by T. S. Eliot and F. R. Leavis take their plausibility (such as it is) from Shakespeare's heaping up of Othello's brutality, stupidity, and unmitigated guilt. But Shakespeare allows Othello a great if partial recovery, in an astonishing final speech:

Soft you, a word or two before you go.
I have done the state some service, and they know't:
No more of that. I pray you, in your letters,
When you shall these unlucky deeds relate,
Speak of me as I am. Nothing extenuate,
Nor set down aught in malice. Then must you speak
Of one that loved not wisely, but too well;
Of one not easily jealous, but, being wrought,
Perplexed in the extreme; of one whose hand,
Like the base Judean, threw a pearl away
Richer than all his tribe; of one whose subdued eyes,
Albeit unused to the melting mood,
Drops tears as fast as the Arabian trees
Their medicinable gum. Set you down this,
And say besides that in Aleppo once,
Where a malignant and a turbaned Turk
Beat a Venetian and traduced the state,
I took by th' throat the circumcised dog
And smote him—thus! *He stabs himself.*

[V.ii.336–54]

This famous and problematic outburst rarely provokes any critic to agree with any other, yet the Eliot–Leavis interpretation, which holds that Othello essentially is "cheering himself up," cannot be right. The Moor remains as divided a character as Shakespeare ever created; we need give no credence to the absurd blindness of "loved not wisely, but too well," or the outrageous self-deception of "one not easily jealous." Yet we are moved by the truth of "perplexed in the extreme," and by the invocation of Herod, "the base Judean" who murdered his Maccabean wife, Mariamme, whom he loved. The association of Othello with Herod the Great is the more shocking for being Othello's own judgment upon himself, and is followed by the Moor's tears, and by his fine image of weeping trees. Nor should a fair critic fail to be impressed by Othello's verdict upon himself: that he has become an enemy of Venice, and as such must be slain. His suicide has nothing Roman in it: Othello passes sentence upon himself, and performs the execution. We need to ask what Venice would have done with Othello, had he allowed himself to survive. I venture that he seeks to forestall what might have been their politic decision: to preserve him until he might be of high use again. Cassio is no Othello; the state has no replacement for the Moor, and might well have used him again, doubtless under some control. All of the rifts in Othello that Iago sensed and exploited are present in this final speech, but so is a final vision of judgment, one in which Othello abandons his nostalgias for glorious war, and pitifully seeks to expiate what cannot be expiated—not, at least, by a farewell to arms.

# 25

# KING LEAR

King *Lear*, together with *Hamlet*, ultimately baffles commentary. Of all Shakespeare's dramas, these show an apparent infinitude that perhaps transcends the limits of literature. *King Lear* and *Hamlet*, like the Yahwist's text (the earliest in the Pentateuch) and the Gospel of Mark, announce the beginning and the end of human nature and destiny. That sounds rather inflated and yet merely is accurate; the *Iliad*, the Koran, Dante's *Comedy*, Milton's *Paradise Lost* are the only rival works in what still could be called Western tradition. This is to say that *Hamlet* and *King Lear* now constitute either a kind of secular scripture or a mythology, peculiar fates for two stage plays that almost always have been commercial successes.

The experience of reading *King Lear*, in particular, is altogether uncanny. We are at once estranged and uncomfortably at home; for me, at least, no other solitary experience is at all like it. I emphasize reading, more than ever, because I have attended many stagings of *King Lear*, and invariably have regretted being there. Our directors and actors are defeated by this play, and I begin sadly to agree with Charles Lamb that we ought to keep rereading *King Lear* and avoid its staged travesties. That pits me against the scholarly criticism of our century, and against all the theater people that I know, but in this matter opposition is true friendship. In the pure good of theory, the part of Lear should be playable; if we cannot accomplish it, the flaw is in us, and in the authentic decline of our cognitive and literate culture. Assaulted by films, television, and computers, our inner and outer ears have difficulty apprehending Shakespeare's hum of thoughts evaded in the mind. Since *The Tragedy of King Lear* well may be the height of literary experience, we cannot afford to lose our capability for confronting it. Lear's torments are central to us, almost to all of us, since the sorrows of generational strife are necessarily universal.

Job's sufferings have been suggested as the paradigm for Lear's ordeal; I once gave credence to this critical commonplace, but now find it unpersuasive. Patient Job is actually not very patient, despite his theological reputation, and Lear is the pattern of all impatience, though he vows otherwise, and movingly urges patience on the blinded Gloucester. The pragmatic disproportion between Job's afflictions and Lear's is rather considerable, at least until Cordelia is murdered. I suspect that a different biblical model was in Shakespeare's mind: King Solomon. I do not mean Solomon in all his glory—in Kings, Chronicles, and obliquely in the Song of Songs—but the aged monarch, at the end of his reign, wise yet exacerbated, the supposed preacher of Ecclesiastes and of the Wisdom of Solomon in the Apocrypha, as well as the putative author of the Proverbs. Presumably Shakespeare was read aloud to from the Bishop's Bible in his youth, and later read the Geneva Bible for himself in his maturity. Since he wrote *King Lear* as a servant of King James I, who had the reputation of being the wisest fool in Christendom, perhaps Shakespeare's conception of Lear was influenced by James's particular admiration for Solomon, wisest of kings. I admit that not many among us instantly associate Solomon and Lear, but there is crucial textual evidence that Shakespeare himself made the association, by having Lear allude to the following great passage in the Wisdom of Solomon, 7:1–6.

> I Myself am also mortal and a man like all other, and am come of
> him that was first made of the earth.
>
> And in my mothers womb was I facioned to be flesh in ten mon-
> eths: I was broght together into blood of the sede of man, and by
> the pleasure that cometh with slepe.
>
> And when I was borne, I received the cõmune aire, and fel upon
> the earth, which is of like nature, crying & weping at the first as all
> other do.

I was nourished in swadling clothes, and with cares.

For there is no King that had anie other beginning of birth.

All men then have one entrance unto life, and a like going out.

[Geneva Bible]

That is the unmistakable text echoed in Lear's shattering sermon to Gloucester:

*Lear.* If thou wilt weep my fortunes, take my eyes;
   I know thee well enough; thy name is Gloucester;
   Thou must be patient; we came crying hither:
   Thou know'st the first time that we smell the air
   We wawl and cry. I will preach to thee: mark.
            *[Lear takes off his crown of weeds and flowers.]*
*Glou.* Alack, alack the day!
*Lear.* When we are born, we cry that we are come
   To this great stage of fools.

[IV.vi.174–81]

After Solomon the kingdom was divided, as it was by Lear. Yet I don't think that Shakespeare in part founds Lear upon the aged Solomon because of the catastrophes of kingdoms. Shakespeare sought what we tend now not to emphasize in our accounts of Lear: a paradigm for greatness. These days, in teaching the play, I begin by insisting on Lear's foregrounding in grandeur, because my students are unlikely at first to perceive it, patriarchal sublimity now being not much in fashion. Lear is at once father, king, and a kind of mortal god: he is the image of male authority, perhaps the ultimate representation of the Dead White European Male. Solomon reigned for fifty years, and was James I's wished-for archetype: glorious, wise, wealthy, even if Solomon's passion for women was not exactly shared by the sexually ambiguous James. Lear is in no way a portrait of James; Shakespeare's royal patron in all likelihood sympathized but did not empathize with the kingdom-dividing Lear. But Lear's greatness would have mattered to James: he too considered himself every inch a king. I think he would have recognized in the aged Lear the aged Solomon, each in their eighties, each needing and wanting love, and each worthy of love.

When I teach *King Lear*, I have to begin by reminding my students that Lear, however unlovable in the first two acts, is very much loved by Cordelia, the Fool, Albany, Kent, Gloucester, and Edgar—that is to say, by every benign character in the play—just as he is hated and feared by Goneril, Regan, Cornwall, and Oswald, the play's lesser villains. The play's great villain, the superb and uncanny Edmund, is ice-cold, indifferent to Lear as he is even to his own father Gloucester, his half brother Edgar, and his lovers Goneril and Regan. It is part of Shakespeare's genius not to have Edmund and Lear address even a single word to each other in the entire play, because they are apocalyptic antitheses: the king is all feeling, and Edmund is bare of all affect. The crucial foregrounding of the play, if we are to understand it at all, is that Lear is lovable, loving, and greatly loved, by anyone at all worthy of our own affection and approbation.

Of course, whoever you may be, you can be loved and loving and still demand more. If you are King Lear, and have ever but slenderly known yourself, then you are almost apocalyptically needy in your demand for love, particularly from the child you truly love, Cordelia. The play's foreground comprehends not only Lear's benignity, and the resentment of Goneril and Regan, weary of their being passed over for their sister, but most crucially Cordelia's recalcitrance in the face of incessant entreaties for a total love surpassing even her authentic regard for her violently emotional father. Cordelia's rugged personality is something of a reaction formation to her father's overwhelming affection. It is one of the many peculiarities of Shakespeare's double plot that Cordelia, despite her absolute importance to Lear himself, is much less central to the play than is her parallel, Edgar. Shakespeare leaps over several intervening reigns in order to have Edgar succeed Lear as king of Britain. Legend, still current in Shakespeare's time, assigned to King Edgar the melancholy distinction that he rid Britain of wolves, who overran the island after the death of Lear.

There are four great roles in *The Tragedy of King Lear*, though you might not know that from most stagings of the play. Cordelia's, for all her pathos, is not one of them, nor are Goneril's and Regan's of the same order of dramatic eminence as the roles of Lear and of the Fool. Edmund and Edgar, antithetical half brothers, require actors as skilled and powerful as do Lear and the Fool. I have seen a few appropriate Edmunds, best of all Joseph Wiseman many years ago in New York, saving an otherwise ghastly production in which Louis Calhern, as Lear, reminded me only of how much more adequate he had been as Ambassador Trentino in the Marx Brothers' *Duck Soup.* Wiseman played Edmund as an amalgam of Leon Trotsky and Don Giovanni, but it worked quite brilliantly, and there is much in the play's text to sustain that curious blend.

Many readers and auditors of Shakespeare become as dangerously enthralled by Edmund as they are by Iago, yet Edgar, recalcitrant and repressed, actually is the larger enigma, and is so difficult to play that I have never once seen a passable Edgar. The title page of the first Quarto edition of *King Lear* assigns a prominence to Edgar rarely afforded him in our critical studies:

M. William Shak-speare: His True Chronicle Historie of the life and death of King Lear and his three Daughters. With the unfortunate life of Edgar, sonne and heire to the Earle of Gloster, and his sullen and assumed humor of Tom of Bedlam . . .

"Sullen" in Shakespeare has the strong meaning of melancholia or depression, a variety of madness assumed by Edgar in his disguise as Tom of Bedlam. The Earl of Kent disguises himself as Caius, to serve Lear. Edgar, in parallel flight, abases himself, sinking below even the bottom of the social scale. Why does Edgar assume the lowest possible disguise? Is he punishing himself for his own credulity, for sharing his father's inability to see through Edmund's brilliant deceptions? There is something so profoundly disproportionate in Edgar's self-abnegation throughout the play that we have to presume in him a recalcitrance akin to Cordelia's, but far in excess of hers. Whether as bedlamite or as poor peasant, Edgar refuses his own identity for more than practical purposes. The most extraordinary manifestation of this refusal is his consistent unwillingness to reveal himself to Gloucester, his father, even as he rescues the blinded Earl from murder by the despicable Oswald, and from suicide, after the defeat of Lear and Cordelia. Only when he is on the verge of regaining his own rank, just before challenging Edmund to mortal combat, does Edgar identify himself to Gloucester, so as to ask a paternal blessing for the duel. The recognition encounter, which kills Gloucester, is one of Shakespeare's great unwritten scenes, being confined as it is to Edgar's narrative account, delivered to Albany after Edmund has received his death wound. Why did Shakespeare choose not to dramatize the event?

A theatrical answer might be that the intricacies of the double plot already seemed so substantial that Shakespeare declined to risk yet further complexity. The Shakespearean audacity is so immense that I doubt such an answer. Lear wakes up sane to be reconciled with Cordelia, a scene in which we all delight. Edgar and Gloucester reconciling, even though the intense affect kills the blind sufferer, could have been nearly as poignant a staged vision. Though we tend to assign greater prominence to the Fool, or to the frighteningly seductive Edmund, the subtitle of the play rightly guides us to Edgar, who will inherit the ruined kingdom. Shakespeare's dramatic self-denial in not writing the scene of Edgar's self-revelation to Gloucester necessarily places the emphasis more upon Edgar, who tells the tale, than upon his father. We learn even more about Edgar's personality and character than we would have known, though we know a great deal already about a role that exemplifies the pathos and value of filial love far more comprehensively than Cordelia's can, because of the necessities of Shakespeare's plot. I return therefore to the voluntary overimmersion in humiliation that Edgar compels himself to undergo.

If we could speak of a poetic rather than dramatic center to the tragedy, we might choose the meeting between the mad King Lear and blind Gloucester in Act IV, Scene vi, lines 80–185. Sir Frank Kermode rightly remarks that the meeting in no way advances the plot, though it may well be the summit of Shakespeare's art. As playgoers and readers, we concentrate on Lear and Gloucester, yet Edgar is the interlude's chorus, and he has set the tonality of Act IV, in its opening lines, with their keynote in "The lamentable change is from the best; / The worst returns to laughter." The entry of the blinded Gloucester darkens that desperate comfort, compelling Edgar to the revision "the worst is not / So long as we can say 'This is the worst.' " It will be the worst only when "the worst" is already dead in our hearts. Gloucester, blinded and cast forth, is a paternal image suggestive enough to reilluminate even Lear's outcast madness. Madness and blindness become a doublet profoundly akin to tragedy and love, the doublet that binds together the entire play. Madness, blindness, love, and tragedy amalgamate in a giant bewilderment.

"But what if excess of love / Bewildered them until they died?" Yeats asks in his "Easter, 1916." Whatever that meant in regard to MacDonagh and MacBride, and Connolly and Pearse, Yeats's question is appropriate to Lear himself. Love, whether it be Lear's for Cordelia, or Edgar's for his father, Gloucester, and for his godfather, Lear, is pragmatically a waste in this most tragic of all tragedies. Lust does no better; when the dying Edmund muses that in spite of all, he was beloved, his sudden capacity for affect superbly surprises us, but we would choose another word rather than "beloved" for the murderous passion of Goneril and Regan.

In Hamlet's play there is a central consciousness, as there is in Macbeth's. In Othello's play, there is at least a dominant nihilist. But Lear's play is strangely divided. Before he goes mad, Lear's consciousness is beyond ready understanding: his lack of self-knowledge, blended with his awesome authority, makes him unknowable by us. Bewildered and bewildering after that, Lear seems less a consciousness than a falling divinity, Solomonic in his sense of lost glory, Yahweh-like in his irascibility. The play's central consciousness perforce is Edgar's, who actually speaks more lines than anyone except Lear. Edmund, more brilliant even than Iago, less of an improviser and more a strategist of evil, is further into nihilism than Iago was, but no one—hero or villain—can be dominant in Lear's tragedy. Shakespeare, *contra* historicists old and new, burns through every context, and never more than in this play. The figure of excess or overthrow never abandons Shakespeare's text; except for Edmund, everyone either loves or hates too much.

Edgar, whose pilgrimage of abnegation culminates in vengeance, ends overwhelmed by the helplessness of his love, a love progressively growing in range and intensity, with the pragmatic effect of yielding him, as the new king, only greater suffering. Edmund, desperately attempting to do some good, despite what he continues to insist is his own nature, is carried off stage to die, not knowing whether Cordelia has been saved or not. No formalist or historicist would be patient with my asking this, but in what state of self-knowledge does Edmund find himself as he dies? His sense of his own identity, powerful until Edgar overcomes him, wavers throughout the long scene of his dying. Lear and Edgar have shared enormous bewilderments of identity, which appear to be further manifestations of excessive love. Shakespeare's intimation is that the only authentic love is between parents and children, yet the prime consequence of such love is only devastation. Neither of the drama's two antithetical senses of nature, Lear's or Edmund's, is sustained by a close scrutiny of the changes the protagonists undergo in Acts IV and V. Edgar's "ripeness is all" is misconstrued if we interpret it as a Stoic comfort, let alone somehow a Christian consolation. Shakespeare deliberately echoes Hamlet's "The readiness is all," itself an ironical reversal of Simon-Peter's sleepiness provoking Jesus's "The spirit is ready, but the flesh is weak." If we must endure our going hence even as our coming higher, then "ripeness is all" warns us how little "all" is. Soon enough, as W. R. Elton observed, Edgar will tell us "that endurance and ripeness are not all." His final wisdom is to submit to "the weight of this sad time," a submission that involves his reluctant assumption of the crown, with the ghastly historical mission of clearing a Britain overrun by wolves.

Love, Samuel Johnson once remarked, is the wisdom of fools and the folly of the wise. The greatest critic in our tradition was not commenting on Lear's tragedy, but he might as well have been, since his observation is both Shakespearean and prudential, and illuminates the limitations of love in the play. Edgar has become wise when the play ends, yet love is still his folly by engendering his inconsolable grief for his two fathers. The great stage of fools has only three survivors standing upon it at the end: Kent willingly soon will join his master, Lear, while the much shaken Albany abdicates his interest to Edgar. The marriage between Albany and Goneril would have been more than enough to exhaust a stronger character than Albany, and Kent is only just barely a survivor. Edgar is the center, and we can wonder why we are so slow to see that it is, except for Lear, Edgar's play after all. Lear's excessive love for Cordelia inevitably sought to be a controlling love, until the image of authority was broken, not redeemed, as Christianizers of this pagan play have argued. The serving love of Edgar prepares him to be an unstoppable avenger against Edmund, and a fit monarch for a time of troubles, but the play's design establishes that Edgar's is as catastrophic a love as Lear's. Love is no healer in *The Tragedy of King Lear;* indeed, it starts all the trouble, and is a tragedy in itself. The gods in *King Lear* do not kill men and women for their sport; instead they afflict Lear and Edgar with an excess of love, and Goneril and Regan with the torments of lust and jealousy. Nature, invoked by Edmund as his goddess, destroys him through the natural vengeance of his brother, because Edmund is immune from love, and so has mistaken his deity.

Dr. Johnson said that he could not bear Act V of the play because it outraged divine justice and so offended his moral sense, but the great critic may have mistaken his own reaction. What the drama of *King Lear* truly outrages is our universal idealization of the value of familial love—that is to say, both love's personal and love's social value. The play manifests an intense anguish in regard to human sexuality, and a compassionate despair as to the mutually destructive nature of both paternal and filial love. Maternal love is kept out of the tragedy, as if natural love in its strongest form would be too much to bear, even for this negative sublimity. Lear's queen, unless she were a Job's wife, laconically suggesting that Lear curse the gods and die, would add an intolerable burden to a drama already harrowing in the extreme.

Hazlitt thought that it was equally impossible to give either a description of the play itself or of its effect upon the mind. Rather strikingly, for so superb a psychological critic, Hazlitt remarks, "All that we can say must fall far short of the subject; or even of what we ourselves conceive of it." Hazlitt touches on the uncanniest aspect of *Lear:* something that we conceive of it hovers outside our expressive range. I think this effect ensues from the universal wound the play deals to the value of familial love. Laboring this point is painful, but everything about the tragedy of *Lear* is painful. To borrow from Nietzsche, it is not that the pain is meaningful but that meaning itself becomes painful in this play. We do them wrong to speak of Lear's own permutations as being redemptive; there can be no re-generation when love itself becomes identical with pain. Every attempt to mitigate the darkness of this work is an involuntary critical lie. When Edgar says of Lear, "He childed as I father'd," the tragedy is condensed into just five words.

Unpack that gnomic condensation, and what do you receive? Not, I think, a parallel between two innocences (Lear's and Edgar's) and two guilts (Lear's elder daughters' and Gloucester's) because Edgar does not consider his father to be guilty. "He childed as I father'd" has in it no reference whatsoever to Goneril and Regan, but only to the parallel between Lear–Cordelia and Edgar–Gloucester. There is love, and only love, among those four, and yet there is tragedy, and only tragedy, among them. Subtly, Edgar indicates the link between his own rugged recalcitrance and Cordelia's. Without Cordelia's initial recalcitrance, there would have been no tragedy, but then Cordelia would not have been Cordelia. Without Edgar's stubborn endurance and self-abnegation, the avenging angel who strikes Edmund down would not have been metamorphosed out of a gullible innocent. We can wonder at the depth and prolongation of the self-abasement, but then Edgar would not have been Edgar without it. And there is no recompense; Cordelia is murdered, and Edgar despair-ingly will resign himself to the burden of kingship.

Critics have taken a more hopeful stance, to argue for redemptive love, and for the rough justice visited upon every villain in the play. The mon-sters in the deep all achieve properly bad ends: Edgar cudgels Oswald to death; the servant, defending Gloucester, fatally wounds Cornwall; Goneril poisons Regan, and then stabs herself in the heart; Edgar cuts Edmund down, as the audience knows Edgar is fated to do. But there is no satisfac-tion for us in this slaughter of the wicked. Except for Edmund, they are too barbaric to be tolerated, and even Edmund, fascinating as he is, would de-serve, like the others, to be indicted for crimes against humanity. Their deaths are meaningless—again, even Edmund's, since his belated change fails to save Cordelia. Cordelia's death, painful to us beyond description, nevertheless has only that pain to make it meaningful. Lear and Gloucester, startlingly, both die more of joy than of grief. The joy that kills Lear is delusional: he apparently hallucinates, and beholds Cordelia either as not having died or as being resurrected. Gloucester's joy is founded upon reality, but pragmatically the extremes of delight and of anguish that kill him are indistinguishable. "He childed as I father'd": Lear and Gloucester are slain by their paternal love; by the intensity and authenticity of that love. War between siblings; betrayal of fathers by daughters and by a natural son; tormented misunderstanding of a loyal son and a saintly daughter by noble patriarchs; a total dismissal of all sexual congress as lechery: what are we bequeathed by this tragedy that we endlessly moralize? There is one valid form of love and one only: that at the end, between Lear and Cordelia, Gloucester and Edgar. Its value, casting aside irrelevant transcendental moralizings, is less than negative: it may be stronger than death, but it leads only to death, or to death-in-life for the extraordinary Edgar, Shakespeare's survivor of survivors.

No one would regard *The Tragedy of King Lear* as a Shakespearean aberration: the play develops out of aspects of *Hamlet, Troilus and Cressida, Measure for Measure,* and *Othello,* and clearly is prelude to aspects of *Macbeth, Antony and Cleopatra,* and *Timon of Athens.* Only *Hamlet,* of all the plays, seems more central to Shakespeare's incessant concerns than *King Lear* is, and in their ultimate implications the two works interlock. Does Hamlet love anyone as he dies? The transcendental aura that his dying moments evoke, our sensation of his charismatic freedom, is precisely founded upon his having become free of every object attachment, whether to father, mother, Ophelia, or even poor Yorick. There is only one mention of the word *father* by Hamlet in all of Act V, and it is in reference to his father's signet, employed to send Rosencrantz and Guildenstern to extinction. The only reference by Hamlet to his father the person is when he speaks of Claudius as having killed "my king" and whored his mother. Hamlet's farewell to Gertrude is the not very affectionate "Wretched Queen, adieu!" There is, of course, Horatio, whose love for Hamlet brings him to the verge of suicide, from which Hamlet saves him, but solely for the purpose of having a survivor who will clear his wounded name. Nothing whatsoever that happens in the tragedy *Hamlet* gives love itself anything except a wounded name. Love, in any of its modes, familial or erotic or social, is transformed by Shakespeare, more than by any other writer, into the greatest of dramatic and aesthetic values. Yet more than any other writer, Shakespeare divests love of any supposed values of its own.

The implicit critique of love, by Shakespeare, hardly can be termed a mere skepticism. Literary criticism, as I have learned from Dr. Johnson, is the art of making the implicit finely explicit, and I accept the risk of apparently laboring what may be to many among us quite obvious, once we are asked to ponder it. "We cannot choose whom we are free to love," a celebrated line of Auden's, may have been influenced by Freud, but Sigmund Freud, as time's revenges will show, is nothing but belated William Shakespeare, "the man from Stratford" as Freud bitterly liked to call him, in support of that defrauded genius, the Earl of Oxford. There is love that can be avoided, and there is a deeper love, unavoidable and terrible, far more central to Shakespeare's invention of the human. It seems more accurate to call it that, rather than reinvention, because the time before Shakespeare had his full influence upon us was also "before we were wholly human and knew ourselves," as Wallace Stevens phrased it. Irreparable love, destructive of every value distinct from it, was and is a Romantic obsession. But the representation of love, in and by Shakespeare, was the largest literary contamination that produced Romanticism.

A. D. Nuttall, more than any other twentieth-century critic, has clarified some of the central paradoxes of Shakespearean representation. Two of Nuttall's observations always abide with me: Shakespeare is out ahead of us, illuminating our latest intellectual fashions more sharply than they can illuminate him, and Shakespeare enables us to see realities that may already have been there but that we would not find it possible to see without him. Historicists—old, new, and burgeoning—do not like it when I add to Nuttall the realization that the difference between what Shakespeare knew and what we know is, to an astonishing extent, just Shakespeare himself. He is what we know because we are what he knew: he childed as we fathered. Even if Shakespeare, like all of his contemporaries and like all of ours, is only a socially inscribed entity, histrionic and fictive, and so not at all a self-contained author, all the better. Borges may have intended a Chestertonian paradox, but he spoke a truth more literal than figurative: Shakespeare is everyone and no one. So are we, but Shakespeare is more so. If you want to argue that he was the most precariously self-fashioned of all the self-fashioned, I gladly will agree. But wisdom finally cannot be the product of social energies, whatever those are. Cognitive power and an understanding heart are individual endowments. Wittgenstein rather desperately wanted to see Shakespeare as a creator of language rather than as a creator of thought, yet Shakespeare's own pragmatism renders that a distinction that makes no difference. Shakespeare's writing creates what holds together language and thought in a stance that neither affirms nor subverts Western tradition. What that stance is, though, hovers still beyond the categories of our critiques.

Social domination, the obsession of our School of Resentment, is only secondarily a Shakespearean concern. Domination maybe, but that mode of domination is more personal than social, more internal than outward. Shakespeare's greatest men and women are pragmatically doom-eager not because of their relation to state power but because their inner lives are ravaged by all the ambivalences and ambiguities of familial love and its displacements. There is a drive in all of us, unless we are Edmund, to slay ourselves upon the stems of generation, in Blake's language. Edmund is free of that drive, but is caught in the closed circle that makes him another of the fools of time. Time, Falstaff's antagonist and Macbeth's nemesis, is antithetical to nature in Lear's play. Edmund, who cannot be destroyed by love, which he never feels, is destroyed by the wheel of change that he has set spinning for his victimized half brother. Edgar, stubborn sufferer, cannot be defeated, and his timing becomes exquisite the moment he and Gloucester encounter the bullying Oswald.

The best principle in reading Shakespeare is Emerson's: "Shakespeare is the only biographer of Shakespeare; and even he can tell nothing, except to the Shakespeare in us." I myself deviate a touch from Emerson, since I think only Shakespeare has placed the Shakespeare in us. I don't believe I am that horrid thing, much deprecated by our current pseudo-Marxist Shakespeareans, an "essentialist humanist." As a gnostic sect of one, I blink at a supposed Shakespeare who is out to subvert Renaissance ideology and who hints at revolutionary possibilities. Essentialist Marxists or feminists or Franco-Heideggerians ask me to accept a Shakespeare rather in their own image. The Shakespeare in me, however placed there, shows me a deeper and more ancient subversion at work—in much of Shakespeare, but in the four high tragedies or domestic tragedies of blood in particular.

Dostoevsky founded Svidrigailov and Stavrogin upon Iago and Edmund, while Nietzsche and Kierkegaard discovered their Dionysiac forerunner in Hamlet, and Melville came to his Captain Ahab through Macbeth. The nihilist questers emerge from the Shakespearean abyss, as Freud at his uncanniest emerged. I do not offer a nihilistic Shakespeare or a gnostic one, but skepticism alone cannot be the origin of the cosmological degradation that contextualizes the tragedies *King Lear* and *Macbeth*. The more nihilistic Solomon of Ecclesiastes and the Wisdom of Solomon tells us, in the latter, Apocryphal work, that "we are borne at all adventure, and we shall be hereafter as though we had never been." The heretic Milton did not believe that God had made the world out of nothing; we do not know what Shakespeare did not believe. Lear, as charted by W. R. Elton, is neither an Epicurean materialist nor a skeptic; rather he is "in rejecting creation *ex nihilo* a pious pagan but a skeptical Christian," as befits a pagan play for a Christian audience. Lear, we always must remind ourselves, is well past eighty, and his world wears out to nothing with him. As in *Macbeth*, an end time is suggested. The resurrection of the body, unknown to Solomon, is also unknown to Lear, who dies in his evident hallucination of Cordelia's revival from the dead.

*King Lear* is Lear's play, not Edmund's, but as I've continued to say, it is also Edgar's play, and ironically the later Edgar is Edmund's unintended creation. The sullen or assumed humor of Tom O'Bedlam is the central emblem of the play: philosopher, fool, madman, nihilist, dissembler—at once all of these and none of these. There is a horror of generation that intensifies as the tragedy grows starker, and Edgar, harsher as he proceeds, shares it with Lear. Nothing sweetens Edgar's imagination of sexuality, whereas Edmund, icy libertine, is deliciously indifferent: "Which of them shall I take? / Both? one? or neither?" A double date with Goneril and

Regan might faze even King Richard III or Aaron the Moor, but it is second nature to Edmund, who attributes his vivacity, freedom from hypocrisy, and power of plotting to his bastardy, at once provocation to his pride and to some uneasiness of spirit:

> Why brand they us
> With base? with baseness? bastardy? base, base?
> Who in the lusty stealth of nature take
> More composition and fierce quality
> Than doth, within a dull, stale, tired bed,
> Go to th'creating a whole tribe of fops,
> Got 'tween asleep and wake?
>
> [I.ii.9–15]

That is Edmund in his "fierce quality," not the mortally wounded man who has the continued accuracy to say, " 'Tis past, and so am I." Edgar, at that moment, takes an opposite view of that "lusty stealth of nature":

> The Gods are just, and of our pleasant vices
> Make instruments to plague us;
> The dark and vicious place where thee he got
> Cost him his eyes.
>
> [V.iii.169–72]

The dying Edmund accepts this, but it can be judged very disconcerting, since that "dark and vicious place" does not appear to be an adulterous bed but is identical with what Lear stigmatizes in his madness:

> Down from the waist they are Centaurs,
> Though women all above:
> But to the girdle do the Gods inherit,
> Beneath is all the fiends': there's hell, there's darkness,
> There is the sulphurous pit—burning, scalding,
> Stench, consumption.
>
> [IV.vi.123–28]

Admirable son of Gloucester and admirable godson of Lear, approved avenger and future king, Edgar nevertheless emerges impaired in many respects from his long ordeal of abnegation. Not least of these impairments is his evident horror of female sexuality, "the dark and vicious place." A high price has been exacted for the long descent into the sullen and assumed humor of Tom O' Bedlam. The cost of confirmation for Edgar is a savage wound in his psyche, but the entire play is more of a wound than the critical tradition has cared to acknowledge. Feminist critics, and those influenced by them, at least address themselves to the rhetoric of male trauma and hysteria that governs the apparent misogyny of Lear's drama. I say "apparent" because the revulsion from all sexuality by Lear and by Edgar is a mask for an even more profound alienation, not so much from excessive familial love as from bewilderment by such love. Edmund is brilliant and resourceful, but his prime, initial advantage over everyone else in the play is his total freedom from all familial affect, a freedom that enhances his fatal fascination for Goneril and Regan.

Are Shakespeare's perspectives in *Lear* incurably male? The only woman in the play who is not a fiend is Cordelia, whom some recent feminist critics see as Lear's own victim, a child he seeks to enclose as much at the end as at the beginning. Such a view is certainly not Cordelia's perspective on her relationship with her father, and I am inclined to credit her rather than her critics. Yet their sense of being troubled is an authentic and accurate reaction to a play that divests all of us, male and female auditors and readers alike, of not less than everything. Dr. Johnson's inability to sustain the murder of the virtuous Cordelia is another form of the same reaction. When Nietzsche said that we possess art lest we perish of the truth, he gave a very equivocal homage to art, and yet his apothegm is emptied out by *King Lear*, where we do perish of the truth. The Freudian, witty oxymoron of "family romances" loses its wit in the context of King Lear, where familial love offers you only a choice between destructions. You can live and die as Gloucester, Lear, and Cordelia do, or as Goneril, Regan, and Edmund do, or you can survive as Edgar does, a fate darker than that of all the others.

The noun *value* in Shakespeare lacks our high-mindedness: it means either an "estimation" of worth, or a more speculative "estimate," both being commercial terms rather bluntly carried over into human relations. Sometimes I think that our only certain knowledge of the man Shakespeare is that his commercial shrewdness rivaled or overtopped every other author's, before or since. Economy in Shakespeare extends to the noun *love*, which can mean "lover" but also means "friend," or a "kind act," and sometimes *for love's sake* means "for one's own sake." Johnson wonderfully tells us that, unlike every other dramatist, Shakespeare refuses to make love a universal agent:

> but love is only one of many passions, and as it has no great influence upon the sum of life, it has little operation in the dramas of a poet, who caught his ideas from the living world, and exhibited only what he saw before him. He knew, that any other passion, as it was regular or exorbitant, was a cause of happiness or calamity.

Johnson speaks of sexual love, rather than familial love, a distinction that Shakespeare taught Freud partly to void. Repressed incestuous desire for Cordelia, according to Freud, causes Lear's madness. Cordelia, again according to Freud, is so darkly silent at the play's opening because of her continued desire for her father. Certainly the family romance of Sigmund and Anna Freud has its effect in these rather too interesting weak misreadings. Lear's excessive love transcends even his attachment to Cordelia: it comprehends the Fool and others. The worship of Lear by Kent, Gloucester, Albany, and most of all his godson Edgar is directed not only at the great image of authority but at the central emblem of familial love, or patriarchal love (if you would have it so). The exorbitant passion or drive of familial love both in Lear and in Edgar is the cause of calamity. Tragedy at its most exorbitant, whether in Athens or at the Globe, must be domestic tragedy, or tragedy of blood in both senses of blood. We don't want to come away from a reading or performance of *King Lear* murmuring to ourselves that the domestic is necessarily a tragedy, but that may be the ultimate nihilism of this play.

2

Leo Tolstoy raged against *King Lear,* partly because he accurately sensed the drama's profound nihilism, but also out of creative envy, and perhaps, too, he had the uncanny premonition that Lear's scenes upon the heath would approximate his own final moments. For those who believe that divine justice somehow prevails in this world, *King Lear* ought to be offensive. At once the least secular and yet the least Christian of all Shakespeare's plays, Lear's tragedy shows us that we are all "fools," in the Shakespearean sense, except for those among us who are outright villains. "Fools" in Shakespeare can mean "dupes," "beloved ones," "madmen," "court jesters," or most of all, "victims." Lear's suffering is neither redeemable nor redeemed. Carefully stationing his play nine centuries before Christ (the time of Solomon), Shakespeare knows he has a (more or less) Christian audience, and so gives them a pagan, legendary king who loses all faith in the gods. If you were King James I, you could be provoked by *King Lear* to the idea that Christian revelation was implied as a deep human need by the hopelessness of Shakespeare's play. But I would think that skeptical Jacobeans (and there were more such than modern criticism concedes) could be stimulated to just the opposite conclusion: Faith is absurd or irrelevant in regard to this dark vision of reality. Shakespeare, as always, stands apart from such reductiveness, and we cannot know what he believed or disbelieved, and yet the burden of *King Lear* allows us finally only four perspectives: Lear's own, the Fool's, Edmund's, Edgar's. You have to be a very determined Christianizer of literature to take any comfort from this most tragic of all tragedies. The play is a storm, with no subsequent clearing.

Lear himself is Shakespeare's most sublime and most demanding character. Hamlet is incommensurate with us, because he is both charismatic and superbly intelligent, and yet we at least comprehend our distance from Hamlet. Lear, beyond us in grandeur and in essential authority, is still a startlingly intimate figure, since he is an emblem of fatherhood itself. Outrageously hyperbolical, insanely eloquent, Lear nevertheless always demands more love than can be given (within the limitations of the human), and so he scarcely can speak without crossing into the realms of the un-sayable. He is thus Hamlet's contrary: we feel that Hamlet says everything that can be said, much more than we can say, whoever we are. Lear over-whelms us, by Shakespearean design, because he somehow succeeds in say-ing what no one else, not even Hamlet, ever could say. From his first words ("Meantime, we shall express our darker purpose") through his last ("Do you see this? Look on her, look, her lips, / Look there, look there!"), he can-not speak without disturbing us. Lear's rhetorical power itself largely ren-ders Cordelia mute and recalcitrant: "Unhappy that I am, I cannot heave / My heart into my mouth." Upon the malevolences Goneril and Regan, it has the contrary effect: everything they speak is stilted, pompous, hollow, false, quite hateful, as we see in Goneril's "A love that makes breath poor and speech unable" and Regan's "I am alone felicitate / In your dear highness' love."

Lear's verbal force almost always preempts all spontaneity of speech in others. The exception is his Fool, the uncanniest character in Shakespeare, and the third, with Cordelia and Lear, in the play's true family, its com-munity of love. In *Hamlet*, the prince's authentic family ties are to Yorick, in the past, and to Horatio, in the play's present time. One function of Lear's Fool is precisely that of Hamlet's Horatio: to mediate, for the audi-ence, a personage otherwise beyond our knowing, Hamlet being too far beyond us, and Lear being blindingly close. Much of what we know in Hamlet we receive from Horatio, just as the Fool similarly humanizes Lear, and makes the dread king accessible to us. Horatio survives Hamlet, much against his own will. The Fool bewilderingly vanishes, another Shake-spearean ellipsis that challenges the audience to reflect upon the meanings of this strangest of characters. A fascinating presence that provokes Lear further into madness, the Fool becomes an absence still provocative, though then to the audience, not to the king. The Fool, again like Hora-tio, is a chorus, which is to be something other than a character in a play. You could remove the Fool and Horatio and not alter much in the way of plot structures, but you would remove our surrogates from these plays, for the Fool and Horatio are the true voices of our feelings. Horatio loves Hamlet; his only other attribute is a capacity for surmise, of woe or of won-der. The Fool loves Lear and Cordelia, and he is loved by them; otherwise he is an amazing blend of bitter wisdom and witty terror. Horatio is a comfort to us, but the Fool drives us a little mad even as he pushes Lear further into madness, so as to punish the King for his great folly. Shakespeare uses the Fool in many ways, and one of them clearly involves Erasmus's preference for folly over knowing. Blake may have been thinking of Lear's Fool in the Proverb of Hell: "If the Fool would persist in his folly, he would become wise."

Lear loves him and treats him as a child, but the Fool is of no determinate age, though clearly he will not grow up. Is he altogether human, or a sprite or changeling? His utterances differ sharply from those of any court fool in Shakespeare; he alone seems to belong to an occult world. Yet his acute ambivalence toward Lear, founded upon an outrage at Cordelia's exile and Lear's self-destructiveness, is one of Shakespeare's crucial inventions of human affect. We do not encounter the Fool until Scene iv of the play, when Lear notes his two-day absence and is told, "Since my young Lady's going into France, Sir, the Fool hath much pined away." "Nothing will come of nothing: speak again," Lear's earlier warning to Cordelia, echoes in the Fool's questioning of Lear ("Can you make no use of nothing, Nuncle?") and in the king's reply ("Why no, boy; nothing can be made out of nothing"). These are pagans speaking, yet they almost seem to mock the Christian doctrine of creation out of nothing. "Thou hast pared thy wit o'both sides, and left nothing i'th'middle," one of the Fool's most reverberatory observations, holds the kernel of the play's troubles; Lear fails to maintain the middle ground of his sovereignty, by dividing Cordelia's central portion of the kingdom between Goneril's northern realm and Regan's southern tyranny. Lear, who was everything in himself, is now nothing:

*Lear.* Does any here know me? This is not Lear:
  Does Lear walk thus? speak thus? Where are his eyes?
  Either his notion weakens, his discernings
  Are lethargied—Ha! waking? 'tis not so.
  Who is it that can tell me who I am?
*Fool.* Lear's shadow.

[I.iv.223–28]

From nothing, Lear rises to madness, spurred to it by the Fool's continuous taunts:

> *Lear.* O me! my heart, my rising heart! but, down!
> *Fool.* Cry to it, Nuncle, as the cockney did to the eels when she put
> 'em i'th'paste alive; she knapp'd 'em o'th'coxcombs with a stick,
> and cried 'Down, wantons, down!' 'Twas her brother that, in pure
> kindness to his horse, buttered his hay.

> [II.iv.118–23]

Lear's madness is much debated: his revulsion from Goneril and Regan becomes an involuntary horror of female sexuality, and the king appears to equate his own torments with female elements he senses in his own nature. In the best commentary on this difficult matter, Janet Adelman (in her *Suffocating Mothers*, 1992) goes so far as to say that Shakespeare himself rescues a "threatened masculinity" by murdering Cordelia. On that argument, subtle and extreme, Flaubert does the same to Emma Bovary, and even the protofeminist Samuel Richardson violates his Clarissa Harlowe into her suicidal decline and demise. Adelman is the most accomplished and formidable of all those who now emphasize Lear's own culpability for his disasters. I find it a curious irony that feminist criticism has taken up the Fool's ambivalence toward Lear, and in doing so has gone beyond the Fool, who after all never ceases to love the King. To feminist critics, Lear is a man more sinning than sinned against. If you really cannot see Goneril and Regan as monsters of the deep, then it must be that your ideology constrains you to believe all males are culpable, Shakespeare and Lear included. But we are back in the fundamental dilemma of School of Resentment criticism of Shakespeare, whether feminist, Marxist, or historicist (Foucault-inspired). The contextualizations are never distinctly appropriate to Shakespeare; they do as well or as badly for minor writers as for major, and if the governing designs are feminist, then they work equally well or badly for all male writers whatsoever. That Shakespeare, another mere male, is also afflicted by fantasies of maternal origin in no way helps explain how and why *King Lear* is arguably the most powerful and inescapable of literary works. The Fool remains a better critic of Lear than all later resenters of the king, because he accepts Lear's sublimity and uniqueness and they cannot.

From the Fool's perspective, Lear indeed is culpable, but only because he was not patriarchal enough to accept Cordelia's recalcitrance at expressing her love. On that view, Lear is condemned for having forsaken his own fatherhood: to divide his kingdom and betray royal authority was also to abandon Cordelia. The Fool's visionary terror is neither antifeminist nor feminist; it is curiously Nietzschean in that it, too, insists upon the image of fatherhood as being the necessary middle ground that alone can keep origins and ends from turning into each other. And the Fool is accurate, certainly in regard to Lear's fall into division and despair, and also in his terror that the cosmos centered upon Lear itself undergoes degradation with the king. Precisely apocalyptic in his forebodings, the Fool ironically is understood only by the audience (and Kent) but almost never by Lear, who listens yet never hears, and cannot identify himself with the bungler the Fool evokes. Yet what drives the Fool? Once Lear has divided Cordelia's portion between Goneril and Regan, it is simply too late for warnings and admonishments to make any pragmatic difference, and the Fool knows this. Ambivalence runs wild in the Fool: yet punishing Lear by increasing his madness can do no good, except to drama itself:

> *Fool.* If thou wert my Fool, Nuncle, I'd have thee beaten for being old
>    before thy time.
> *Lear.* How's that?
> *Fool.* Thou should'st not have been old till thou hadst been wise.
> *Lear.* O! let me not be mad, not mad, sweet heaven;
>    Keep me in temper; I would not be mad!
>
> [I.v.38–44]

The Fool and Lear sing trios with the undertaker, in this great spiritual chorus of things falling apart. When a Gentleman tells Kent, at the start of Act III, that the Fool labors to outjest Lear's heart-stricken injuries, we feel that this is wrong. As Kent leads Lear and the Fool to a hovel-shelter from the storm, Shakespeare allows the Fool a prophecy premonitory of William Blake:

> This is a brave night to cool a courtezan.
> I'll speak a prophecy ere I go:
> When priests are more in word than matter;
> When brewers mar their malt with water;
> When nobles are their tailors' tutors;
> No heretics burn'd, but wenches' suitors;
> When every case in law is right;
> No squire in debt, nor no poor knight;
> When slanders do not live in tongues;
> Nor cut-purses come not to throngs;
> When usurers tell their gold i'th'field;
> And bawds and whores do churches build;
> Then shall the realm of Albion
> Come to great confusion:
> Then comes the time, who lives to see't,
> That going shall be us'd with feet.
> The prophecy Merlin shall make; for I live before his time.
>
> [III.ii.79–95]

Weird and wonderful, this exuberant chant transcends Lear's anguished situation and the Fool's childlike fury. Who is the Fool to utter this, and what inspires Shakespeare to such an outburst? After his prophesying, the Fool ceases to madden Lear, and becomes touchingly waiflike, until soon enough he mysteriously vanishes from the play. Shakespeare probably thought he was parodying Chaucer in the opening lines of the Fool's verses, and directly quoting the same passage (wrongly ascribed to Chaucer) in lines 91–92, yet he goes well beyond parody into an obliquely powerful condemnation of a Jacobean England where priests, brewers, nobles, and tailors all cheerfully are condemned. This goes along merrily enough, and the "great confusion" of an Albion where matters are righted is genially ironic, ensuing in the grand anticlimax of Englishmen employing their feet for walking! "This prophecy Merlin shall make; for I live before his time" concludes a fine chant of nonsense, while associating the Fool with Merlin's magic. Though trapped in Lear's endgame, the Fool is also free of time, and presumably drifts out of the play into another era, with a final echo in Lear's brokenhearted "And my poor fool is hang'd!" that begins the king's own dying speech, where the identities of Cordelia and the Fool blend in Albion's confusion.

3

A decade or so back, I had to defend Lear against the dislike of many of my women students, but that time is past. Feminist critics will be unhappy with the mad old king for perhaps another decade. I suspect they will make fewer converts in the early twenty-first century, though, since Lear is very much a fit protagonist for the millennium and after. His catastrophe doubtless sends him into rages against the mother within. Nevertheless, he is aware of his need to "sweeten" his "imagination"—the return of Cordelia heals him, and not through mere selfishness. It isn't Shakespeare who destroys Cordelia but Edmund (too belatedly rescinding his order), and he is anything but Shakespeare's surrogate. I will argue that Edmund is a representation of Christopher Marlowe, Shakespeare's troublesome forerunner and rival, whose influence effectually ended much earlier, with the advent of the Bastard Faulconbridge, Bottom, Shylock, Portia, and overwhelmingly, Falstaff. Marlowe returns brilliantly in Edmund, but as a shadow strongly controlled by Shakespeare, and so Lear's antithesis, who cannot even speak to the magnificent king. Edmund fascinates; he out-Iagos Iago, being a strategist rather than an improviser. He is the coldest personage in all Shakespeare, just as Lear is emotionally the most turbulently intense, but Gloucester's Bastard is madly attractive, and not just to the infatuated Goneril and Regan, who die for him. Properly played, he is the sublime of Jacobean villains, icily sophisticated and frighteningly disinterested for a Machiavel who would have secured supreme power but for Edgar's triumphant return as accuser and avenger. Edmund and Edgar are the most interesting set of brothers in Shakespeare: I have already discussed Edmund's unintended and ironic re-creation of Edgar, but since each is the other's undersong, I will keep the play's ultimate hero in mind as I consider its principal villain. Edmund outplots everyone in the play, easily duping Edgar, but the purgatory of Edgar's impersonating Tom O'Bedlam and of guiding his blinded father produces an implacable champion whose justice cuts down Edmund with inevitable ease as the wheel comes full circle. The interplay of Edmund and Edgar strikingly becomes the dialectic of Lear's fate (and of England's) more than of Gloucester's, since Edgar is Lear's godson and involuntary successor, while Edmund is the point-for-point negation of the old king.

One need not be a Goneril or a Regan to find Edmund dangerously attractive, in ways that perpetually surprise the unwary reader or playgoer. William R. Elton makes the suggestion that Edmund is a Shakespearean anticipation of the seventeenth-century Don Juan tradition, which culminates in Molière's great play (1665). Elton also notes the crucial difference between Edmund and Iago, which is that Edmund paradoxically sees himself as overdetermined by his bastardy even as he fiercely affirms his freedom, whereas Iago is totally free. Consider how odd we would find it had Shakespeare decided to present Iago as a bastard, or indeed given us any information at all about Iago's father. But Edmund's status as natural son is crucial, though even here Shakespeare confounds his age's expectations. Elton cites a Renaissance proverb that bastards by chance are good but by nature bad. Faulconbridge the Bastard, magnificent hero of *The Life and Death of King John*, is good not by chance, but because he is very nearly the reincarnation of his father, Richard Lionheart, whereas the dreadful Don John, in *Much Ado About Nothing*, has a natural badness clearly founded upon his illegitimacy. Edmund astonishingly combines aspects of the personalities of Faulconbridge and of Don John, though he is even more attractive than Faulconbridge, and far more vicious than Don John of Aragon.

Though Edmund, unlike Iago, cannot reinvent himself wholly, he takes great pride in assuming responsibility for his own amorality, his pure opportunism. Don John in *Much Ado* says, "I cannot hide what I am," while Faulconbridge the Bastard affirms, "And I am I, howe'er I was begot."

Faulconbridge's "And I am I" plays against Iago's "I am not what I am." Edmund cheerfully proclaims, "I should have been that I am had the maidenliest star in the firmament twinkled on my bastardizing." The great "I am" remains a positive pronouncement in Edmund, and yet he is as grand a negation, in some other ways, as even Iago is. But because of that one positive stance toward his own being, Edmund will change at the very end, whereas Iago's final act of freedom will be to pledge an absolute muteness as he is led away to death by torture. Everything, according to Iago, lies in the will, and in his case everything does.

In Act V, Scene iii, Edmund enters with Lear and Cordelia as his prisoners. It is only the second time he shares the stage with Lear, and it will be the last. We might expect that he would speak to Lear (or to Cordelia), but he avoids doing so, referring to them only in the third person in his commands. Clearly Edmund does not wish to speak to Lear, because he is actively plotting the murder of Cordelia, and perhaps of Lear as well. Yet all the intricacies of the double plot do not in themselves explain away this remarkable gap in the play, and I wonder why Shakespeare avoided the confrontation. You can say he had no need of it, but this drama tells us to reason not the need. Shakespeare is our Scripture, replacing Scripture itself, and one should learn to read him the way the Kabbalists read the Bible, interpreting every absence as being significant. What can it tell us about Edmund, and also about Lear, that Shakespeare found nothing for them to say to each other?

Edmund, for all his sophisticated and charismatic charm, inspires no one's love, except for the deadly and parallel voracious passions of Goneril and Regan. And Edmund does not love them, or anyone else, even himself. Perhaps Lear and Edmund cannot speak to each other because Lear is bewildered by the thwarting of his excess of love for Cordelia, and by the hatred for him of Goneril and Regan, unnatural daughters, as he must call them. Edmund, in total contrast, hardly regards love as natural, even as he grimly exults in being the natural son of Gloucester. But even that contrast hardly accounts for the curious sense we have that Edmund somehow is not in the same play as Lear and Cordelia.

When Goneril kisses Edmund (Act IV, Scene ii, line 22), he gallantly

accepts it as a kind of literal kiss of death, since he is too grand an ironist
not to appreciate his own pledge: "Yours in the ranks of death." Still more
remarkable is his soliloquy that closes Act V, Scene i:

> To both these sisters have I sworn my love;
> Each jealous of the other, as the stung
> Are of the adder. Which of them shall I take?
> Both? one? or neither? Neither can be enjoy'd
> If both remain alive: to take the widow
> Exasperates, makes mad her sister Goneril;
> And hardly shall I carry out my side,
> Her husband being alive. Now then, we'll use
> His countenance for the battle; which being done,
> Let her who would be rid of him devise
> His speedy taking off. As for the mercy
> Which he intends to Lear and to Cordelia,
> The battle done, and they within our power
> Shall never see his pardon; for my state
> Stands on me to defend, not to debate.

So cool a negativity is unique, even in Shakespeare. Edmund is superbly sincere when he asks the absolutely open question "Which of them
shall I take? / Both? one? or neither?" His insouciance is sublime, the questions being tossed off in the spirit of a light event, as though a modern
young nobleman might ask whether he should take two princesses, one, or
none out to dinner? A double date with Goneril and Regan should daunt
any libertine, but the negation named Edmund is something very enigmatic. Iago's negative theology is predicated upon an initial worship of
Othello, but Edmund is amazingly free of all connection, all affect,
whether toward his two adder- or sharklike royal princesses, or toward his
half brother—or toward Gloucester, in particular. Gloucester is in the way,
in rather the same sense that Lear and Cordelia are in the way. Edmund evidently would just as soon not watch his father's eyes be put out, but this
delicacy does not mean that he cares at all about the event, one way or the

other. Yet, as Hazlitt pointed out, Edmund does not share in the hypocrisy of Goneril and Regan: his Machiavellianism is absolutely pure and lacks an Oedipal motive. Freud's vision of family romances simply does not apply to Edmund. Iago is free to reinvent himself every minute, yet Iago has strong passions, however negative. Edmund has no passions whatsoever; he has never loved anyone, and he never will. In that respect, he is Shakespeare's most original character.

There remains the enigma of why this cold negation is so attractive, which returns us usefully to his absolute contrast with Lear, and with Lear's uncanny Fool. Edmund's desire is only for power, and yet one wonders if *desire* is at all the right word in connection with Edmund. Richard III lusts for power; Iago quests for it over Othello, so as to uncreate Othello, to reduce the mortal god of war into a chaos. Ulysses certainly seeks power over Achilles, in order to get on with the destruction of Troy. Edmund is the most Marlovian of these grand negations, a will to power with no particular purpose behind it, since the soldier Macbeth does not so much will to usurp power as he is overcome by his own imagination of usurpation. Edmund accepts the overdetermination of being a bastard, indeed he overaccepts it, and glorifies in it, but he accepts nothing else. He is convinced of his natural superiority, which extends to his command of manipulative language, and yet he is not a Marlovian rhetorician, like Tamburlaine, nor is he intoxicated with his own villainy, like Richard III and Barabas. He is a Marlovian figure not in that he resembles a character in a play by Marlowe, but because I suspect he was intended to resemble Christopher Marlowe himself. Marlowe died, aged twenty-nine, in 1593, at about the time that Shakespeare composed *Richard III*, with its Marlovian protagonist, and just before the writing of *Titus Andronicus*, with its Marlovian parody in Aaron the Moor. By 1605, when *King Lear* was written, Marlowe had been dead for twelve years, but *As You Like It*, composed in 1599, is curiously replete with wry allusions to Marlowe. We have no contemporary anecdotes connecting Shakespeare to Marlowe, but it seems quite unlikely that Shakespeare never met his exact contemporary, and nearest precursor, the inventor of English blank-verse tragedy. Edmund, in the pre-Christian context of *King Lear*, is certainly a pagan atheist and libertine naturalist, as Elton emphasizes, and these are the roles that Marlowe's life exemplified for his contemporaries. Marlowe the man, or rather Shakespeare's memory of him, may be the clue to Edmund's strange glamour, the charismatic qualities that make it so difficult for us not to like him.

Whether or not an identification of Marlowe and Edmund is purely my critical trope, even as trope it suggests that Edmund's driving force is Marlovian nihilism, revolt against authority and tradition for revolt's own sake, since revolt and nature are thus made one. Revolt is heroic for Edmund, and he works his plots so that his natural superiority will make him king, whether as consort either to Regan or to Goneril, or as solitary figure, should they slay each other. After Goneril first has murdered Regan, and then killed herself, Edmund undergoes his radical transformation. What is exposed first is his acute overdetermination by his status as bastard. On knowing that his death wound is from Edgar, at least his social equal, he begins to be reconciled to the life being left behind him, the great line of acceptance being the famous "The wheel is come full circle; I am here."

"I am here" reverberates with the dark undertone that here I started originally, that to have been born a bastard was to start with a death wound. Edmund is quite dispassionate about his own dying, but he is not doom-eager, unlike Goneril and Regan, both of whom seem to have been in love with him precisely because they sought a death wound. Nowhere else, even in Shakespeare, are we racked by the Hitchcockian suspense that attends Edmund's slow change as he dies, a change that comes too late to save Cordelia. Edmund, reacting to Edgar's extraordinary account of their father's death, confesses to being moved, and hesitates on the verge of reprieving Cordelia. He does not get past that hesitation until the bodies of Goneril and Regan are brought in, and then his reaction constitutes the paradigmatic moment of change in all of Shakespeare:

> Yet Edmund was belov'd:
> The one the other poison'd for my sake,
> And after slew herself.
>
> [V.iii.238–40]

Out of context this is outrageous enough to be hilarious. The dying nihilist reminds himself that in spite of all he was and did, he *was* beloved.
He does not say that he cared for either, or for anyone else, and yet this
evidence of connection moves him. In context, its mimetic force is enormous. An intellect as cold, powerful, and triumphant as Iago's is suddenly
startled by overhearing itself, and the will to change comes upon Edmund.
The good he means to do will be "despite of mine own nature," he tells us,
so that his final judgment must be that he has not changed, more a Marlovian than a Shakespearean stance. And yet he is finally mistaken, for his nature has altered, too late to avoid the play's tragic catastrophe. Unlike
Iago, Edmund has ceased to be a pure or grand negation. It is an irony of
Shakespearean representation that we like Edmund least when he turns so
belatedly toward good. The change is persuasive, but by it Edmund ceases
to be Edmund. Hamlet dies into apotheosis; Iago will die stubbornly Iago,
in silence. We do not know who Edmund is as he dies, and he does not
know either.

4

The double plot of *King Lear* adds considerable complexity to what would
already be the most emotionally demanding of Shakespeare's plays, even
if the grim story of Gloucester, Edgar, and Edmund did not complement
the ordeal of Lear and his daughters. Suffering is the true mode of action
in *King Lear*: we suffer with Lear and Gloucester, Cordelia and Edgar, and
our suffering is not lessened as, one by one, the evil are cut down: Cornwall, Oswald, Regan, Goneril, and finally Edmund. I think that Shakespeare allows us no choice but suffering, because Lear's immense (though
waning) vitality possesses such a capacity for pathos from which we cannot exclude ourselves (unless we have started with a good morning's resentment of Lear, ideologically motivated). To trace the giant fluctuations
of affect in Lear is a harrowing project, but the play's greatness cannot fully
be apprehended without it, since a close reading will find in Lear's suffering a kind of order, though no idea of order; it is only entropy, human and
natural, that is formalized. No vision—neither Montaigne's skepticism nor

Christian redemption—is appropriate to this surging on of superior vitality into copious suffering and meaningless death. You can deny the pragmatic nihilism of *King Lear* or of *Hamlet* if you are a firm enough theist, but you will be rather beside the point, for Shakespeare neither challenges nor endorses your hopes for a personal resurrection. Suffering achieves its full reality of representation in *King Lear;* hope receives none. Hope is named Cordelia, and she is hanged at Edmund's command; Edgar survives to battle wolves, and to endure a heroic hopelessness. And that, rather than ripeness, is all.

A drama so comfortless succeeds because we cannot evade its power, of which the largest element is Lear's terrible greatness of affect. You can deny Lear's authority, as some now do, but you still must apprehend that in him the furnace comes up at last. Nothing I know of in the world's literature, sacred or secular (a distinction this play voids), hurts us so much as Lear's range of utterances. Criticism risks irrelevance if it evades confronting greatness directly, and Lear perpetually challenges the limits of criticism. Lear also demands our love: "That we our largest bounty may extend / Where nature doth with merit challenge." I have not located any criticism worthy of Lear that did not start with love, difficult as we (with Cordelia) may find it to express such love. The significant action of *King Lear* is mostly suffering, domestic more even than political. How do you convert even intensely dramatic suffering into aesthetic pleasure, without merely gratifying the audience's sadism? Shakespeare's Jacobean followers—the playwrights Webster, Tourneur, and Ford—rely entirely on their indubitable eloquence, and the consequence is a moderately triumphal sadomasochism. A more or less normative audience does not experience sexual excitation from watching Gloucester's eyes gouged out, or from seeing Lear stumble onto the stage with the hanged Cordelia in his arms. Love redeems nothing—on that Shakespeare could not be clearer— but the powerful representation of love askew, thwarted, misunderstood, or turned to hatred or icy indifference (Goneril, Regan, Edmund) can become an uncanny aesthetic value. Lear, surging on through fury, madness, and clarifying though momentary epiphanies, is the largest figure of love desperately sought and blindly denied ever placed upon a stage or in print. He is the universal image of the unwisdom and destructiveness of paternal love at its most ineffectual, implacably persuaded of its own benignity, totally devoid of self-knowledge, and careening onward until it brings down the person it loves best, and its world as well.

I am aware that the sentence just concluded is inadequate, because it would apply almost as well to Arthur Miller's *Death of a Salesman* (post-Ibsenite *Lear*) as to Shakespeare's incommensurate tragedy. The difference is that Lear is one of Chesterton's "great souls in chains," as are Hamlet, Othello, Macbeth, Cleopatra, and—utterly distinct—the Falstaff rejected by Prince Hal. King Lear is also the ultimate image of royal, legitimate authority, and more mysteriously the image of the wayward, frightening Yahweh of the J writer, earliest of Hebrew authors. The death of Lear is the end of the father, of the king, and of that part of the godhead that is father-king, Blake's Urizen. Nothing, in Shakespeare or in life, goes down for a final time, but after Lear something vanishes from Western literary representations of the father-king-God. Aesthetic and spiritual defenses of Milton's God in *Paradise Lost* are never persuasive, and the culprit is as much Shakespeare as the Milton whom he overinfluenced, despite Milton's rugged wariness. I have a permanent affection for the Satan of *Paradise Lost*, and yet he shamelessly imitates his intellectual superior, Iago. Milton's God, I find unbearable: he is a cursing scold, bellowing against "ingrates," shamefully imitating King Lear, without in any way sharing in the mad king's furies of love demanded and love rejected. Lear drowns the stage in a rigorously modulated pathos; Milton's God is an avalanche of self-congratulatory provocations to defensive satire.

There is no King Lear in our time; individual scale has become too diminished. Lear's largeness is now part of his enormous value for us, but Shakespeare severely limits that largeness. The death of Lear cannot be an atonement for us, any more than it serves as an atonement for Edgar, Kent, and Albany. For Edgar, it is the final catastrophe; his godfather and his father both are gone, and the contrite Albany (who has much to be contrite for) abdicates the crown to the hapless Edgar, Shakespeare's most reluctant royal successor, at least since the childlike Henry VI. The remorseful Albany and the aged Kent, soon to join his master Lear in death, do not represent the audience: Edgar the survivor does, and his despairing accents send us out of the theater unconsoled.

Shakespeare denies Lear's death the transcendental aura that he imparted to the dying Hamlet. Horatio invokes flights of angels to sing the prince to his rest, while Lear's survivors stand dazed and shattered, confronting what must be termed their loss of love. I have mentioned my difficulty as a teacher during the academic feminist seventies and eighties, attempting to convey to skeptical or even hostile women students that Lear, in Shakespeare's darkest paradox, supremely incarnated love. The worst of those difficulties have vanished in these apocalyptic nineties, but I remain ruefully grateful for the chastening experience, since that precisely is Lear's endless relevance: to expose love at its darkest, even its most unacceptable, yet also at its most inevitable. It is fascinating that initially Lear attributes Cordelia's recalcitrance to join in her sisters' pompous hyperboles to "pride, which she call plainness." Lear and all three daughters suffer from a plethora of prides, though Cordelia's legitimate concern is with what John Keats would have called the holiness of her heart's affections. Freud most peculiarly thought that Lear burned with repressed lust for Cordelia, perhaps because the great analyst did for his Anna. Lear, however, seems incapable of repressing anything whatsoever. He is simply, by light-years, the most violent expressionist in all Shakespeare:

Let it be so; thy truth then be thy dower:
For, by the sacred radiance of the sun,
The mysteries of Hecate and the night,
By all the operation of the orbs
From whom we do exist and cease to be,
Here I disclaim all my paternal care,
Propinquity and property of blood,
And as a stranger to my heart and me
Holds thee from this for ever. The barbarous Scythian,
Or he that makes his generation messes
To gorge his appetite, shall to my bosom
Be as well neighbour'd, pitied, and reliev'd,
As thou my sometime daughter.

[I.i.107–19]

This is so horrible as to court grotesque comedy, if anyone other than Lear shouted it forth. The foregrounding of this play would involve a long career of outbursts, which presumably helped convert Regan and Goneril into mincing hypocrites, and the favorite Cordelia into someone who has learned the gift of patient silence. I have suggested that the models for Lear were the darker Solomons of Ecclesiastes and the Wisdom of Solomon, two saturnine expressionists weary of eros, and of all else. "Better thou / Hadst not been born than not t'have pleased me better," Lear's vicious remark to Cordelia, is apt prelude to a drama in which everyone would have been better had they not been born. It is not so much that all is vanity; all is nothing, less than nothing.

Is this Lear's culpability, or is he merely the genius of his realm and era? "He hath ever but slenderly known himself," Regan says to Goneril, who replies: "The best and soundest of his time hath been but rash." Of the dozen principal roles in *King Lear*, eight are dead by the final curtain (Lear, Cordelia, Edmund, Gloucester, Goneril, Regan, Cornwall, Oswald) and the Fool has vanished. The survivors Edgar and Albany are of the younger time; Kent, soon to take his last journey, doubtless would be considered "rash" by Goneril, who appears to mean "wholehearted" rather than "impetuous" or "ill-tempered." Lear's rashness, at its most destructive, remains a wholeheartedness, in constant contrast to Edmund's cunning brilliance. Though Lear's most frequent metaphors tend to be hyperboles, tempests in his mind, they are partly redeemed by their largeness, fit for the king's capacious soul. I specify the redemption of figures of speech, because no person, not even Lear, is redeemed in this harshest of dramas. Cordelia, tragic heroine, requires no redemption, and Lear's enormous changes, his flashes of compassion and of social insight, essentially are emanations of his wholeheartedness, rather than the transformations Bradley and most subsequent critics have judged them to be. Edmund follows the Shakespearean paradigm of changing at last through self-overhearing, but Lear is something different, even for Shakespeare: he is the most awesome of all the poet's originals.

No one else in Shakespeare is so legitimate a representation of Authority, indeed of supreme authority. An Age of Resentment, which has exalted poor Caliban, is baffled and unhappy with Lear, who nevertheless remains the West's dominant emblem of fatherhood. With the shrewdness of genius, Shakespeare gives Lear only daughters, and the blinded Gloucester only sons. Lear has done badly enough with daughters; what would he have done with a son? What would Shakespeare have done with Queen Lear? Would she, like Job's laconic wife, have advised her outraged husband: "Curse God, and die"? Wisely, she is deceased, before the play opens, and receives only one mention by Lear, to add panache to one of his frequent curses against daughters. Lear is not a study in redemption but in outrageousness and in being outraged; he is Shakespeare's perfection in the poetics of outrage, surpassing even Macbeth at evoking the audience's involuntary identification. Mortality is the ultimate outrage we all of us must endure, and Lear's authentic prophecy is not against filial ingratitude but against nature, despite his insistence that he speaks for nature.

Perpetually outraged, except for the brief idyll of his reconciliation with Cordelia, Lear appeals primordially to the universal outrage of all those acutely conscious of their own mortality. Resentment, justified or not, is part of social psychology; the sense of being outraged need have no social component whatsoever. We die as individuals, however generous or benighted our public sympathies may be. Lear's peculiar intimacy with us, as our dead father, partly depends upon this shared sense of outrage. Hamlet, always beyond us, consorts with supernal powers, for all his skepticism and our own. Lear is overwhelming because he is so close, despite his magnitude. Unless you have firm transcendental beliefs (and Lear loses his), then all you can place against mortality (besides heroic stoicism) is love, whether familial or erotic. Love in this play, as I observed in discussing Edgar, is catastrophic. The confusions of domestic love destroy Lear and Gloucester; the murderous and suicidal lust for Edmund of Goneril and Regan could prompt only the dying Edmund, most estranged of souls, to the conclusion that he was beloved. Shakespeare remorselessly makes love itself both outrageous and outraged, in a cosmos centered upon Lear's needy greatness.

I suppose it is my own outrageousness that tells me Shakespeare's two supreme visions of advanced old age are Lear and Falstaff, an insane jux-taposition. Lear laments his antiquity; Falstaff transcends denying it by af-firming his endless youth. Gamboling about on the battlefield, cavorting with Doll Tearsheet, puffing up Gadshill as a highwayman, enacting mar-velous skits in a tavern: is this the style of old age? Perhaps Shakespeare early apprehended that he would never reach more than fifty-two? I am nineteenth-century enough to find in Falstaff the portrait of the artist as an old man: supremely intelligent, furiously comic, benign enough, alive be-yond belief, heartbrokenly in love in the mode of the poet of the Sonnets, rejected and forlorn. Lear, composed much later, is anything but an auto-biographical projection. Even the Fool (especially the Fool?) cannot move Lear to laughter. In Falstaff, old age is defeated, until erotic defeat renders Sir John a child again, dying as he plays with flowers. Lear's crowning of himself with flowers is a triumph of his madness, another episode in an old age that is a shipwreck.

Whenever Lear reminds himself that he is past eighty, the contrast with Falstaff is enhanced, and Shakespeare thereby increases the distance between Lear and himself. Falstaff, even just after his rejection, does his best not to further internalize his suffering, while Lear seems to have no de-fenses against his own pathos. He is the heart of his world, as Arthur Kirsch emphasized, in his comparison of Lear to the Solomonic Koheleth, the preacher of Ecclesiastes, who always searches his own heart and finds there, as well as in the world, also the vanity of vanities. The greatheart-edness of Lear is surely his most attractive quality, but it is supremely im-portant that we recognize his other grand aspects, lest we see him finally as a tower of pathos and not as the most tragic of all stage personages. He is the great image of authority, but he himself impairs that image with high deliberation: "A dog's obey'd in office." His true greatness is else-where: appallingly wrongheaded, he remains always totally honest, and his example teaches his godson Edgar to "Speak what we feel, not what we ought to say," two lines away from the play's close. Endlessly furious, Lear also is infinitely frank: his enormous spirit harbors no duplicities. Every inch a king, he is less of a Machiavel than any other king in Shakespeare, except for Henry VI, who was better suited to be a hermit than a monarch.

Shakespeare risks the paradox that his worst politician is his most awe-

some ruler. Lear is too great to dissemble, as is Cordelia, his true daughter. Their common greatness is their mutual tragedy, where all best things
are thus confused to ill. That seems one of the secrets of Shakespearean
tragedy: we are beyond good and evil because we cannot make a merely
natural distinction between them, even though both Lear and Edmund, in
their opposite ways, believe otherwise. Lear's magnificent generosity of
spirit, which makes him love too much, also prompts him to demand too
much love. Other fashions will roll over current theatrical and academic
ideologies, and Lear will emerge again as the greatest of Shakespeare's
skeptics, surpassing even Hamlet as death's ambassador to us.

Charles Lamb, my precursor in believing that "Lear is essentially impossible to be represented on a stage," insisted that the greatness of Lear
was a matter of intellectual dimension, as when the king identifies his age
with that of the heavens themselves. What Lamb implied was that Lear's
imagination, even when diseased, remains healthier than Macbeth's, while
possessing something like the proleptic force of Macbeth's imagination.
The great king is not one of Shakespeare's overwhelming intellects; in this
play, that is reserved for Edmund. But Lear's imagination, and the language
it engenders, is both the largest and the most normative in all Shakespeare.
What Lear imagines, he imagines well, even in madness, in the rages of his
self-invoked hell. Without Lear, Shakespeare's invention of the human
would have fallen short of Shakespeare's full capacities for representation.
How can criticism categorize the quality of largeness or greatness in a literary character? Turned ideological, criticism no longer tries, but a cognitive and affective response adequate to Shakespeare must confront
greatness, both in his protagonists and in their creator. *King Lear*, the modern touchstone for the sublime, hollows out if Lear's greatness is scanted
or denied.

In life, we frequently are deceived; the greatness of friends and of public figures alike dissolves upon closer scrutiny. You can fail to perceive
Lear's greatness, if your program does not allow for such a quality's existence. But then, who or what are you, if you lack even the dream of greatness? Dr. Johnson loved Falstaff both because the great critic had that
dream and because Falstaff banished melancholy, Johnson's demon. No

one among us can love Lear: we are not Cordelia, Edgar, the Fool, Gloucester, Kent, or even the rather culpable Albany. Yet I marvel that anyone
among us could fail to apprehend Lear's sublimity. Shakespeare lavishes his
own genius, at its most exuberant, upon Lear's greatness, a splendor surpassing that of the biblical Solomon's. Lear's utterances establish a standard
of measurement that no other fictive personage can approach; the limits of
human capacity for profound affect are consistently transcended by Lear.
To feel what Lear suffers strains us as only our own greatest anguishes
have hurt us; the terrible intimacy that Lear insists upon is virtually unbearable, as Dr. Johnson testified. I have argued already that this intimacy
stems from Lear's usurpation of everyone's experience of ambivalence toward the father, or toward fatherhood. In the rest of this discussion, I will
center upon adumbrating this argument. Lear the father, thanks to Shakespeare's audacity, endlessly evokes God the Father, a Western metaphor
now repudiated in all of our academies and in our more enlightened
churches. I hardly expect feminist critics (male and female) to accept these
evocations, but to repudiate Lear utterly is a very expensive gesture, since
more than the patriarchy goes down with Lear's ruin. There is no truer
voice of feeling than Lear's in all of imaginative literature, the Bible included, and to lose Lear's greatness is also to abandon a part of our own capacity for significant emotion.

Lear's language achieves its apotheosis in his astonishing exchanges
with the blinded Gloucester (Act IV, Scene vi, lines 86–185), after the
mad king enters, "fantastically dressed with wild flowers." These hundred
lines constitute one of Shakespeare's assaults on the limits of art, largely because their pathos is unprecedented. After Gloucester recognizes Lear's
voice, the king chants an attack upon womankind so extreme that he himself calls for balm to sweeten his diseased sexual imagination:

> Ay, every inch a king:
> When I do stare, see how the subject quakes.
> I pardon that man's life. What was thy cause?
> Adultery?
> Thou shalt not die: die for adultery! No:

The wren goes to't, and the small gilded fly

Does lecher in my sight.

Let copulation thrive; for Gloucester's bastard son

Was kinder to his father than my daughters

Got 'tween the lawful sheets. To't, Luxury, pell-mell!

For I lack soldiers. Behold yond simp'ring dame,

Whose face between her forks presages snow;

That minces virtue, and does shake the head

To hear of pleasure's name;

The fitchew nor the soiled horse goes to't

With a more riotous appetite.

Down from the waist they are Centaurs,

Though women all above:

But to the girdle do the Gods inherit,

Beneath is all the fiend's: there's hell, there's darkness,

There is the sulphurous pit—burning, scalding,

Stench, consumption; fie, fie, fie! pah, pah!

Give me an ounce of civet, good apothecary,

To sweeten my imagination.

There's money for thee.

[IV.vi.107–31]

Shakespeare, hardly a hater of women, risks this extremity precisely because Lear's troubled authority has foundered where he thought it most absolute: in the relationship with his own daughters. Goneril and Regan have usurped authority; their nature is akin to Edmund's idea of nature, rather than Lear's, and so the mad king's revulsion is from nature itself, not an idea but the fundamental fact of sexual difference. Shakespeare's audience, women and men alike, jocularly accepted the slang of "hell" for the vagina, but Lear may have startled even those happy to be entertained by the representation of madness. No exorcism applied only to women could solve Lear's difficulties; every old man, as Goethe shrewdly wrote, is King Lear, exorcised by nature itself. "Sweeten my imagination" is the deepest pathos of this passage, because it manifests the same Lear who soon proclaims to

Gloucester, "There than might'st behold / The great Image of Authority: / A dog's obey'd in office."

This Lear is mad only as William Blake was mad: prophetically, against both nature and society. Edgar, agonizing at his godfather's sufferings, cries, "Reason in madness," but that is not necessarily the audience's perspective. Again as with Blake, Lear's prophecy fuses reason, nature, and society into one great negative image, the inauthentic authority of this great stage of fools. We enter crying at our birth, knowing with Lear that creation and fall are simultaneous. This realization will continue in *Macbeth*, where again the action takes place in the world that ancient Gnostics called the *kenoma*, or "emptiness." What can fatherhood be in the *kenoma*? Mirrors and fatherhood alike are abominable, according to the modern gnostic Borges, because both multiply the images of men and of women. Lear's terrible wisdom, far from being patriarchal, is as anti-patriarchal as the Wisdom of Solomon and as Ecclesiastes, whose "vanity" is similar to the "emptiness" of the Gnostics. "Nothing begets nothing" could be the pragmatic motto of fatherhood in Lear's play. Only Cordelia could refute that despair, and Lear also prophesies the drama's greatest darkness when he emerges from madness to see Cordelia and to say, "You are a spirit, I know; where did you die?"

# 26

# MACBETH

Theatrical tradition has made *Macbeth* the unluckiest of all Shakespeare's plays, particularly for those who act in it. Macbeth himself can be termed the unluckiest of all Shakespearean protagonists, precisely because he is the most imaginative. A great killing machine, Macbeth is endowed by Shakespeare with something less than ordinary intelligence, but with a power of fantasy so enormous that pragmatically it seems to be Shakespeare's own. No other drama by Shakespeare—not even *King Lear*, *A Midsummer Night's Dream*, or *The Tempest*—so engulfs us in a phantasmagoria. The magic in *A Midsummer Night's Dream* and *The Tempest* is crucially effectual, while there is no overt magic or witchcraft in *King Lear*, though we sometimes half expect it because the drama is of such hallucinatory intensity.

The witchcraft in *Macbeth*, though pervasive, cannot alter material events, yet hallucination can and does. The rough magic in *Macbeth* is wholly Shakespeare's; he indulges his own imagination as never before, seeking to find its moral limits (if any). I do not suggest that Macbeth represents Shakespeare, in any of the complex ways that Falstaff and Hamlet may represent certain inner aspects of the playwright. But in the Renaissance sense of imagination (which is not ours), Macbeth may well be the emblem of that faculty in Shakespeare, a faculty that must have frightened Shakespeare and ought to terrify us, when we read or attend *Macbeth*, for the play depends upon its horror of its own imaginings. Imagination (or fancy) is an equivocal matter for Shakespeare and his era, where it meant both poetic furor, as a kind of substitute for divine inspiration, and a gap torn in reality, almost a punishment for the displacement of the sacred into the secular. Shakespeare somewhat mitigates the negative aura of fantasy in his other plays, but not in *Macbeth*, which is a tragedy of the imagination. Though the play triumphantly proclaims, "The time is free," when Macbeth is killed, the reverberations we cannot escape as we leave the theater or close the book have little to do with our freedom.

Hamlet dies into freedom, perhaps even augmenting our own liberty, but Macbeth's dying is less of a release for us. The universal reaction to Macbeth is that we identify with him, or at least with his imagination. Richard III, Iago, and Edmund are hero-villains; to call Macbeth one of that company seems all wrong. They delight in their wickedness; Macbeth suffers intensely from knowing that he does evil, and that he must go on doing ever worse. Shakespeare rather dreadfully sees to it that *we are* Macbeth; our identity with him is involuntary but inescapable. All of us possess, to one degree or another, a proleptic imagination; in Macbeth, it is absolute. He scarcely is conscious of an ambition, desire, or wish before he *sees* himself on the other side or shore, already having performed the crime that equivocally fulfills ambition. Macbeth terrifies us partly because that aspect of our own imagination is so frightening: it seems to make us murderers, thieves, usurpers, and rapists.

Why are we unable to resist identifying with Macbeth? He so dominates his play that we have nowhere else to turn. Lady Macbeth is a powerful character, but Shakespeare gets her off the stage after Act III, Scene iv, except for her short return in a state of madness at the start of Act V. Shakespeare had killed off Mercutio early to keep him from stealing *Romeo and Juliet*, and had allowed Falstaff only a reported death scene so as to prevent Sir John from dwarfing the "reformed" Hal in *Henry V*. Once Lady Macbeth has been removed, the only real presence on the stage is Macbeth's. Shrewdly, Shakespeare does little to individualize Duncan, Banquo, Macduff, and Malcolm. The drunken porter, Macduff's little son, and Lady Macduff are more vivid in their brief appearances than are all the secondary males in the play, who are wrapped in a common grayness. Since Macbeth speaks fully a third of the drama's lines, and Lady Macbeth's role is truncated, Shakespeare's design upon us is manifest. We are to journey inward to Macbeth's heart of darkness, and there we will find ourselves more truly and more strange, murderers in and of the spirit.

The terror of this play, most ably discussed by Wilbur Sanders, is deliberate and salutary. If we are compelled to identify with Macbeth, and he appalls us (and himself), then we ourselves must be fearsome also. Working against the Aristotelian formula for tragedy, Shakespeare deluges us with fear and pity, not to purge us but for a sort of purposiveness without purpose that no interpretation wholly comprehends. The sublimity of Macbeth and of Lady Macbeth is overwhelming: they are persuasive and valuable personalities, profoundly in love with each other. Indeed, with surpassing irony Shakespeare presents them as the happiest married couple in all his work. And they are anything but two fiends, despite their dreadful crimes and deserved catastrophes. So rapid and foreshortened is their play (about half the length of *Hamlet*) that we are given no leisure to confront their descent into hell as it happens. Something vital in us is bewildered by the evanescence of their better natures, though Shakespeare gives us emblems enough of the way down and out.

*Macbeth* is an uncanny unity of setting, plot, and characters, fused together beyond comparison with any other play of Shakespeare's. The drama's cosmos is more drastic and alienated even than *King Lear*'s, where nature was so radically wounded. *King Lear* was pre-Christian, whereas *Macbeth*, overtly medieval Catholic, seems less set in Scotland than in the *kenoma*, the cosmological emptiness of our world as described by the ancient Gnostic heretics. Shakespeare knew at least something of gnosticism through the Hermetic philosophy of Giordano Bruno, though I think there can be little or no possibility of a direct influence of Bruno on Shakespeare (despite the interesting surmises of Frances Yates). Yet the gnostic horror of time seems to have infiltrated *Macbeth*, emanating from the not-less-than-universal nature of Shakespeare's own consciousness. The world of *Macbeth* is one into which we *have been thrown*, a dungeon for tyrants and victims alike. If *Lear* was pre-Christian, then *Macbeth* is weirdly post-Christian. There are, as we have seen, Christian intimations that haunt the pagans of *Lear*, though to no purpose or effect. Despite some desperate allusions by several of the characters, *Macbeth* allows no relevance to Christian revelation. Macbeth is the deceitful "man of blood" abhorred by the Psalms and elsewhere in the Bible, but he scarcely can be assimilated to biblical villainy. There is nothing specifically anti-Christian in his crimes; they would offend virtually every vision of the sacred and the moral that human chronicle has known. That may be why Akira Kurosawa's *Throne of Blood* is so uncannily the most successful film version of *Macbeth*, though it departs very far from the specifics of Shakespeare's play. Macbeth's tragedy, like Hamlet's, Lear's, and Othello's, is so universal that a strictly Christian context is inadequate to it.

I have ventured several times in this book my surmise that Shakespeare intentionally evades (or even blurs) Christian categories throughout his work. He is anything but a devotional poet and dramatist; there are no *Holy Sonnets* by Shakespeare. Even Sonnet 146 ("Poor soul, the centre of my sinful earth") is an equivocal poem, particularly in its crucial eleventh line: "Buy terms divine in selling hours of dross." One major edition of Shakespeare glosses "terms divine" as "everlasting life," but "terms" allows several less ambitious readings. Did Shakespeare "believe in" the resurrection of the body? We cannot know, but I find nothing in the plays or poems to suggest a consistent supernaturalism in their author, and more perhaps to intimate a pragmatic nihilism. There is no more spiritual comfort to be gained from *Macbeth* than from the other high tragedies. Graham Bradshaw subtly argues that the *terrors* of *Macbeth* are Christian, yet he also endorses Nietzsche's reflections on the play in Nietzsche's *Daybreak* (1881). Here is section 240 of *Daybreak*:

> *On the morality of the stage.*—Whoever thinks that Shakespeare's theatre has a moral effect, and that the sight of Macbeth irresistibly repels one from the evil of ambition, is in error: and he is again in error if he thinks Shakespeare himself felt as he feels. He who is really possessed by raging ambition beholds this its image with *joy;* and if the hero perishes by his passion this precisely is the sharpest spice in the hot draught of this joy. Can the poet have felt otherwise? How royally, and not at all like a rogue, does his ambitious man pur-

sue his course from the moment of his great crime! Only from then on does he exercise 'demonic' attraction and excite similar natures to emulation—demonic means here: in defiance *against* life and advantage for the sake of a drive and idea. Do you suppose that Tristan and Isolde are preaching *against* adultery when they both perish by it? This would be to stand the poets on their head: they, and especially Shakespeare, are enamoured of the passions as such and not least of their death-welcoming moods—those moods in which the heart adheres to life no more firmly than does a drop of water to a glass. It is not the guilt and its evil outcome they have at heart, Shakespeare as little as Sophocles (in Ajax, Philoctetes, Oedipus): as easy as it would have been in these instances to make guilt the lever of the drama, just as surely has this been avoided. The tragic poet has just as little desire to take sides *against* life with his images of life! He cries rather: 'it is the stimulant of stimulants, this exciting, changing, dangerous, gloomy and often sun-drenched existence! It is an adventure to live—espouse what party in it you will, it will always retain this character!'— He speaks thus out of a restless, vigorous age which is half-drunk and stupefied by its excess of blood and energy—out of a wickeder age than ours is: which is why we need first to *adjust* and *justify* the goal of a Shakespearean drama, that is to say, not to understand it.

Nietzsche links up here with William Blake's adage that the highest art is immoral, and that "Exuberance is beauty." *Macbeth* certainly has "an excess of blood and energy"; its terrors may be more Christian than Greek or Roman, but indeed they are so primordial that they seem to me more shamanistic than Christian, even as the "terms divine" of Sonnet 146 impress me as rather more Platonic than Christian. Of all Shakespeare's plays, *Macbeth* is most "a tragedy of blood," not just in its murders but in the ultimate implications of Macbeth's imagination itself being bloody. The usurper Macbeth moves in a consistent phantasmagoria of blood: blood is the prime constituent of his imagination. He *sees* that what opposes him is blood in one aspect—call it nature in the sense that he opposes nature—

and that this opposing force thrusts him into shedding more blood: "It will have blood, they say: blood will have blood."

Macbeth speaks these words in the aftermath of confronting Banquo's ghost, and as always his imaginative coherence overcomes his cognitive confusion. "It" is blood as the natural—call that King Duncan—and the second "blood" is all that Macbeth can experience. His usurpation of Duncan transcends the politics of the kingdom, and threatens a natural good deeply embedded in the Macbeths, but which they have abandoned, and which Macbeth now seeks to destroy, even upon the cosmological level, if only he could. You can call this natural good or first sense of "blood" Christian, if you want to, but Christianity is a revealed religion, and Macbeth rebels against nature *as he imagines it.* That pretty much makes Christianity as irrelevant to *Macbeth* as it is to *King Lear,* and indeed to all the Shakespearean tragedies. Othello, a Christian convert, does not fall away from Christianity but from his own better nature, while Hamlet is the apotheosis of all natural gifts, yet cannot abide in them. I am not suggesting, here as elsewhere in the book, that Shakespeare himself was a gnostic, or a nihilist, or a Nietzschean vitalist three centuries before Nietzsche. But as a dramatist, he is just as much all or any of those as he is a Christian. *Macbeth,* as I have intimated before, is anything but a celebration of Shakespeare's imagination, yet it is also anything but a Christian tragedy. Shakespeare, who understood everything that we comprehend and far more (humankind never will stop catching up to him), long since had exorcised Marlowe, and Christian tragedy (however inverted) with him. Macbeth has nothing in common with Tamburlaine or with Faustus. The nature that Macbeth most strenuously violates is his own, but though he learns this even as he begins the violation, he refuses to follow Lady Macbeth into madness and suicide.

2

Like *A Midsummer Night's Dream* and *The Tempest, Macbeth* is a visionary drama, and difficult as it is for us to accept that strange genre, a visionary tragedy. Macbeth himself is an involuntary seer, almost an occult medium, dreadfully open to the spirits of the air and of the night. Lady Macbeth, initially more enterprising than her husband, falls into a psychic decline for causes more visionary than not. So much are the Macbeths made for sublimity, figures of fiery eros as they are, that their political and dynastic ambitions seem grotesquely inadequate to their mutual desires. Why do they want the crown? Shakespeare's Richard III, still Marlovian, seeks the sweet fruition of an earthly crown, but the Macbeths are not Machiavellian over-reachers, nor are they sadists or power-obsessed as such. Their mutual lust is also a lust for the throne, a desire that is their Nietzschean revenge against time and time's irrefutable declaration: "It was." Shakespeare did not care to clarify the Macbeths' childlessness. Lady Macbeth speaks of hav-ing nursed a child, presumably her own but now dead; we are not told that Macbeth is her second husband, but we may take him to be that. He urges her to bring forth men children only, in admiration of her "manly" resolve, yet pragmatically they seem to expect no heirs of their own union, while he fiercely seeks to murder Fleance, Banquo's son, and does destroy Mac-duff's children. Freud, shrewder on *Macbeth* than on *Hamlet,* called the curse of childlessness Macbeth's motivation for murder and usurpation. Shake-speare left this matter more uncertain; it is a little difficult to imagine Mac-beth as a father when he is, at first, so profoundly dependent on Lady Macbeth. Until she goes mad, she seems as much Macbeth's mother as his wife.

Of all Shakespeare's tragic protagonists, Macbeth is the least free. As Wilbur Sanders implied, Macbeth's actions are a kind of falling forward ("falling in space," Sanders called it). Whether or not Nietzsche (and Freud after him) were right in believing that we are lived, thought, and willed by forces not ourselves, Shakespeare anticipated Nietzsche in this convic-tion. Sanders acutely follows Nietzsche in giving us a Macbeth who prag-matically lacks any will, in contrast to Lady Macbeth, who is a pure will until she breaks apart. Nietzsche's insight may be the clue to the different ways in which the Macbeths desire the crown: she wills it, he wills noth-ing, and paradoxically she collapses while he grows ever more frightening, outraging others, himself outraged, as he becomes the nothing he projects. And yet this nothingness remains a negative sublime; its grandeur merits the dignity of tragic perspectives. The enigma of *Macbeth*, as a drama, always will remain its protagonist's hold upon our terrified sympathy. Shakespeare surmised the guilty imaginings we share with Macbeth, who is Mr. Hyde to our Dr. Jekyll. Stevenson's marvelous story emphasizes that Hyde is younger than Jekyll, only because Jekyll's career is still young in villainy while old in good works. Our uncanny sense that Macbeth somehow is younger in deed than we are is analogous. Virtuous as we may (or may not) be, we fear that Macbeth, our Mr. Hyde, has the power to realize our own potential for active evil. Poor Jekyll eventually turns into Mr. Hyde and cannot get back; Shakespeare's art is to suggest we could have such a fate.

Is Shakespeare himself—on any level—also a Dr. Jekyll in relation to Macbeth's Mr. Hyde? How could he not be, given his success in touching a universal negative sublime through having imagined Macbeth's imaginings? Like Hamlet, with whom he has some curious affinities, Macbeth projects an aura of intimacy: with the audience, with the hapless actors, with his creator. Formalist critics of Shakespeare—old guard and new—insist that no character is larger than the play, since a character is "only" an actor's role. Audiences and readers are not so formalistic: Shylock, Falstaff, Rosalind, Hamlet, Malvolio, Macbeth, Cleopatra (and some others) seem readily transferable to contexts different from their dramas. Sancho Panza, as Kafka demonstrated in the wonderful parable "The Truth About Sancho Panza," can become the creator of Don Quixote. Some new and even more Borgesian Kafka must rise among us to show Antonio as the inventor of Shylock, or Prince Hal as the father of Sir John Falstaff.

To call Macbeth larger than his play in no way deprecates my own favorite among all of Shakespeare's works. The economy of *Macbeth* is ruthless, and scholars who find it truncated, or partly the work of Thomas Middleton, fail to understand Shakespeare's darkest design. What notoriously dominates this play, more than any other in Shakespeare, is time, time that is not the Christian mercy of eternity, but devouring time, death nihilistically regarded as finality. No critic has been able to distinguish between death, time, and nature in *Macbeth*; Shakespeare so fuses them that all of us are well within the mix. We hear voices crying out the formulae of redemption, but never persuasively, compared with Macbeth's soundings of night and the grave. Technically, the men in *Macbeth* are "Christian warriors," as some critics like to emphasize, but their Scottish medieval Catholicism is perfunctory. The kingdom, as in *King Lear*, is a kind of cosmological waste land, a Creation that was also a Fall, in the beginning.

*Macbeth* is very much a night piece; its Scotland is more a mythological Northland than the actual nation from which Shakespeare's royal patron emerged. King James I doubtless prompted some of the play's emphases, but hardly the most decisive, the sense that the night has usurped the day. Murder is the characteristic action of *Macbeth*: not just King Duncan, Banquo, and Lady Macduff and her children are the victims. By firm implication, every person in the play is a potential target for the Macbeths. Shakespeare, who perhaps mocked the stage horrors of other dramatists in his *Titus Andronicus*, experimented far more subtly with the aura of murderousness in *Macbeth*. It is not so much that each of us in the audience is a potential victim. Rather more uneasily, the little Macbeth within each theatergoer can be tempted to surmise a murder or two of her or his own.

I can think of no other literary work with *Macbeth*'s power of *contamination*, unless it be Herman Melville's *Moby-Dick*, the prose epic profoundly influenced by *Macbeth*. Ahab is another visionary maniac, obsessed with what seems a malign order in the universe. Ahab strikes through the mask of natural appearances, as Macbeth does, but the White Whale is no easy victim. Like Macbeth, Ahab is outraged by the equivocation of the fiend that lies like truth, and yet Ahab's prophet, the Parsi harpooner Fedallah, himself is far more equivocal than the Weird Sisters. We identify with Captain Ahab less ambivalently than we do with King Macbeth, since Ahab is neither a murderer nor a usurper, and yet pragmatically Ahab is about as destructive as Macbeth: all on the *Pequod*, except for Ishmael the narrator, are destroyed by Ahab's quest. Melville, a shrewd interpreter of Shakespeare, borrows Macbeth's phantasmagoric and proleptic imagination for Ahab, so that both Ahab and Macbeth become world destroyers. The Scottish heath and the Atlantic Ocean amalgamate: each is a context where preternatural forces have outraged a sublime consciousness, who fights back vainly and unluckily, and goes down to a great defeat. Ahab, an American Promethean, is perhaps more hero than villain, unlike Macbeth, who forfeits our admiration though not our entrapped sympathy.

3

Hazlitt remarked of Macbeth that "he is sure of nothing but the present moment." As the play progresses to its catastrophe, Macbeth loses even that certitude, and his apocalyptic anxieties prompt Victor Hugo's identification of Macbeth with Nimrod, the Bible's first hunter of men. Macbeth is worthy of the identification: his shocking vitality imbues the violence of evil with biblical force and majesty, giving us the paradox that the play seems Christian not for any benevolent expression but only insofar as its ideas of evil surpass merely naturalistic explanations. If any theology is applicable to *Macbeth*, then it must be the most negative of theologies, one that excludes the Incarnation. The cosmos of *Macbeth*, like that of *Moby-Dick*, knows no Savior; the heath and the sea alike are great shrouds, whose dead will not be resurrected.

God is exiled from *Macbeth* and *Moby-Dick*, and from *King Lear* also. Exiled, not denied or slain; Macbeth rules in a cosmological emptiness where God is lost, either too far away or too far within to be summoned back. As in *King Lear*, so in *Macbeth*: the moment of creation and the moment of fall fuse into one. Nature and man alike fall into time, even as they are created.

No one desires *Macbeth* to lose its witches, because of their dramatic immediacy, yet the play's cosmological vision renders them a little redundant.

Between what Macbeth imagines and what he does, there is only a temporal gap, in which he himself seems devoid of will. The Weird Sisters, Macbeth's Muses, take the place of that will; we cannot imagine them appearing to Iago, or to Edmund, both geniuses of the will. They are not hollow men; Macbeth is. What happens to Macbeth is inevitable, despite his own culpability, and no other play by Shakespeare, not even the early farces, moves with such speed (as Coleridge noted). Perhaps the rapidity augments the play's terror; there seems to be no power of the mind over the universe of death, a cosmos all but identical both with Macbeth's phantasmagoria and with the Weird Sisters.

Shakespeare grants little cognitive power to anyone in *Macbeth*, and least of all to the protagonist himself. The intellectual powers of Hamlet, Iago, and Edmund are not relevant to Macbeth and to his play. Shakespeare disperses the energies of the mind, so that no single character in *Macbeth* represents any particular capacity for understanding the tragedy, nor could they do better in concert. Mind is elsewhere in *Macbeth*; it has forsaken humans and witches alike, and lodges freestyle where it will, shifting capriciously and quickly from one corner of the sensible emptiness to another. Coleridge hated the Porter's scene (II.iii), with its famous knocking at the gate, but Coleridge made himself deaf to the cognitive urgency of the knocking. Mind knocks, and breaks into the play, with the first and only comedy allowed in this drama. Shakespeare employs his company's leading clown (presumably Robert Armin) to introduce a healing touch of nature where *Macbeth* has intimidated us with the preternatural, and with the Macbeths' mutual phantasmagoria of murder and power:

*Porter.* Here's a knocking, indeed! If a man were Porter of Hell Gate, he should have old turning the key. (*Knocking.*) Knock, knock, knock. Who's there, i' th' name of Belzebub?—Here's a farmer, that hang'd himself on th' expectation of plenty: Come in time-server; have napkins enow about you; here you'll sweat for't. (*Knocking.*) Knock, knock. Who's there, i' th' other devil's name?—Faith, here's an equivocator, that could swear in both the scales against either scale; who committed treason enough for God's sake, yet could not equivocate to heaven: O! come in, equivocator. (*Knocking.*) Knock, knock, knock. Who's there?—Faith, here's an English tailor come hither for stealing out of a French hose: come in, tailor; here you may roast your goose. (*Knocking.*) Knock, knock. Never at quiet! What are you?—But this place is too cold for Hell. I'll devil-porter it no further: I had thought to have let in some of all professions, that go the primrose way to th' everlasting bonfire. (*Knocking.*) Anon, anon: I pray you, remember the Porter.

[II.iii.1–22]

Cheerfully hungover, the Porter admits Macduff and Lennox through what indeed is now Hell Gate, the slaughterhouse where Macbeth has murdered the good Duncan. Shakespeare may well be grimacing at himself on "a farmer, that hang'd himself on th' expectation of plenty," since investing in grain was one of Shakespeare's favorite risks of venture capital. The more profound humor comes in the proleptic contrast between the Porter and Macbeth. As keeper of Hell Gate, the Porter boisterously greets "an equivocator," presumably a Jesuit like Father Garnet, who asserted a right to equivocal answers so as to avoid self-incrimination in the Gunpowder Plot trial of early 1606, the year *Macbeth* was first performed. Historicizing *Macbeth* as a reaction to the Gunpowder Plot to me seems only a compounding of darkness with darkness, since Shakespeare always transcends commentary on his own moment in time. We rather are meant to contrast the hard-drinking Porter with Macbeth himself, who will remind us of the Porter, but not until Act V, Scene v, when Birnam Wood comes to Dunsinane and Macbeth begins: "To doubt th' equivocation of the fiend, / That lies like truth." De Quincey confined his analysis of the knocking at the gate in Macbeth to the shock of the four knocks themselves, but as an acute rhetorician he should have attended more to the Porter's subsequent dialogue with Macduff, where the Porter sends up forever the notion of "equivocation" by expounding how alcohol provokes three things:

> *Porter.* Marry, Sir, nose-painting, sleep, and urine. Lechery, Sir, it pro-
> vokes, and unprovokes: it provokes the desire, but it takes away
> the performance. Therefore, much drink may be said to be an
> equivocator with lechery: it makes him, and it mars him; it sets
> him on, and it takes him off; it persuades him, and disheartens
> him; makes him stand to, and not stand to: in conclusion, equivo-
> cates him in a sleep, and giving him the lie, leaves him.
> [II.iii.28–37]

Drunkenness is another equivocation, provoking lust but then denying the male his capacity for performance. Are we perhaps made to wonder whether Macbeth, like Iago, plots murderously because his sexual capacity has been impaired? If you have a proleptic imagination as intense as Macbeth's, then your desire or ambition outruns your will, reaching the other bank, or shoal, of time all too quickly. The fierce sexual passion of the Macbeths possesses a quality of baffled intensity, possibly related to their childlessness, so that the Porter may hint at a situation that transcends his possible knowledge, but not the audience's surmises.

Macbeth's ferocity as a killing machine exceeds even the capacity of such great Shakespearean butchers as Aaron the Moor and Richard III, or the heroic Roman battle prowess of Antony and of Coriolanus. Iago's possible impotence would have some relation to the humiliation of being passed over for Cassio. But if Macbeth's manhood has been thwarted, there is no Othello for him to blame; the sexual victimization, if it exists, is self-generated by an imagination so impatient with time's workings that it always overprepares every event. This may be an element in Lady Macbeth's taunts, almost as if the manliness of Macbeth can be restored only by his murder of the sleeping Duncan, whom Lady Macbeth cannot slay because the good king resembles *her* father in his slumber. The mounting nihilism of Macbeth, which will culminate in his image of life as a tale signifying nothing, perhaps then has more affinity with Iago's devaluation of reality than with Edmund's cold potency.

A. C. Bradley found in *Macbeth* more of a "Sophoclean irony" than anywhere else in Shakespeare, meaning by such irony an augmenting awareness in the audience far exceeding the protagonist's consciousness that perpetually he is saying one thing, and meaning more than he himself understands in what he says. I agree with Bradley that *Macbeth* is the masterpiece of Shakespearean irony, which transcends dramatic, or Sophoclean, irony. Macbeth consistently says more than he knows, but he also imagines more than he says, so that the gap between his overt consciousness and his imaginative powers, wide to begin with, becomes extraordinary. Sexual desire, particularly in males, is likely to manifest all the vicissitudes of the drive when that abyss is so vast. This may be part of the burden of Lady Macbeth's lament before the banquet scene dominated by Banquo's ghost:

Nought's had, all's spent,
Where our desire is got without content:
'Tis safer to be that which we destroy,
Than by destruction dwell in doubtful joy.

[III.ii.4–7]

The madness of Lady Macbeth exceeds a trauma merely of guilt; her husband consistently turns from her (though never against her) once Duncan is slain. Whatever the two had intended by the mutual "greatness" they had promised each other, the subtle irony of Shakespeare reduces such greatness to a pragmatic desexualization once the usurpation of the crown has been realized. There is a fearful pathos in Lady Macbeth's cries of "To bed," in her madness, and a terrifying proleptic irony in her earlier outcry "Unsex me here." It is an understatement to aver that no other author's sense of human sexuality equals Shakespeare's in scope and in precision. The terror that we experience, as audience or as readers, when we suffer *Macbeth* seems to me, in many ways, sexual in its nature, if only because murder increasingly becomes Macbeth's mode of sexual expression. Unable to beget children, Macbeth slaughters them.

4

Though it is traditional to regard *Macbeth* as being uniquely terrifying among Shakespeare's plays, it will appear eccentric that I should regard this tragedy's fearsomeness as somehow sexual in its origins and in its dominant aspects. The violence of *Macbeth* doubtless impresses us more than it did the drama's contemporary audiences. Many if not most of those who attended *Macbeth* also joined the large crowds who thronged public executions in London, including drawings-and-quarterings as well as more civilized beheadings. The young Shakespeare, as we saw, probably heaped up outrages in his *Titus Andronicus* both to gratify his audience and to mock such gratification. But the barbarities of *Titus Andronicus* are very different in their effect from the savageries of *Macbeth*, which do not move us to nervous laughter:

For brave Macbeth (well he deserves that name),
Disdaining Fortune, with his brandish'd steel,
Which smok'd with bloody execution,
Like Valour's minion, carv'd out his passage,
Till he fac'd the slave;
Which ne'er shook hands, nor bade farewell to him,
Till he unseam'd him from the nave to th' chops,
And fix'd his head upon our battlements.

[I.ii.16–23]

I cannot recall anyone else in Shakespeare who sustains a death wound from the navel all the way up to his jaw, a mode of unseaming that introduces us to Macbeth's quite astonishing ferocity. "Bellona's bridegroom," Macbeth is thus the husband to the war goddess, and his unseaming strokes enact his husbandly function. Devoted as he and Lady Macbeth palpably are to each other, their love has its problematic elements. Shakespeare's sources gave him a Lady Macbeth previously married, and presumably grieving for a dead son by that marriage. The mutual passion between her and Macbeth depends upon their dream of a shared "greatness," the promise of which seems to have been an element in Macbeth's courtship, since she reminds him of it when he wavers. Her power over him, with its angry questioning of his manliness, is engendered by her evident frustration—certainly of ambition, manifestly of motherhood, possibly also of sexual fulfillment. Victor Hugo, when he placed Macbeth in the line of Nimrod, the Bible's first "hunter of men," may have hinted that few of them have been famous as lovers. Macbeth sees himself always as a soldier, therefore not cruel but professionally murderous, which allows him to maintain also a curious, personal passivity, almost more the dream than the dreamer. Famously a paragon of courage and so no coward, Macbeth nevertheless is in a perpetual state of fear. Of what? Part of the answer seems to be his fear of impotence, a dread related as much to his overwhelming power of imagination as to his shared dream of greatness with Lady Macbeth.

Critics almost always find an element of sexual violence in Macbeth's murder of the sleeping and benign Duncan. Macbeth himself overdetermines this critical discovery when he compares his movement toward the murder with "Tarquin's ravishing strides" on that tyrant's way to rape the chaste Lucrece, heroine of Shakespeare's poem. Is this a rare, self-referential moment on Shakespeare's own part, since many in Macbeth's audience would have recognized the dramatist's reference to one of his nondramatic works, which was more celebrated in Shakespeare's time than it is in ours? If it is, then Shakespeare brings his imagination very close to Macbeth's in the moment just preceding his protagonist's initial crime. Think how many are murdered onstage in Shakespeare, and reflect why we are not allowed to watch Macbeth's stabbings of Duncan. The unseen nature of the butchery allows us to imagine, rather horribly, the location and number of Macbeth's thrusts into the sleeping body of the man who is at once his cousin, his guest, his king, and symbolically his benign father. I assumed that, in *Julius Caesar,* Brutus's thrust was at Caesar's privates, enhancing the horror of the tradition that Brutus was Caesar's natural son. The corpse of Duncan is described by Macbeth in accents that remind us of Antony's account of the murdered Caesar, yet there is something more intimate in Macbeth's phrasing:

> Here lay Duncan,
> His silver skin lac'd with his golden blood;
> And his gash'd stabs look'd like a breach in nature
> For ruin's wasteful entrance.
>
> [II.iii.111–14]

Macbeth and "ruin" are one, and the sexual suggestiveness in "breach in nature" and "wasteful entrance" is very strong, and counterpoints itself against Lady Macbeth's bitter reproaches at Macbeth's refusal to return with the daggers, which would involve his seeing the corpse again. "Infirm of purpose!" she cries out to him first, and when she returns from planting the daggers, her imputation of his sexual failure is more overt: "Your constancy / Hath left you unattended," another reminder that his firmness has abandoned him. But perhaps desire, except to perpetuate himself in time, has departed forever from him. He has doomed himself to be the "poor player," an overanxious actor always missing his cues. Iago and Edmund, in somewhat diverse ways, were both playwrights staging their own works, until Iago was unmasked by Emilia and Edmund received his death wound from the nameless knight, Edgar's disguise. Though Iago and Edmund also played brilliantly in their self-devised roles, they showed their genius primarily as plotters. Macbeth plots incessantly, but cannot make the drama go as he wishes. He botches it perpetually, and grows more and more outraged that his bloodiest ideas, when accomplished, trail behind them a residuum that threatens him still. Malcolm and Donalbain, Fleance and Macduff—all flee, and their survival is for Macbeth the stuff of nightmare.

Nightmare seeks Macbeth out; that search, more than his violence, is the true plot of this most terrifying of Shakespeare's plays. From my childhood on, I have been puzzled by the Witches, who spur the rapt Macbeth on to his sublime but guilty project. They come to him because preternaturally they *know* him: he is not so much theirs as they are his. This is not to deny their reality apart from him, but only to indicate again that he has more implicit power over them than they manifest in regard to him. They place nothing in his mind that is not already there. And yet they undoubtedly influence his total yielding to his own ambitious imagination. Perhaps, indeed, they are the final impetus that renders Macbeth so ambiguously passive when he confronts the phantasmagorias that Lady Macbeth says always have attended him. In that sense, the Weird Sisters are close to the three Norns, or Fates, that William Blake interpreted them as being: they gaze into the seeds of time, but they also act upon those they teach to gaze with them. Together with Lady Macbeth, they persuade Macbeth to his self-abandonment, or rather they prepare Macbeth for Lady Macbeth's greater temptation into unsanctified violence.

Surely the play inherits their cosmos, and not a Christian universe. Hecate, goddess of spells, is the deity of the night world, and though she calls Macbeth "a wayward son," his actions pragmatically make him a loyal associate of the evil sorceress. One senses, in rereading *Macbeth*, a greater preternatural energy within Macbeth himself than is available to Hecate or to the Weird Sisters. Our equivocal but compulsive sympathy for him is partly founded upon Shakespeare's exclusion of any other human center of interest, except for his prematurely eclipsed wife, and partly upon our fear that his imagination is our own. Yet the largest element in our irrational sympathy ensues from Macbeth's sublimity. Great utterance continuously breaks through his confusions, and a force neither divine nor wicked seems to choose him as the trumpet of its prophecy:

> Besides, this Duncan
> Hath borne his faculties so meek, hath been
> So clear in his great office, that his virtues
> Will plead like angels, trumpet-tongu'd against
> The deep damnation of his taking-off;
> And Pity, like a naked new-born babe,
> Striding the blast, or heaven's Cherubins, hors'd
> Upon the sightless couriers of the air,
> Shall blow the horrid deed in every eye,
> That tears shall drown the wind.
>
> [I.vii.16–25]

Here, as elsewhere, we do not feel that Macbeth's proleptic eloquence is inappropriate to him; his language and his imaginings are those of a seer, which heightens the horror of his disintegration into the bloodiest of all Shakespearean tyrant-villains. Yet we wonder just how and why this great voice breaks through Macbeth's consciousness, since clearly it comes to him unbidden. He is, we know, given to seizures; Lady Macbeth remarks, "My Lord is often thus, / And hath been from his youth." Visionary fits come upon him when and as *they* will, and his tendency to second sight is clearly allied both to his proleptic imaginings and to the witches' preoccupation with him. No one else in Shakespeare is so occult, not even the hermetic magician, Prospero.

This produces an extraordinary effect upon us, since we *are* Macbeth, though we are pragmatically neither murderers nor mediums, and he is. Nor are we conduits for transcendent energies, for visions and voices; Macbeth is as much a natural poet as he is a natural killer. He cannot reason and compare, because images beyond reason and beyond competition overwhelm him. Shakespeare can be said to have conferred his own intellect upon Hamlet, his own capacity for more life upon Falstaff, his own wit upon Rosalind. To Macbeth, Shakespeare evidently gave over what might be called the passive element in his own imagination. We cannot judge that the author of *Macbeth* was victimized by his own imagination, but we hardly can avoid seeing Macbeth himself as the victim of a beyond that surmounts anything available to us. His tragic dignity depends upon his contagious sense of unknown modes of being, his awareness of powers that lie beyond Hecate and the witches but are not identical with the Christian God and His angels. These powers are the tragic sublime itself, and Macbeth, despite his own will, is so deeply at one with them that he can contaminate us with sublimity, even as the unknown forces contaminate him. Critics have never agreed as to how to name those forces; it seems to me best to agree with Nietzsche that the prejudices of morality are irrelevant to such daemons. If they terrify us by taking over this play, they also bring us joy, the utmost pleasure that accepts contamination by the daemonic.

5

*Macbeth,* partly because of this uncanniness, is fully the rival of *Hamlet* and of *King Lear,* and like them transcends what might seem the limits of art. Yet the play defies critical description and analysis in ways very different from those of *Hamlet* and *Lear.* Hamlet's inwardness is an abyss; Lear's sufferings finally seem more than human; Macbeth is all too human. Despite Macbeth's violence, he is much closer to us than are Hamlet and Lear. What makes this usurper so intimate for us? Even great actors do badly in the role, with only a few exceptions, Ian McKellen being much the best I've attended. Yet even McKellen seemed haunted by the precariousness of the role's openness to its audience. I think we most identify with Macbeth because we also have the sense that we are violating our own natures, as he does his. *Macbeth,* in another of Shakespeare's startling originalities, is the first Expressionist drama. The consciousness of Hamlet is wider than ours, but Macbeth's is not; it seems indeed to have exactly our contours, whoever we are. And as I have emphasized already, the proleptic element in Macbeth's imagination reaches out to our own apprehensiveness, our universal sense that the dreadful is about to happen, and that we have no choice but to participate in it.

When Malcolm, at the play's end, refers to "this dead butcher, and his fiend-like Queen," we are in the odd position both of having to agree with Duncan's son and of murmuring to ourselves that so to categorize Macbeth and Lady Macbeth seems scarcely adequate. Clearly the ironies of *Macbeth* are not born of clashing perspectives but of divisions in the self—in Macbeth and in the audience. When Macbeth says that in him "function is smother'd in surmise," we have to agree, and then we brood on to what more limited extent this is true of ourselves also. Dr. Johnson said that in Macbeth "the events are too great to admit the influence of particular dispositions." Since no one feared more than Johnson what he called "the dangerous prevalence of the imagination," I have to assume that the greatest of all critics wished not to acknowledge that the particular disposition of Macbeth's proleptic imagination overdetermines the events of the play. Charting some of the utterances of this leaping-ahead in Macbeth's mind ought to help us to leap ahead in his wake.

In a rapt aside, quite early in the play, Macbeth introduces us to the extraordinary nature of his imagination:

> This supernatural soliciting
> Cannot be ill; cannot be good:—
> If ill, why hath it given me earnest of success,
> Commencing in a truth? I am Thane of Cawdor:
> If good, why do I yield to that suggestion
> Whose horrid image doth unfix my hair,
> And make my seated heart knock at my ribs,
> Against the use of nature? Present fears
> Are less than horrible imaginings.
> My thought, whose murther yet is but fantastical,
> Shakes so my single state of man
> That function is smother'd in surmise,
> And nothing is, but what is not.

[I.iii.130–42]

"My single state of man" plays upon several meanings of "single": unitary, isolated, vulnerable. The phantasmagoria of murdering Duncan is so vivid that "nothing is, but what is not," and "function," the mind, is smothered by "surmise," fantasy. The dramatic music of this passage, impossible not to discern with the inner ear, is very difficult to describe. Macbeth speaks to himself in a kind of trance, halfway between trauma and second sight. An involuntary visionary of horror, he *sees* what certainly is going to happen, while still knowing this murder to be "but fantastical." His tribute to his own "horrible imaginings" is absolute: the implication is that his will is irrelevant. That he stands on the border of madness may seem evident to us now, but such a judgment would be mistaken. It is the resolute Lady Macbeth who goes mad; the proleptic Macbeth will become more and more outraged and outrageous, but he is no more insane at the close than he is here. The parameters of the diseased mind waver throughout Shakespeare. Is Hamlet ever truly mad, even north-by-northwest? Lear, Othello, Leontes, Timon all pass into derangement and (partly) out again, but Lady Macbeth is granted no recovery. It might be a relief for us if Macbeth ever went mad, but he cannot, if only because he represents all our imaginations, including our capacity for anticipating futures we both wish for and fear.

At his castle, with Duncan as his royal guest, Macbeth attempts a soliloquy in Hamlet's mode, but rapidly leaps into his own:

> If it were done, when 'tis done, then 'twere well
> It were done quickly: If th' assassination
> Could trammel up the consequence, and catch
> With his surcease, success; that but this blow
> Might be the be-all and the end-all—here,
> But here, upon this bank and shoal of time,
> We'd jump the life to come.

[I.vii.1–7]

"Jump" partly means "risk," but Shakespeare carries it over into our meaning also. After the great vision of "Pity, like a naked new-born babe"

descends upon Macbeth from some transcendent realm, the usurping host
has another fantasy concerning his own will:

> I have no spur
> To prick the sides of my intent, but only
> Vaulting ambition, which o'erleaps itself
> And falls on th' other—

[I.vii.25–28]

Lady Macbeth then enters, and so Macbeth does not complete his
metaphor. "The other" what? Not "side," for his horse, which is all will, has
had its sides spurred, so that ambition evidently is now on the other shoal
or shore, its murder of Duncan established as a desire. That image is central in the play, and Shakespeare takes care to keep it phantasmagoric by
not allowing us to see the actual murder of Duncan. On his way to this
regicide, Macbeth has a vision that takes him even further into the realm
where "nothing is, but what is not":

> Is this a dagger, which I see before me,
> The handle toward my hand? Come, let me clutch thee:—
> I have thee not, and yet I see thee still.
> Art thou not, fatal vision, sensible
> To feeling, as to sight? or art thou but
> A dagger of the mind, a false creation,
> Proceeding from the heat-oppressed brain?
> I see thee yet, in form as palpable
> As this which now I draw.
> Thou marshall'st me the way that I was going;
> And such an instrument I was to use.—
> Mine eyes are made the fools o' th' other senses,
> Or else worth all the rest: I see thee still;
> And on thy blade, and dudgeon, gouts of blood,
> Which was not so before.—There's no such thing.
> It is the bloody business which informs

Thus to mine eyes.—Now o'er the one half-world
Nature seems dead, and wicked dreams abuse
The curtain'd sleep: Witchcraft celebrates
Pale Hecate's off'rings; and wither'd Murther,
Alarum'd by his sentinel, the wolf,
Whose howl's his watch, thus with his stealthy pace,
With Tarquin's ravishing strides, towards his design
Moves like a ghost.—Thou sure and firm-set earth,
Hear not my steps, which way they walk, for fear
Thy very stones prate of my where-about,
And take the present horror from the time,
Which now suits with it.—Whiles I threat, he lives:
Words to the heat of deeds too cold breath gives.
                    *A bell rings.*
I go, and it is done: the bell invites me.
Hear it not, Duncan; for it is a knell
That summons thee to Heaven, or to Hell.

                                        [II.i.33–64]


This magnificent soliloquy, culminating in the tolling of the bell, always has been judged to be an apotheosis of Shakespeare's art. So accustomed is Macbeth to second sight that he evidences neither surprise nor fear at the visionary knife but coolly attempts to grasp this "dagger of the mind." The phrase "a false creation" subtly hints at the gnostic cosmos of *Macbeth*, which is the work of some Demiurge, whose botchings made creation itself a fall. With a wonderful metaphysical courage, admiration for which helps implicate us in Macbeth's guilts, he responds to the phantasmagoria by drawing his own dagger, thus acknowledging his oneness with his own proleptic yearnings. As in *King Lear*, the primary meaning of *fool* in this play is "victim," but Macbeth defiantly asserts the possibility that his eyes, rather than being victims, may be worth all his other senses together.

This moment of bravura is dispersed by a new phenomenon in Macbeth's visionary history, as the hallucination undergoes a temporal transformation, great drops of blood manifesting themselves upon blade and handle. "There's no such thing," he attempts to insist, but yields instead to one of those openings-out of eloquence that perpetually descend upon him. In that yielding to Hecate's sorcery, Macbeth astonishingly identifies his steps toward the sleeping Duncan with Tarquin's "ravishing strides" toward his victim in Shakespeare's narrative poem *The Rape of Lucrece*. Macbeth is not going to ravish Duncan, except of his life, but the allusion would have thrilled many in the audience. I again take it that this audacity is Shakespeare's own signature, establishing his complicity with his protagonist's imagination. "I go, and it is done" constitutes the climactic prolepsis; we participate, feeling that Duncan is dead already, before the thrusts have been performed.

It is after the next murder, Banquo's, and after Macbeth's confrontation with Banquo's ghost, that the proleptic utterances begin to yield to the usurper's sense of being more outraged than outrageous:

> Blood hath been shed ere now, i' th' olden time,
> Ere humane statute purged the gentle weal;
> Ay, and since too, murthers have been perform'd
> Too terrible for the ear: the time has been,
> That, when the brains were out, the man would die,
> And there an end; but now, they rise again,
> With twenty mortal murthers on their crowns,
> And push us from our stools. This is more strange
> Than such a murther is.

> [III.iv.74–82]

Since moral contexts, as Nietzsche advised us, are simply irrelevant to *Macbeth*, its protagonist's increasing sense of outrage is perhaps not as outrageous as it should be. The witches equivocate with him, but they are rather equivocal entities in any case; I like Bradshaw's remark that they "seem curiously capricious and infantile, hardly less concerned with pilots and chestnuts than with Macbeth and Scotland." Far from governing the *kenoma*, or cosmological emptiness, in which *Macbeth* is set, they seem much punier components of it than Macbeth himself. A world that fell even as it was created is anything but a Christian nature. Though Hecate has some potency in this nature, one feels a greater Demiurgical force at loose in this play. Shakespeare will not name it, except to call it "time," but that is a highly metaphorical time, not the "olden time" or good old days, when you bashed someone's brains out and so ended them, but "now," when their ghosts displace us.

That "now" is the empty world of *Macbeth*, into which we, as audience, *have been thrown*, and that sense of "thrownness" *is* the terror that Wilbur Sanders and Graham Bradshaw emphasize in *Macbeth*. When Macduff has fled to England, Macbeth chills us with a vow: "From this moment, / The very firstlings of my heart shall be / The firstlings of my hand." Since those firstlings pledge the massacre of Lady Macduff, her children, and all "unfortunate souls" related to Macduff, we are to appreciate that the heart of Macbeth is very much also the heart of the play's world. Macbeth's beheading by Macduff prompts the revenger, at the end, to proclaim, "The time is free," but we do not believe Macduff. How can we? The world is Macbeth's, precisely as he imagined it; only the kingdom belongs to Malcolm. *King Lear*, also set in the cosmological emptiness, is too various to be typified by any single utterance, even of Lear's own, but Macbeth concentrates his play and his world in its most famous speech:

She should have died hereafter:
There would have been a time for such a word.—
To-morrow, and to-morrow, and to-morrow,
Creeps in this petty pace from day to day,
To the last syllable of recorded time;
And all our yesterdays have lighted fools
The way to dusty death. Out, out, brief candle!
Life's but a walking shadow; a poor player,
That struts and frets his hour upon the stage,
And then is heard no more: it is a tale
Told by an idiot, full of sound and fury,
Signifying nothing.

[V.v.17–28]

Dr. Johnson, rightly shocked that this should be Macbeth's response to the death of his wife, at first insisted that "such a word" was an error for "such a world." When the Grand Cham retreated from this emendation, he stubbornly argued that "word" meant "intelligence" in the sense of "information," and so did not refer to "hereafter," as, alas, it certainly does. Johnson's moral genius was affronted, as it was by the end of *King Lear*, and Johnson was right: neither play sees with Christian optics. Macbeth has the authority to speak for his play and his world, as for his self. In Macbeth's time there is no hereafter, in any world. And yet this is the suicide of his own wife that has been just reported to him. Grief, in any sense we could apprehend, is not expressed by him. Instead of an elegy for Queen Macbeth, we hear a nihilistic death march, or rather a creeping of fools, of universal victims. The "brief candle" is both the sun and the individual life, no longer the "great bond" of Macbeth's magnificent invocation just before Banquo's murder:

> Come, seeling night,
> Scarf up the tender eye of pitiful Day,
> And, with thy bloody and invisible hand,
> Cancel, and tear to pieces, that great bond
> Which keeps me pale!—Light thickens; and the crow
> Makes wing to th' rooky wood;
> Good things of Day begin to droop and drowse,
> Whiles Night's black agents to their preys do rouse.
> Thou marvell'st at my words: but hold thee still;
> Things bad begun make strong themselves by ill.
>
> [III.iii.46–55]

There the night becomes a royal falcon rending the sun apart, and Macbeth's imagination is wholly apocalyptic. In the "To-morrow, and to-morrow, and to-morrow" chant, the tenor is postapocalyptic, as it will be in Macbeth's reception of the news that Birnam Wood has come to Dunsinane:

I 'gin to be aweary of the sun,
And wish th' estate o' th' world were now undone.—

[V.v.49–50]

Life is a walking shadow in that sun, a staged representation like the bad actor whose hour of strutting and fretting will not survive our leaving the theater. Having carried the reverberation of Ralph Richardson as Falstaff in my ear for half a century, I reflect (as Shakespeare, not Macbeth, meant me to reflect) that Richardson will not be "heard no more" until I am dead. Macbeth's finest verbal coup is to revise his metaphor; life suddenly is no longer a bad actor, but an idiot's story, nihilistic of necessity. The magnificent language of Macbeth and of his play is reduced to "sound and fury," but that phrase plays back against Macbeth, his very diction, in all its splendor, refuting him. It is as though he at last refuses himself any imaginative sympathy, a refusal impossible for his audience to make.

6

I come back, for a last time, to the terrible awe that Macbeth provokes in us. G. Wilson Knight first juxtaposed a reflection by Lafew, the wise old nobleman of *All's Well That Ends Well*, with *Macbeth*:

> *Laf.* They say miracles are past; and we have our philosophical persons to make modern and familiar, things supernatural and causeless. Hence is it that we make trifles of terrors, ensconcing ourselves into seeming knowledge, when we should submit ourselves to an unknown fear.

[II.iii.1–6]

Wilbur Sanders, acknowledging Wilson Knight, explores *Macbeth* as the Shakespearean play where most we "submit ourselves to an unknown fear." My own experience of the play is that we rightly react to it with terror, even as we respond to *Hamlet* with wonder. Whatever *Macbeth* does otherwise, it certainly does not offer us a catharsis for the terrors it evokes.

Since we are compelled to internalize Macbeth, the "unknown fear" finally is of ourselves. If we submit to it—and Shakespeare gives us little choice—then we follow Macbeth into a nihilism very different from the abyss-voyages of Iago and of Edmund. They are confident nihilists, secure in their self-election. Macbeth is never secure, nor are we, his unwilling cohorts; he childers, as we father, and we are the only children he has.

The most surprising observation on fear in *Macbeth* was also Wilson Knight's:

> Whilst Macbeth lives in conflict with himself there is misery, evil, fear; when, at the end, he and others have openly identified himself with evil, he faces the world fearless: nor does he appear evil any longer.

I think I see where Wilson Knight was aiming, but a few revisions are necessary. Macbeth's broad progress is from proleptic horror to a sense of baffled expectations, in which a feeling of having been outraged takes the place of fear. "Evil" we can set aside; it is redundant, rather like calling Hitler or Stalin evil. When Macbeth is betrayed, by hallucination and foretelling, he manifests a profound and energetic outrage, like a frantic actor always fated to miss all his cues. The usurper goes on murdering, and achieves no victory over time or the self. Sometimes I wonder whether Shakespeare somehow had gotten access to the Gnostic and Manichaean fragments scattered throughout the Church Fathers, quoted by them only to be denounced, though I rather doubt that Shakespeare favored much ecclesiastical reading. Macbeth, however intensely we identify with him, is more frightening than anything he confronts, thus intimating that we ourselves may be more dreadful than anything in our own worlds. And yet Macbeth's realm, like ours, can be a ghastly context:

> *Old Man.* Threescore and ten I can remember well;
> Within the volume of which time I have seen
> Hours dreadful, and things strange, but this sore night
> Hath trifled former knowings.

*Rosse.* Ha, good Father,
　Thou seest the heavens, as troubled with man's act,
　Threatens his bloody stage: by th' clock 'tis day,
　And yet dark night strangles the travelling lamp.
　Is 't night's predominance, or the day's shame,
　That darkness does the face of earth entomb,
　When living light should kiss it?
*Old Man.* 'Tis unnatural,
　Even like the deed that's done. On Tuesday last,
　A falcon, towering in her pride of place,
　Was by a mousing owl hawk'd at and kill'd.
*Rosse.* And Duncan's horses (a thing most strange and certain)
　Beauteous and swift, the minions of their race,
　Turn'd wild in nature, broke their stalls, flung out,
　Contending 'gainst obedience, as they would make
　War with mankind.
*Old Man.* 'Tis said, they eat each other.
*Rosse.* They did so; to th' amazement of mine eyes,
　That look'd upon 't.

[II.iv.1–20]

This is the aftermath of Duncan's murder, yet even at the play's opening a wounded captain admiringly says of Macbeth and Banquo: "they/
Doubly redoubled strokes upon the foe: / Except they meant to bathe in
reeking wounds, / Or memorize another Golgotha, / I cannot tell—."
What does it mean to "memorize another Golgotha"? Golgotha, "the place
of skulls," was Calvary, where Jesus suffered upon the cross. "Memorize"
here seems to mean "memorialize," and Shakespeare subtly has invoked a
shocking parallel. We are at the beginning of the play, and these are still
the *good* captains Macbeth and Banquo, patriotically fighting for Duncan
and for Scotland, yet they are creating a new slaughter ground for a new
Crucifixion. Graham Bradshaw aptly has described the horror of nature in
*Macbeth,* and Robert Watson has pointed to its gnostic affinities. Shakespeare throws us into everything that is not ourselves, not so as to induce

an ascetic revulsion in the audience, but so as to compel a choice between Macbeth and the cosmological emptiness, the *kenoma* of the Gnostics. We choose Macbeth perforce, and the preference is made very costly for us.

Of the aesthetic greatness of *Macbeth*, there can be no question. The play cannot challenge the scope and depth of *Hamlet* and *King Lear*, or the brilliant painfulness of *Othello*, or the world-without-end panorama of *Antony and Cleopatra*, and yet it is my personal favorite of all the high tragedies. Shakespeare's final strength is radical internalization, and this is his most internalized drama, played out in the guilty imagination that we share with Macbeth. No critical method that works equally well for Thomas Middleton or John Fletcher and for Shakespeare is going to illuminate Shakespeare for us. I do not know whether God created Shakespeare, but I know that Shakespeare created us, to an altogether startling degree. In relation to us, his perpetual audience, Shakespeare is a kind of mortal god; our instruments for measuring him break when we seek to apply them. *Macbeth*, as its best critics have seen, scarcely shows us that crimes against nature are repaired when a legitimate social order is restored. Nature *is* crime in *Macbeth*, but hardly in the Christian sense that calls out for nature to be redeemed by grace, or by expiation and forgiveness. As in *King Lear*, we have no place to go in *Macbeth*; there is no sanctuary available to us. Macbeth himself exceeds us, in energy and in torment, but he also represents us, and we discover him more vividly within us the more deeply we delve.

# 27

# ANTONY AND CLEOPATRA

A.C. Bradley considered only four of Shakespeare's characters to be "inexhaustible": Hamlet, Cleopatra, Falstaff, and Iago. Readers and playgoers might wonder why no role from *King Lear* is on that shortlist: Lear himself, Edmund, Edgar, or the Fool. Perhaps Shakespeare divided his genius between the four in *King Lear*, which is certainly as inexhaustible as *Hamlet*, among all the plays. Of Shakespearean representations of women, Cleopatra's is the most subtle and formidable, by universal consent. Critics never can agree on very much about her: Shakespeare's control of the various perspectives on her is so astute in this play, more perhaps than in any other, that the audience is given an enigmatic range of possible judgments and interpretations. Since Antony clearly does not understand her, are we likely to do any better? Rosalie Colie made the nice point that we never see Antony and Cleopatra alone together. Actually we do, just once, but only for a moment, and when he is dangerously enraged against her. What were they like when they were, more or less, in some harmony? Did they go on acting, each taking the other as audience? With Hamlet, Falstaff, and Iago, they are the most intensely theatrical personages in Shakespeare, and Cleopatra at last wears Antony out: it would take Hamlet or Falstaff not to be upstaged by her. Cleopatra never ceases to play Cleopatra, and her perception of her role necessarily demotes Antony to the equivocal status of her leading man. It is her play, and never quite his, since he is waning well before the curtain goes up, and she cannot allow herself to wane. The archetype of the star, the world's first celebrity, she is beyond her lovers—Pompey, Caesar, Antony—because they are known only for their achievements and their final tragedies. She has and needs no achievements, her death is triumphant rather than tragic, and she forever is known best for being well known.

After the four high tragedies of domesticity and blood, *Antony and Cleopatra* breaks out into the great world of the struggle of East versus West, of dissolving vistas and innumerable scenes. Dr. Johnson oddly judged that "no character is very strongly discriminated" in *Antony and Cleopatra*, an observation more fit for *Macbeth*, where only the Macbeths do not fade into a common grayness. Everyone in *Antony and Cleopatra* is distinct, from the choric Enobarbus through the Clown who at the close brings Cleopatra the fatal asps. There are a dozen sharply etched minor roles aside from Antony's ex-ally Caesar and Antony's closest subordinate Enobarbus.

So vast and intense are Cleopatra and Antony as personalities that they seem to conclude the major phase of Shakespeare's preoccupation with the inner self, which had begun at least twelve years before with Faulconbridge in *King John*, Richard II, Portia, and Shylock (however unintentional) and then had flowered in Falstaff, a decade before Cleopatra. Coriolanus, who follows Cleopatra, is a "lonely dragon" with an abyss within, and the protagonists of the late romances are something other than realistic representations. Doubtless it is simplistic to suggest that the fourteen consecutive months in which *King Lear*, *Macbeth*, and *Antony and Cleopatra* were composed wore out even William Shakespeare. I am the most Bardolatrous of critics and yet even I find that after Antony's collapse and Cleopatra's apotheosis, Shakespeare was wary of further quests into the interior.

John Dryden, in the Preface to his popular revision of *Antony and Cleopatra*, under the title *All for Love* (1678), allowed himself to sound mildly censorious concerning his illustrious protagonists:

That which is wanting to work up the pity to a greater heighth, was not afforded me by the story: for the crimes of love which they both

committed, were not occasion'd by any necessity, or fatal ignorance, but were wholly voluntary, since our passions are, or ought
to be, within our power.

I doubt that Dryden himself "pitied" Antony and Cleopatra, though he
clearly regarded their mutual passion as reprehensible and catastrophic. I
don't know that it is at all useful to characterize the relationship between
Cleopatra and Antony as mutually destructive, though Shakespeare certainly shows that it helps destroy them. Still, in their high-stakes cosmos
of power and treachery, Octavius doubtless would have devoured them
both anyway, at a perhaps more leisurely pace. *All for Love*, Dryden's exuberant title, would not have done for Shakespeare's play; even *All for Lust*
misses the mark. Antony and Cleopatra are, both of them, charismatic
politicians; each of them has so great a passion for himself and herself that
it becomes marvelous for them actually to apprehend each other's reality,
in even the smallest degree. Both of them take up all the space; everyone
else, even Octavius, is reduced to part of their audience. There is, to be
sure, a ghost who never appears in this play: Julius Caesar, who alone ever
reduced *them* to supporting cast, though never to mere audience. Perhaps
it was from Shakespeare's *Julius Caesar*, play and character, that Shakespeare's Antony and Cleopatra learned their endearing trait of never listening to what anyone else says, including each other. Antony's death
scene is the most hilarious instance of this, where the dying hero, making
a very good end indeed, nevertheless sincerely attempts to give Cleopatra some advice, while she keeps interrupting, at one point splendidly responding to his "let me speak a little" with her "No, let me speak." Since his
advice is quite bad anyway, as it has been throughout the play, this makes
little difference, except that Antony, just this once, almost stops acting the
part of Antony, Herculean hero, whereas Shakespeare wishes us to see
that Cleopatra never stops acting the part of Cleopatra. That is why it is
so wonderfully difficult a role for an actress, who must act the part of
Cleopatra, and also portray Cleopatra acting the part of Cleopatra. I recall
the young Helen Mirren doing better with that double assignment than
any other Cleopatra that I have seen.

Are Antony and Cleopatra "in love with each other," to use our language, which for once is not at all Shakespearean? Are we in love with one another? It was Aldous Huxley, in one of his essays, who remarked that we use the word *love* for the most amazing variety of relationships, ranging from what we feel for our mothers to what we feel for someone we beat up in a bordello, or its many equivalents. Juliet and Romeo indeed are in love with each other, but they are very young, and she is astonishingly good-natured, with a generosity of spirit unmatched in all of Shakespeare. We certainly can say that Cleopatra and Antony do not bore each other, and clearly they are bored, erotically and otherwise, by everyone else in their world. Mutual fascination may not be love, but it certainly is romance in the defining sense of imperfect, or at least deferred, knowledge. Cleopatra in particular always has her celebrated remedies for staleness, famously extolled by Enobarbus. Antony, also a mortal god, has his aura, really a kind of astral body, that departs with the music of Hercules, the oboes under the stage. There is no replacement for him, as Cleopatra realizes, since with his death the age of Julius Caesar and Pompey is over, and even Cleopatra is very unlikely to seduce the first great Chief Executive Officer, the Emperor Augustus.

The question therefore becomes: What is the value of mutual fascination, or of romantic love, if you want to call it that? Certainly it is less of a bewilderment, less of a vastation, than the familial love that afflicts Lear and Edgar. With monstrous shrewdness, Shakespeare modified Plutarch by having Antony abandoned by the god Hercules, rather than by Bacchus. A Dionysiac hero cannot be consigned to the past, as Hamlet's more-than-Nietzschean career continues to demonstrate. A Herculean hero was not as archaic for Shakespeare's contemporaries as he is for us, but clearly Antony is already a belated figure. Lear and Edgar are not as exposed to the audience's range of perspectives as are Cleopatra and Antony. Whore and her aging gull is a possible perspective upon them, if you yourself are a savage reductionist, but then why would you want to attend or read this play? A Dionysiac Antony would call every value, whether erotic or social, more into question than a Herculean Antony is capable of doing. If there is a critique of value in the play, it must be embodied in Cleopatra, who is raised to an apotheosis after Antony breaks apart. He ceases to be a god, and then she becomes one.

What are we to do with an Egyptian goddess, even if we are free enough of Roman reductiveness that we do not fall into the operatic trap of seeing her as a gypsy whore? If my interpretation of *King Lear* has any imaginative accuracy, then familial love, far from being a value, is exposed as an apocalyptic nightmare. Romantic love can be said to have hastened Antony's Osiris-like dismantling, yet it would be difficult, as I have been intimating, to demonstrate it either as value or as catastrophe, on the basis of his decline and fall. But Cleopatra is altogether another story, and her story certainly involves an augmentation of value. Is it the value of love? That seems to be a most difficult question, and a true challenge to what we used to call *literary* criticism. You could argue that the Cleopatra of Act V is not only a greater actress than she was before, but also that she becomes a playwright, exercising a talent released in her by Antony's death. The part that she composes for herself is very complex, and one strand in it is that she was and still is in love with Antony, and so is more than bereft. Indeed, she marries him as she dies, which is sublimely poignant, though it may remind us of Edmund's reaction to beholding the corpses of Goneril and Regan: "All three / Now marry in an instant."

Existence, we cannot forget Nietzsche's observing, is justified only as an aesthetic phenomenon. I would hesitate, wicked old aesthete though I be, to judge that for Shakespeare, love is justified only as an aesthetic value, but that does seem (to me) to be the burden of *The Tragedy of Antony and Cleopatra*, at least as Cleopatra rewrites it in the act where she has no rival in usurping all the space. Her would-be competitive dramatist, George Bernard Shaw, who asserted that he felt only disdain for the mind of Shakespeare when he compared it with his own, is quite cutting but weirdly off-center in his preface to his own *Caesar and Cleopatra*:

> I have a technical objection to making sexual infatuation a tragic theme. Experience proves that it is only effective in the comic spirit. We can bear to see Mrs. Quickly pawning her plate for love of Falstaff, but not Antony running away from the battle of Actium for love of Cleopatra.

One can grant that Shaw seizes upon one of the least persuasive episodes in Antony's degradation, but surely *Antony and Cleopatra* hardly is a tragedy as *King Lear* and *Othello* are tragedies. More even than the rest of Shakespeare, the play has no genre, and the comic spirit has a large share in it. Enobarbus gives the answer to Shaw when he calls Cleopatra a wonderful piece of work. He means Cleopatra's daemonic drive, her narcissistic exuberance, the vitality of which approaches Falstaff's. Shaw abominated Falstaff, and associated Shakespeare's Cleopatra with Falstaff, which is to make the right linkage for the wrong reason. Cleopatra, essentially an ironic humorist, even a parodist, presumably educated Antony in laughter even as Falstaff educated Hal, with the difference that Falstaff does not trade in sexual love, and Cleopatra does. Antony certainly is past his earlier glory almost throughout the play, except for sudden revivals or epiphanies, but Shakespeare was improving upon the model of decline he had established with his own Julius Caesar. And with Cleopatra, how can we, or even Cleopatra herself, ever establish the demarcation between her inwardness and her outwardness? She is surely the most theatrical character in stage history, far surpassing Pirandello's experiments in the same mode. We need not ask if her love for Antony ever is love indeed, even as she dies, because the lack of distinctiveness in the play is between the histrionic and the passionate. The value of familial love in Shakespeare is overwhelming but negative; the value of passionate love in the most mature Shakespeare depends upon a fusion of theatricality and narcissistic self-regard. The art itself is nature, and the value of love becomes wholly artful.

2

Though the splendors of *Antony and Cleopatra* commence with Shakespeare's loving farewell to his own invention of the human, the play is endlessly various, returning to *Hamlet* in that regard. In *Hamlet*, Shakespeare necessarily has to ram most of the variety into his infinite hero, while in *Antony and Cleopatra*, for all Cleopatra's myriad guises, the variousness lies primarily in one historical world's replacing another, with extraordinary persuasiveness and exuberance. An heroic age—the era of Julius Caesar—yields to the oncoming discipline of Augustan Rome. Shakespeare, as we learn al-

ways, does not let us see whether he himself prefers one side or the other,
but the contrast among the perpetual intensity of Cleopatra, the dying
music of Antony, and the grumpy efficiency of Octavius Caesar can lead
us to a probable surmise on the poet's preferences. In *Macbeth*, Shakespeare
gives us no option but to journey into the interior with his hero-villain.
*Antony and Cleopatra*, written directly afterward, allows us little intimacy
with the doomed lovers, and sweeps us outward into the world's perspectives upon them, and our perspectives upon their world. This movement
away from inwardness is established immediately in the angry complaint
of Philo to Demetrius, both of them Antony's officers:

> Nay, but this dotage of our general's
> O'erflows the measure: those his goodly eyes,
> That o'er the files and musters of the war
> Have glow'd like plated Mars, now bend, now turn
> The office and devotion of their view
> Upon a tawny front: his captain's heart,
> Which in the scuffles of great fights hath burst
> The buckles on his breast, reneges all temper,
> And is become the bellows and the fan
> To cool a gipsy's lust.
> *Flourish. Enter ANTONY, CLEOPATRA, her Ladies, the Train, with Eunuchs*
> *fanning her.*
> Look, where they come:
> Take but good note, and you shall see in him
> The triple pillar of the world transform'd
> Into a strumpet's fool: behold and see.
>
> [I.i.1–13]

Whether we behold dotage and a lustful gypsy depends upon whether
there is something in us that would not make us very good Roman soldiers:

> *Cleo.* If it be love indeed, tell me how much.
> *Ant.* There's beggary in the love that can be reckon'd.

*Cleo.* I'll set a bourn how far to be belov'd.

*Ant.* Then must thou needs find out new heaven, new earth.

[I.i.14–17]


She teases, he is grandiose, and his ensuing declarations are unconvincing:


Let Rome in Tiber melt, and the wide arch
Of the rang'd empire fall! Here is my space,
Kingdoms are clay: our dungy earth alike
Feeds beast as man.

[I.i.33–36]


To mean that, you need to fuse the outlooks of Falstaff and of Hamlet; Antony may not be merely on Egyptian holiday, yet he certainly sounds like it. Roman thoughts, as Cleopatra complains, suddenly strike him, each time another messenger shows up. All through the play the messengers are both frequent and invariably truthful: they are the inviolable rules of the game. Reflecting accurately that he "must from this enchanting queen break off," Antony departs for Rome, but only after Cleopatra plays her first great scene, matador to Antony's bull:


*Cleo.*                              Play one scene
    Of excellent dissembling, and let it look
    Like perfect honour.
*Ant.*                         You'll heat my blood: no more.
*Cleo.* You can do better yet; but this is meetly.
*Ant.* Now, by my sword,—
*Cleo.*                         And target. Still he mends.
    But this is not the best. Look, prithee, Charmian,
    How this Herculean Roman does become
    The carriage of his chafe.
*Ant.* I'll leave you, lady.

*Cleo.*                    Courteous lord, one word:
   Sir, you and I must part, but that's not it:
   Sir, you and I have lov'd, but there's not it;
   That you know well, something it is I would,—
   O, my oblivion is a very Antony,
   And I am all forgotten.
*Ant.*                    But that your royalty
   Holds idleness your subject, I should take you
   For idleness itself.
*Cleo.*                    'Tis sweating labour,
   To bear such idleness so near the heart
   As Cleopatra this. But sir, forgive me,
   Since my becomings kill me, when they do not
   Eye well to you. Your honour calls you hence,
   Therefore be deaf to my unpitied folly,
   And all the gods go with you! Upon your sword
   Sit laurel victory, and smooth success
   Be strew'd before your feet!
*Ant.*                    Let us go. Come;
   Our separation so abides, and flies,
   That thou, residing here, goes yet with me,
   And I, hence fleeting, here remain with thee.
   Away!

[I.iii.78–105]

This is an appropriate place to ask: How does Antony appear to Cleopatra, even at the best of their time? Leeds Barroll subtly argues that:

of the heavens . . . she sees him as a sight. Not great but gigantic; not compelling but picturesque: not powerful but loud: visible, decorous giant of the world. Not the striving god Hercules, but the static god Atlas, colossal in his changeless holding.

I welcome this, but think it very doubtful, unless we take it as Cleopatra's widowed vision of her self-slain lover. In the passage I have quoted, Antony is a striving Hercules, who can be played with but remains always dangerous, at once a mortal god and a Roman politician. Following the pattern of Pompey and of Julius Caesar, Antony's erotic relationship with Cleopatra is also an unstable political alliance, to be sold out, by either party, when and if the price is right. In this greatly savage play, you do not betray your love by bargaining it away: you honor it by being well compensated for your erotic loss by a gain in power. Though they both keep denying this, Cleopatra and Antony know well the rules of the game. She never does break them; he does, but not because his love for her surpasses her regard for him.

Antony is a man upon whom the sun is going down: his genius wanes in the presence of Octavius Caesar. A swordsman, Antony is hopelessly outclassed by the first imperial bureaucrat, who has inherited the canniness, though not the generosity, of his uncle and adoptive father, Julius Caesar. The audience senses a weariness in Antony, a psychic fatigue with Rome and all things Roman. Once astute at politics (as in Shakespeare's own *Julius Caesar*), Antony has become a bungler, who cannot take or give good advice. His major error is to renegotiate his ostensible alliance with Octavius on the absurdly unstable basis of a dynastic marriage with Octavia, sister to the future Roman emperor. That changes the political game to a version of Russian roulette, in which Antony is bound to shoot himself—that is to say, to get back to Cleopatra at much too high a cost. Fascinated as he is by her, and bored with Octavia, Antony will not lose all for love (or lust) but for changes in himself that he scarcely can hope to understand. I might have thought that no one in Shakespeare could go beyond Falstaff, Hamlet, Iago, and Lear in change founded upon self-overhearing, but Antony—who certainly matches none of them in self-consciousness—is the largest instance of such metamorphic susceptibility in all of Shakespeare. Generally, scholars overlook that Shakespeare's Cleopatra is closer to North's version of Plutarch than is Shakespeare's Antony, partly because Plutarch (for family reasons) did not much like the historical Antony, even though he admits some of the hero's better qualities.

For Plutarch, Antony's failure at the Battle of Actium was partly motivated by cowardice, a nasty judgment totally alien to Shakespeare's Antony, whose courage never wanes, in grand comparison to his judgment, political skill, and erotic self-control.

Though the play's Antony necessarily cannot match its Cleopatra, Shakespeare creates a magnificent ruin, who becomes only more sublime as he falls. Doubtless, this Mark Antony is too multiform to be a strictly tragic figure, just as Cleopatra is too varied and too close to quasi-divinity for us to find in her a tragic heroine, a Cordelia or a Lady Macbeth. In his decline and fall, Antony transcends his personal limitations, and is humanized with a sumptuousness lavish even for Shakespeare. Pathos and grandeur mingle inextricably as the prodigal Antony shatters, in what must be Shakespeare's greatest catastrophe creation, a fecund breaking of the vessels without parallel elsewhere in all of Western literature. The sublime music of Antony's self-destruction would be the play's largest poetic achievement, except that nothing could surpass the immense harmonies of Cleopatra's own death scene, which can be said to have changed Shakespeare himself once and for all. After *Antony and Cleopatra*, something vital abandons Shakespeare.

Plutarch's Antony, whatever real brutalities and malfeasances he commits, is always distinguished by his love of honor, and by his capacity to arouse affection in common soldiers. Yet Antony, in Plutarch's judgment, was the most self-indulgent of the Romans of his era, and succumbed to Cleopatra as the ultimate indulgence:

> The love for Cleopatra which now entered his life came as the final and crowning mischief which could befall him. It excited to the point of madness many passions which had hitherto lain concealed, or at least dormant, and it stifled or corrupted all those redeeming qualities in him which were still capable of resisting temptation.

I cite Plutarch only to emphasize that Shakespeare does not exclude this as one of a myriad of perspectives available to his audience as they confront the Antony–Cleopatra relationship, though I hardly view it as a very helpful judgment in itself. One of Shakespeare's most beautiful ironies is that Antony is at his most interesting, and appealing, when he loses his sense of self-identity:

*Ant.* Eros, thou yet behold'st me?

*Eros.*                                      Ay, noble lord.

*Ant.* Sometime we see a cloud that's dragonish,
    A vapour sometime, like a bear, or lion,
    A tower'd citadel, a pendent rock,
    A forked mountain, or blue promontory
    With trees upon 't, that nod unto the world,
    And mock our eyes with air. Thou hast seen these signs,
    They are black vesper's pageants.

*Eros.*                                      Ay, my lord.

*Ant.* That which is now a horse, even with a thought
    The rack dislimns, and makes it indistinct
    As water is in water.

*Eros.*                          It does, my lord.

*Ant.* My good knave Eros, now thy captain is
    Even such a body: Here I am Antony,
    Yet cannot hold this visible shape, my knave.

                                      [IV.xiv. 1–14]

How extraordinary it is that Antony, swaggering swordsman and rev-eler, should sound momentarily like Hamlet! Eros is not Polonius, but then Antony is not being parodistic. Overhearing his own puzzlement, as to whether Eros still recognizes him as Antony, the hero broods upon his cloudlike wavering of self-identity. Antony's doubt is the consequence not of a single reversal, but of the entire process of transformation he has undergone throughout four acts of dissolution, preludes to his suicide. This dying music is the most prolonged in Shakespeare, and may be the richest study of the nostalgias given us by any of the plays. It is another of the great Shakespearean inventions, a funeral music so prolonged and var-ied as to have no rival in all subsequent Western literature. To sustain our involvement, Shakespeare must persuade himself, and us, that his Herculean hero is grand enough to merit these obsequies. Plutarch's Antony could never provoke such magnificence. Shakespeare shows us that a world goes down with Antony, and has Octavius say it best:

> The breaking of so great a thing should make
> A greater crack. The round world
> Should have shook lions into civil streets,
> And citizens to their dens. The death of Antony
> Is not a single doom; in the name lay
> A moiety of the world.
>
> [V.i.14–19]

Octavius's "moiety" is the Eastern half of the Roman world, but the breaking here relates more to a temporal than a spatial entity. With Antony's death, the age of Julius Caesar and of Pompey is over, an age that began with the death of Alexander the Great. For Shakespeare, it is the Herculean or heroic age, and, as I have remarked, Antony—in the play—is already archaic, reflective of a time when charismatic flamboyance still could overcome every obstacle. A demagogue and brutal politician as well as a conqueror, Antony was Shakespeare's final triumph over Marlowe's shouting cartoon, Tamburlaine the Great. Iago undid Barabas, Jew of Malta; Antony outshines Tamburlaine, and Prospero will transcend Doctor Faustus, as Shakespeare sweeps Marlowe off the boards. Antony's death, ironically bungled to begin with, is allowed to achieve an absolute music in contradistinction to Tamburlaine's pathetic defiance of the necessity of dying. And yet I do not believe that audiences receive Antony's death as tragic: this is not the death of Hamlet or of Lear, or the death of Falstaff as related by Mistress Quickly in *Henry V.* There is immense pathos when Antony dies, desperately trying to give Cleopatra sound advice, and recovering something of his dignity, largely through his authentic concern for her. Whether in some sense he has been dying since the play opens we well may wonder, and a four-act decline and fall necessarily disperses any tragic effect upon us. Still, Shakespeare is careful to show us the gap cut in reality by Antony's death—most of all for Cleopatra, but for everyone else in the drama as well.

Is she deceived? Are they? As with Falstaff and with Hamlet, though Antony is not of their surpassing splendor, such questions return us to a central question in Shakespeare: What is the value of personality, particularly when the power of personality is as palpable as it is in Antony? The fate of Antony is catastrophic, because he is so often humiliated before he dies, while Cleopatra transcends any potential for humiliation by her ritually measured death. And yet Antony's personality is a Shakespearean triumph: this Herculean hero's intricate balance of qualities hardly could be more persuasively represented. Marvelous as Antony's most characteristic gestures can be, the audience shares in the play's given premise, which is that Antony's vitality exceeds his actions, even when these are rancid. Hamlet's infinite charisma, because it is intellectual and spiritual, is beyond Antony's charismatic endowment, but Hamlet is isolated, except for Horatio. Antony is the grandest of Shakespeare's captains—Othello and Coriolanus included—because his personality dominates every aspect of his world, even the consciousness of his enemy Octavius. And that personality, like Cleopatra's, is exuberantly comic: extraordinarily, this tragedy is funnier than any of the great Shakespearean comedies. Shakespeare's genius, remorseless in *Lear*, *Othello*, and *Macbeth*, totally and wonderfully indulges itself in *Antony and Cleopatra*, which is certainly the richest of all the thirty-nine plays. Poetry itself constitutes much of that wealth, and the personalities of Antony and of Cleopatra constitute a great poem, Herculean and erotic, each an idea of order in that a violent disorder is also an order. Cleopatra, having more mind, wit, and guile, is closer, as I've remarked, to Falstaff, but Antony surpasses everyone in the essential gaudiness of his poetry. I cannot believe that any other male character in Shakespeare so fascinated his playwright, not even Hamlet and Falstaff. Antony is Shakespeare's desire to be different, his wish to be elsewhere: he is the *otherness* of Shakespeare's art carried to its farthest limit at representing the variety possible for a merely heroic male, whose inwardness is endlessly mobile, though lacking the intellectual force of Hamlet and of Falstaff. Gusto, comical and yet godlike, is the essence of Antony.

3

*Antony and Cleopatra,* as a play, is notoriously excessive, and keeping up with it, in a good staging or a close reading, is exhilarating but exhausting. Teaching the play, even to the best of classes, is for me a kind of glorious ordeal. Hamlet, Falstaff, Iago all demand an energetic response, but their plays have a few flats, or resting places. *Antony and Cleopatra* surges on, prodigal of its inventiveness, daemonic in the varied strength of its poetry. Critics rightly tend to agree that if you want to find everything that Shakespeare was capable of doing, and in the compass of a single play, here it is. I can think of no other play, by anyone, that approaches the range and zest of *Antony and Cleopatra.* If the greatest of all Shakespeare's astonishing gifts was his ability to invent the human, and clearly I think it was, then this play, more than *Hamlet* or *King Lear,* might be considered his masterwork, except that its kaleidoscopic shifting of perspectives bewilders us. A critical description or a performance of either Cleopatra or Antony seems doomed always to leave out too much, but Shakespeare would have it that way, as if he had grown impatient both of players and of audiences. A drama with a remarkable quantity of scene shifts, *Antony and Cleopatra* seems to have no minor or dispensable episodes or sequences, even when neither Antony nor Cleopatra is on stage. Janet Adelman sensibly argues that this augments the patterns of uncertainty in the play, and she suggests that Shakespeare deliberately makes aspects of both major characters opaque to us. This may be, and yet the converse is equally plausible; since no privileged perspective is granted to the audience, the dramatic ironies proliferate and cannot be controlled by us. The uncertainties multiply because the highly histrionic protagonists themselves rarely know whether they are being themselves or acting themselves. Their characters are in that one sense transparent: they are role players, with all the world for audience. The world is always on their minds: the word *world* is a refrain throughout *Antony and Cleopatra.* If you cease to know when you impersonate yourself, then you are likely to seem more opaque than you are.

Falstaff dominates his plays, though scholarly critics crusade to reduce his magnitude. Hamlet encounters less critical resistance in pervading his drama, while Iago can be said to improvise *Othello* as he goes along. So varied and exuberant is *Antony and Cleopatra* that its protagonists never dominate; the world prevails, and the play, more than any other by Shakespeare, is itself a heterocosm. Cleopatra and Antony are parts of a world; they desire to *be* the world, and that alone is their tragedy. Octavius wins because he represents Rome, and Rome will ingest much of the world. Shakespeare neither endorses nor protests the Roman imperialism; when the victorious Octavius proclaims, "The time of universal peace is at hand," our own perspective will determine what degree of Shakespearean irony we hear. The new Caesar ends the play with an ambiguous tribute to his dead enemies:

> She shall be buried by her Antony.
> No grave upon the earth shall clip in it
> A pair so famous: high events as these
> Strike those that make them: and their story is
> No less in pity than his glory which
> Brought them to be lamented. Our army shall
> In solemn show attend this funeral,
> And then to Rome. Come, Dolabella, see
> High order, in this great solemnity.
>
> [V.ii.356–64]

What exactly is Octavius saying? Essentially, he is praising the glory of his own victory, while graciously allowing "pity" for the most famous, he thinks, of all couples. One could remark that he had hoped to exhibit at least Cleopatra, if not Antony also, in his triumphal procession upon returning to Rome, and his inability to do so is the actual pity of it, for him. But whether Shakespeare desires the audience to be so little receptive to the Roman victor, we cannot know. Even if history permitted it, how could we accommodate a vision of Antony and Cleopatra as Emperor and Empress first of the East, and then of the world? There would be no play, and Shakespeare exults in the opportunities afforded him by his two titanic exuberances, each rammed with life, and careless of the costs of their flamboyancies. The world's report, in regard to both, is of blemishes, and the audience cannot say that the world is wholly wrong. The great ones of this play—Antony, Octavius, even the younger Pompey—never speak for the world and the audience. It is their subordinates, military and at court, with whom we can identify, as in this dialogue between Antony's chief man, Enobarbus, and Menas, who serves Pompey:

> *Men.*          —You and I have known, sir.
> *Eno.* At sea, I think.
> *Men.* We have, sir.
> *Eno.* You have done well by water.
> *Men.* And you by land.
> *Eno.* I will praise any man that will praise me, though it cannot be de-
>      nied what I have done by land.
> *Men.* Nor what I have done by water.
> *Eno.* Yes, something you can deny for your own safety: you have been
>      a great thief by sea.
> *Men.* And you by land.
> *Eno.* There I deny my land service. But give me your hand, Menas: if our
>      eyes had authority, here they might take two thieves kissing.
>                                                   [II.vi.83–96]

"I will praise any man that will praise me" is, in context, great comedy, and out of it, a dark wisdom. Antony, Octavius, and Pompey cut their deals and divide up their world; the admirals and generals who execute their orders have a wonderful, instructive comradeship, voiding their leaders' grand rhetorics, and happily acknowledging land piracy and sea piracy. Their perspective is the world's: the quarrel between East and West, Cleopatra-Antony and Octavius, is a vast dispute between pirates on a sublime scale. The center of *Antony and Cleopatra* is neither the relation between the celebrated lovers, nor their struggle with Octavius: wavering and varied, the circles that serve them mingle perspectives with the audience. The world is the center, personified by everyone in the drama who is not the supreme commander of an empire, or at least of a faction (Pompey).

Octavia, dealt by her brother to Antony in political marriage, becomes an image of the world, as Antony watches her reluctant farewell to her brother:

> Her tongue will not obey her heart, nor can
> Her heart inform her tongue—the swan's down feather,
> That stands upon the swell at the full of tide,
> And neither way inclines.
>
> [III.ii.47–50]

The world, like Octavia, is powerless to choose between full tide and ebb tide: she, and the world, are "the swan's down feather" that "neither way inclines." Antony's metaphor, with its generous detachment, testifies to his endless capacity for empathy, and helps explain the love he evokes in his troops. Yet the metaphor's implications do not favor him, or Octavius, or Cleopatra. Enobarbus, told that Caesar has eliminated Lepidus and Pompey, again speaks for the audience:

> Then, world, thou hast a pair of chaps, no more;
> And throw between them all the food thou hast,
> They'll grind the one the other.
>
> [III.v.13–15]

"Chaps" here are "chops," jaws, and after devouring all the food the world affords they will seek to swallow one another. Like the world, something in us will not wholly take sides; Shakespeare takes great care to prevent this, for all the vitalism he assigns to Cleopatra and her Antony. When Antony returns from his final, desperate, and momentary victory against Octavius, Cleopatra greets him with her usual magnificence:

> O infinite virtue, com'st thou smiling from
> The world's great snare uncaught?
>
> [IV.viii.17–18]

It will be only a step beyond this that Antony and Cleopatra's fleet sells out to Octavius, provoking the final Herculean rage of Antony. What then is "the world's great snare," that must catch even the "infinite virtue," or matchless courage, of the descendant of Hercules? Is it the war, or a Cleopatran plot with Octavius, or simply the mutability of the world, its insatiability as an audience? The world does not choose Octavius, but in this most theatrical of plays we are given theater of the world, and the audience, glutted with Shakespearean richness, must finally be allowed its peace, in the death of its two heroes, before it returns for quite another play, a *Coriolanus* or a *Pericles*. If you require the world as audience, and Cleopatra and Antony will accept no less, then at last you must burn out, like Antony, or choose a private theater for your apotheosis, as Cleopatra does. No one has given more to the drama than Shakespeare, and here he is at his most prodigal, but he begins also to sense that the audience is a snare for him and soon will require less, rather than his more. Once Shakespeare loved the world; later in his career, Falstaff's is a scornful love, one that scoffs the world aside, and bids it pass. The poet of *Antony and Cleopatra* neither loves nor hates the world, nor the theater; he has begun to weary of them both. The glory of *Antony and Cleopatra* is neither its ambivalence nor its ambiguities: of all Shakespeare's dramas, it is the greatest as poem. It plays superbly still, when properly directed and acted, but as a reverberation it is too large for any stage, though still better perceived upon the right stage than in even the most acute study.

4

Cleopatra, indisputably the peer of Falstaff and of Hamlet, is the most vital woman in Shakespeare, surpassing even Rosalind. Antony cannot be fully known, because of Shakespeare's highly deliberate distancing. Cleopatra, even if the perspectives dissolved, would finally be unknowable anyway, for many of the same reasons that cause us to begin early on to know Falstaff, and then always to have to begin again. In the most brilliantly drastic of recent critical interpretations, Janet Adelman finds in Cleopatra Shakespeare's reimagining of "the female mystery of an endlessly regenerating source of supply, growing the more it is reaped." Upon that mystery, in Adelman's view, Shakespeare founds Antony's "fully masculine selfhood that can overflow its own rigid boundaries." These are impressive contentions, but do they not idealize? Antony dies well, with a loving concern for Cleopatra, but Shakespeare keeps the hero within the boundaries of Roman selfhood: "a Roman, by a Roman / Valiantly vanquish'd." Falstaff's death, playing with flowers and smiling upon his finger's end, childlike and with a reverberation of the Twenty-third Psalm, overflows all boundaries, though some critics (Wyndham Lewis, Auden, and also Empson) have questioned whether Falstaff's selfhood was fully masculine. A good Roman death, Antony's, but it resembles more the deaths of Brutus and Cassius than those of Falstaff and of the transcendent Hamlet. Perhaps one could agree that Cleopatra indeed endlessly regenerates herself, but her power is not transferable, whether to Antony or to the audience.

Shakespeare invented our realization that we grow most aware of lovers only when our distance from them suddenly increases, and that when we have lost them, particularly to death, we can be visited by an ecstasy that masks as their enlargement but actually constitutes a reduction. Proust was Shakespeare's greatest pupil in this ironic process, when Albertine becomes the narrator's Antony, a lost and enigmatic sublime. Some commentators observe that Cleopatra is only in love with Antony throughout Act V, when he is dead. That seems to me a little unkind, but her devotion to him does not begin to touch its height until the end of Act IV, when he dies, rather cumbersomely, in her arms. As a politician and as a dynastic ruler, she has strong concerns for Egypt and for her children, considerations set aside when she ponders the consequences, for Egypt and for them, of her enduring the humiliation of being exhibited to the males of Rome. Historically (according to Plutarch), Octavius executed only Antony's eldest son, but in Act V, Scene ii, lines 123–32, Octavius threatens Cleopatra with the destruction of all her children if she thwarts his triumph by her suicide. Despite Hollywood's gaudy depictions of Roman triumphs, many of us still lack the realization of the ordeals these constituted for defeated monarchs and generals, exposed first to the viciousness of the populace and then to the likelihood of brutal executions. Cleopatra, in Octavius's plan, is not for execution, but is to become a perpetual circus act for his glory: "For her life in Rome / Would be eternal in our triumph." Shakespeare takes a particular zest in Cleopatra's rejection of this infamy:

> *Cleo.*                                    Now, Iras, what think'st thou?
>     Thou, an Egyptian puppet shalt be shown
>     In Rome as well as I: mechanic slaves
>     With greasy aprons, rules, and hammers, shall
>     Uplift us to the view. In their thick breaths,
>     Rank of gross diet, shall we be enclouded,
>     And forc'd to drink their vapour.
> *Iras.*                                    The gods forbid!
> *Cleo.* Nay, 'tis most certain, Iras: saucy lictors
>     Will catch at us like strumpets, and scald rhymers
>     Ballad us out o' tune. The quick comedians
>     Extemporally will stage us, and present
>     Our Alexandrian revels: Antony
>     Shall be brought drunken forth, and I shall see
>     Some squeaking Cleopatra boy my greatness
>     I' the posture of a whore.
>
> [V.ii.206–20]

Shakespeare must have known that the Roman theaters, like the continental playhouses of his own era, were not compelled to employ boys for women's parts; do we hear his ruefulness that his Serpent of old Nile had to endure the travesty of some squeaker boying her greatness upon stage at the Globe itself? A play that imagistically identifies Cleopatra with earth and water will allow her, at the close, to exult, "I am fire, and air," thus escaping Octavius, "the universal landlord." The world, let alone Octavius, wants its triumph over Cleopatra, but Shakespeare at last takes sides, and denies the world its sadism, by appropriating Cleopatra for his play's triumph alone. No one else in Shakespeare makes so fine an end, in a personal ritual of exaltation. We are moved when Fortinbras commands that

Hamlet's body be taken up for a military funeral, on the grounds that Hamlet would have been another Fortinbras or Hamlet Senior, an assumption absurd enough to arouse our irony even as we welcome an apotheosis at which we know Hamlet would have scoffed. Prince of ironies, he would not have begrudged the audience its comfort. Cleopatra's transmogrification is quite another matter; Shakespeare leaps to compose his most extraordinary dying music. But which is his Cleopatra? What precisely is being celebrated in her ritual?

Cleopatra dies as the representative of the ancient god-rulers of Egypt, though Shakespeare knew what we know, which is that she was wholly Macedonian in ancestry, being descended from one of the generals of Alexander the Great. Still, only the panoply of her dying is hieratic; its purpose is simple and unbearably poignant: reunion with Antony. Here her art is that of the dramatist; her elegy for Antony is only partly personal, since she laments lost greatness, her public passion:

> Noblest of men, woo't die?
> Hast thou no care of me? Shall I abide
> In this dull world, which in thy absence is
> No better than a sty? O, see, my women:
> The crown o' the earth doth melt. [*Antony dies.*]
> My lord?
> O, wither'd is the garland of the war,
> The soldier's pole is fall'n: young boys and girls
> Are level now with men: the odds is gone,
> And there is nothing left remarkable
> Beneath the visiting moon.

> [IV.xv.59–68]

"The odds is gone" means that value, which depends upon distinctions, has been lost, the fallen soldier's pole having been the standard of measurement. Cleopatra's longing for a lost sublime hardly indicates that we have a new transcendental woman replacing the histrionic masterwork we have known. She is still actress enough to play her last and greatest scene, for which the dead Antony is the occasion and provocation. This is not to question their closeness, now forever enhanced by his absence, but to renew our awareness that like Antony, and like Cleopatra herself, we cannot disentangle her passion from her self-portrayal. Shakespeare, cunning beyond man's thought, loads every psychic rift with ore, and we are left wondering by even her most poignant utterances:

> No more, but e'en a woman, and commanded
> By such poor passion as the maid that milks,
> And does the meanest chares. It were for me
> To throw my sceptre at the injurious gods,
> To tell them that this world did equal theirs,
> Till they had stol'n our jewel. All's but naught:
> Patience is sottish, and impatience does
> Become a dog that's mad: then is it sin,
> To rush into the secret house of death,
> Ere death dare come to us? How do you, women?
> What, what, good cheer! Why, how now, Charmian?
> My noble girls! Ah, women, women! Look,
> Our lamp is spent, it's out. Good sirs, take heart,
> We'll bury him: and then, what's brave, what's noble,
> Let's do it after the high Roman fashion,
> And make death proud to take us. Come, away,
> This case of that huge spirit now is cold.
> Ah, women, women! come, we have no friend
> But resolution, and the briefest end.

[IV.xv.73–91]

Where are the limits of the histrionic here? Cleopatra's audience is made up of Iras and Charmian, and the audience itself, but most of all she is now her own audience, since she lacks Antony, her most appreciative fan (herself excepted). Iris and Charmian, and we, are very moved by her, but perhaps she surpasses us, since she moves herself so extraordinarily that the effect itself becomes an added aesthetic grace. We cannot reach the inmost level of Cleopatra's ever-burgeoning inner self. That helps account for

Shakespeare's dismissal of inwardness, after its infinite development in the four high tragedies. Even with Macbeth we knew the limits of his self-dramatization, and could shudder at our involuntary identification with his powerful imaginings. With Cleopatra, we can never know where the performing self ends, and so we admire, while refusing identification. This does not lessen Cleopatra, but it estranges her, even where she most fascinates. Shakespeare knew what he wrought; as almost always, we are slow to catch up. Cleopatra's comic intensities vie with her erotic energies; to regard her as a tragic heroine loses too much of her. When a hapless messenger informs her that Antony has married Octavia, she remembers Antony's earlier declaration: "Let Rome in Tiber melt," and replies with: "Melt Egypt into Nile." Shakespeare does not show us Antony's return to Egypt, and to Cleopatra. We ought to surmise why, since their reunion belongs to their public history, and not to their private encounters, which exclude us. It may be that Shakespeare prefers to show us their strained relationship by events, including Cleopatra's catastrophic insistence upon taking part in the sea battle at Actium, and even more, her remarkable performance with Octavius's ambassador, Thidias:

> *Cleo.*                                Most kind messenger,
>     Say to great Caesar this in deputation:
>     I kiss his conquering hand: tell him, I am prompt
>     To lay my crown at's feet, and there to kneel.
>     Tell him, from his all-obeying breath I hear
>     The doom of Egypt.
> *Thid.*                                'Tis your noblest course.
>     Wisdom and fortune combating together,
>     If that the former dare but what it can,
>     No chance may shake it. Give me grace to lay
>     My duty on your hand.
> *Cleo.*                                Your Caesar's father oft,
>     When he hath mus'd of taking kingdoms in,
>     Bestow'd his lips on that unworthy place,
>     As it rain'd kisses.
>
> [III.xiii.73–84]

One suspects that this is not so much treachery to Antony as payback time, since Cleopatra can assume that Antony will storm in (as he does), order Thidias soundly whipped, and salute the Empress of Egypt as "half blasted ere I knew you," "a boggler" (an artist at shifting allegiances), and most nastily:

> I found you as a morsel, cold upon
> Dead Caesar's trencher: nay, you were a fragment
> Of Gnaeus Pompey's, besides what hotter hours,
> Unregister'd in vulgar fame, you have
> Luxuriously pick'd out. For I am sure,
> Though you can guess what temperance should be,
> You know not what it is.

[III.xiii.116–22]

They are too entangled to part, though they have bought and sold each other, and neither believes any longer that anything will end well for them. Their greatest mutual scene comes at the monument, where Cleopatra has taken refuge, and where the dying Antony is hoisted up to her. An astonishing medley of outrageous comedy and terrible pathos, their dialogue defies critical description:

> *Ant.* I am dying, Egypt, dying; only
>     I here importune death awhile, until
>     Of many thousand kisses, the poor last
>     I lay upon thy lips.
> *Cleo.*                 I dare not, dear,
>     Dear my lord, pardon: I dare not,
>     Lest I be taken: not the imperious show
>     Of the full-fortun'd Caesar ever shall
>     Be brooch'd with me, if knife, drugs, serpents, have
>     Edge, sting, or operation, I am safe:
>     Your wife Octavia, with her modest eyes,
>     And still conclusion, shall acquire no honour

Demuring upon me: but come, come, Antony,—

Help me, my women,—we must draw thee up:

Assist, good friends.

*Ant.*                         O quick, or I am gone.

*Cleo.* Here's sport indeed! How heavy weighs my lord!

Our strength is all gone into heaviness,

That makes the weight. Had I great Juno's power,

The strong-wing'd Mercury should fetch thee up,

And set thee by Jove's side. Yet come a little,

Wishers were ever fools, O, come, come, come.

               *They heave ANTONY aloft to CLEOPATRA.*

And welcome, welcome! Die where thou hast liv'd,

Quicken with kissing: had my lips that power,

Thus would I wear them out.

*All.* A heavy sight!

*Ant.* I am dying, Egypt, dying.

Give me some wine, and let me speak a little.

*Cleo.* No, let me speak, and let me rail so high,

That the false huswife Fortune break her wheel,

Provok'd by my offence.

                                        [IV.xv.18–44]

Cleopatra is never more outrageously funny, or more vulnerable to a moralizing perspective that distorts her beyond measure. Poor Antony wants a final kiss, but she is afraid to descend, which is understandable enough, except that her taste and timing are more than dubious in bringing Octavia into this grotesque and terrible moment. Bad taste and worse timing are transcended when Antony repeats his gorgeous line—"I am dying, Egypt, dying"—and begs for wine so he can "speak a little," only to have Cleopatra cry out, "No, let me speak," and then vault into a fustian rant, her most purely histrionic. Dr. Johnson angrily termed "That the false huswife Fortune break her wheel" a "despicable line," but the great moral critic did not want to catch the play's strange hilarity. Antony dies with as much dignity as he can summon up, in the face of a raving Cleopatra, and with the knowledge that he has bungled even his own suicide. The world is there, always, and Shakespeare negotiates a final division of honors between Cleopatra and the world in Act V, in which Antony, a great shadow's last embellishment, is more present by being wholly absent, grander in memory than when we have seen him on stage.

5

Never easy to interpret, Cleopatra in Act V is at her subtlest in her dialogue with Dolabella, whom she half-seduces, as is her style. She begins with her "dream" of Antony, a godlike catalogue that stresses his munificence: "His delights / Were dolphin-like, they show'd his back above / The element they lived in." This is the prelude to the crucial interchange that determines Cleopatra's suicide:

> Cleo. Think you there was, or might be such a man
>       As this I dreamt of?
> Dol.                    Gentle madam, no.
> Cleo. You lie up to the hearing of the gods.
>       But if there be, or ever were one such,
>       It's past the size of dreaming: nature wants stuff
>       To vie strange forms with fancy, yet to imagine
>       An Antony were nature's piece 'gainst fancy,
>       Condemning shadows quite.
> Dol.                          Hear me, good madam:
>       Your loss is as yourself, great; and you bear it
>       As answering to the weight: would I might never
>       O'ertake pursued success, but I do feel,
>       By the rebound of yours, a grief that smites
>       My very heart at root.
> Cleo.                      I thank you, sir:
>       Know you what Caesar means to do with me?
> Dol. I am loath to tell you what I would you knew.
> Cleo. Nay, pray you, sir,—

*Dol.*                        Though he be honourable,—
*Cleo.* He'll lead me then in triumph.
*Dol.* Madam, he will, I know 't.

                                                  [V.ii.93–110]

Dolabella, we sense, would be her next lover, if time and circumstances permitted it, but Shakespeare's time will not relent. In Dryden's *All for Love*, Dolabella and Cleopatra undergo a strong mutual attraction, and Dryden for good measure throws in a flirtation between Ventidius and Cleopatra. Shakespeare's Dolabella, an ambitious politician, as he was in Plutarch, is so smitten by Cleopatra's passionate grief that he risks his own career by confirming her nightmare vision of being led in triumph. She is at her canniest in the subsequent scene with Octavius, persuasively enacting her outrage at being exposed as holding back half her wealth from the conqueror. Thus assured that she intends to live, Octavius withdraws, and her opportunity for death and transfiguration is preserved. "Again for Cydnus, / To meet Mark Antony," she calls for her "best attires."

The summit of this magnificent play comes in the interlude with the Clown just before the apotheosis of Cleopatra's suicide, an interlude that sustains Janet Adelman's contention that Shakespeare's "insistence upon scope, upon the infinite variety of the world, militates against the tragic experience." Uncanny perspectives abound throughout *Antony and Cleopatra*, but the Clown's is the most unnerving. He dominates the interchange with Cleopatra, as her charm first melts his misogyny and then resolidifies it when he fails to persuade her against her resolve. Few exchanges in the world's literature are as poignant and as subtle as these, in which the Clown offers Cleopatra the fatal asp:

*Clown.* Very good: give it nothing, I pray you, for it is not worth the feeding.
*Cleo.* Will it eat me?

How difficult it is to categorize that childlike "Will it eat me?" Perhaps Cleopatra, before mounting into death and divine transfiguration, needs a final return to the playful element in her self that is her Falstaffian essence, the secret to her seductiveness. In the Clown's repetition of "I wish you joy o' the worm," we hear something beyond his phallic misogyny, a prophecy perhaps of Cleopatra's conversion of the painful ecstasy of her dying into an erotic epiphany of nursing both Antony and her children by her Roman conquerors. Her artfulness and Shakespeare's fuse together in a blaze of value that surmounts the equivocations of every mode of love in Shakespeare.

Cleopatra's best epitaph is more impressive for being spoken by Octavius, far unlikelier than Dolabella to be captured by the enchantress:

> she looks like sleep,
> As she would catch another Antony
> In her strong toil of grace.
>
> [V.ii.344–46]

Not at all "another Antony," Octavius surpasses himself in this tribute to her seductive prowess. By now, the audience very likely is, or should be, the world, and is crowded by multiple perspectives. "Will it eat me?" jostles with "I wish you joy o' the worm," and both are set a little to one side by our hope, against hope, that there is one more Antony for her to catch.

# PART VIII

# TRAGIC EPILOGUE

# 28

# CORIOLANUS

The insolence of power is stronger than the plea of necessity. The tame submission to usurped authority or even the natural resistance to it, has nothing to excite or flatter the imagination: it is the assumption of a right to insult or oppress others that carries an imposing air of superiority with it. We had rather be the oppressor than the oppressed. The love of power in ourselves and the admiration of it in others are both natural to man: the one makes him a tyrant, the other a slave. Wrong dressed out in pride, pomp, and circumstance, has more attraction than abstract right. Coriolanus complains of the fickleness of the people: yet, the instant he cannot gratify his pride and obstinacy at their expense, he turns his arms against his country.

—William Hazlitt

*C*oriolanus, more even than *Julius Caesar* and *Henry V,* is Shakespeare's political play. That interests me less than its experimental nature, since it appears to be a deliberate departure from the modes of the five high tragedies: *Hamlet* (1601), *Othello* (1604), *King Lear* (1605), *Macbeth* (1606), and *Antony and Cleopatra* (1606). Shakespeare turned forty after having written the last three of those plays in just over a year. *Coriolanus* (1607) has as its protagonist a battering ram of a soldier, literally a one-man army, the greatest killing machine in all of Shakespeare. That Coriolanus is not totally unsympathetic (whatever one's politics) is a Shakespearean triumph, since of all major figures in the plays, this one has the most limited consciousness.

Notoriously the victim of his dominating and devouring mother, Coriolanus is an overgrown child. Anywhere except upon a battlefield, he is, at best, a disaster waiting to happen. Confronting the mob of Roman plebeians, he is guaranteed to insult them into an absolute fury. Shakespeare, as Anne Barton brilliantly demonstrates, is careful to distinguish the Roman commoners of *Coriolanus* from the crowds in *Julius Caesar* or the followers of Jack Cade in *Henry VI.* Barton says of the plebeians in *Coriolanus:* "They care about motivation, their own and that of their oppressors, and they are by no means imperceptive." They are not a rabblement, and Shakespeare does not take sides against them. Caius Martius (to give Coriolanus his actual name) would be better suited as a general of the Volscians, Rome's warlike enemies, than he is as a Roman leader, an irony that Shakespeare enforces throughout. From Caius Martius's perspective, the common people of Rome deserve neither bread nor circuses. In their view, he is a menace to their survival. Shakespeare, as Hazlitt would not admit, allows some justice to the people's side of this clash. They are fearful and irascible, but Caius Martius is dangerously provocative, and they are more right than not to banish him. His worship of "honor" grants no value whatsoever to their lives. Still, he is more his own enemy than he is theirs, and his tragedy is not the consequence of their fear and anger, but of his own nature and nurture.

As noted before, in fourteen consecutive months Shakespeare had created Lear and the Fool, Edgar and Edmund, Macbeth and Lady Macbeth, and Antony and Cleopatra. Compared with that eightfold, in personality or in character Caius Martius scarcely exists. Had Shakespeare wearied of the labor of reinventing the human, at least in the tragic mode? There is little inwardness in Caius Martius, and what may be there is accessible neither to us nor to anyone in the play, including Caius Martius himself. What, then, was Shakespeare attempting to do for himself, as a dramatist, by composing *Coriolanus?* Norman Rabkin, in a lucid interpretation of the play, sees Martius as essentially congruous with prior tragic protagonists:

In accepting the name Coriolanus, Martius accepts public recognition for what he has done, and necessarily compromises himself.

Like Lear, Macbeth, Brutus, and Hamlet, Coriolanus makes us realize here how much the hero is created by what he has accomplished, defined by the events through which he has passed.

But are Lear and Macbeth, Brutus and Hamlet, so created and defined?
There is a substance in them that prevails; in contrast, Coriolanus is quite
empty. Lear's passion, Macbeth's imagination, Brutus's nobility, Hamlet's infinite consciousness precede accomplishments and outlast events. We cannot envision Coriolanus in any contexts or circumstances other than his
own, and yet he cannot survive his context or his circumstance. That precisely is his tragedy, and that, rather than politics, is Shakespeare's principal concern in this play. To invoke again Chesterton's phrase that always
haunts me, Shakespeare's most vital protagonists are "great spirits in
chains."

Coriolanus is in chains, because of his nature and his situation, yet he
is anything but a great spirit. Raised by his mother to be an infant Mars,
he always remains just that, despite his ceaseless drive toward autonomy.
When the crowd banishes him, he defies them in his most memorable
speech:

> You common cry of curs! whose breath I hate
> As reek o'th'rotten fens, whose loves I prize
> As the dead carcasses of unburied men
> That do corrupt my air: I banish you!
> And here remain with your uncertainty!
> Let every feeble rumour shake your hearts!
> Your enemies, with nodding of their plumes,
> Fan you into despair! Have the power still
> To banish your defenders, till at length
> Your ignorance—which finds not till it feels,
> Making but reservation of yourselves,
> Still your own foes—deliver you as most
> Abated captives to some nation
> That won you without blows! Despising

For you the city, thus I turn my back.
There is a world elsewhere!

[III.iii.120–35]

Out of context, this is magnificent; within the play, it may be more pathetic than heroic. Coriolanus should indeed have gone into exile; he might then have matured in "a world elsewhere." Instead, as Hazlitt noted with grim satisfaction, Coriolanus goes to the Volscians, and leads them against Rome, hardly an honorable enterprise, unless "honor" means only the battle prowess of the individual, whatever his cause. Anne Barton almost uniquely maintains that Coriolanus does find a home among the Volscians, because they are more archaic than the Romans and universally worship war. I find this puzzling, since the play's pragmatic point is that Coriolanus ends homeless: he cannot bear to return to Rome, and he cannot stay in the service of the Volscians. Barton's contention is that Coriolanus has learned the truth that the commons have rights also, but dies before he can "rebuild his life." Hazlitt seems to me closer to the play's realities when he observes that Coriolanus lives and dies in "the insolence of power." The tragedy of Coriolanus is that there is absolutely no place for him in the world of the commonal and the communal, whether among Volscians or Romans. But why Shakespeare chose to write so curious a tragedy is still the question I wish to address.


2


T. S. Eliot famously preferred *Coriolanus* to *Hamlet*, weirdly insisting that *Coriolanus* was Shakespeare's best tragedy. I assume that Eliot was being perverse, even if he sincerely believed that *Hamlet* was "an aesthetic failure." Shakespeare's rhetorical art is deliberately subdued in *Coriolanus*; on the scale of *King Lear* or *Macbeth* or *Antony and Cleopatra*, this later tragedy scarcely exists at all. It fascinates because it is so large a departure from the creative ecstasy of the fourteen months of composition just preceding. In my many years of incessantly teaching Shakespeare, I have encountered much initial resistance to *Coriolanus*, which for readers and playgoers is something of an acquired taste.

Read or seen in sequence with the high tragedies, *Coriolanus* may seem more problematical than it is. Shakespeare, here and in the evidently unfinished *Timon of Athens*, experimented with essentially unsympathetic protagonists, though his genius found ways of making them sympathetic despite themselves. Coriolanus is no Brutus; Roman patriotism counts for little to Martius, compared with a purely personal honor. Shakespeare had explored the uses of a protagonist's sense of outrage with the hero-villain Macbeth. Coriolanus's concept of his own honor has been outraged by his banishment, while Timon's outrage stems from an all-but-universal ingratitude. Both Coriolanus and Timon are outrageous, but because of their conviction that they have been outraged, we join ourselves with them at crucial moments. This is another of Shakespeare's originalities, another way of inventing the human.

Eugene Waith and A. D. Nuttall, in very different yet complementary ways, have alerted other critics to the remarkable vision of Coriolanus leading the Volscians on, which is conveyed by the Roman general Cominius to the fearful tribunes who exiled the Herculean hero:

> He is their god. He leads them like a thing
> Made by some other deity than nature,
> That shapes man better; and they follow him
> Against us brats, with no less confidence
> Than boys pursuing summer butterflies,
> Or butchers killing flies.
>
> [IV.vi.91–96]

Waith speaks of Coriolanus's "superhuman bearing," thus returning us to the paradoxes of this strange figure: at once a god and a child, an infant Mars indeed! Nuttall, in a suggestion I find extraordinarily useful for all of Shakespeare, points to the Hermetist myth of man as a mortal god in "like a thing / made by some other deity than nature." I have sketched this myth—of man as a mortal god—as Shakespeare's likeliest cosmology in my introductory chapters, and follow Nuttall in citing it again here. Coriolanus, "a kind of nothing," hopes to "stand / As if a man were author of himself / And knew no other kin." Because of his mother, and her peculiar nurture of him, this ultimately will not be possible for him. And yet his authentic heroism is his hermetic endeavor to be the mortal god Coriolanus, and not the perpetually infantile Caius Martius. Barren inwardly, almost empty, he nevertheless possesses a desperately heroic will.

That last sentence almost could refer to Iago, but Coriolanus is anything but a villain, even a hero-villain. He is so oddly original a character that description of him is very difficult. Kenneth Burke suggested that we regard this play as a "grotesque tragedy." *Timon of Athens* certainly fits that phrase, but the enormous pathos that Coriolanus provokes in us seems other than grotesque. Shakespeare subtly does not offer us any acceptable alternatives to Coriolanus's sense of honor, even as we are shown how limited and crippling that sense becomes when it is challenged. The hero's mother, his friends, and his enemies, both Roman and Volscian, move us to no sympathy whatsoever. No one, except perhaps T. S. Eliot, has been able to identify with Coriolanus. Hazlitt—who remarked, "We are Hamlet"—might also have insisted that only the Duke of Wellington could confuse himself with Coriolanus.

Coriolanus, I would venture, is Shakespeare's reaction-formation, or belated defense, against his own Antony, a much more interesting Herculean hero. Since *Coriolanus* was composed just after *Antony and Cleopatra*, Shakespeare would have been peculiarly aware of the discontinuity between the two Herculean protagonists. Antony, very much in decline, nevertheless retains all of the complexities, and some of the virtues, that made him a superb personality. Insofar as Coriolanus has any personality at all, it is quite painful, to himself as well as to others. Cleopatra, more even than Antony, touches and transcends the limits of personality. From *Coriolanus* on, Shakespeare retreats from personality: Timon is closer to Ben Jonson's satiric ideograms than he is to Shakespearean representation from Launce in *The Two Gentlemen of Verona* through Cleopatra. And the mode critics have named "Shakespeare's late romances" itself seems to take precedence over human mimesis: even Imogen, Leontes, and Prospero are on the border between realistic personality and symbolic being. Perhaps Caliban and Ariel are personalities, but then Caliban is only half-human, and Ariel is a sprite. Part of the immense fascination of *Coriolanus*, for me, is that in it

Shakespeare experienced a sea change, and abandoned what had been the center of his dramatic art. No one from Coriolanus on is a free artist of himself or herself. Cleopatra, an astonishing act of human invention, was Shakespeare's farewell to his richest gift, and I wish we could surmise why this was, or perhaps had to be. Was Shakespeare weary of his own enormous success at inventing the human? Inwardness, Shakespeare's largest legacy to the Western self, vanishes in Coriolanus, and never quite makes it back in later Shakespeare. Cleopatra's vast inner self dies no ordinary death; she is transmogrified, and so we are left with no occasion for grief or regret. One way of seeing the change in Shakespeare is to contrast Cleopatra's question regarding the fatal asp—"Will it eat me?"—with Coriolanus's "Alone I did it," his final vaunt to the Volscians. Cleopatra's whimsical, childlike question is endless to meditation, and charms us, and fills us with fresh wonder at her personality; Coriolanus's boast is childish, and its poignance is infinitely more limited.

In all questions as to his development, we return to surmise about Shakespeare, the most enigmatic of all dramatists. The poetry of *Coriolanus* is properly harsh, even strident, since so much of the play is tirade. Shakespeare is in perfect control of his form and his material, perhaps in too perfect a control. Not even Shakespeare can subdue *King Lear, Macbeth,* and *Antony and Cleopatra* to ordinary designs: wildness keeps breaking out. Lear and Edmund, Macbeth and Cleopatra, all get away from their creator, just as Falstaff, Hamlet, and Iago are instances of Hobgoblin run off with the garland of Apollo. There are no transcendental energies whirling about in *Coriolanus;* Caius Martius himself has very little mind, and no imagination whatsoever. The play is the assertion of an immensely professional dramatist over his *materia poetica*: we feel that Coriolanus does exactly what Shakespeare wants him to do. Shrewd and powerful as it is, *Coriolanus* is not one of the enlargements of life. It is almost as though Shakespeare had set out to defeat Ben Jonson upon his rival's own chosen ground, since *Coriolanus* is in many ways the work that Jonson failed to write in *Sejanus his Fall* (1605), itself an inadequate attempt to correct and overgo *Julius Caesar.* *Coriolanus* continues to move scholars and critics, but not the generality of readers and playgoers, who are less impressed by its perfection as neoclassic tragedy. Yet Jonson was never a shadow for Shakespeare, as Marlowe had been for so long, and more of a personal recoil from his own achievement has to be ascribed to the playwright of *Coriolanus*. Shakespeare had outdone himself in the five great tragedies; into that abyss of the self even he did not care to venture further. Starting back from inwardness gave him (and us) *Coriolanus*, which is surely the strangest of all Shakespeare's thirty-nine plays. I mean strangeness in a double sense: uncanniness and also a new kind of aesthetic splendor, reduced yet unique. Giving up a great deal, Shakespeare achieves formal perfection, of a sort he never repeated.

3

The pathos of the formidable Coriolanus augments whenever we, or Shakespeare, consider the hero in conjunction with his ferocious mother, Volumnia, who must be the most unpleasant woman in all of Shakespeare, not excluding Goneril and Regan. Since Volumnia, like everyone else in the play, has only an outward self, we have few clues as to how an early Roman matron became Strindbergian (a nice comparison by Russell Fraser). In Shakespeare's strangest play, Volumnia remains the most surprising character, not at all readily assimilable to your average devouring mother. She boasts of having sent Caius Martius off to battle when he was still very young (one remembers Othello as a child warrior) and she delights in blood, though it be her son's:

> it more becomes a man
> Than gilt his trophy. The breasts of Hecuba
> When she did suckle Hector, look'd not lovelier
> Than Hector's forehead when it spit forth blood
> At Grecian sword contemning.
>
> [I.iii.39–44]

This pathological grotesquerie cannot be far away from satire, like so much else in *Coriolanus*. With such a mother, Coriolanus, nasty as he can be, must be forgiven by the audience. I have never seen this tragedy played for laughs, like *Titus Andronicus*, but one has to wonder just what Shakespeare is at, as when the next hero-to-be, Coriolanus's son, is described at play:

> *Val.* How does your little son?
> *Vir.* I thank your ladyship; well, good madam.
> *Vol.* He had rather see the swords and hear a drum, than look upon
> his schoolmaster.
> *Val.* O'my word, the father's son! I'll swear 'tis a very pretty boy. O'my
> troth, I looked upon him o'Wednesday half an hour together. 'has
> such a confirmed countenance. I saw him run after a gilded but-
> terfly, and when he caught it, he let it go again, and after it again,
> and over and over he comes, and up again, catched it again; or
> whether his fall enraged him, or how 'twas, he did so set his teeth
> and tear it. Oh, I warrant how he mammocked it!
> *Vol.* One on's father's moods.
> *Val.* Indeed, la, 'tis a noble child.
> 
> [I.iii.53–67]

Tearing butterflies to shreds with your teeth ("mammocked it") may well be a good training for getting into your father's battle mood, but it will not recommend you to civil society. Possibly that is Shakespeare's point; the Roman rabble, in a dozen years or so, will have to contend with an-other Caius Martius. In the meantime, as the current hero marches home, his mother and his friend greedily count up his wounds, to be shown to the people when he stands for the office of consul:

> *Men.* True? I'll be sworn they are true. Where is he wounded? [*To the*
> *Tribunes*] God save your good worships! Martius is coming home:
> he has more cause to be proud. Where is he wounded?
> *Vol.* I'th'shoulder, and i'th'left arm: there will be large cicatrices to
> show the people, when he shall stand for his place. He received
> in the repulse of Tarquin seven hurts i'th'body.
> *Men.* One i'th'neck, and two i'th'thigh—there's nine that I know.

*Vol.* He had, before this last expedition, twenty-five wounds upon
   him.
*Men.* Now it's twenty-seven: every gash was an enemy's grave.

                                            *A shout and flourish*

   Hark, the trumpets!

                                            [II.i.140–56]

Can this be performed, except as comedy? Shakespeare modulates
quickly into the scene in which Coriolanus and the plebes banish one another, confrontations just over the border from comedy. It is difficult to
judge precisely how to take Volumnia, who owes a grim debt to Virgil's
frightening Juno. Shakespeare makes this lineage explicit when Volumnia
declines a supper invitation:

Anger's my meat: I sup upon myself
And so shall starve with feeding. [*To Virgilia*] Come, let's go.
Leave this faint puling, and lament as I do,
In anger, Juno-like. Come, come, come!

                                            [IV.ii.50–53]

Like mother, like son; he too sups upon himself and so shall starve with
feeding. This is not funny only because, like Juno in the *Aeneid*, it is so scary.
What is not at all comic, but at last truly tragic, is the confrontation between Coriolanus and Volumnia when she exhorts him to turn back as he
leads his Volscians against Rome:

*Vol.*                          There's no man in the world
   More bound to's mother, yet here he lets me prate
   Like one i'th'stocks.

                                            [V.iii.158–60]

Volumnia's most unpleasant moment, this transcends nastiness because
pragmatically it murders Coriolanus, as he informs his mother:

O mother, mother!
What have you done? Behold, the heavens do ope,
The gods look down, and this unnatural scene
They laugh at. O my mother, mother! O!
You have won a happy victory to Rome:
But for your son, believe it, O believe it,
Most dangerously you have with him prevail'd,
If not most mortal to him. But let it come.

[V.iii.182–89]

As tragedy, this seems to me more than grotesque, and perhaps its un-canniness places it upon the other side of tragedy. Janet Adelman, in a brilliant reading of this scene, concludes that "dependency here brings no rewards, no love, no sharing with the audience; it brings only the total collapse of the self, the awful triumph of Volumnia." Where there is no consolation, even if it is only the sharing of grief, can we still have the aesthetic experience of tragedy? In *Coriolanus* and in *Timon of Athens*, Shakespeare gives us the twilight of tragedy. Nothing is got for nothing, and the five great tragedies can be surmised to have cost Shakespeare a great deal. Reading *King Lear* and *Macbeth* attentively, or seeing them well performed (very rare), are shattering experiences, unless you are too cold or closed-off to care anymore. Writing *King Lear* and *Macbeth* is at the least a demonstration that you are neither chilled nor solipsistic. In the transition to *Coriolanus* and *Timon of Athens*, Shakespeare acknowledged that he had transcended a limit, and discovered he was as done with tragedy as with un-mixed comedy.

# 29

# TIMON OF ATHENS

Shakespeare appears to have abandoned *Timon of Athens*, for reasons still unclear. He never staged it, and parts of it are less finished than others. Some recent scholars assign several scenes of the play to Thomas Middleton, but their evidence is not at all persuasive, and one or two of them would be glad to give much of *Macbeth* to Middleton, which arouses absolute distrust in me. Rough as some of it is, *Timon of Athens* can be very effective in the theater. There is a marvelous score for it by Duke Ellington, which accompanied Shakespeare's text when last I saw it in performance, superbly acted by Brian Bedford. I find that the play stages better than it reads; it is intensely dramatic, but very unevenly expressed. Shakespeare gives over much of the later part of the drama to Timon's curses, which are considerably more pungent than Coriolanus's tirades. Perhaps the curses wearied the playwright; they tire one on the page, but Bedford thrilled with them in the theater. As with *Troilus and Cressida*, which also was never staged, Shakespeare seems to have underestimated his dramatic art. *Timon of Athens*, unlike *Troilus and Cressida*, is not a great poem, but the two plays work equally well in performance. Shakespeare was so adroit a professional man of the theater that he must have known both dramas were highly actable. Politics, as we saw, may have kept *Troilus and Cressida* off stage. With *Timon of Athens*, I suspect that Shakespeare experienced a personal revulsion at what he was finishing, and turned away from it to do some play doctoring upon what became *Pericles*, thus inaugurating his final mode of visionary dramas, or romances.

Though regarded as a tragedy, *Timon of Athens* is somewhere between satire and farce. Just as *Coriolanus* may have started as an overgoing of Jonson's *Sejanus his Fall, Timon of Athens* also seems to have begun as an attempt to outdo Jonson as moral satirist. Coriolanus and Volumnia, as I intimated, are not persons but Jonsonian ideograms; Timon is not even that, being a caricature or a cartoon. Several scholars have emphasized Timon's uniqueness in Shakespeare: he has no family connections. Without father, mother, wife, or child, or even a mistress, Timon also has no origins. We learn later in the play that he once saved Athens, with his sword and with his money. Evidently, Timon began as a soldier, and was once a general; where he gained his first fortune, we never are told. His attitude toward sexuality goes from initial indifference to later horrified recoil; the play, alone in Shakespeare, has no female roles whatsoever except for whores.

As Bloom Brontosaurus Bardolater, an archaic survival among Shakespearean critics, I do not hesitate to find an immense personal bitterness in *Timon of Athens*, including a fierce animus against sexual indulgence. Timon, when he raves to Alcibiades's whores, is outrageously obsessed with venereal infection, as Pandarus was in the Epilogue to *Troilus and Cressida*. There is an excessive fury that pervades *Timon of Athens*, a near-madness that transcends Timon's outrage at ingratitude. The distance that Shakespeare cultivated in *Coriolanus* has vanished in *Timon of Athens*; the play in some crucial respects is an open wound. As always, we know nothing about Shakespeare's inner life, and so we cannot know if the wound was his own. Yet in *Timon of Athens*, more even than in *King Lear*, Shakespeare anticipates the savage indignation of Jonathan Swift. The play exists for no other purpose but to attain that stance, though whether Timon's outrage is the manifestation of a defrauded idealist or of a gullible fool remains ambiguous throughout. Hazlitt, possibly reacting against Dr. Johnson's moral disapproval of Timon's prodigality, began the Romantic tradition of exalting Timon:

> . . . Timon, who neither loves to abhor himself nor others. All his vehement misanthropy is forced, up-hill work. From the slippery turns of fortune, from the turmoils of passion and adversity, he wishes to sink into the quiet of the grave. On that subject his thoughts are in-

tent, on that he finds time and place to grow romantic. He digs his own grave by the sea-shore; contrives his funeral ceremonies amidst the pomp of desolation, and builds his mausoleum of the elements.

Hazlitt's Timon is exactly contemporary with the poor daemon of Mary Shelley's *Frankenstein*, and this passage would serve equally well for Frankenstein's creature if it were moved from the Greek shore to the Arctic icecaps. This High Romantic Timon has been very influential, from Hazlitt (1816) through Swinburne (1880) and on to its culmination in G. Wilson Knight's *The Wheel of Fire* (1930):

In no other play is a more forceful, a more irresistible, mastery of technique—almost crude in its massive, architectural effects— employed. But then, no play is so massive, so rough-hewn into Atlantean shapes from the mountain rock of the poet's mind or soul, as this of Timon. . . . No technical scaffolding in Shakespeare has to stand so weighty and shattering a stress. For this play is *Hamlet*, *Troilus and Cressida*, *Othello*, *King Lear*, become self-conscious and universal; it includes and transcends them all.

It would be wonderful to believe this, but Wilson Knight's generous overpraise cannot be sustained by Shakespeare's text. I had the privilege, in my youth, of attending Wilson Knight's performance of selected scenes from *Timon of Athens*; the critic-actor invested Timon with all the sublimity of Lear, but the reverberation did not follow me out of the theater, and was heard no more. I have had sensitive students who associated Timon with Lear, but this cannot survive analysis. *Timon of Athens* is an amazing torso, powerfully expressionistic, yet Shakespeare evidently concluded that it was a mistake, and he was right. Playable as it has proved to be, it remains the graveyard of Shakespeare's tragic art. As a dramatized fable, with a burden, supposedly, of ingratitude, it would lack Shakespearean resonance except that the elegiac intensity recalls the great tragic sequence that Shakespeare created against the grain, since his native genius was for comedy. Falstaff and Rosalind came out of the primal exuberance of Shakespeare's being; Hamlet and Lear were painful births. *Timon of Athens* is anything but a culmination; its final mausoleum is also the resting place of the first great European tragedies since ancient Athens.

## 2

Timon is the most vivid cartoon in his play, and almost the only one who matters. There is his faithful steward, Flavius; Apemantus the Cynic, described in the list of characters as "a churlish philosopher"; and there is Alcibiades, much diminished from his appearances in Plato and in Plutarch. All the rest are sycophants, flatterers, and whores; not even Macbeth so centers his drama as Timon does. Coriolanus lacks inwardness, but not in comparison with Timon, who lacks not less than everything until he cascades into his first rage in Act III, Scene iv, when he instructs his steward to invite all the flatterers, leeches, and false friends to a final feast, which will consist of lukewarm water and stones in covered dishes. After throwing the water in the faces of his guests and pelting them out with stones, Timon at last touches a rancorous eloquence in his farewell to Athens:

> Let me look back upon thee. O thou wall
> That girdles in those wolves, dive in the earth
> And fence not Athens! Matrons, turn incontinent!
> Obedience fail in children! Slaves and fools,
> Pluck the grave wrinkled Senate from the bench,
> And minister in their steads! To general filths
> Convert, o' th' instant, green virginity!
> Do 't in your parents' eyes! Bankrupts, hold fast;
> Rather than render back, out with your knives,
> And cut your trusters' throats! Bound servants, steal!
> Large-handed robbers your grave masters are,
> And pill by law. Maid, to thy master's bed;
> Thy mistress is o' th' brothel! Son of sixteen,
> Pluck the lin'd crutch from thy old limping sire;
> With it beat out his brains! Piety and fear,

Religion to the gods, peace, justice, truth,
Domestic awe, night-rest and neighbourhood,
Instruction, manners, mysteries and trades,
Degrees, observances, customs and laws,
Decline to your confounding contraries;
And yet confusion live! Plagues incident to men,
Your potent and infectious fevers heap
On Athens, ripe for stroke! Thou cold sciatica,
Cripple our senators, that their limbs may halt
As lamely as their manners! Lust and liberty
Creep in the minds and marrows of our youth,
That 'gainst the stream of virtue they may strive,
And drown themselves in riot! Itches, blains,
Sow all th' Athenian bosoms, and their crop
Be general leprosy! Breath infect breath,
That their society, as their friendship, may
Be merely poison! Nothing I'll bear from thee
But nakedness, thou detestable town!
Take thou that too, with multiplying bans!
Timon will to the woods, where he shall find
Th' unkindest beast more kinder than mankind.
The gods confound—hear me, you good gods all—
Th' Athenians both within and out that wall;
And grant, as Timon grows, his hate may grow
To the whole race of mankind, high and low!
Amen.

[IV.i.1–41]

Long as this speech is, it would be difficult to parcel out in quotations, and indeed it comes as a rhetorical release, after three rather inadequate acts. Since Timon now will curse his way through two remaining acts, he will weary us, but this first outburst certainly has both powers and pleasures. Since Timon is only a caricature with a speech floating over his head in a balloon, it is perfectly legitimate to substitute Athens for London, and

the fortyish Shakespeare for the noble Athenian. London in 1607 is "ripe
for stroke," where all value will "decline to your confounding contraries; / And yet confusion live!" I don't mean to suggest that Shakespeare
like Timon is off to the woods, but the zest of civic denunciation is his and
not Timon's. When Lear curses, we are not likely to mistake the great king
for Shakespeare, because Lear's inwardness is endless, and we have been allowed to naturalize ourselves in it. Lear's passions are larger than our own,
and yet they are also our own; Timon's rages are wholly apart from us, and
Shakespeare has made not the slightest effort to personalize Timon for us.
More even than in *Coriolanus*, Shakespeare is in flight from tragedy and its
perpetually growing inner selves. When next we hear Timon roar, we are
little more persuaded that a distinct person speaks:

> O blessed breeding sun, draw from the earth
> Rotten humidity; below thy sister's orb
> Infect the air! Twinn'd brothers of one womb,
> Whose procreation, residence and birth
> Scarce is dividant—touch them with several fortunes,
> The greater scorns the lesser. Not nature,
> To whom all sores lay siege, can bear great fortune,
> But by contempt of nature.
> Raise me this beggar, and deny 't that lord,
> The senators shall bear contempt hereditary,
> The beggar native honour.
> It is the pasture lards the brother's sides,
> The want that makes him lean. Who dares, who dares,
> In purity of manhood stand upright,
> And say this man's a flatterer? If one be,
> So are they all, for every grize of fortune
> Is smooth'd by that below: The learned pate
> Ducks to the golden fool; all's obliquy;
> There's nothing level in our cursed natures
> But direct villainy. Therefore be abhorr'd
> All feasts, societies, and throngs of men!

His semblable, yea himself, Timon disdains.
Destruction fang mankind! Earth, yield me roots.

[IV.iii.1–23]

As a lifelong university teacher, I never forget "The learned pate / Ducks
to the golden fool." Brilliant and scabrous, this address to nature has a fine
edge of desperation to it, and is properly answered by the irony that, digging for roots, Timon finds gold:

Who seeks for better of thee, sauce his palate
With thy most operant poison. What is here?
Gold? Yellow, glittering, precious gold?
No, gods, I am no idle votarist.
Roots, you clear heavens! Thus much of this will make
Black, white; foul, fair; wrong, right;
Base, noble; old, young; coward, valiant.
Ha, you gods! Why this? What this, you gods? Why, this
Will lug your priests and servants from your sides,
Pluck stout men's pillows from below their heads.
This yellow slave
Will knit and break religions, bless th'accurs'd,
Make the hoar leprosy ador'd, place thieves,
And give them title, knee and approbation
With senators on the bench. This is it
That makes the wappen'd widow wed again:
She whom the spital-house and ulcerous sores
Would cast the gorge at, this embalms and spices
To th' April day again. Come, damn'd earth,
Thou common whore of mankind, that puts odds
Among the rout of nations, I will make thee
Do thy right nature.

[IV.iii.24–45]

Again the powerful cogency of this is indisputable, and it is difficult to
get out of one's head: "Come, damn'd earth, / Thou common whore of

mankind." Critics have pointed out the link to Lear's parallel diatribes that combine visions of financial corruption and of rampant sexuality, but Lear has the humanity to cry out for perfume to "sweeten my imagination." Timon, confronting Alcibiades' "brace of harlots," goes even further to indulge a poisoned sexual imagination:

> Be a whore still. They love thee not that use thee.
> Give them diseases, leaving with thee their lust.
> Make use of thy salt hours; season the slaves
> For tubs and baths; bring down rose-cheek'd youth
> To the tub-fast and the diet.
>
> [IV.iii.84–88]

Before surpassing even this, Shakespeare-Timon (what else can we truly call him?) urges Alcibiades to a grand general slaughter of London-Athens:

> That by killing of villains
> Thou was born to conquer my country.
> Put up thy gold. Go on. Here's gold. Go on.
> Be as a planetary plague, when Jove
> Will o'er some high-vic'd city hang his poison
> In the sick air. Let not thy sword skip one.
> Pity not honour'd age for his white beard:
> He is an usurer. Strike me the counterfeit matron:
> It is her habit only that is honest,
> Herself's a bawd. Let not the virgin's cheek
> Make soft thy trenchant sword: for those milk-paps,
> That through the window-bars bore at men's eyes,
> Are not within the leaf of pity writ,
> But set them down horrible traitors. Spare not the babe
> Whose dimpled smiles from fools exhaust their mercy:
> Think it a bastard, whom the oracle
> Hath doubtfully pronounc'd thy throat shall cut,
> And mince it sans remorse. Swear against objects.
> Put armour on thine ears and on thine eyes

Whose proof nor yells of mothers, maids, nor babes,
Nor sight of priests in holy vestments bleeding
Shall pierce a jot. There's gold to pay thy soldiers.
Make large confusion; and, thy fury spent,
Confounded by thyself! Speak not, be gone.

[IV.iii.107–30]

This is so sublimely outrageous as to cross over into the grotesque, as Shakespeare clearly recognizes. The satire begins to bite backwards, against Timon and his creator, when we hear the exuberant suggestion that the dimpled babe be minced "sans remorse." Shakespeare is not done with us, and returns to Timon's horror of sexuality. After urging Alcibiades's camp followers to "be whores still," Timon surpasses himself with a litany of venereal invective that makes me believe, with the late Anthony Burgess, that Shakespeare had endured something of this:

Consumptions sow
In hollow bones of man; strike their sharp shins,
And mar men's spurring. Crack the lawyer's voice,
That he may never more false title plead,
Nor sound his quillets shrilly. Hoar the flamen,
That scolds against the quality of flesh,
And not believes himself. Down with the nose,
Down with it flat, take the bridge quite away
Of him that, his particular to foresee,
Smells from the general weal. Make curl'd-pate ruffians bald,
And let the unscarr'd braggarts of the war
Derive some pain from you. Plague all,
That your activity may defeat and quell
The source of all erection. There's more gold.
Do you damn others, and let this damn you,
And ditches grave you all!

[IV.iii.153–68]

This hymn to syphilis is unmatched and unmatchable. Wilson Knight, carried away by a visionary enthusiasm, commends "the unity of his curses: he is violently antagonized by human health, bodily or social." Much as I still revere Wilson Knight, I blink in astonishment, and I would hope that Shakespeare also, whatever his possible agony, mastered this madness by expressing it so magnificently. In the power of Timon's utterance, we are halfway between scourging prophecy and self-satire, but that is Timon's perpetual dilemma, and the expressive genius of this extreme drama. Lear's curses, even at their wildest, maintained a certain royal decorum; Timon is beyond any restraints, social or political, and he has no inwardness to check him. What can we do with such hatred, particularly when Shakespeare has done nothing to foreground or otherwise account for Timon's zeal against sexuality? All of us doubtless respond to the denunciations of the crooked lawyer, and the false priest (flamen), and braggart nonsoldiers, but the graphic reductions of syphilis seem disproportionate to the sin of ingratitude. Shakespeare does little to distance us, or himself, from Timon. Alcibiades, though an honorable enough soldier, is certainly one of Shakespeare's few failures of representation; the charisma of Socrates's would-be lover is never located by Shakespeare. Where we might expect an Athenian Prince Hal or at least a Hotspur, we get an earnest plodder. That leaves only the Cynic philosopher Apemantus, but he also fails to inspire Shakespeare to much zest. Apemantus arrives, in order to see for himself whether Timon has become a true Cynic or merely a complainer. Wit deserts Shakespeare, as these two codgers rail away at each other, making us long for Rosalind, whom Apemantus parodies by offering Timon a medlar:

> *Apem.* The middle of humanity thou never knewest, but the extremity
> of both ends. When thou wast in thy gilt and thy perfume, they
> mocked thee for too much curiosity; in thy rags thou know'st
> none, but art despis'd for the contrary. There's a medlar for thee;
> eat it.
> *Tim.* On what I hate I feed not.
> *Apem.* Dost hate a medlar?

*Tim.* Ay, though it look like thee.

*Apem.* An th' hadst hated meddlers sooner, thou shouldst have loved
    thyself better now. What man didst thou ever know unthrift that
    was beloved after his means?

*Tim.* Who, without those means thou talk'st of, didst thou ever know
    belov'd?

*Apem.* Myself.

*Tim.* I understand thee; thou hadst some means to keep a dog.

*Apem.* What things in the world canst thou nearest compare to thy
    flatterers?

*Tim.* Women nearest, but men—men are the things themselves.

[IV.iii.301–22]


That is the height of their exchanges, which decline into shouting insults at each other. This has a certain liveliness on the stage, but yields little as language or insight.

Fortunately, Shakespeare rallies to grant Timon two final excursions
into eloquence before his apparently self-willed and mysterious death.
The first is his last benediction for Athens:


Come not to me again; but say to Athens,
Timon hath made his everlasting mansion
Upon the beached verge of the salt flood,
Who once a day with his embossed froth
The turbulent surge shall cover. Thither come,
And let my grave-stone be your oracle.
Lips, let four words go by and language end:
What is amiss, plague and infection mend!
Graves only be men's works and death their gain;
Sun, hide thy beams, Timon hath done his reign.

[V.i.213–22]


The two epitaphs Timon writes for himself are useless doggerel in contrast to that. When Cordelia and Lear die, we are more moved than Dr.

Johnson could tolerate; Timon's vanishing rests our ears, in or out of the theater. Shakespeare, a great self-critic, probably made an aesthetic judgment upon this play, and so dismissed it as largely unworthy of him. Perhaps he glanced back at the best lines spoken by a Poet at the play's start:

Our poesy is as a gum which oozes
From whence 'tis nourish'd. The fire i' th' flint
Shows not till it be struck.

[I.i.21–23]

Not enough of the fire of poetry is shown to redeem *Timon of Athens* from its furies. It was time for Shakespeare to embark upon the "unpath'd waters, undreamed shores" of his final, visionary phase.

# PART IX

# THE LATE ROMANCES

# 30

# PERICLES

Shakespeare was occupied with *Pericles* in the winter of 1607–8, though scholars are not able to define the precise nature of that occupation. The first two acts of the play are dreadfully expressed, and cannot have been Shakespeare's, no matter how garbled in transmission. We have only a very bad quarto, but the inadequacy of so much of the text is probably not the reason why *Pericles* was excluded from the First Folio. Ben Jonson had a hand in editing the First Folio, and he had denounced *Pericles* as "a mouldy tale." Presumably Jonson and Shakespeare's colleagues also knew that one George Wilkins was the primary author of the first two acts of the play. Wilkins was a lowlife hack, possibly a Shakespearean hanger-on, and Shakespeare may have outlined Acts I and II to Wilkins and told him to do the writing. Even by the standards of Shakespeare's London, Wilkins was an unsavory fellow—a whoremonger, in fact, a very relevant occupation for a coauthor of *Pericles*, though the superb brothel scenes are Shakespeare's work.

*Pericles* is not only uneven (and mutilated) but very peculiar in genre. It features choral recitations by a presenter, the medieval poet John Gower, who is atrocious in the first two acts but improves markedly thereafter. The play resorts to frequent dumb show, in the manner of *The Murder of Gonzago*, revised by Hamlet into *The Mousetrap*. Most oddly, it has only a sporadic continuity: we are given episodes from the lives of Pericles, his wife Thaisa, and their daughter Marina. The episodes do not necessarily generate one another, as they would in history, tragedy, and comedy, but Shakespeare had exhausted all of those modes. After *Antony and Cleopatra,* we have seen the retreat from inwardness in *Coriolanus* and in *Timon of Athens.*

It would be absurd to ask, What sort of personality does Shakespeare's Pericles possess? Libraries have been written on the personality of Hamlet, but Pericles has none whatsoever. Even Marina has every virtue but no personality: there cannot be that individual a pathos in the emblematic world of *Pericles, Prince of Tyre.* Shakespeare was not in flight from the human, but he had turned to representing something other than the shared reality of Falstaff and Rosalind, Hamlet and Cleopatra, Shylock and Iago. Pericles and Marina are a universal father and daughter; his only importance is that he is her father, who loses her and then receives her back again, and she matters only as a daughter, who suffers separation from her father, and then is restored to him. I am not suggesting that they are archetypes or symbols, but only that their relationship is all that interests Shakespeare. Lear is everything and nothing in himself, and Cordelia, in much briefer compass, also contains multitudes. Pericles is just real enough to suffer trauma, and Marina is strong enough to resist being debauched, but both scarcely exist as will, cognition, desire. They are not even passive beings. In that sense alone, the jealous Ben Jonson was right: Pericles and Marina are figures in a moldy tale, an old story always being retold.

Both performances of *Pericles* that I have attended, some thirty years apart, were student productions, and both confirmed what many critics long have maintained: even the first two acts are quite playable. Except for the astonishing recognition scene between Pericles and Marina in Act V, and the two grotesquely hilarious brothel scenes in Act IV, very little in the play can be judged dramatic, and yet performance somehow transfigures even the ineptitudes of George Wilkins. This puzzles me, because bad direction and bad acting have converted me to Charles Lamb's party: it is, alas, better, especially now, to read Shakespeare than to see him travestied and deformed. *Pericles* is the exception; it is the only play in Shakespeare I would rather attend again than reread, and not just because the text has been so marred by transmission. Perhaps because he declined to compose the first two acts, Shakespeare compensated by making the remaining three acts into his most radical theatrical experiment since the mature *Hamlet* of 1600–1601. *Pericles* consistently is strange, but it has nothing as startling as the gap in representation that Shakespeare cuts into *Hamlet* from Act II, Scene ii, through Act III, Scene ii. But then *what* is being represented in the last three acts of *Pericles*?

Gower, speaking the Epilogue, tells us that Pericles, Thaisa, and Marina are "Led on by heaven, and crown'd with joy at last," so that the play represents the triumph of virtue over fortune, thanks to the intercession of "the gods," which must mean Diana in particular. Shakespeare, in his final phase, frequently seems a rather belated acolyte of Diana. No dramatist, though, would have understood better than Shakespeare how impossible it is to bring off a staged representation of triumphant chastity, virginal or married. Shakespeare's poem *The Phoenix and the Turtle* is exactly relevant on this subject:

> Love hath reason, reason none,
> If what parts, can so remain.

Whether the heart's reasons can be staged was always Shakespeare's challenge, and kept his art a changing one. How to represent the mystery of married chastity—"If what parts, can so remain"—remained a perplexity to the end. Shakespeare's Gower and *Pericles* so remove us from our world (except for the whorehouse scenes!) that the play indeed answers the Bawd's rhetorical question: "What have we to do with Diana?" (IV.ii.148).

Essentially, there are only two deities in *Pericles*, Neptune and Diana, and Diana wins. What are we to make of that victory? Neptune has oppressed Pericles, almost in the pattern of Poseidon's operations against Odysseus. Northrop Frye, noting the processional form of *Pericles*, remarks that the play's manner of presenting its action makes it one of the world's earliest operas, and then compares it to Eliot's *The Waste Land*, and necessarily also to Eliot's "Marina." I suppose that Diana's triumph is operatic enough, as is Marina's victory over both the staff and the clientele of the brothel. Frye's reading of the play, rather like Wilson Knight's more baroque interpretation, seems to me a little remote from *Pericles*'s curious and deliberate emptiness, akin to much of *The Waste Land* and Eliot's "Marina."

Such an emptying-out of Shakespeare's characteristic richness is a *kenosis* of sorts; the most sophisticated of all poet-playwrights surrenders his greatest powers and originalities—God becoming man, as it were. Frye calls *Pericles* "psychologically primitive," but this is true only in the sense of Shakespeare's knowing abnegation of inwardness, not in asking the audience for a primitive response. Our participation is not uncritical; we give up the Shakespearean lifelike, but not the Shakespearean selfsame. Gower is there to keep telling us that this is a play, but so redundant a message takes us back from Pericles and Marina not to "mouldy tales" and the authority of the archetypal, but to Shakespeare himself. The audience does not attend without the foregrounding of knowledge as to who the playwright is, and how different *Pericles* is from the more than thirty plays preceding it. Nor can anyone now read *Pericles* without the awareness that the creator of Hamlet, Falstaff, and Cleopatra is giving us a protagonist who is merely a cipher, a name upon the page. Wonder is always where one starts and ends with Shakespeare, and Shakespeare himself, as poet-playwright, is the largest provocation to wonder in *Pericles*. One suspects that the scenario for the play originated with Shakespeare, but that he had some distaste for what was to go into the first two acts and casually assigned them to a crony, Wilkins.

*Pericles* begins at Antioch, where its founder and ruler, Antiochus the Great, gleefully piles up the heads of suitors for his unnamed daughter, executing them for not solving a riddle whose solution would reveal his ongoing incest with her. Getting the riddle right, Pericles of Tyre flees for his life. After making a voyage to Tharsus, to relieve starvation there, the colorless hero suffers his first shipwreck, and then finds himself ashore at Pentapolis, where he marries Thaisa, daughter of the local king. All this out of the way, Shakespeare himself takes over to start Act III. Pericles and Thaisa, who is about to deliver their infant daughter Marina, are voyaging back to Tyre; Neptune acts up, and we rejoice to hear Shakespeare's great voice as Pericles invokes the gods against the storm:

The god of this great vast, rebuke these surges,
Which wash both heaven and hell; and thou that hast
Upon the winds command, bind them in brass,
Having call'd them from the deep! O, still
Thy deaf'ning, dreadful thunders; gently quench
Thy nimble sulphurous flashes!

[III.i.1–6]

That is Herman Melville's Shakespeare, though Ahab, if he spoke these lines, would convert them to defiance. Pericles is no Ahab, and endures the apparent death of Thaisa in giving birth to Marina. He then yields to the sailors' superstition that a corpse on board will sink the ship, meaning that his wife's coffin must go overboard. The farewell of Pericles to his bride also found its way to Melville's imagination:

A terrible childbed hast thou had, my dear;
No light, no fire: th'unfriendly elements
Forgot thee utterly; nor have I time
To give thee hallow'd to thy grave, but straight
Must cast thee, scarcely coffin'd, in the ooze;
Where, for a monument upon thy bones,
And e'er-remaining lamps, the belching whale
And humming water must o'erwhelm thy corpse,
Lying with simple shells.

[III.i.56–64]

Resolute to forfeit mimetic realism, Shakespeare never lets us know whether Thaisa is dead indeed. When, in the next scene, the lady is either revived or resurrected by Cerimon of Ephesus, where her coffin apparently has landed, she comes awake with the outcry "O dear Diana," thus invoking the particular goddess of the Ephesians. In the next scene, at Tharsus, commending the infant Marina's care and upbringing to the governor, Cleon, and his wife, Dionyza (whom Pericles had rescued from famine), the Prince of Tyre vows "by bright Diana" to remain unshorn until Marina be married. Subsequently, the restored Thaisa goes off to abide at the temple of Diana in Ephesus as the goddess's high priestess. The play's final reconciliations will conclude there, and I think it important to observe that Shakespeare avoids the patterns of Christian miracle plays in thus exalting Diana of the Ephesians. It is as though St. Paul never came to Ephesus: the divinity that haunts Shakespeare's late romances is located by him outside the Christian tradition. Shakespeare, in his dying, may have returned to his father's Catholicism, but like Wallace Stevens's reputed deathbed conversion, this would have been another instance of the imaginative achievement going one way and the personal life quite another.

When I think of *Pericles*, I remember first not the final scene in Diana's temple, where Thaisa is reunited with Pericles and Marina, but the two superbly vivid episodes of Marina's defiance in the brothel, and then the sublime recognition scene between Marina and Pericles on board ship at the onset of Act V. If the remainder of *Pericles* were worthy of these great confrontations, then the play would stand with the strongest of Shakespeare's, which, alas, it does not. Act IV, at its best and worst, reads like a Jacobean *Perils of Pauline*, with Marina always on the verge of being either murdered or raped. For the crime of outshining their natural daughter, Marina's guardians arrange for Marina to be slaughtered by the seaside. In the nick, pirates arrive and rescue her, but only to sell Marina to a brothel in Mytilene. The great Flaubert, in his final days, is reported to have been considering for his next novel the ideal setting "a whorehouse in the provinces." Returning to the spirit of the wonderfully rancid *Measure for Measure*, Shakespeare surpasses all possible rivals in the gusto with which he portrays the oldest profession:

*Pand.* Boult!

*Boult.* Sir?

*Pand.* Search the market narrowly; Mytilene is full of gallants. We lost too much money this mart by being too wenchless.

*Bawd.* We were never so much out of creatures. We have but poor three, and they can do no more than they can do; and they with continual action are even as good as rotten.

*Pand.* Therefore let's have fresh ones, whate'er we pay for them. If
there be not a conscience to be us'd in every trade, we shall never
prosper.

*Bawd.* Thou say'st true; 'tis not our bringing up of poor bastards, as I
think I have brought up some eleven—

*Boult.* Ay, to eleven; and brought them down again. But shall I search
the market?

*Bawd.* What else, man? The stuff we have, a strong wind will blow it
to pieces, they are so pitifully sodden.

*Pand.* Thou sayest true; there's two unwholesome, a' conscience. The
poor Transylvanian is dead, that lay with the little baggage.

*Boult.* Ay, she quickly pooped him; she made him roast-meat for
worms. But I'll go search the market.

[IV.ii. 1–23]

Only in the brothel scenes does Shakespeare's mimetic art return, wonderfully refreshing in the stiff world of *Pericles*. Pandar, Bawd, and Boult
have personalities; Pericles, Marina, and Thaisa do not. Before the formidable, indeed divine (being Diana-like) virtue of Marina, these splendid
disreputables must yield, while inaugurating a mode of irony frequently imitated since. Pandar presages the stance of Peachum and Lockit in Gay's *The
Beggar's Opera*: "If there be not a conscience to be us'd in every trade, we
shall never prosper." The wind of mortality blows upon overworked
whores and their Transylvanian client, and upon Shakespeare also (by
some accounts). Anticipating a high market—a wealthy prospective
client—for Marina, the Bawd makes the most poetic remark of the play: "I
know he will come in our shadow, to scatter his crowns in the sun." But
they do not know that Marina is in fact their nemesis. Men march out of
the brothel asking one another, "Shall's go hear the vestals sing?," and soon
enough the three worthies are in the position of the unhappy kidnappers
in O. Henry's "The Ransom of Red Chief":

*Pand.* Well, I had rather than twice the worth of her she had ne'er
come here.

*Bawd.* Fie, fie upon her! she's able to freeze the god Priapus, and undo
a whole generation. We must either get her ravish'd or be rid of
her. When she should do for clients her fitment and do me the
kindness of our profession, she has me her quirks, her reasons,
her master-reasons, her prayers, her knees; that she would make a
puritan of the devil, if he would cheapen a kiss of her.
*Boult.* Faith, I must ravish her, or she'll disfurnish us of all our cavalle-
ria, and make our swearers priests.

[IV.vi.1–12]

They are already defeated, and they know it; their comic despair exceeds their bravado, and neither they nor we believe that Boult will ever
ravish her. The governor of Mytilene, Lysimachus, arrives, intending to be
the designated taker of Marina's maidenhead, and departs in love with her,
and in revulsion at his own purpose. Boult next falls before her, and goes
forth to advertise to Mytilene that Marina will teach singing, weaving,
sewing, and dancing, after she is lodged "amongst honest women," as soon
she is. Clearly we have to regard Marina's chastity as being mystical or occult; it cannot be violated, because Diana protects her own. Marina, after
her family's reunion, can be married to Lysimachus, both because he now
knows that her social rank is at least as high as his own, and also because
Diana (in *Pericles*) accepts married chastity as an alternative for her votaress.
The comedy in the brothel scenes is among Shakespeare's most advanced;
only the irony of Marina's invulnerable status maintains the dramatic structure's coherence, since we observe three sensible sexual pragmatists confronted by a magical maiden whom they cannot suborn, that being well
beyond their power. They discover that indeed they have to do with Diana
(to answer the Bawd's earlier question), who necessarily undoes them.

What remains is the summit of *Pericles*, the magnificent recognition
scene between father and daughter, the one crucial event toward which the
entire play has been plotted. Pericles, having been told by Cleon that Marina is dead, is in trauma. Unkempt and barely nourished, he lies on the
deck of his ship, rather like Kafka's undead Hunter Gracchus on his death
ship. But Gracchus is the Wandering Jew or Flying Dutchman, caught for-

ever in cycle, and Pericles at last is on the verge of release from his passive yielding to a procession of catastrophes. Critics rather oddly compare Pericles and Marina to Antiochus the Great and his incestuous paramour, the nameless daughter, the supposed point being that Pericles and Marina evade incest. The danger is only in the critics, and not in the play, since it is Lysimachus who authorizes Marina to act as therapist for Pericles, and the reformed governor both is in love with the maiden and hardly desires to join himself to the profession of the gaudy trio of Pandar, Bawd, and Boult. It is in her mystical vocation as votaress of Diana that Marina approaches the comatose Prince of Tyre. Doubtless there is an implied contrast between incest and chaste father-daughter love, but it is too obvious for critical labor.

The 150 lines of the recognition scene (V.i.82–233) are one of the extraordinary sublimities of Shakespeare's art. From Marina's first address to her father—"Hail, sir! my lord, lend ear"—and his first traumatic response of pushing her back, through to Pericles's falling asleep to the music of the spheres, Shakespeare holds us rapt. I use that archaic phrase because of my experience as a teacher, observing the intense reaction of my students, which parallels my own. It is a lesson in delayed response that Shakespeare teaches, in this prolonged revelation of kinship. As the dialogue goes forward, it crests initially in Pericles's gathering awareness of the resemblance between his lost wife and the young woman standing before him:

> I am great with woe
> And shall deliver weeping. My dearest wife
> Was like this maid, and such a one
> My daughter might have been: my queen's square brows;
> Her stature to an inch; as wand-like straight;
> As silver-voic'd; her eyes as jewel-like
> And cas'd as richly; in pace another Juno;
> Who starves the ears she feeds, and makes them hungry
> The more she gives them speech.
>
> [V.i.105–13]

This begins by recapitulating the spirit of Marina's birth at sea, with the apparent death of Thaisa. But the accents of a man permanently in love with his wife's eyes, gait, voice break through in curiously Virgilian cadence (deliberate, I would think), and prepare us for a further tribute both to mother and to daughter:

> yet thou dost look
> Like Patience gazing on kings' graves, and smiling
> Extremity out of act.
>
> [V.i.137–39]

"Extremity" sums up all of Pericles's catastrophes; awe is a proper response to the tribute father makes to daughter, as her smile undoes the whole history of his calamities. Both here and ongoing, it is remarkable that Shakespeare never once allows Marina any affective reaction as the mutual recognition progresses. Pericles weeps as the names, first of Marina and then of Thaisa, are spoken by his daughter in her all-but-final lines in the play. But Marina remains grave, formal, and priestess-like, somberly saying, "Thaisa was my mother, who did end / The minute I began." By now we have accepted her occult status, and Pericles at least comes alive:

> O Helicanus, strike me, honour'd sir!
> Give me a gash, put me to present pain,
> Lest this great sea of joys rushing upon me
> O'erbear the shores of my mortality,
> And drown me with their sweetness. O, come hither,
> Thou that beget'st him that did thee beget;
> Thou that wast born at sea, buried at Tharsus,
> And found at sea again. O Helicanus,
> Down on thy knees! thank the holy gods as loud
> As thunder threatens us: this is Marina.
>
> [V.i.190–99]

It is as though, emerging from trauma, he requires a proof of his own fleshly mortality. His subsequent vision of Diana bids him on to Ephesus, and to a second scene of recognition, where he gratifies us by crying out to his wife, "O come, be buried / A second time within these arms." Here, at last, Marina expresses emotion, when she kneels to her mother: "My heart / Leaps to be gone into my mother's bosom." That formal kneeling somewhat qualifies her sentiment, since to kneel is not quite to leap into one's mother's arms. Still, Shakespeare has exhausted himself, and us, with the epiphany of Marina to Pericles, and wisely the play subsides with the announcement that Marina will marry Lysimachus, and the two will reign in Tyre. Pericles, after destroying Cleon and his wicked wife Dionyza, will take up royal rule in Pentapolis, where Thaisa's father has conveniently died. Gower comes on to wish us "New joy wait on you," and this inauguration of Shakespeare's late romances has reached conclusion. As M. C. Bradbrook observed, *Pericles* is "half spectacle and half vision." That is a very problematical formula, and Shakespeare took a high risk with this play. But what remained for him to accomplish? He had revived European tragedy, and vastly perfected comedy and dramatic chronicle. What remained was vision, tempered by the necessities of stage presentation. He went well beyond *Pericles* in the romances that followed it, but this play was the school where he learned his final art.

# 31

# CYMBELINE

A difficult play to stage, at least in our time, *Cymbeline* puzzles as frequently as it enchants. Romantic critics were greatly moved by it, and, as a belated representative of that critical tradition, I too am fascinated by this ornate drama. Hazlitt and Tennyson fell in love with Imogen, who almost alone in Shakespeare's late romances is represented with something of the inwardness that had been the playwright's greatest strength. Caliban, in *The Tempest*, indeed has his curious complexities, but he is only half-human, if that, despite the absurd recent tendency to render him as an ideological rebel, a supposedly black freedom fighter. Principal figures in Shakespeare's romances tend to be baroquely wrought in ways we do not yet wholly understand. Leontes in *The Winter's Tale* begins as what we now call a "case history," rather like Edmund Spenser's Malbecco, "who quite / Forgot he was a man, and Jealousy is hight." Shakespeare's anti-Faust, Prospero, is somewhat veiled from us (and himself) as long as he is the master of his hermetic art. When he breaks his staff and drowns his book, he deepens, but the play ends, and we can only surmise the personality of the restored ruler who will return to Milan, where every third thought shall be his grave. In *Cymbeline*, Imogen's husband, Posthumus, holds back from an inwardness that might deluge him, and remains a borderline figure, always on the verge of self-overhearing.

*Cymbeline* is a very uneven play, with much in it that can seem hasty or even perfunctory. Yet all of it does seem Shakespeare's, and sometimes we hear unmistakable overtones of his personal distaste for the London of 1609–10. Russell Fraser may overstate this when he observes that "in *Cymbeline* the gap narrows between the playwright and his players," but no biographer of Shakespeare matches Fraser at bringing the man and the work together, and unsavoriness hovers on the margins of the romances, though it rarely dominates. Something, though, is askew in *Cymbeline*, more than in the subsequent *Winter's Tale* and *The Tempest*. Dr. Johnson, perhaps annoyed by intimations of Shakespeare's perturbed spirit, famously dismissed *Cymbeline*:

> The play has many just sentiments, some natural dialogue, and some pleasing scenes, but they are obtained at the expense of much incongruity. To remark the folly of the fiction, the absurdity of the conduct, the confusion of the names, and manners of different times, and the impossibility of the events in any system of life, were to waste criticism upon unresisting imbecility, upon faults too evident for detection, and too gross for aggravation.

Johnson was both right and wrong: the incongruities are blatantly there, but they are more than usually deliberate, even for Shakespeare. It does jar us when Posthumus is exiled from ancient Britain to Renaissance Italy, but Shakespeare wants us to remark his freestyle audacity, his improviser's freedom from the scruples that sank without trace Ben Jonson's laborious tragedies. Jonson, in his Preface to the Quarto publication of *The Alchemist*, stressed the "great difference between those that . . . utter all they can, how ever unfitly; and those that use election, and a meane." It was an old quarrel between the two friends and rivals, and Shakespeare's response in *Cymbeline* was to utter all he could, more than ever, with sublime disregard for Jonsonian "Election." Nothing fits, anything goes in this wild play, where Shakespeare really does seem to let himself range. That may be why Imogen (happily) got away from Shakespeare and carries us back to his richly inward characters, even though *Cymbeline* is not that kind of a play.

But what sort of play is it? My question does not concern genre, since mature Shakespeare almost always is beyond genre. Though we classify *Cymbeline* with the other "late romances," it does not share much with *The Winter's Tale* and *The Tempest,* let alone with *Pericles.* Imogen has little in common with Marina, Perdita, and Miranda, beyond her restoration (with two brothers to boot) to her father at play's end. There are wonders enough in *Cymbeline,* and yet it is not a drama built upon wild surmise. No one in our century (myself included) thinks it as eminent a work as *The Winter's Tale* and *The Tempest,* Shakespearean masterpieces. Though it abounds with self-borrowings from earlier plays by Shakespeare, it scarcely resembles *Othello,* to which it owes most, particularly in its "little Iago," Iachimo, a mere trifler compared with the more-than-Satanic greatness of Othello's destroyer. Part of the fascination of *Cymbeline* is the reader's (and playgoer's) sense that something is wayward about this drama; it will not abide a steady contemplation. One cannot even be certain that it behaves like a play: the plot is a chaos, and Shakespeare never bothers to be probable. Nor can we say how Imogen found herself in the world of the villains Cloten and Iachimo, who exist on a different level of representation from her mimetic realism. Perhaps Shakespeare was in a contrary mood and decided that this time he would please himself, and yet others were then pleased as well. *Cymbeline* is more a dramatic poem than it is a play, and more than any other stage work by Shakespeare it seems to insist implicitly on the autonomy of the aesthetic. That may be why its Rome is at once ancient and modern, and its Britain both Jacobean and archaic. Shakespeare had wearied of history, even as he had come to the end of both comedy and tragedy.

2

*Cymbeline* begins with a conversation at court between two unnamed gentlemen, one a stranger, thus allowing Shakespeare to foreground the play. We are told that King Cymbeline had two sons, both abducted from their nursery some twenty years before and not seen since. His remaining child, Imogen, a daughter and heir to the throne, has declined the advances of her stepmother's loutish son, and instead has secretly married the worthy

Posthumus, an orphan brought up with her as a king's ward. Furious at this disobedience, Cymbeline (a cipher throughout the drama) banishes Posthumus, provoking Imogen's characteristic lament:

> There cannot be a pinch in death
> More sharp than this is.

> [I.ii.61–62]

Cloten, the wicked Queen-stepmother's nasty son, whose name admirably suggests his clottish nature, is introduced to us as a noisome braggart. So far, we could be in any corrupt royal court, like that of James I, Shakespeare's patron. Now, suddenly, we move to contemporary Rome, where the vicious Iachimo meets the exiled Posthumus, and wagers that he has the Italian art to seduce Imogen. Improbably, Posthumus accepts the bet, which stems from Iachimo's general estimate of womankind: "If you buy ladies' flesh at a million a dram, you cannot preserve it from tainting." We are given no time to wonder at Posthumus's folly before we are back in Britain, where the wicked Queen, proleptic of Browning's woman poisoner, believes she has obtained a death draught for Imogen, though it is merely a sleeping potion because of a doctor's sensible distrust of so obvious a Wicked Stepmother.

What, besides Imogen, keeps us attentive, Shakespeare must have known, but I cannot account for it. The egregious Iachimo (who should be played only by the late Danny Kaye) shows up at the British court, denounces Posthumus to Imogen as having been unfaithful to her in Rome, and offers himself to the princess as the means to her revenge betwixt the sheets. Shakespeare, who knows how impatient his audience is becoming, has his little Iago shift course when Imogen threatens to inform Cymbeline of this attempted assault. The audience can only blink in astonishment when Iachimo changes tactics and insists he was only testing Imogen, out of his supposed esteem for Posthumus. Since Imogen suddenly begins to accept the varlet's overpraise of her exiled husband, we might suspect that Imogen is mindless, or that Shakespeare is sublimely confident that we will accept any nonsense from him, which is almost true. We are given the absurd Trojan Horse strategy, when Iachimo urges Imogen to keep safe for him, in her bedchamber, a trunk supposedly containing precious gifts for the Roman emperor, but that actually will hold the bouncing Iachimo. When Imogen consents to this nonsense, we wrongly decide that she is beautiful though dumb, and rightly decide that Shakespeare's new motto might well be "Outrage, outrage, always give them outrage!"

Before Iachimo pops out of the box to survey the sleeping beauty and her chamber, it is useful to slow down and ask, Does Shakespeare get away with this? We could be back in the Plautine *Comedy of Errors*, or forward with the late Zero Mostel in the equally Plautine *A Funny Thing Happened on the Way to the Forum*. Does *Cymbeline* only lack more music, and an all-but-nude chorus line? Doubtless some director will attempt it, but is *Cymbeline*, then, a kind of zany romance, akin to the peculiarly effective erotic comedy in *Twelfth Night*? No one, at least since Swinburne, would consider *Cymbeline* a play as eminent as *Twelfth Night*, one of Shakespeare's twelve to fifteen or so masterworks.

Everything about *Cymbeline* is madly problematical, as Shakespeare, in a willful mood, evidently intended. Iachimo and Cloten are comic villains, Posthumus is a husbandly dolt, and Cymbeline is thickheaded enough to deserve his tiresomely wicked Queen. Imogen ought to be in a play worthier of her aesthetic dignity, but Shakespeare seems too troubled to give her the context she deserves, at least in the first two acts. Grotesquerie swirls about her, and yet Imogen remains always the sublime, antithetical to the grotesque. Radically experimental, Shakespeare establishes what might be a new mode of drama in *Cymbeline*, one we have trouble recognizing, since his remaining plays do not resemble it, and our modern theater has nothing like this juxtaposition of aesthetic dignity with the absurd. We have had absurdist dramas in profusion, but their protagonists tend to be as grotesque as their contexts, even in Pirandello. The enchanting Imogen, with whom Hazlitt and Tennyson fell in love, is not possible upon our stages.

Shakespeare gives a very vivid instance of antithetical technique in Act II, Scene ii, set in Imogen's bedchamber, where she falls asleep reading Ovid, and Iachimo, Jack-in-the-box, comes out of the trunk to slip a bracelet off her arm (without waking her!) and gloatingly takes inventory of both the room and the sleeping princess. He notes that the leaf of Imogen's book is turned down at the rape of Philomela by Tereus, but this comedian is no Ovidian rapist, but only Peeping Tom, who duly remarks, "On her left breast / A mole cinque-spotted."

Wilson Knight, wildly off even for this wild work, thought Iachimo comparable to Iago and Edmund, which is to read a symbolically idealized play, and not Shakespeare's *Cymbeline*. There is nothing in Iachimo that goes beyond the powers of any Jacobean playwright awash with Italianate villains. To call Iachimo even a "comic villain" overrates him; Iago and Edmund are abysses of nihilism, endless to meditation. Iachimo is a zany, like the ridiculously unpleasant Cloten. Critics have argued that he is shrewd enough to deceive Posthumus, who is not, alas, very clever, and who joins that large company of Shakespearean husbands and lovers totally unworthy of their women. Confronting Iachimo's "evidence" of Imogen's supposed infidelity, Posthumus becomes a parody-Othello, whose soliloquy at the end of Act II is interesting only for what it hints at in Shakespeare's own consciousness. Something is here too strong for Posthumus:

Is there no way for men to be, but women
Must be half-workers? We are all bastards,
And that most venerable man, which I
Did call my father, was I know not where
When I was stamp'd. Some coiner with his tools
Made me a counterfeit: yet my mother seem'd
The Dian of that time: so doth my wife
The nonpareil of this. O vengeance, vengeance!
Me of my lawful pleasure she restrain'd,
And pray'd me oft forbearance: did it with
A pudency so rosy, the sweet view on't
Might well have warm'd old Saturn; that I thought her
As chaste as unsunn'd snow. O, all the devils!
This yellow Iachimo, in an hour, was't not?
Or less; at first? Perchance he spoke not, but

Like a full-acorn'd boar, a German one,
Cried "O!" and mounted; found no opposition
But what he look'd for should oppose and she
Should from encounter guard. Could I find out
The woman's part in me—for there's no motion
That tends to vice in man, but I affirm
It is the woman's part: be it lying, note it,
The woman's: flattering, hers; deceiving, hers:
Lust, and rank thoughts, hers, hers: revenges, hers:
Ambitions, covetings, change of prides, disdain,
Nice longing, slanders, mutability;
All faults that name, nay, that hell knows, why, hers
In part, or all: but rather all. For even to vice
They are not constant, but are changing still;
One vice, but of a minute old, for one
Not half so old as that. I'll write against them,
Detest them, curse them: yet 'tis greater skill
In a true hate, to pray they have their will:
The very devils cannot plague them better.

[II.iv.153–86]

It is astonishing that the plodding, though virtuous, Posthumus utters this tirade, with its self-contradictory excesses. Why does Shakespeare assign this dreadfully unsympathetic outburst to Posthumus? Though gullible, Imogen's husband is supposed to be honorable, sane, and deserving of his widely acclaimed esteem, and of his superb wife and her devotion. Subsequently, this hero sends a letter to his servant Pisanio, ordering him to murder Imogen.

There is no way, one might think, that Posthumus is salvageable, though Shakespeare insouciantly does not care. Meredith Skura, in a brilliant application of psychoanalysis to the play's dilemmas, argues that Posthumus cannot find himself as a husband until he gets back to himself as a son, in relation to his lost family, available to him only in a dream-vision. As Skura notes, identities are very unstable in *Cymbeline* (I would except Imogen), perhaps more than elsewhere in Shakespeare: "The exaggerated complications in *Cymbeline* make us realize with even more force than usual that 'reality' finally lies in the enrichment, and the truth lies in the excess." I myself am more than wary of Freudian interpretations of Shakespeare, but Skura shrewdly psychoanalyzes the play's dilemmas, and not the play or its characters.

*Cymbeline* is a pungent self-parody on Shakespeare's part: we revisit *King Lear, Othello, The Comedy of Errors,* and a dozen other plays, but we see them now through a distorting lens. So skewed are our optics that I honor Skura's suggestion, though the wretched Posthumus seems to me unredeemable, and I find him acceptable only in his penultimate phase, when he longs for death, so that he can expiate his guilt in sentencing Imogen to the death she does not die. Even the sacred Shakespeare cannot have it every which way, and he redeems Posthumus at a high cost to the audience's sensibilities. Yet self-parody demands such expense, and so I wish to alter the question of *Cymbeline*'s "excess" to the question of Shakespeare himself. What was he trying to do for himself as a maker of plays by the heap of self-parodies that constitute *Cymbeline*?

3

Posthumus, even as an ideogram, is no fun. Shakespeare knew that a play must give pleasure, yet he portrays Posthumus as a very painful character, whose name refers both to having been ripped from a dying mother's womb and to being the only survivor of a family. What Imogen finds in Posthumus we are not shown, but if Cloten (rhyming with "rotten") is the alternative, that tells us enough. Shakespeare is his own worst enemy in *Cymbeline*: he is weary of making plays. The miasma of fatigue and disgust that hovers on the edges of the high tragedies and the problem comedies has drifted to the center of *Cymbeline*, where Shakespeare cannot bear to murder another Cordelia in the wonderful Imogen. After composing perhaps three dozen dramas, Shakespeare had not exhausted his resources, but he craved distancing from what he was doing. You can say of *Cymbeline* that nothing works or that everything does, because the play is a large ellipsis, with too much left out; Shakespeare would not bother anymore to put it in.

Posthumus is not a cipher, like Cymbeline, but he is rather too much of a self-parody for us to feel that Iachimo and Cloten are *his* parodies. What does it mean to parody the self in a nausea of the spirit, a question that returns me to Posthumus's soliloquy. The cry of "O vengeance, vengeance!" parodies an Othello who himself had become a parody of the Noble Moor. Posthumus adds to this a graver illness when he yearns to isolate "the woman's part in me," a yearning that parodies Lear in his madness yielding to the *hysteria passio*. Some scholars suggest that Shakespeare casts an ironic eye upon the satirists of his day when Posthumus, hardly a scribbler, vows literary revenge upon women: "I'll write against them, / Detest them, curse them." It cannot be accidental that those who detest and curse women are always the lovesick, or the depraved, or insane husbands whose dementia is their horror of being cuckolded. We never feel that Shakespeare himself catches the disease that afflicts Troilus, Othello, Posthumus, Leontes, and many others. And yet Posthumus reads to me as something bordering upon Shakespearean self-punishment.

Authorial self-parody is a defense, one not at all easy to categorize. *The Old Man and the Sea* is Hemingway's *Cymbeline;* Faulkner has too many to list. Through patriotic rant, in *Cymbeline* Shakespeare shockingly parodies his John of Gaunt, Faulconbridge the Bastard, and Henry V, by assigning the British defiance of Rome in Act III, Scene i, to the wicked Queen and the rotten Cloten. The Queen in particular is a Shakespearean self-chastisement for his earlier indulgences in patriotic bombast:

> That opportunity,
> Which then they had to take from's, to resume
> We have again. Remember, sir, my liege,
> The kings your ancestors, together with
> The natural bravery of your isle, which stands
> As Neptune's park, ribb'd and pal'd in
> With rocks unscaleable and roaring waters,
> With sands that will not bear your enemies' boats,
> But suck them up to th' topmast. A kind of conquest
> Caesar made here, but made not here his brag
> Of "Came, and saw, and overcame:" with shame

(The first that ever touch'd him) he was carried
From off our coast, twice beaten: and his shipping
(Poor ignorant baubles) on our terrible seas,
Like egg-shells mov'd upon their surges, crack'd
As easily 'gainst our rocks. For joy whereof
The fam'd Cassibelan, who was once at point
(O giglot fortune!) to master Caesar's sword,
Made Lud's town with rejoicing-fires bright,
And Britons strut with courage.

[III.i.15–34]

"Neptune's park" is a bit much, and the Queen's parentheses give away
the rest to outrageousness. The Roman armada's cracking like eggshells is
a fine grotesquerie, and Shakespeare's irony shows through "And Britons
strut with courage." Shakespeare's unwholesome mode continues in the
next scene, where the faithful servant Pisanio is properly shocked that the
wretched Posthumus commands him to murder Imogen, once she has set
forth upon the journey to Milford Haven, where Posthumus pretends he
will meet her. Each time Imogen speaks in *Cymbeline*, self-parody stops and
the beautiful voice that reinvented the human returns to us:

O, for a horse with wings! Hear'st thou, Pisanio?
He is at Milford-Haven: read, and tell me
How far 'tis thither. If one of mean affairs
May plod it in a week, why may not I
Glide thither in a day? Then, true Pisanio,
Who long'st, like me, to see thy lord; who long'st
(O let me bate) but not like me yet long'st:
But in a fainter kind. O, not like me:
For mine's beyond beyond; say, and speak thick,
(Love's counsellor should fill the bores of hearing,
To th' smothering of the sense) how far it is
To this same blessed Milford. And by th' way
Tell me how Wales was made so happy as

T' inherit such a haven. But, first of all,
How we may steal from hence: and for the gap
That we shall make in time, from our hence-going
And our return, to excuse: but first, how get hence.
Why should excuse be born or ere begot?
We'll talk of that hereafter. Prithee speak,
How many score of miles may we well rid
'Twixt hour and hour?

[III.ii.49–69]

Who could hear this without loving the speaker? And yet the overtones are dark: to wish for Pegasus is to risk the fate of Icarus, while the accents of a woman authentically in love beat against our memories of Posthumus's ghastly soliloquy. As Imogen departs to meet Posthumus, Shakespeare at his play's midpoint bestows upon us the marvelous theatrical coup of taking us to Wales, where we are placed before the cave of the rugged outdoorsman Belarius and his two adopted sons, the long-ago abducted princes Guiderius and Arviragus, all now known respectively as Morgan, Polydore, and Cadwal. Morgan salutes the glories of the hunter's life as being preferable to that of the courtier and the soldier, in which he suffered, but the young men are rueful, longing for the unlived life of power and battle. Polydore, heir to Britain though he does not know it, rather fiercely protests the difference between age and youth:

Haply this life is best
(If quiet life be best) sweeter to you
That have a sharper known, well corresponding
With your stiff age; but unto us it is
A cell of ignorance, travelling a-bed,
A prison, or a debtor that not dares
To stride a limit.

[III.iii.29–35]

The image of the confined debtor is a dark one for a king's son, and has the poignance here of a changeling's fantasy that is no fantasy. The

younger brother Cadwal is more poignant as he de-idealizes the hunter's
life:

> What should we speak of
> When we are old as you? When we shall hear
> The rain and wind beat dark December? How
> In this our pinching cave shall we discourse
> The freezing hours away? We have seen nothing:
> We are beastly: subtle as the fox for prey,
> Like warlike as the wolf for what we eat:
> Our valour is to chase what flies: our cage
> We make a quire, as doth the prison'd bird,
> And sing our bondage freely.
>
> [III.iii.35–44]

I suppose these laments are refreshing primarily because they have broken through the prevalent mode of self-parody. Morgan's bitterness, in response, speaks for Shakespeare's long observation, through his own life and
Southampton's, of the squalors of city and of court:

> How you speak!
> Did you but know the city's usuries,
> And felt them knowingly: the art o' th' court,
> As hard to leave as keep: whose top to climb
> Is certain falling: or so slipp'ry that
> The fear's as bad as falling: the toil o' th' war,
> A pain that only seems to seek out danger
> I' th' name of fame and honour, which dies i' th' search,
> And hath as oft a sland'rous epitaph
> As record of fair act. Nay, many times,
> Doth ill deserve by doing well: what's worse,
> Must court'sy at the censure. O boys, this story
> The world may read in me: my body's mark'd
> With Roman swords; and my report was once
> First, with the best of note. Cymbeline lov'd me,

And when a soldier was the theme, my name
Was not far off: then was I as a tree
Whose boughs did bend with fruit. But in one night,
A storm, or robbery (call it what you will)
Shook down my mellow hangings, nay, my leaves,
And left me bare to weather.

[III.iii.44–64]

This is purged of self-parody, and surely reflects Shakespeare's observations of a lifetime. Himself a usurer, he does not exempt his experiential guilt: "but know the city's usuries, / And felt them knowingly." The speech is wonderfully subtle: "The art o' th' court, / As hard to leave as keep." Antithetical wisdom takes away with both hands: "The fear's as bad as falling"; "fame and honour, which dies i' th' search"; "ill deserve by doing well." Belarius-Morgan is not a consciousness, unlike Imogen; the reflections can only be Shakespeare's own. Amiable relief as these three Welsh hunters are, Shakespeare grants them little individuality, and Act III, Scene iii, works largely as a theatrical surprise.

What follows in Scene iv is much finer, Imogen being the center. Having read Posthumus's murderous letter to Pisanio, she suffers a suicidal impulse, but recovers admirably, and agrees to the shrewd plan of yet another Shakespearean double self-parody. Her death will be reported to Posthumus, and disguised as a young man she will go forth, eventually to find service as a page to the Roman general Lucius, whose demand for tribute Cymbeline has refused. Another parodistic recycling is tacked on: Pisanio gives Imogen the wicked Queen's potion, advertised for seasickness or indigestion, but actually just a powerful sedative. Shakespeare overloads us with plot, but to some purpose: Imogen, for us to know her best, must be reunited with her lost brothers, as part of *Cymbeline*'s occult design of familial reconciliations. I suspect also that the plot complexities, luxuriantly crowded from now to the end, are themselves a parody, since after *Cymbeline* Shakespeare will seem as weary of plot as of characterization. *The Winter's Tale* has a much simpler design, and *The Tempest* is virtually plotless.

From Imogen's assumption of male garb onward, *Cymbeline* explodes into an excess of plot. The horrible Cloten departs for Milford Haven, maliciously attired in Posthumus's garments, determined to slay Posthumus and ravish Imogen. She happily stands in front of the Cave of Belarius, where she delights us with one of her best speeches:

> I see a man's life is a tedious one,
> I have tir'd myself: and for two nights together
> Have made the ground my bed. I should be sick,
> But that my resolution helps me: Milford,
> When from the mountain-top Pisanio show'd thee,
> Thou was within a ken. O Jove! I think
> Foundations fly the wretched: such, I mean,
> Where they should be reliev'd. Two beggars told me
> I could not miss my way. Will poor folks lie,
> That have afflictions on them, knowing 'tis
> A punishment, or trial? Yes; no wonder,
> When rich ones scarce tell true. To lapse in fulness
> Is sorer than to lie for need: and falsehood
> Is worse in kings than beggars. My dear lord,
> Thou art one o' th' false ones! Now I think on thee,
> My hunger's gone; but even before, I was
> At point to sink, for food.—But what is this?
> Here is a path to 't: 'tis some savage hold:
> I were best not call; I dare not call: yet famine,
> Ere clean it o'erthrow Nature, makes it valiant.
> Plenty and peace breeds cowards: hardness ever
> Of hardiness is mother. Ho! who's here?
> If any thing that's civil, speak: if savage,
> Take, or lend. Ho! no Answer? Then I'll enter.
> Best draw my sword; and if mine enemy
> But fear the sword like me, he'll scarcely look on't.
> Such a foe, good heavens!

[III.vi.1–27]

The charm of this is immense, and would enhance a better play than the parodistic *Cymbeline*, which retains the good taste never to render Imogen a parody. Her own gentle irony, replete with grace under pressure, is directed primarily against herself, yet does not spare her husband, her father, and males in general. Yet what is most wonderful here is tone; Imogen maintains the only distinctive voice in the play. Her concluding "Such a foe, good heavens!" in reference to herself, is the best comic moment in *Cymbeline*, where the glint rarely abandons Shakespeare's eye, and yet the almost ceaseless self-mockery rarely induces us to smile. Fortunately, the very next scene cheers Imogen, and her sympathetic audience with her. We know that she is being united with her brothers, though they do not even know that she is a woman. Shakespeare, at last fully himself in this play, writes with superb suggestiveness, as the three siblings fall in love with one another, all of them edging near the truth. Imogen's tribute to the natural courtliness of her brothers reinforces the ceaseless polemic against the nobility that is *Cymbeline*'s unexpected (and effective) undersong:

> Great men,
> That had a court no bigger than this cave,
> That did attend themselves, and had the virtue
> Which their own conscience seal'd them, laying by
> That nothing-gift of differing multitudes,
> Could not out-peer these twain. Pardon me, gods!
> I'ld change my sex to be companion with them,
> Since Leonatus' false.
>
> [III.vii.54–61]

Her speech hardly pays a compliment to the people either, and safely evades incestuous desire. When we go on to Act IV, Shakespeare seems to have steadied himself, and though the two final acts are even more baroque and parodistic, the edge of bitterness is less evident.

4

The audience sighs happily when Polydore-Guiderius, Cymbeline's older
son, beheads Cloten, and then salutes the absurd villain with a fitting
envoi:

> With his own sword,
> Which he did wave against my throat, I have ta'en
> His head from him: I'll throw't into the creek
> Behind our rock, and let it to the sea,
> And tell the fishes he's the queen's son, Cloten,
> That's all I reck.
>
> [IV.ii.149–54]

Since we know that the speaker will live to be King of Britain, that
probably allowed Shakespeare this audacity, for having the head of a
queen's son thrown to the fishes otherwise might have bothered the theatrical censor. Shakespeare intends the headless corpse of Cloten, clad as
it is in Posthumus's clothes, to be put to excellent use, when Imogen awak-
ens from a deathlike sleep into the delusion that her husband's remains lie
next to her. It seems odd that Imogen could mistake the anatomy of Cloten
for her husband's, but then she is in a state of shock. Grieved, she is carried off, kindly enough, by the Roman general Lucius, and will not speak
again until the long recognition scene that concludes the play.

Earlier, believing their friend dead, her bereaved brothers chant over
her what could be judged the finest of all the songs in Shakespeare's plays:

> *Gui.* Fear no more the heat o' th' sun,
>      Nor the furious winter's rages,
>    Thou thy worldly task hast done,
>      Home art gone, and ta'en thy wages.
>    Golden lads and girls all must,
>    As chimney-sweepers, come to dust.

*Arv.* Fear no more the frown o' th' great,
    Thou art past the tyrant's stroke,
Care no more to clothe and eat,
    To thee the reed is as the oak:
The sceptre, learning, physic, must
All follow this and come to dust.

*Gui.* Fear no more the lightning-flash.
*Arv.*      Nor th' all-dreaded thunder-stone.
*Gui.* Fear not slander, censure rash.
*Both.*     Thou hast finish'd joy and moan.
All lovers young, all lovers must
Consign to thee, and come to dust.

*Gui.* No exorciser harm thee!
*Arv.* Nor no witchcraft charm thee!
*Gui.* Ghost unlaid forbear thee!
*Both.* Nothing ill come near thee!
    Quiet consummation have,
    And renowned be thy grave!

                      [IV.ii.258–81]

Beautiful as this is, it is one of the darkest of elegies, centering on "fear no more" as the only consolation for dying. One of my students once re-marked that, for her, *Cymbeline* existed for the sake of this lyric. That it is the finest thing in a peculiarly uneven play, I would grant; it is also a clue to *Cymbeline*'s ethos, which I find both somber and nihilistic, resembling in this Shakespeare's *Funeral Elegy* for Will Peter, composed some two years later, but unfortunately with considerably less aesthetic splendor than is manifested here. Since *Cymbeline*, like *King Lear*, takes us back to archaic Britain, Christian attitudes toward immortality are irrelevant, though where in Shakespeare's plays they do make a difference, I do not know. Since the song "Fear no more" is too grand for its context (Imogen merely sleeps), I have no difficulty hearing in it Shakespeare's own stance toward dying, and regard it as the *locus classicus* of Shakespeare upon death. The two prime Shakespearean values are personality and love, both equivocal at the best, and here, with all else, they come to dust. This poem is a dark comfort, but its extraordinary aesthetic dignity is the only consolation we should seek or find in Shakespeare.

It is more cheering to move on to Act IV, Scene iii, where Cymbeline is told that the Queen is dangerously ill, mourning the disappearance of Cloten, and to the scene after, where Belarius and the still unrecognized princes vow to join their fellow Britons in the battle against the Roman invaders. Posthumus cannot ever show up without making me more mournful, and he is particularly silly in the soliloquy with which he opens Act V, as he contemplates the false "bloody cloth" sent him by Pisanio as evidence of Imogen's murder:

Yea, bloody cloth, I'll keep thee: for I wish'd
Thou shouldst be colour'd thus. You married ones,
If each of you should take this course, how many
Must murder wives much better than themselves
For wrying but a little? O Pisanio,
Every good servant does not all commands:
No bond but to do just ones. Gods, if you
Should have ta'en vengeance on my faults, I never
Had liv'd to put on this: so had you saved
The noble Imogen, to repent, and struck
Me, wretch, more worth your vengeance. But alack,
You snatch some hence for little faults; that's love,
To have them fall no more: you some permit
To second ills with ills, each elder worse,
And make them dread it, to the doers' thrift.
But Imogen is your own, do your best wills,
And make me blest to obey. I am brought hither
Among th' Italian gentry, and to fight
Against my lady's kingdom: 'tis enough
That, Britain, I have kill'd thy mistress: peace,

I'll give no wound to thee: therefore, good heavens,
Hear patiently my purpose. I'll disrobe me
Of these Italian weeds, and suit myself
As does a Briton peasant: so I'll fight
Against the part I come with: so I'll die
For thee, O Imogen, even for whom my life
Is, every breath a death: and thus, unknown,
Pitied, nor hated, to the face of peril
Myself I'll dedicate. Let me make men know
More valour in me than my habits show.
Gods, put the strength o' th' Leonati in me!
To shame the guise o' th' world, I will begin,
The fashion less without, and more within.

[V.i.1–33]

I quote this partly for its peculiar badness, but also to open again the question of Posthumus's unfinished personality. His repentance is in dubious taste, since he continues to believe that his wife betrayed him with Iachimo, but that supposed crime, once so hellish, is now "wrying but a little" and a "little fault." The wonder again is why Shakespeare so consistently labors to make Posthumus so dubious a protagonist, so estranged from the audience that we simply cannot welcome his final reunion with Imogen. It grates us to hear that the gods should have saved Imogen, so that she could repent, and it bothers me even more that Posthumus becomes a parody of Edgar, to be disguised as "a Briton peasant." *Cymbeline* continues to be a revenge by Shakespeare against his own achievements, and Posthumus also is best understood as a prime agent of that parodistic self-vengeance.

This self-parody continues in dumb show at the start of Act V, Scene ii, where Posthumus, in peasant disguise, vanquishes and disarms Iachimo, and then abandons him, in a debasement of the Edgar-Edmund duel. Iachimo, no Edmund and no Iago, blames his slander of Imogen for his defeat by a mere peasant, and begins to repent his career. By the time Belarius, the princes, and Posthumus have rescued Cymbeline, reversed a British

rout, and thoroughly crushed the Romans, we ought to be ready for anything, and yet Shakespeare sees to it that we are surprised, though his
originality for just this once is an equivocal reward, aesthetically considered. Posthumus, reverting to Roman garb, is captured, and awaits execution, in the willing spirit of expiation. He falls asleep in prison, and
Shakespeare grants him a double vision, first of his lost family, and then of
a descent of Jupiter, sitting upon an eagle and throwing thunderbolts at the
family ghosts. Only Wilson Knight, with his customary generosity, has attempted an aesthetic defense of this scene; he once told me that not to appreciate the ghosts and Jupiter was not to understand Shakespeare. Wilson
Knight was a great critic, and a religious Shakespearean, and I have reread
this scene continually, trying to persuade myself that it is not bad, but it is
awful, and I think deliberately so. Why Shakespeare turned to doggerel
here, I do not know, but he certainly made it as bad as possible. This, for
instance, is one of the ghostly brothers, praising Posthumus:

> *First Brother.* When once he was mature for man,
> in Britain where was he
> That could stand up his parallel,
> or fruitful object be
> In eye of Imogen, that best
> Could deem his dignity?
>
> [V.iv.52–57]

That would go very well in my favorite anthology of bad verse, *The
Stuffed Owl*, and has to be a parody of a parody. Something buffoonish
breaks loose in Shakespeare, and Jupiter descends to a verbal music that
sets a new, all-time low in divine epiphanies:

> No more, you petty spirits of region low,
>     Offend our hearing: hush! How dare you ghosts
> Accuse the thunderer, whose bolt (you know)
>     Sky-planted, batters all rebelling coasts?
> Poor shadows of Elysium, hence, and rest

Upon your never-withering banks of flowers:
Be not with mortal accidents opprest,
   No care of yours it is, you know 'tis ours.
Whom best I love I cross; to make my gift,
   The more delay'd, delighted. Be content,
Your low-laid son our godhead will uplift:
   His comforts thrive, his trials well are spent:
Our Jovial star reign'd at his birth, and in
   Our temple was he married. Rise, and fade.
He shall be lord of lady Imogen,
   And happier much by his affliction made.
This tablet lay upon his breast, wherein
   Our pleasure his full fortune doth confine,
And so away: no farther with your din
Express impatience, lest you stir up mine.
Mount, eagle, to my palace crystalline.

[V.iv.93–113]

There is no way that Shakespeare, keenest of ears, does not apprehend the absurdity of this. The puzzle is insoluble, if we insist on taking this seriously. But it is certainly an outrageous parody of the descent of any god from a machine, and we are expected to sustain it as travesty. Posthumus, waking up, finds a prophetic text promising good fortune, and reacts to it by a parody of Theseus in *A Midsummer Night's Dream*:

'Tis still a dream: or else such stuff as madmen
Tongue, and brain not: either both, or nothing,
Or senseless speaking, or a speaking such
As sense cannot untie. Be what it is,
The action of my life is like it, which
I'll keep, if but for sympathy.

[V.iv.146–51]

Shakespeare cannot stop himself, in his run-on self-parodies; we are suddenly back in *Measure for Measure* with the jovial Pompey, bawd turned executioner's assistant, exuberantly informing Barnardine that the ax is upon the block. A cheerful gaoler tells the more-than-willing Posthumus that he is about to be hanged:

A heavy reckoning for you sir: but the comfort is you shall be called to no more payments, fear no more tavern-bills; which are often the sadness of parting, as the procuring of mirth: you come in faint for want of meat, depart reeling with too much drink: sorry that you have paid too much, and sorry that you are paid too much: purse and brain, both empty: the brain the heavier for being too light; the purse too light, being drawn of heaviness. O, of this contradiction you shall now be quit. O, the charity of a penny cord! It sums up thousands in a trice: you have no true debitor and creditor but it: of what's past, is, and to come, the discharge: your neck, sir, is pen, book, and counters; so the acquittance follows.

[V.iv.158–73]

Compulsive self-parody does not exist elsewhere in Shakespeare; in *Cymbeline* it passes all bounds. Shakespeare probably cannot stop, or if he will not stop, that hardly alters the critical question: Why is the self-travesty so unrelenting? Posthumus is quite out of character in Act V, Scene iv; he seems to become a surrogate for Shakespeare in replies to the gaoler that welcome mortality. Just before the gaolers come for him, Posthumus is given the play's most obscure speech, which Dr. Johnson thought too thin to be understood, and yet its resonance disputes Johnson's judgment. I quote it a second time, for its importance:

'Tis still a dream: or else such stuff as madmen
Tongue and brain not: either both, or nothing,
Or senseless speaking, or a speaking such
As sense cannot untie. Be what it is,
The action of my life is like it, which
I'll keep, if but for sympathy.

[V.iv.146–51]

Shakespeare may be going beyond even his limits of expression, and I doubt Johnson's paraphrase, which does not confront: "which / I'll keep, if but for sympathy." Through Posthumus, I hear Shakespeare observing that the action of our lives is lived for us, and that the desperate best we can do is to accept ("keep") what happens as if we performed it, if but for ironic sympathy with ourselves. It is another of those uncanny recognitions in which Shakespeare is already beyond Nietzsche.

5

Act V, Scene i, of *Cymbeline* is almost five hundred lines in length, and rivals *Measure for Measure*'s final scene in complexity and delayed recognitions. The rivalry may be deliberate; self-parody is again an element, and the inverted moralism of *Measure for Measure*'s conclusion has its echoes in *Cymbeline*'s ending. Shaw, Shakespeare's jealous descendant, rewrote the final act as *Cymbeline Refinished*, particularly mangling the last scene. Imogen becomes a Shavian woman, unrecognizably so, and though I sometimes am baffled by the end of *Cymbeline*, I prefer bafflement to Shaw's mutilation. The last scene opens cheerfully with the announcement that the Queen, herself a parody of Lady Macbeth, ended "with horror, madly dying," like Queen Macbeth. Unlike that grand personage, *Cymbeline*'s queen dies saying she never loved her husband.

The Roman captives are brought in, with Lucius, his page Fidele (Imogen), Iachimo, and Posthumus among them. Since Belarius and the princes stand as honored victors among the Britons, we rightly expect a full panoply of recognitions, restorations, and explanations. Cymbeline compounds matters by taking Fidele as his own page. While Cymbeline and the disguised Imogen converse apart, Belarius and her brothers see "the same dead thing alive" but do not proclaim their find. Shakespeare turns us to Iachimo, who confesses and repents so profusely that we badly miss the true Iago, who defies the coming torture and will not speak. The wordy Iachimo all but recapitulates the entire play, and declines from being Iago's parody to being the travesty of a chorus. And yet Shakespeare's dramatic shrewdness has not abandoned him: Iachimo's collapse exposes how far below Iago's negative greatness we can descend and still find ourselves embodied in a villain. Iago, like Hamlet and Macbeth, is beyond us, but *we are Iachimo*. Our bravado, malice, fearfulness, confusion are all in Iachimo, who is not much worse than we are, and whom Shakespeare intends to spare. About two years before *Cymbeline*, Shakespeare would have attended Ben Jonson's masterpiece *Volpone*, where the savagely moralistic Jonson shocks us at the end of his play (or at least me) by harshly punishing Volpone and Mosca, two marvelously likable rogues. Iachimo's reprieve by Posthumus seems to me another of Shakespeare's smiling rejoinders to Jonson's ethical ferocity.

Shakespeare's self-travesty enters again when Posthumus knocks Imogen down even as she attempts to reveal herself to him, a clear parody of Pericles's roughly pushing Marina back when she begins to address him. Posthumus (surely Shakespeare's most tiresome hero) finally speaks eloquently when he knows he embraces his restored wife:

> Hang there like fruit, my soul,
> Till the tree die.
>
> [V.v.263–64]

Even Cymbeline is allowed memorable utterance, when all three of his children are given back to him at once:

> O, what, am I?
> A mother to the birth of three? Ne'er mother
> Rejoic'd deliverance more.
>
> [V.v.369–71]

The general pardon extended by Cymbeline to all his Roman captives follows fittingly upon this joy. But Shakespeare, seemingly unable to cease from travesty, here as at the close of *Measure for Measure*, confounds us by Cymbeline's further gesture, which reduces much of the play to sheer idiocy, confirming Dr. Johnson's irritation. After bloodily defeating the Roman Empire, in a war prompted by his refusal to continue paying tribute, Cymbeline suddenly declares that he will pay the tribute anyway! Shakespeare has shown us the valor and battle prowess of Posthumus, Belarius, and the princes, and now in a Falstaffian reversal he tells us again, "There's honour for you!" After that gesture, one wonders if Shakespearean irony does not also hover as Cymbeline begins the play's final speech:

> Laud we the gods,
> And let our crooked smokes climb to their nostrils
> From our blest altars.
>
> [V.v.477–79]

What do those "crooked smokes" of sacrifice praise in the gods? *King Lear* was a pagan play for a Christian audience, and undid all consolations, pagan and Christian. *Cymbeline*, more a mixed travesty than a romance, tempers its final reconciliations and restorations with wariness. No other play by Shakespeare, not even *Measure for Measure* or *Timon of Athens*, shows the playwright so alienated from his own art as *Cymbeline* does. *Troilus and Cressida* may be more overtly rancid than *Cymbeline*, but we seem to confront the author's sickness of spirit in Imogen's play, akin to the malaise that pervaded *Hamlet*. This is only another way of explaining why the context of *Cymbeline* is so alien to Imogen, who deserves to have been in a better play. Shakespeare hardly can repress his greatness, even in *Cymbeline*, but for once it is a power that he scarcely can tolerate or forgive.

# 32

# THE WINTER'S TALE

After the aesthetic self-wounding of *Cymbeline, The Winter's Tale* surges with Shakespeare's full power, though changed altogether from any of its earlier displays. I would judge *The Winter's Tale* to be Shakespeare's richest play since *Antony and Cleopatra,* and prefer it to the more problematical *Tempest.* Yet *The Winter's Tale* has its authentic difficulties, born of its strong originality. I ardently wish that the tradition had not termed Shakespeare's last plays his "romances," though nothing can change that nomenclature now. What the idea of "romance" gives with one hand, it takes away with the other, and Shakespeare, as I keep insisting, writ no genre. *The Taming of the Shrew* looks like farce, and yet it isn't; Falstaff's "histories" are tragicomedies; and *Hamlet,* "poem unlimited," is simply the norm, not the exception, among Shakespeare's plays. *The Winter's Tale,* like *Twelfth Night* and *King Lear,* is yet another "poem unlimited." We cannot come to the end of Shakespeare's greatest plays, because every time we achieve a new perspective, other fresh vistas appear that evade our expectations.

*The Winter's Tale* is a vast pastoral lyric, and it is also a psychological novel, the story of Leontes, an Othello who is his own Iago. Most critics also discover in it a mythic celebration of resurrection and renewal, a judgment I find a little unwarranted, though all the *materia poetica* that stimulates such interpretations is there in equivocal profusion. No poet, not even Shakespeare, purges time of its destructiveness, and winter's tales by their very name render homage to repetition and to change. Wilson Knight, subtly evading his own inveterate transcendentalism, judged the play's deity to be neither biblical nor classical, but rather what he called "Life itself," rightly testifying to *The Winter's Tale*'s naturalism, marvelous in its scope. *Realism* is a very difficult term to employ in discussions of imaginative literature, but to me *The Winter's Tale* is far more realistic than *Sister Carrie* or *An American Tragedy*. Dreiser is more the romancer, while Shakespeare is the truest poet of things as they are.

Ideologues do not cluster around *The Winter's Tale*, as they do around *The Tempest*, so neither performance nor commentary is much politicized, even in these bad days. I treasure my memory of seeing John Gielgud as Leontes in Edinburgh in the summer of 1951, superbly incarnating the madness of sexual jealousy, while subtly hinting that his paranoia stemmed from too close an identity with Polixenes. My inner ear still retains Gielgud's troubled rasping of the monosyllables that constitute Leontes's first words in the play, spoken to Polixenes, supposedly to delay his departure to his kingdom of Bohemia:

> Stay your thanks a while,
> And pay them when you part.
>
> [I.ii.9–10]

The crucial foregrounding of *The Winter's Tale* emerges from a famous declaration of Polixenes that describes the boyhood he shared with Leontes:

> We were as twinn'd lambs that did frisk i' the sun,
> And bleat the one at the other: what we chang'd
> Was innocence for innocence: we knew not
> The doctrine of ill-doing, nor dream'd
> That any did. Had we pursu'd that life,
> And our weak spirits ne'er been higher rear'd
> With stronger blood, we should have answer'd heaven
> Boldly 'not guilty', the imposition clear'd
> Hereditary ours.
>
> [I.ii.67–75]

What was this "innocence for innocence"? The "imposition . . . / Hereditary ours" has to be Original Sin. Does Polixenes know exactly what he is saying? Presumably he means that, could they have been cleared of the sin where they began, which Christianity insists is their sin, though it was done long before them by Adam, then they could have pled "not guilty" to heaven. But Shakespeare has Polixenes say more than he means, and an actual freedom from Adam's sin thus is suggested. The love between the two pre-adolescent boys seems not to have marked Polixenes, but it may well be the root of Leontes's madness. Leontes's wife Hermione playfully suggests that "Your queen and I are devils," hardly the opinion of Polixenes, but we wonder about Leontes, who asks his wife, "Is he won yet?" She jests about their courtship, but the equivocal quality is there again in Leontes's response:

> Why, that was when
> Three crabbed months had sour'd themselves to death,
> Ere I could make thee open thy white hand,
> And clap thyself my love; then didst thou utter
> 'I am yours for ever.'
>
> [I.ii.101–5]

There is a sly grudge still in that "crabbed" and "sour'd," and the image of the betrothal handshake immediately grates against the image of Hermione's hand extended to Polixenes in friendship. Leontes's aside inaugurates the true action of the play:

> Too hot, too hot!
> To mingle friendship far, is mingling bloods.
> I have *tremor cordis* on me: my heart dances,
> But not for joy—not joy. This entertainment
> May a free face put on, derive a liberty
> From heartiness, from bounty, fertile bosom,
> And well become the agent: 't may, I grant:
> But to be paddling palms, and pinching fingers,
> As now they are, and making practis'd smiles

As in a looking-glass, and then to sigh, as 'twere
The mort o' th' deer—O, that is entertainment
My bosom likes not, nor my brows. Mamillius,
Art thou my boy?

[I.ii.108–20]

Leontes, quite mad with the illness of sexual jealousy, represents a more
refined version of that grand malady than Othello manifested. Shakespeare, the world's obsessive authority on cuckoldry, perhaps was a little
mad on the subject himself. Proust, who went to school with Shakespeare
to perfect his own comedy of sexual jealousy, surpasses even Shakespeare
in the humor of the obsession, but not in the murderous madness of it:

Affection! thy intention stabs the centre:
Thou dost make possible things not so held,
Communicat'st with dreams;—how can this be?—
With what's unreal thou coactive art,
And fellow'st nothing: then 'tis very credent
Thou mayst co-join with something; and thou dost,
(And that beyond commission) and I find it,
(And that to the infection of my brains
And hard'ning of my brows).

[I.ii.138–46]

"Affection" here means both lustful desire and sexual jealousy, each active enough to encourage Leontes's deep need for betrayal. "Nothing" is the
key; the repressed longing for, and active horror of, betrayal by Hermione
with Polixenes is founded upon a nihilistic sense of the abyss of personal
nothingness. Nothing is but what is not, and dream yields an amalgam of
imposture and irreality. "Your actions are my dreams," Hermione will be
told by her husband. Leontes advances on both Iago and Edmund in his nihilistic worship of what is not. Shakespeare evokes both our horror of
falling into the hell of jealousy and our fellow feeling with Leontes's sense
of having been outraged, even though he alone is the outrager:

Gone already!
Inch-thick, knee-deep; o'er head and ears a fork'd one.
Go, play, boy, play: thy mother plays, and I
Play too; but so disgrac'd a part, whose issue
Will hiss me to my grave: contempt and clamour
Will be my knell. Go, play, boy, play. There have been,
(Or I am much deceiv'd) cuckolds ere now,
And many a man there is (even at this present,
Now, while I speak this) holds his wife by th' arm,
That little thinks she has been sluic'd in 's absence
And his pond fish'd by his next neighbour, by
Sir Smile, his neighbour: nay, there's comfort in't,
Whiles other men have gates, and those gates open'd,
As mine, against their will. Should all despair
That have revolted wives, the tenth of mankind
Would hang themselves. Physic for't there's none;
It is a bawdy planet, that will strike
Where 'tis predominant; and 'tis powerful, think it,
From east, west, north, and south; be it concluded,
No barricado for a belly. Know't,
It will let in and out the enemy,
With bag and baggage: many thousand on 's
Have the disease, and feel 't not.

[I.ii.185–207]

The wonderfully dreadful zest of this is infectious; the energy of Leontes's diseased sexual imagination is endowed by Shakespeare with an irresistible force. Male fear and resentment of women emerge with comic genius in the vicious eloquence of

That little thinks she has been sluic'd in 's absence
And his pond fish'd by his next neighbour, by
Sir Smile, his neighbour.

[I.ii.194–96]

Leontes, in his rage, gives all crazed husbands their permanent mottos: "It is a bawdy planet," and the vivid "No barricado for a belly." His nihilistic transport, at once a frenzy and an ecstasy, reaches its sublime in a litany of nothings:

> Is whispering nothing?
> Is leaning cheek to cheek? is meeting noses?
> Kissing with inside lip? stopping the career
> Of laughing with a sigh (a note infallible
> Of breaking honesty)? horsing foot on foot?
> Skulking in corners? wishing clocks more swift?
> Hours, minutes? noon, midnight? and all eyes
> Blind with the pin and web, but theirs, theirs only.
> That would unseen be wicked? is this nothing?
> Why then the world, and all that's in't, is nothing,
> The covering sky is nothing, Bohemia nothing,
> My wife is nothing, nor nothing have these nothings,
> If this be nothing.
>
> [I.ii.284–96]

Leontes's tonalities have a rising intensity matchless even in Shakespeare. Though he will subside into sanity and repentance in Act III, Scene ii, his enormous interest for audiences and readers is what vivifies the first half of the play. The second half will have Autolycus, and Perdita, but until we touch the seacoast of Bohemia (created to infuriate Ben Jonson), Leontes carries *The Winter's Tale*. Whether his madness or his nihilism counts as the truer starting point, he is one of Shakespeare's high priests of "nothing," a worthy successor to Iago and to Edmund. Frank Kermode rightly speaks of "the more intellectual torments of Leontes" as compared with the inarticulate sufferings of Othello. Leontes is intellectual enough to have become a nihilist, but why does Shakespeare also confer upon the King of Sicilia the dark distinction of being the outstanding misogynist in all of the plays? The alliance of misogyny and nihilism is one of the greater Shakespearean insights into male nature, and prompted aspects of Nietzsche's uncannier broodings. Leontes, in his greatest tirade, opens with "Is whispering nothing?" and then follows with ten more rhetorical questions before the word *nothing* returns in the twelfth question: "Is this nothing?" His answer will give us seven more nothings in three and a half lines:

> Why then the world, and all that's in't, is nothing,
> The covering sky is nothing, Bohemia nothing,
> My wife is nothing, nor nothing have these nothings,
> If this be nothing.
>
> [I.ii.293–96]

Leontes, nothing himself (as he secretly fears), beholds what is not there, as well as the nothing that is. Shakespeare's winter's tale gives us a mind of winter unable to cease its reductions until the deaths of others (deaths both real and apparent) shock it back to reality. I remember Gielgud, needing to cope with the decline of his role into endless repentance, playing Leontes in Act V with a kind of gingerly alertness that brilliantly suggested a man who fears sudden engulfment by a tidal wave of nothingness. Whether or not there is repressed homosexuality in Leontes's aberration, Shakespeare's principal clue to us for the king's jealous madness is the idea of tyranny, which is the judgment of Leontes's courtiers, and of the oracle of Apollo at Delphos:

> *Off.* [*Reads*] Hermione is chaste; Polixenes blameless; Camillo a true
>     subject; Leontes a jealous tyrant; his innocent babe truly begot
>     ten; and the king shall live without an heir, if that which is lost be
>     not found.
>
> [III.ii.132–36]

To see sexual jealousy and metaphysical nihilism as modes of tyranny has its own interest, but it still leaves dark the cause of Leontes's madness. Cause and effect are fictions, according to Nietzsche, who again follows in Shakespeare's wake. As our profoundest student of the dangerous prevalence of the imagination, Shakespeare takes a final step beyond Macbeth's proleptic genius in Leontes's phantasmagoria. Where there is nothing, everything is possible. Schlegel, made uneasy by this irrationality, presumed to lecture Shakespeare on his omission of some provocation for Leontes: "In fact, the poet might perhaps have wished slightly to indicate that Hermione, though virtuous, was too warm in her efforts to please Polixenes." Coleridge was nearer the mark in saying that Shakespeare's description of Leontes's jealousy was "perfectly philosophical," which I take to mean that Shakespeare had isolated the metaphysical basis of sexual jealousy, the fear that there will not be space enough and time enough for oneself. Proust charmingly compared the passion of the jealous lover to the zeal of the art historian. The tyranny of an insatiable curiosity becomes an obsession with the possible, in which one tries to fend off one's own mortality and thereby risks the hideous immortality of Spenser's Malbecco, whose fate Shakespeare certainly had pondered:

> Yet can he never dye, but dying lives,
> And doth himselfe with sorrow new sustaine,
> That death and life attonce unto him gives.
> And painefull pleasure turnes to pleasing paine.
> There dwels he ever, miserable swaine,
> Hatefull both to himselfe, and every wight;
> Where he through privy griefe, and horrour vaine,
> Is waxen so deform'd, that he has quight
> Forgot he was a man, and Gealosie is hight.

## 2

The great advocate for the "law and process of great nature" in *The Winter's Tale* is the fierce and courageous Paulina, to be widowed when her unfortunate husband Antigonus falls victim to Shakespeare's most famous stage direction: *Exit, pursued by a bear.* Antigonus thus becomes one of the two fatalities brought about through Leontes's madness, the other being the young Prince Mamillius, heir to his father's throne. Hermione and Perdita, wife and daughter, survive, though the question of Hermione's supposed death is appropriately left ambiguous by Shakespeare, who refused to clarify whether indeed she had died, and was later resurrected, or whether she was spirited away by Paulina, and maintained for sixteen years. Since Leontes is sanely contrite for that entire time, it would seem rather harsh that he be kept ignorant of his wife's continued existence and proximity, except that the Delphic Oracle must first be fulfilled. Presumably Shakespeare wished his audience—or a large part of it—to believe in the miracle of Hermione's resurrection, and yet he gives some hints that he is himself skeptical of this wonder, though he postpones these clues until Act V.

Shakespeare presumably had learned from *Pericles* that one recognition scene is enough, since the meeting of Pericles and Marina has a strength that dissipates the subsequent reunion with Thaisa. In *Cymbeline*'s last scene, the plethora of recognitions is heaped pell-mell, but we have seen how often Shakespeare edges over into farce in that strange play. Rather than dim the restoration of Hermione, Shakespeare allows the reunion of Leontes and Perdita to be narrated by three anonymous gentlemen of the court, one of whom intimates that Paulina was watching over more than a statue in the sixteen years since Hermione's apparent death:

I thought she had some great matter there in hand; for she hath privately twice or thrice a day, ever since the death of Hermione, visited that removed house.

[V.ii.104–7]

Hermione, gazing upon her daughter, speaks a touch more ambiguously, but still in the mode of one who has not known death:

for thou shalt hear that I,
Knowing by Paulina that the Oracle
Gave hope thou wast in being, have preserv'd
Myself to see the issue.

[V.iii.125–28]

Hermione (or Shakespeare) has forgotten that she has heard the Oracle for herself; her slip indicates considerable consultation between two old friends during sixteen years of visits twice or thrice a day. It is amiably like

Shakespeare to want to have both a supernatural resurrection and a skeptical awareness that nature is otherwise engaged. Having it both ways,
Shakespeare hints also that we ought to look closely at Hermione's ordeal
throughout Act II and the first two scenes of Act III, a somewhat (critically)
neglected sequence, if only because as readers we are so pleased to reach
the seacoast of Bohemia, bears and all, since Leontes's dementia, while
never tedious, nevertheless exhausts us. Once Polixenes and his courtier
Camillo, on the latter's sound advice, have fled Sicilia for their lives,
Leontes's murderous madness takes on fresh urgency and a really frightening rhetorical violence:

> How blest am I
> In my just censure! in my true opinion!
> Alack, for lesser knowledge! how accurs'd
> In being so blest! There may be in the cup
> A spider steep'd, and one may drink, depart,
> And yet partake no venom (for his knowledge
> Is not infected); but if one present
> Th' abhorr'd ingredient to his eye, make known
> How he hath drunk, he cracks his gorge, his sides,
> With violent hefts. I have drunk, and seen the spider.
> Camillo was his help in this, his pander:
> There is a plot against my life, my crown;
> All's true that is mistrusted: that false villain,
> Whom I employ'd, was pre-employ'd by him:
> He has discover'd my design, and I
> Remain a pinch'd thing; yea, a very trick
> For them to play at will.

[II.i.36–52]

Since Leontes had commanded Camillo to poison Polixenes, this scary
speech is even crazier than it sounds. Even for Shakespeare's absolute genius at metaphor, the spider in the cup is astonishing; paranoia achieves its
masterpiece when Leontes intones, "I have drunk, and seen the spider." He

has imbibed deeply the wine of jealousy, and the "spider steep'd" is the emblem of his own madness. The late William Seward Burroughs, in his best sentence, affirmed that "paranoia means having all the facts," the credo of another who had seen the spider in the cup.

Leontes is shocked back to sanity by his son's death and his wife's apparent demise, in what must be the most incredible transition in *The Winter's Tale*, if not in all of Shakespeare. Even Gielgud seemed to me overmatched by Act III, Scene ii, where the startled release from paranoia is enacted. The dramatic problem results from Shakespeare's lavishing of his art on Leontes's madness, which is too persuasive to be cured so suddenly. Yet this is a winter's tale, an old story retold by the hearth, to a haggling of wind and weather. Shakespeare wants us to grant him the storyteller's absolute authority, and perhaps (like us) he finds Leontes sane considerably less interesting than Leontes berserk. Before we can protest what seems a lapse in dramatization, we are carried off to that outrageous seacost of Bohemia, where *The Winter's Tale* ventures on to its truest greatness, with Perdita, princess of shepherdesses, and Autolycus, prince of thieves.

3

*The Winter's Tale* has an extraordinary amplitude; the wonderful Autolycus, most amiable of all Shakespearean rogues, is just as essential to the play as are Leontes and Perdita. The nineteenth-century Irish critic Edward Dowden first applied the term *romance* to Shakespeare's final plays, and we are now trapped with it, but *The Winter's Tale* is a romantic comedy, if we adopt the perspective of Autolycus. That stance has a long tradition; Homer says that Autolycus was the foremost thief among men, while Ovid makes him the son of Hermes, the mercurial trickster god. Shakespeare's Autolycus greatly enhances the tradition: he is a minstrel as well as a thief, and the splendid songs in the play are his. But best of all, he has a vital and unique personality, and received Dr. Johnson's approbation: "The character of *Autolycus* is very naturally conceived, and strongly represented." I cannot improve upon that, but always delight in expounding Johnson, and begin by observing that, with Imogen and Caliban, Autolycus is the strongest representation in late Shakespeare. We do not encounter Autolycus until Act IV, Scene iii, where he enters magnificently, singing:

When daffodils begin to peer,
    With heigh! the doxy over the dale,
Why, then comes in the sweet o' the year,
    For the red blood reigns in the winter's pale.

The white sheet bleaching on the hedge,
    With heigh! the sweet birds, O how they sing!
Doth set my pugging tooth an edge;
    For a quart of ale is a dish for a king.

The lark, that tirra-lirra chants,
    With heigh! with heigh! the thrush and the jay,
Are summer songs for me and my aunts,
    While we lie tumbling in the hay.

[IV.iii.1–12]

The contrast between Leontes and Autolycus is very vivid: Leontes has been the pale or enclosure of winter, while Autolycus proclaims that "the red blood reigns in the winter's pale." There may be an image of pale, wintry cheeks changing to summery ruddiness, with a subtle transition from pale faces to the white sheets that Autolycus perpetually pilfers. But the contrast is between Leontes's nasty fantasies of adulterous "skulking in corners" and Autolycus's tumbling in the hay with his "aunts" (the doxy over the dale) to the joyous summer songs of lark, thrush, and jay. Autolycus, no Bohemian but an English pastoral Villon, follows his song with his boisterous credo, culminating in the whoop of "A prize!" when he spots the rustic Clown, son of the Shepherd who is Perdita's foster father:

My traffic is sheets; when the kite builds, look to lesser linen. My father named me Autolycus; who, being as I am, littered under Mercury, was likewise a snapper-up of unconsidered trifles. With die and drab I purchased this caparison, and my revenue is the silly cheat. Gallows and knock are too powerful on the highway: beating and hanging are terrors to me: for the life to come, I sleep out the thought of it. A prize! a prize!

[IV.iii.23–31]

No highwayman, Autolycus loathes violence, and happily credits "die and drab," dicing and whores, for his ragged tinker's costume. His dupes are his income, and this world is good enough for him, as befits a natural man. Pickpocket and confidence man, he is also a ballad singer and ballad-monger, and most charmingly a pedlar of fine knacks for ladies, as in this, his best song and one of Shakespeare's finest:

Lawn as white as driven snow,
Cyprus black as e'er was crow,
Gloves as sweet as damask roses,
Masks for faces and for noses:
Bugle-bracelet, necklace amber,
Perfume for a lady's chamber:
Golden quoifs and stomachers
For my lads to give their dears:
Pins, and poking-sticks of steel,
What maids lack from head to heel:
Come buy of me, come! come buy! come buy!
Buy, lads, or else your lasses cry.
Come buy!

[IV.iv.220–32]

Who in the audience can resist so melodious a pedlar? As a song sales-man, Autolycus is at his merriest:

*Clo.* What hast here? ballads?
*Mop.* Pray now, buy some: I love a ballad in print, a life, for then we are
sure they are true.

*Aut.* Here's one, to a very doleful tune, how a usurer's wife was
  brought to bed of twenty money-bags at a burden, and how she
  longed to eat adders' heads and toads carbonadoed.

*Mop.* Is it true, think you?

*Aut.* Very true, and but a month old.

*Dor.* Bless me from marrying a usurer!

*Aut.* Here's the midwife's name to 't, one Mistress Tale-porter, and five
  or six honest wives that were present. Why should I carry lies
  abroad?

*Mop.* Pray you now, buy it.

*Clown.* Come on, lay it by: and let's first see moe ballads: we'll buy the
  other things anon.

*Aut.* Here's another ballad of a fish that appeared upon the coast on
  Wednesday the fourscore of April, forty thousand fathom above
  water, and sung this ballad against the hard hearts of maids: it
  was thought she was a woman, and was turned into a cold fish for
  she would not exchange flesh with one that loved her. The ballad
  is very pitiful, and as true.

*Dor.* Is it true too, think you?

*Aut.* Five justices' hands at it, and witnesses more than my pack will
  hold.

[IV.iv.260–85]

The pack of Autolycus contains Shakespeare at his most exuberant,
mocking the absurdities of broadside street ballads. As parodistic song
writer, Autolycus blends into Shakespeare, immensely enjoying his fantasies of usurers' wives (Shakespeare himself being a usurer) and the metamorphosis of a woman "turned into a cold fish for she would not exchange
flesh with one that loved her." The pleasure of all this is enhanced for an
audience that has suffered the jealous, flesh-hating diatribes of Leontes,
and thus appreciates all the more Autolycus's sly benignity. Later, after ex-
changing garments with Prince Florizel so that Florizel and "his clog,"
Perdita, can escape from Polixenes, Autolycus wins us yet more securely by
declaring his Villon-like ethos:

The prince himself is about a piece of iniquity (stealing away from his father with his clog at his heels): if I thought it were a piece of honesty to acquaint the king withal, I would not do 't: I hold it the more knavery to conceal it; and therein am I constant to my profession.

[IV.iv.678–83]

As a force for benevolence, Autolycus rivals Paulina in *The Winter's Tale*, since he saves Perdita just as Paulina rescues Hermione. The mode of operation is delightfully different, since we rightly prefer the comic to the tragicomic. Autolycus pragmatically solves the secret of Perdita's birth and brings the Shepherd and the Clown, with their proofs, to Polixenes. We are left a little sad, perhaps, when we last see Autolycus, who is to reenter the service of Prince Florizel with a promise to be honest, but we cheer up when we reflect that Dr. Johnson was accurate, and so Autolycus, being "very naturally conceived" by Shakespeare, necessarily will return to his true nature and will run away again, stealing bedsheets and hawking his outrageous ballads.

4

A listing of anyone's favorite scenes from Shakespeare always should include Act IV, Scene iv, of *The Winter's Tale*. The scene is amazingly long (840 lines) and contains the most beautiful of all Shakespearean pastoral courtships in its opening sequence, where Perdita and Florizel declare and celebrate their mutual passion. This lovers' ceremony is so extraordinarily beautiful, and so vital to the subtler aspects of *The Winter's Tale*, that I will slow down and interpret it rather closely.

We are at a pastoral festival, celebrating the sheep shearing. Perdita, garlanded with flowers, plays the part of Flora, ancient Italian goddess of fertility, and so the Shepherd's daughter and unknowing Sicilian princess is the hostess of the feast. From the start, Perdita carries about her the suggestion that she is an unfallen Proserpina (Persephone)—daughter of Ceres (Demeter) and Jupiter (Zeus)—whose story Shakespeare knew best from

Ovid. Carried off to the underworld by Pluto (Dis), Proserpina is half-rescued by Ceres, who negotiates her daughter's freedom for spring and summer only. Perdita, as we will see, will not yield to this diminishment, in what we might call her mythological aura. But Shakespeare, rapt by her, renders her as vivid and distinct a personality as Leontes or Autolycus. Even Florizel, under Perdita's influence, comes alive as his father, Polixenes, never does. Florizel begins Act IV, Scene iv, by saluting Perdita with a lover's enthusiasm for the transfiguration of her costume, rather than its transformation of her great beauty:

> These your unusual weeds, to each part of you
> Do give a life: no shepherdess, but Flora
> Peering in April's front. This your sheep-shearing
> Is as a meeting of the petty gods,
> And you the queen on 't.
>
> [IV.iv.1–5]

"To each part of you / Do give a life" has a fine erotic suggestiveness, but Perdita, who dislikes both her dressing up and Florizel's dressing down, does not yield to the compliment:

>      Sir: my gracious lord,
> To chide at your extremes, it not becomes me—
> O pardon, that I name them! Your high self,
> The gracious mark o' th' land, you have obscur'd
> With a swain's wearing, and me, poor lowly maid,
> Most goddess-like prank'd up: but that our feasts
> In every mess have folly and the feeders
> Digest it with a custom, I should blush
> To see you so attir'd; sworn, I think,
> To show myself a glass.
>
> [IV.iv.5–14]

Gently balancing her respect for the crown prince of Bohemia, who is hopelessly beyond her in social rank, with her shrewd rustic's good sense,

Perdita demurs at the feast of fools over which nevertheless she must preside. Attending, in disguise, are Polixenes and Camillo. One of the finest and most profound dialogues in all of Shakespeare takes place between Perdita and Polixenes, after she greets them "with rosemary, and rue":

*Pol.*                                    Shepherdess—
    A fair one are you—well you fit our ages
    With flowers of winter.
*Per.*                              Sir, the year growing ancient,
    Not yet on summer's death nor on the birth
    Of trembling winter, the fairest flowers o' th' season
    Are our carnations and streak'd gillyvors,
    Which some call nature's bastards: of that kind
    Our rustic garden's barren; and I care not
    To get slips of them.
*Pol.*                              Wherefore, gentle maiden,
    Do you neglect them?
*Per.*                              For I have heard it said
    There is an art which, in their piedness, shares
    With great creating nature.
*Pol.*                                    Say there be;
    Yet nature is made better by no mean
    But nature makes that mean: so, over that art,
    Which you say adds to nature, is an art
    That nature makes. You see, sweet maid, we marry
    A gentler scion to the wildest stock,
    And make conceive a bark of baser kind
    By bud of nobler race. This is an art
    Which does mend nature—change it rather—but
    The art itself is nature.
*Per.*                              So it is.
*Pol.* Then make your garden rich in gillyvors,
    And do not call them bastards.
*Per.*                                    I'll not put
    The dibble in earth to set one slip of them;

No more than, were I painted, I would wish
This youth should say 'twere well, and only therefore
Desire to breed by me. Here's flowers for you:
Hot lavender, mints, savory, marjoram,
The marigold, that goes to bed wi' th' sun
And with him rises, weeping: these are flowers
Of middle summer, and I think they are given
To men of middle age. Y'are very welcome.
*[She gives them flowers]*

[IV.iv.77–108]

To say with Polixenes that "the art itself is nature" may be only a Renaissance commonplace, but that is not what is original and powerful about
this civilized and comic mock debate. Nor is it the irony of Polixenes urging in horticulture what he wishes to deny to his son, to "marry / A gen-
tler scion to the wildest stock." The dispute is not between nature and art,
but between the earlier madness of Leontes and the courageous vitalism of
his daughter, who incarnates a heroic naturalism that appears elsewhere in
Shakespeare, but not in so vivacious and winning a form. Jealous paranoia
has yielded to a triumph of exuberant goodness, as stubborn in its way as
the obsession of Leontes. Perdita is very much her father's daughter, and
doubtless Shakespeare means to indicate that her innate royalty breaks
through, just as it does with Polydore and Cadwal in *Cymbeline.*

But her passionate naturalism transcends even her vigorous personality,
and appears to speak for something in Shakespeare himself. I think, contrary to many critics, that the playwright is more on her side than on
Polixenes's, for Polixenes is more in the camp of Ben Jonson than of Shakespeare. Jonson, in his remarkable poem prefacing the First Folio, essentially
says of Shakespeare that "the art itself is nature." Nature, Jonson affirmed,
was proud of Shakespeare's designs, yet "Art / . . . must enjoy a part" of
Shakespeare's eminence. Jonson presages the recent scholarly emphasis
on Shakespeare as a self-reviser, yet implicit in his praise of Shakespeare
is his more characteristic judgment that his more successful rival "wanted
art." Time has awarded the palm to Shakespeare's art, over Jonson's, but the

singularity of Shakespeare is clearly the astonishing fusion of art and nature in some two dozen of his thirty-nine plays. Perdita is not interested
in an art that mends or changes nature; she cries out instead for an unfallen
nature that would be its own art:

> O Proserpina,
> For the flowers now that, frighted, thou let'st fall
> From Dis's waggon! daffodils,
> That come before the swallow dares, and take
> The winds of March with beauty; violets, dim,
> But sweeter than the lids of Juno's eyes
> Or Cytherea's breath; pale primroses
> That die unmarried, ere they can behold
> Bright Phoebus in his strength (a malady
> Most incident to maids); bold oxlips and
> The crown imperial; lilies of all kinds,
> The flower-de-luce being one. O, these I lack,
> To make you garlands of; and my sweet friend,
> To strew him o'er and o'er!

[IV.iv.116–29]

With my characteristic temerity, I assert that Perdita speaks for Shakespeare in this marvelous passage. Had she been Proserpina, Perdita implies,
she would not have experienced the failure in nerve that resulted in our
flowers becoming seasonal. A continual spring and harvesttime would still
exist together if Proserpina had been of Perdita's hardy temperament. In
the exquisite pathos of this speech, Perdita goes beyond the role of
Leontes's daughter, and prophesies the naturalistic sensibility of John
Keats:

> daffodils,
> That come before the swallow dares, and take
> The winds of March with beauty.

The nature itself is art, in Perdita, Shakespeare, and Keats, and challenges us as it does Florizel in Perdita's invitation to her lover. Responding to the prospect of being strewn "o'er and o'er" with flowers of the absent spring, Florizel laughingly protests: "What, like a corpse?" and so provokes Perdita's bold reply:

No, like a bank, for love to lie and play on:
Not like a corpse; or if—not to be buried,
But quick, and in mine arms.

[IV.iv. 130–32]

Abashed at her own forwardness, Perdita ruefully all but chides herself: "sure this robe of mine / Does change my disposition." Florizel, in a remarkable riposte, saves her from embarrassment, and then embarks upon the finest tribute any man in Shakespeare makes to his beloved:

What you do,
Still betters what is done. When you speak, sweet,
I'd have you do it ever: when you sing,
I'd have you buy and sell so, so give alms,
Pray so, and, for the ord'ring your affairs,
To sing them too: when you do dance, I wish you
A wave o' the sea, that you might ever do
Nothing but that, move still, still so,
And own no other function. Each your doing,
So singular in each particular,
Crowns what you are doing, in the present deeds,
That all your acts are queens.

[IV.iv. 135–46]

The ecstasy of this rhapsodic declaration was to prompt Shelley's *Epipsychidion*, but even that great chant of eros cannot match the intricate music with which Shakespeare endows Florizel. Yeats, in his *Last Poems*, particularly in the invocation of Helen of Troy as a young girl in "Long-legged

Fly," approached the sinuous rhythms of this paean to a woman's grace of movement:

> when you do dance, I wish you
> A wave o'the sea, that you might ever do
> Nothing but that, move still, still so,
> And own no other function.

Shakespeare intends the violent shock of our contrasting son and father when Polixenes, later in the scene, addresses Perdita with a brutality that recalls the worst rhetorical violences of crazed Leontes:

> And thou, fresh piece
> Of excellent witchcraft, who, of force, must know
> The royal fool thou cop'st with,—[. . .]
> I'll have thy beauty scratch'd with briers and made
> More homely than thy state. For thee, fond boy,
> If I may ever know thou dost but sigh
> That thou no more shalt see this knack (as never
> I mean thou shalt), we'll bar thee from succession;
> Not hold thee of our blood, no, not our kin,
> Farre than Deucalion off: mark thou my words!
> Follow us to the court. Thou churl, for this time,
> Though full of our displeasure, yet we free thee
> From the dead blow of it. And you, enchantment,—
> Worthy enough a herdsman; yea, him too,
> That makes himself, but for our honour therein,
> Unworthy thee. If ever henceforth thou
> These rural latches to his entrance open,
> Or hoop his body more with thy embraces,
> I will devise a death as cruel for thee
> As thou art tender to 't.

[IV.iv.423–42]

After that, it is more than difficult to like the previously colorless Polixenes, just as Leontes never wins our affection. "Pastoral romance" increasingly seems a very odd description of *The Winter's Tale;* "grotesque comedy" is much apter. Again, Shakespeare writes no genre; extravagance, a wandering beyond limits, is his truest mode. He will not be confined by any convention or by any intellectual enterprise.

5

The return to Sicilia in Act V of *The Winter's Tale* culminates in the famous statue scene, where Hermione is reunited with Leontes and Perdita. Where everything is so problematic, Shakespeare is pleased to remind us that we are watching (or reading) a representation that is more than willing to be aware that it is only a fiction. Paulina sums matters up by telling the restored family, and with them the audience, "Go together, / You precious winners all." Nobody loses in *The Winter's Tale,* at least at the end; Mamillius is long dead of grief, and Antigonus doubtless was thoroughly digested by one of those bears that abound on the seacoast of Bohemia. Paulina, making reasonably clear that she is not a necromancer, is also careful to distance us from realism:

> That she is living,
> Were it but told you, should be hooted at
> Like an old tale: but it appears she lives,
> Though yet she speak not.

[V.iii.115–18]

"If this be magic," Leontes says, "let it be an art / Lawful as eating." Being sixteen years older, Hermione—both as statue and as woman—is somewhat wrinkled, but otherwise much herself. I think we mistake the tone when we find this scene hieratic or portentous, but then why does Shakespeare insist upon a statue at all, let alone one sculpted by Julio Romano? I may be the only critic who finds this scene not one of the glories of *The Winter's Tale* but rather its principal puzzle, since Shakespeare is not self-mocking here. A theatrical coup it certainly is: statues coming to life work well upon stage. The wonders of *The Winter's Tale*, for me, are elsewhere: with Leontes's mad jealousy, Autolycus's singing thievery, and most of all with Perdita and Florizel celebrating each other in a natural ecstasy. Shakespeare, at the close, is rather too deliberately the knowing illusionist, and is skeptical of any credo that the art itself is nature.

## 33

# THE TEMPEST

Of all Shakespeare's plays, the two visionary comedies—*A Midsummer Night's Dream* and *The Tempest*—these days share the sad distinction of being the worst interpreted and performed. Erotomania possesses the critics and directors of the *Dream*, while ideology drives the bespoilers of *The Tempest*. Caliban, a poignant but cowardly (and murderous) half-human creature (his father a sea devil, whether fish or amphibian), has become an African-Caribbean heroic Freedom Fighter. This is not even a weak misreading; anyone who arrives at that view is simply not interested in reading the play at all. Marxists, multiculturalists, feminists, *nouveau* historicists—the usual suspects—know their causes but not Shakespeare's plays.

Because *The Tempest* (1611) was Shakespeare's last play without the col- laboration of John Fletcher, and probably had been a success at the Globe, it heads off the First Folio, printed as the first of the comedies. We know that *The Tempest* was presented at the court of James I, which probably accounts for its masquelike features. The play is fundamentally plotless; its one outer event is the magically induced storm of the first scene, which rather oddly gives the play its title. If there is any literary source at all, it would be Mon- taigne's essay on the Cannibals, who are echoed in Caliban's name though not in his nature. Yet Montaigne, as in *Hamlet,* was more provocation than source, and Caliban is anything but a celebration of the natural man. *The Tempest* is neither a discourse on colonialism nor a mystical testament. It is a wildly experimental stage comedy, prompted ultimately, I suspect, by Marlowe's *Doctor Faustus*. Prospero, Shakespeare's magus, carries a name that is the Italian translation of Faustus, which is the Latin cognomen ("the favored one") that Simon Magus the Gnostic took when he went to Rome. With Ariel, a sprite or angel (the name is Hebrew for "the lion of God"), as his familiar rather than Marlowe's Mephistopheles, Prospero is Shakespeare's anti-Faust, and a final transcending of Marlowe.

Since Caliban, though he speaks only a hundred lines in *The Tempest*, has now taken over the play for so many, I will start with him here. His fortunes in stage history are instructive, and comfort me at our bad moment for *The Tempest*. In Davenant and Dryden's *The Enchanted Isle*, a musical revision that held the London stage on and off between 1667 and 1787, Caliban gets himself so drunk early on that he instigates no plot against Prospero. This Caliban (a different kind of travesty from our current noble rebel) for more than a century provided a prime role for singing comedians. In the High Romantic period, the prancing and yodeling yahoo finally was replaced by Shakespeare's poignant "savage and deformed slave." As the text suggests, Caliban was still represented as half amphibian, but peculiar transformations crowded after that: a snail on all fours, a gorilla, the Missing Link or ape man, and at last (London, 1951) a Neanderthal. In a ghastly Peter Brook version of the 1960s, which I gaped at unbelievingly, Caliban was Java Man, a ferocious primitive who accomplished the rape of Miranda, took over the island, and celebrated his triumph by bumbuggering Prospero. Another modern tradition—now, of course, prevalent—has cast black actors in the role: Canada Lee, Earle Hyman, and James Earl Jones were among the early exemplars whom I saw. In 1970, Jonathan Miller was inspired to set the play in the age of Cortés and Pizarro, with Caliban as a South American Indian field hand, and Ariel as an Indian literate serf. That was bizarre enough to be entertaining, unlike George C. Wolfe's infuriating recent success, in which Caliban and Ariel, both black slaves, vied with one another in hating Prospero. Fashions tire; the early twenty-first century may still have mock scholars moaning about neocolonialism, but I assume that by then Caliban and Ariel will be extraterrestrials—perhaps they are already.

The critical tradition, until recently, has been far more perceptive than the directorial, as regards the role of Caliban. Dryden accurately observed that Shakespeare "created a person which was not in Nature." A character who is half-human cannot be a natural man, whether black, Indian, or Berber (the likely people of Caliban's mother, the Algerian witch Sycorax). Dr. Johnson, no sentimentalist, wrote of "the gloominess of his temper and the malignity of his purposes," while dismissing any notion that Caliban spoke a language of his own. In our century, the poet Auden blamed Prospero for corrupting Caliban, a simplistic judgment, but as always Auden on Shakespeare benefits us by his insight, here in the wonderful prose address "Caliban to the Audience," from *The Sea and the Mirror.* Perhaps because Shelley had identified with Ariel, Auden assimilates Caliban to himself:

> And from this nightmare of public solitude, this everlasting Not Yet, what relief have you but in an ever giddier collective gallop, with bisson eye and bevel course, toward the grey horizon of the bleaker vision; what landmarks but the four dead rivers, the Joyless, the Flowing, the Mournful, and the Swamp of Tears, what goal but the Black Stone on which the bones are cracked, for only there in its cry of agony can your existence find at last an unequivocal meaning and your refusal to be yourself become a serious despair, the love nothing, the fear all?

This is primarily Auden on Auden, heavily influenced by Kierkegaard, but it catches Caliban's dilemma: "The love nothing, the fear all." Between Johnson and Auden on Caliban, the great figure is Browning, in his astonishing dramatic monologue "Caliban upon Setebos." Here the terrible psychic suffering brought about through the failed adoption of Caliban by Prospero is granted fuller expression than Shakespeare allowed:

> Himself peeped late, eyed Prosper at his books
> Careless and lofty, lord now of the isle:
> Vexed, 'stitched a book of broad leaves, arrow-shaped,

Wrote thereon, he knows what, prodigious words;
Has peeled a wand and called it by a name;
Weareth at whiles for an enchanter's robe
The eyed skin of a supple ocelot;
And hath an ounce sleeker than youngling mole,
A four-legged serpent he makes cower and couch,
Now snarl, now hold its breath and mind his eye,
And saith she is Miranda and my wife:
Keeps for his Ariel a tall pouch-bill crane
He bids go wade for fish and straight disgorge;
Also a sea-beast, lumpish, which he snared,
Blinded the eyes of, and brought somewhat tame,
And split its toe-webs, and now pens the drudge
In a hole o'the rock and calls him Caliban;
A bitter heart that bides its time and bites.
Plays thus at being Prosper in a way,
Taketh his mirth with make-believes: so He.

As throughout Browning's poem, Caliban speaks of himself in the third person, except that the final "He" is Setebos, the god of the witch Sycorax. The lumpish sea beast, "a bitter heart that bides its time and bites," is a sick child's tortured plaything. Cast out by Prospero, Caliban bides his time but will be too fearful and inept to bite. What Browning sees is Caliban's essential childishness, a weak and plangent sensibility that cannot surmount its fall from the paradisal adoption by Prospero. Caliban's attempted rape of Miranda is readily explained away by his current academic admirers, but I wonder sometimes why feminist critics join in Caliban's defense. On this matter, the audience's perspective has to be that of Miranda and Prospero, and not Caliban's antic glee that, had he not been prevented, he would have peopled all the isle with Calibans. Half a Wild Man, half a sea beast, Caliban has his legitimate pathos, but he cannot be interpreted as being somehow admirable.

2

A play virtually plotless must center its interest elsewhere, yet Shakespeare in *The Tempest* seems more concerned with what Prospero might intimate than with the coldness of this anti-Faust's personality. Ariel also is more a figure of vast suggestiveness than a character possessing an inwardness available to us, except by glimpses. Part of *The Tempest's* permanent fascination for so many playgoers and readers, in a myriad of national cultures, is its juxtaposition of a vengeful magus who turns to forgiveness, with a spirit of fire and air, and a half-human of earth and water. Prospero seems to incarnate a fifth element, similar to that of the Sufis, like himself descended from the ancient Hermetists. The art of Prospero controls nature, at least in the outward sense. Though his art ought also to teach Prospero an absolute self-control, he clearly has not attained this even as the play concludes. Prospero's Platonism is at best enigmatic; self-knowledge in Neo-Platonic tradition hardly should lead on to despair, and yet Prospero ends in a dark mode, particularly evident in the Epilogue that he speaks.

What was Shakespeare trying to do for himself as a playwright, if not necessarily as a person, by composing *The Tempest?* We can conclude reasonably that he did not intend this drama to be a final work. In 1611, Shakespeare was only forty-seven, and he did write substantial parts, at least, of three more plays: *Henry VIII,* the lost *Cardenio,* and *The Two Noble Kinsmen,* probably all with the collaboration of John Fletcher. Prospero is not more a representation of Shakespeare himself than Dr. Faustus was a self-portrait of Christopher Marlowe. Yet Romantic readers and playgoers felt otherwise, and I am still enough of a Late Romantic to wish to surmise what moved them to their extravagance.

There is an elliptical quality to *The Tempest* that suggests a more symbolic drama than Shakespeare actually wrote. Prospero, unlike Hamlet, does not end saying that he has something more to tell us, but that he must "let it be." We rightly feel that Hamlet could have told us something crucial about what he himself represented, could have plucked the heart out of his mystery, had he had the time and the inclination to do so. Prospero's seems a very different story of the self: Hamlet dies into the truth, while Prospero lives on in what may be a bewilderment or at least a puzzlement. Since Prospero's story is not tragic, but somehow comic, in the old sense of ending happily (or at least successfully), he appears to lose spiritual authority even as he regains political power. I am not suggesting that Prospero loses the prestige we generally ascribe to tragedy, and to Hamlet in particular. Rather, the authority of a counter-Faust, who could purchase knowledge at no spiritual cost, abandons Prospero. Leaving the enchanted isle is not in itself a loss for Prospero, but breaking his staff and drowning his book certainly constitute diminishments to the self. These emblems of purified magic were also the marks of exile: going home to rule Milan purchases restoration at a high price. Prospero, bidding farewell to his art, tells us that he even has raised the dead, a role that Christianity reserves for God and for Jesus. To be Duke of Milan is to be only another potentate; the abandoned art was so potent that politics is absurd in contrast.

The Tempest is more Ariel's play than Caliban's, and much more Prospero's. Indeed Prospero would be a far apter title than The Tempest, which turns me to what seems the play's true mystery: Why does it so slyly invoke the Faust story, only to transform legend beyond recognition? Simon Magus, according to Christian sources (no Gnostic ones being available), suffered the irony of being not "the favored one" at all when he went to Rome. In a contest with Christians, this first Faustus attempted levitation, and crashed down to his death. Most subsequent Fausts sell out to the Devil, and pay with spirit, the grandest exception being Goethe, for his Faust's soul is borne off to heaven by little boy angels whose chubby buttocks so intoxicate Mephistopheles with homoerotic lust that he notices too late the theft of his legitimate prize.

Prospero, the anti-Faust, with the angel Ariel for his familiar, has made a pact only with deep learning of the hermetic kind. Since Marlowe's Dr. Faustus was a failed scholar compared with Prospero, Shakespeare enjoys foregrounding an ironic contrast between his long-defunct rival's protagonist and the magus of The Tempest. Simon Magus was, like Jesus the Magician, a disciple of John the Baptist, and evidently resented that he was not preferred to Jesus, but again we have only Christian accounts of this. Prospero the magician is certainly not in competition with Jesus; Shakespeare takes considerable care to exclude Christian references from *The Tempest*. When a chastened Caliban submits to Prospero at the close, his use of the word *grace* initially startles us:

> Ay, that I will; and I'll be wise hereafter,
> And seek for grace. What a thrice-double ass
> Was I, to take this drunkard for a god,
> And worship this dull fool!
>
> [V.i.294–97]

Yet what can this mean except that Caliban, having substituted Stephano for Setebos as his god, now turns to the god Prospero? It is only after the play ends that the actor who had impersonated Prospero steps before the curtain to speak in terms that are recognizably Christian, yet are still remote enough from that revelation:

> And my ending is despair,
> Unless I be reliev'd by prayer,
> Which pierces so, that it assaults
> Mercy itself, and frees all faults.
> As you from crimes would pardon'd be,
> Let your indulgence set me free.
>
> [Epilogue 15–20]

This is addressed to the audience, whose applause is being solicited:

> But release me from my bands
> With the help of your good hands.
>
> [Epilogue 9–10]

"Indulgence" therefore is audacious wit: the Church pardons, the audience applauds, and the actor is set free only by approbation of his skill. The role of Prospero, within *The Tempest*'s visionary confines, is godlike; even the magus's angry and impatient outbursts parody, at a very safe distance, the irascible Yahweh of the Book of Numbers. *The Tempest* is an elegantly subtle drama and, like several other Shakespearean masterworks, is hard to hold steady in our view. No audience has ever liked Prospero; Ariel (*pace* the director Wolfe) has a wary affection for the magus, and Miranda loves him, but then he has been both benign mother and stern father to his daughter. Why does Shakespeare make Prospero so cold? The play's ethos does not seem to demand it, and the audience can be baffled by a protagonist so clearly in the right and yet essentially antipathetic. Once the neglectful ruler of Milan, Prospero, successful only as magician and as single parent, goes back to Milan, where evidently he again is not likely to shine as an administrator. Northrop Frye once identified Prospero with Shakespeare, but only in a highly ironic sense, finding in Prospero also:

> a harassed overworked actor-manager, scolding the lazy actors, praising the good ones in connoisseur's language, thinking up jobs for the idle, constantly aware of his limited time before his show goes on, his nerves tense and alert for breakdowns while it is going on, looking forward longingly to peaceful retirement, yet in the meantime having to go out and beg the audience for applause.

That is charming enough to be accurate, and perhaps the harried dramatist-director (he had given up acting, evidently just before writing *Othello*) realized that he himself was becoming colder, no longer the "open and free nature" Ben Jonson praised. There is not much geniality in *The Tempest*, or in other later plays by Shakespeare, except for the role of Autolycus in *The Winter's Tale*. Prospero, as Frye remarks, has no transcendental inclinations, for all his trafficking with spirits. What, besides the revenge he throws aside, could Prospero have been seeking in his Hermetic studies, which in any case began in Milan, long before he had anything to avenge? The Renaissance Hermetist, a Giordano Bruno or a Dr. John Dee, was seeking knowledge of God, the quest of all gnosis. Not Prospero, for he gives not a single hint that the eternal mysteries spur him on. Unlike

Bruno, Prospero the anti-Faust is not a heretic; he is indifferent to the Christian revelation, even as he studies an arcane wisdom that other magi either preferred to Christianity (if, with Bruno, they dared) or more frequently hoped to turn to Christian purposes. Again, we abide in a puzzle: Is Prospero's art, like Shakespeare's, aesthetic rather than mystical? That would make Prospero only the enlargement of a failed metaphor, and belie our experience of the play. Though he stages revels, to his own discomfiture, Prospero is not Ben Jonson, nor Shakespeare.

Evidently, Prospero is a true scholar, pursuing wisdom for its own sake, and yet that rarely could be a dramatic activity, and Prospero is a very successful dramatic representation. But of what? His quest is intellectual, we might even say scientific, though his science is as personal and idiosyncratic as Dr. Freud's. Freud, speaking to his disciples, liked to call himself a conquistador, which seems to me a suggestive epithet for Prospero. Like Freud, Prospero really is the favored one: he is bound to win. Freud's triumph has proved equivocal; much of it expires with the twentieth century. Prospero exults as he approaches his total victory, and then he becomes very sad. No one else in Shakespeare is nearly as successful, except King Henry V. Ironical reversal for Falstaff's bad son takes place only in history, just outside the confines of his play, and in *Henry VI*, where the young Shakespeare opens with Henry V's funeral, French uprisings against the English, and forebodings of civil war in England.

Prospero does not wait for his re-entry into history; ironic loss is all but immediate, even as his forgiven enemies—Caliban included—acknowledge his supremacy, both temporal and mystical. The dynastic marriage of Miranda to the Prince of Naples will unite the two realms and thus prevent further political troubles from outside. But what occult powers, if any, does Prospero still possess after he breaks the staff and drowns his book? I think the singular "book" is meant to contrast with Marlowe's Faustus crying out, "I'll burn my books" when Mephistopheles and the other devils carry him off forever. Faustus has only his library, of Cornelius Agrippa and all the others, but Prospero has "my book," which he has written, the crown of his long labors in reading, brooding, and practicing the control of spirits. That clears away part of the puzzle, and vastly increases the poignance when this conquistador drowns his life's work. It is as though an unpublished Freud threw what would have been the Standard Edition into the sea of space and time.

If there is an analogue between Shakespeare and Prospero, it would have to be their mutual eminence, first among poet-playwrights and supreme among white magicians, or Hermetists. Ben Jonson collected his own works, plays included, and published them in 1616, the year of Shakespeare's death. It was not until 1623 that Shakespeare's friends and coworkers brought out his book, the First Folio, which printed eighteen plays for the first time, with *The Tempest* in pride of place, and with a less jealous Ben Jonson proudly assisting in the enterprise, which after all confirmed his refusal to drown his own book. Prospero does perform that suicidal act, one that needs to be clarified if we are to see *The Tempest* more for what it is and less for the legendary auras it has accumulated.

3

Ariel is our largest clue to understanding Prospero, though we have no similar aid for apprehending this great sprite, who has very little in common with Puck, despite the assertions of many critics. Barely mentioned in the Bible, Ariel seems to have been selected by Shakespeare not for the irrelevant Hebrew meaning of his name (he is no "lion of god" in the play, but a spirit of the elements fire and air), but probably for the sound association between Ariel and aireal. Plainly a contrast to Caliban, all earth and water, Ariel comes into the play before Caliban does, and finally is dismissed to his freedom—his last words to Prospero are "Was't well done?" an actor speaking to a director. Ariel's evidently will be endless play, in the air and in the fire. Caliban, despite his current claque, is grumpily re-adopted by a reluctant Prospero—"this thing of darkness I / Acknowledge mine"— and will go off with his foster father (not his slave owner) to Milan to continue his interrupted education. That seems a visionary prospect indeed, but should cause no more shudders than the future of many Shakespearean marriages: Beatrice and Benedick flailing at each other in late middle age is not a happy vista. Ariel's future, in his terms, is a very cheerful one, though it is beyond Shakespeare's understanding, or ours. Shelley associated Ariel with the freedom of Romantic poetic imagination, which is not altogether un-Shakespearean, but which also is now out of fashion. Whatever happens in *The Tempest* is the work of Ariel, under Prospero's direction, yet it is not solitary labor, as presented upon our stages. The sprite is the leader of a band of angels: "to thy strong bidding task / Ariel and all his quality," they being his subordinates and airy spirits like himself. They, too, presumably are working for their freedom, and are not happy about it, if we can believe Caliban.

Ariel and Prospero play an odd comic turn (wonderfully parodied by Beckett's Clov and Hamm in *Endgame*) in which Ariel's anxiety about the terms of his release from hermetic service and Prospero's uncertain temper combine to keep the audience a little on edge, waiting for an explosion that does not take place (except upon politically correct stages). Frank Kermode usefully reminds us that *The Tempest* "is unquestionably the most sophisticated comedy of a poet whose work in comedy is misunderstood to a quite astonishing degree." It was difficult, surely, to surpass *Twelfth Night*, *Measure for Measure*, and *The Winter's Tale* in sophistication, yet Shakespeare managed this so brilliantly that, as Kermode implies, we still cannot apprehend fully the comic achievement. I have only rarely heard anyone laugh at a performance of *The Tempest*, but that is because of the directors, whose moral sensibilities never seem to get beyond their politics. The Prospero–Ariel relationship is delicious comedy, together with much else in the play, as I hope to show. What is not at all comic is the mutual torment of the Prospero–Caliban failed adoption, which I will examine again as I turn to a closer consideration of *The Tempest*.

4

The deliberate absence of images in *The Tempest* may have prompted Auden to call his "commentary" *The Sea and the Mirror*. Auden's Prospero says to Ariel that he surrenders his Hermetic library "To the silent dissolution of the sea / Which misuses nothing because it values nothing." Starting with the storm at sea, and ending with Prospero's promise of "calm seas, auspicious gales," *The Tempest* allows us to be washed free of images, one of the comedy's many gifts. We are Miranda, who is adjured to "Sit still, and hear the last of our sea-sorrow." If the sea values nothing, and swallows all, it also keeps nothing, and casts us back again. Ariel's best and most famous song makes our drowned bones into coral, and translates what Hart Crane calls our "lost morning eyes" into pearls.

Ariel suggests a more radical metamorphosis than anyone in the drama actually undergoes. No one fades away, and yet no particular character, not even Prospero, suffers "a sea-change / Into something rich and strange." Perhaps only the complete work of Shakespeare taken as a whole could sustain that metaphor. I wonder again if *The Tempest* was one of Shakespeare's throwaway titles, another "as you like it," or "what you will." The storm is Ariel's creation (the will being Prospero's), and what matters is that it is a sea fiction, a drenching that at last leaves everyone dry. No one is harmed in the play, and forgiveness is extended to all by Prospero, in response to Ariel's most human moment. Everything dissolves in *The Tempest*, except the sea. From one perspective, the sea is dissolution itself, but evidently not so in this unique play. There is no Imogen or Autolycus in *The Tempest*; personality seems no longer to be a prime Shakespearean concern, and is inapplicable anyway to the nonhuman Ariel and half-human Caliban. A visionary comedy was not a new genre for Shakespeare; *A Midsummer Night's Dream* is Bottom's play, yet also Puck's. Still, *The Tempest*—unlike *Cymbeline* and *The Winter's Tale*—is not at all a recapitulation. Mysteriously, it seems an inaugural work, a different mode of comedy, one that Beckett attempted to rival in *Endgame*, a blending of *Hamlet* with *The Tempest*.

Allegory was not a Shakespearean mode, and I find little in *The Tempest*. W.B.C. Watkins, an admirable critic, noted Spenserian elements in Ariel's harpy scene and in the masque of Ceres, neither of which is one of the glories of the play. *The Tempest* provokes speculation, partly because we expect esoteric wisdom from Prospero, though we never receive any. His awesome art is absurdly out of proportion to his purposes; his adversaries are a sorry lot, and could be defeated by a mere Sycorax, rather than by the mightiest of magi. I suspect that anti-Faustianism is again the best clue to

Prospero; magic scarcely bears dramatic representation, unless a defla-
tionary element is also at work. Shakespeare was interested in everything,
and yet cared far more about inwardness than about magic. When his own
so potent art turned aside from inwardness, after the extraordinary fourteen
months in which he composed *King Lear, Macbeth,* and *Antony and Cleopatra,*
a kind of emptying-out of the self pervaded *Coriolanus* and *Timon of Athens.*
The apparent influx of myth and miracle that scholars celebrate in the last
plays is more ironic and even farcical than we have taken it to be. Prospero's magic is not always a persuasive substitute for the waning inwardness, and Shakespeare gives signs that he is cognizant of this trouble.

Prospero is nearly as nervous about missed cues and temporal limitations as Macbeth was, and his absolute magic is jumpily aware that its
sway cannot be eternal, that its authority is provisional. Authority seems
to me the play's mysterious preoccupation. I say "mysterious" because Prospero's authority is unlike anyone else's in Shakespeare. To say what it is not
is easy enough: not legal power, even though Prospero was legitimate
Duke of Milan. Nor is it precisely moral: Prospero is not truly anxious to
justify himself. Perhaps it has a link to what Kent implies when, in the disguise of Caius, he again seeks service with his master, Lear, but Prospero
does not have much in him of Lear's divine majesty. Prospero seeks a kind
of secularized spiritual authority, and he finally attains something like it,
though at considerable human expense to himself. Gerald Hammond, in
his wonderful study of seventeenth-century English poetry and poems,
*Fleeting Things* (1990), makes a fine observation on how even the opening
scene introduces the problem of authority: *"The Tempest* begins its explo-
ration of the uses and abuses of authority with a foundering ship on which
passengers and crew are at odds." The honest old Gonzalo admonishes the
forthright Boatswain to remember whom he has aboard, and receives a
wonderful reply:

> None that I more love than myself. You are a counsellor; if you can
> command these elements to silence, and work the peace of the pres-
> ence, we will not hand a rope more; use your authority: if you can-
> not, give thanks you have lived so long, and make yourself ready in

your cabin for the mischance of the hour, if it so hap. Cheerly, good hearts! Out of our way, I say.

[I.i.20–27]

The ironic authority has been usurped by Prospero, who commanded these elements to storm. When we first encounter Prospero, in the next scene, we hear him urging Miranda to "be collected" and cease to be distracted by tempest and shipwreck, since he assures us that no one has been hurt in the slightest. This is so endlessly suggestive that an audience has to be somewhat bewildered. If the overwhelming storm—which totally convinced the experienced Boatswain of its menace—is unreal, then what in the play can be accepted when it appears? A. D. Nuttall describes much of *The Tempest* as "pre-allegorical," a phenomenal sheen that encourages us both to marvel and to be skeptical. Prospero, though he later seems to be influenced by Ariel's concern for the victims of the mage's illusions, would seem to have decided upon "the rarer action" of forgiving his enemies even before he plots to get them under his control.

Since Prospero, through Ariel and his lesser daemons, controls nature on, and near, the island, the audience never can be sure what it is that they behold. When Prospero tells us that "bountiful Fortune" has brought his enemies to his shore, we can only wonder at the cosmological intelligence service that is at play. Ariel's first entrance (in advance of Caliban's) dissolves no ambiguities. This all-powerful spirit had been imprisoned in a pine tree by the witch Sycorax, and would be there still had not Prospero's Art liberated him. Evidently Ariel has not the resources to fend off magic, which is thus assigned a potency greater than that of the angelic world. Fire and air, like Caliban's earth and water, yield to the Fifth Element of hermetic sages and North African witches. The pleasantly teasing relationship between Prospero and Ariel contrasts with the fury of hatred between Prospero and Caliban, and yet Ariel, no more than Caliban, has the freedom to evade Prospero's will. Before Act I closes, that potent will charms Prince Ferdinand into a frozen stasis, demonstrating that the human, like the supernatural and the preternatural, is subject to Prospero's Art.

5

We hardly recognize that *The Tempest* is a comedy whenever Prospero is on stage. That may be only a consequence of our acting and directing traditions, which have failed to exploit the contrasts between the anti-Faust's authority and the antics of his hapless enemies. Since Prospero makes no appearance in Act II, the delicious humor comes through, even in some of our current ideological jamborees that pass for productions of *The Tempest*. Shakespeare is subtly genial and shrewd in the dialogues given to his castaways:

> *Adr.* Though this island seem to be desert,—
> *Ant.* Ha, ha, ha!
> *Seb.* So: you're paid.
> *Adr.* Uninhabitable, and almost inaccessible,—
> *Seb.* Yet,—
> *Adr.* Yet,—
> *Ant.* He could not miss't.
> *Adr.* It must needs be of subtle, tender and delicate temperance.
> *Ant.* Temperance was a delicate wench.
> *Seb.* Ay, and a subtle; as he most learnedly deliver'd.
> *Adr.* The air breathes upon us here most sweetly.
> *Seb.* As if it had lungs, and rotten ones.
> *Ant.* Or as 'twere perfumed by a fen.
> *Gon.* Here is everything advantageous to life.
> *Ant.* True; save means to live.
> *Seb.* Of that there's none, or little.
> *Gon.* How lush and lusty the grass looks! how green!
> *Ant.* The ground, indeed, is tawny.
> *Seb.* With an eye of green in 't.
> *Ant.* He misses not much.
> *Seb.* No; he doth but mistake the truth totally.

[II.i.34–55]

Partly, this works as an intricate allusion to the prophet Isaiah's vision of the destruction of Babylon:

Come downe and sit in the dust: a virgine, daughter Babel, sit on the grounde: there is no throne, O daughter of the Chaldeans: for thou shalt no more be called, Tendre and delicate.

[Geneva Bible, Isaiah 47:1]

Temperance, a woman's name among the Puritans, meaning both "calm" and "chaste," is also a word for a moderate climate. Antonio, Prospero's usurping brother, and Sebastian, would-be usurper of his brother, Alonso, King of Naples, are the unredeemable villains of the play. Gonzalo and Adrian, more amiable, are the butts of this nasty duo, but the jokes, on their deeper level, go against the scoffers, since the Isaiah allusion is a warning of the fall that awaits evildoers. The immediate comedy is that Gonzalo and Adrian have the truer perspective, since the isle (though they cannot know this) is enchanted, while Antonio and Sebastian are savage reductionists, who themselves "mistake the truth totally." The audience perhaps begins to understand that perspective governs everything on Prospero's island, which can be seen either as desert or as paradise, depending upon the viewer.

Isaiah and Montaigne fuse in Gonzalo's subsequent rhapsody of an ideal commonwealth that he would establish upon the isle, were he king of it. The taunts of Sebastian and Antonio at this charming prospect prepare us for their attempt to murder the sleeping Alonso and Gonzalo, who are saved by Ariel's intervention, an episode more melodramatic than the comic contest allows us to apprehend seriously. Comedy returns in the meeting between Caliban and King Alonso's jester, Trinculo, and his perpetually intoxicated brother, Stephano. Poor Caliban, hero of our current discourses on colonialism, celebrates his new freedom from Prospero by worshiping Trinculo as his god:

No more dams I'll make for fish
  Nor fetch in firing

At requiring;
Nor scrape trenchering, nor wash dish:
    'Ban, 'Ban, Cacaliban
Has a new master:—get a new man.


Freedom, high-day! high-day, freedom! freedom,
high-day, freedom!


The complexities of Caliban multiply in Act III, where his timid brutality and hatred of Prospero combine in a murderous scheme:

Why, as I told thee, 'tis a custom with him
I' th' afternoon to sleep: there thou mayst brain him,
Having first seiz'd his books; or with a log
Batter his skull, or paunch him with a stake,
Or cut his wezand with thy knife. Remember
First to possess his books; for without them
He's but a sot, as I am, nor hath not
One spirit to command: they all do hate him
As rootedly as I. Burn but his books.

[III.ii.85–93]


The viciousness of this contrasts with the aesthetic poignance of Caliban's reaction to the invisible Ariel's music:

Be not afeard; the isle is full of noises,
Sounds and sweet airs, that give delight and hurt not.
Sometimes a thousand twangling instruments
Will hum about mine ears; and sometimes voices,
That, if I then had wak'd after long sleep,
Will make me sleep again: and then, in dreaming,
The clouds methought would open, and show riches
Ready to drop upon me; that, when I wak'd,
I cried to dream again.

[III.ii.133–41]

What reconciles the two passages is Caliban's childishness; he is still very young, and his uncompleted education yielded to the trauma of failed adoption. Shakespeare, inventing the half-human in Caliban, astonishingly blends together the childish and the childlike. As audience, we are repelled by the childish, gruesome fantasies of battering Prospero's skull, or paunching him with a stake, or cutting his windpipe with a knife. Yet only a few moments on, we are immensely moved by the exquisite, childlike pathos of Caliban's Dickensian dream. Far from the heroic rebel that our academic and theatrical ideologues now desire him to become, Caliban is a Shakespearean representation of the family romance at its most desperate, with an authentic changeling who cannot bear his outcast condition.

As a victim of that condition, Caliban is the ironic forerunner of the state of traumatized confusion that Prospero and Ariel will impose upon all of the castaway princes and nobles. Hounded by Ariel in the guise of a Harpy, they at last are herded into a grove near Prospero's cell, to await his judgment. First, the magus celebrates the betrothal of Miranda and Ferdinand with a visionary masque performed by spirits at his command. Poetically, this entertainment seems to me the nadir of *The Tempest*, and I suggest it may be, in some places, a deliberate parody of the court masques that Jonson was composing for James I at the moment that Shakespeare's play was written. Far more important than the masque itself is the manner of its disruption, when Prospero suddenly suffers the crucial trial of his Art. He starts suddenly, and when he speaks, the masque vanishes:

> I had forgot that foul conspiracy
> Of the beast Caliban and his confederates
> Against my life: the minute of their plot
> Is almost come.
>
> [IV.i.139–42]

Few theatrical coups, even in Shakespeare, match this. On edge throughout the play to seize the propitious moment, Prospero has so lulled himself with the showman's aspect of his Art that he, and all his, nearly are undone. Critics tend to slight Prospero's perturbation here, question its necessity, as if they were so many Ferdinands, finding it "strange." Miranda refutes them when she observes that "Never till this day / Saw I him touch'd with anger, so distemper'd." His anger is not just with "the beast Caliban," discarded foster son, but with himself for failing in alertness, in the control of consciousness. A lifetime of devotion to the strict discipline of Hermetic lore has only barely prevailed, and something in Prospero's self-confidence is forever altered.

I am not at all clear as to why critics should find this a mystery: Shakespeare invents the psychology of overpreparing the event, from which the majority of us suffer. I think of Browning's Childe Roland, one of Shakespeare's heirs, who suddenly comes upon the Dark Tower and chides himself: "Dunce, / Dotard, a-dozing at the very nonce, / After a life spent training for the sight!" Prospero's mastery depends upon a strictly trained consciousness, which must be unrelenting. His momentary letting-go is more than a danger signal and provides his most memorable utterance, addressed to Ferdinand, his prospective son-in-law, and so heir both to Naples and to Milan:

> You do look, my son, in a mov'd sort,
> As if you were dismay'd: be cheerful, sir.
> Our revels now are ended. These our actors,
> As I foretold you, were all spirits, and
> Are melted into air, into thin air:
> And, like the baseless fabric of this vision,
> The cloud-capp'd towers, the gorgeous palaces,
> The solemn temples, the great globe itself,
> Yea, all which it inherit, shall dissolve,
> And, like this insubstantial pageant faded,
> Leave not a rack behind. We are such stuff
> As dreams are made on; and our little life
> Is rounded with a sleep. Sir, I am vex'd;
> Bear with my weakness; my old brain is troubled:
> Be not disturb'd with my infirmity:
> If you be pleas'd, retire into my cell,
> And there repose: a turn or two I'll walk,
> To still my beating mind.

[IV.i.146–63]

A tradition of interpretation, now little credited, read this as Shakespeare's overt farewell to his art. That is certainly rather too reductive, yet one wonders at "the great globe itself," which may contain an ironic reference to Shakespeare's own theater. Whether or not there is a personal element here, Prospero's great declaration confirms the audience's sense that this is a magus without transcendental beliefs, whether Christian or Hermetic–Neo-Platonic. Prospero's vision and the London of towers, palaces, and the Globe itself shall dissolve, not to be replaced by God, heaven, or any other entity. Nor do we appear to have any resurrection: "our little life / Is rounded with a sleep." What the audience sees upon the stage is insubstantial, and so is the audience itself. What vexes Prospero indeed is his infirmity, his lapse of attention, and the murderousness of Caliban, but what might vex the audience is the final realization that this powerful wizard pragmatically is a nihilist, a kind of benign Iago (an outrageous phrase!), whose project of necessity must end in his despair. When he urgently summons Ariel, and says, "Spirit, / We must prepare to meet with Caliban," the telling reply is:

> Ay, my commander: when I presented Ceres,
> I thought to have told thee of it; but I fear'd
> Lest I might anger thee.

> [IV.i.167–69]

Since Ariel and Prospero rather easily drive out Caliban, Stephano, and Trinculo, who flee before spirit hounds, we are left to wonder what Ariel might have done had Prospero not roused himself. Not once in the play does Ariel act without a specific order from Prospero, so perhaps the danger from Caliban's plot was more real than many critics concede. There is a certain air of relief in Prospero's language as he addresses Ariel to open Act V, when the culmination is at hand:

> Now does my project gather to a head:
> My charms crack not; my spirits obey; and time
> Goes upright with his carriage. How's the day?

> [V.i.1–3]

After ordering Ariel to release the King of Naples and the other worthies, Prospero achieves the zenith of his anti-Faustianism in a great speech
of renunciation, which nevertheless provides more fresh queries than answers:

> Ye elves of hills, brooks, standing lakes, and groves;
> And ye that on the sands with printless foot
> Do chase the ebbing Neptune, and do fly him
> When he comes back; you demi-puppets that
> By moonshine do the green sour ringlets make,
> Whereof the ewe not bites; and you whose pastime
> Is to make midnight mushrooms, that rejoice
> To hear the solemn curfew; by whose aid—
> Weak masters though ye be—I have bedimm'd
> The noontide sun, call'd forth the mutinous winds,
> And 'twixt the green sea and the azur'd vault
> Set roaring war: to the dread rattling thunder
> Have I given fire, and rifted Jove's stout oak
> With his own bolt; the strong-bas'd promontory
> Have I made shake, and by the spurs pluck'd up
> The pine and cedar: graves at my command
> Have wak'd their sleepers, op'd, and let 'em forth
> By my so potent Art. But this rough magic
> I here abjure; and, when I have requir'd
> Some heavenly music—which even now I do,—
> To work mine end upon their senses, that
> This airy charm is for, I'll break my staff,
> Bury it certain fathoms in the earth,
> And deeper than did ever plummet sound
> I'll drown my book.

[V.i.33–57]

The poetic strength of *The Tempest*, perhaps even of Shakespeare,
touches a limit of art in this apparent *kenosis*, or emptying-out, of Prospero's

mortal godhood. If I say "apparent," it is because the unholy powers of the magus surpass anything we could have expected, and we wonder if this declaration really can undo his acquired nature, which itself is art. The spirits supposedly being dismissed are deprecated as "weak masters," and we have to ask when and why Prospero roused the dead. That art indeed would have been so much more than potent that to term it "rough magic" is altogether inadequate. Which book will be drowned, out of the number in Prospero's library, or is this not his own manuscript?

Prospero's abjuration sounds more like a great assertion of power than like a withdrawal from efficacy. Nothing Prospero says severs him more from Shakespeare than this speech. We are listening not to a poet-playwright but to an uncanny magician whose art has become so internalized that it cannot be abandoned, even though he insists it will be. The single scene that is Act V will continue for some 250 lines, during which Prospero's authority suffers no diminishment. Why do Antonio and Sebastian, who express no repentance whatsoever, take no action against Prospero, if he no longer commands spirits? When Prospero, in an aside to Sebastian and Antonio, says that he knows of their plot against King Alonso, yet "at this time / I will tell no tales," why do they not cut him down? Sebastian only mutters, in an aside, "The devil speaks in him," and indeed from the perspective of the villains, the devil does inhabit Prospero, who terrifies them. Prospero may yet attempt to abandon his art, but it is not at all clear that his supernatural authority ever will abandon him. His deep melancholy as the play closes may not be related to his supposed renunciation.

Most of what we hear in the remainder of *The Tempest* is triumph, restoration, some reconciliation, and even some hints that Prospero and Caliban will work out their dreadful relationship, but much also is left as puzzle. We are not told that Caliban will be allowed to stay on the island; will he accompany Prospero "to my Milan, where / Every third thought shall be my grave"? The thought of Caliban in Italy is well-nigh unthinkable; what is scarcely thinkable is Antonio in Milan, and Sebastian in Naples. Presumably the marriage of Ferdinand and Miranda will ensure both Naples and Milan against usurpers, though who can say? In some respects, Prospero in

Milan as restored ruler is as unsettling a prospect as Caliban continuing his education in that city. Gonzalo, in a remarkable speech, tells us that Ferdinand:

> found a wife
> Where he himself was lost, Prospero his dukedom
> In a poor isle, and all of us ourselves
> When no man was his own.
>
> [V.i.210–13]

Gonzalo encompasses more than he intends, for Prospero's true dukedom may always be that poor isle, where "no man was his own," since all were Prospero's, and only he was his own. How can the magus, whatever his remaining powers may be, find himself his own in Milan?

# 34

# HENRY VIII

My experience of rereading *Henry VIII* makes me doubt the hypothesis that a considerable portion of it could be by John Fletcher. Though it is a better dramatic poem than a play, *Henry VIII* seems remarkably unified, with only a few touches that suggest Fletcher. An experiment in pageantry, *Henry VIII* offers grand roles—Wolsey, Katherine, Henry—rather than characters, and its principal fascination (at least for me) is Shakespeare's detachment from all the protagonists, who interest him only when they are on their way down and out (Buckingham, Wolsey, Katherine, very nearly Cranmer) but who then move the poet, and us, to considerable sympathy.

The puzzle of the play is the king, who is not the Holbein–Charles Laughton Henry VIII, and always remains ambiguous. Shakespeare, with his customary political caution, avoids any suggestion that Henry is particularly culpable when his favorites fall, though the playwright also never quite exonerates the king. Even the Catholic–Protestant confrontation is so muted that Shakespeare hardly appears to take sides. The play is eloquently plangent, though it purports to conclude with a celebratory patriotism when Cranmer prophesies the glorious reign of the just-born Queen Elizabeth. The audience has to reflect that Queen Anne Bullen (Boleyn) joined Cromwell and Thomas More (mentioned in the play as replacing Wolsey) in being beheaded, and that Cranmer is spared by Henry only to be burned alive at a later time. No one in the drama is endowed with any inwardness; they are heraldic pictures with beautiful voices, which is all that Shakespeare wants them to be. Only the king is not a speaking portrait; whether he is more or less than that is beyond judgment, because of Shakespeare's evasiveness. Henry, with all-but-absolute power, somehow escapes responsibility for the evil he has sanctioned in Wolsey, and perpetrated against Buckingham and Katherine. We are not even offered conflicting perspectives on the king; he lacks the nasty consistency that might have made him interesting. A director and an actor can do about anything they wish with the part; every staging I've seen did not abandon the Holbein-Laughton archetype, though there is little in the text to support it.

Why did Shakespeare write *Henry VIII*? The alternating title, *All Is True*, is capable of various interpretations, none of them particularly persuasive. Some is true, some isn't, as Shakespeare probably realized. The representation of the king would be unlikely, except that it scarcely exists. Henry at first is not at all clever; he is Wolsey's gull, and is enlightened only when the wicked Cardinal-Chamberlain gets careless in correspondence. A different Henry saves Cranmer late in the play, but we are told nothing about why the king's judgment has improved. We cannot even know whether Henry discards Katherine because of his insatiable temperament, though blaming it on Wolsey is implausible. Shakespeare accepts everything. "All is true" translates into: Don't make moral judgments; they are neither safe nor helpful. Look at this grand pageant; listen to these elegiac laments; share the nostalgia for the glory that was Elizabeth.

*Henry VIII* is a processional, a reversion to pre-Shakespearean theater. Shakespeare, weary of his own genius, here undoes most of what he had invented. We are not upon the stage in *Henry VIII*, except insofar as any of us believes that she or he has fallen from greatness. A dramatic poem of things-in-their-farewell, this is a performance piece, perhaps a last hurrah (though Fletcher and Shakespeare's *The Two Noble Kinsmen* followed it). Russell Fraser, commending Shakespeare for having "mastered the noblest rhetoric ever fashioned in English," wryly also notes that the protagonists of *Henry VIII* "dance to the same tune when the last fit of their greatness is on them." Going down, everyone indeed is equally noble in this play;

Shakespeare's "distincts" are gone. Dr. Johnson thought that "the genius of Shakespeare comes in and goes out with Katherine," a judgment that surprises me, since the last fits of Buckingham and of Wolsey remarkably resemble the laments of Katherine. Still, Johnson, the great moralist, was moved by "the meek sorrows and virtuous distress" of the cast-off queen, and Buckingham is hardly meek or Wolsey virtuous. This dramatic poem went a little to one side of Johnson, who loved Cordelia best of Shakespeare's heroines. And yet *Henry VIII*, considered for its poetry alone, deserves more aesthetic esteem than it has been accorded. Like *The Two Noble Kinsmen, Henry VIII* marks a new and original style, one that transcends the stage images who chant it. We hear its first culmination when Buckingham goes to his "long divorce of steel," and compares his fate to his father's, murdered by Richard III's command:

When I came hither I was Lord High Constable
And Duke of Buckingham: now poor Edward Bohun;
Yet I am richer than any base accusers,
That never knew what truth meant: I now seal it,
And with that blood will make 'em one day groan for't.
My noble father Henry of Buckingham,
Who first rais'd head against usurping Richard,
Flying for succour to his servant Banister,
Being distress'd, was by that wretch betray'd,
And without trial fell; God's peace be with him.
Henry the Seventh succeeding, truly pitying
My father's loss, like a most royal prince
Restor'd me to my honours; and out of ruins
Made my name once more noble. Now his son,
Henry the Eighth, life, honour, name and all
That made me happy, at one stroke has taken
For ever from the world. I had my trial,
And must needs say a noble one; which makes me
A little happier than my wretched father:
Yet thus far we are one in fortunes; both

Fell by our servants, by those men we lov'd most:
A most unnatural and faithless service.
Heaven has an end in all; yet you that hear me,
This from a dying man receive as certain:
Where you are liberal of your loves and counsels,
Be sure you be not loose; for those you make friends
And give your hearts to, when they once perceive
The least rub in your fortunes, fall away
Like water from ye, never found again
But where they mean to sink ye. All good people
Pray for me; I must now forsake ye; that last hour
Of my long weary life is come upon me:
Farewell;
And when you would say something that is sad,
Speak how I fell. I have done, and God forgive me.

[II.i.102–36]

Shakespeare's own obsession with betrayal by a friend seems very strong in this, reminding us of the situation of the Sonnets, and of the Player King's speech on the contrariness of wills and fates in *Hamlet*. There is also an affinity with the *Funeral Elegy* for Will Peter, composed just before *Henry VIII*, where the poet's bitterness at having been slandered is pungently conveyed, with several anticipations of the play's laments. Perhaps Shakespeare himself felt that he was only "a little happier than his wretched father." We do not know, nor are we at all certain whether the Blatant Beast of gossip had impugned the poet with regard to Will Peter, perhaps for a relationship like that conveyed by the Sonnets. There is a spiritual music in the formal complaints of *Henry VIII* that carries an undersong of personal sorrow, at least to my ear. Wolsey's great orations of loss are almost too magnificent for so venal a person; their sonority again hints at a private grief:

So farewell, to the little good you bear me.
Farewell? a long farewell to all my greatness.

This is the state of man; to-day he puts forth
The tender leaves of hopes, to-morrow blossoms,
And bears his blushing honours thick upon him:
The third day comes a frost, a killing frost,
And when he thinks, good easy man, full surely
His greatness is a-ripening, nips his root,
And then he falls as I do. I have ventur'd
Like little wanton boys that swim on bladders,
This many summers in a sea of glory,
But far beyond my depth: my high-blown pride
At length broke under me, and now has left me,
Weary and old with service, to the mercy
Of a rude stream that must for ever hide me.
Vain pomp and glory of this world, I hate ye;
I feel my heart new open'd. O how wretched
Is that poor man that hangs on princes' favours!
There is betwixt that smile we would aspire to,
That sweet aspect of princes, and their ruin,
More pangs and fears than wars or women have;
And when he falls, he falls like Lucifer,
Never to hope again.

[III.ii.350–72]

It is not possible for the auditor or reader to care about Wolsey, a mean-souled cleric who deserves anything that exposure and humiliation bring to him. Again like the *Funeral Elegy*, the melody of disgrace seems intensely close. Is the prince here truly not Henry VIII but Henry Wriothesley, third Earl of Southampton? The question, though unanswerable, has its critical use, if only because the poetry of Wolsey's fall is so grandly in excess of what so mean a role merits. The problem is not Wolsey's wickedness but his littleness. This is no Iago or Macbeth, just a crooked administrator, an archetypal politician. Wolsey cannot fall like Lucifer; he is no morning star gone down to perdition. And yet the astonishing resources of Shake-speare's most mature style are summoned up to hymn a mere hypocrite's discomfiture. A pageant is a pageant, however, commercially speaking, and the strongest style in the language might lavish its exuberance where it would. Wolsey, addressing his aide, Cromwell, urges this loyal servant to abandon him, in accents enormously beyond the decorum of a politician's fall:

> Let's dry our eyes; and thus far hear me Cromwell,
> And when I am forgotten, as I shall be,
> And sleep in dull cold marble, where no mention
> Of me more must be heard of, say I taught thee;
> Say Wolsey, that once trod the ways of glory,
> And sounded all the depths and shoals of honour,
> Found thee a way (out of his wrack) to rise in,
> A sure and safe one, though thy master miss'd it.
> Mark but my fall, and that that ruin'd me:
> Cromwell, I charge thee, fling away ambition,
> By that sin fell the angels; how can man then,
> The image of his maker, hope to win by it?
> Love thyself last, cherish those hearts that hate thee;
> Corruption wins not more than honesty.
> Still in thy right hand carry gentle peace
> To silence envious tongues. Be just, and fear not;
> Let all the ends thou aim'st at be thy country's,
> Thy God's and truth's: then if thou fall'st, O Cromwell,
> Thou fall'st a blessed martyr.
> Serve the king: and prithee lead me in:
> There take an inventory of all I have,
> To the last penny, 'tis the king's. My robe,
> And my integrity to heaven, is all
> I dare now call mine own. O Cromwell, Cromwell,
> Had I but serv'd my God with half the zeal
> I serv'd my king, he would not in mine age
> Have left me naked to mine enemies.

[III.ii.431–57]

Eloquent beyond eloquence, this sublimity certainly is not applicable to Shakespeare himself, whose worldly ambitions did not exceed the renewal of a gentleman's coat of arms and the comfortable affluence of his final return to Stratford. Nor does the godly zeal suit Shakespeare, though there is a curious medley of defensive piety and skeptical doubt of resurrection in the *Funeral Elegy* for William Peter. The playwright perhaps felt "naked to mine enemies" in 1612–13, since that is the aura of the *Funeral Elegy*, but if those enemies existed at all, we again do not know who they were. Shakespeare, nearing his fiftieth birthday, may have been physically ill, or somewhat traumatized by slander, or both. We reflect that, unlike Marlowe or Ben Jonson, he always in his right hand had carried "gentle peace / To silence envious tongues." One need not be the great and good Dr. Samuel Johnson to be immensely moved by Queen Katherine's final lines:

> When I am dead, good wench,
> Let me be us'd with honour; strew me over
> With maiden flowers, that all the world may know
> I was a chaste wife to my grave: embalm me,
> Then lay me forth; although unqueen'd, yet like
> A queen, and daughter to a king inter me.
> I can no more.
>
> [IV.ii.167–73]

And yet it is the lines that touch us; poor Katherine is too pathetic to sustain this hushed harmony, and we can wonder again why Shakespeare should be so inspired. Paradoxically, he had attained a condition in which drama, from which he had become estranged, still kindled his powers, while the sincere grief of the *Funeral Elegy* provoked a poem so frequently banal (though not always) that many scholars reject the authorship as not being good enough for him.

I cannot solve the puzzle of *Henry VIII*, and I have trouble responding to the rapture and exultation of Cranmer's concluding prophecy concerning the infant Elizabeth. Dead at fifty-two, Shakespeare never experienced old age, and yet the style of old age dominates *Henry VIII*. Falstaff, one of Shakespeare's prime surrogates—more so, perhaps, than Hamlet—refused to acknowledge his years and is all the more heroically funny for it. The world seems very old in *Henry VIII*, and in the scenes Shakespeare wrote for *The Two Noble Kinsmen*. Through his uncanniness, Shakespeare knew the end of his era, whatever we now choose to call that time. *Henry VIII* is an elegy for Shakespeare's world-altering achievement in poetic drama, and consciously bids farewell to the playwright's highest powers.

# 35

# THE TWO NOBLE KINSMEN

Ultimately the supremacy of Shakespeare consists in his unmatched power of thinking. Since this is poetic thinking, and usually dramatic in its nature, we tend to consider it as imaging rather than arguing. But here too Shakespeare-as-inventor encloses us. His is the largest form of representing thought, as well as action, that we have known. Can we truly distinguish his thinking from his representations of thinking? Is it Shakespeare or Hamlet who thinks not too much but much too well? Hamlet is his own Iago just as he is his own Falstaff, because Shakespeare has made Hamlet the freest of all his "free artists of themselves," to use Hegel's phrase. Shakespeare's eminence among all strong poets is that, compared even with Dante or Chaucer, he enjoys and manifests the greatest degree of freedom in fashioning his free artists of self. Nietzsche implied that the Dionysian Hamlet perished of the truth, presumably after abandoning art. The Hamlet of Act V is certainly not the poet-playwright-director of Acts II and III, and Shakespeare allows the dying prince to hint that he possesses a new kind of knowledge not yet available to us. Such knowledge would have come from a different thinking that began with Hamlet's sea change, on the abortive voyage to England. Our only evidence for differences in Shakespeare's own thinking ensues from intimations that his greatest plays induced sea changes in their own author. The experience of composing *Hamlet* and *King Lear, Macbeth* and *Antony and Cleopatra, The Winter's Tale* and *The Tempest* left traces available to us in his final work, *The Two Noble Kinsmen*, of a new Shakespeare, who chose to abandon writing after touching, and transgressing, the limits of art, and perhaps also of thought.

As far as we can know, the Shakespearean portions of *The Two Noble Kinsmen* (1613) constitute the final writing of any sort by the author of *Hamlet* and *King Lear.* I have never seen a performance of *The Two Noble Kinsmen*, and don't particularly want to, since Shakespeare's contributions to the play are scarcely dramatic. Critics of *The Two Noble Kinsmen* generally disagree, but I find Shakespeare's style, in this final work, to be subtler and defter than ever, though very difficult to absorb. His purposes here are very enigmatic; he abandons his career-long concern with character and personality and presents a darker, more remote or estranged vision of human life than ever before. Pageant, ritual, ceremony, whatever one chooses to call it, Shakespeare's share in *The Two Noble Kinsmen* is poetry astonishing even for him, but very difficult poetry, hardly suitable for the theater. It contrasts oddly with the rest of the play, written by John Fletcher, in perhaps the third collaboration between the two. Since we do not have their *Cardenio*, and since Fletcher may have written relatively little or even none of *Henry VIII*, *The Two Noble Kinsmen* is their only certain joint enterprise. Shakespeare's colleagues, editing the First Folio, included *Henry VIII* but not the final play, thus conceding it to Fletcher (then their resident playwright, as Shakespeare's successor). Scholars now mostly agree that Shakespeare wrote Act I, the first scene of Act III, and Act V (excluding the second scene). Three-fifths of the play is evidently Fletcher's, and is both lively and rather silly. Shakespeare's two-fifths is somber and profound, and perhaps gives us a better entrance into Shakespeare's inner life, in his final phase, than is provided by *Cymbeline*, *The Winter's Tale*, and *The Tempest*.

More lyrical than dramatic, *The Two Noble Kinsmen*'s Shakespearean portions manifest little action and minimal character portrayal. Instead we hear a voice, hardly, as in *Henry VIII*, in "the style of old age" (Shakespeare being forty-nine) and yet more than a little weary of great passions, and of the sufferings of what Chesterton was to call "great spirits in chains." Prospero, Shakespeare's anti-Faust, was his last great spirit. Theseus, who by the close of *The Two Noble Kinsmen* is almost Shakespeare's surrogate, is in himself only a voice, one remarkably unlike that of the Theseus of *A Midsum-*

*mer Night's Dream.* The earlier Theseus was Hippolyta's inferior; this final Theseus is at least her equal. He is Shakespeare's last poet, possibly reflecting what I suppose must be called the playwright's staggered and uneasy retirement. Shakespeare seems to have gone home again, to Stratford, in late 1610 or early 1611, but then to have returned intermittently to London until sometime in 1613. After that, in the nearly three years before his death, he was in Stratford, writing nothing. The rest was silence, but why?

Only conjecture is available to us, and I suspect our best clues are in *The Two Noble Kinsmen.* Shakespeare's abandonment of his art is virtually unique in the annals of Western literature, nor can I think of a major composer or painter who made a similar retreat. Tolstoy gave up his true work for a time, and wrote religious tracts instead, but returned magnificently at the end with his short novel *Hadji Murad.* There are poets who should have stopped and didn't; Wordsworth after 1807 and Whitman after 1865 wrote very badly indeed. Molière died at fifty just after writing, directing, and acting the lead part in *The Imaginary Invalid.* Shakespeare possibly gave up acting as early as 1604, in his later thirties, and presumably directed all his plays through *Henry VIII,* though he may have stopped earlier, perhaps in 1611, since by then he lived mostly in Stratford. We can only guess whether he supervised *The Tempest* in 1611, or whether he was on hand to see the Globe Theater burn down during a performance of *Henry VIII* on June 29, 1613. Biographers surmise some of Shakespeare's familial and financial activities during the last three years of his life, but they cannot help us to speculate as to why he chose to end after a dramatist's career of a quarter century. Russell Fraser, my favorite Shakespeare biographer, wryly repeats Theodore Spencer's fantasy that a deputation of the King's Men called upon their old friend and urged him to leave the writing to John Fletcher, who by 1613 had begun to be much more the mode than the old-fashioned Shakespeare. Indeed, I can imagine the players reacting with great puzzlement and frustration to the speeches provided them by Shakespeare in *The Two Noble Kinsmen.* Yet they would have known that Fletcher was an inkblot in comparison to Shakespeare, whose enormous success had been their fortune also.

In his final effort, the endlessly fecund experimenter goes beyond romance or tragicomedy into a strange new mode, which he founds upon Chaucer, his truest precursor, and still his only authentic rival in the language. Shakespeare returns to *The Knight's Tale*, which had helped inform *A Midsummer Night's Dream*, and this time he engages it much more directly. Chesterton, who had a shrewd sense of the relationship between Chaucer and Shakespeare, remarked of *The Knight's Tale* that

> Chaucer does not himself go to prison with Palamon and Arcite, as Shakespeare does in some sense go to prison with Richard the Second. Nay, to some extent, and in some subtle fashion, Shakespeare seems to identify himself with Hamlet who finds Denmark a prison or the whole world a prison. We do not have this sense of things closing in upon the soul in Chaucer, with his simple tragedies; one might almost say, his sunny tragedies. In his world misfortunes are misfortunes, like clouds in the sky; but there is a sky.

But by *The Two Noble Kinsmen*, Shakespeare has no interest in going to prison (or anywhere else) with Palamon and Arcite, and the play (or Shakespeare's part in it) is all clouds and no sky. Where Shakespeare based his own Theseus in *A Midsummer Night's Dream* more on Chaucer's Knight than on Chaucer's Theseus, the Theseus of *The Two Noble Kinsmen* is a harsh figure throughout, until at the close he seems to modulate into someone rather like Shakespeare himself. Chaucer's Knight and Shakespeare's earlier Theseus are chivalric skeptics; the final Theseus might be called a brutal nihilist, who nevertheless plays at maintaining the outer forms of chivalry. The ethos of Chaucer's poem is condensed by one of the Knight's couplets:

It is ful fair a man to bare him evene,
For alday meeteth men at unset stevene.

My old friend, the great Chaucerian Talbot Donaldson, superbly paraphrased this as:

It is a good thing for a man to bear himself with equanimity, for one
is constantly keeping appointments one never made.

That is not quite the stance of Theseus in the final lines of *The Two Noble
Kinsmen*, as far as we know the last lines of serious poetry that Shakespeare
ever wrote:

> O you heavenly charmers,
> What things you make of us! For what we lack
> We laugh; for what we have are sorry; still
> Are children in some kind. Let us be thankful
> For that which is, and with you leave dispute
> That are above our question. Let's go off,
> And bear us like the time.
>
> [V.iv.131–37]

I will return to this passage when I conclude this chapter, but for now
note only that to "bear us like the time" alludes to "bare him evene," while
swerving away from the Chaucerian equanimity. Chaucer, a genial satirist,
is also a very good-humored ironist; the ironies of *The Two Noble Kinsmen*, as
we will see, are savage. One might have thought that Shakespeare had
touched the limits of bitterness in *Troilus and Cressida* and *Measure for Measure*,
but he extends those limits in his final play. Mars and Venus govern *The Two
Noble Kinsmen*, and it would be difficult to decide which deity is more reprehensible, or whether indeed it is pragmatically responsible to distinguish
between the two. "Make love, not war!," a popular chant of the sixties, becomes sublimely inane in *The Two Noble Kinsmen*, since Shakespeare at forty-
nine scatters organized violence and eros into a confusion not to be
resolved.

In temperament and visions of reality, Shakespeare's work from about
1588 through *Twelfth Night* in 1601 was profoundly Chaucerian. The
dramatist of the problem plays, the high tragedies, and the late romances
still rendered a kind of homage to Chaucer, but the final resort to this
greatest of precursors hints at a third Shakespeare, from whom the genial

spirit, even in irony, has departed. Had there been a theater to write for, perhaps Shakespeare would have left us another three or four plays, but he evidently sensed that no theater would or could have played them, and one can doubt that even *his* prestige would find a theater now for a nihilism surpassing *The Two Noble Kinsmen's*, even if such a darkness were possible. *The Knight's Tale* evades the abyss of nihilism, though its implications are dark enough: pure caprice governs all of life.

Chaucer's heroes, Palamon and Arcite, are sworn brothers and chivalric idealists, until they gaze upon the superb Emily, the sister of Hippolyta, now married to Theseus of Athens. From that fatal falling-in-love onward, they are sworn rivals, determined to cut each other down, so that the survivor can possess Emily. Theseus sets up a grand tournament to settle the matter, but Arcite's victory proves ironic, since he falls off his horse during a victory canter and is mortally injured. Palamon therefore gets the girl, and Theseus delivers an oration that insists all this was divinely ordained.

But Theseus does not speak for the narrating Knight, nor does the Knight speak for the poet Chaucer, though the differences between the three are subtle. For the Knight, love is an accident, and all life is accidental, including the ruin of the friendship of Palamon and Arcite. Talbot Donaldson interprets Chaucer as implying that pure chance governs everything, including love and death, which does not leave much of Theseus's theodicy but bears out the Knight's stoic acceptance of keeping appointments one has never made. Since Palamon and Arcite are virtually indistinguishable, while poor Emily is passive, the reader might not much care if it were not for Chaucer's own subtle negations. Palamon, Arcite, and Emily pray respectively in the temples of Venus, Mars, and Diana, all of which are chapels of pain, replete with representations of victims and victimization. The Knight describes these with bland cheerfulness, but we shudder, and Chaucer clearly intends that we are to be appalled.

Talbot Donaldson wryly notes that "whereas the horrors in Chaucer seem mostly charged to the gods above, Shakespeare puts them back where they started, in the hearts of people." For *The Two Noble Kinsmen*, that is an understatement: eros is the authentic horror, the never-ending and ultimate illness, universal and afflicting all ages of men and women, once they have left childhood for the sorrows of sexual life. In fact, Shake-

speare's part of *The Two Noble Kinsmen* might make us doubt that life is anything except sorrows. Act I opens with three mourning Queens throwing
themselves down at the feet, respectively, of Theseus, Hippolyta, and
Emilia. These women in black are the widows of three kings among the
Seven Against Thebes, whose rotting corpses surround the walls of Creon's
city, for the tyrant refuses them burial. The Queens' supplicating laments
are ritualistic, essentially baroque in their elaborations:

> We are three queens, whose sovereigns fell before
> The wrath of cruel Creon; who endured
> The beaks of ravens, talons of the kites,
> And pecks of crows in the foul fields of Thebes.
> He will not suffer us to burn their bones,
> To urn their ashes, nor take th' offence
> Of mortal loathsomeness from the blest eye
> Of holy Phoebus, but infects the winds
> With stench of our slain lords. O, pity, Duke!
> Thou purger of the earth, draw thy feared sword
> That does good turns to th' world; give us the bones
> Of our dead kings, that we may chapel them;
> And of thy boundless goodness take some note
> That for our crowned heads we have no roof,
> Save this which is the lion's and the bear's,
> And vault to everything.

> [I.i.39–54]

One could fit the matter of their plea into ten fewer lines, but the man-
nerism of their speech is more important. The luxuriance, not so much of
grief, but of outrage, dominates. Outrageousness is the rhetorical tonality
of Shakespeare's final mode, where most voices carry the burden of having been outraged: by injustice, by time, by eros, by death. Thomas De
Quincey, the Romantic critic most attuned to rhetoric, found in Acts I
and V of *The Two Noble Kinsmen* "the most superb work in the language," and
commended Shakespeare's "more elaborate style of excellence." What are
the poetic motives of such extraordinary elaboration? Theodore Spencer,

puzzling out these "slow rhythms" and this "formal grace," suggested a choral effect, distanced from action:

> There are, in the Shakespearean parts of *The Two Noble Kinsmen*, an unmistakable incantation, tone, and order: the incantation which accepts illusion, the tone which has forgotten tragedy, and an order melted at the edges into a larger unity of acceptance and wonder.

Spencer, whose own lyrics closely imitated Yeats's, seems to me to be describing late Yeats, not late Shakespeare. Illusion, acceptance, and wonder are neither the matter nor the manner of *The Two Noble Kinsmen*. The style of old age suits the Yeats of *Last Poems and Plays* or the Hardy of *Winter Words*, or the Stevens of *The Rock*, but not Shakespeare in this final play. If this greatest of poets is weary of passion, he is also estranged from the enormous panoply of styles he has previously created. Ellipsis becomes a favorite rhetorical figure, which is bewildering in so baroque a style; to elaborate while leaving out is a strange mode, yet it is perfectly appropriate for this play of destructive desire and obliterated friendship. Theseus reacts to the first queen's litany by remembering the long-ago day of her wedding to the slain Capaneus:

> you were that time fair;
> Not Juno's mantle fairer than your tresses,
> Nor in more bounty spread her; your wheaten wreath
> Was then nor threshed nor blasted; Fortune at you
> Dimpled her cheek with smiles.
>
> [I.i.62–66]

Himself about to be married, Theseus abruptly laments (rather unflatteringly to her face) the loss of the first Queen's beauty:

> O grief and time,
> Fearful consumers, you will all devour!
>
> [I.i.69–70]

It is that sense of loss, more than the entreaties of the Queens, and even of Hippolyta and Emilia, that makes Theseus decide to postpone his marriage, in order to march against Creon and Thebes. This first scene of heraldic intensity yields to an equally deliberate second, the introduction of Palamon and Arcite. Shakespeare wastes no art in rendering them at all distinct from each other; they seem, indeed, as inseparable cousins, to share the same high, somewhat priggish moral character, and to exhibit no personality whatsoever. Their interest for Shakespeare, and for us, is as a polemical thrust against the London of 1613, the city the playwright had abandoned for Stratford, and yet rather uneasily, since he kept a foot in the capital. In 1612, heretics and witches were still being executed, while in the next year Sir Thomas Overbury was poisoned in the Tower of London, at the behest of the Countess of Essex, whose marriage to James I's catamite, Robert Carr, Overbury had protested. As always, the circumspect Shakespeare kept his comments both recondite and indefinite, though Creon's Thebes rather clearly is the rancid London of James I:

> *Arc.*                          this is virtue,
>    Of no respect in Thebes. I spake of Thebes,
>    How dangerous, if we will keep our honours,
>    It is for our residing, where every evil
>    Hath a good colour; where every seeming good's
>    A certain evil; where not to be even jump
>    As they are, here were to be strangers, and
>    Such things to be, mere monsters.
>
>                                   [I.ii.35–42]

To be "even jump," or "exactly," with the way things are in Thebes-London is to descend rapidly from the state of innocence that Palamon and Arcite continue to celebrate. Moral warriors, estranged nephews of Creon, they rejoice mutually in their "gloss of youth," and in being "yet unhardened in / The crimes of nature." Yet they are patriotic young men, and rally to Thebes when informed that Theseus marches against it, however noble his cause. Shakespeare, more grimly than ever before, declines to

glorify war, and gives us a truly shocking speech by the Amazon Hippolyta, as she and her sister Emilia bid farewell to Pirithous, cousin and
closest friend of Theseus, as he goes off to join the Duke in battle:

> We have been soldiers, and we cannot weep
> When our friends don their helms, or put to sea,
> Or tell of babes broached on the lance, or women
> That have sod their infants in—and after ate them—
> The brine they wept at killing 'em.

[I.iii.18–22]

If one cannot weep at mothers boiling, in their own salt tears, their own
infants for dinner, one can perhaps laugh, in psychological self-defense.
Since this grotesque vision is cause for neither woe nor wonder on Hippolyta's part, we can surmise that Shakespeare again achieves an alienation effect, in the mode of his own *Titus Andronicus* of two decades before.
But that play was an outrageous send-up of Marlowe and Kyd. What is this
sentiment doing in *The Two Noble Kinsmen*? Neither Hippolyta herself nor
Emilia seems to take this hideous image as other than merely factual, which
is another mark of Shakespearean distancing in this uncanny play. It would
be at least as difficult to gauge Hippolyta's lack of jealousy when she considers the depth of the Pirithous–Theseus relationship:

> They two have cabined
> In many as dangerous as poor a corner,
> Peril and want contending; they have skiffed
> Torrents whose roaring tyranny and power
> I'th' least of these was dreadful; and they have
> Fought out together where death's self was lodged;
> Yet fate hath brought them off. Their knot of love,
> Tied, weaved, entangled, with so true, so long,
> And with a finger of so deep a cunning,
> May be outworn, never undone. I think
> Theseus cannot be umpire to himself,

Cleaving his conscience into twain and doing
Each side like justice, which he loves best.

[I.iii.35–47]

To say that your marriage may outwear but never outdo your husband's relation to his closest male companion is again to manifest an uncanny dispassionateness, particularly since Hippolyta evidently does not care which one Theseus loves best. Emilia's reply is both polite and even more dispassionate: "Doubtless / There is a best, and reason has no manners / To say it is not you." Unless Shakespeare means to parody his major excursions into jealousy, including *Othello* and *The Winter's Tale*, he is giving us an entrance into an Amazonian consciousness very different from anything he has portrayed in his women. All this is prelude to the most moving account that Shakespeare ever rendered of love between young girls. Rosalind and Celia, as their respective lusts for Orlando and Oliver evidence, were early inseparables of a very different order than were the older Emilia and the departed Flavina, lost when each lady was just eleven:

*Emil.* You talk of Pirithous' and Theseus' love;
　　Theirs has more ground, is more maturely seasoned,
　　More buckled with strong judgement, and their needs
　　The one of th'other may be said to water
　　Their intertangled roots of love. But I
　　And she I sigh and spoke of were things innocent,
　　Loved for we did, and like the elements
　　That know not what, nor why, yet do effect
　　Rare issues by their operance, our souls
　　Did so to one another. What she liked
　　Was then of me approved, what not, condemned,
　　No more arraignment; the flower that I would pluck
　　And put between my breasts—O, then but beginning
　　To swell about the blossom—she would long
　　Till she had such another, and commit it
　　To the like innocent cradle, where phoenix-like

They died in perfume; on my head no toy
But was her pattern; her affections—pretty,
Though happily her careless wear—I followed
For my most serious decking; had mine ear
Stolen some new air, or at adventure hummed one
From musical coinage, why, it was a note
Whereon her spirits would sojourn—rather dwell on—
And sing it in her slumbers. This rehearsal—
Which every innocent wots well comes in
Like old emportment's bastard—has this end,
That the true love 'tween maid and maid may be
More than in sex dividual.

[I.iii.55–82]

We see why Emilia, more even than Chaucer's Emily, will be so despairingly passive as to whether she will be awarded to Arcite or to Palamon. The length, weightedness, and complexity of this declaration is unique in Shakespeare, and deserves to be better known as the *locus classicus* in defense of such love in the language. Emilia's speech is much Shakespeare's most passionate in the play, as Hippolyta dryly observes. Hippolyta's courtly irony cannot lessen the poignance of Emilia's paean to the dead Flavina, or more precisely to the perfect love of the two pre-adolescent girls, each finding her entire identity in the other. The contrast between this union of serenities and the murderous violence of the Palamon-Arcite strife for Emilia could not be more persuasive. With a mordant wit, Shakespeare concludes the scene with a sisterly debate as gravely courteous as it is disquieting:

*Hipp.*                    You're out of breath,
  And this high-speeded pace is but to say
  That you shall never—like the maid Flavina—
  Love any that's called man.
*Emil.*                    I am sure I shall not.
*Hipp.* Now alack, weak sister,
  I must no more believe thee in this point,

Though in't I know thou dost believe thyself,
Than I will trust a sickly appetite
That loathes even as it longs. But sure, my sister,
If I were ripe for your persuasion, you
Have said enough to shake me from the arm
Of the all-noble Theseus, for whose fortunes
I will now in and kneel, with great assurance
That we, more than his Pirithous, possess
The high throne in his heart.

*Emil.*                                   I am not
Against your faith, yet I continue mine.

[I.iii.82–98]

The key phrasing is "a sickly appetite / That loathes even as it longs," a superb expression of acute ambivalence. It is difficult not to conclude that the ambivalence is very much that of the forty-nine-year-old Shakespeare, who seems to intimate his own newfound freedom—if not from desire, then from its tyranny—and seems also to manifest a nostalgia for other modes of love. Shakespeare's sexual complexity, which may have chastised itself in the elegy for Will Peter, breaks bounds in *The Two Noble Kinsmen*, if only in some ironic grace notes, since he avoids celebrating anything like the Emilia–Flavina ecstasy of oneness in his accounts of the Pirithous–Theseus and Palamon–Arcite relationships.

The victorious Theseus, having captured the wounded Palamon and Arcite, vows to heal them and then to hold them prisoner, for reasons that Shakespeare keeps implicit but that have about them a touch of sadistic and homoerotic possessiveness, a pride at having in one's power two such superb defeated warriors. Shakespeare's first act comes full circle, with the reappearance of the three Queens, now burying the remnants of their husbands, and keening a memorably enigmatic couplet:

This world's a city full of straying streets,
And death's the market-place, where each one meets.

[I.v.15–16]

This may be Shakespeare's most direct response to *The Knight's Tale*'s warning that we are always keeping appointments we have never made. We then go off to prison with Palamon and Arcite, but since this is part of John Fletcher's share in the play, we can evade it, except for noting that the cousins fall in love with Emilia at first sight, thus destroying their own friendship forever, as in Chaucer. Shakespeare began writing again by supplying a first scene to Act III, where Arcite, long since liberated by old acquaintance with Theseus's friend Pirithous, is wandering lovelorn in the woods, while everyone else is off a-maying. On this fateful Mayday, the still-shackled Palamon, freshly escaped from prison, confronts Arcite, and the two agree on a fight to the death, the winner take Emilia. The scene has a mad, irrealistic charm, as Shakespeare juxtaposes their high rhetoric of chivalry with their mutually insane, regretful need to immolate one another. It is difficult to describe the comedy of their encounter, parallels being few, but some lines of Arcite's catch the flavor:

> Honour and honesty
> I cherish and depend on, howsoe'er
> You skip them in me, and with them, fair coz,
> I'll maintain my proceedings. Pray be pleased
> To show in generous terms your griefs, since that
> Your question's with your equal, who professes
> To clear his own way with the mind and sword
> Of a true gentleman.
>
> [III.i.50–57]

This intricate mix of pomposity and courtesy disappears when Fletcher takes over for the duel, which is interrupted by Theseus and his entourage, Emilia included. After the furious Duke threatens the two erotic madmen with the prospects of death or banishment, a tournament is agreed upon, each duelist to be backed by three knights of his choice, the victor to receive Emilia, the loser (and his supporters) to suffer beheading, so that Theseus is bound to achieve his dubious satisfaction. Shakespeare thus gets to write Act V (except for Fletcher's weak second scene), and to improve on Chaucer only by giving both Arcite and Palamon wonderfully outrageous prayers delivered respectively to Mars and to Venus before the tournament begins. These two ghastly invocations are followed by Emilia's chaste prayer to Diana, which can hardly compete with a Shakespeare wholly bent upon mischief in the prior effusions. Arcite begins with a preliminary virtual cheerleading, urging his knights ("yea, my sacrifices!") to ready themselves for invoking Mars:

> Our intercession, then,
> Must be to him that makes the camp a cistern
> Brimmed with the blood of men; give me your aid,
> And bend your spirits towards him.
>
> [V.i.45–48]

"A cistern / Brimmed with the blood of men" prepares us for the climax of Arcite's rhapsody, where a Shakespeare who clearly enjoys being wicked goes almost too far to be funny:

> O great corrector of enormous times,
> Shaker of o'er-rank states, thou grand decider
> Of dusty and old titles, that healest with blood
> The earth when it is sick, and curest the world
> O'th'plurisy of people; I do take
> Thy signs auspiciously, and in thy name
> To my design march boldly. Let us go.
>
> [V.i.63–69]

Shakespeare's disgust with the London of James I, from which he is self-exiled, peeps through these hyperboles, which would have been excessive even for Marlowe's Tamburlaine the Great. The "enormous" times are at once disorderly and unnatural, and the "o'er-rank states" include James's notorious court, so overripe that it is rotten. To heal "with blood" refers to the bad medicine of bloodletting, and the memorable phrase "plurisy of people" plays upon both overpopulation and inflammation, a nation both too many and too diseased. The Falstaffian Shakespeare, subtle in his ironies in *Henry V,* overreaches here to considerable effect, yet only as a warm-up to his most unsavory utterance, surpassing his own Thersites in *Troilus and Cressida,* and yet all an idealistic paean. Here is Palamon celebrating Venus:

> Hail, sovereign queen of secrets, who hast power
> To call the fiercest tyrant from his rage
> And weep unto a girl; that hast the might
> Even with an eye-glance to choke Mars's drum
> And turn th'alarm to whispers; that canst make
> A cripple flourish with his crutch, and cure him
> Before Apollo; that mayst force the king
> To be his subject's vassal, and induce
> Stale gravity to dance; the polled bachelor,
> Whose youth, like wanton boys through bonfires,
> Have skipped thy flame, at seventy thou canst catch,
> And make him, to the scorn of his hoarse throat,
> Abuse young lays of love. What godlike power
> Hast thou not power upon? To Phoebus thou
> Addest flames hotter than his; the heavenly fires
> Did scorch his mortal son, thine him; the huntress
> All moist and cold, some say began to throw
> Her bow away and sigh. Take to thy grace
> Me thy vowed soldier, who do bear thy yoke
> As 'twere a wreath of roses, yet is heavier
> Than lead itself, stings more than nettles.
> I have never been foul-mouthed against thy law;
> Ne'er revealed secret, for I knew none; would not,
> Had I kenned all that were; I never practiced
> Upon man's wife, nor would the libels read
> Of liberal wits. I never at great feasts
> Sought to betray a beauty, but have blushed
> At simpering sirs that did; I have been harsh
> To large confessors, and have hotly asked them

If they had mothers—I had one, a woman,
And women 'twere they wronged. I knew a man
Of eighty winters—this I told them—who
A lass of fourteen brided. 'Twas thy power
To put life into dust; the aged cramp
Had screwed his square foot round,
The gout had knit his fingers into knots,
Torturing convulsions from his globy eyes
Had almost drawn their spheres, that what was life
In him seemed torture. This anatomy
Had by his young fair fere a boy, and I
Believed it was his, for she swore it was,
And who would not believe her? Brief, I am
To those that prate and have done, no companion;
To those that boast and have not, a defier;
To those that would and cannot, a rejoicer.
Yea, him I do not love that tells close offices
The foulest way, nor names concealments in
The boldest language; such a one I am,
And vow that lover never yet made sigh
Truer than I. O then, most soft sweet goddess,
Give me the victory of this question, which
Is true love's merit, and bless me with a sign
Of thy great pleasure.

> *[Here music is heard and doves are seen to flutter. They*
> *fall again upon their faces, then on their knees.]*

O thou that from eleven to ninety reignest
In mortal bosoms, whose chase is this world
And we in herds thy game, I give thee thanks
For this fair token, which, being laid unto
Mine innocent true heart, arms in assurance
My body to this business. Let us rise
And bow before the goddess. [*They bow.*]

> Time comes on.

[V.i.77–136]

At sixty-seven, I wince as I read this, its visions of seventy, eighty, and ninety partly reminding me that Shakespeare, at forty-nine, does not seem either to anticipate or to welcome reaching such gladsome stages of existence. This astonishing hymn to Venus is beyond irony, and is a negatively sublime coda to Shakespeare's quarter century of dramatic poetry. How does one catch up to Shakespeare in what looks like a new mode even for him, and one that he declined to develop? No critical method will aid us to confront and absorb this perpetually new poetry, the farewell voice of the poet so much stronger than all others ever that his difference in degree from them works as a pragmatic difference in kind. And if men wince as they read Palamon's prayer (and they should), it must be because it activates an all-but-universal guilt and shame. No passage in all of Shakespeare impresses me as being at once so painful and so personal, since Palamon speaks only for innocents like himself, and not for the rest of us, Shakespeare included. Suddenly, Palamon is endowed with personality, and is radically distinguished from Arcite, and from the male audience, except for some tiny saving remnant, if they are there. We live now in what is at once a shame culture and a guilt culture, and this uncannily powerful speech certainly will provoke both shame and guilt in many of us, if we have inner ears left after the visual assault that is our era. I am not exactly a moral critic, and my Bardolatry emanates from an aesthetic stance, so I turn now to a more purely aesthetic appreciation of this superb speech.

The terrible power of Venus is described here almost entirely in grotesque and catastrophic images, and yet Venus is being absolved of victimizing us, even as our wretchedness is so memorably portrayed. Chaucer has taught Shakespeare a final lesson beyond mere irony; Palamon is wholly admirable, but he does not quite know what he is saying, and only an authentic exemplar of the chivalric code could speak with his peculiar authority and not sound absurd. If Venus is not culpable, and only we are responsible for the insanity she provokes in us, then we need to ask (as Palamon will not) why we are unable to sustain her sway without disasters and disgrace. Palamon may possess original virtue, but most of us between eleven and ninety do not, and nothing in this play or in all the rest of Shakespeare gives support to a Pauline-Augustinian doctrine of an erotic original sin. On the probable evidence of *The Two Noble Kinsmen* and the *Funeral Elegy* for Will Peter, Shakespeare himself was well enough battered to be glad to be out of it all, but simply to urge "true love's merit" upon us does not seem suitable for the ambivalent husband of Anne Hathaway. Palamon is an erotic realist, who precisely estimates and describes Venus's dreadful power over, and terrible effects on, males from eleven to ninety, even as he rightly protests his merit as her chaste votary. Shakespeare does not allow one nuance within the speech to betray its grandest more-than-irony: like Emilia just after him, Palamon might as well be invoking Diana, since she is really his goddess.

Palamon has a double vision of Venus; Shakespeare, like most of us, is an erotic monist, and though he preserves Palamon's speech from any shadows of rhetorical irony, he takes care to give us an undersong that severely qualifies this paean to a guiltless and flawless Venus. Chaucer, for all his ironic mastery, might not have trusted his auditors (to whom he read aloud, at court and elsewhere) as much as Shakespeare seems to trust the audience here, though I think it likelier that Shakespeare had despaired of all audiences by now, and composes the paradox of Palamon's speech for himself and a few confidants. Such an attitude would lead to no more plays, and this indeed is Shakespeare's prelude to the three years of dramatic silence that concluded his life. Chance is the presiding deity of *The Knight's Tale;* Venus rather than Mars or Diana is the tyrant governing *The Two Noble Kinsmen.* In regard to Palamon's grand oration, we should trust the song and not the singer, totally devout as this young warrior thinks himself to be. His Venus destroys inwardly, as Mars does outwardly; the litany of obliterations is absolute as Venus hunts all of us down. Wasted old men ("stale gravity") perform the dance of death. Bald bachelors of seventy hoarsely sing love songs. Cripples cast their crutches aside. Phoebus Apollo dotingly allows his son Phaethon to drive the sun's chariot, a fatal venture. Diana falls in love with Endymion and discards her bow. Best of all is the "anatomy" of eighty with his bride of fourteen; here we are given the parody of God creating Adam in Venus's "power / To put life into dust," resulting in a deliberate ugliness surpassing anything like it in Shakespeare:

the aged cramp
Had screwed his square foot round,
The gout had knit his fingers into knots,
Torturing convulsions from his globy eyes
Had almost drawn their spheres, that what was life
In him seemed torture.

[V.i.108–13]

Eyeballs popping, feet and hands distorted, the lust-driven "aged cramp" appears more a victim of torture than an enjoyer of pleasure. Palamon's accent registers scorn, yet we feel terror. The angriest reaction to this provocative passage was that of Talbot Donaldson:

What part of Palamon's prayer is not devoted to Venus' power to humiliate and corrupt is devoted to praise of himself for never having conspired sexually against women or made lewd jokes about them, constantly reminding himself, like a good boy, that he had a mother.

It is certainly a question of Shakespearean distancing, which here evaded a Chaucerian ironist. Following Chaucer, Shakespeare grants victory to Arcite, and Theseus implacably prepares to execute Palamon and his three champions. But Arcite's horse throws the triumphant rider, and the fatally injured disciple of Mars graciously yields Emilia to Palamon. Since Shakespeare has emphasized that the heroine's heart is in the grave with the eleven-year-old Flavina, we hardly rejoice at this turn of fortune. The last words are given to Theseus, who seems finally to be aware of the absurdity of it all, thus merging himself with Shakespeare:

A day or two
Let us look sadly, and give grace unto
The funeral of Arcite, in whose end
The visages of bridegrooms we'll put on
And smile with Palamon; for whom an hour,
But one hour since, I was as dearly sorry

As glad of Arcite, and am now as glad
As for him sorry.

[V.iv.124–31]

This amiable revisionism yields to the wonderful closing passage, in which Theseus seems to have vanished, and Shakespeare himself says goodbye to us forever:

O you heavenly charmers,
What things you make of us! For what we lack
We laugh; for what we have we are sorry; still
Are children in some kind. Let us be thankful
For that which is, and with you leave dispute
That are above our question. Let's go off,
And bear us like the time.

[V.iv.131–37]

Those "heavenly charmers" scarcely seem Venus, Mars, and Diana; something more whimsical is being evoked. Palamon, Arcite, Emilia, Theseus— all these cartoons have been dismissed, and what remains is Shakespeare and ourselves. He has learned to laugh for what he lacks, and to be sorry for what he has: both lack and possession are very light, as in our own best moods when we were, or still are, children. The rest is not quite silence, nor is it being equable while we keep appointments we have never made, for bearing us like the time means sustaining not just a particular moment but whatever time still remains. No concluding lines elsewhere in Shakespeare seem to me nearly as comforting.

# CODA:
# THE SHAKESPEAREAN
# DIFFERENCE

If there is validity to my surmise that Shakespeare, by inventing what has become the most accepted mode for representing character and personality in language, thereby invented the human as we know it, then Shakespeare also would have modified severely our ideas concerning our sexuality. The late Joel Fineman, questing to understand Shakespeare's "subjectivity effect," found in the Sonnets a paradigm for all of Shakespeare's (and literature's) bisexualities of vision. Setting aside Fineman's immersion in the critical fashions that ascribe everything to "language" rather than to the authorial self, he nevertheless had an authentic insight into the link between Shakespeare's portraits of the ever-growing inner self, and Shakespeare's preternatural awareness of bisexuality and its diguises.

Here, as ever, Shakespeare is the original psychologist, and Freud the belated rhetorician. The human endowment, Shakespeare keeps intimating, is bisexual: after all, we have both mothers and fathers. Whether we "forget" either the heterosexual or the homosexual component in our desire, or "remember" both, is in the Sonnets and the plays not a question of choice, and only rarely a matter for anguish. Antonio's melancholy in *The Merchant of Venice* seems the largest exception, since his sorrow at losing Bassanio to Portia has suicidal overtones. Shakespeare was, at the least, a skeptical ironist, and so his representations of bisexuality hardly could forgo an ironic reserve, more ambiguous than ambivalent.

Nietzsche ambiguously followed Hamlet in telling us that we could find words only for what was already dead in our hearts, so that there was always a kind of contempt in the act of speaking. Before Hamlet taught us how *not* to have faith either in language or in ourselves, being human was much simpler for us but also rather less interesting. Shakespeare, through Hamlet, has made us skeptics in our relationships with anyone, because we have learned to doubt articulateness in the realm of affection. If someone can say too readily or too eloquently how much they love us, we incline not to believe them, because Hamlet has gotten into us, even as he inhabited Nietzsche.

Our ability to laugh at ourselves as readily as we do at others owes much to Falstaff, the cause of wit in others as well as being witty in himself. To cause wit in others, you must learn how to be laughed at, how to absorb it, and finally how to triumph over it, in high good humor. Dr. Johnson praised Falstaff for his almost continuous gaiety, which is accurate enough but neglects Falstaff's overt desire to teach. What Falstaff teaches us is a comprehensiveness of humor that avoids unnecessary cruelty, because it emphasizes instead the vulnerability of every ego, including that of Falstaff himself.

Shakespeare's wisest woman may be Rosalind in *As You Like It*, but his most comprehensive is Cleopatra, through whom the playwright taught us how complex eros is, and how impossible it is to divorce acting the part of being in love and the reality of being in love. Cleopatra brilliantly bewilders us, and Antony, and herself. Mutability is incessant in her passional existence, and it excludes sincerity as being irrelevant to eros. To be more human in love is, now, to imitate Cleopatra, whose erotic variety makes staleness impossible, and certitude just as unlikely.

Four centuries have only augmented Shakespeare's universal influence; it seems accurate to observe that many more have read the plays, for themselves or in schools, than have attended performances, or even seen versions in movie houses and on television. Will that change in the new century, since deep reading is in decline, and Shakespeare, as the Western canon's center, now vanishes from the schools with the canon? Will generations to come believe current superstitions, and so cast away genius, on the grounds that all individuality is an illusion? If Shakespeare is only a product of social processes, perhaps any social product will seem as good as any other, past or present. In the culture of virtual reality, partly prophesied by Aldous Huxley, and in another way by George Orwell, will Falstaff and Hamlet still seem paradigms of the human? A journalist, scorning what he called any "lone genius," recently proclaimed that the three leading "ideas" of our moment were feminism, environmentalism, and structuralism. That is to mistake political and academic fashions for ideas, and stimulates me to ask again, Who besides Shakespeare can continue to inform an authentic idea of the human?

Had Shakespeare been murdered at twenty-nine, like Christopher Marlowe, then his career would have ended with *Titus Andronicus* or *The Taming of the Shrew,* and his masterpiece would have been *Richard III.* Social processes would have coursed on under Elizabeth and then under James, but the twenty-five plays that matter most would not have come out of Renaissance Britain. Cultural poetics doubtless could be as well occupied with George Chapman or Thomas Heywood, since a social energy is a social energy, if that is your standard for value or concern. We all of us might be gamboling about, but without mature Shakespeare we would be very different, because we would think and feel and speak differently. Our ideas would be different, particularly our ideas of the human, since they were, more often than not, Shakespeare's ideas before they were ours. That is why we do not have feminist Chapman, structuralist Chapman, and environmentalist Chapman, and may yet, alas, have environmentalist Shakespeare.

2

Shakespeare has had the status of a secular Bible for the last two centuries. Textual scholarship on the plays approaches biblical commentary in scope and intensiveness, while the quantity of literary criticism devoted to Shakespeare rivals theological interpretation of Holy Scripture. It is no longer possible for anyone to read everything of some interest and value that has been published on Shakespeare. Though there are indispensable critics of

Shakespeare—Samuel Johnson, William Hazlitt, perhaps Samuel Taylor Coleridge, certainly A. C. Bradley—most commentary upon Shakespeare at best answers the needs of a particular generation in one country or another. Those needs vary: directors and actors, audiences and common readers, scholar-teachers and students do not necessarily seek the same aids for understanding. Shakespeare is an international possession, transcending nations, languages, and professions. More than the Bible, which competes with the Koran, and with Indian and Chinese religious writings, Shakespeare is unique in the world's culture, not just in the world's theaters.

This book—*Shakespeare: The Invention of the Human*—is a latecomer work, written in the wake of Shakespeare critics I most admire: Johnson, Hazlitt, Bradley, and their mid-twentieth-century disciple, Harold Goddard. I have sought to take advantage of my belatedness by asking always, Why Shakespeare? He already was the Western canon, and is now becoming central to the world's implicit canon. As I assert throughout, Hamlet and Falstaff, Rosalind and Iago, Lear and Cleopatra are clearly more than great roles for actors and actresses. It is difficult sometimes not to assume that Hamlet is as ancient a hero as Achilles or Oedipus, or not to believe that Falstaff was as historical a personality as Socrates. When we think of the Devil, we are as likely to reflect on Iago as on Satan, while the historical Cleopatra seems only a shadow of Shakespeare's Egyptian mesmerizer, the Fatal Woman incarnate.

Shakespeare's influence, overwhelming on literature, has been even larger on life, and thus has become incalculable, and seems recently only to be growing. It surpasses the effect of Homer and of Plato, and challenges the scriptures of West and East alike in the modification of human character and personality. Scholars who wish to confine Shakespeare to his context—historical, social, political, economic, rational, theatrical—may illuminate particular aspects of the plays, but are unable to explain the Shakespearean influence on us, which is unique, and which cannot be reduced to Shakespeare's own situation, in his time and place.

If the world indeed can have a universal and unifying culture, to any degree worthy of notice, such a culture cannot emanate from religion. Judaism, Christianity, and Islam have a common root, but are more diverse than similar, and the other great religious traditions, centered upon China and India, are very remote from the Children of Abraham. The universe increasingly has a common technology, and in time may constitute one vast computer, but that will not quite be a culture. English already is the world language, and presumably will become even more so in the twenty-first century. Shakespeare, the best and central writer in English, already is the only universal author, staged and read everywhere. There is nothing arbitrary in this supremacy. Its basis is only one of Shakespeare's gifts, the most mysterious and beautiful: a concourse of men and women unmatched in the rest of literature. Iris Murdoch, whose high but impossible ambition has been to become a Shakespearean novelist, once told an interviewer, "There is of course the great problem—to be able to be like Shakespeare—create all kinds of different people quite unlike oneself."

What Shakespeare himself was like, we evidently never will know. We may be incorrect in believing we know what Ben Jonson and Christopher Marlowe were like, and yet we seem to have a clear sense of their personalities. With Shakespeare, we know a fair number of externals, but essentially we know absolutely nothing. His deliberate colorlessness may have been one of his many masks for an intellectual autonomy and originality so vast that not only his contemporaries but also his forerunners and followers have been considerably eclipsed by comparison. One hardly can overstress Shakespeare's inward freedom; it extends to the conventions of his era, and to those of the stage as well. I think we need to go further in recognizing this independence than we ever have done. You can demonstrate that Dante or Milton or Proust were perfected products of Western civilization, as it had reached them, so that they were both summits and epitomes of European culture at particular times and particular places. No such demonstration is possible for Shakespeare, and not because of any supposed "literary transcendence." In Shakespeare, there is always a residuum, an excess that is left over, no matter how superb the performance, how acute the critical analysis, how massive the scholarly accounting, whether old-style or newfangled. Explaining Shakespeare is an infinite exercise; you will become exhausted long before the plays are emptied out. Allegorizing or ironizing Shakespeare by privileging cultural anthropology or theatrical history or religion or psychoanalysis or politics or Foucault or Marx or feminism works only in limited ways. You are likely, if you are shrewd, to achieve Shakespearean insights into your favorite hobbyhorse, but you are rather less likely to achieve Freudian or Marxist or feminist insight into Shakespeare. His universality will defeat you; his plays know more than you do, and your knowingness consequently will be in danger of dwindling into ignorance.

Can there be a Shakespearean reading of Shakespeare? His plays read one another, and a double handful of critics have been able to follow the plays in that project. I would like to believe that there still could be a Shakespearean staging of Shakespeare, but it is quite a long time now since I last encountered one. This book offers what it intends as a Shakespearean reading of the characters of his plays, partly by employing one character to interpret another. Sometimes, I have resorted to a few characters by other authors, particularly by Chaucer and Cervantes, but going outside Shakespeare to apprehend Shakespeare better is a dangerous procedure, even if you confine yourself to the handful or fewer of writers who are not destroyed by being compared with the creator of Falstaff and of Hamlet. Juxtaposing Shakespeare's characters to those of his contemporary rival dramatists is ludicrous, as I have indicated throughout this book. Literary transcendence is now out of fashion, but Shakespeare so transcends his fellow playwrights that critical absurdity hovers near when we seek to confine Shakespeare to his time, place, and profession. These days, critics do not like to begin by standing in awe of Shakespeare, but I know of no other way to begin with him. Wonder, gratitude, shock, amazement are the accurate responses out of which one has to work.

Jacob Burckhardt, a rather distinguished Old Historicist, has just one mention of Shakespeare in his masterwork, *The Civilization of the Renaissance in Italy* (1860), but it is quite devastating to Renaissance Italy, and to its Spanish overlords. That Shakespeare's timing and location were immensely fortunate has to be granted, but then several dozen other dramatists in his generation had the same advantages. Burckhardt's true point was "that such a mind is the rarest of heaven's gifts." Together with his younger colleague at Basel, Friedrich Nietzsche, Jacob Burckhardt revived for us the ancient

Greek sense of the agonistic, the vision of literature as an incessant and on-going contest. Shakespeare, though he had to begin by absorbing and then struggling against Marlowe, became so strong with the creation of Falstaff and Hamlet that it is difficult to think of him as competing with anyone, once he had fully individuated. From *Hamlet* on, Shakespeare's contest primarily was with himself, and the evidence of the plays and their likely compositional sequence indicates that he was driven to outdo himself.

Charles Lamb, admirable critic, has been much denigrated in this century for insisting that it was better to read Shakespeare than to watch him acted. If one could be certain that Ralph Richardson or John Gielgud or Ian McKellen was to do the acting, then argument with Lamb would be possible. But to see Ralph Fiennes, under bad direction, play Hamlet as a poor little rich boy, or to sustain George C. Wolfe's skilled travesty of *The Tempest,* is to reflect upon Lamb's wisdom. When you read, then you can direct, act, and interpret for yourself (or with the help of Hazlitt, A. C. Bradley, and Harold Goddard). In the theater, much of the interpreting is done for you, and you are victimized by the politic fashions of the moment. Harry Berger, Jr., in a wise book, *Imaginary Audition* (1989), gives us a fine irony:

> It is no doubt perverse to find that desire of theater burning through Shakespeare's texts is crossed by a certain despair of theater, of the theater that seduces them and the theater they seduce; a despair inscribed in the auditory voyeurism with which the spoken language outruns its auditors, dropping golden apples along the way to divert the greedy ear that longs to devour its discourse.

Presumably, this ironic perversity stems from Shakespeare's apparent fecklessness as to the survival of his plays' texts. The creative exuberance of Shakespeare doubtless suggested carelessness to the superbly labored Ben Jonson, at least in some of his moods, but ought not to mystify us. There is indeed a bad current fashion among some Shakespearean scholars to reduce the poet-dramatist to the crudest texts that somehow can be deemed authentic; Sir Frank Kermode has protested eloquently against this destructive practice, which can be seen at its worst in the Oxford Edition of Gary Taylor. Charles Lamb was amiably seconded by Rosalie Colie, who reminded us of the advice given by the editors of the First Folio, Shakespeare's fellow actors, Heminges and Condell: "Read him, therefore, and againe, and againe." Colie added the fine reminder that "no excuse is needed for treating Chaucer's work as read material, although we know he read it *aloud*, as performance, at the time."

Shakespeare directing Shakespeare, at the Globe, hardly could supervise performances of *Hamlet* or *King Lear* in their full, bewildering perplexity. As director, even Shakespeare had to choose to emphasize one perspective or another, the limitation of every director and of every actor. With dramas almost infinite in their amplitude, Shakespeare (with whatever suffering, or whatever unconcern) had to reduce the range of possible interpretation. The critical reading of Shakespeare, *not* by academics but by the authentic enthusiasts in his audience, had to have begun as a contemporary concern, since those early quartos—good and bad—were offered for sale, sold, and reprinted. Eighteen of Shakespeare's plays had appeared in separate volumes before the First Folio of 1623, starting with *Titus Andronicus* in 1594, the year of its first performance, when Shakespeare turned thirty. Falstaff's advent (under his original name, Oldcastle), in 1598, was attended by two quarto printings, with reprintings in 1599, 1604, 1608, 1613, and 1622, and two more quartos followed the First Folio, in 1632 and 1639. Hamlet, Falstaff's only rival in contemporary popularity, sustained two quartos within two years of his first stage appearance. The point is that Shakespeare knew he *had* early readers, less numerous by far than his audience, but more than just a chosen few. He wrote primarily to be acted, yes, but he wrote also to be read, by a more select group. This is not to suggest that there are two Shakespeares, but rather to remind us that the one Shakespeare was subtler and more comprehensive than certain theatrical reductionists care to acknowledge.

William Hazlitt, in 1814, wrote a brief essay called "On Posthumous Fame—Whether Shakespeare Was Influenced by a Love of It?" One can wonder at Hazlitt's conclusion, which was that Shakespeare was wholly free of such egotism. Nowadays, many critics like to think of Shakespeare as the Andrew Lloyd Webber of his day, coining money and allowing posterity to care for itself. This seems very dubious to me; Shakespeare was not Ben Jonson, but he was much in Jonson's company, and probably he had too keen a sense of his own powers to share in Jonson's or George Chapman's anxieties about literary survival. The Sonnets of Shakespeare are very divided on this, as on most matters, but the aspiration for literary permanence figures strongly in them. Perhaps Coleridge, in his transcendental intensity, got this best: "Shakespeare is the Spinozistic deity—an omnipresent creativeness."

Spinoza said that we should love God without expecting that God would love us in return. Perhaps Shakespeare, as such a godhead, accepted his audience's homage without giving it anything in return; perhaps indeed Hamlet is Shakespeare's authentic surrogate, provoking the audience's love precisely because Hamlet palpably does not need or want its love, or anyone's love. Shakespeare may have been strong enough not to need the poet-dramatist's equivalent of love, an intimation of the applause of eternity. Yet so ruthless an experimenter, who increasingly declined to repeat himself, who used the old almost always to make something radically new, seems as a playwright to have consistently quested for his own inward interests, even as he took care to stay ahead of the competition. The essence of poetry, according to Dr. Johnson, was invention, and no poetry that we have approaches Shakespeare's plays as invention, particularly as invention of the human.

There is the heart of the matter, at once the subject of this book and the mark of my difference from nearly all current Shakespearean criticism, whether academic, journalistic, or theatrical. It is most possible that Shakespeare was unaware of his originality at the representation of human nature—that is to say, of human *action*, and the way such action frequently was antithetical to human words. Marlowe and Jonson, in their different but related ways, can be said to have valued words over action, or perhaps rather to have seen the playwright's proper function as showing that words were the authentic form of action. Shakespeare's apparent skepticism, the opening mark of his difference from Marlowe and Jonson alike, asks us to observe that we act very unlike our words. The central principle of Shakespearean representation at first seems a more-than-Nietzschean skepticism, since Hamlet knows that what he can find words for is already dead in his heart, and consequently he scarcely can speak without contempt for the act of speaking. Falstaff, who gives all to wit, can speak without contempt, but he speaks always with ironies that transcend even his pupil Hal's full apprehension. Sometimes I reflect that not Hamlet and Falstaff, but Iago and Edmund are the most Shakespearean characters, because in them, and by them, the radical gap between words and action is most fully exploited. *Skepticism*, as a term, fits Montaigne or Nietzsche better than it does Shakespeare, who cannot be confined to a skeptical stance, however widely (or wildly) we define it. The best analyst of this Shakespearean freedom has been Graham Bradshaw, in his admirable *Shakespeare's Skepticism* (1987), one of the half-dozen or so best modern (since A. C. Bradley, that is) books about Shakespeare.

For Bradshaw, Shakespeare's mastery of ironic distancing is one of the poet-dramatist's central gifts, creating a pragmatic skepticism in regard to all questions of "natural" value. I would alter this only by swerving away from such skepticism, as I think Shakespeare himself did, by giving up all rival accounts of nature through an acceptance of the indifference of nature. We can surmise that Shakespeare, with nature's largeness *in* him, testified to nature's indifference, and so at last to death's indifference. Yet Shakespeare, with art's greater largeness also in him, is neither indifferent nor quite skeptical, neither a believer nor a nihilist. His plays persuade all of us that *they* care, that their characters *do* matter, but never for, or to, Eternity.

Sometimes these personages matter to others, but always finally to themselves—even Hamlet, even Edmund, even the wretched Parolles of *All's Well That Ends Well* and the rancid Thersites of *Troilus and Cressida*. Value in Shakespeare, as Jane Austen admirably learned from him, is bestowed upon one character by or through another or others and only because of the hope of shared esteem. We are skeptical of Hamlet's final estimate of Fortinbras, even as we are somewhat quizzical as to Hamlet's perpetual overestimation of the faithful but colorless Horatio. We are not at all skeptical of Hamlet's own value, despite his own despair of it, because everyone in the play, even Hamlet's enemies, somehow testifies to it.

We cannot get enough perspectives on Hamlet, and always want still more, because Hamlet's largeness and his indifference do not so much merge him into nature as they confound nature with him. Falstaff's equal circumference of consciousness suggests that nature can achieve mind only by associating itself with Falstaff, and thus acquiring something of his wit. Edmund mistakenly invokes nature as his goddess, whereas his actual, negative achievement is to render nature into a devouring entity, a mind (of sorts) that excludes very nearly all affect. Iago, more accurately invoking a "divinity of hell," succeeds in his brilliant project of destroying the only ontological reality he knows, organized warfare, as epitomized by the war god Othello, and replacing it with an anarchic incessant warfare of all against all. Iago does this in the name of a nothingness that can compensate him for his own wound, his sense of having been passed over and rejected by the only value he has ever known, Othello's martial glory.

Shakespeare's representation of the human is not a return to nature, despite the startled sense that has prevailed from Shakespeare's contemporaries to the present, which is that Shakespeare's men, women, and children are somehow more "natural" than other dramatic and literary characters. If you believe, as so many apostles of "cultural studies" assert they do, that the natural ego is an obsolete entity, and that individual style is an outmoded mystification, then Shakespeare, like Mozart or Rembrandt, is likely to seem interesting primarily for qualities that all artists share, whatever their relative eminence. Disbelief in a self of one's own is a kind of elitist secular heresy, perhaps only available to the sect of "cultural studies." The death of the author, Foucault's post-Nietzschean invention, convinces academic partisans gathered under Parisian banners, but means nothing to the leading poets, novelists, and dramatists of our moment, who almost invariably assure us that their quest is to develop further their own selfish innovations. I don't want to blame postmodernist Paris upon Freud, but I suspect that the master's sublime confidence at inventing inner agencies, and ascribing independent existence to such gorgeous fictions, is the foreground to the "death of the subject" in the poststructural prophets of Resentment. If the ego can be predicated or voided with equal ease, then selves can be shuffled off with high cultural abandon.

What happens to Sir John Falstaff if we deny him an ego? The question is doubly funny, since some of us would shrug and say, "After all, he is just language," and a few of us might want to say that the vivid representation of so strong a selfhood dismisses all skepticism as to the reality of the ego. Sir John himself certainly feels no self-skepticism; his gusto precludes Hamletian waverings as to whether we are too full or too empty. There is an abyss of potential loss in Falstaff; he senses that he will die of betrayed affection. Empson, determined not to be sentimental about fat Jack, wanted us to think of the great comedian as a dangerously powerful Machiavel. Empson was a great critic, but nevertheless he forgot that Shakespeare's major Machiavels—Iago and Edmund—know themselves to be ontologically nil, which is not exactly a Falstaffian malady. In vitalistic self-awareness, Falstaff truly is the Wife of Bath's child. He would have liked Henry V to fill his purse, but his killing grief at being rejected is not primarily a worldly catastrophe.

3

Is it possible to account for Shakespeare's universalism, for our sense of his uniqueness? I grant that America's Shakespeare is not Britain's, nor Japan's, nor Norway's, but I recognize also something that really is Shakespeare's, and that always survives his successful migration from country to country. Against all of our current demystifications of cultural eminence, I go on insisting that Shakespeare invented us (whoever we are) rather more than we have invented Shakespeare. To accuse Shakespeare of having invented, say, Newt Gingrich or Harold Bloom is not necessarily to confer any dramatic value upon either Gingrich or Bloom, but only to see that Newt is a parody of Gratiano in *The Merchant of Venice* and Bloom a parody of Falstaff. A *nouveau* historicizer would dismiss that as a politics of identity, but I dare say it was the praxis of the audience at the Globe, and of Shakespeare himself, who gave us Ben Jonson as Malvolio, Kit Marlowe as Edmund, and William Shakespeare as— There you take your choice. The playwrights in Shakespeare are inspired amateurs: Peter Quince, Falstaff and Hal, Hamlet, Iago, Edmund, Prospero—and I suspect that the highly professional Shakespeare has no surrogate in that rather various group. The only parts we know for sure that he acted were the Ghost in *Hamlet* and old Adam in *As You Like It.* One gathers he was available to play older men, and we can wonder how many English kings he portrayed. A number of critics suggestively have called Shakespeare a Player King, haunted by images akin to those assumed by Falstaff and Hal when they alternate the role of Henry IV in their improvised skit. Perhaps Shakespeare played Henry IV; we do not know. To be a player clearly was for Shakespeare an equivocal fate, one that involved some social chagrin. We do not know how closely to integrate Shakespeare's life and his sonnet sequence, but critics have intimated, to me convincingly, that Falstaff's relation to Hal has a parallel in the poet's relation, in the Sonnets, to his patron and possible lover, the Earl of Southampton. Whatever it was that Shakespeare experienced with Southampton, it clearly had a negative side, and too searingly reminded him that he was indeed a player and not a king.

Why Shakespeare? He childed as we fathered; he cannot have intended to make either his characters or his audience into his children, but he fathered much of the future, and not of the theater alone, not even of literature alone. Almost the only lasting human concern that Shakespeare can be said to have *not* affected is religion, whether as praxis or as theology. Though his care was to avoid politics and faith alike, for his neck's sake, he has influenced politics considerably, though far less than he has shaped psychology and morals (circumspect as he was as to morality, at least in his fashion). As much a creator of selves as of language, he can be said to have melted down and then remolded the representation of the self in and by language. That assertion is the center of this book, and I am aware that it will seem hyperbolical to many. It is merely true, and has been obscured because we now assert far too little for the effect of literature upon life, at this bad time when the university teachers of literature teach everything except literature, and discuss Shakespeare in terms scarcely different from those employed for television serials or for the peerless Madonna. What runs on television, or with Madonna, is akin to Elizabethan bear baitings and public executions; Shakespeare indeed was and is popular, but was not "popular culture," whether then or now, at least not in our curious, current sense of what increasingly has become an oxymoron.

Why Shakespeare? Who could replace him, as a representer of persons? Dickens has something of Shakespeare's global universalism, but Dickens's grotesques, and even his more normative figures, are caricatures, more in the mode of Ben Jonson than of Shakespeare. Cervantes is closer to an authentic rival: Don Quixote matches Hamlet, and Sancho Panza could confront Falstaff, but where are Cervantes's Iago, Macbeth, Lear, Rosalind, Cleopatra? Chaucer, I suspect, comes closest, and Chaucer is Shakespeare's authentic precursor, more truly influential on Falstaff and Iago than Marlowe (and Ovid) ever could be on any Shakespearean character. Doubtless we read, and even go to the theater, in quest of more than personalities, but most human beings are lonely, and Shakespeare was the poet of loneliness and of its vision of mortality. Most of us, I am persuaded, read and attend theater in search of other selves. In search of one's own self, one prays, or meditates, or recites a lyric poem, or despairs in solitude. Shakespeare matters most because no one else gives us so many other selves, larger and more detailed than any closest friends or lovers seem to be. I hardly think that makes Shakespeare a substitute for life, which, alas, so often seems an inadequate substitution for Shakespeare. Oscar Wilde, with his canny observation that nature imitates Shakespeare, as best as it can, is the proper guide to these matters. The world has grown melancholy, Oscar murmured, because a puppet, Hamlet, was sad. Other poets have made a heterocosm or second nature, Spenser and Blake and Joyce among them. Shakespeare is a third realm, neither nature nor second nature. This third kingdom is imaginal, rather than given or imaginary.

By "the imaginal," I here mean Shakespeare's idea of the play, which has been subtly expounded by a number of critics since Anne Barton. Even as a growing uneasiness gradually removed much of Shakespeare's pride in the theater, an implicit confidence in his own power of characterization partly took the place of a waning contact with his audience. Acting and harlotry blend into each other in Shakespeare's disillusionment, and he recoils from the mix only to suggest that plays themselves, as deceits, are ghostlike imitations of sordid realities. But what of those greater shadows, the men and the women of the "dark comedies," the high tragedies, and the tragicomedies that we (not Shakespeare) call "late romances"? To turn against representation is to renew Plato's polemic against the poets, yet we do not sense any transcendental element in Shakespeare's dialectical revulsion from shadows. Transcendentalism, in Shakespeare, tends to be available only in its withdrawal and departure, as when we hear the music of the god Hercules abandoning his favorite, Antony. Shakespeare, even at his darkest, is reluctant to abandon his protagonists. We cannot imagine Shakespeare, like Ben Jonson, collecting his own plays in a large folio entitled *The Works of William Shakespeare*, and yet Prospero is hardly a figure of diminishment, however he chooses to conclude. We do not see the Shakespearean magus very plainly on our stage these days, because more often than not he is presented as a baffled white colonialist who does not know how to cope with a heroic black insurgent (or even two, if George C. Wolfe's fancy about Ariel as a defiant black woman should prove contagious). Still, Prospero abides as an image of Shakespeare's pride (somewhat equivocal) in his own magic of creating persons.

4

Leeds Barroll, in a persuasive revision of Shakespearean chronology, argues that Shakespeare produced *King Lear, Macbeth,* and *Antony and Cleopatra* in about a year and two months, in 1606–7. This extraordinary pace, again according to Barroll, was also standard for Shakespeare, who wrote twenty-seven plays in the decade from 1592 to 1602. Still, it is a kind of shock to envision the composition of *King Lear, Macbeth,* and *Antony and Cleopatra* in just fourteen months. And yet, each time I read *King Lear,* I am startled that any single human being could compose so vast a cosmological catastrophe in any time span. I think we are returned to the basis for now unfashionable Bardolatry: we find something preternatural about Shakespeare, as we do about Michelangelo or Mozart. Shakespeare's facility, marked by his contemporaries, seems to us something more. Whatever the social and economic provocations that animated him, they could scarcely differ, in kind or in degree, from the precisely parallel stimuli upon, say, Thomas Dekker or John Fletcher. The mystery of Shakespeare, as Barroll implies, is not the composition of three tragedies in sixty weeks but that the three comprised *Lear, Macbeth,* and *Antony and Cleopatra.*

I have been chided by my old friend Robert Brustein, the director of the American Repertory Theatre at Harvard, for suggesting that we might be better off with public readings of Shakespeare, on screen as on stage. Ideally, of course, Shakespeare should be acted, but since he is now almost invariably poorly directed and inadequately played, it might be better to *hear* him well rather than *see* him badly. Ian McKellen would be a splendid Richard III, but if his director insists that McKellen portray Richard as Sir Oswald Mosley, the English would-be Hitler, then I would prefer to hear this remarkable actor read the part aloud instead. Laurence Fishburne is an impressive-looking personage, but consider for how long one could *listen* to his reading of Othello's part aloud. Shakespeare's texts indeed are somewhat like scores, and need to be adumbrated by performance, but if our theater is ruined, would not public recitation be preferable to indeliberate travesty?

It is a commonplace that there is even more commentary on Shakespeare than there is on the Bible. For us, now, the Bible is the most difficult of books. Shakespeare is not; paradoxically, he is open to everyone, and provocative to endless interpretation. The prime reason for this, put most simply, is Shakespeare's endless intelligence. His major characters are rich in multiform qualities, and a mixed few of them abound as intellects: Falstaff, Rosalind, Hamlet, Iago, Edmund. They are more intelligent than we are, an observation that will strike a formalist or historicist critic as Bardolatrous nonsense. But the creatures directly reflect their creator: his intelligence is more comprehensive and more profound than that of any other writer we know. The aesthetic achievement of Shakespeare cannot be separated from his cognitive power. I suspect that this accounts for his mixed effect on philosophers: Hegel and Nietzsche celebrated him, but Hume and Wittgenstein regarded him as overesteemed, possibly because a human being as intelligent as Falstaff or Hamlet seemed not possible to them. Falstaff is at once a cosmos and a person; Hamlet, more enigmatic, is a person and a potential king. The equivocal Machiavel, Prince Hal, is certainly a person, and becomes a formidable king, but he is considerably less of a world-in-himself than are Falstaff and Hamlet, or even Rosalind. Iago and Edmund each is an abyss in himself, fevering to a false creation.

A. D. Nuttall, one of my heroes of Shakespearean criticism, wonderfully tells us that Shakespeare was not a problem solver, and cleared up no difficulties (which may be why Hume and Wittgenstein undervalued the maker of Falstaff and Hamlet). Like Kierkegaard, Shakespeare enlarges our vision of the enigmas of human nature. Freud, wrongly desiring to be a scientist, gave his genius away to reductiveness. Shakespeare does not reduce his personages to their supposed pathologies or family romances. In Freud, we are overdetermined, but always in much the same way. In Shakespeare, as Nuttall argues, we are overdetermined in so many rival ways that the sheer wealth of overdeterminations becomes a freedom. Indirect communication, the mode of Kierkegaard, so well expounded by Roger Poole, was learned by Kierkegaard from Hamlet. Perhaps Hamlet, like Kierkegaard, came into the world to help save it from reductiveness. If Shakespeare brings us a secular salvation, it is partly because he helps ward off the philosophers who wish to explain us away, as if we were only so many muddles to be cleared up.

I remarked earlier that we ought to give up the failed quest of trying to be right about Shakespeare, or even the ironic Eliotic quest of trying to be wrong about Shakespeare in a new way. We can keep finding the meanings of Shakespeare, but never *the* meaning: it is like the search for "the meaning of life." Wittgenstein, and the formalist critics, and the theatricalists, and our current historicizers, all join in telling us that life is one thing and Shakespeare another, but the world's public, after four centuries, thinks otherwise, and they are not easily refuted. Ben Jonson, Shakespeare's shrewdest friend and contemporary, began by insisting that Shakespeare wanted art, but after Shakespeare's death, Jonson felt differently. Advising the actors on how to edit the First Folio of Shakespeare, Jonson must have read about half of the plays for the first time, and he seems to have come around to Shakespeare's own view that "the art itself is nature." David Riggs, Jonson's biographer, defends Jonson from Dryden's accusation of insolence toward Shakespeare, and shows rather that the more neoclassical poet-playwright changed his mind when the full range of Shakespeare was made available to him. What Jonson discovered, and celebrated, is what common readers and common playgoers keep discovering, which is that Shakespeare's personages are so artful as to seem totally natural.

5

Nothing is more difficult for scholars of Shakespeare to apprehend and acknowledge than his cognitive power. Beyond any other writer—poet, dramatist, philosopher, psychologist, theologian—Shakespeare thought everything through again for himself. This makes him as much the fore-runner of Kierkegaard, Emerson, Nietzsche, and Freud as of Ibsen, Strind-berg, Pirandello, and Beckett. Working as a playwright under Elizabeth I, and then under James I, Shakespeare necessarily presents his thoughts obliquely, only rarely allowing himself a surrogate or spokesperson among his dramatic personages. Even when one may appear, we cannot know who it is. The late novelist Anthony Burgess judged Sir John Falstaff to be Shakespeare's prime surrogate. Myself a devout Falstaffian, with a passion against the novelists who lack gratitude for Falstaff, I want to think that Burgess was right, but I cannot know this. I tend to find Shakespeare in Edgar, perhaps because I locate Christopher Marlowe in Edmund, but I do not wholly persuade myself. It may be that no character—not Hamlet, nor Prospero, nor Rosalind—speaks "for" Shakespeare himself. Perhaps the ex-traordinary voice we hear in the Sonnets is as much a fiction as any other voice in Shakespeare, though I find that very difficult to believe.

Shakespeare, canny *and* uncanny, played with almost every "received" concept that was available to him, but may have been persuaded by none of them whatsoever. If you reread his plays incessantly, and ponder every performance you attend, you are not likely to think of him either as a Protestant or as a Catholic, or even as a Christian skeptic. His sensibility is secular, not religious. Marlowe, the "atheist," had a more religious tem-perament than Shakespeare possessed, while Ben Jonson, though as secu-lar a dramatist as Shakespeare, was personally more devout (by fits and starts, anyway). We know that Jonson preferred Sir Francis Bacon to Mon-taigne; we suspect that Shakespeare might not have agreed with Jonson. Montaigne may be a kind of tenuous link between Shakespeare and Molière: Montaigne would be all that they might have had in common. His motto, "What do I know?," is a fit epigraph for both playwrights.

Whatever it was that Shakespeare knew (and it seems not less than everything), he had generated most of it for himself. His relation to Ovid and to Chaucer is palpable, and his contamination by Marlowe was considerable, until it was worked out by the triumphant emergence of Falstaff. Except for those three poets, and for a purely allusive relationship to the Bible, Shakespeare did not rely on authorities, or on authority. When *we* confront the greatest of his tragedies—*Hamlet, Othello, King Lear, Macbeth, Antony and Cleopatra*—we are alone with Shakespeare. We enter a cognitive realm where our moral, emotional, and intellectual preconceptions will not aid us in apprehending sublimity. When acute scholars pratfall into the trap of assuring us that Shakespeare somehow trusted in "a universal moral order which cannot finally be defeated," they lose their way in *King Lear* or *Macbeth*, which are set in no such order. The man Shakespeare, cautious and diffident, wrote only one play taking place in Elizabethan England, the not-very-subversive farce *The Merry Wives of Windsor*. Shakespeare was too circumspect to set a play in Jacobean England or Scotland: *King Lear* and *Macbeth* keep an eye upon James I, while *Antony and Cleopatra* avoids any too close resemblances to James's rather dubious court. The death of Christopher Marlowe was a lesson Shakespeare never forgot, while the torture of Thomas Kyd and the incarceration of Ben Jonson doubtless also hovered always in Shakespeare's consciousness. There is little authentic evidence, *in the plays*, that Shakespeare strove either to uphold or to subvert, however covertly, the established order.

The Sonnets seem to manifest a profound chagrin at being what we call an entertainer, but I think that Shakespeare might have felt even more chagrin had he found himself to be what we call a moralist. Insofar as Marlowe was his forerunner, Shakespeare desired to hold an audience even more firmly than Marlowe held them. Shakespeare railed against the actors, but never—like Ben Jonson—against the audience. Jonson's trauma was that his tragedy *Sejanus* had been hooted off the stage at the Globe. Shakespeare, acting in the play, must have reflected that he had had no similar experience, and he never would. His audience loved Falstaff and Hamlet from the start. Doubtless, the groundlings hissed *Sejanus* for some of the same reasons that caused Jonson to be summoned before the Council, there to be accused of "popperie and treason," but probably they also found it as boring as we do. Jonson—a magnificent comic playwright in *Volpone, The Alchemist,* and *Bartholomew Fair*—alas was a pedant of a tragedian. Shakespeare, who bored none, took care also not to offend "the virtuous" in his England; that came later, and has achieved its apotheosis now, in our humorless academy. That Shakespeare reigns still as the world's universal entertainer, multicultural and amazingly metamorphic, returns us to the unsolved secret of what it is, in him, that transcends history.

To call Shakespeare a "creator of language," as Wittgenstein did, is insufficient, but to call Shakespeare also a "creator of characters," and even a "creator of thought," is still not enough. Language, character, and thought all are part of Shakespeare's invention of the human, and yet the largest part is the passional. Ben Jonson remained closer to Marlowe's mode than to Shakespeare's in that Jonson's personages also are cartoons, caricatures without inwardness. That is why there is no intergenerational contest in Jonson's plays, no sense of what Freud called "family romances." The deepest conflicts in Shakespeare are tragedies, histories, romances, even comedies: of blood. When we consider the human, we think first of parents and children, brothers and sisters, husbands and wives. We do not think of these relationships in terms of Homer and of Athenian tragedy, or even of the Hebrew Bible, because the gods and God are not primarily involved. Rather, we think of families as being alone with one another, whatever the social contexts, and that is to think in Shakespearean terms.

6

Change—of fortune, and in time—is Shakespeare's largest commonplace. Death, the final form of change, is the overt concern of Shakespeare's tragedies and histories, and the hidden preoccupation of his comedies. His tragicomedies—or romances, as we now call them—treat death more originally even than do his high tragedies. Perhaps all sonnets, being ultimately erotic, tend to be elegiac; Shakespeare's appear as the shadows of death itself. Death's ambassador to us uniquely is Hamlet; no other figure, fictive or historic, is more involved with that undiscovered country, unless you desire to juxtapose Jesus with Hamlet. Whether you subsume Shakespeare under nature or art, his peculiar distinction prevails: he teaches us the nature of dying. Some have said this is because Shakespeare approximates a secular scripture. It does seem more adequate, to me, to take Shakespeare (or Montaigne) as such a text than it would be to take Freud or Marx or Franco-Heideggerians or Franco-Nietzscheans. Shakespeare, almost uniquely, is both entertainment and wisdom literature. That the most pleasure-giving of all writers should be also the most intelligent is almost a bewilderment to us. So many of our "cloven fictions" (as William Blake called them) are dissolved by Shakespeare that even a brief listing may be instructive: affective versus cognitive; secular versus sacred; entertainment versus instruction; roles-for-actors versus characters and personalities; nature versus art; "author" versus "language"; history versus fiction; context versus text; subversion versus conservatism. Shakespeare, in cultural terms, constitutes our largest contingency; Shakespeare is the cultural history that overdetermines us. This complex truth renders vain all our attempts to *contain* Shakespeare within concepts provided by anthropology, philosophy, religion, politics, psychoanalysis, or Parisian "theory" of any sort. Rather, Shakespeare contains us; he always gets there before us, and always waits for us, somewhere up ahead.

There is a fashion among some current academic writers on Shakespeare that attempts to explain away his uniqueness as a cultural conspiracy, an imposition of British imperialism, and so a weapon of the West against the East. Allied to this fashion is an even sillier contention: that Shakespeare is no better or worse a poet-playwright than Thomas Middleton or John Webster. After this, we are taken over the verge into lunacy: Middleton wrote *Macbeth*, Sir Francis Bacon or the Earl of Oxford wrote all of Shakespeare, or whole committees of dramatists wrote Shakespeare, commencing with Marlowe and concluding with John Fletcher. Though academic feminism, Marxism, Lacanianism, Foucaultianism, Derrideanism, and so on are more respectable (in the academies) than the Baconians and Oxfordians, it is still the same phenomenon, and contributes nothing to a critical appreciation of Shakespeare. This book commenced by turning away from almost all current Anglo-American writing about, and teaching of, Shakespeare; I mentioned it as rarely as possible, because it cannot aid any open and honest reader or playgoer in the quest to know Shakespeare better.

The wheel of fortune, time, and change turns perpetually in Shakespeare, and accurate perception of him must begin by viewing these turnings, upon which Shakespeare's characters are founded. Dante's characters can evolve no further; Shakespeare's, as I have noted, are much closer to Chaucer's, and seem to owe more to Chaucer's mutable visions of men and women than to anyone's else's, including biblical portrayals or those of Shakespeare's favorite Latin poet, Ovid. Tracing Ovid's effect upon Shakespeare in his study *The Gods Made Flesh*, Leonard Barkan observes: "Many of the great figures of Ovid's poem define themselves by their struggle to invent new languages." Metamorphoses in Shakespeare are almost always related to the playwright's endless quest to find distinct language for every major and many a minor character, language that can change even as they change, wander even as they wander. Turning around, in Shakespeare, frequently takes on the traditional image of wheeling, the wheel sometimes being Fortune's emblem of extravagance: of roaming beyond limits.

Shakespeare's own audiences chose Falstaff as their favorite, even above Hamlet. Fortune's wheel seems to have little relevance to others; Falstaff is ruined by his hopeless, misplaced paternal love for Prince Hal. Hamlet dies after a fifth act in which he has transcended all his earlier identities in the play. Falstaff is thus love's fool, not fortune's, while Hamlet can only be regarded as his own fool or victim, replacing his father surrogate, the clown Yorick. It is appropriate that the antithetical figures of Lear and Edmund both invoke the image of the wheel, but to opposite effects and purposes. Shakespeare's plays are the wheel of all our lives, and teach us whether we are fools of time, or of love, or of fortune, or of our parents, or of ourselves.

# A WORD AT THE END:
## FOREGROUNDING

I greet you at the beginning of a great career, which yet must have had a long foreground somewhere, for such a start.

—Emerson to Whitman, 1855

The "foreground" Emerson sees in Whitman's career is not, as he makes clear by his strange and original use of the word, a background. That latter term has been employed by literary historians during the twentieth century to mean a context, whether of intellectual, social, or political history, within which works of literature are framed. But Emerson means a temporal foreground of another sort, a precursory field of poetic, not institutional, history; perhaps one might say that its historiography is written in the poetry itself. *Foregrounding*, the verb, means to make prominent, or draw attention to, particular features in a literary work.

What is the long foreground of Sir John Falstaff, or of Prince Hamlet, or of Edmund the Bastard? A formalist or textualist critic might say there is none, because these are men made out of words. A contextualist or historicist critic might say, There is background but no foreground. I have argued throughout this book that Shakespeare invents (or perfects, Chaucer being there before him) a mode of representation that depends on his foregrounding of his characters. Shakespeare calls upon the audience to surmise just how Falstaff and Hamlet and Edmund got to be the way they are, by which I mean: their gifts, their obsessions, their concerns. I am not going to ask what made Falstaff so witty, Hamlet so skeptical, Edmund so icy. The mysteries or enigmas of personality are a little to one side of Shakespearean foregrounding.

Shakespeare's literary art, the highest we ever will know, is as much an art of omission as it is of surpassing richness. The plays are greatest where they are most elliptical. Othello loves Desdemona, yet seems not to desire her sexually, since evidently he has no knowledge of her palpable virginity and never makes love to her. What are Antony and Cleopatra like when they are alone together? Why are Macbeth and his fierce lady childless? What is it that so afflicts Prospero, and causes him to abandon his magical powers, and to say that in his recovered realm every third thought shall be of his grave? Why does no one behave other than zanily in *Twelfth Night*, or other than madly in *Measure for Measure*? Why must Shylock be compelled to accept Christian conversion, or Malvolio be so outrageously tormented? Foregrounding is necessary to answer these questions. I will begin with *Hamlet*, partly because I will argue that Shakespeare all but began with him, since there is no *Ur-Hamlet* by Thomas Kyd, and probably there was a *Hamlet* by Shakespeare as early as 1588. Another reason for starting with *Hamlet* is that the play, *contra* T. S. Eliot, indeed is Shakespeare's masterpiece, cognitively and aesthetically the farthest reach of his art.

In the final *Hamlet*, the prince we first encounter is a student home from Wittenberg, where his companions included Rosencrantz, Guildenstern, and Horatio. It is less than two months since the sudden death of his father, and only a month since his mother's marriage to his uncle, who has assumed the crown. Critics have been too ready to believe that Hamlet's melancholia results from these traumas, and from the Ghost's subsequent revelation that Claudius bears the mark of Cain. Yet the long foreground of Hamlet in Shakespeare's life and career, and of Hamlet in the play, suggests quite otherwise. This most extraordinary of all the Shakespearean characters (Falstaff, Iago, Lear, Cleopatra included) is, amidst much else, a despairing philosopher whose particular subject is the vexed relationship between purpose and memory. And his chosen mode for pursuing that relationship is the theater, of which he will display a professional's knowledge and an active playwright's strong opinions. His Wittenberg is pragmatically London, and his university must certainly be the London stage. We are allowed to see his art in action, and in the service of his philosophy, which transcends the skepticism of Montaigne and, by doing so, invents Western nihilism.

Hamlet's aptest disciple is Iago. As I have already noted, Harold Goddard, a now greatly neglected Shakespearean critic who possessed true insight, remarked that Hamlet was his own Falstaff. I would add that Hamlet also was his own Iago. A. C. Bradley suggested that Hamlet was the only Shakespearean character who could have written the play in which he appears. Again, I would add that Hamlet was capable of composing *Othello*, *Macbeth*, and *King Lear*. There is pragmatically something very close to a fusion of Hamlet and Shakespeare the tragedian, by which I do not mean that Hamlet was any more a representation of William Shakespeare than Ophelia was, or whom you will, but rather that Hamlet, in taking on Shakespeare's function as playwright-actor, assumes also the power of making Shakespeare his mouthpiece, his Player King who takes instruction. This is very different from Hamlet's serving as Shakespeare's mouthpiece. Rather, the creature usurps the creator, and Hamlet exploits Shakespeare's memory for purposes that belong more to the Prince of Denmark than to Shakespeare the man. Paradoxical as this must sound, Hamlet "lets be" Shakespeare's empirical self, while taking over the dramatist's ontological self. I do not think that this was Shakespeare's design, or his overt intention, but I suspect that Shakespeare, apprehending the process, let it be. Foregrounding Hamlet, as I will show, depends entirely on conclusions and inferences drawn only from the play itself; the life of the man Shakespeare gives us very few interpretative clues to help us apprehend Hamlet. But Hamlet, fully foregrounded, and Falstaff are clues to what, in a Shakespearean term, we could call the "selfsame" in Shakespeare. That sense of "selfsame" is most severely tested by the character of Hamlet, the most fluid and mobile of all representations ever.

Presumably, Shakespeare had read Montaigne in Florio's manuscript version. Nothing seems more Shakespearean than the great, culminating essay, "Of Experience," composed by Montaigne in 1588, when I suspect that Shakespeare was finishing his first *Hamlet*. Montaigne says that we are all wind, but the wind is wiser than we are, since it loves to make a noise and move about, and does not long for solidity and stability, qualities alien to it. As wise as the wind, Montaigne takes a positive view of our mobile selves, metamorphic yet surprisingly free. Montaigne, like Shakespeare's greatest characters, changes because he overhears what he himself has said. It is in reading his own text that Montaigne becomes Hamlet's precursor at representing reality in and by himself. He becomes also Nietzsche's forerunner, or perhaps melds with Hamlet as a composite precursor whose mark is always upon the aphorist of *Beyond Good and Evil* and *The Twilight of the Idols*. Montaigne's experiential man avoids Dionysiac transports, as well as the sickening descents from such ecstasies. Nietzsche unforgettably caught this aspect of Hamlet in his early *The Birth of Tragedy*, where Coleridge's view that Hamlet (like Coleridge) thinks too much is soundly repudiated in favor of the truth, which is that Hamlet thinks too well. I quote this again because of its perpetual insight:

> For the rapture of the Dionysian state with its annihilation of the ordinary bounds and limits of existence contains, while it lasts, a *lethargic* element in which all personal experiences of the past become immersed. This chasm of oblivion separates the worlds of everyday reality and of Dionysian reality. But as soon as this everyday reality re-enters consciousness, it is experienced as such, with nausea: an ascetic, will-negating mood is the fruit of these states.
>
> In this sense the Dionysian man resembles Hamlet: both have once looked truly into the essence of things, they have gained *knowledge*, and nausea inhibits action; for their action could not change anything in the eternal nature of things; they feel it to be ridiculous or humiliating that they should be asked to set right a world that is out of joint. Knowledge kills action; action requires the veils of illusion: that is the doctrine of Hamlet, not that cheap wisdom of Jack the Dreamer who reflects too much and, as it were, from an excess of possibilities does not get around to action. Not reflection, no— true knowledge, an insight into the horrible truth, outweighs any motive for action, both in Hamlet and in the Dionysian man.

To see that for Hamlet knowledge kills action is to repeat the nihilist arguments that Hamlet composes for the Player King (quite possibly spoken by Shakespeare himself, upon stage at the Globe, doubling the role with the Ghost's). In his later *Twilight of the Idols*, Nietzsche returned to the Dionysiac Hamlet, though without mentioning him. Recalling the "O what a rogue and peasant slave am I!" soliloquy, where Hamlet denounces himself as one who "Must like a whore unpack my heart with words," Nietzsche arrives at a formulation that is the essence of Hamlet: "That for which we find words is something already dead in our hearts. There is always a kind of contempt in the act of speaking." With faith neither in language nor in himself, Hamlet nevertheless becomes a dramatist of the self who surpasses St. Augustine, Dante, and even Montaigne, for that is Shakespeare's greatest invention, the inner self that is not only ever-changing but also ever-augmenting.

J. H. Van den Berg, a Dutch psychiatrist from whom I've learned much, disputes Shakespeare's priority as the inventor of the human by assigning "the birth date of the inner self" to 1520, two generations before *Hamlet*. For Van den Berg, that undiscovered country was found by Martin Luther, in his discourse on "Christian Freedom," which distinguishes the "inner" man from the physical one. It is the inner man who has faith, and who needs only the Word of God. Yet that Word does not dwell within man, as it did for Meister Eckhart and Jakob Böhme, mystics extraordinary, and must come from above. Only the Ghost's word comes to Hamlet from above, and for Hamlet it both does and does not have authority. If you scorn to unpack your heart with words, then why have faith in the Ghost's act of speaking? The deadness in Hamlet's heart long precedes the Ghost's advent, and the play will show us that it has been with Hamlet since early childhood. Foregrounding Hamlet is crucial (and anguishing), because it involves the prehistory of the first absolutely inner self, which belonged not to Martin Luther but to William Shakespeare. Shakespeare allowed something very close to a fusion between Hamlet and himself in the second quarter of the tragedy, which begins with the advent of the players in Act II, Scene ii, and continues through Hamlet's antic glee when Claudius flees *The Mousetrap* in Act III, Scene iii.

We are overfamiliar with *Hamlet*, and we therefore neglect its wonderful outrageousness. The Prince of Denmark evidently is a frequent truant from Wittenberg and haunts the London playhouses; he is eager to hear all the latest gossip and fireworks of Shakespeare's theatrical world, and happily is brought up to date by the Player King. Clearly referring to Shakespeare and his company, Hamlet asks, "Do they hold the same estimation they did when I was in the city? Are they so followed?" and the Globe audience is free to roar when Rosencrantz answers, "No, indeed, are they not." The war of the theaters is discussed with great gusto in Elsinore, just down the street from the Globe. A greater outrageousness comes just a touch later when Hamlet becomes Shakespeare, admonishing the players to act what he has written. Not Claudius but the clown Will Kemp becomes the drama's true villain, and revenge tragedy becomes Shakespeare's revenge against poor players. Ophelia, in her lament for Hamlet, elegizes her lover as courtier, soldier, and scholar; as I have already mentioned, she might have added playwright, actor, and theater manager, as well as metaphysician, psychologist, and lay theologian. This most various of heroes (or hero-villains, as a few would hold) is more interested in the stage than all Shakespeare's other personages taken together. Playing a role is for Hamlet anything but a metaphor; it is hardly *second* nature, but indeed is Hamlet's original endowment. Fortinbras, crying out for military honors because Hamlet, had he ascended the throne, would have merited them, has gotten it all wrong. Had he lived, on or off a throne, Hamlet would have written *Hamlet*, and then gone on to *Othello*, *King Lear*, and *Macbeth*. Prospero, Shakespeare's redeemed Faustus, would have been Hamlet's final epiphany.

Shakespeare might have been everyone and no one, as Borges suggested, but from Act II, Scene ii, through Act III, Scene iii, Shakespeare can be distinguished from Hamlet only if you are resolved to keep the Prince and the actor-dramatist apart. Hamlet's relationship to Shakespeare precisely parallels the playwright's stance toward his own *Ur-Hamlet*; one can say that the Prince revises Shakespeare's career even as the poet revises the earlier protagonist into the Prince. It cannot be accidental that nowhere else in his work can we find Shakespeare risking so deliberate a conflation of life and art. The Sonnets dramatize their speaker's rejection, akin to the pathos of Falstaff's ruin, while no intrusion from the life of the theater is allowed in *Henry IV, Part Two*. It would make no sense to speak of "intrusions" in the "poem unlimited," *Hamlet*, where all is intrusion, and nothing is. The play as readily could have been expanded into a two-part work, because it could absorb even more of Shakespeare's professional concerns. When Hamlet admonishes and instructs the players, neither he nor the play is the least out of character: *The Mousetrap* is as natural to the world of *Hamlet* as is the crooked duel arranged by Claudius between Hamlet and Laertes.

But what does that tell us about Hamlet in his existence before the play begins? We cannot avoid the information that this was always a man of the theater, as much a critic as an observer, and very possibly more of an actual than a potential playwright himself. Foregrounding Hamlet will teach us his greatest paradox: that long before his father's murder and mother's seduction by Claudius, Hamlet was already a self-dramatizing genius of the theater, driven to it out of his contempt for the act of speaking what was already dead in his heart. The apocalyptic self-consciousness of this charismatic personality could have led to dangerous action, a murderousness prophetic of Macbeth's, had it not been for the outlet of this theatrical vocation. Hamlet is only secondarily a courtier, soldier, and scholar; primarily he is that anomaly (and knows it): a royal playwright, "The play's the thing" in every possible sense. Of all Shakespeare's works, this is the play of plays because it is the play of the play. No theory of the drama takes us further than the sequence from Act II, Scene ii, through Act III, Scene iii, if we realize that compared with it, everything that comes before and after in *Hamlet* is interruption. The mystery of Hamlet and the enigma of Shakespeare are centered here.

Backgrounding Shakespeare is a weariness, because it does nothing to explain Shakespeare's oceanic superiority to even the best of his contemporaries, Marlowe and Ben Jonson. Marlowe's Faustus is a cartoon; Shakespeare's Faustus is Prospero. Dr. Faustus in Marlowe acquires Mephistopheles, another cartoon, as familiar spirit. Ariel, Prospero's "sprite," though necessarily other than human, has a personality nearly as distinct as that of the great magus. What Shakespeare shared with his era can explain everything about Shakespeare, except what made him so different in degree from his fellows that at last it renders him different in kind. Foregrounding Shakespeare's characters begins by noting what Shakespeare himself implied about them; it cannot conclude by compiling what they imply about Shakespeare. We can make surmises, particularly in regard to Hamlet and Falstaff, who seem in many ways to live at the limits of Shakespeare's own consciousness. With just a handful of Shakespearean roles—Hamlet, Falstaff, Rosalind, Iago, Macbeth, Lear, Cleopatra—we sense infinite potential, and yet we cannot surpass Shakespeare's employment of them. With Lear—as to a lesser degree with Othello and Antony—we feel that Shakespeare allows us to know their limits as what Chesterton called "great spirits in chains." Perhaps the Falstaffian Chesterton thought of Hamlet as another such figure, since from a Catholic perspective Hamlet (and Prospero) are purgatorial souls at best. Dante foregrounds only Dante the Pilgrim; all others in him no longer can change, since those souls sustaining Purgatory only can be refined, not fundamentally altered. It is because of his art of foregrounding that Shakespeare's men and women are capable of surprising changes, even at the final moment, as Edmund changes at the close of *King Lear.* Unless you are adequately foregrounded, you can never quite overhear yourself.

Shakespeare is a great master of beginnings, but how far back does a Shakespearean play begin? Prospero foregrounds *The Tempest* in his early conversation with Miranda, but does the drama truly commence with his expulsion from Milan? Most would say it starts with the storm that rather oddly gives the play its title, a tempest that ends after the first scene. Since there is almost no plot—any summary is maddening—we are not surprised that scholars tell us there is no source for the plot. But the foreground begins with Shakespeare's subtle choice of a name for his protagonist, Prospero, which is the Italian translation of the Latin Faustus, "the favored one." Presumably Shakespeare, like Marlowe, knew that the name Faustus began as the cognomen that Simon Magus of Samaria took when he went to Rome, there to perish in an unlikely flying contest with St. Peter. *The*

*Tempest*, most peculiarly, is Shakespeare's *Dr. Faustus*, all unlike Marlowe's last play. Think how distracting it would be had Shakespeare named his Mage Faustus, not Prospero. There is no devil in *The Tempest*, unless you argue with Prospero that poor Caliban is one, or at least a sea devil's child. The ultimate foregrounding of *The Tempest* is its magician's name, since its substitution for Faust means that Christianity is not directly relevant to the play. A distinction between "white" and "black" magic is not crucial; an art, Prospero's, is opposed to the sale and fall of a soul, Faustus's.

Hamlet, Prospero, Falstaff, Iago, Edmund: all have evolved through a foretime that itself is the implicit creation of Shakespeare's imaginings. While Hamlet and Prospero intimate dark sensibilities that preceded their catastrophes, Falstaff suggests an early turning to wit, even as Hamlet turned to theater and Prospero to hermetic magic. The despair of having thought too well too soon seems shared by Hamlet and by Prospero, while Falstaff, a professional soldier who long ago saw through chivalry and its glories, resolutely resolves to be merry, and will not despair. He dies of brokenheartedness, according to his fellow scamps, and so Hal's rejection does seem the Falstaffian equivalent of Hamlet's rejection of, and by, life itself.

It seems appropriate that I conclude this book with Falstaff and with Hamlet, as they are the fullest representations of human possibility in Shakespeare. Whether we are male or female, old or young, Falstaff and Hamlet speak most urgently for us and to us. Hamlet can be transcendent or ironic; in either mode his inventiveness is absolute. Falstaff, at his funniest or at his most reflective, retains a vitalism that renders him alive beyond belief. When we are wholly human, and know ourselves, we become most like either Hamlet or Falstaff.